The Massachusetts Historical Society

A Bicentennial History

1791–1991

1154 Boylston Street. Photo by David Bohl, 1991.

The Massachusetts Historical Society

A Bicentennial History

1 7 9 1 – 1 9 9 1

Louis Leonard Tucker

1 9 9 5

Boston, Massachusetts

Published by the Society

DISTRIBUTED BY NORTHEASTERN UNIVERSITY PRESS, BOSTON

Library of Congress Cataloging-in-Publication Data

Tucker, Louis Leonard, 1927–
    The Massachusetts Historical Society : a bicentennial history,
1791–1991 / by Louis Leonard Tucker.
        p.   cm.
    Includes bibliographical references (p.   ) and index.
    ISBN 0-934909-68-7
    1. Massachusetts Historical Society—History.   I. Title.
F61.M43T83   1996
974.4'006—dc20   96-3155
                                                              CIP

Designed by David Ford

Published at the charge of the Publication Fund

This book is dedicated to

Jeremy Belknap

who valued history and loved

his native New England,

the United States of America,

and the

Massachusetts Historical Society.

Contents

Contents

Acknowledgments

UNLIKE A WORK of art, an historical publication is a cooperative enterprise. An author depends upon many others to achieve his goal. I was helped by a host of kind people and am pleased to acknowledge their assistance.

My largest debt was to the efficient staff of the Massachusetts Historical Society, who assisted me in numerous ways, from locating documents, books, and photographs, to deciphering difficult manuscripts. The following were especially helpful: Katherine Griffin, Brenda Lawson, Daniel McCormack, Richard Ryerson, Virginia Smith, Chris Steele, Celeste Walker, and Donald Yacovone.

Peter Drummey, Conrad E. Wright, and Henry Lee, president of the Society, made the ultimate sacrifice by consenting to read the entire manuscript. They provided me with an abundance of insightful critical comments, many of which I accepted. My son Professor Mark Tucker, of Columbia University, also reviewed the manuscript and offered sage advice on style and content.

I owe a special debt of gratitude to the Council of the Society for granting me a six-month sabbatical leave in 1993 so that I could be relieved of burdensome administrative duties and concentrate on writing this book.

In conjunction with my sabbatical, I benefited greatly from a five-month fellowship at the Huntington Library (San Marino, California), where the bulk of the manuscript was written. I offer my special thanks to President Robert A. Skotheim and Director of Research Robert (Roy) Ritchie of the Huntington Library for their many courtesies while I was at that heavenly site.

The following professional colleagues also assisted me in various ways: Rodney Armstrong, director of the Boston Athenaeum; Professor

Acknowledgments

Donald L. Greene of Piedmont College; Harley Holden, director of the Harvard University Archives; James Maloney, treasurer of the City of Cambridge; Professor Raymond Robinson of Northeastern University; Professor John A. Schutz (emeritus) of the University of Southern California; John C. Van Horne, director of the Library Company of Philadelphia; Ronald York of the Cambridge Public Library.

Finally, there are not words adequate to express my appreciation to Edward Hanson of the Society's Division of Publications, who edited this book. He uncovered and corrected errors in the text and footnotes, tightened and refined my bulky narrative, and made significant organizational changes, all of which considerably improved the work. Let it be understood, however, that, if there are still errors in the text and footnotes, structural weaknesses, or interpretive deficiencies, I alone bear the responsibility for these failings.

Preface

FOR THE NEARLY two hundred members and friends of the Massachusetts Historical Society who gathered in the handsome headquarters of the American Academy of Arts and Sciences in Cambridge on the balmy evening of May 17, 1991, to celebrate the organization's bicentennial, it was a time to reflect upon the Society's founding and small beginnings and its growth into one of the nation's premier research centers for the study of American history. The formal program that followed a reception and dinner focused upon the manifold achievements of the Society and its contributions to American historical scholarship. These themes were stressed by an array of distinguished speakers: former President Thomas Boylston Adams; the Reverend Peter Gomes, chaplain of Memorial Church, Harvard University; historians Bernard Bailyn and Oscar Handlin of Harvard University and Pauline Maier of the Massachusetts Institute of Technology; R. Michael Robbins, a former president of the Society of Antiquaries in London; and United States Senator Edward M. Kennedy.

Since it was an evening of high celebration, the speakers appropriately accentuated the positive, eliminated the negative, and remained in the realm of generalization. The fact is that none of the speakers, including the historians, was in a position to provide an incisive, detailed analysis of the institution's two-hundred-year history. To do so would have required research in a publication that traced the Society's history from 1791 to 1991, and no such study existed then.

This book is designed to correct that deficiency. It is intended not only for speakers at future commemorations but for current and future members and friends of the Society and for students of American cultural and educational history.

Let it be underscored that a history of the Massachusetts Historical

Preface

Society is not a provincial story. Through its incomparable library and publications, and the writings of its illustrious members, such as Jeremy Belknap, Francis Parkman, William Hickling Prescott, and Samuel Eliot Morison, the Society has made—and continues to make—a profound impact upon the cultural and educational history of the United States. Let it further be noted that the Society holds the distinction of being the first institution to collect Americana in a systematic manner and publish the basic sources of American history.

The Society holds one other distinction. It was the first historical society founded in the United States and, as such, is the precursor of the more than 10,000 historical societies currently operating. This fact alone connotes its significance to our national heritage.

Short Title List

Published works

A.A.S., *Procs.*
Proceedings of the American Antiquarian Society, 1812–1880; new ser. (1880/81-present).

Adams, *Autobiography*
Adams, Charles F., *Charles Francis Adams, 1835–1915, An Autobiography*. Boston, 1916.

Bentley, *Diary*
Bentley, William, *The Diary of William Bentley, D.D.*, 4 vols. Salem, Mass., 1905–1914.

Butterfield, "Ford, Editor"
Lyman H. Butterfield, "Worthington Chauncey Ford, Editor," M.H.S., *Procs.*, 83(1971):46–82.

Butterfield, "Papers of the Adams Family"
Lyman H. Butterfield, "The Papers of the Adams Family: Some Account of Their History," M.H.S., *Procs.*, 71(1953–1957):328–356.

Drummey, ed., "Bates-Riley Correspondence"
Peter Drummey, ed., " 'As If I Never Was Away': The Letters of Eleanor Bates to Stephen T. Riley, 1944–1945," M.H.S., *Procs.*, 104(1992):148–193.

Kirkland, *Adams*
Edward C. Kirkland, *Charles Francis Adams, Jr., 1835–1915: The Patrician at Bay*. Cambridge, Mass., 1965.

Landsberg, *John Dos Passos' Correspondence*
Melvin Landsberg, ed., *John Dos Passos' Correspondence with Arthur K. McComb; or "Learn to Sing the Carmagnole."* Niwot, Col., 1991.

M.H.S., *Colls.*
Collections of the Massachusetts Historical Society (1792-present).

M.H.S., *Procs.*
Proceedings of the Massachusetts Historical Society (1791–present).

Mitchell, *Handbook*
Stewart Mitchell, *Handbook of the Massachusetts Historical Society, 1791–1948*. Boston, 1949.

Short Title List

Nagel, *Descent from Glory*
>Paul C. Nagel, *Descent From Glory: Four Generations of the John Adams Family*. New York, 1983.

Nagel, "The Ice Age"
>Paul C. Nagel, " 'The Ice Age . . . Passed Away': Adams Family Meditations Upon Republican New England," in Conrad Edick Wright, ed., *Massachusetts and the New Nation*. Boston, 1992.

NEHGR
>*New England Historical and Genealogical Register* (1847-present).

Riley, *Years of Stewardship*
>*Stephen Thomas Riley: The Years of Stewardship*. Boston, 1976.

Russell, *Adams*
>Francis Russell, *Adams: An American Dynasty*. New York, 1976.

Schutz, *A Noble Pursuit*
>John A. Schutz, *A Noble Pursuit: The Sesquicentennial History of the New England Historic Genealogical Society, 1845–1995*. Boston, 1995.

Sibley's Harvard Graduates
>*Biographical Sketches of Those Who Attended Harvard College*, by John L. Sibley and Clifford K. Shipton. Boston and Cambridge, Mass., 1873–1975. 17 vols. to date.

Tucker, *Clio's Consort*
>Louis Leonard Tucker, *Clio's Consort: Jeremy Belknap and the Founding of the Massachusetts Historical Society*. Boston, 1990.

Van Tassel, *Recording America's Past*
>David D. Van Tassel, *Recording America's Past*. Chicago, 1960.

Wheeler, "Fifty Years"
>Warren Gage Wheeler, "Fifty Years on Boylston Street," M.H.S., *Procs.*, 78(1966):38–49. A limited edition of this work was printed at Dedham, Mass., in 1966.

Whitehill, *Independent Historical Societies*
>Whitehill, Walter M., *Independent Historical Societies: An Enquiry into Their Research and Publication Functions and Their Financial Future*. Boston, 1962.

Witness to America's Past
>*Witness to America's Past: Two Centuries of Collecting By the Massachusetts Historical Society*. Boston, 1991.

Manuscripts

C.F. Adams Papers
>Charles Francis Adams II (1835–1915) Papers, Massachusetts Historical Society.

Adams, "Random Sketches"
>John Adams, "Random Sketches Over Eighty Years," Part II, M.H.S., *Procs.*, vol. 72 (1957–1960), in Editorial Correspondence, Nov. 1959. M.H.S. Archives.

Bolton, Journal
>Journal of Charles K. Bolton, 13 vols., 1875–1950. Charles Knowles Bolton Papers, M.H.S.

Short Title List

Faÿ File
    The Case of Bernard Faÿ, 1943–1946, in the Stewart Mitchell Records, M.H.S. Archives
Ford-Lodge Correspondence
    Ford-Lodge Correspondence, in the Henry Cabot Lodge (1850–1924) Papers, M.H.S.
Mitchell Papers, Boston Athenaeum
    Stewart Mitchell Papers, 1839–1957. Boston Athenaeum, Boston, Mass.
Mitchell Records, M.H.S. Archives
    Stewart Mitchell Records, M.H.S. Archives

List of Illustrations

Frontispiece.

1154 Boylston Street, Boston, headquarters of the Massachusetts Historical Society

Following page 298

List of Illustrations

No historical society, I venture to say, has contributed more to the knowledge of the American past [than the Massachusetts Historical Society]. For two centuries the rich collections of this society have attracted students, nourished scholars, generated books, and nobly advanced the great adventure of history.

Arthur M. Schlesinger, Jr., "Text vs. Context," M.H.S., *Procs.*, 103(1991):1.

The truth is Massachusetts has always been remarkable for the number of its chroniclers, annalists and historical contributors. It is the only state in the Union which possesses elaborate histories contemporaneous in their authorship with all the epochs and incidents through which it has passed in two centuries and nearly a half. One is amazed to notice how large a proportion of all our existing literature of native production is historical—and how uniformly it is spread over all the years that lie between us and the beginnings of things here. Diaries, journals, and letter-books and pamphlets—sprinkled in between such books as Mather's, Hutchinson and Minot's Histories— afford us rich materials which leave but few gaps in our ancient records. From the beginning it is plain that Massachusetts was intended to have a History—and not a day has been passed by white men on this soil on which the pen has not recorded some event, experience or fact that has since been gathered by the annalist.

George E. Ellis to Rev. Samuel Osgood (New-York Historical Society, Domestic Corresponding Secretary), April 27, 1855 (New-York Historical Society manuscript collections).

The Massachusetts
Historical Society

A Bicentennial History

1791–1991

Chapter 1

Belknap
and the Beginning

THE MASSACHUSETTS Historical Society was founded in 1791 in Boston, but its origins can be traced to the rustic community of Dover, New Hampshire. There, in the early 1770s, the Reverend Jeremy Belknap, minister of that town's First Congregational Church, began research on what was to become a three-volume history of the Granite State. It was while undertaking this study that Belknap conceived the idea of an historical repository of Americana.[1]

Born in Boston on June 4, 1744, Belknap was a fifth-generation New Englander. He was educated in the classical tradition at the Boston Latin School and Harvard College, from which he graduated in 1762. Belknap's pious parents had pointed him in the direction of the Congregational ministry from birth, and the dutiful son, a serious, industrious youngster, willingly followed that path. "It has been my constant, habitual thought, ever since I was capable of judging," he wrote in 1766, "that I should preach the gospel." In 1767, after five years of teaching school and reading theology, he was called to the pulpit in Dover. He remained there for nearly twenty years, until late 1786.

Shortly after settling in Dover, Belknap decided to write a history of New Hampshire in his spare time. He proceeded "to learn what I can from printed books and manuscripts, and the information of aged and intelligent persons of the former state and affairs of this town and province."

---

[1] Information in this chapter not otherwise acknowledged is derived from Louis Leonard Tucker, *Clio's Consort: Jeremy Belknap and the Founding of the Massachusetts Historical Society* (Boston, 1990). The reader should consult this work for specific citations and for further details on Belknap's career as an historian and the founding of the Society.

The Massachusetts Historical Society

That Belknap should have undertaken such a study was not surprising. He had a love of history in general, and American history in particular. His intense interest can be attributed to at least four factors.

First and foremost, he was deeply influenced by his Puritan heritage, which placed a transcendent value on the study of human history. The Puritans had a profound historical sense, viewing their exodus from England in the early seventeenth century and subsequent settlement in Massachusetts as part of God's master plan for the human race. They regarded themselves as key participants in an epochal event of world history. In the well-known words of their leader, John Winthrop: "We must always consider that we shall be as a city upon a hill—the eyes of all people are upon us." Puritan parents emphasized this unique historical mission to their offspring, and the clergy reinforced the theme in their sermons, other public pronouncements, and counseling. Accordingly, Belknap developed an "inquisitive disposition in historical matters" and a "natural curiosity to enquire into the original settlement, progress and improvement of the country which gave him birth."

Young Belknap's minister at the Old South Church, the Reverend Thomas Prince, was a second major influence upon his historical conditioning. One of early New England's most accomplished historians, Prince had "a zeal of laying hold on every Book, Pamphlet, and Paper, both in Print and Manuscript," which might "have any Tendency to enlighten our History." He became Belknap's intellectual, as well as spiritual, preceptor. He transmitted his distinctive historical values to his protégé: a passion for factual accuracy; a penchant for original sources; a zeal for thorough research. Belknap later acknowledged his debt to his mentor, writing that he was "educated" by Prince, "whose memory he [Belknap] shall always revere." Prince was an omnivorous collector of books and manuscripts, "either pertaining to New England or pertaining to its History and Public affairs." Belknap, too, became a gatherer of historical materials relating to New England in his adult years.

Harvard College also played a role in stimulating Belknap's interest in history. The young scholar became an avid reader of historical works as he studied Greek, Roman, and European history. One of his favorite authors was Laurence Echard, the seventeenth-century English writer who specialized in Roman history. One Echard sentence, in particular, made a strong impression upon Belknap: "There are required so many

Belknap and the Beginning

Qualifications and Accomplishments in an Historian, and so much care and niceness in writing an History, that some have reckon'd it One of the Most Difficult Labours Human Nature is capable of.'' Belknap copied this statement in his commonplace book and, in later years, when someone demeaned historians or the writing of history, he cited it in refuting these charges.

Finally, the American Revolution and the powerful nationalistic surge that accompanied this event had a marked effect upon Belknap's historical conditioning. A young minister when the war broke out, he quickly developed into a "warm friend of the Revolution." He became a prominent member of New England's "black regiment," as the Loyalists and British referred to the pro-Revolution Congregational clergy. When the Americans achieved victory in 1783, Belknap celebrated along with the other Whigs. Subsequently, he became an ardent cultural nationalist, proclaiming the virtues of the fledgling nation and forecasting a glorious future for it. His historical writings, all of which related to the United States, were literary manifestations of his intense nationalism.

Soon after beginning research on his history of New Hampshire, Belknap realized he had undertaken a labor of vast dimensions. As a disciple of Prince, he was committed to using original sources, but there was no corpus of such materials in New Hampshire. No one had had the foresight, interest, or energy to collect documentary sources pertaining to New Hampshire's past and store them in a repository. Belknap had to travel throughout the province to locate relevant documents. This was an arduous task, requiring both time and finances beyond a minister's means. Nonetheless, Belknap made the effort. Deeply motivated, he was prepared to make sacrifices to achieve his goal. The Latin phrase *Nil magnum sine labore* (Nothing great is done without labor) served as his creed.

Whenever he could arrange it, Belknap traveled through New Hampshire and spent many hours in public offices and "in the garrets and rat-holes of old houses." He was doggedly persistent in his research. "I am willing even to scrape a dunghill," he wrote in 1783, "if I may find a jewel at the bottom."

Realizing that he did not have sufficient time to canvass the entire state, Belknap turned to an expedient Prince had employed while writing his history of New England. He composed and distributed a printed "circular," or questionnaire, to the "several Clergymen, and other gentlemen of public character" in New Hampshire. In a postscript, he appealed for documents and information relevant to his study. He also used the technique of oral history, interviewing "aged and intelligent" residents of the state and "many persons who have been employed in surveying, masting, hunting and scouting; as well as in husbandry, manufactures, merchandise, navigation and fishery."

Belknap's research experience convinced him of the critical need for an historical repository, not only in New Hampshire but elsewhere as well. He was keenly aware that Americans intent upon researching and writing history were seriously disadvantaged because of a lack of sources.

The young nation was not without libraries, but those few that existed held little of value to historical researchers. Most were subscription libraries, committed to collecting *belles lettres*, not historical source materials. Among these were the Library Company of Philadelphia, founded by Benjamin Franklin in 1731, the Library Company of Charleston, South Carolina, and New York Society Library. Even in New England, the most culturally advanced region of the United States, there were only three libraries of note: the Harvard and Yale college libraries, used almost entirely by the students and faculty, and the Redwood Library in Newport, Rhode Island, a subscription library. None of these concentrated on collecting primary historical sources.

The nation's two learned societies—the American Philosophical Society in Philadelphia and the American Academy of Arts and Sciences in Boston—both focused on discussions and publications, not on developing a library. Moreover, their principal interest was natural science, not history.

It was very different for European historians. In England, for example, researchers had access to the British Museum, the Royal Society, the Society of Antiquaries of London, British governmental offices, and the celebrated university libraries at Cambridge and Oxford. Continental scholars were similarly blessed with a rich supply of well-stocked repositories, from the Académie des Inscriptions et Belles Lettres in Paris to the Real Academia de la Historia in Madrid to the Royal Library in Berlin.

For Belknap, what really underscored the need for repositories in America was the rapid—and alarming—loss of important documents and other historical materials. He emphasized the crisis in a letter to

Belknap and the Beginning

John Adams in 1789: "The want of public repositories for historical materials as well as the destruction of many valuable ones by fire, by war and by the lapse of time has long been a subject of regret in my mind. Many papers which are daily thrown away may in future be much wanted, but except here and there a person who has a curiosity of his own to gratify, no one cares to undertake the collection and of this class of Collectors there are scarcely any who take care for securing what they have got together after they have quitted the stage."

Belknap was especially distressed by the losses of his native state over a period of years. Fires had destroyed the court house in Boston in 1747 and the Harvard College library in 1764; in both cases, nothing of historical value survived. A band of "patriots" had sacked Lt. Gov. Thomas Hutchinson's elegant home in Boston in 1765, during the Stamp Act crisis, scattering or destroying many valuable documents pertaining to Massachusetts's colonial era; Hutchinson had painstakingly collected these for use in his history of the Massachusetts Bay Colony. British troops had ransacked the Court of Common Pleas as they were preparing to evacuate Boston in 1776 and thrown numerous legal documents in the adjoining streets.

The most painful blow of all to Belknap was the damage sustained by Thomas Prince's incomparable collection called the "New England Library." After Prince's death, his books and manuscripts were stored in the steeple of the Old South Church, in the heart of the city. It was not an appropriate repository for this outstanding collection. Even before the Revolution, it had suffered the effects of neglect and unauthorized removals. Books and documents disappeared, and the remaining items fell into a state of disarray. Belknap informed a correspondent in 1774 that he intended to travel to Boston to consult "the papers of the late Mr. Prince, of which there is a vast number lying in a most shamefully chaotic state."

During the Revolution, British troops occupied the Old South Church and dispersed the "greater part" of Prince's "noble collection of manuscripts." Belknap blamed the king's soldiers for the "irretrievable loss," calling it a "sacrifice to British barbarity." Wrote Belknap: "Had we suffered it by the hands of Saracens, the grief had been less poignant."

While Belknap formulated the idea of an historical library during his residence in Dover, he had no intention of implementing his plan in that town. He knew it could not be done there. Dover was a provincial community with a population of only 1,600 residents. It lacked a sufficient nucleus of learned citizens who would use and support such a facility.

Then, too, Belknap held a low opinion of Dover and its inhabitants. He once described the area as "the semi-barbarous region of the North." In 1783, in a letter to a friend, he delivered this scathing indictment of Dover and its people:

> I have long thought, and do still think it one of the greatest misfortunes of my life to be obliged to rear a family of children in a place and among a people where insensibility to the interests of the rising generation, and an inveterate antipathy to literature, are to be reckoned among the prevailing vices; where there is not so much public spirit as to build a school-house; where men of the first rank let their children grow up uncultivated as weeds in the highway; where grand jurors pay no regard to their oaths; and where a judge on the bench has publicly instructed them to invent subterfuges and evasions to cheat their consciences and prevent the execution of the laws for the advancement of learning.

Belknap's disdain for Dover was undoubtedly linked to the severe problems he was experiencing in his ministry. His final decade there was a miserable period, both for him and for his parishioners. He engaged in a prolonged, bitter dispute with his church over his salary. By 1786, it was apparent to both pastor and parish that their differences were irreconcilable and a separation was in the best interest of both parties. Belknap applied for, and received, his release from the First Church. The following year, 1787, at the age of forty-two, he returned to Boston and became minister of the Long Lane Church. He was overjoyed to be back in his native town, and, no doubt, Doverites were glad to be rid of him.

After assuming his new position, Belknap continued to work on the history of New Hampshire. At the same time, he developed a renewed interest in the matter of establishing a repository. He was certain that the Boston area could sustain such a program. He concluded that the most expedient course of action was to append the facility to the Harvard College library in nearby Cambridge.

This was not a new idea for Belknap. He had projected a similar plan as early as 1774 in a draft of a letter to a close friend in Boston. Displaying remarkable prescience, he proposed that an effort be made to collect sources relevant to the growing Anglo-American controversy and that these be deposited in the college library for a "future historian."

Belknap and the Beginning

Belknap asserted "that the present Times exhibit so critical and important a Scene as must make a distinguished figure in the Eyes of posterity and thence arises a necessity that a properly authenticated Series of information impartially collected should descend to them." He further noted that there were in the "Libraries and Custody of Gentlemen of the present age many materials which are now neglected and which may soon be scattered the loss of which posterity may regret as much as we do now the carelessness of former Times."

Belknap also listed the items he regarded as having value for a future researcher:

> Political pamphlets, Newspapers, Letters, funeral and Election Sermons and many other papers which are now regarded only as beings of a day may if preserved give posterity a better idea of the Genius and Temper of the present age (and of our most material Transactions) than can be derived from any other source.

Since Belknap was then residing in Dover, he could not take an active role in the project he had proposed. For the effort to be successful, someone in Boston or its environs would have to organize and direct it. Such catalysts, however, were not in abundant supply, and Belknap's idea languished.

In 1780, at the height of the Revolution, Harvard officials sought to achieve what Belknap had suggested in 1774. The Board of Overseers voted that the Corporation should consider acquiring for the library "every thing that has been written that is worth preserving, relative to the present controversy between Great Britain and this country." But once again there was no subsequent action.

At this point, the Reverend William Gordon entered the proceedings. An English clergyman and Whig historian, Gordon had emigrated to the colonies in 1770 and in 1772 took a pulpit in nearby Roxbury. In 1775, "struck with the scenes that were opening upon the world," the far-sighted Gordon began to collect documents on the Anglo-American crisis. He believed he was witnessing one of the epochal historical events of his era and planned to write an account of it.

When the war finally erupted, Gordon proposed to the Harvard officials the exact plan Belknap had contemplated in 1774: the college should appoint a committee to collect "written and printed materials, for the use of some future historian, and deposit them in the library." The officials approved the scheme and urged Gordon to head the committee. A "bustling busybody," as John Adams described him, Gordon agreed to do it, but that became the extent of his involvement. It was a stillborn effort. When Gordon returned to England in 1786, the project once more was abandoned.

Harvard officials revived the plan again in 1787. Belknap, now a resident of Boston and serving on the Board of Overseers, sensed that he would be asked to direct the project:

> Some of the gentlemen in the government of the College are anxious to revive the matter; and, if they put it forward, I shall expect that part of the business will fall upon me, for I have often experienced that, where there is much labour and little profit, I am not out of employ; and you know there is a set of men who, when they see a person willing to work, will always put enough upon him to do.

Belknap's hunch proved correct. The officials "put it forward," and he accepted the assignment. Through the spring and summer of 1787 he worked diligently to acquire materials. On one occasion, he entered into negotiations with Ebenezer Hazard of New York City, an old friend, who was seeking to sell his extensive and significant collection of American newspapers and pamphlets. This would have formed an important base for the enterprise.

When Belknap submitted Hazard's proposed price to the college officials, they met him with indifference. He persisted, but there was still no response. Finally, he became exasperated. As he informed Hazard: "it was allowed to be an object worthy of attention, but no body seemed in earnest about prosecuting it—say and do you know are 2 things." And further: "I imagine it would be a long-winded, and perhaps ineffectual business, to set on foot a collection of dead materials for the use of a future historian. They acknowledge the utility of such a thing, and that is all."

Harvard's failure to act with dispatch and honor its stated intention apparently led Belknap to rethink the issue of a repository. Attaching this endeavor to the Harvard library appeared now to be unrealistic. Nor was there any other prospective institution in Boston or Cambridge to which an historical library could be linked.

Belknap discounted the American Academy of Arts and Sciences, which John Adams and a few other learned men had founded in Boston in 1780. As an active member of this organization, Belknap knew that its principal focus was upon natural history and the sciences, notwithstanding the statement in its charter that the Academy was also founded "to promote and encourage the Knowledge of the Antiquities of America." There was little likelihood that the Academy would establish a library to house historical sources.

Belknap concluded that the most sensible plan was to assemble a group of historically minded men from the Boston area and establish an independent organization, a "Society of Antiquarians." This was a vision much broader than the one he had held earlier. He now contemplated not only a library but a membership organization, much like the American Academy of Arts and Sciences or American Philosophical Society.

The model for this type of institution was located in Great Britain: the Society of Antiquaries of London, the oldest historical body in the world. Since Belknap was closely attuned to British cultural affairs, especially in London, there can be no question that he was familiar with the Society of Antiquaries. By the 1780s, it was well-known throughout Great Britain. The Society had a membership of nearly four hundred and shared quarters in newly rebuilt Somerset House, a "magnificent and noble structure," with two of London's most prestigious cultural organizations, the Royal Society and Royal Academy.

While its antecedents extended back to the late sixteenth century, the London Society really took root in the early eighteenth century. Beginning in 1707, a "few gentlemen, well-wishers to Antiquities," met weekly at various taverns in the Strand and along Fleet Street to engage in conversation about antiquarian matters. In time, they produced some publications, thereby strengthening their association. In 1753, the Society acquired its first permanent quarters, a library-cabinet room in Chancery Lane. The institution now began to take hold. Sponsoring meetings for its members, maintaining a library and cabinet, and publishing—these became the three staple elements of the London Society's agenda, and this is precisely what Belknap envisioned for the organization he sought to establish.

Belknap earnestly "wished that a beginning could be made," but events conspired against him. Throughout 1788 and 1789, his attention was diverted by two critical public issues: Shays's Rebellion and the ratification of the federal constitution in Massachusetts.

Shays's revolt shocked and terrified Belknap. It augured the disintegration of the United States and the end of the "noble experiment." He closely monitored developments in western Massachusetts and was elated when the troops of the Commonwealth, dispatched by Gov. James Bowdoin, suppressed the "insurgents" and quashed the rebellion.

The constitutional ratifying convention followed on the heels of the Shays episode. A Federalist, Belknap was an ardent supporter of the Constitution. His interest in this issue intensified when the convention decided to conduct its meetings in his commodious Long Lane Church. As the nominal host, Belknap was in almost constant attendance. He was a keen observer of this memorable historical proceeding. Reflecting his strong historical bent, he took notes on the debates; his document has become a prime source for the convention.

When these two momentous issues were resolved, Belknap again turned his thoughts to establishing an historical organization. In August 1789, John Pintard of New York City came to Boston on business and, in the course of his stay, met with Belknap. As later events would confirm, this meeting would have a profound effect upon the cultural and intellectual history of the United States.

A "lively, chearful" man of boundless energy and enthusiasm, Pintard was "one of the first characters of New York City." A "singular mixture of heterogeneous particles," he was a successful entrepreneur, a merchant prince who also engaged in a myriad of civic, cultural, and charitable activities. The consummate urban booster, he was constantly prodding and encouraging other wealthy merchants to contribute their time, talents, services, and funds to improve the cultural and intellectual life of New York City.

While his range of cultural interests was broad, Pintard had a particular "passion for American history." In this regard, he was a soul mate to Belknap. He, too, was an avid collector of documentary sources and aspired to be a writer of history. He, too, was deeply disturbed by the loss and wanton destruction of historical materials. During the American Revolution, he personally castigated the British troops who pillaged the King's College library in New York City. He, too, staunchly believed that primary sources were vital for the writing of first-rate history. In words strongly reminiscent of Belknap's view on the subject, Pintard wrote: "Without the aid of original records and authentic documents, history will be nothing more than a well-combined series of ingenious conjectures and amusing fables."

Pintard also shared Belknap's vision of founding an historical organization. He was intent upon establishing what he called an "American Antiquarian Society." Having heard of Belknap's plan from a mutual friend, Ebenezer Hazard, and having read and been impressed by his first volume of the history of New Hampshire, Pintard arranged to meet the minister-historian during his visit to Boston. It was a union of kindred spirits.

Neither man left an account of what they discussed, but references in Belknap's subsequent correspondence to friends suggest that, in addition to exchanging thoughts on American history, and books and authors, they talked about founding historical organizations in their respective cities. They also projected a broader conception, the establishment of similar programs in every state of the fledgling nation, in short, a national network of such facilities. Each would collect materials and sponsor publications. All would freely exchange their publications. The net result of such a system would be the diffusion of historical information throughout the United States. It was a bold vision, far in advance of its time.

The immediate goal was to make a beginning in Boston and New York City. Pintard was the first to set his plan in motion. Upon returning to New York City, he went to work, aided and abetted by one Gardiner Baker, also a man of many parts and enormous energy.

While wishing to establish an independent organization, Pintard took a more pragmatic approach and "engrafted an antiquarian scheme of a museum" upon a newly formed institution, the Sons of St. Tammany Society. Pintard had inspired the founding of this Society in 1789; Baker was also actively involved in the effort. At its creation, Tammany was merely a fraternal, patriotic, and social club with a pronounced democratic flavor; it was formed in response to the establishment of the aristocratic Society of Cincinnati. Tammany had not yet developed into a potent political organization.

Pintard and Baker established their appendage in June 1790.[2] They called it the "American Museum," rather than the "American Antiquarian Society," as Pintard had suggested earlier. Baker, who had a far different conception than Pintard, may have influenced the change of name. While he did not publicize it at this time, Baker was intent upon developing a facility that featured a collection of historical "curiosities" and oddments and attracted visitors willing to pay an admission fee to

[2] This was the first step in the founding of the New-York Historical Society, the early history of which is traced in Pamela Spence Richards, *Scholars and Gentlemen: The Library of the New-York Historical Society, 1804–1982* (New York, 1984).

view such displays. He had no interest in a library and historical research. The "snub-nosed, pock-pitted, bandy-legged, fussy, good-natured" Baker was, in reality, a precursor of Phineas T. Barnum, a master of hokum. If Pintard was aware of Baker's true intentions, he made no issue of them at this time. He was not likely to provoke a dispute since he was indebted to Baker for his assistance in persuading the more recalcitrant members of the Tammany Society that the museum was a worthwhile project and merited their financial support.

In Pintard's view, the principal purpose of the museum was to collect and preserve "whatever may relate to the history of our country, and serve to perpetuate the same, as also all American curiosities of nature and art." In a letter to Thomas Jefferson in 1790 requesting "supernumerary papers, Gazettes, etc." for his museum, Pintard stressed the historical orientation of the new facility: "The plan is a patriotic one and if prosecuted may prove a public benefit by affording a safe deposit for many fugitive tracts which serving the purpose of a day, are generally afterwards consigned to oblivion tho' ever so important in themselves, as useful to illustrate the manners of the time."

Even though the museum was as yet a facility in name only, Pintard began the laborious process of collecting historical materials. He deposited these in the Tammany's headquarters, the "Wigwam," a small, two-story structure on Broad Street in Lower Manhattan. He solicited contributions from friends and other potential donors. Belknap responded to his appeal with a gift of John Eliot's Indian Bible, a massive achievement of linguistic scholarship.

As the collection grew, there arose an inevitable need for larger quarters. In September 1790 the Society petitioned the Common Council for a room in City Hall. The Council quickly acceded to this request, consigning a room that was being vacated by the Federal Congress, then in the process of moving the capital from New York City to Philadelphia.

The American Museum became operational in the spring of 1791. Baker was appointed its keeper, a paid position. In June, the trustees drew up a set of laws and regulations. The museum opened its doors to visitors on Tuesday and Friday afternoons.

It soon became apparent to Pintard that his vision of the museum as an historical repository and center of research was in jeopardy with Baker at the helm. "New York's First Museum Proprietor, Menagerie Keeper, and Promoter Extraordinary" promptly took control of the fa-

Belknap and the Beginning

cility and began to develop it into a center of entertainment and a commercial peep show. In so doing, he subverted Pintard's attempt to found an historical society.

Why did not Pintard challenge Baker and fight for the implementation of his plan? As a trustee and secretary of the museum, he was well positioned to do so. In ordinary times, Pintard might have raised his voice in opposition to Baker's actions. But this was not an ordinary time. In late 1791, Pintard suddenly began to experience serious financial problems. Within a few months, he lost his entire fortune in a crash of stock speculations and was reduced to the status of a pauper. He was forced to flee New York City to avoid imprisonment. The character and future of the museum were no longer important to the beleaguered Pintard. Financial survival became his principal objective, leaving Baker a free hand in the operation of the museum.

Belknap fared much better in his effort to found an historical organization. In the months following his meeting with Pintard, he continued to discuss his plan with four Bostonians who shared his interest in American history and establishing a repository: John Eliot, Peter Thacher, William Tudor, and James Winthrop. Eliot, minister of the New North Church, was Belknap's closest friend and the cousin of his wife. Thacher, minister of the prestigious Brattle Street Church, had been a student of Belknap's when the latter had taught at Milton, prior to entering the ministry; he regarded Belknap as a "friend and father." Tudor, a leading lawyer of Boston, had trained in John Adams's law office and served as a judge advocate in the army during the American Revolution. Winthrop, a member of New England's most prominent family and the son of the eminent scientist-scholar, Professor John Winthrop of Harvard College, served as librarian of the Cambridge school. All four were Harvard graduates and relatively young: Eliot and Winthrop were thirty-seven, Thacher thirty-eight, and Tudor forty. Eliot, Thacher, and Winthrop also collected documents and were prospective donors to the proposed repository.

On August 27, 1790, Belknap prepared a draft of a "Plan of an Antiquarian Society." The late Julian Boyd, the distinguished historical editor and Jeffersonian scholar, called this plan "the charter of the historical society movement in the United States."

Belknap's momentous document contained a number of key provisions, which offer insight into his conception of the proposed organization. He wrote that the Society was to be formed for the purpose of "collecting and communicating the Antiquities of America." It is interesting to note that he first inserted "Historical" after "communicating" but then drew a line through it and added "the Antiquities of America." The final word, America, bears special significance since it connotes the national scope of the program. Belknap underscored this point in elaborating on the duties of members: each member "shall engage to use his utmost endeavors to collect and communicate to the Society manuscripts, printed books, and pamphlets, historical facts, biographical anecdotes, observations in natural history, specimens of natural and artificial curiosities, and any other matters which may elucidate the natural and political history of America from the earliest times to the present day."

As noted above, with its reference to collecting of "specimens of natural and artificial curiosities," Belknap's plan also embodied a museum component or "cabinet." But Belknap never intended to develop a museum designed to attract patrons who paid admissions, as Gardiner Baker had done. For Belknap, the cabinet was to be an adjunct and subordinate unit. The library was to be the heart of his organization; it was to be a research center.

Belknap also had definite ideas on membership. He affirmed that membership be limited to "not more than *seven at first*...." with a slight increase to follow. Both then and later, he held firmly to the conviction that the Society should have few members, and elect only those who had a sincere interest in the organization and would work to strengthen it. He had no patience for those who joined an organization and then made no contribution to it.

Belknap also reaffirmed the plan of a national network of societies that he and Pintard had discussed in their meeting one year earlier. The members of the Boston Society were to write "gentlemen in each of the United States requesting them to form similar societies and a correspondence shall be kept up between them for the purpose of communicating discoveries and improvements to each other." Each society was to publish periodic communications of a uniform size, and there would be a free exchange of these publications among all thirteen organizations.

For the next four months, there was no substantive progress. Belknap sought to initiate some movement but, for various reasons, his confreres were not able to focus on the project.

In early January 1791 there was a flurry of activity. Belknap was able to organize a meeting for January 24. He and his colleagues decided to invite five others as prospective members. These were: James Sullivan, the attorney general of the Commonwealth and an enthusiastic historian in his spare time; George Richards Minot, who had published two reputable historical treatises on the Commonwealth and Shays's Rebellion; Thomas Wallcut, an eccentric bachelor and ardent bibliophile, who had amassed an enormous collection of historical works, especially pamphlets; the Reverend James Freeman of King's Chapel, the first Unitarian church in the New World; and Dr. William Baylies, a physician of Dighton, who "delighted much in fictitious history."

All agreed to participate in the enterprise. Belknap asked Minot and Sullivan to prepare a draft of a constitution for circulation among the group prior to the meeting. The official founding would take place at this gathering.

On January 24, eight of the ten assembled at Tudor's imposing home on present-day Court Street, then called Prison Row. The first order of business was to select officers. It was not a competitive election. The selection was by mutual agreement, and all eight were assigned positions of authority. The group chose Sullivan for the presidency.[3] Tudor became treasurer, Eliot assumed the dual position of librarian-cabinet keeper, and Thacher, Winthrop, and Minot were placed on the "Annual Committee." Belknap took the position of corresponding secretary. The officers were not to be compensated for their services, as this was to be a purely voluntary effort.

The next item of business was the constitution. The preamble set forth the purposes of the Society:

The preservation of books, pamphlets, manuscripts and records, containing historical facts, biographical anecdotes, temporary projects, and beneficial

---

[3] A native of Berwick, Maine, and of Irish Catholic parentage, Sullivan studied law with his brother and later practiced law in Maine and Massachusetts. He received an honorary degree from Harvard in 1780. He was an amateur historian, specializing in legal history. After a long career as attorney general of the Commonwealth, he was elected governor and served from 1807 to 1808. For further biographical data on Sullivan, see Thomas C. Amory, *Life of James Sullivan*, 2 vols. (Boston, 1859); M.H.S., *Colls.*, 2d ser., 1(1818):252–254.

speculations, conduces to mark the genius, delineate the manners, and trace the progress of society in the United States, and must always have a useful tendency to rescue the true history of this country from the ravages of time, and the effects of ignorance and neglect.

A collection of observations and descriptions in natural history and topography, together with specimens of natural and artificial curiosities, and a selection of every thing which can improve and promote the historic knowledge of our country, either in a physical or political view, has long been considered as a desideratum; and as such a plan can be best executed by a society whose sole and special care shall be confined to the above objects: We the subscribers do agree to form such an institution, and to associate for the above purposes.

Membership was a sensitive issue since there was a divergence of opinion among the eight founders. Belknap and Eliot favored a mere handful, while others urged broader representation. They finally decided on a maximum of thirty resident (from the Commonwealth of Massachusetts) and thirty corresponding members.

For Belknap, a prospective member had to fulfill two criteria: he had to have a deep-seated interest in the Society and its mission; and he had to devote time, energy, and financial resources to the organization. Belknap preferred "doers" to "joiners." Shortly after the founding of the Society, when additional members were being considered, Belknap exhorted his colleagues to select only those disposed to "become active workers in that field; in order that it should not be tempted to elect members for the sake of bestowing upon them *a feather*, and become pursy and heavy by numbers, without proportionate activity, and power of progress."

John Eliot, another founder who vibrated in tune with Belknap on every aspect of the Society, echoed his sentiment in a letter to Benjamin Trumbull of Connecticut on December 11, 1790: "We have added five Members, and mean to increase our number still, tho' never to exceed 25. . . . By making the number extensive, or very *honourable*, it may be less useful. By *honourable* . . . I mean such members as are chosen into other Societies merely to do honor unto the institution, or to receive honor from it. Every person shall be under obligations to assist in the business of the Society." Belknap and Eliot projected the ideal. Only a few new members, however, met their standards.

The founders next established a dues structure. There was to be a $5 admission fee for resident members and annual dues of $2. A resident member could become a life member, and be exempt from annual dues, by paying an additional $34. There were to be no financial assessments for corresponding members. This was to be an honorific designation.

It should be noted that the constitution deviated from Belknap's skeletal plan in a number of important ways. The most significant difference was in the choice of title. Belknap's "Antiquarian Society" was replaced by "The Historical Society," although this alteration assuredly had Belknap's approval. The change in title was prompted by the group's determination to provide a direct historical focus to the newly-founded organization and to draw a sharp distinction between themselves and the American Academy of Arts and Sciences. In his letter to Benjamin Trumbull, John Eliot affirmed the group's decision to stress its historical mission by naming the nascent organization "the Historical Society, because it comprehends every thing relating to this country,—its antiquities, its history, civil, natural, and ecclesiastical. We confine our attention here, and hence are we different from the Academy and other literary societies. To pursue one particular subject is the only way of succeeding. We mean to confine our attention to this business of collecting things which will illustrate the history of our country."

"We have now formed our Society," a pleased Belknap notified Ebenezer Hazard on February 19, 1791, "and it is dubbed, not the Antiquarian, but the 'Historical Society.' It consists at present of only 8, and is limited to 25.[4] We intend to be an active, not a passive, literary body; not to lie waiting, like a bed of oysters, for the tide (of communication) to flow in upon us, but to seek and find, to preserve and communicate literary intelligence, especially in the historical way. We are not, however, quite ripe for action."

---

[4] There are two inexplicable errors in Belknap's statement. The organization consisted of 10, not 8 members; and, according to the "regulations" voted at the first meeting, membership was not to exceed 30 members.

Chapter 2

Building
a Good Repository

THE FIRST objective of the founders of the fledgling organization was to gather a collection of historical materials, but this required them to consider a permanent headquarters to house a library and also serve as a meeting site. Conducting business in the homes of the officers, as they originally did, could only be a temporary expedient. For the present, though, a modest-sized room was sufficient to fulfill both goals.

At their first meeting, the founders appointed a standing committee and charged it with the responsibility of finding permanent quarters. Lacking funds to purchase or rent a building, they had to appeal to likely benefactors. Their first target was the state government. At its second formal sitting, the Society appointed a small delegation to meet with the governor and the lieutenant governor, to apprise them of the founding of the organization and its "views and designs," and to solicit their aid in securing an "apartment." The record does not show whether or not this meeting took place.

At the same time, the Society appealed to the Massachusetts Bank for assistance with its housing needs.[1] This effort was successful. Founded in 1784 by a handful of Boston entrepreneurs, the bank occupied a "handsome large brick building" called the Manufactory, located in the center of the city at the northeast corner of Hamilton Place and Tremont Street,

---

[1] On the early history of the bank, see: Ben Ames Williams, Jr., *Bank of Boston 200: A History of New England's Leading Bank, 1784–1984* (Boston, 1984), 3–24; N.S.B. Gras, *The Massachusetts First National Bank of Boston, 1784–1934* (Cambridge, Mass., 1937), passim.

opposite the Granary Burial Ground.[2] The structure originally had been built for the manufacture of linen, "which was begun here with a spirit exerted too violently to continue long"—and it did not, surviving for only "three or four years." Subsequently, worsted hose and other products were made there, but these, too, were short-lived enterprises.[3]

After purchasing the building in 1784 for its headquarters, the bank undertook a complete renovation, from cellar to roof, and added a vault and other essential accessories—"a midling sized Bell," for example, "in case of Fire or an attempt to rob the Bank."

The bank's directors already had displayed a degree of civic concern for eleemosynary groups, as well as a keen sense of public relations, by permitting the Medical Society to meet in the "Stockholders Chamber" four times a year, provided such gatherings did not "interfere with any Business of the Bank." They also responded positively to the Historical Society's appeal, allowing the members free use of its "Chamber over the Directors Room." They set forth only two conditions: the Society could "have recourse thereto only in Bank hours" and it was responsible for furnishing the room.[4]

The Society quickly accepted this offer and moved the donations received from the founders into the room on June 30, 1791.[5] This marked the beginning of the library and cabinet. Next it took steps to furnish the room. Dipping into its meager treasury, which held only the admittance fees and annual dues of the founders, the Society purchased "twelve chairs, a plain pine table painted, with a draw & lock & key, also an Inkstand."[6] The cost was 4 pounds, 16 shillings; or $16.

The Society remained in the Manufactory for only one year. The

---

[2] The Manufactory House is depicted in *Here We Have Lived: The Houses of the Massachusetts Historical Society* (Boston, 1967); all the other homes of the Society, including 1154 Boylston Street, also are shown in this picture book, which was published by the Society.

[3] For a description of the Manufactory House, see M.H.S., *Colls.*, 1st ser., 3(1794):252–253.

[4] Gras, *First National Bank*, 252, 343.

[5] M.H.S., *Procs.*, 1(1791–1835):13. Judge William Tudor may have been instrumental in persuading the bank's directors to permit the Society to use the library. He became one of its directors in 1792.

[6] M.H.S. Recording Secretary Minutes, June 30, 1791 (M.H.S. Archives). One of these chairs still survives. See, *Witness to America's Past: Two Centuries of Collecting by the Massachusetts Historical Society* (Boston, 1991), 38–39.

bank's directors, feeling compelled to relocate to State Street—then the center of the city's fast-growing commercial, banking, and insurance industries—decided to convert the Manufactory into residential apartments. Accordingly, on May 29, 1792, they notified the Society that its stockholders "can no longer accommodate the Society with a room for their Library &c."[7]

Forced to move, the Society in June 1792 rented a small room in the northwest corner of the attic of stately Faneuil Hall.[8] Below were the spacious chamber which served as a town hall for Bostonians and a room used as an office by the city's selectmen. At the base of the building was the bustling public market, including the odorous meat market, sausage racks and all. The Society's apartment was an inadequate facility, small and difficult to reach. In the judgment of a contemporary, its location was "as retired and recondite as explorers into the recesses of antiquity could think of visiting." Because of this, most meetings were held in the homes of members.[9] The Society could not hope to flourish in such a poor physical setting.

The Society's stay in Faneuil Hall was also brief, less than two years. But, another opportunity for housing providentially surfaced and the Society was quick to grasp it.

On December 31, 1793, William Scollay, Charles Bulfinch, and Charles Vaughan, three prominent Bostonians then engaged in constructing the Tontine Crescent, a sizable real estate development on present Franklin Street between Hawley and Devonshire streets, notified President James Sullivan by letter: "In erecting the centre building of the Crescent it was our intention to accommodate the Historical Society with a convenient room. We now request you to communicate

---

[7] M.H.S., *Procs.*, 1(1791–1835):35; Gras, *First National Bank*, 355.

[8] For the early history of Faneuil Hall, see Abram English Brown, *Faneuil Hall and Faneuil Hall Market or Peter Faneuil and His Gift* (Boston, 1900). There is no available information on the size of the Society's room.

[9] Years later, in an address before the Society, Edward Everett stated that the Society met in the office of Judge George R. Minot in its first two years. The fact that Everett had the Society first quartered in Faneuil Hall and next in the Manufactory leads to the conclusion that his research on the history of the early years was faulty. See Edward Everett, "Anecdotes of Early Local History," *Orations and Speeches on Various Occasions* (Boston, 1850), 2:107–108.

to the Society, at their next meeting, our offer of the upper apartment in its present state with the addition of stairs and windows." The developers set forth but two minor conditions: the Society must pay a token fee of five shillings to occupy the room "for ever"; and the Society was responsible for finishing and furnishing the chamber.[10]

Here was a handsome offer. For all practical purposes, the Society was to receive free quarters in perpetuity in what was planned to be the most beautiful and fashionable residential complex in eighteenth-century Boston and the United States. This was the "first architectural crescent in the New World."[11]

While Scollay and Vaughan were key agents in this ambitious real estate scheme, Bulfinch was the mainspring of the venture.[12] The former two, both merchants, were essentially speculators. Their prime objective was a liberal return upon their investment. Bulfinch's main motivation was aesthetic. He was intent upon transforming provincial Boston into the most beautiful city in America. His model was mid-Georgian London. A self-taught architect, Bulfinch was original, daring, and endowed with excellent taste. The Tontine Crescent, which he alone designed, was an essential part of his grand conception. It was also Bulfinch who had proposed the novel idea of devoting the two rooms of the central pavilion to public purposes. This was perhaps the first time in American history that a private real estate developer committed a portion of his project to a public cultural use.

While on an eighteen-month architectural study tour of Europe, Bulfinch had observed the crescent form in Bath, England (Wood's "Circles"), and in London, where the Adam brothers had designed two half circles of connecting houses as an extension to Portland Place in the Belgravia section. Returning to Boston in 1787, the soon-to-be "architect of Federal Boston" embarked upon his innovative project.

The Tontine Crescent was Bulfinch's first major architectural project

[10] M.H.S., *Procs.*, 1(1791–1835):58n., 65; M.H.S. Corresponding Secretary, letterbook, 22 (M.H.S. Archives).

[11] Harold and James Kirker, *Bulfinch's Boston: 1787–1817* (New York, 1964), 54.

[12] On Bulfinch's life and architectural career, see ibid., and Charles A. Place, *Charles Bulfinch: Architect and Citizen* (Boston, 1925).

and one of his loveliest creations.[13] Building on land recently reclaimed from a swamp, Bulfinch began construction of sixteen brick houses, three stories in height, shaped in the form of a semicircle. The complex was to be 480 feet in length. In front of these elegant row houses, he laid out a 300-foot-long, grassy open space, which was 100 feet wide at the center and 50 feet wide at the ends. Surrounding this embellishment were trees and a large chain fence. The park was "supposed to serve the purposes of health by purifying the air, at the same time that it adds a natural ornament to artificial beauty." Bulfinch's ultimate plan was to construct a second and complementary crescent on the north side of the park so as to complete the ellipse, but this did not materialize.[14]

The central pavilion of the Crescent, under which was an archway for the passage of carriages, contained two rooms. They were forty feet long, twenty-five feet wide, and twenty feet high. It was the upper chamber that Bulfinch had earmarked for the Society.[15]

At a special meeting on January 11, 1794, Sullivan notified the members of the developers' offer, which they hastily accepted. Wrote Sullivan: "nothing could be more congenial to our wishes, or acceptable to our interest, than the generous offer you have made."[16] A deed was drawn up and approved by both parties on May 1.[17] The Society held its first meeting in the Tontine Crescent on June 11. The Reverend William Bentley of Salem visited the Society on February 16, 1795, and provided a description of the work still underway on the Society's "apartment, which is to be finished in a Square. Several natural Curiosities are already collected, and a foundation is laid for a good Library upon the plan of their institution. The principal Books respecting America have

[13] For contemporary descriptions of the Tontine Crescent, see *Columbian Centinel*, July 6, July 31, Nov. 23, Dec. 4, 1793; *Massachusetts Magazine*, 6(1794):67; *Boston Directory* (1796), 6. See also Amory, *James Sullivan*, 1:357–358; and *Old-Time New England* 36(1945):2–4, 37(1947):60–66.

[14] While an aesthetic success, the project became Bulfinch's financial downfall, forcing him into bankruptcy. See Kirker and Kirker, *Bulfinch's Boston*, 66–69; Place, *Bulfinch*, 56–75.

[15] The lower room was reserved for the Boston Library Society, which was founded in 1794 and by 1817 had acquired 5,000 volumes. See Kirker and Kirker, *Bulfinch's Boston*, 215–216.

[16] M.H.S., *Procs.*, 1(1791–1835):58–59n.

[17] The "substance" of the deed is printed in M.H.S., *Procs.*, 1(1791–1835):65n.

already been collected but their number is small. Piles of Gazettes afford the eye little entertainment. Their table is of an oval form and suits the general appearance of the Room."[18] The Society would remain in these quarters for the next thirty-nine years.[19]

Two days before it received the offer of space in the Crescent, the Society had appointed a committee to draw up an act of incorporation and present it to the General Court at its next session. Apparently President Sullivan, then serving as attorney general of the Commonwealth and concerned about the non-legal status of the Society, proposed this action. The committee, headed by Sullivan, drafted the bill, which the legislature passed with dispatch and which Gov. Samuel Adams approved on February 19, 1794.[20]

The most significant change effected by the act of incorporation was the alteration of the Society's name: the "Historical Society" became the "Massachusetts Historical Society." Another revision involved increasing the limit of resident members from thirty to sixty.[21] The wordy statement of purpose of the original constitution was reduced to a pithy: "Whereas the collection & preservation of materials for a political and natural history of the United States is a desireable object, and the institution of a Society for those purposes will be of public utility." The annual income from any real estate held by the Society could not exceed £500, and its personal estate, excluding its historical holdings, could not exceed the value of £2,000. The act also provided that members of both houses of the legislature could "have free access to the Library and Museum."[22]

Perhaps for symbolic reasons, the Society held its first meeting, as a newly incorporated body, in the senate chamber of the Old State House.

---

[18] *The Diary of William Bentley, D.D.*, 4 vols. (Salem, Mass., 1905–1914), 2:127.

[19] On July 13, 1801, a grateful Society expressed its appreciation to Bulfinch by electing him a resident member and waiving his admission fee and annual dues. M.H.S., *Procs.*, 1(1791–1835):143–144.

[20] The petition was submitted to the House on Jan. 21 and received its first reading on Jan. 31. After its third reading on Feb. 7, it passed to the Senate to be engrossed. On Feb. 12 the Senate passed the bill to be engrossed with an amendment and returned it to the House. The House then read the amended bill and passed it to be enacted on Feb. 17 (House Journal and Senate Journal, Massachusetts State Archives).

[21] There was no reference to corresponding members in the act; the 1791 constitution provided for a maximum of thirty corresponding members.

[22] *Acts and Resolves of Massachusetts, 1792–1793.* Acts, 1793—Chapter 36. Approved Feb. 19, 1794.

The main business was electing a slate of officers. Sullivan and his fellow officers of the *ancien regime* retained their positions; Sullivan held the presidency from 1791 to 1806.[23]

The act of incorporation granted the Society authority to make "orders and by-laws for governing its members and property." The Society promptly established a committee to draw up "laws and regulations," and these were adopted at the June 11 meeting at the Tontine Crescent.

Securing a headquarters, achieving incorporation, fashioning a comprehensive set of by-laws and regulations for the administration of the Society and the library—these were fundamental foundation stones in establishing a solid base for the institution. But the two essential building blocks were the library-museum and the publications program. For the Society to grow and prosper, these two vital components had to be successful. Otherwise, it would be nothing more than a discussion group.

Jeremy Belknap assumed responsibility for accomplishing both objectives. He devoted the remaining six and one-half years of his life to these tasks. The founder also became the master builder of the Society.

When planning the Society, Belknap had proposed to the nine fellow founders that each donate materials from his personal historical collections to establish a nucleus for the library. The materials Belknap had in mind were historical sources, such as books, pamphlets, manuscripts, maps, broadsides—that is, paper materials. These items were of paramount importance to him.

Belknap also was committed to establishing a museum or cabinet. As a son of the Enlightenment, he implicitly believed in the unity of all knowledge. History was simply one branch of a universal science. The purpose clause in the Society's constitution of 1791 underscored the need to collect "specimens of natural and artificial curiosities," in addition to "books, pamphlets, manuscripts, and records." "Historical knowledge" embraced a "physical or political view."[24] Thus, Belknap

[23] The Rev. William Bentley wrote in Sept. 1808 that the Federalist-dominated membership of the Society "thrust" the Jeffersonian-Republican Sullivan from the presidency and voted in Christopher Gore, who served as governor from 1809 to 1810 (Bentley, *Diary*, 3:38).

[24] M.H.S., *Procs.*, 1(1791–1835):2.

approved the collecting of ostrich eggs, shark jaws, a "very large Fla-mingo," and other oddities of the natural realm. But in his personal scale of values as an historian, such materials were of secondary importance. In his own work he drew exclusively from paper sources.

All but one of the ten founders made contributions to the library. Perhaps wishing to lead by example, Belknap made the most substantial donation. He gave a number of books and a large body of manuscripts, many of which he had collected during his years in Dover while re-searching his *History of New Hampshire*. Some of the manuscripts dated from the seventeenth century, but most were eighteenth-century documents, such as the correspondence of Gov. William Shirley of Mas-sachusetts, Governors Benning and John Wentworth of New Hamp-shire, and Gen. William Pepperrell, the hero of the Louisbourg campaign of 1745. By any standard, the gifts of Belknap and the other founders represented an impressive base for the library. Once this cornerstone was established, Belknap embarked upon a one-man crusade to enlarge the collection. As he wrote: "Let it be remembered that this Society is formed, not for the purpose of *waiting* for communications, but that the spirit of the Society is *active*." Belknap best summarized his aggressive collecting attitude in 1795: "There is nothing like having a *good repos-itory*, and keeping a *good look-out*, not waiting at home for things to fall into the lap, but prowling about like a wolf for the prey."[25]

Belknap's quest had no geographical limits. It extended from Boston to Europe and beyond. Residents of the Boston area became his primary targets. He badgered members of the Society and every local figure who either had participated in significant historical events or had achieved a degree of historical eminence, from John, Abigail, and Samuel Adams to John Hancock and Paul Revere.

As corresponding secretary of the Society, he maintained a close contact with all corresponding members living outside of Massachusetts. His frequent letters to these distinguished men, who resided in every section of the nation and a few foreign countries, almost always included an appeal for donations to the library. Belknap himself had nominated many of these men for membership, and it is apparent that his selections

[25] Belknap to Ebenezer Hazard, Aug. 21, 1795. Printed in M.H.S., *Colls.*, 5th ser., 3:356–357.

were based upon their capability to provide gifts for the library, either from personal holdings or through solicitation of others—or both.

Belknap also targeted congressional officials for donations to the library. He was intent upon adding federal documents to the collection. He made requests to the United States Congress for copies of "printed acts, journals, reports, treaties, letters, proceedings of courts-martial and other papers relative to the public affairs of the United States, civil and military, foreign and domestic." He then reinforced these appeals by writing to congressmen who were members of the Society, imploring them to monitor his requests and make certain they were implemented.

Belknap also cast his net to Europe. From his days in Dover, he had carried on a brisk correspondence with learned men in Great Britain, and with the German bibliophile Christoph Daniel Ebeling of Hamburg. The Society received a number of gifts from these sources.

Belknap's relationship with Ebeling was especially productive. The German scholar had become enamored of the United States and taught a course on the history of the new nation. In preparation for writing a history and geography of the United States, which took him over twenty years to complete, he had amassed a vast collection of Americana, one of the largest private holdings in the world at that time.

Belknap regarded Ebeling as a prime potential donor. He arranged to have him elected a corresponding member, serving as his sponsor, and then set out to reduce his library. He was not a subtle solicitor. Over a period of years, Ebeling made some notable contributions to the Society but retained the bulk of his holdings, much to Belknap's dismay. After Ebeling's death in 1817, his remarkable collection was auctioned off and came to rest in Massachusetts—but in Cambridge, not Boston. Israel Thorndike, a wealthy Boston merchant, outbid the king of Prussia, acquiring the library for $6,500 and donating it to Harvard College.

In his solicitations to correspondents, members and non-members, Belknap inserted a "Circular Letter of the Historical Society." This was a printed document containing a prefatory segment that explained the Society and its purposes, a detailed questionnaire requesting basic historical information on the community in which the recipient resided, and an appeal for contributions to the library-museum: "Any books, pamphlets, manuscripts, maps or plans which may conduce to the accomplishment of the views of the Society; and any natural or artificial productions which may enlarge its museum, will be accepted with thanks."

Belknap's "Circular Letter" was patterned after a questionnaire the Reverend Thomas Prince had devised and distributed in the early eighteenth century when he was writing his *Chronological History of New England*. Because of his close relationship with Prince in his youth, Belknap was familiar with the minister's tactic for compiling historical data and materials. He also had employed this technique successfully in New Hampshire when he began research on the early history of the Granite State. He sent a similar questionnaire to "men of learning" throughout the state. Since there was no historical society in Dover, Belknap kept custody of the materials sent to him. They became his personal property. Prince had done likewise, which accounts for his incomparable New England Library.

Belknap (and the Society) produced two editions of the "Circular Letter," the first in 1791 and the second in 1795. While he designed them for "every Gentleman of Science in the Continent and Islands of America," he also sent them to European correspondents and, in the judgment of one authority, "to persons almost at the ends of the earth." All he sought from non-American correspondents was a positive response to his request for donations to the library-museum.

Was the "Circular Letter" a successful device? The frequent gifts to the library from donors from all areas of the nation and western Europe, which were reported at Society meetings, strongly suggest that Belknap's tactic was a resounding success.

In sum, Belknap's role in building a base for the Society's historical warehouse was of major dimensions. While it is not possible to quantify the full extent of his contributions, one statistic pertaining to his personal benefaction illustrates his impact upon this facility. Of the 1,010 items listed in the Society's printed *Catalogue* of the library in 1796, Belknap personally contributed 171, or nearly 15 percent.

Belknap's voluminous correspondence with historically-minded men in other states not only led to the acquisition of gifts for the library. It also enhanced the Society's reputation as the first among American historical societies. Thus, when these men contemplated forming their own societies in the early nineteenth century, they turned to the Boston organization for advice and direction, soliciting a copy of its charter, rules and regulations, and an outline of its views and purposes.[26]

Building a library was a relatively simple task, once a storage facility had been acquired. Many people were willing to emulate the founders and donate items to the collection. There was no financial outlay involved in this type of philanthropy.

Launching a publications program, however, was a more difficult undertaking. For this the Society needed hard cash. Where would the Society get these discretionary funds? How could it sustain such an expensive enterprise over a period of years?

There were other niggling problems. What types of publications should the Society produce? Who would do the editorial work? What would its content be, its format? What would appeal to a Boston audience? Who would serve as printer and distributor?

Belknap did not have answers to all of these questions, but he did have a clear conception of the nature of his proposed publication. First and foremost, he intended to print transcriptions of manuscripts acquired by the Society. He was profoundly concerned about the preservation of historical information contained in these one-of-a-kind sources. He also knew that libraries could be destroyed by fires or natural disasters, or their holdings depleted by the "ravages of unprincipled or mercenary men"; he had witnessed the destruction wrought upon Thomas Prince's priceless collection in the Old South Church by British soldiers during the Revolution.

Belknap believed that printing was the best way to preserve documentary information. As he wrote in 1792: "There is no sure way of preserving historical records and materials, but by *multiplying the copies*. The art of printing affords a mode of preservation more effectual than Corinthian brass or Egyptian marble; for statues and pyramids which have long survived the wreck of time, are unable to tell the names of their sculptors, or the date of their foundations." "Multiply the copies" became the clarion call. If this were done, future historians would never be lacking in documentary sources.

Belknap also had a secondary motive: the desire to disseminate historical information among the general populace in Boston. As an ardent

[26] See Leslie W. Dunlap, *American Historical Societies, 1790–1860* (Madison, Wisc., 1944), 10–11, 127.

cultural nationalist of the first order, he believed that every citizen should have full knowledge of how the United States began and developed. They would acquire this knowledge, in his view, by reading documents of the past. As he wrote in 1792: "Not only names, dates, and facts may be thus handed down to posterity; but principles and reasonings, causes and consequences, with the manner of their operation, and their various connexions, may enter into the mass of historical information."

But how to achieve his objective? The practical problems seemed insuperable. Then, in late 1791, a development took place that offered him an opportunity to realize his plan. His son, Joseph, and Alexander Young, another young Bostonian, pooled their meager financial resources, established a printing firm, and announced that they planned to publish a weekly periodical to be called the *American Apollo*.

Coincidental with this announcement, Jeremy proposed to the Society that it should make an arrangement with the printers to prepare a 4- to 8-page historical supplement to the periodical containing transcriptions of manuscripts from its library. He volunteered to select and prepare the documents for publication. In sum, he would serve as the editor of the supplement—without compensation, of course.

Belknap may not have regarded a newspaper supplement as the ideal historical publication, but he was a realist and knew that this was the only available option. Besides, he had a broader plan in mind. He foresaw other ways in which the newspaper could bring benefits to the Society, exclusive of the supplement. He could use it to promote all the activities of the Society. For example, he would be able to insert appeals for donations to the library-museum in the main segment of the journal. And when gifts were made, he could acknowledge them, listing both the contribution and donor. Belknap had a keen sense of public relations and a perceptive understanding of human nature. He knew that most people liked to see their names in print.

The Society readily approved Belknap's plan and, shortly thereafter, consummated the deal with the printers. Believing that this partnership would lead to an appreciable increase in subscriptions, the printers agreed to underwrite the cost of the supplement and provide the Society with fifty complimentary copies. They set an annual charge of $2 for a subscription to the enlarged publication.

The project began with a rush. Over 1,200 Bostonians, an unusually large number for that period, subscribed to the innovative journal, which had been heavily promoted by Belknap and other Society members.

The first issue of *American Apollo* appeared on January 6, 1792. For his initial offering in the supplement, Belknap selected a set of documents pertaining to the Cape Breton expedition of 1745 and the capture of Louisbourg, the vaunted French fortress. He described this episode as "one of the most remarkable events in the history of this country."

It was an excellent choice of subject matter and shrewd marketing strategy on Belknap's part. He pandered to provincial pride. For nearly half a century, Massachusetts residents had gloried in this legendary victory over the hated French. The feat had been achieved by a colonial American force consisting largely of Massachusetts troops.

The Cape Breton issue was well received by subscribers, but subsequent supplements failed to stimulate, much less excite, readers. The public could not generate overwhelming enthusiasm for documents relating to such subjects as "Morrell's *Nova-Anglia*" (1625), "Births and Deaths in the third precinct of Brookfield," and "A Trip to Niagara, 1792." The basic weakness of the publication was obvious: a reader's interest could not be sustained by a random assortment of documents. The public craved a "regular history of America," not documentary snippets.

Interest in the supplement rapidly waned. Within three months, subscriptions dropped 50 percent. The supplement became a financial albatross to the printers, and soon tensions developed between them and the Society. Relations also became strained between the printer-partners, with Joseph wishing to continue the relationship despite the financial loss and his partner opting to break with the Society.

The constant feuding of the printer-partners led to a predictable split up in May 1792. Joseph Belknap purchased the interest of his disgruntled colleague and joined forces with Thomas Hall, another printer.[27]

In January 1793, the Society appointed a two-man committee, consisting of the Reverend James Freeman and John Eliot, "to procure to be bound . . . twenty copies of the first volume of the Collections."[28] With this 288-page tome was born the *Collections* series, which eventually

---

[27] This union was also short-lived, and in July 1794 Joseph bought out this partner as deficits continued to mount.

[28] M.H.S., *Procs.*, 1(1791–1835):49.

became one of the seminal sources for the study of American history.[29] Perpetuating the series became an obsession with Belknap for the remainder of his life.

The supplement continued as a separate monthly throughout 1793 and 1794 with Jeremy Belknap selecting and editing the entries. But public apathy persisted, and subscriptions continued to decline.

Joseph Belknap finally dissolved his relationship with the Society at the end of 1794. He informed them: "I found I must necessarily be a looser if I continued the publication at my own risk."[30] On December 24, 1794, the *American Apollo* came to an end.

Through all of these developments, Jeremy Belknap conscientiously conducted his editorial work, remaining aloof from the strife between the two contending elements; his relationship to Joseph dictated such a prudent course of action. He concentrated on preparing and producing two more volumes of the *Collections*. Somehow, the Society managed to dredge up the necessary funds to pay for the printing.

The Society entered into a contract with a new printer in 1795, but by mid-year the situation had become hopeless. Belknap and a few others were still intent upon producing volumes of *Collections*, but no funds were available. The Society appointed Belknap chairman of a committee that was to investigate and report "measures to increase the means of the Society to publish their *Collections*." Belknap's committee decided to appeal to the public for financial support, preparing the following statement for the Boston newspapers: "When it is considered that these Collections will consist of historical and biographical memoirs, geographical and topographical descriptions, accounts of new discoveries and improvements in travel, navigation, manufactures, and commerce, scarce and valuable pamphlets and manuscripts respecting the antiquities of America, and other subjects which daily arrest the attention of the curious and inquisitive, and promise a great increase of science and fund of entertainment, they cannot but hope that a generous and candid public will enable them to carry their views into effect, and assist them in their endeavors to do real service to the community."[31]

---

[29] Pages 1–208 appeared in weekly supplements of the *American Apollo*. Beginning in September, the historical supplement appeared monthly, a pattern continued through volume 3. Volumes 4 and 5 were originally issued in quarterly segments.

[30] Records of the Recording Secretary, 1791–1813, vol. 1 (M.H.S. Archives).

[31] M.H.S., *Procs.*, 1(1791–1835):xxx-xxxi.

A "generous and candid" public, however, showed no interest in the *Collections*. Rebuffed by the populace, Belknap directed an impassioned appeal to the Society's members, both resident and corresponding. "It is in our power to furnish the public with much information," he wrote one corresponding member, "by republishing scarce and valuable pieces, and communicating original matter, which frequently comes into our hands, and would come more frequently, if the publication could be renewed and continued."

Belknap's appeal was a partial success, and the Society managed to raise additional funds to publish volume four of the *Collections*. But this seemed to be the end of the program. The financial problem remained insoluble. The committee appointed to oversee the printing of the *Collections* reported to the Society at its annual meeting in 1796 "that it is not expedient to continue the publication at present"; possibly because he favored continuing the series, Belknap had resigned from the committee at the March 25 meeting.

His health rapidly declining, Belknap terminated his editorial work on the *Collections* series after the publication of volume four. If he had not fully accomplished his objective, he had established a sturdy foundation upon which his successors would continue to build. His contemporaries acknowledged his achievement. Professor Ebeling spoke for many when he wrote: "The Collection[s] of the Historical Society, I say without flattery, is the only source wherein one *may drink deep*, as Pope says."[32]

Belknap wanted to quench the historical thirst not only of Society members but of the masses as well. The founders, and particularly Belknap, were committed to the purpose of "public utility." Collecting and preserving the sources of American history were but the means to a greater end. On occasion, the Society's zeal to assist worthwhile historical projects would lead to a temporary loss of significant library holdings. For example, in October 1828, the Society voted to assist the federal commissioners who were seeking to resolve the boundary dispute between Maine and New Brunswick. The Society provided the commissioners with three maps, an atlas, and Jedidiah Morse's *American Geography*.[33]

The commissioners failed to return the borrowed materials. The So-

[32] *American Apollo*, Aug. 24, 1792.
[33] M.H.S., *Procs.*, 1(1791–1835):415–416.

ciety finally recovered one map in 1841, but two others remained missing. In 1852, Edward Everett became secretary of state and ordered a full-scale search of the State Department files. The missing maps were found and returned to the Society, but no mention was made of the atlas and Morse's work.[34]

Belknap also held the conviction that the Society should sponsor public lectures on history to educate the citizenry. He was the main agent in organizing a lecture program to commemorate the 300th anniversary of Christopher Columbus's discovery of the New World and volunteered to deliver the address.

The Tammany Society of New York City had sponsored a public observance of Columbus's first voyage on October 12. This was the first public commemoration of the event in the history of the young nation. After conducting research on the date, Belknap concluded that October 23 was the proper day for the celebration, allowing for the discrepancy between the Julian calendar in use in the fifteenth century and the modern Gregorian calendar, which the British adopted in 1752.[35]

On October 23, after holding their regular Society meeting at the parsonage of the Reverend Peter Thacher of the Brattle Street Church, the members trooped to the minister's spacious meetinghouse, there to be joined by a host of citizens. Nathaniel Cutting, who attended the event, recorded in his diary:

> At 11 o'clock, A.M., repaired to the Meeting House in Brattle Street, where I found a respectable audience assembled to hear a discourse in commemoration of the first Discovery of America by Christopher Columbus. The Rev. Mr. Belknap, one of the members of the Historical Society, was the orator. He gave a very concise & comprehensive narrative of the most material circumstances which led to, attended, or were consequent on the Discovery of America. The subject was so interesting and so extremely well handled that the audience paid the most profound attention, and gave evident signs of being exceedingly well entertained. For my own part, I never heard any thing of the kind that gave me so much pleasure. This is designed as a beginning to celebrate the centenary of the Discovery of America. It is just 300 years since that important event took place. The

[34] M.H.S., *Procs.*, 2(1835–1855):11, 214, 215, 218, 219, 221, 224, 491, 492, 510, 512, 524, 525.

[35] Later research revealed that Belknap was in error. The difference was actually 11 days. In 1492, the discrepancy was 9 days. See M.H.S. *Miscellany* No. 52 (Autumn 1992), 3.

ceremony was conducted much in the style of a common lecture. The celebration commenced with an anthem. Mr. Thatcher made an excellent prayer, part of a psalm was then sung, and then Mr. Belknap delivered his discourse, which was succeeded by a prayer from Mr. Eliot. Mr. Thatcher then read an Ode composed for the occasion by Mr. Belknap, which was sung by the choir; this finished the ceremony. The celebration was under the auspices of the Massachusetts Historical Society.[36]

Belknap portrayed Columbus as the quintessential hero, as was to be expected. In a provocative address before the Society in 1992, in which she analyzed Belknap's presentation, Lilian Handlin concluded that his portrayal symbolized "humanity's triumph over history—just what Americans thought they were doing in 1776."[37]

Belknap remained active in Society affairs until 1798, when he suffered two slight strokes. He reduced both his ministerial duties and his activities with the Society, but he continued to solicit materials for the Society. On June 14, he wrote to Abigail Adams, requesting information on Gen. John Skey Eustace, who had served in the American army during the Revolutionary War, and inquiring whether her husband, John, "owned Thurloe's State Papers." Six days later, he suffered an attack of apoplexy which left him paralyzed and speechless. He died later that morning at the age of fifty-four. He was buried in the Granary Burying Ground, the resting place of his family and many other Boston worthies, a short distance from his birthplace and beloved historical society.

From Belknap's death in 1798 to 1833, when the Society moved to new quarters on Tremont Street, the history of the organization seemed to have a static character. There was a seamless sameness to these thirty-five years. There were no major developments, no sudden surges of activity or great leaps forward. Nor were there any aggres-

---

[36] M.H.S., *Procs.*, 2d ser., 12(1871–1873):65.

[37] "The Massachusetts Historical Society and Its Columbuses," M.H.S., *Procs.*, 104(1992):12–13. Handlin's thesis is that, through the writings and pronouncements of five of its members, the Society was "partly responsible for Columbus's fortunes in American consciousness" in the nineteenth century. The five were: Belknap; Washington Irving, "codifier of the Columbus myth as we know it"; Edward Everett; Edward Everett Hale; and Charles F. Adams, Jr. "No other scholarly organization has been more influential than the M.H.S. in articulating the Columbus image for its contemporaries."

sive, commanding, Belknap-type leaders who manifested his sense of commitment and were willing to devote endless hours to Society activities.

Four times a year, on the last Tuesday of January, April, July, and October, eight to fifteen resident members made the arduous two-story climb up the steep, narrow, winding staircase to the Tontine Crescent chamber, convened in formal session, and conducted a wide range of routine, prosaic, institutional business: recording donations to the library and cabinet; nominating and electing resident and corresponding members, and officers at the annual business meeting in April; making decisions on deaccessioning materials from the library and cabinet; reviewing requests of non-members to use the library and of members to borrow materials; appointing committees for special assignments and responding to their reports; listening to carefully prepared memoirs of deceased members, both resident and corresponding. It was a time of small beginnings.

From its founding in 1791 to April 1833, when it moved to Tremont Street, the Society, with few exceptions, continued to meet but four times each year. There were seven meetings during the first year, but each was designated a "special" meeting. The constitution of 1791 called for four quarterly meetings, each beginning on the last Tuesday of January, April, July, and October. The annual meeting, at which officers were elected and reports presented, was held in April.

Upon occupying its Tremont Street quarters, the Society altered its laws and regulations. A major change was the scheduling of nine monthly meetings from October to June. There were no meetings in July, August, and September, when most members left Boston for vacation sites.

This new schedule, plus a change in physical character of its headquarters, led to greater visitation of the Society by members. Prior to 1833, few members set foot inside its quarters on non-meeting days. The only likely visitors were the librarian and cabinet-keeper, who had assigned responsibilities for the collections, and, possibly, those members at work on a volume of *Collections* or conducting personal research. Prior to 1833, the quarters were basically storage facilities, not clubhouses. Moreover, it was difficult to gain entry because only the librarian had a key.

Because of the limited space in all of its pre-1833 quarters, many of the regular meetings were held in members' homes. Attendance at these meetings was usually ten to fifteen; the maximum number of resident members was sixty.

From 1791 to 1861, the meetings began at high noon for, as Stewart Mitchell has written: "those were the gracious days when gentlemen earned their livings in the morning—if they had to earn them at all—lunched late, and devoted the remainder of their waking hours to leisure, to learning, and to the art of life."[38] From 1861 to 1879, they began at 11 A.M. From 1879 to 1895 (and beyond to 1945), they took place at 3 P.M. The changes in time were caused by low attendance, a constant concern of the officers. In 1862, the Society experimented with evening meetings, but the idea was abandoned after three months. Only for special meetings did the attendance rise appreciably.

One persistent lament suffused the early meetings: a lack of financial resources to accomplish such vital projects as publishing new volumes of *Collections*.[39] The Society's financial condition remained uniformly weak during this period. The standing committee that reviewed the treasurer's reports at the annual meetings always found his statistics "well kept, correctly cast, and properly vouched" but tactfully refrained from commenting on the appallingly small balances, which rarely exceeded $100—not that it was the treasurer's responsibility to serve as a fund raiser for the Society.

A regular feature of Society meetings throughout the years has been the election of new members. Until 1815, candidates for membership in the Society were voted upon by ballot.[40] At the August 29, 1815, meeting, Joseph McKean moved that "the law and custom of our forefathers be

---

[38] Stewart Mitchell, *Handbook of the Massachusetts Historical Society, 1791–1948* (Boston, 1949), 5.

[39] The *Collections* were published on a fairly regular basis, the 10 volumes of the first series appearing between 1792 and 1809. By 1810, there was sufficient interest to require reprinting the first 3 volumes. For details on the contents of each volume and subsequent publishing history, see *Massachusetts Historical Society Handbook of the Publications and Photostats, 1792–1935*, 2d ed. (Boston, 1937).

[40] For an illuminating examination of the voting process in the early nineteenth century, see Worthington C. Ford, "Voting with Beans and Corn," M.H.S., *Procs.*, 57(1923–1924):230–239. See also, M.H.S., *Procs.*, 2d ser., 8(1892–1894):341.

adopted, as it stands in the Statute of Elections, 1643, *mutatis mutandis*, 'For the yearly choosing of assistants, the freemen shall use Indian corn and beans, the Indian corn to manifest election, and the beans contrary.' '' This motion was approved. McKean had based his motion upon an action taken by the Massachusetts General Court in September 1643: "It is ordered, that for the yearly choosing of Assistants for the time to come, instead of papers the freemen shall use Indian beanes, the white beanes to manifest election, the black for blanks." Thus, as Worthington C. Ford pointed out in an article on the subject in 1924, McKean's scholarship was deficient. The 1643 act specified only Indian white and black beans. It made no reference to corn. No matter. The Society began to use corn and black beans.

Where did the Society acquire its corn and beans? According to George E. Ellis, "some of the veritable kernels of Indian corn and the beans which were sent in from the neighboring towns as affirmative and negative votes in the old colonial times, and King Philip's succotash bowl, serve for these formalities."

King Philip's "samp bowl," as it is traditionally known, served as the ballot box from 1815 through most of the nineteenth century.[41] A carved elm burl, this beautiful example of Algonquian craftsmanship was donated to the Society by one of its members, Isaac Lothrop, in 1803; he had purchased the bowl for eight dollars. One of the earliest gifts to the Society, it ranks as one of its rarest treasures.

On October 26, 1855, Edward Everett delivered an oration in Boston on "Vegetable and Mineral Gold" before the United States Agricultural Society. In the course of his address, Everett held up an ear of corn, which had come from Lexington, and stated:

> Drop a grain of our gold, of our blessed gold, into the ground, and lo! a mystery. In a few days it softens, it swells, it shoots upwards, it is a living thing. It is yellow itself, but sends up a delicate spire, which comes peeping, emerald green, through the soil; it expands to a vigorous stalk; revels in the air and sunshine; arrays itself more glorious than Solomon, in its broad, fluttering, leafy robes, whose sound, as the west wind whispers through them, falls as pleasantly on the husbandman's ear, as the rustle of his sweetheart's garment; still towers aloft, spins its verdant skeins of vegetable floss, displays its dancing tassels, surcharged with fertilizing dust, and

[41] At some undetermined date, the Society switched to two formal ballot boxes.

at last ripens into two or three magnificent batons like this (an ear of Indian corn,) each of which is studded with hundreds of grains of gold, every one possessing the same wonderful properties as the parent grain, every one instinct with the same marvellous reproductive powers. There are seven hundred and twenty grains on the ear which I hold in my hand.

On the ride home from the dinner, Everett gave the ear of corn to President Robert C. Winthrop. The latter stripped some of the kernels to replenish the Society's supply.[42]

From its founding to its removal to Boylston Street, the Society expelled only three of its members. Edmund Randolph, the eminent Virginian who served as attorney general of the United States and secretary of state, and William Blount, a delegate to the continental congress from North Carolina, and, later, a United States senator from Tennessee, were jointly banished in 1797. Nominated by Belknap, Randolph had been elected a corresponding member in October 1792.[43] Blount was elected a corresponding member in October 1796.[44]

Both were banished because of alleged political misdeeds. While serving in the United States Senate, Blount had been accused of plotting with Indians to assist the British in evicting the Spanish from Florida and Louisiana. The Senate expelled him and the Society followed suit. Randolph was belatedly removed from the Society's rolls because of his alleged involvement in an "obscure scandal" that occurred in 1795, which forced his resignation as secretary of state. In its vote of expulsion, the Society did not particularize. It merely affirmed that the two "are, in our opinion, unworthy of our confidence."[45]

Samuel Turell was the third member to be ejected. Because he was a resident member and a Bostonian, his expulsion was a more serious matter than the dismissal of Blount and Randolph. Nominated by Belknap, Turell was elected a resident member in 1793 and served as cabinet-keeper from 1793 to 1808. A watchmaker by profession, he was "a man of intelligence, and a great lover of books." Turell also had a passion for natural history and a yen to operate a museum. Securing permission from the Society to borrow some of its natural history spec-

---

[42] The corn and beans are still in use at meetings at this writing (1994). The Society has also preserved the ear of corn in its museum collection.

[43] M.H.S., *Procs.*, 1(1791–1835):43–44.

[44] M.H.S., *Procs.*, 1(1791–1835):101.

[45] M.H.S., *Procs.*, 1(1791–1835):106.

imens for a museum he and "other Societies and individuals" accomplished his objective. The Reverend William Bentley, who described Turell as an "ingenious man," visited the museum in 1802 and was duly impressed. "Many articles have been indulged Mr. Turell from the Collections of the Historical Society," wrote Bentley. He has some minerals, insects, and medals, many Indian Curiosities, and has many wishes for his success." In 1805, Bentley described Turell's "Cabinet" as the "best ever shewn in that Capital."[46]

For unknown reasons, the Society's officers did not share Bentley's enthusiasm for Turell or his museum. They were more concerned with the loss of Society materials. In 1807, the Society appointed a committee "to demand of Mr. Turell, Cabinet-Keeper, the various articles belonging to the Society which have been in his possession, and to see that they are returned to the Cabinet." Turell failed to respond to the "demand." Two years later, the Society repeated the exercise. This time its committee consisted of the librarian and newly appointed Cabinet-Keeper Timothy Alden. There was still no response. More than two years later, the Society's patience came to an end. Because Turell had failed to comply with its edict and "whereas he has otherwise acted unworthily as a member," the Society expelled him on August 27, 1811.[47]

Outside of its members-only meetings, the Society took seriously its responsibility to stimulate public interest in American history. In particular, it took an active role in commemorating significant historical events relating to Massachusetts and the Revolutionary War, such as the landing of the Pilgrims at Plymouth and the Battle of Bunker Hill. It often served as the catalyst for these celebrations.

In January 1830, for example, the Society appointed a committee to consult with city officials about organizing an appropriate public observance of the bicentennial of Boston's settlement. From the consultations there emerged a comprehensive program.

The celebrations opened with a formal ceremonial program at 8 A.M. at the old State House, attended by the city fathers and local dignitaries, and featuring an address of "considerable length" by Mayor Harrison

---

[46] Bentley, *Diary*, 2:433., 3:191.

[47] M.H.S., *Procs.*, 1(1791–1835):222. It is not known if Turell ever returned the items he had borrowed.

Gray Otis. At 9:30 A.M., there was a parade of sizable proportions. Members of the Historical Society, dressed in their usual dark suits, were grouped as one unit. Led by the colorfully attired Ancient and Honorable Artillery Company, a fixture at all civic celebrations, the units marched up Beacon Street and entered the Common, where they passed through two lines of several thousand cheering school children who were accompanied by their teachers. The parade ended at the storied Old South Meetinghouse, where Josiah Quincy delivered an oration, Charles Sprague read a poem, and the Reverend John Pierpont presented an ode, a standard format for historical commemorations.

Since it was now time for lunch, a large group gathered in Faneuil Hall, where a "collation was prepared for their entertainment." In the late afternoon, as dinnertime approached, "about a hundred gentlemen," including "many members" of the Historical Society, assembled at the Exchange Coffee-House. Lt.-Gov. Thomas L. Winthrop, a direct descendant of Gov. John Winthrop and a leading member of the Historical Society,[48] presided as chairman of the affair, and a "truly convivial spirit animated by the recollections which the exercises of the day excited, prevailed on the occasion." The dinner party was an event of "high intellectual entertainment," marked by a number of florid speeches and toasts. Following this repast, Winthrop sponsored a "large reception" at his home on Beacon Street. This was the final event of a long and arduous day of celebration.[49]

The most significant development in these three and one-half decades was the steady growth of the library and, to a lesser extent, the cabinet. The library held 225 volumes in 1793; 450 volumes in 1794; about 1,000 volumes in 1800; about 2,000 volumes in 1810; about 4,600 volumes in 1839. There was a similar marked increase in pamphlets, newspapers, and other printed materials. There was also an appreciable increase of manuscripts, many of which were created in the seventeenth and eighteenth centuries. In time, manuscripts would become the library's major resource.

The expansion of the library can be tracked in the lists of acquisitions which were reported at many of the Society meetings. At the gathering

[48] He served as president from 1835 to 1841.
[49] M.H.S., *Procs.*, 1(1791–1835):434–435n.

of January 31, 1809, to cite but one example, the following donations were recorded:

For the Collections:—

An Account of the Capture of the Ship "Hope," . . . by Captain Mugford, in June 1776, with a List of Naval Commanders belonging to that town who distinguished themselves in the Revolutionary War. From John Prince, Esq.

A file of Papers, containing a Letter of King Charles II. to Governor Winthrop, 1661; a Letter of Sir Edmund Andros, 1668; of Governor Coxe, 1690; of Jeremiah Dummer, 1711; of William Bollan, Esq., 1750 and 1758; and copy of a Letter to the Agents of the Colonies, 1758. From the Heirs of Thomas Fayerweather, Esq.

An original Letter of Richard Henry Lee to Samuel Adams, Feb. 5, 1781. From a Friend.

Memoirs of Rev. Charles Morton, of Charlestown, by Rev. Dr. Holmes.

Memoirs of Rev. John Lothrop, the first minister of Barnstable, by Rev. Dr. Lothrop.

Obituary of the Town of Middleborough, by Hon. Isaac Thomson, Esq.

A Letter from Rev. Habijah Weld to Mr. Prince, being in answer to certain queries for his Annals; an Historical Narrative of Newspapers in New Hampshire; a file of Letters from Dr. Kennicot, Court de Gebelin, and Mr. Hollis; an original Indenture, Thomas Danforth on one part, John Davis and others, trustees, on behalf of New York, &c., 1684. From Rev. Timothy Alden, Jr.

A curious Manuscript, in short hand, written in 1732, containing Texts, Heads of Sermons, &c. From Dr. Allman, of Halifax.

For the Library:—

Grotius de Origine Gentium Americanarum; Historia Vinlandiæ, a Thermodo de Torfeo, Historico Regio; Histoire du Cap Breton; Voyages aux Côtes du Chili, du Pérou, et Brésil, par M. Frezier, 1712, 1713, 1714; and Lawson's Voyages to South Carolina. From Mr. Obadiah Rich.

Laws of the State of New York, three volumes, from Hon. Stephen Van Renssellaer, Esq.

Documents of the First Session of the Tenth Congress, and Documents of the Session from November, 1808, to March, 1809. From Hon. Josiah Quincy, Esq.

The Works of Fisher Ames, from Hon. George Cabot, Esq.

Harris's Tour to the Territory north-west of the Alleghany Mountains; Volume of Sermons addressed to Freemasons; and Sermon on the Landing of the Fathers at Plymouth, preached Dec. 22, 1808. From the author.

Pharmacopoeia; Report on Vaccination; and Medical Papers, Nos. 1, 2, and 3. From the Massachusetts Medical Society.

Georgical Papers, from the Trustees of the Agricultural Society.

Adams's Defence of the American Constitutions, from Thomas Adams, Esq.

Eulogy upon President McKeen, with the President's Inaugural Address; and a Sermon Preached at the Festival of John the Baptist, 1807. From the author, Rev. William Jenks.

Humphrey's Account of the Missionary Societies, from Mr. Samuel Jenks.

Holmes's Sermon before the Society for Propagating the Gospel, 1808; and Holmes's Fast Sermon, 1809. From the author.

Buckminster's Sermon upon the Death of Governor Sullivan. From the author.

Questio Physica Inauguralis de Somno, quam Eruditorum Examini subjecit Thomas Brown, Britannus; Questio de Mania, Johannes Wharton, Virginiensis. From Rev. Charles Lowell.

A volume of occasional Sermons, from Rev. William Emerson.

Allen's Election Sermon, 1808; and Allen's Historical Sketch of Berkshire and the Town of Pittsfield. From the author.

Norton's Discourse on 1 Tim. II.4, from the author.

Thomson's Reply to Norton's Sermon, and Relly's Cherubimical Mystery, from a Friend.

Josselyn's Rarieties of New England, from Mr. Joseph Coggswell.

Address of the Philadelphia Bible Society, and first Report read, May 1, 1809; and Extracts from the Minutes of the General Assembly of the Presbyterian Church of the United States, 1809. From Ebenezer Hazard, Esq.

A collection of Pamphlets published by the Portland Committee of Safety, January, 1809, from Mr. Calvin Day.

Wood's History of President Adams's Administration; Rules and Orders of Massachusetts House of Representatives; Election Sermon, 1809; and Artillery Election Sermon, 1809. From a Friend.

Review of the Works of Fisher Ames, Esq.; Essay on the Rights of Nations relative to Fugitives from Justice; Inadmissible Principles of the King of England's Proclamation, by the late President Adams; and White's Oration, July 4, 1809. From David Everett, Esq.

Remarkables of Dr. Increase Mather, from a Friend.

Two volumes of Miscellanies, neatly bound; volume of Manuscript Sermons, preached at the First Church in Boston, 1652 and 1653, written by Seaborn Cotton; Connecticut Election Sermons, 1801, 1802, 1803; First three numbers of the American Magazine, 1743; Report of the Opinion of the Court in the case of Penhallow *versus* Doane, 1795; and several Sermons and other Pamphlets, &c. From Rev. Timothy Alden.

Dunbar's Ordination Sermon at Canton, with Historic Documents of that Town, from the author.

Hancock's Election Sermon, 1722, from Rev. Thomas Gray.

Two volumes of the Worcester Magazine; thirty volumes of the Massachusetts Spy, neatly bound in seventeen. From Isaiah Thomas, Esq.

Baring's Inquiry into the Orders of Council; A Faithful Picture of New Orleans; Gallatin's View of the Public Debt, &c.; The Yankee Farmer's Inquiry about the Affair of the Chesapeake; several Pamphlets relative to the same business; Embargo Laws; Pickering's Correspondence; Report of the Committee on the Exchange Bank, Rhode Island; five Sermons before the Humane Society; and Missionary and other Sermons, to the number of twenty. From a Friend.

Centinel, 1808, from Major Russell.

Chronicle, 1808, from Adams & Rhoades.

Palladium, 1808, from Young & Minns.

Boston Gazette, 1808, from Russell & Cutler.

Repertory, 1808, from Dr. John Park.

Patriot, 1808, from David Everett, Esq.

New York Spectator, 1808, from E. Belden & Co.

For the Cabinet:—

An Impression on Copper from the Gold Medal which was presented by Congress to Commodore Preble, from Hon. Robert Smith.

Specimens of Sand, Marble, Schistus, Sulphuret of Iron, from various parts of the United States; specimens of Gypsum, from St. George's; Tourmaline, from Brattleborough; Nautilus, and other Shells, from the Feejee Islands; Basement of a Pillar, from ancient Syracuse; specimens of Lava, from St. Vincent; a remarkable Knife, dug up at Wakefield, New Hampshire. From Rev. Timothy Alden.

Specimens of Garnet, found imbedded in a rock at Bedford, from Rev. Samuel Stearns.

Part of the Monumental Stone erected in Sudbury, where an Indian battle was fought, 1676, from a Friend.

A Silver Instrument for branding Negroes, from a Friend.

Six Copper Coins of Roman Emperors; ten Copper Coins of the United States; six Silver Coins of England; and Bills of the old Paper Money in 1714, and of Massachusetts and old Continental emission, from one dollar to twenty. From a Friend.[50]

Meeting after meeting, year after year, the librarian reported acquisitions similar to these. The historical treasure house grew larger and larger. While welcomed by the members, these newly acquired items ex-

---

[50] M.H.S., *Procs.*, 1(1791–1835):200–203.

acerbated an increasingly acute storage problem. The wound was self-inflicted since the Society did not have an acquisitions policy and accepted every donation, whatever its character. This lack of discrimination, especially with respect to artifacts and natural history specimens, worked to the detriment of the Society.[51] By 1820, if not sooner, the Tontine Crescent room was crammed full with an astonishing array of materials, all "buried under the dust of ages," in the caustic judgment of one severe critic of the Society.[52] Items were stored willy nilly. Anyone conducting research had a difficult time locating specific items among the clutter.

The concentration of historical holdings in one room provoked fear and anxiety among the officers and other members. They were particularly terrified by the thought of a fire, which could result in the total destruction of their irreplaceable collection. These men had long memories. Almost all were graduates of Harvard and knew of the conflagration on a snowy and bitterly cold January night in 1764 that leveled the college library in a matter of hours. Over 5,000 books, the largest collection in the American colonies, were destroyed.

The members also knew from painful, personal experience that Boston was vulnerable to a similar calamity.[53] "The evil in our architecture," one commentator wrote in 1794, "lies principally in this, that we build with wood."[54] Since many of the buildings in the densely populated city were of wooden construction, the smallest fire could quickly race out of control, expand into an inferno, and engulf a wide section. The city's volunteer fire-fighting force, with its primitive equipment, was no match for a large blaze.

A fire in 1825 underscored the potential danger for the Society.[55] While this particular blaze was confined to an area some distance from

---

[51] As a special museum committee reported in 1959: "Stuffed possums, spiders, Madagascar bats and centipedes in alcohol seem for some time to have been a favorite gift for members to bestow upon the Society, and this was quite proper since one of the original purposes of the Society was to collect 'specimens of natural history and artificial curiosities.' " M.H.S. Council Records, May 11, 1959 (M.H.S. Archives).

[52] Samuel G. Drake, *Narrative Remarks, Expository Notes and Historical Criticisms* (Albany, N.Y., 1874), 13.

[53] On the history of major fires in Boston in the early years, see M.H.S., *Colls.*, 1st ser., 3:268–273, 4:188–190.

[54] M.H.S., *Colls.*, 1st ser., 3:273.

[55] For a contemporary account of the fire, see *Boston Daily Advertiser and Repertory*, Nov. 11, 1825.

the Tontine Crescent and did not touch the Society directly, it did destroy some of the organization's significant holdings.

The fire began shortly after midnight on Thursday, November 10, in William Brown's hatter shop on the ground floor of 10 Court Street. This was in the heart of the city. It spread quickly to the second and third stories, which housed the offices of a number of lawyers, and then moved to adjoining structures. Before it was brought under control, "nine or ten large buildings, and several smaller ones" were in ruins. Twenty-five law offices and twenty mercantile shops were destroyed.

Aroused by the night fire watch, the city's fire brigades rushed to the scene but, as the *Daily Advertiser* reported, "the men were handicapped by a great deficiency in the supply of water, and a very little disposition on the part of a great portion of the persons assembled to afford the least aid." The newspaper did commend the firemen for a gallant effort: "Many, if not all of the fire companies, conducted with spirit, and they certainly deserve credit for preventing a further spread of the fire."

Several fire companies from neighboring towns came to assist. One of these was the high-spirited Harvard College student company which "came with their engine from Cambridge, and stationed themselves where they could render effectual service, but no measure being taken to supply them with water, we are told they went fifteen times to a wharf at considerable distance to fill their engine, and returned with it each time to the fire, to the great applause of crowds of bystanders who did nothing."

One of the law offices consumed by the fire was that of James Savage, treasurer of the Society and an avid antiquarian-historian in his spare moments.[56] On occasion, Savage took books and manuscripts from the library (with permission) and kept them in his law office, where he did his research and writing; borrowing was a common practice by members. At the time of the fire, Savage had physical custody of five Society items: the first volume of Ebenezer Hazard's *Historical Collections*, the first volume of Abiel Holmes's *Annals*, a volume of Thomas Hutchinson's *Curious Collections*, the nineteenth volume of Gov. Jonathan Trumbull's collection of manuscripts, and the second volume of Gov. John Winthrop's three-volume manuscript, "The History of New En-

[56] *Boston Daily Advertiser*, Nov. 12, 1825.

gland." The loss of the Hazard, Holmes, and Hutchinson works, while regrettable, was not tragic since they were published accounts and other copies were extant.

Not so in the case of the Trumbull and Winthrop volumes. These were irreplaceable manuscripts. The destruction of the Winthrop work was especially grievous. The governor's magisterial history was one of the seminal sources for the settlement of Massachusetts and New England by the Puritans. Savage had borrowed it because he was then preparing for publication a new edition of the work.

Also lost in the fire was the Society's entire reserve stock of *Collections*, more than 2,000 volumes. These back issues had been stored in the rooms of the Society's printer, Phelps and Farnham, adjacent to Savage's office. Every copy of volumes VII and VIII of the second series was destroyed, and "almost every copy" of volumes IV and V of the first series and IX of the second series. In a letter to President John Davis on May 1, 1826, a remorseful Savage itemized the Society's losses in the "sad fire," expressed his "deep and sincere regret," and noted the destruction of his personal collection of historical works, "not one was saved."[57]

Utilizing all available reserve funds, the Society reprinted some copies of two of the lost volumes of *Collections*, but it was unable to reproduce the "remaining three volumes thus deficient" because its "pecuniary means are exhausted." To raise money for this project, the Society embarked upon a subscription program in 1828. It solicited orders from the general public for all of their *Collections*. It offered the first series, containing ten volumes, at $1.50 each; the second series, also with ten volumes, at $1.50 each, with the exception of the tenth volume, which was priced at $2; the third series, which consisted of two volumes, at $1.50 each.[58]

The promotion was an abysmal failure. Bostonians showed little interest in the *Collections*. The treasurer's report of 1829 noted a mere $60 taken in for the sale of books.[59]

[57] M.H.S., *Procs.*, 1(1791–1835):393n. Following the destruction of his office, Savage abandoned the legal profession and devoted himself to historical pursuits. See also, ibid., 16(1878):137.

[58] M.H.S. circular, "Historical Collections," May 1, 1828 (M.H.S. Archives).

[59] M.H.S., *Procs.*, 1(1791–1835):419n.

Building a Good Repository

The Society was shocked by the losses it sustained in the fire of 1825. Now, more than ever, it recognized the vulnerability of its Tontine Crescent quarters. If a fire developed on either side, it "must necessarily expose to utter destruction all their accumulations." The members concluded that they must leave their rent-free home and seek safer quarters. The rapid growth of the collection and the resultant lack of space were also factors prompting a new facility. "Difficulty of access" and the "uncomfortable" character of the site were additional reasons for a move.

In 1825, officials of the Society, Boston Athenaeum, American Academy of Arts and Sciences, and the Massachusetts Medical Society began to discuss jointly constructing a building "additional to the Athenaeum, which shall afford the Societies convenient rooms for their libraries and their private meetings."[60] The plan called for each organization to contribute $3,000 for the structure. The Society agreed to participate in the venture. It appointed a committee and authorized it to accept donations. The deliberations continued into 1826, but nothing materialized.[61]

In April 1827, the Society struck out on its own, appointing a committee "to inquire whether a more safe and suitable room can be provided for the use of the Society, free of expense." Josiah Quincy, then serving as president of Harvard University, was appointed chairman of the committee.[62]

Nothing developed in the next five years. Then, in 1832, a promising opportunity for new quarters materialized. The Provident Institution for Savings Bank began construction of a three-story building at 30 Tremont Street. Possibly because James Savage was one of its principal officers (he was also serving on the Society's committee to find new quarters), the bank offered the Society the use of the second story and one-half of the attic and set forth two options. The Society either could rent this space for a ten-year period, with the prospect of purchasing a "permanent interest" in time, or it could buy the two units outright.

Although an unprepossessing architectural specimen, the Tremont Street structure had a number of features which appealed to the members. Most importantly, the suite of rooms on the second floor provided

---

[60] The Athenaeum was then located on Pearl Street.

[61] M.H.S., *Procs.*, 1(1791–1835):384, 386, 419–420.

[62] M.H.S., *Procs.*, 1(1791–1835):399.

more space than the Tontine Crescent. Because there were no append-
ages on three of its sides, the building posed less of a fire threat than the
Tontine Crescent room. Also, there were "many advantages of light and
air, of central position, and convenient access."[63]

While not a factor of transcendent importance, there was a symbolic
propriety in the Society being located in a section of Boston which provided "many hallowed associations of remote and of recent history." The
site of the new quarters had once held the home of the Reverend Henry
Caner, the prominent rector of King's Chapel who remained a Tory during the pre-Revolution crisis and, along with many members of his congregation, fled with the British forces to Halifax, Nova Scotia, in March
1776. Adjacent to the northern side of the bank building was the King's
Chapel Burial Ground, "a spot hallowed in history and romance," which
held the remains of many of Boston's earliest ministers and magistrates,
including Massachusetts Bay Colony's first governor, John Winthrop,
and the distinguished Puritan clerics John Cotton and John Davenport.[64]

When newly-elected member Charles Francis Adams looked out upon
the ancient graveyard, he was deeply moved: "we seemed on that spot
to clasp hands across the years with the fathers, and almost with the
colonial period."[65] Next to the cemetery was King's Chapel, the first
Anglican church in Puritan Boston, a loyalist religious stronghold before
the American Revolution and, after independence had been achieved, the
first Unitarian church in the United States. Designed by Peter Harrison
of Newport, Rhode Island, this stone structure was one of Boston's most
beautiful and historic churches. A short distance down Tremont Street,
on the opposite side, was the Old Granary Burial Ground, the final
resting place of a host of Boston's leading citizens, including such Revolutionary War worthies as Samuel Adams, John Hancock, James Otis,
Paul Revere, and Robert Treat Paine. The founder of the Society, Jeremy
Belknap, also was buried there.

---

[63] President Robert C. Winthrop told the members in 1871 that the Society selected the
Tremont Street site because of the "earnest desire" and "pecuniary assistance of the late
Lieutenant-Governor William Phillips, whose noble mansion, [still stood] on the opposite
side of the street." M.H.S., *Procs.*, 2d ser., 12(1871–1873):132.

[64] M.H.S., *Procs.*, 2d ser., 11(1896–1897):411, 12(1871–1873):132.

[65] M.H.S., *Procs.*, 2d ser., 11(1896–1897):411.

Building a Good Repository

Since it did not have the necessary funds to purchase the building, the Society authorized its committee to enter into a contract with the bank for a ten-year lease. Before the contract was drawn up, the Society confronted the problem of raising funds for the annual rental fee. The committee decided on a public subscription and set a lofty goal of $5,000. Society officials had little optimism that they would raise such an amount. They were hoping for a sum of sufficient size, which would yield interest equal to the annual rental fee. The committee prepared the subscription paper on October 15, 1832, and circulated it among the gentry of Boston and members of the Society.

Perhaps to the amazement of these officials, the response was positive. Between November 6, 1832, and April 11, 1833, sixty-four people subscribed, including nineteen Society members, and the returns approximated the target: $5,000. The major contributors were Samuel Appleton, James Bowdoin, Peter Chardon Brooks, and Jonathan Phillips, son of the lieutenant-governor. Each gave $300. Interestingly, only Bowdoin was a member.

Heartened, if not elated, by this affirmation of support, the Society's officers decided to abandon the option of rental and, instead, purchase the two areas of the building, "with a privilege in the entries and stairways." The bank's original price had been $7,000 and the Society was now faced with a $2,000 shortfall. A meeting with James Savage, however, produced the good news that the bank would be willing to reduce the purchase price to $6,500; Savage was wearing an assortment of "hats" at this point.

On March 18, the Society approved an indenture with the bank, which had been drawn up by a special committee two weeks earlier. It also authorized its treasurer, the ubiquitous Savage, to borrow the additional $1,500, presumably from his own bank, "on interest, payable semi-annually."[66]

And so the Society acquired "another establishment with happier accommodations." In late March, Librarian James Bowdoin and Cabinet-

---

[66] For details on this transaction, including the successful subscription, see: M.H.S., *Procs.*, 1(1791–1835):454–457, 462, 465. The indenture is printed on p. 461. The Society has a manuscript copy of the document in its archives. See also, ibid., 2d ser., 11(1896–1897):308–313.

Keeper Redford Webster arranged for the transfer of the collection from the Tontine Crescent to the new quarters. At the same time, the Society authorized these officials to refine the holdings and deposit in the Society of Natural History "such articles in the Museum, relating to that subject."[67] The Society also appointed a committee to arrange for the sale or rental of the vacated room.[68]

---

[67] M.H.S., *Procs.*, 1(1791–1835):467.

[68] It was leased to the Boston Phrenological Society for a time, then, in 1839, the Boston Library Society purchased it for $1,500. M.H.S., *Procs.*, 2(1835–1855):132.

Chapter 3

A New Life
on Tremont Street

THE SOCIETY'S first meeting at the Tremont Street quarters took place on June 5, 1833. Eleven members assembled in the "east room," which was furnished in Spartan fashion. They sat on long settees and the green Windsor chairs purchased at the founding. President John Davis presided at a large oblong table at the head of the room. The cost of furnishing the room had been modest, less than $500. This meeting marked the beginning of a new era in the Society's history—the advent of the gentlemen's history club.[1]

The Society celebrated its semi-centennial on October 31, 1844, the Council deciding to use the year of incorporation (1794) as the founding date.[2] The program was a low-key affair, consisting of an afternoon address by the Reverend John G. Palfrey at the Masonic Temple, located a few blocks from the Society's quarters. The general public was invited to attend.

Palfrey's presentation, while appropriate for the occasion, was not memorable. It was standard filiopietistic fare, a studied cluster of clichés. He heaped praise upon the founders and other early leaders, recorded the organization's achievements in its first half century, and lauded the character and efforts of the Pilgrims and Puritans. His closing statements reflected the formulaic rhetoric of the address: "The founders of New England left a rich inheritance to their children, but in nothing so

---

[1] M.H.S., *Procs.*, 1(1791–1835):470.

[2] M.H.S., *Procs.*, 2(1835–1855):267, 289, 292. The plans were drawn up in 1843–1844. There was mild debate about designating 1791 as the founding date, but the council ultimately settled upon 1794 for this commemoration.

precious as in the memory of their wise and steady virtue. May there never be baseness to affront that memory! May there never be indifference to lose or disregard it! May its ennobling appeal never fail of a quick response in the hearts of any generation of dwellers on this honored soil!"[3]

On the following day, the *Boston Daily Advertiser* reported that there had been a "large and highly discriminating audience" in attendance, including "a full representation of the Society, among whose members we noticed the venerable John Quincy Adams, and many ladies were present."[4]

The membership in which former President Adams found himself had changed considerably since the Society's inception. As the Society settled into its new quarters, membership increasingly became an issue of consequence. Initially, Belknap had envisioned a small body. In his 1790 "Plan of an Antiquarian Society," he proposed "not more than seven at first." After the founding had taken place, he and his colleagues settled on the figure of thirty resident and thirty corresponding members. In 1794, with the passage of its charter, the Society raised resident membership, the critical category, to sixty.[5]

Further moves to increase resident membership began in the 1840s. The Society was then well established on Tremont Street and fast developing the reputation of being one of Boston's most exclusive organizations. The city was growing rapidly in these years. Boston's population had risen from 43,000 in 1820 to 61,000 in 1830 to 100,000 in 1842. This steady growth provided a larger pool of potential candidates for membership. A growing number of Bostonians coveted an association with the Society.

To the more progressive members of the Society, the sixty-member limit was no longer realistic. As Josiah Quincy wrote: "With the number of sixty, the Society labored during more than fifty years, published about thirty volumes, and obtained a character and celebrity which rendered admission into it a subject of desire, especially by those who

[3] Palfrey's address is printed in M.H.S., *Colls.*, 3d ser., 9:165–168. After the program, senior member Robert C. Winthrop hosted a reception for his colleagues at his nearby home.

[4] *Boston Daily Advertiser*, Nov. 1, 1844. See also, M.H.S., *Procs.*, 2(1835–1855):284.

[5] The charter called for 60 corresponding and 10 honorary members.

had congenial historical sympathies. In process of time, men of this class arose in Massachusetts, adapted and disposed to unite in the same labors, extremely desirous to become members of the Society, but into which they could not enter on account of the restriction contained in the Act of Incorporation. Men of this description gradually multiplied. Some of these, who hoped for admission, were disappointed when vacancies occasionally happened, and which were filled by others. Some of these were said to have had the mortification of being rejected when others were elected."[6]

President James Savage, a zealous maverick on many matters, led a movement for enlargement. He favored one hundred members. At the December 1845 meeting, he introduced a motion calling for the standing committee to consider the "expediency of applying to the Legislature for an alteration of the charter, so as to allow an increase in the number of members." The motion passed but not without stern opposition. George Ticknor, another formidable personality, was the leading member of the group favoring the status quo.[7]

The committee did not deliver its report until the January 1846 meeting. Both protagonists, Savage and Ticknor, were in attendance together with an unusually large number of members (twenty-three), who had been attracted by the impending report of the committee and the anticipated verbal fireworks.[8] The committee's report did not address Savage's request directly. Rather, it recommended that the Society apply to the General Court for an act repealing the clause that restricted membership to sixty and inserting one authorizing the Society "to regulate, from time to time, the number of its members by its own By-Laws."[9]

Savage strenuously supported the recommendation, while Ticknor "was very adverse to the proposed change." Charles F. Adams, who was not at the meeting, noted, "considering the characteristics of the two men, the discussion between him and Mr. Savage . . . was not improbably marked with animation."[10] When the dust had settled, Ticknor's faction emerged the victors. In the understated words of the Society's

[6] M.H.S., *Procs.*, 2d ser., 10(1895–1896):316–317.

[7] M.H.S., *Procs.*, 2d ser., 10(1895–1896):321–324.

[8] The previous meeting attracted 13, which was an average attendance for a monthly meeting. The subsequent annual meeting drew only 18.

[9] Charles F. Adams, "Confidential Paper on Special Meeting of Jan. 18, 1877" (M.H.S. Archives).

[10] Adams, "Confidential Paper."

scribe, the report "was taken up, and, after discussion, was rejected."[11]

The battle for enlargement began again in 1855 when Robert C. Winthrop assumed the presidency. Winthrop would not have gone as far as the first president of the Historical Society of Pennsylvania, who asserted in his inaugural address: "The members of an historical society ought to be numerous, perhaps unlimited. All who feel a strong interest in its general views ought to be admissable, and every inhabitant of our state ought to feel that interest."[12] Winthrop firmly believed, however, that the Society should not be limited to sixty members. His first target was a membership of one hundred. He was keenly aware that almost all of the historical organizations established after the founding of the Boston Society, especially those outside of New England, had liberal provisions on membership and were more inclusive than exclusive. Almost all had no numerical limit.[13]

Knowing that a majority of the members strongly opposed expansion, Winthrop and his supporters attempted an act of subterfuge to achieve their objective. One of the Society's endowment funds, the Appleton Fund, exceeded in nominal amount the limit of personal property the Society was allowed to hold by its charter. A committee appointed by the members prepared an application to the General Court for an amendment enlarging the sum to $100,000. This was a perfunctory proposal and had the support of the entire membership. The committee then saw fit to attach a rider to this innocuous application, increasing the number of members from sixty to one hundred.[14] "This raised quite a breese," as Charles F. Adams noted in his diary. Ticknor vigorously opposed the rider. And, surprisingly, so did Savage, who made a curious and inexplicable turnabout from his position a decade earlier. The debate, again, was spirited, but the proponents for expansion were doomed to defeat. Winthrop failed to "stem the tide." The opposition voted down the rider, postponing consideration of expansion until the next year. "I sat

[11] Adams, "Confidential Paper"; M.H.S., Procs., 2(1835–1855):335.

[12] Williams Rawle, "An Inaugural Discourse, Delivered on the 5th of November, 1825, before the Historical Society of Pennsylvania," Memoirs of the Historical Society of Pennsylvania, 1(1826):29.

[13] See Dunlap, American Historical Societies, ch. 4. In 1860, the New-York Historical Society, the nation's second oldest historical society, had 1,500 members (p. 38).

[14] Charles F. Adams, "Confidential Paper on Special Meeting of Jan. 8, 1877" (M.H.S. Archives).

a silent and not unamused witness of all this commotion," wrote Adams.[15]

Undeterred by this defeat, Winthrop laid plans for the next round. He was determined to achieve his objective. His first step was to weaken the opposition by splintering its leadership. He targeted the volatile Savage as a prospective ally. His efforts apparently were successful for, in March 1857, Savage experienced another "rapid change of heart" and, once again, became an exponent of expansion. Functioning as Winthrop's shadow, he introduced a resolution calling for an application to the legislature to increase the membership to one hundred. The motion passed "with only a few dissenting votes." The General Court quickly approved the measure.[16]

Winthrop had done his work with consummate skill. Not only had he defused his critics by winning the support of Savage, he had also manifested a shrewd sense of timing. He coupled his effort for expansion with the opening of the beautiful Dowse library. It was a clever bit of manipulation, befitting a person with his rich political experience. As Charles F. Adams astutely observed, "the increase of 1857 was carried through the influence of Mr. Winthrop at the time of the opening of the Dowse Library, in recognition of the increased life and activity he had then already infused into the organization."[17]

In 1849, President James Savage nominated "Miss F.M. Caulkins" of Norwich, Connecticut, as a corresponding member of the Historical Society. This was a momentous precedent, for never before in the history of the Society had a female been proposed for membership, resident or corresponding.

The Society's nominating committee endorsed Savage's recommendation and submitted her name to the council for review and presentation to the members. The Council approved the committee's choice and, at the subsequent gathering of the members, Savage himself announced the governing body's decision. If they were stunned or protested the

[15] Charles F. Adams, Diary, May 10, 1855 (Adams Papers, M.H.S.). For an analysis of these events in 1855 by Adams, see M.H.S., *Procs.*, 10(1895–1896):323–323.

[16] Charles F. Adams, "Confidential Paper on Special Meeting of Jan. 18, 1877" (M.H.S. Archives).

[17] Adams, "Confidential Paper."

decision, the recording secretary refrained from noting it in his minutes. The twenty-one men who attended the April annual meeting voted Caulkins into membership. Again, the minutes of the meeting make no mention of any discussion of the matter.[18]

It is not likely that any member openly challenged Savage on this issue, as he was a strong-minded individual, "a man of strong and even intense prejudices." A polemical porcupine, he would fight fiercely to win his case. When he developed an opinion, he held to it. As Robert C. Winthrop stated: "His impulsive and even explosive utterances of such opinions were never to be forgotten by those who witnessed them."[19]

Savage also had a violent temper and profane tongue when he became angry. He "hated Cotton Mather with a deadly hatred," and his opinion of Hancock was no better. Charles Deane remembered "how once, at a late hour in the evening, he was returning from some entertainment in company with Mr. Savage, when the latter suddenly stopped before the old John Hancock house, then still overlooking Beacon Street, and, with minatory gestures expressive of hatred and contempt, proceeded to wake the echoes of night by objurgating the former owner of the mansion through forms of speech quite unconventionally profane."[20]

---

[18] M.H.S., *Procs.*, 2(1835–1855):425.

[19] For biographical data on this colorful character and accomplished amateur historian-editor, see M.H.S., *Procs.*, 12(1871–1873):433–442, 16(1878):133–134, 2d ser., 20(1906–1907): 235–244. Charles Francis Adams painted this word portrait of Savage: "In some respects Mr Savage is a valuable man. His integrity is great, his industry extraordinary, and his acuteness considerable. But on the other hand, he is tedious, bigoted and inconsequential—full of Boston notions engrafted upon old John Bull prejudices." Charles F. Adams, Diary, Mar. 8, 1855 (Adams Papers, M.H.S.).

[20] M.H.S., *Procs.*, 12(1871–1873):441; 2d ser., 20(1906–1907):241. Savage's disputatious character is further illustrated by an encounter he had with John Quincy Adams in 1843. Adams had agreed to present a public bicentennial lecture on the New England Confederation. Two weeks before the lecture, President Savage visited Adams. "I had a long conversation with him," Adams recorded in his diary, "chiefly upon a question fit only to make a learned body ridiculous by forming a subject for divided opinions, and even of controversy—that is, on the day of the ceremony. The day of the Confederation was 19th May 1643. The day chosen for the celebration is the 29th of May, because at that time the difference between the calendars was only ten days. But the difference is now two days more: and I told Mr. Savage that as the 19th of May of old style of the present year is the 31st of the new style, I thought they should take the 31st for the celebration. But he and Judge Davis [U.S. District Court Judge Isaac P. Davis, the Society's cabinet-keeper] have settled the point between themselves on principle. He argued it with me, astronomically

A New Life on Tremont Street

The vote came on Caulkins's fifty-fifth birthday. The minutes failed to remark on the historic significance of her election and made only the pithy notation: "Miss F.M. Caulkins of Norwich, Connecticut, was chosen Corresponding Member."[21]

Who was this unlikely member? Frances Manwaring Caulkins was born in New London on April 26, 1795.[22] Her family had been pioneers of that area, having settled there near its founding. She was educated in Norwich schools and, for a period, studied under Lydia Huntley Sigourney, later to achieve modest fame as the "Sweet singer of Hartford." From youth, she was an "insatiable reader" and collector of historical and genealogical information, and displayed an "earnest enthusiasm" for historical research. She spent seven years in her uncle's home in New London, where she read extensively in his well-stocked library and wrote articles on local history and local personalities for newspapers. To earn a livelihood, she became a teacher in a girls' school in Norwich and, later, a principal of a similar institution in New London. She never married.

Because of her profound interest in religion, she became an author of inspirational pamphlets for the American Tract Society in New York City. In the late 1850s, she also produced six volumes of Bible studies for children. Perhaps reflecting the influence of Sigourney, she dabbled in verse, but history was really her primary interest and she became an avid exponent of it in the 1840s. In 1845, she published a *History of Norwich*; she re-wrote much of this work and produced a second edition in 1866. In 1852, she wrote a *History of New London*; she slightly revised this work and issued a second edition in 1860. Both of these admirable volumes were of extremely high quality. A modern authority, Malcolm Freiberg, has written a glowing assessment of these two books: "Remarkable for their time and remarkable even by today's sterner standards, these two studies remain classics of how local history can be

---

and politically, with such lucid illustration that I lost the thread of his syllogism, and finally did not understand him at all." Charles F. Adams, ed., *Memoirs of John Quincy Adams*, 12 vols. (Philadelphia, 1874–1877), 11:375. Adams presented his lecture on May 29, not May 31.

[21] M.H.S., *Procs.*, 2(1835–1855):425.

[22] For further detail on Caulkins, see the biographical sketch by Malcolm Freiberg, in Edward James, Janet W. James, Paul S. Boyer, eds., *Notable American Women, 1607–1950* (Cambridge, Mass., 1971), 1:313–314.

written. For they are local history writ large, without parochialism (if with a gentle local pride), and with an unswerving reliance on what the original records had to say. Neither title has been superseded."[23]

Apparently, Savage had been much taken by her historical, as well as genealogical, achievements. This is clearly suggested in a letter he wrote on February 19, 1849, in which he praised Caulkins's writings and added: "I wish in some way to get into the lady's good graces."[24] The following month, he nominated her for membership, and within another month she was duly elected.

However, during her two decades of membership, Caulkins never visited the Society or attended a meeting; nor did she submit any contributions to the *Proceedings*. Stewart Mitchell wrote in 1949: "Just how this lady managed to crash the select masculine circle of the Society may never be known, but there she remained for twenty years in solitary confinement."[25] Not until 1966, 117 years later, did another female "crash the select masculine circle of the Society."[26]

After its incorporation in 1794, the Society decided to develop a seal. Belknap apparently had given some thought to this issue shortly after founding the organization. A document in his personal papers, dated 1791, related to a seal: "For the Historical Society a Beehive—supported by two Beavers Nil Magnum sine labore Nothing great is done without labour." But he did not prepare a sketch of the beehive and beavers or submit his idea for formal consideration.[27]

In December of 1794, the Society designated James Winthrop a committee of one to design a seal. The son of the distinguished Hollis Professor of Mathematics of Harvard and himself part-time librarian at the college, "troublesome James" was an erratic personality, who "would get drunk at unexpected moments and then make mischief."[28] This time, though, he got right to the task and submitted a sketch the following month. It consisted of:

[23] *Notable American Women*, 1:313.

[24] James Savage Papers, M.H.S. The correspondent was probably Sylvester Judd, an historian-antiquarian from Northampton, Mass.

[25] Mitchell, *Handbook*, 11.

[26] See Chapter 16.

[27] Tucker, *Clio's Consort*, 103.

[28] Mitchell, *Handbook*, 3–4.

A New Life on Tremont Street

An antiquary sitting on a ruin, and copying an inscription from the pedestal of an obelisk. Beyond the obelisk appears an ancient wall and gateway, and behind the wall a pyramid, and are seen, together with some scattered fragments of columns, behind the antiquary. The legend, 'Massachusetts Historical Society, 1794. *E Vestutate Lux.*'[29]

The members were less than enthusiastic over Winthrop's proposal, as reflected by their subsequent vote: "that the subject be referred to the next meeting of the Society; and that, in the mean time, each member turn his attention to it."[30] Winthrop's idea did not even receive a second review.

Belknap retained a strong interest in the subject. He wrote in his diary in December 1796: "Device and motto for a Seal for Historical Society a flying *eagle*—a ranging *wolf*—and a *shark*—all seeking their prey." Thus, Belknap replaced bees and beavers with more predatory creatures. For reasons unknown, he also failed to present his new conception to the members, and so the idea died aborning.

Nothing further developed on the seal until the Society moved into its Tremont Street quarters in 1833. On August 27, the members appointed President John Davis a committee of one to "prepare a device for a seal for the Society" and report at the next meeting. Davis submitted his report on February 27, 1834.[31]

A devotee of classical literature, he sought inspiration from a "well-known anecdote" involving Virgil and Caesar Augustus. The latter had sponsored a series of shows and games for the populace of Rome. Virgil, then a young, unknown poet, as the story went, anonymously composed two flattering verses, in which he equated Caesar with Jupiter:

Nocte pluit tota, redeunt spectacula mane,
Divisum imperium cum Jove Caesar habet.

(It rains all night, the games return with day,
Caesar with Jove thus holds divided sway.)

Virgil posted his distich on a wall of the Forum. The composition attracted considerable attention and there was a call for the poet to step

---

[29] A facsimile of Winthrop's "Report of a Seal for the Historical Society," which contains his "rought sketch," is in M.H.S., *Procs.*, 1(1791–1835): between 338 and 339.

[30] Tucker, *Clio's Consort*, 103.

[31] On Davis's contribution and attendant developments, see: M.H.S., *Procs.*, 1(1791–1835):483–485, 15(1876–1877):256–258.

forward and be recognized. Virgil was too modest to do so. Not so a "wretched poetaster" named Bathyllus, who claimed the authorship and was duly honored by an unsuspecting Augustus.

Virgil was understandably annoyed by Bathyllus's act of deceit. He took revenge by writing and posting the following five verses below the two verses he had written earlier:

> Hos ego versiculos feci, tulit alter honores;
>> Sic vos non vobis fertis aratra boves;
>> Sic vos non vobis mellificatis apes;
>> Sic vos non vobis vellera fertis oves;
>> Sic vos non vobis nidificatis aves.

> [I wrote these lines; another has borne away the honor -
>> Thus do ye, oxen, for others bear the yoke;
>> Thus do ye, bees, for others make honey;
>> Thus do ye, sheep, wear fleeces for others;
>> Thus do ye, birds, for others build nests.]

Davis extracted the motto for the Society's seal—"Sic vos non vobis"—from Virgil's offering and added a beehive to round out the symbolism (did he resurrect Belknap's beehive?). In the impish words of Stewart Mitchell, former librarian and director of the Society:

> The President had found his source of inspiration, but the use of it required discretion. It was obvious that it would never do to liken the Members to oxen under the yoke—dragging a plow, perhaps. Nor would it be proper to think of them as sheep about to be sheared. Least of all could they be birds and build nests for cuckoos. Only the bees remained out of the verses of Virgil, but bees had always had a good reputation for the sweetness and light of their honey and their wax. The most savage critic of humanity had made this famous. So the good judge introduced a hive into his design to illustrate the motto *Sic vos non vobis*. Promptly, and with appreciation, the Society accepted his suggestion for its seal, and the thought has survived all the changes and chances of more than a century. Thus it was the *Sic vos non vobis* prevailed over erratic James Winthrop's *E Vestutate Lux*.[32]

Davis dated the origin of the Society from the year of its founding (1791) whereas Winthrop had used the date of incorporation (1794).

Davis's creation came under question in 1857 by certain members and

[32] Mitchell, *Handbook*, 8.

the Society appointed a committee to review a new design submitted by
fellow member Nahum Mitchell. Taking a conservative tack, the committee concluded that the "old seal, although inferior in beauty to the
sketch, made by Mr. Mitchell, and defective also, in point of sharpness
and depth, yet gives an impression sufficiently clear, distinct, and otherwise good for all practical purposes. To discard it for a new one, merely
because the latter is better suited to the present advanced state of art,
would afford a precedent for continued changes, in order to keep pace
with the progress of improvement. Such changes weaken the confirma-
tive proof derived from a corporate seal and might even bring its identity
or genuineness into question, to the detriment or hazard of corporate
interests. There is besides, a certain degree of respect, commonly enter-
tained for the antiquity of a seal, which should be cherished by a Society
like ours."[33]

Thus, tradition triumphed over modernity. All remained quiet on the
seal front until the annual meeting of 1881, when Henry W. Haynes,
an avid student of the classics, read a paper in which he challenged Virgil's
authorship of the Society's motto. Haynes marshalled a formidable list
of scholarly authorities to support his allegation and concluded: "Although I acknowledge the merits of this father of Latin grammarians
[Donatus], I think that his authority ought no longer to be invoked to
prove Vergil's authorship of our motto; and I fear that its paternity,
instead of being as respectable as has been imagined, is in fact rather
dubious."[34] If any member saw fit to challenge Haynes's contention, the
recording secretary failed to note it. The issue did not surface again
and Society publications continued to ascribe attribution of the motto to
Virgil.

From its founding until the mid-nineteenth century, the Society was a
hardscrabble institution. Its endowment may not have been as thin as
the homeopathic soup made from the shadow of a pigeon that had
starved to death, to recall Abraham Lincoln's well-known apothegm, but

[33] M.H.S. Recording Secretary, Records, 2:114 (M.H.S. Archives).

[34] M.H.S., *Procs.*, 18(1880–1881):402–404. Haynes was a man of many talents and
interests. He was a lawyer, archaeologist, classical scholar, and taught Latin and Greek at
the University of Vermont. He once presented a paper at the Society on the "custom of
driving a pin or nail in a building." See his memoir, ibid., 48(1914–1915):128–132.

it was small, less than a million dollars excluding the value of its property. The Society's basic source of support was members' entrance fees, annual dues, and, on rare occasion, life memberships. Because of its low membership, entrance fees and annual dues did not produce a large amount of income.[35] In 1791, the entrance fee was set at $5 and annual dues at $2. A life membership cost $34. These sums remained in effect until 1839, when the annual dues were increased to $3 "for the purpose of having the Library kept open, and to meet the additional expense thereof and of warming the room."[36]

The charges were altered during the remainder of the century, with increases taking place in most categories:

1853
Entrance fee $8
Annual dues 3
Life membership 30

1873
Entrance fee $20
Annual dues 10
Life membership 150

1857
Entrance fee $10
Annual dues 5
Life membership 60

1881
Entrance fee $25
Annual dues 10
Life membership 150

1864
Entrance fee $10
Annual dues 7
Life membership 60

[35] Some of the members became notorious delinquents in the payment of dues. The Rev. William Bentley is a case in point. After becoming involved in a heated dispute with the Society over a publication issue, Bentley refused to attend meetings or pay his dues. On Sept. 3, 1808, he reported in his diary the receipt of a "letter for dues from [Treasurer Josiah] Quincy which I did not notice. I have now a bill for 12 years due and a vote of the Society that all delinquent members after three months shall be sued. So much for the Historical Society" (Bentley, *Diary*, 3:381).

Daniel Webster was another delinquent. In 1847, the treasurer had the "painful duty" of reporting that Webster was "more than three years overdue" on his dues and, therefore, he removed him from the Society's rolls. Webster finally paid his dues in 1848 and was reinstated. He never attended a Society meeting. See M.H.S., *Procs.*, 64(1930–1932): 47–48.

[36] M.H.S., *Procs.*, 2(1835–1855):143.

A New Life on Tremont Street

While the Society did not expect to receive financial aid from the state legislature, it did hope to secure sturdy support from its members. But the hope was not realized. Despite its high reputation as a learned society and a membership which, while small, included many men of means, the Society was not the recipient of major gifts. Nor did the Society press members for large donations. George E. Ellis, a future president of the Society, underscored this point in 1855: "It is remarkable that while some of the very richest men in the city are members of the Society who on occasion might contribute a million of dollars without being deprived of a single comfort or even luxury of life, we probably do less in the way of pecuniary demand or outlay—than any similar society in the world."[37]

Member Robert C. Winthrop, Jr., informed Charles C. Smith in 1888 that he refused to write a memoir of John C. Gray I because, "altho' he left a large property and neither wife nor child, he did not leave a dollar to a Society of which he had been 40 years a member."[38]

An article in the *Boston Evening Transcript* on April 16, 1852, underscored the Society's financially impoverished condition. After presenting a positive assessment of the Society, "one of the oldest and most efficient literary institutions in the country," the contributor decried its lack of finances which worked a severe hardship upon the library, in particular: "The society, unfortunately, has no funds to purchase books or even to pay the salary of a librarian. Its whole income is derived from an assessment of three dollars a year on its members, amounting to a hundred and eighty dollars annually, which is barely sufficient to pay its incidental expenses."

The writer then presented the novel notion that the general citizenry of Boston and the Commonwealth should provide support for the Society: "A *working* society like this, which has already accomplished so much, is certainly deserving of the patronage of an intelligent community; and it is greatly to be desired that some of the surplus wealth of the city and state might be turned into this channel, so that the society's rooms might be kept constantly open for study, and a librarian be

[37] Ellis to Samuel Osgood, Apr. 27, 1855 (New-York Historical Society). Osgood was the domestic corresponding secretary of the New York society.

[38] Robert C. Winthrop, Jr., to Charles C. Smith, June 17, 1888 (Charles C. Smith Papers, M.H.S.).

always on the spot to facilitate the investigations of that growing class of inquirers—the students of American history."

This strong appeal did not result in a rash of public contributions. The Society received its first major gift in 1854 and, interestingly, it came from a non-member, Samuel Appleton, a prominent Boston business-man. The gift, a bequest, was $10,000 in stock and was presented by the three trustees of Appleton's estate "in accordance with what we believe to have been his wish."[39] The gift was to be placed in an endowment fund with the accumulated income to be used for "procuring, preservation, preparation, and publication of historical papers." The Society sold the stock and realized a sum of $12,203, which became the principal fund.

The Appleton bequest established the precedent. In subsequent years, the Society received additional modest gifts, which were also established as endowment funds. David Sears created The Massachusetts Historical Trust Fund in 1855 with a $2,000 donation; Sears and Nathaniel Thayer later supplemented this fund. Dowse, another non-member, contributed $10,000 in 1857, along with his library. George Peabody also gave $22,123 in 1857, and James Savage, a former president, bequeathed $6,000 in 1873.[40]

During the 1840s, the Society became embroiled in heated disputes with both the State of Connecticut and the Commonwealth of Massachusetts over the return of manuscript collections. Acting at the direction of Gov. Roger S. Baldwin, the Connecticut secretary of state, Daniel P. Tyler, sent the Society a resolution from the General Assembly in September 1845, which stated that the "numerous official letters and valuable cor-respondence intimately connected with executive and legislative acts of this State, during an important and interesting period of its history" by Gov. Jonathan Trumbull belonged in the office of the Connecticut sec-retary of state, not the Massachusetts Historical Society. This was a

---

[39] M.H.S., *Procs.*, 2(1835–1855):597–601, 605. Only one of the trustees, Nathan Ap-pleton, was a member of the Society. The remaining two, Nathaniel L. Bowditch and William Appleton, joined the ranks later when openings developed; Bowditch was elected in 1856 and Appleton in 1868.

[40] Information on these funds is contained in the published minutes of the Society in the *Proceedings*. All funds were listed in the treasurer's reports at annual meetings.

collection Jeremy Belknap had acquired in 1794. Tyler demanded the return of the documents.

The Society categorically rejected Tyler's claim of replevin. Connecticut renewed its effort in 1846 and, again, the Society stood its ground, asserting "that it is their duty to preserve the same in their own Library, in conformity with the will of the donors." The Society's response emphasized that Trumbull's son, David, had made the donation on the basis of his father's desire to place his papers in a "public library, as materials for future historians." They also inserted this key statement from David's letter: "Had the Massachusetts Historical Society existed during his life, there is no doubt but he would have chosen to give them to an institution, whose patriotic views they would so directly subserve, in preference to a collegiate or other library, where they probably would soon become 'food for worms.' "[41]

In 1850, the Society became involved in an effort relating to its role as an institution of public benefit. It led a movement to preserve the local records of the Commonwealth. Becoming increasingly concerned about the "insecure and decaying condition of many of the municipal records of our towns, etc.," it appointed a three-man committee, chaired by George F. Hoar, to study the problem and recommend suggestions for improvement. These would then be incorporated into a memorial to the General Court. The ultimate objective was to enact legislation to alleviate or correct the problem.

At the December meeting, Hoar, who took all of his assigned responsibilities seriously, went far beyond his charge. He presented not only a draft of a memorial but a draft of statutory provisions as well. In his memorial, Hoar emphasized the need to preserve Massachusetts's local records, stressing the fundamental principles which Belknap had enunciated in the eighteenth century. "The careful preservation of public records and documents throughout the Commonwealth," he began, "presents an object worthy the attention of an enlightened gov-

---

[41] On the Trumbull Papers issue, see M.H.S., *Procs.*, 2(1835–1855): 322, 323, 328, 330–333, 343–346, 355, 357, 359. The battle between the Society and the State of Connecticut raged, intermittently until 1921, when the Bostonians finally capitulated and transferred the documents to the Connecticut State Library. See Chapter 13.

ernment. Such records possess a high and increasing interest as memorials of the Fathers and Founders of the Commonwealth, to be preserved with reverential care. But as materials for illustrating its history, general or local, they are invaluable, and should be guarded, as far as possible, by the protection of the public law against the decay of time, or the mutilation, injury, or loss to which indifference or neglect may expose them. No adequate security, it is believed, is now provided for these important historical documents in the existing statutes of the Commonwealth."

Hoar went on to propose statutory provisions for a significant program of documentary preservation for the Commonwealth. He recommended that local and county officials be required (1) to maintain and safeguard all records within their custody; (2) to create copies of endangered records; (3) to keep records within their jurisdiction and not allow them to be removed, "except upon summons in due form of law"; (4) to keep all county, city, or town records open to public inspection; (5) to provide repositories for records of defunct townships or common lands; (6) to allow any county, city, or town the right to make copies of records in the custody of other jurisdictions; (7) to penalize any town clerk for not conforming to the regulations; and (8) to mandate that records of disbanded churches or religious societies, which "not have been otherwise provided for in due form of law," be turned over to the town or city clerk of the municipality involved.[42]

The Society approved Hoar's report and promptly appointed Richard Frothingham, Jr., a committee of one to present the memorial to the General Court and "use his efforts to enforce the same."[43] Frothingham was an excellent choice for this assignment. A resident of Charlestown, he had been a member of the house of representatives for a decade and was highly respected as a political leader and amateur historian. He had an extensive record of historical publications and was frequently selected to deliver addresses at commemorative programs.[44]

Frothingham was eminently successful in his assignment. The General Court enacted legislation "covering the principal points" of the

---

[42] M.H.S., *Procs.*, 2(1835–1855):461–463, 466.

[43] M.H.S., *Procs.*, 2(1835–1855):463.

[44] For Frothingham's memoir, see M.H.S., *Procs.*, 2d ser., 1(1884–1885): 381–393.

draft statement. This was the first major action taken by the Commonwealth to develop a state-wide program to preserve local public records.

The Society also sponsored public lecture programs. The purpose was educational, and the intended audience was the local citizenry. At its final meeting at the Tontine Crescent on May 30, 1833, the Society appointed a committee to organize a series of public lectures that fall and winter. All speakers were to be drawn from the membership and there was to be an admission charge.[45] The series was fully organized after the Society moved to Tremont Street. Diverse in subject matter, the lectures were held at the Athenaeum on Monday evenings and featured some of the more talented literati of the membership:

Edward Everett	Introductory
Alexander H. Everett	The Life of Columbus
Jared Sparks	The Treason of Arnold
John Pickering	Indian Languages
Joseph Willard	Life, Character, and Services of General Oglethorpe
James Savage	The Different Principles on which the European Colonies in America were founded
William Sullivan	Notices of some Eminent Men who have deceased within the last Fifty Years
Joseph B. Felt	The Prevailing Fashion of Dress in New England, from its first settlement to the present time
George Bancroft	The Origin of Puritanism
Convers Francis	The Regicide Judges
Leverett Saltonstall	The Colonial Charter and Laws of Massachusetts
John G. Palfrey	Progress of American Periodical Literature

The Society derived a profit of $146.16 from this series.[46]

---

[45] M.H.S., *Procs.*, 1(1791–1835):470–472, 477, 478n., 480. Those who purchased tickets to the lectures were permitted to visit the library and cabinet on Thursday afternoons from 3 P.M. "till evening."

[46] For the 1833 series, see M.H.S., *Procs.*, 1(1791–1835):471, 473, 477–478, 488n.

The Massachusetts Historical Society

Buoyed by this success, the Society laid plans for another series in 1835–1836. There were fourteen lectures in this program:

Edward Everett	Mexico
Edward Everett	Peru
William Sullivan	The Feudal Law
John G. Palfrey	The Capture of Louisburg
Alexander H. Everett	The French Revolution
Alexander H. Everett	The Revolution of the Three Days
Charles W. Upham	Sir George Downing (in two parts)
Joseph B. Felt	Sir Edmund Andros's Administration in Massachusetts
Francis C. Gray	The History of the Pilgrims (in two parts)
James T. Austin	The First Provincial Congress in Massachusetts
John Pickering	The Islands in the Indian Ocean, as connected with the Original Population of the American Continent
John G. King	The Sources and Uses of History[47]

The following year, the Society presented another series of fourteen lectures:

James T. Austin	The Siege of Boston (in two parts)
William Sullivan	The Use of History, Tradition, Boston Fifty Years Ago, and on the Changes in Boston within Fifty Years (in two parts)
Alden Bradford	The Commissioners of Charles II as a Court of Appeals in Massachusetts in 1664
Alexander H. Everett	The Constitution of the United States
Joseph B. Felt	Rival Chiefs, D'Aulnay and La Tour, Governors of Nova Scotia
William Lincoln	French Neutrals
Alexander Young	The Pequot War, 1637
Alden Bradford	The Character of the Patriots of the Revolution
Convers Francis	The Character of Father Rale
Samuel Swett	The Life of Governor Winthrop

[47] M.H.S., *Procs.*, 2(1835–1855):33–34. Ticket sales yielded $867; expenses were $251; the net profit was $616. These lectures were presented at the Masonic Temple.

A New Life on Tremont Street

O.W.B. Peabody   The Life of General Putnam
Charles W. Upham   The Career and Character of Timo-
                                 thy Pickering[48]

Charles Francis Adams attended Felt's lecture and made these comments in his diary: "Mr. Brooks took tea with us and dragged me out afterwards to a Lecture. He seemed so desirous of having some companion that in order to please him rather than myself I went. I was the more induced to this as the lecturer was Mr. Felt, a sort of relation of ours whom I somewhat respected. He is an Antiquary and withal not being very attractive either as preacher or Lecturer would not be likely to draw full houses. His Lecture was upon the intrigues of the French Officers in Nova Scotia during the early part of the seventeenth century and particularly the feud between La Tour and d'Aulnay. The subject was a more fruitful one of romantic incident than I expected and in the hands of an Orator would have paid largely. As it was Mr. Felt was far from dull."[49]

The Society sponsored yet another series in 1841–1842. The leadoff speaker was former President John Quincy Adams. His topic was "The War Between Britain and China," and it drew a throng of listeners. "We never saw such an audience," one reporter commented:

> . . . It seemed to us, as we cast our eyes around upon the multitude, that all the eminence of the city had congregated there to do honor to the venerable and learned ex-President, and to receive instruction from his eloquent lips. We can hardly think of a man in Boston or its vicinity, distinguished in literature, science, politics, or commerce, whom we did not see there . . . the spacious room was literally crammed, and hundreds who had calculated on purchasing tickets at the door, went away, unable to obtain admission.[50]

The other speakers and their topics were:

Joseph B. Felt   Historical View of the Fasts and
                                   Thanksgivings of New England
Alden Bradford   The Discovery of North American and
                                   First Settlement of Massachusetts

---

[48] M.H.S., *Procs.*, 2(1835–1855):79–80. Ticket sales brought in $449.50; expenses were $237.67; the net profit was $211.83. These lectures also were delivered at the Masonic Temple.

[49] Marc Friedlaender et al., eds., *Diary of Charles Francis Adams* (Cambridge, Mass., 1986), 7:158, 159n.

[50] *Salem Register*, Nov 29, 1841.

William Jenks	Reflections on some Peculiarities in Character, Circumstances, and Conduct of the Early Fathers of New England
Henry Giles	The Spirit of Irish History and English Dominion
Charles Burroughs	Life of Sir William Pepperell, with an Account of the Siege of Louisburg in 1745 (in two parts)
Francis Baylies	The Expedition against Quebec under General Wolfe
William Cogswell	The History of Education in the United States
Charles Francis Adams	The Origin of Society
Emory Washburn	The Life and Times of William Stoughton
John Lord	The German Barbarians
Convers Francis	The Visit of Bishop Berkeley to America[51]

With the ticket charge set at $1 for the series, these lectures grossed $885. After expenses, the Society netted $643.65. The committee printed a total of 1,050 tickets, sold 885, and provided the lecturers with 30 free tickets; 135 tickets were unsold. Giles, who was not a member of the Society, was the only speaker to receive an honorarium ($15).[52]

In the next few years, the Society considered sponsoring additional series, but it was not able to organize these programs.[53]

The bicentennial of the first confederation of the New England colonies (1643) prompted the Society to sponsor a special public lecture at the First Church on May 29, 1843.[54] It persuaded John Quincy Adams to serve as principal speaker. The former president of the United States proved to be a strong drawing card. Despite being scheduled for 11 A.M. on a Monday, the lecture drew a sizable audience. The Society had extended invitations to historical organizations in New England and

[51] M.H.S., *Procs.*, 2(1835–1855):226–227.

[52] See the advertisement for the series in *Boston Evening Transcript*, Sept. 4, 1841; M.H.S., *Procs.*, 2(1835–1855):226–227.

[53] On the importance of the "lecture-series system" in the cultural life of nineteenth-century Boston, see Martin Green, *The Problem of Boston: Some Readings in Cultural History* (New York, 1966), 75–76.

[54] The confederation was a loose union formed among the colonies of Massachusetts Bay, Plymouth, Connecticut, and New Haven. It lasted for forty years.

throughout the United States. The New Hampshire Historical Society sent seven delegates; the American Antiquarian Society, eight; the New-York Historical Society, eight; the Georgia Historical Society, one; the Connecticut Historical Society also had representation at the meeting.[55]

Adams was pleased with his performance. He noted in his diary: "I then delivered my address, beginning at twenty minutes past eleven and closing at five minutes past one, one hour and three-quarters, omitting about one-eighth of what I had written. It was very well received, and there was no manifestation of what I most dreaded,—a sense of weariness on the part of the auditory. The attention was general and unremitting to the last. The house was well filled, but not crowded; excepting the members of the Society, about as many women as men."[56]

The final lecture series the Society sponsored during its residence at Tremont Street occurred in 1869. These were presented at the Lowell Institute[57] and dealt entirely with aspects of Massachusetts history, an idea conceived by George E. Ellis. Each was limited to one hour.[58]

Robert C. Winthrop	Massachusetts and its Early History-Introductory Lecture
George E. Ellis	The Aims and Purposes of the Founders of the Massachusetts Colony
George E. Ellis	Treatment of Intruders and Dissentients by the Founders of Massachusetts
Samuel F. Haven	History of Grants under the Great Council for New England
William Brigham	The Colony of New Plymouth and its Relations to Massachusetts
Emory Washburn	Slavery as it once prevailed in Massachusetts

[55] M.H.S., *Procs.*, 2(1835–1855):254.

[56] Quoted in M.H.S., *Procs.*, 2(1835–1855):254n.

[57] The Lowell Institute was founded in 1836 through the munificence of John Lowell, Jr. It provided funds for public lectures on science, religion, and literature by the leading thinkers of the day "for the sole purpose of generating ideas in Boston." Lowell's objective was an enlightened citizenry. He set the condition that a male Lowell was always to be the trustee of the Institute. See Edward Weeks, *The Lowells and Their Institute* (Boston, 1966). Also of value is Harriet Knight Smith, *The History of the Lowell Institute* (Boston, 1898).

[58] M.H.S., *Procs.*, 11(1869–1870):33; M.H.S. Scrapbook, M.H.S. Archives, Boston and New York City newspaper clippings on the "admirable course of lectures."

Charles W. Upham	Records of Massachusetts under its First Charter
Oliver Wendell Holmes	The Medical Profession in Massachusetts
Samuel Eliot	Early Relations With the Indians
Chandler Robbins	The Regicides Sheltered in New England
Joel Parker	The First Charter and the Early Religious Legislation of Massachusetts
Edward E. Hale	Puritan Politics of England and New England
George B. Emerson	Education in Massachusetts: Early Legislation and History

The series was enormously successful, and the Society decided to publish the lectures, which was done in 1869.

The unusual interest in this series led the Society to consider plans for a followup set in the succeeding year. It did not materialize, however, due to the difficulty of organizing such an elaborate program.

In a cumulative sense, the Society's lecture programs, more than its publications, sharply increased the reputation and visibility of the organization in the Boston area. Newspaper reports of these programs aided in this process. After the Lowell Institute series, the standing committee stated in its report to the membership: "The interest taken in these lectures encourages us to hope that they have strengthened the hold of the Society upon the community."[59]

If the members had been pleased by the new quarters on Tremont Street in 1833, their pleasure was short-lived. Within a decade, the perennial and predictable space problem surfaced. The five rooms of the Society became stuffed to bursting with books, newspapers, pamphlets, documents, portraits, and assorted historical bric-a-brac. The librarian and cabinet-keeper found it necessary to use even the hallways for storage. They constantly shuffled materials from room to room, from hallway to hallway, seeking to open up some free space for the ever-expanding collection. Shelf space for the books, in particular, became a premium.

In 1844, the Society appointed a committee to consider "extending the

---

[59] M.H.S., *Procs.*, 11(1869–1870):33.

accommodations for the Library and to report a plan." The plan called for the partitioning of the "front room," with the rear portion becoming a storage area for newspapers and other items. It was implemented.[60]

This renovation provided only temporary relief, since the Society continued to collect aggressively. In 1852, a local resident with a boosterish temperament took to the public press and scolded the Society for the unkempt appearance of its quarters, calling specific attention to the poor housing of the portraits of the "solid men of Boston":

> Through your valuable paper I wish to draw the attention of the public to the shabby condition of the rooms of the Massachusetts Historical Society, and of the pictures in their collection. The rooms are unworthy to invite a stranger to visit, and altogether unsuitable to the reported liberality of the rich men of Boston. They are a reproach to the memory of the departed. A very few of the *thousands* spent upon illegitimate and foolish schemes, would make those pictures and rooms as they should be—time-honored and of inestimable value to the city of Boston. Many of those pictures are likenesses of the true and real 'solid *men* of Boston;' words now so often referred to with great unction. As works of art many of these likenesses might not be valuable, but they are valuable and without price, as representations of truly great men,—not of men, the mere agents and demi-gods of a faction. As works of art no one can ever decide on their merit until they have been put into the hands of the picture-restorer. If they were worth receiving and being kept in a room with a *name*, they are, without doubt, worth preserving: but if not soon put into the hands of a judicious restorer, they will be lost to posterity, and to the future history of Boston and America.[61]

By mid-century, the space problem had reached the critical stage. This resulted in the appointment of another committee, a three-member body. The officers directed this group to begin negotiations with the Provident Institution for Savings Bank for the purchase of the third story. These deliberations were not successful, and in 1853 the Society enlarged the committee's charge, empowering it "to obtain such accommodation in this or other estate in this city; and, for that purpose, may sell and convey the right and property of this Society in the premises to said Provident Institution, and by indenture of lease, or otherwise, may procure the desired benefit."[62]

[60] M.H.S., *Procs.*, 2(1835–1855):270, 285.
[61] *Boston Evening Transcript*, Nov. 17, 1852.
[62] M.H.S., *Procs.*, 2(1835–1855):467–468, 476, 547–548, 549.

In addition to the lack of space and their "dingy" character, the Tremont Street quarters also gave off an odor caused by the "many natural curiosities,—plants, insects, birds, &c., supposed to be in a state of 'preservation,'" but which "either from neglect or from their succumbing to the law of things earthly, [they] turned to dust, and a musty odor from them . . . pervaded the apartments." The quarters also were bitterly cold in the winter months. "There was an old drum stove, called air-tight," although the members "used to think sometimes it was also heat-tight."[63]

Thus, after only twenty years, the Society was prepared to sell its portion of 30 Tremont Street to the bank, if it could acquire more spacious and affordable quarters elsewhere.

Then an important development took place. As the Society began the search for a new home, the bank decided to vacate its quarters and relocate in nearby Temple Place. This opened the promising possibility of the Society acquiring the entire building at Tremont Street. The Society's committee and bank officials met in 1854 and 1855 and exchanged correspondence on real estate matters, but nothing conclusive came from their contacts. At one point, the bank offered the Society the option of leasing the second story of its newly-acquired building in Temple Place, but the committee decided that this site was not suited to the Society's purposes.

In 1855, the Society expanded the committee to ten members and directed it to examine another potential headquarters, "the church-building in Freeman Place, and any other buildings or places fit for the Society's use." After inspecting the church, the committee concluded that it was "not prepared to recommend an abandonment of the present premises."[64] President Robert C. Winthrop, who had served on the three-member committee, later recalled that he and his colleagues had "visited many localities, and considered many schemes; but these gentlemen at length decided that we ought not to abandon the old hive where so much precious honey had been made and stored, and where so many historical and personal associations were clustered."[65]

The issue came to a head in late 1855. The original committee of three

---

[63] Comments by George E. Ellis in 1873. M.H.S., *Procs.*, 13(1873–1875):21–22.
[64] M.H.S., *Procs.*, 3(1855–1858):42–43, 44–45.
[65] M.H.S., *Procs.*, 12(1871–1873):133.

met with the trustees of the bank and offered to purchase its portion of 30 Tremont Street, including the land on which the structure stood. After further negotiations, the deal was completed in February 1856. The purchase price was $35,000. The Society raised $7,500 from resident members and a few wealthy Bostonians, and borrowed $27,500 from the Suffolk Savings Bank for Seamen.[66]

On March 1, 1856, the Society leased the lower floor to its mortgage-holder, the Suffolk Savings Bank, for fifteen years at an annual rate of $2,200. This was done out of financial expediency. The Society also leased the third floor to the Massachusetts Charitable Mechanic Association at a rent of $300 per year. This transaction was only a verbal agreement which the Society could abrogate "at will." The Society knew that this would be a short-term rental since the Mechanic Association was intent upon constructing its own quarters and had purchased land for this purpose that same year. The rental turned out to be even briefer in duration than apparently contemplated by both parties. A month later, on April 12, the president of the Mechanic Association informed his fellow trustees that the Historical Society had requested that they vacate the rooms they then occupied "on account of some contemplated alterations in the building."[67] This involved plans to convert the hall on the third floor into a library area, complete with bookshelves. Portraits also were to be stored there.

When the Mechanic Association moved, the Society occupied both top floors and the entire attic. It now had space to house the extant collection. More importantly, it was committed to 30 Tremont Street for the foreseeable future.

---

[66] For details of this transaction, see M.H.S., *Procs.*, 3(1855–1858):47–48, 49, 64–67. The key documents can be found in M.H.S. Recording Secretary, Records, 1814–1857, 2:81 (M.H.S. Archives).

[67] *Annals of the Massachusetts Charitable Mechanic Association, 1852 to 1860* (1860), 493.

Chapter 4

The Dowse Library
and Gentlemen's
History Club

T H E S O C I E T Y remained at 30 Tremont
Street for six and one-half decades, from 1833 to 1897. During this
period, it came of age and developed into one of Greater Boston's most
prestigious cultural organizations. Its greatest surge of development
occurred during the lengthy presidency of Robert C. Winthrop, 1855–
1885.[1]

The "Providential President," as George Ellis once called Winthrop,
revolutionized the Society.[2] While his achievements were not monumental in scope, they were substantive and markedly altered the character of the organization. He increased the membership from sixty to
one hundred, which led to a tripling of attendance at meetings. Exer-
cising decisive influence, he brought into the membership a host of
distinguished men of letters, many of whom had national reputations.[3]
These two accomplishments led to more vibrant and stimulating meetings. He had a hand in securing the Dowse Library in 1857 and estab-

[1] For biographical data on Winthrop, see M.H.S., *Procs.*, 2d ser., 2(1885–1886):80–84;
9(1894–1895):218–241 (eulogies by Charles C. Smith, Samuel A. Green, and Charles F.
Adams); 3d ser., 1(1907–1908):97–100.

[2] M.H.S., *Procs.*, 2d ser., 2(1885–1886):82; 3d ser., 1(1907–1908):99.

[3] In the contentious pre-Civil War era, Winthrop made it a point to exclude from
membership anyone sympathetic to the Southern cause. An ardent Whig, he upheld the
Union. Much to the displeasure of Charles F. Adams, during his presidency Winthrop
blocked the membership of Charles Sumner because of his political views. See Charles F.
Adams, Diary, Dec. 10, 1857; Mar. 11, Dec. 9, 1858; Feb. 1, 1859 (Adams Papers).

lishing the room that housed this gift. He took the leading role in instituting a new serial publication, the *Proceedings*, in 1859. He personally secured the George Peabody endowment fund of $20,000 in 1867, the Society's largest gift to that point. Finally, he can be credited with the enlargement of the Tremont Street quarters in 1872–1873. Because of these multiple achievements, his successor, George Ellis, acclaimed Winthrop's presidency the "golden period" of the Society's history.[4] Winthrop, in sum, gave the Society "form, consistence, character, dignity, momentum."[5]

Winthrop was a powerful leader whose presence was strongly felt when the members assembled. He was an arresting personality, a man of marked individuality, a magnetic center. Charles F. Adams, who also possessed these traits, called him "our first and most prominent member," the "head of our roll."[6] Worthington C. Ford offered this assessment of Winthrop's stature in the Society: "Winthrop, courtly, formal and polished, was a Mandarin-like personage before whom the Society burned incense, and in another age would have canonized."[7]

Winthrop shone on the rostrum. When he rose to speak, the members fell into a hush and came to attention. He was a gifted speaker, "a finished orator," a virtuoso of the spoken word.[8] He was blessed with a mellifluous voice and had a dignified and courtly bearing. He had refined his oratorical style in the political arena, in the Massachusetts General Court and the United States Congress; he had been speaker of both the state and federal lower houses.

A "master of commemorative oratory," he served as the main speaker at numerous local and national historical events.[9] He was selected to deliver the oration at the laying of the cornerstone of the Washington Monument on July 4, 1848, and was again chosen to be the main speaker at the completion of the giant structure on February 22, 1885, thirty-seven years later.[10]

---

[4] M.H.S., *Procs.*, 2d ser., 2(1885–1886):84. These many achievements are discussed in more depth later in this chapter.

[5] Charles F. Adams's phrase. M.H.S., *Procs.*, 2d ser., 9(1894–1895):237.

[6] M.H.S., *Procs.*, 2d ser., 9(1894–1895):234. See also, ibid., 56(1922–1923):221–222.

[7] M.H.S., *Procs.*, 48(1914–1915):419.

[8] M.H.S., *Procs.*, 2d ser., 9(1894–1895):221.

[9] M.H.S., *Procs.*, 2d ser., 9(1894–1895):220.

[10] M.H.S., *Procs.*, 2d ser., 2(1885–1886):67.

While an Olympian figure, Winthrop was but one of many talented members of the Society. The roster during the Tremont Street era, the golden age of gentlemen-scholars in Greater Boston, was an extraordinary assembly of literati. Every major author of what has come to be known as the "Massachusetts School of Historians," the group that dominated American historiography for most of the nineteenth century and educated countless millions of Americans (as well as Europeans) on the history of New England and the United States, was affiliated with the Boston society. No other historical organization in the nation could match this illustrious group.[11]

After attending a meeting of the Society in 1859, John Langdon Sibley, the librarian of Harvard University, recorded in his diary:

> It is a remarkable fact that there seems to be no prominent man of letters in Europe or America with whom more or less of the members of the Society are not acquainted personally. Is there any society in the world except the Massachusetts Historical Society, of which this can be said, considering the small number of its members? And what a memorable year 1859, Prescott, Hallam, De Tocqueville, Irving, Macauley. Has there ever been such an era of historical writers? Add to this Humboldt, Sparks, Bancroft, Hildreth, Parkman, Motley, etc. etc.[12]

[11] Some historians from other sections of the nation have resented the dominance and challenged the competence of the Massachusetts writers. As Arthur Schlesinger, Jr., has written: "Scholars to the south and west have often rather irritably found a Yankee bias in the writing of American history—what it would be politically correct these days . . . to call New Englandcentrism." M.H.S., *Procs.*, 103(1991):1. The southern historian Ulrich B. Phillips was one of these anti-Massachusetts critics. "The history of the United States," he wrote in 1903, "has been written by Boston and largely written wrong." Phillips to G.J. Baldwin, May 2, 1903, in Peter Novick, *That Noble Dream: The "Objectivity Question" and the American Historical Profession* (New York, 1988), 73.

[12] John Langdon Sibley, Journal, 1846–1865 (Harvard University Archives). Sibley considered both resident and corresponding members. The year 1859 was not an aberration. Reporting for the Council for the 1884–1885 annual report, Clement H. Hill noted that: Parkman produced two volumes on Montcalm and Wolfe as part of his "France and England in North America" *magnum opus*; Sibley completed the third volume of his *Biographical Sketches of Harvard Graduates*; Oliver Wendell Holmes published his *Life of Emerson* for the "American Men of Letters" series; Henry Cabot Lodge edited the first volume of a new edition of the *Works of Alexander Hamilton*; John T. Morse, Jr., added a *Life of John Adams* volume to the "Lives of American Statesmen" series; Justin Winsor edited volumes 3 and 4 of his *Narrative and Critical History of America*; Horace E. Scudder published a popular *History of the United States*; Samuel A. Green produced

The Dowse Library and Gentlemen's History Club

In eulogizing Robert C. Winthrop in 1894, Charles F. Adams, Jr., stated that he had viewed a photograph of the Society's resident members, taken in the early 1860s at the spacious Brookline estate of Winthrop, then president. He reflected upon the high intellectual quality of these men, citing in particular his father, Winthrop, George S. Hillard, Richard Frothingham, Charles Deane, Francis Parkman, John Lothrop Motley, Oliver Wendell Holmes, Henry Wadsworth Longfellow, Jacob Bigelow, Richard Henry Dana, Russell Lowell, Edmund Quincy, Rockwood Hoar, and Ralph Waldo Emerson. "No society," stated Adams, "whether in the New World or in the Old could boast a choicer array. Orators, statesmen, and diplomats; historians, poets and conversationalists; wits, jurists, philanthropists, philosophers,—they were, and they remain, a galaxy the brilliancy of which time will only enhance."[13]

Even some of the lesser lights were unusually talented. John Torrey Morse, Jr., described one of them:

> I think that the most picturesque member of the Society during the earlier years of my membership was William Everett, the son of Edward Everett. He was a genuine character. Charles Lamb could have immortalised him with one of those inimitable descriptions of Elia. He had certain unfortunate personal traits which interfered with his success in life, but he really was a man of astonishing acquirements, a scholar in the old-fashioned sense of that word. Greek and Roman literature were as familiar to him as the literature of England, and this he knew by heart. He would have chattered with Erasmus in Latin, very fluently. If you asked him for a quotation, even the most recondite, he not only at once placed it for you but probably would repeat the whole page in which it occurred. He had one of those astonishing memories which are incapable of ever forgetting anything. He read voraciously, and the result was that it seemed as though he could have compiled out of his own head the whole *Encyclopaedia Britannica*, barring only the scientific parts, for which department he had no taste. He was an orator, to speak after the fashion of those olden times when oratory was impetuous, dramatic and elaborate. I remember an entertaining incident in illustration of this; that is to say, I remember it, but with one embarrassing hiatus in my memory. Some literary man had

---

seven more tracts on the history of Groton; and other members issued an assortment of ephemeral writings—1884–1885 was also a very productive year for Society authors. M.H.S., *Procs.*, 2d ser., 2(1885–1886):68.

[13] M.H.S., *Procs.*, 2d ser., 9(1894–1895):240–241.

recently died, in England I think, and he was of such eminence that his death was mentioned by our president; and precisely here comes my unfortunate failure to recall who the decedent was! To call him Mr. Blank or Mr. A.B. is a woful bathos, yet inevitable, unless I would lose my little story, and that I will not do; so I limp on. Now Everett was a reverential admirer of this illustrious Unknown and was profoundly afflicted by the decease. Accordingly, after the mention by the chair, he rose to speak, apparently quite extemporaneously; in fact, he had had no opportunity for preparation. He stood for a moment silent, and looked around upon the assemblage impressively. Then throwing out both arms, he exclaimed in tragic tones: *"And is — dead?"* Then again for a moment he gazed upon us, as if adequate expression failed him. But forthwith recovering his command of speech, he poured forth an amazing volume of eloquence, I think I may say, of real eloquence. The tears ran down his cheeks as he spoke. He recited to us, from memory, a whole ode of Horace, of course in the original Latin, and several stanzas from Longfellow. It was really a very striking oratorical display. Although some may have smiled at his ardor—not at the moment, but afterward—yet it was truly effective.[14]

In 1857, the Society acquired title to a majestic private library of 4,665 volumes, one of the finest collections in New England.[15] This massive and unexpected gift from Thomas Dowse of Cambridge not only substantially elevated the quality and scope of the Society's holdings, but also led to a major renovation of its quarters.

Dowse was an unlikely benefactor of the Massachusetts Historical Society.[16] While his roots in the Commonwealth reached back to the colonial past, he was not of the social or economic elite. Born in Charlestown on December 28, 1772, he was "brought up in narrow circumstances." According to his long-time friend Edward Everett, he was "born in the lower walks of life; one might almost say, the lowest of those removed from actual dependence and penury." His father was a tanner and leather dresser.

After losing their Charlestown home in a fire set by British troops

---

[14] M.H.S., *Procs.*, 60(1926–1927):166–167.

[15] *Catalogue of the Private Library of Thomas Dowse of Cambridge, Mass., Presented to the Massachusetts Historical Society, July 30, 1856* (Boston, 1856).

[16] The prime source for Dowse's biography is Edward Everett, "Eulogy on Thomas Dowse," M.H.S., *Procs.*, 3(1855–1858):361–398. Unless otherwise noted, all quotations concerning Dowse are taken from this source. See also Walter M. Whitehill, "The Centenary of the Dowse Library," M.H.S., *Procs.*, 71(1953–1957):167–178.

during the battle of Bunker Hill, the Dowses moved to Holliston and, after a brief stay, settled in Sherborn, the ancestral home of the family, where the father plied his trade.

At age six, Thomas was injured in a fall from an apple tree. The injury, coupled with a later bout with rheumatic fever, left him lame for life. Unable to participate in vigorous physical activities, the sickly child turned to books for "occupation and amusement." He became an omnivorous reader, spending his every cent on books. He came to idolize Sir Walter Scott, the celebrated Scottish poet and novelist. Perhaps he identified with Scott because the author also had suffered from lameness. Dowse later said that "lameness drove us both to books,—him to making them, and me to reading them." Although he "enjoyed scarcely the humblest advantages of education," the "poor lame boy" developed a wide range of knowledge through his extensive reading. "His lameness," wrote Everett, "was the most earnest and successful teacher."

The youngster emulated his father and decided to earn his livelihood as a tanner and leather dresser. He learned the rudiments of the trade from his father. After a ten-year apprenticeship in Roxbury, he established residence in Cambridgeport in 1803 and opened his own business.

"Industrious, punctual, energetic, intelligent, and upright," as Everett said of him, Dowse prospered in his trade. The humble mechanic accumulated sufficient funds to build a substantial three-story wooden structure in 1814. His workshop was on the ground floor and his dwelling place on the two upper floors.[17] The most imposing room in his home was the library, where Dowse spent much of his leisure time. He read before and after work and on Sundays, foregoing church.

A shy bachelor, Dowse began to collect books. He committed all funds not needed for his business and basic living to his library. He bought steadily from Boston book shops and, on occasion, from London dealers. Lacking a reading knowledge of foreign languages, he collected mostly English literature. A contemporary, who surveyed private libraries in New England, wrote of Dowse's collection: "The writer can barely say, that he has glanced at the library that seems to be the richest and fullest in *English literature* of any owned by a private individual in New En-

---

[17] The building still stands at the corner of Massachusetts Avenue and Prospect Street but has been altered to the point of non-recognition (Cambridge Historical Commission, *Survey of Architectural History in Cambridge* [Cambridge, Mass., 1971], 3:106).

gland."[18] Dowse also bought translations of Latin and Greek classics, and German, French, Italian, Spanish, and Portuguese literary works; and "with a few exceptions, the works of nearly every standard English and American author, with a copious supply of illustrative and miscellaneous literature." A contemporary estimated that he spent over $40,000 on his library.

Everett, who befriended Dowse and occasionally visited him while serving as president of Harvard University, underscored the richness of his collection as well as his distinctive qualities as a self-made man:

> I scarce know if I may venture to adduce an instance, nearer home, of the most praiseworthy and successful cultivation of useful knowledge on the part of an individual, without education, busily employed in mechanical industry. I have the pleasure to be acquainted, in one of the neighboring towns, with a person who was brought up to the trade of a leather dresser, and has all his life worked, and still works, at this business. He has devoted his leisure hours, and a portion of his honorable earnings, to the cultivation of useful and elegant learning. Under the same roof which covers his workshop, he has the most excellent library of English books, for its size, with which I am acquainted. The books have been selected with a good judgment, which would do credit to the most accomplished scholar, and have been imported from England by himself. What is more important than having the books, their proprietor is well acquainted with their contents.

While interested primarily in content, Dowse also sought books with beautiful bindings. Having tanned skins for Boston bookbinders, he had a keen knowledge and appreciation of fine bindings. As his collection grew, his reputation as a connoisseur of books correspondingly increased. He became known in local bookish circles as the "literary leather dresser." He was also considered somewhat of an eccentric. He was frequently asked: "How many volumes have you in your collection?" Dowse's standard reply was a laconic: "Never counted them."[19]

In the 1850s, as Dowse entered his eighties, he became increasingly concerned about the disposition of his beloved library, "containing the dearest earthly objects of his affections, the friends of many years, his guides in youth, his support in manhood, his solace in old age." He arranged for a printed catalogue of his collection. Then he focused his

[18] Luther Farnham, *A Glance at Private Libraries* (Boston, 1855; reprint, Weston, Mass., 1991), 60.

[19] M.H.S., *Procs.*, 10(1867–1869):433–434.

thought on a permanent home for the books. Some years earlier, President Josiah Quincy of Harvard had proposed to him that he should donate the collection to the university. He offered to build a fire-proof building on the campus to house it and agreed to other provisions for its safe-keeping. Dowse did not accept this offer.

In September 1853, Dowse experienced some setbacks in his health, and this gave him cause for concern. He asked George Livermore, his neighbor, trusted friend, and one of the two men he selected as executors of his estate, to approach Harvard on an informal basis and ascertain if the university would be willing to renew the offer President Quincy had made earlier.[20] Livermore conferred with President James Walker. The Harvard official coveted the collection but could not assure Dowse of a separate building because it would involve considerable expense. Walker informed Livermore that, if the donation were made, an arrangement could be worked out to segregate the collection within the main library collection in Gore Hall, but this was not acceptable to Dowse.[21]

At one point, Dowse offered his collection to Livermore, who refused it. Livermore grew fearful that Dowse would die before making a decision on the disposition of the library and the books would "come to the hammer," that is, be auctioned off by his estate.

Then, in 1856, using Livermore as an intermediary, Dowse offered his library to the Massachusetts Historical Society on two conditions: that the books remain together in one room "for ever," and that they be used only in that room. Livermore was an appropriate choice for the assignment since he had been a member of the Society since 1848.

On July 26, Livermore notified Winthrop of Dowse's decision and conditions. Without consulting other Society officers, Winthrop accepted the gift and so informed Livermore. The latter responded:

> I called on our venerable friend Mr. Dowse, on Saturday evening, and read to him your letter respecting his proposal for giving his library to the Massachusetts Historical Society. . . . He desired me to have a paper drawn up in due form, conveying all his books to the Historical Society; and witnesses were summoned to be present at the signing of the same, this morning. But Mr. Dowse found himself so weak, and his hand so stiff, that he could not hold a pen. At his request, I read aloud to him and to the witnesses—Dr.

[20] Livermore's memoir is in M.H.S., *Procs.*, 10(1867–1869):415–468.
[21] M.H.S., *Procs.*, 10(1867–1869):457–458.

W.W. Wellington, Messrs. S.P. Heywood and O.W. Watriss—your letter, and the paper conveying the library to the Society. Mr. Dowse then stated to the witnesses above named, that, being unable to write his name, he then, in their presence, gave outright to the Massachusetts Historical Society all the books composing his library named in the catalogue now in the press of Messrs. J. Wilson and Son.[22]

On July 30, accompanied by his "valued friend" Livermore, Winthrop visited Dowse to convey his personal thanks and inspect the library. He was deeply impressed. Dowse presented Winthrop with a volume of his rare, five-volume 1625 edition of *Purchase his Pilgrimage, or Relations of the World and the Religions observed, in all Ages and Places, etc.* as "an earnest and evidence of my having given the whole of my library to said Massachusetts Historical Society."

Why did Dowse select the Society, instead of Harvard or the Boston Public Library, then in the process of formation? He never answered this question. A modern author, Walter Muir Whitehill, has written that Livermore persuaded him to take this action.[23] Yet at the special dedicatory ceremony for the Dowse Library in April 1857, Livermore stated to the members: "Perhaps I may now be pardoned if I frankly confess, that a feeling of fond pride and interest in the place of my birth had oftentimes led me to hope that Mr. Dowse would leave his library to some public institution in the city of Cambridge."[24] This would seem to exclude Livermore as a source of influence. Nonetheless, he agreed to serve as conduit of the transaction.

From available evidence, it seems that Dowse made an independent decision. This would be in character. In a letter to Robert C. Winthrop, the Society's president, on July 28, Livermore made these revealing statements; he had informed Dowse that the Society was prepared to accept his offer and abide by his two conditions. Dowse

> expressed himself very much gratified that you had received his proposition so favorably; and remarked, in substance, that, as he had long been familiar with the character of the Society, and was personally acquainted with many of the members, he felt sure, that, in their keeping, his books which had been for many years his choice and cherished friends, would be carefully preserved and properly used according to the conditions which he had named, and which I communicated to you. . . . As Mr. Dowse has for

[22] M.H.S., *Procs.*, 3(1855–1858):102. See also 100–109.
[23] Whitehill, "Centenary of Dowse Library," 173.
[24] M.H.S., *Procs.*, 3(1855–1858):164.

several years past honored me with his friendship, and communicated to me freely his plans and purposes in regard to his property, I can assure you that the disposition which he has been pleased to make of his library is the deliberate decision to which he has come, after having for a long time considered the subject.[25]

President Winthrop had a different explanation for Dowse's decision. A few times each year, the Society held "social meetings" in the homes of members. One of these gatherings, called a "strawberry festival," was held in the spring. In the spring of 1856, Livermore invited the members to his Cambridge home. As a courtesy, he also invited Dowse, thinking that he would enjoy mingling with such distinguished literati as Josiah Quincy, James Savage, Jared Sparks, George Ticknor, Charles F. Adams, Francis Parkman, Oliver Wendell Holmes, J. Lothrop Motley, and Henry Wadsworth Longfellow as well as his friend Edward Everett. Dowse respectfully declined the invitation because of "age and infirmities."[26] Livermore could not have been surprised. He knew of Dowse's sensitivity about his lameness. As Everett noted: "His lameness, which increased with the advance of age, caused him to have rather a morbid disinclination for company abroad; and he had pursued his taste for books and art without sympathy at home." Livermore also knew that Dowse was painfully shy and ill at ease in social settings. "He has never," Everett commented, "coined the rich ore of his really genial nature into that bright currency of affable demonstration, which adds so much to the ease and spirit of social intercourse."[27]

Winthrop, nonetheless, was convinced that Livermore's invitation to Dowse to partake of strawberries with the members had been the determining factor in his decision. Winthrop later informed the members: "Cambridge strawberries have ever since had a peculiar flavor for us—not Hovey's Seedling, though that too was a Cambridge product, but what I might almost call the Livermore Seedling or the Dowse Graft, which were the immediate fruits of our social meeting at Mr. Livermore's."[28]

---

[25] M.H.S., *Procs.*, 3(1855–1858):102–103.

[26] M.H.S., *Procs.*, 2d ser., 3(1886–1887):53.

[27] Everett, "Eulogy on Dowse," M.H.S., *Procs.*, 3(1855–1858):361–398.

[28] M.H.S., *Procs.*, 2d ser., 3(1886–1887):53–54. Charles F. Hovey was one of the principal dry-goods merchants in Boston in the nineteenth century. He instituted such practices as the one-price system and early closing. See M.H.S., *Procs.*, 46(1912–1913):212–214.

Whatever the motivation, Dowse made the gift. And so, a man who had never been considered for membership in the Society became its "greatest benefactor." Dowse apparently never coveted membership. Had he been elected a member, there is a strong possibility he would have declined the honor. Dowse was not a clubbable person. In Everett's words: "He kept no company, he joined no clubs, belonged to no mutual-admiration societies, talked little, wrote less, published nothing."[29]

On August 5, Winthrop convened a special meeting of the Society to make "an announcement of a most interesting character." He informed the members of the gift and requested their approval of his unilateral action. A committee, hastily formed and led by Everett, prepared five resolutions which the members unanimously approved. After endorsing their president's action and agreeing to honor Dowse's conditions, the members voted to designate the collection "the Dowse Library of the Massachusetts Historical Society" and place an appropriate book-plate in each volume. They also offered to Dowse their "most grateful and heart-felt acknowledgments for so noble a manifestation of his confidence in the Society, and of his regard for the cause of literature and learning," and asked him to sit for a portrait "to be hung for ever in the room which shall be appropriated to his Library."[30] The members directed President Winthrop to present Dowse with a copy of the resolutions with "the cordial wishes of every member that the best blessings of Heaven may rest upon the close of his long, honorable, and useful life."[31]

The Society's action of arranging for a portrait came none too soon for, on November 4, Dowse died. Just weeks before his sitter's death, Moses Wright completed the portrait and delivered it to 30 Tremont Street.[32]

The Society now owned Dowse's books. It next had to decide where to store them. It was obligated to devote an entire room of its meager and already congested quarters to this gift. But it was a concession willingly made since the members recognized the value of the collection

[29] M.H.S., *Procs.*, 3(1855–1858):393.

[30] The portrait was Edward Everett's idea. Dowse "consented with the hesitation inspired by his characteristic diffidence and humility."

[31] M.H.S., *Procs.*, 3(1855–1858):109.

[32] M.H.S., *Procs.*, 3(1855–1858):115–122.

and especially its aesthetic merits. Many of the books were richly bound in calf and morocco and were a delight to the eye.

Because of the significance of these works and their beautiful bindings, the Society decided to make the room housing them the centerpiece of its otherwise drab quarters. As a spokesman for the committee appointed to oversee the transaction asserted: "the Society owe it to themselves and the memory of Mr. Dowse, that his splendid gift should be so placed and arranged as that its full extent, value, and importance can be at once seen and appreciated, and in a room made attractive, agreeable, and interesting,—a room in which we should have some pride in exhibiting it to strangers, and into which we should not be ashamed to introduce Mr. Dowse himself, were he to return to earth, or had we the power to show him the disposition we had made of the treasures, so precious to himself, which he had intrusted to our care."[33]

What the official had failed to state was that the funds for embellishing the Dowse Library were to be provided by the benefactor's estate. Executor Livermore authorized a gift of $3,000 for this purpose.[34]

Before the books were to be moved to the Society, the committee inspected the collection in Dowse's home. After taking measurements, it discovered that the library was too small to fill any of the "three large rooms" and too large for either of the "two small rooms." It concluded that the volumes should be housed in special book cases in the "inner back room of the second floor," one of the three larger rooms.

The committee supervised the furnishing of the Dowse Library. It arranged for the construction of handsome, glassed black walnut book cases. At the base of the cases were large drawers for the storage of "choice manuscripts, the important papers of the Society, and various articles belonging to its cabinet." The committee also purchased a large, oval table and a "sumptuous official chair" for the president. These were placed in the center of the room, opposite the door. The committee hung Wright's "speaking portrait" of Dowse on the wall directly behind the president's chair, the "principal niche of the room."

Dowse had displayed only two art works in his library, a marble bust of Sir Walter Scott by Sir Francis Legatt Chantrey and an unfinished

[33] M.H.S., *Procs.*, 3(1855–1858):127.

[34] M.H.S., *Procs.*, 3(1855–1858):128, 169, 172–173. Livermore also served on the Society's committee handling the transaction.

portrait of Edward Everett as a young man by Gilbert Stuart. He had treasured these items for personal reasons. Out of respect for the donor, the committee placed both in the Dowse Library, positioning them at key focal points. It also added busts of Shakespeare, Milton, Washington, Franklin, and other literary and historical luminaries "whose writings or whose lives were especially dear to Mr. Dowse." Among American historical figures, Franklin was, without question, Dowse's favorite because of his status as the quintessential self-made man. The busts were placed on top of the bookcases. When the committee completed its task, it had created a "beautiful apartment."[35]

The Society formally dedicated the Dowse Library at its annual meeting in April 1857. "A very large attendance," Charles F. Adams noted, "and it was quite evident that we were to have another show day." After electing new officers in the grungy old library room, the usual meeting site, Livermore presented the key to the Dowse Library to President Winthrop and made appropriate remarks. The members then moved one floor below, to the entrance of the Dowse Library. After opening the door, Winthrop invited the two senior members, Josiah Quincy and James Savage, to lead the officers and members into their new meeting room. It was a ceremonial entry. When all were seated, Winthrop rose from his imposing presidential chair and delivered a characteristic, florid address ("to-day it [the Society] is permitted to display plumage and pinions. . . ."). One of his remarks bore the ring of prophecy:

> I can hardly be mistaken in thinking, that this occasion is destined to be long remembered as an epoch in the history of our Society, and that from the opening of yonder folding doors, I might almost say, 'on golden hinges turning,' through which we have been admitted to the enjoyment of these ample accommodations and these priceless treasures, will be dated a new era of its existence.[36]

The opening of the Dowse Library was indeed a pivotal event in the history of the Society as well as the cultural life of nineteenth-century Boston. This spacious and attractively appointed room changed the physical character of the Society and made it a more inviting place for the members. As Charles Francis Adams noted in his diary, "nobody would recognize, in this Dowse library, the dirty, ordinary, ill-kept and poor

[35] M.H.S., *Procs.*, 3(1855–1858):126–128.
[36] M.H.S., *Procs.*, 3(1855–1858):163–173.

provisioned room in which it used to hold very small and very dull monthly meetings. It is now rich, comparatively, and a great deal more active, at least in appearance."[37]

The Dowse Library soon became a central gathering place for the patrician-historians. It developed into the social and intellectual nerve center of the Society. "With its cheerful afternoon outlook, towards the western sky, over the King's Chapel burying-ground," it provided a restful haven for social intercourse, scholarly pursuits, and intellectual musings.[38]

Even on non-meeting days, when members found themselves in the vicinity of the Society with time to spare in the afternoon, they gravitated to their historical clubroom, gathered about the long oval table and discussed and debated historical issues or examined newly acquired books, manuscripts, and artifacts. Samuel A. Green, the Society's librarian from 1868 to 1918, recalled in 1909: "It was formerly the custom of a few of the members, who were generally spoken of as 'The Saints,' to meet around the Dowse table near midday and talk over historical matters, at the same time discussing whatever was uppermost in their minds. In this group Mr. Winthrop was easily first in leading the informal conversation; and Dr. Ellis usually was present, together with Mr. Frothingham, Dr. Robbins, Mr. Deane, Mr. T.C. Amory, Dr. Shurtleff, Mr. Sabine, and others," all broadly cultivated amateurs with a serious interest in history.[39] Another "Saint," Charles C. Smith, frequently dropped in after two o'clock, "the close of his business hours, . . . to join the group of members, that gathered at midday for a social hour or so, now and then with no lack of story-telling."[40]

On one occasion, Dr. Oliver Wendell Holmes passed through the inner swinging doors, made the "strenuous ascent" up the iron stairs, reached the Dowse Library, and found only one of the "Saints" at the large table, Charles Deane. Holmes was "full of wit and humor, was always bubbling over with his inimitable expressions of interest, in persons and things, and a variety of causes." He sat opposite to Deane and began to talk. Julius Tuttle, assistant to the librarian, who was in the

---

[37] M.H.S., *Procs.*, 2d ser., 10(1895–1896):323.

[38] M.H.S., *Procs.*, 2d ser., 12(1897–1899):56.

[39] M.H.S., *Procs.*, 42(1908–1909):175. See, also, 2d ser., 7(1891–1892):87.

[40] M.H.S., *Procs.*, 51(1917–1918):350–351.

room attending to his duties, reported: "It seemed to me to be fully an hour before he had finished his most fascinating discourse, without a word from his listener."[41]

In 1927, seventy-seven-year-old John Torrey Morse, Jr., reminisced about his early years as a member of the Society: "As my memory runs back to those remote old meetings of fifty years ago they seem to me a little—not very much—but distinctly a little, different from those which we have to-day. In those days there was more social solidarity. . . . The members all knew each other, more or less intimately. When we came together there was a general shaking of hands and familiar saluting of friends. The effect was really quite that of a Club. Of course with the great expansion in society which has taken place since then, that condition is no longer to be expected. A splitting of groups has been inevitable. But it was rather pleasant then to feel intimate with each other's idiosyncrasies and to anticipate the way in which one member would accept or repudiate what another member was saying."[42]

The Dowse Library became to these historical devotees what the Turk's Head Inn in London's Soho had been to the members of "The Club," the celebrated literary association formed by Dr. Samuel Johnson and his coterie in 1764.

Dowse's death created a minor dilemma for the Society. Because of his significant gift, the Society felt obliged to "pay a tribute to the memory of so munificent a benefactor." But a vexing question arose. Should the Society break tradition and memorialize a non-member?

At the Society meeting in November, shortly after Dowse's death, Edward Everett introduced a resolution calling for the appointment of a committee by the president to "prepare for the Records of the Society such a commemorative notice of Mr. Dowse as shall do justice to the feelings of gratitude and respect which the Members of the Society unanimously cherish for his memory."

After considering the niggling problems provoked by the issue, and Everett's resolution, Winthrop and the members decided to discard tradition and honor Dowse in the usual manner for a member. Taking his direction from Everett's resolution, Winthrop designated him as a com-

[41] M.H.S., *Procs.*, 61(1927–1928):99–100.
[42] M.H.S., *Procs.*, 60(1926–1927):166.

mittee of one to prepare Dowse's memoir.[43] Because of his longstanding friendship with Dowse, Everett was a logical candidate for the assignment.

It was a fortunate choice for Dowse, since the sixty-two-year-old Everett, who had had a notable academic and public career, was one of the most accomplished orators in the nation, often called the "Cicero of America."[44] For this reason he would be selected in 1863 to deliver the principal address at the consecration of the Gettysburg Cemetery, while the president of the United States would be limited to "a few appropriate remarks."[45] As it turned out, Everett became known as the orator who gave the "other speech" at Gettysburg. Dowse was certain to receive a lengthy and memorable eulogy.

Everett's oratorical skills had been evident as early as 1814, when the youthful Harvard graduate was installed as minister of the venerable Brattle Street Church. With the passage of time and as he moved into other responsible positions and achieved greater maturity, he honed his oratorical talents and became highly sought after to speak at large public gatherings, especially historical commemorations. Ceremonial oratory was Everett's forte. A classical rhetorician, he could hold a mass audience in thrall, even though his speeches lasted from one and one-half to two and one-half hours. Contemporaries generally acknowledged that Everett and Daniel Webster, who was also a member of the Society, were among the nation's premier orators. Everett "was sometimes described as the Raphael among orators while Webster was called the Michaelan-

---

[43] M.H.S., *Procs.*, 3(1855–1858):122.

[44] On Everett's life and career, see: Paul Revere Frothingham, *Edward Everett: Orator and Statesman* (Boston, 1925); Ronald F. Reid, *Edward Everett: Unionist Orator* (New York, 1990); Ronald F. Reid, "Edward Everett and Neoclassical Oratory in Genteel America" in Gregory Clark and S. Michael Halloran, eds., *Oratorical Culture in Nineteenth-Century America: Transformations in the Theory and Practice of Rhetoric* (Carbondale, 1993), 29–56; M.H.S., *Procs.*, 2d ser., 18(1903–1904):91–117; Paul A. Varg, *Edward Everett: The Intellectual in the Turmoil of Politics* (Selinsgrove, Pa., 1992), ch. 8.

Everett served as Harvard's first professor of Greek language and literature, 1819–1825; U.S. congressman, 1825–1835; governor of Massachusetts, 1836–1839; minister to Great Britain, 1841–1845; president of Harvard, 1846–1849; secretary of state, 1852–1853; and U.S. senator, 1853–1854.

[45] For discussions of Everett's speech at Gettysburg, see *Edward Everett at Gettysburg* (Boston, 1963); Garry Wills, *Lincoln at Gettysburg: The Words That Remade America* (New York, 1992), 31–34.

gelo. The latter was more rugged, forceful, natural, while Everett was always graceful and delicate—with an excess, however, of sweeping line and brilliant color."[46]

Everett's greatest asset as a speaker was his strong, melodic voice. In the words of a contemporary: "The timbre of Mr. Everett's voice resembled very closely that of the bells which have in their metal the largest proportion of silver. Several years ago, in listening to the bells of Moscow, which have the maximum of silver, and are kept ringing a large part of the time, I was perpetually reminded of Mr. Everett's oratory."[47]

Aside from his voice, Everett captivated his audiences by speaking without a text in hand. He did prepare texts for his speeches but did not use them. He placed the document on the lectern in full view of his audience but did not turn a page. He diligently researched his subject and meticulously selected appropriate figures of speech, anecdotes, and allusions to classical literature.[48] Then he memorized his entire address!

Everett's final step was to practice the gestures with which he planned to enhance his delivery. Each sentence, each phrase, each word could provoke a particular physical movement by Everett. As his biographer has written: "Hand, voice, and eye acted in harmony. He was an exquisitely adjusted machine." And further: "he left nothing to chance—nothing to what is often foolishly described as 'the inspiration of the moment.' Everything with this man was carefully worked out, studied, and perfected, sometimes even to the minutest details."[49]

Oratory in Everett's time was a theatrical event and Everett was a consummate actor, as polished and professional as an Edwin Booth or Laurence Olivier. Not that he was without critics, even in Boston. Some of his fellow Society members affirmed that his style was more impressive than his content. Some considered his orations "artificial and affected." After Everett had spoken at Lexington in 1835, Ralph Waldo Emerson wrote in his journal: "He is all art, & I find him nowadays maugre all his gifts & great merits more to blame than praise. He is not

[46] Frothingham, *Everett*, 393.

[47] Frothingham, *Everett*, 399–400. The contemporary was Andrew P. Peabody.

[48] Two days before delivering his speech at Gettysburg, Everett inspected the battlefield to learn where the major actions had taken place. During his speech, he pointed to these sites as he described them. See Wills, *Lincoln at Gettysburg*, 33.

[49] For an analysis of Everett's method as an orator, see Frothingham, *Everett*, 391–400.

content to be Edward Everett, but would be Daniel Webster. This is his mortal distemper."[50] Despite his critics, Everett always attracted a throng when he spoke.[51]

Everett's career as a speaker flourished after 1854 when he resigned from the United States Senate and returned to Boston, "broken in spirits and in health—a disappointed and defeated man."[52] On February 22, 1856, under the sponsorship of the Mercantile Library Association of Boston, he delivered a one-hour-and-forty-minute address on "The Character of Washington," to mark the 124th anniversary of the re-nowned Virginian's birth and the centennial of Washington's first visit to Boston.

The lecture was a resounding success and led to a national speaking tour to raise funds for the Mount Vernon Ladies Association to restore Washington's home. He traveled across the East, South, and Midwest, packing the halls wherever he spoke. It was a triumphal trip but a grueling physical experience for a man not in the best of health. Everett was energized by the adulation he received from his responsive audi-ences and by the satisfaction of knowing he was performing a significant patriotic task. From 1856 to 1858, he gave the Washington lecture 136 times and raised nearly $90,000 for the restoration. The admission fee was twenty-five cents.[53]

With all of these activities consuming his time, Everett was delayed in

[50] Emerson's Journal, Apr. 22, 1835. Published in Merton M. Sealts, ed., The Journals and Miscellaneous Notebooks of Ralph Waldo Emerson (Cambridge, Mass., 1965), 5:32–33.

[51] Charles Francis Adams, Everett's brother-in-law, aggressively disliked him and com-mented that Everett's oratorical style employed "brilliant contrasts, happy allusions, strik-ing anecdotes, but there is no *depth* or maturity of thought, no greatness of view, no ingredients that make the Statesman or the Philosopher. As a popular festival Orator he will be unrivalled, but I doubt his success as a name for futurity." Marc Friedlaender and L.H. Butterfield, eds., Diary of Charles Francis Adams (Cambridge, Mass., 1974), 5:380.

[52] Frothingham, Everett, 373.

[53] Everett also participated in another program, beginning in 1858, which further ben-efitted Mount Vernon. Robert Bonner, editor and owner of the New York Ledger, a weekly newspaper, asked him to write fifty-three weekly articles; the paper had a circulation of 300,000 and a reading audience of 1,000,000. If Everett accepted, Bonner agreed to con-tribute $10,000 to the Mt. Vernon program. Everett accepted. He published his first article in November 1858 and his last one in the fall of 1859. The subject matter was varied, ranging from biographical sketches of William Hickling Prescott, Henry Hallam, and William Bond to brief accounts and descriptions of European cities. These articles were later combined and issued as a book entitled Mount Vernon Papers.

preparing his memoir of Dowse for the Historical Society. In late 1858, nearly two years after accepting the assignment, he began to apply himself to the task.

The Dowse Institute now enters the story. By his will, after making special bequests and providing $25,000 for his relatives, Dowse placed the residue of his estate in trust, to be administered by his executors, Livermore and Ebenezer Dale. Dowse had instructed his executors to apply and distribute these funds to "literary, scientific, and charitable purposes."

With this guideline in mind, the executors offered to the City of Cambridge $10,000 "for the establishment and support of an annual course of Public Lectures in Cambridge, under the name of The Dowse Institute." They proposed paying this sum on the condition that the City grant an annual sum of $600 to the institute "in every year for ever." They also proposed the appointment of three residents of Cambridge, plus the mayor and president of the Common Council, as trustees of the institute. The trustees were invested with the authority of administering the lecture program and the City Council was to serve as a board of visitors. A day later, the City accepted the offer.[54]

The trustees held their first meeting on June 14, with the executors also present. They made but one decision: they voted to invite Everett to deliver the inaugural lecture on a date to be determined. Subsequently, having learned of Everett's forthcoming eulogy of Dowse before the Historical Society, the trustees asked him to present a "commemorative sketch of the life of the esteemed and lamented donor" in Cambridge City Hall on December 7. They deemed this subject to be appropriate for the commencement of the institute program.

As a courtesy, the trustees notified the Historical Society of their plan and secured its approval. Everett was only too happy to accept the assignment. He knew that he would be speaking to a sizable audience, always a factor of considerable importance to him. Moreover, a second address would justify his heavy investment of time and energy in preparing the eulogy.

The institute offer led Everett to reflect upon his Historical Society obligation. An idea came to mind. Rather than repeat his oration to the usual handful of members, possibly twenty to twenty-five, in the small-

[54] Dowse Institute, *Organization of the Institute, and By-laws Adopted by the Trustees* (Cambridge, Mass., 1858).

ish Dowse Library, why not ask the Society to sponsor a public program in a large hall in Boston and charge admission? In this way, he and the Society would be performing a useful educational service and, at the same time, be raising badly needed funds for the Society. Everett submitted his proposal at the Society's October meeting. The members quickly approved it and delegated the standing committee to work out "all necessary arrangements."[55]

On December 7, Everett delivered his Dowse Institute oration to an "overflowing audience." A *Boston Daily Evening Transcript* reporter noted that "large numbers were disappointed at not being able to obtain seats." He also wrote that it was an "eminently brilliant production." In length, it was a vintage Everett presentation, lasting one and one-half hours.[56]

The following evening Everett repeated his address in Boston for the Society. The building chosen by the Society was the cavernous Music Hall, the largest auditorium in New England. Called "Boston's Temple of Music," the architecturally undistinguished structure was built in 1852 to serve as the site for major musical and civic programs. The hall was 130 feet in length, 78 feet in width, 65 feet in height, and had excellent acoustics. It featured an enormous organ and was lighted by hundreds of gas jets along the cornice. There was a smaller auditorium below the main hall, called Mumstead Hall, which seated "about 300" and was used primarily for rehearsals, meetings of the Handel and Haydn Society, and billiard matches.[57]

As Everett, President Winthrop, and the Reverend William Jenks, "the senior clerical member of the Society," sat on the stage awaiting the beginning of the program, they gazed upon an assemblage of about 2,500 people, "the Hall being completely filled with the exception of a portion of the upper balcony." Many dignitaries were present, including Gov. Nathaniel P. Banks, former Gov. Emory Washburn, Chief Justice Lemuel Shaw and a number of other judges, nearly all of the ministers of the city, Boston Mayor Frederic W. Lincoln, Jr., and about sixty members of the Society. What prompted such an outpouring of cus-

---

[55] M.H.S., *Procs.*, 4(1858–1860):124–125, 134.

[56] *Boston Daily Evening Transcript*, Dec. 8, 1858, which provides a long account of the speech.

[57] For a description of the hall, see *King's Handbook of Boston* (Cambridge, Mass., 1878), 228–229.

tomers and dignitaries? The attraction was assuredly Everett, not a eulogy of the virtually unknown Dowse.

After the Reverend Mr. Jenks opened the program with an "impressive prayer," Winthrop delivered introductory remarks. An accomplished orator in his own right, he began by noting that only four times in the history of the Society had it sponsored a "public and formal commemoration." On October 23, 1792, it had celebrated the 300th anniversary of Columbus's first trip to the new world with an address by Jeremy Belknap. On December 22, 1813, it had commemorated the 193rd anniversary of the landing of the "Pilgrim Fathers" at Plymouth; Judge John Davis delivered an oration suitable to the occasion. On May 29, 1843, John Quincy Adams had spoken on the bicentennial anniversary of the New England Confederation. On October 31, 1844, John Gorham Palfrey had delivered an address commemorating the fiftieth anniversary of the Society.

In setting the stage for Everett's tribute to Dowse, Winthrop next cited some of the earlier prominent benefactors of the Society, such as James Sullivan, Christopher Gore, Samuel Appleton, and Belknap. He also held up for public view the "sumptuous" folio edition of *Purchas his Pilgrimage*, which Dowse had given to him as a surety on July 30, 1856. In introducing Everett, he stressed the speaker's close personal friendship with Dowse, reflected by the fact that the latter had only one painting in his library, Gilbert Stuart's striking portrait of a youthful Everett.

When Everett rose, he was "greeted with enthusiasm by the audience." Curiously, he began with these words: "Mr. President and Gentlemen of the Massachusetts Historical Society." He failed to acknowledge the presence of the dignitaries and vast body of nonmembers. It was as though he were addressing the members in the Dowse Library.

Everett gave another virtuoso presentation. In the words of a newspaper reporter, he "enchained the attention of his hearers throughout the performance, which occupied an hour and forty minutes, and during which time the distinguished orator did not recur at all to his notes."[58] In the course of his address, Everett cited 180 painters and writers

[58] For detailed accounts of the lecture, see M.H.S., *Procs.*, 3(1855–1858):355–398; *Boston Daily Evening Transcript*, Dec. 10, 1858.

in nearly every ancient and modern language, a prodigious feat of memory.[59]

Charles F. Adams, who attended the affair, rendered this report:

The address was marked by the usual characteristics of that gentleman. Great beauty of finish, occasional touches of eloquence, skill in the disposition of his topic, and extraordinary facility of memory. I admire the beauty of the work, but with as little emotion as I should feel in looking over the finest of Mechlin lace or the ivory Chinese balls skillfully carved one within another. In this instance he had a most unpromising topic, for Dowse was nothing but a respectable leather dresser who had a fancy for pretty books. But he did what he could to show him possessed of good and great qualities, and then wove in many incidental matters to relieve the tedium of common places.[60]

The Society realized a sum of $700 from Everett's oration. In its report to the membership at the April 1859 annual meeting, the standing committee noted a deficit in the operating budget for the fiscal year. It concluded with this comment: "It should be gratefully remembered, that this deficit would have been much more serious but for the timely aid which our treasury received in the proceeds of the 'Eulogy on Mr. Dowse,' by our distinguished associate, Mr. Everett, whose remarkable accomplishments and gifts, while they have enriched so many other associations, have not passed over our own, without leaving substantial and memorable results."[61]

The growing prestige and influence of the Society upon Boston's cultural community after it had relocated on Tremont Street was underscored in 1860 when it was placed on the schedule of the Prince of Wales during his visit to the city. Canada had extended an invitation to Queen Victoria to visit Victoria, British Columbia, to dedicate a bridge named in her honor. The queen declined but sent her eldest son, the heir apparent to the throne, in her stead. The Queen's problem child, the future King Edward VII, arrived in Canada in July. When he reached Boston on October 17, the nineteen-year-old crown prince was nearing

[59] Mark A. DeWolfe Howe wrote: "If that was a heavy load for a speech to carry, it had, at least, an extraordinary interest as a feat of memory." *Boston: The Place and the People* (New York, 1903), 303–304.

[60] Charles F. Adams, Journal, Dec. 9, 1858 (Adams Papers).

[61] M.H.S., *Procs.*, 4(1858–1860):240–242, 251.

the end of a triumphant, but strenuous, North American tour. He was to tour Boston on October 18 and 19 and leave on the morning of October 20, a Saturday.[62]

On October 18, the prince was feted from morning to late evening. The climactic event was a huge banquet in his honor. Wherever he appeared, thousands of Bostonians gathered for a glance. He was a weary young man when he finally reached his quarters in the Revere House late that evening.

On the following day, "the Prince was allowed to take a full measure of repose after the excitements of Thursday, and a late breakfast was served in his apartments yesterday." About 11 A.M. the whirlwind schedule began again. Seated in an elegant barouche pulled by four horses and accompanied by a delegation of dignitaries from Boston and Cambridge, also in barouches, the prince and his entourage moved through the city and across the Charles River into Cambridge. A contingent of smartly dressed mounted police from Boston led the way. Three Society representatives, Robert C. Winthrop, Edward Everett, and George Ticknor, were part of the official delegation.

When the convoy reached Cambridge, a squad of mounted police from that city relieved the Boston security force. The group's first destination was Harvard University. After an extended visit to the school, which included a tour, a ceremonial program with faculty and students, and a lavish luncheon, the royal procession and company moved slowly down Brattle Street, Cambridge's most fashionable avenue with its large, stately eighteenth-century homes. The party traveled to Mt. Auburn Cemetery, America's first garden cemetery, where the prince planted two trees, a purple ash and a mountain elm.

Moving "post-haste," the company retraced its steps through Cambridge and crossed into Charlestown to the Bunker Hill Monument, which commemorated the Americans' storied defense on June 17, 1775, rather than Great Britain's pyrrhic victory.

Returning to Boston, the prince and his delegation drove to the Society's quarters, alighted from their carriages, and climbed the steep, forty-nine iron stairs to the Dowse Room. It was now four o'clock and

[62] For the prince's visit to Boston and the Society, see: M.H.S., *Procs.*, 5(1860–1862):97–98, 42(1908–1909):231–232. The *Boston Daily Advertiser*, Oct. 18, 20, 1860, offers a full account of the visit.

the dull rays of the setting sun were striking the ancient gravestones in the King's Chapel Cemetery, casting shadows on the walls of the Society's building.

In a role in which he excelled, President Winthrop served as the host and guide for the prince, who was accompanied by the Duke of Newcastle; the Earl of St. Germans; Lord Lyons, the British minister at Washington; Maj. Gen. Robert Bruce, the governor of the prince; and other attendants. Society officials included Gov. Emory Washburn, George Livermore, Charles Deane, and Samuel A. Green.

While in the Dowse Room, the prince made perfunctory, complimentary remarks about Dowse's portrait and examined a few of "the most sumptuous volumes" of the collection. He also inspected the manuscript of Gov. John Winthrop's "Journal of New England" and George Washington's epaulets, which the commander-in-chief had worn during the siege of Yorktown in 1781 and on the day he had resigned his military commission in Annapolis in 1783. It is reasonable to assume that Winthrop did not remind the prince and his retinue that the next day marked the anniversary of Cornwallis's stunning defeat and surrender at Yorktown, when the "world turned upside down" for the British.

While leafing through the manuscript copy of the great Virginian's "Newburgh Address," the prince "intimated a disposition to possess an autograph of Washington." Winthrop made a mental note of this remark.

As the prince ambled about, he gazed at the swords of Miles Standish and other Pilgrim Fathers, and at the portraits of the Winslows and Winthrops and other early New England worthies. He "glanced in passing" at a few artifacts on display, including a sample of the tea which Samuel Adams and his fellow "Indians" had thrown into the harbor during the celebrated Boston Tea Party.

The prince "paused longer" before the "crossed swords" tablet and listened intently as Winthrop explained the background and symbolic significance of this unique artifact. One of the swords had been worn by Col. William Prescott, commander of the American forces at Breed's Hill during the battle of Bunker Hill. The second belonged to Capt. John Linzee of the Royal Navy, who had commanded the British sloop-of-war *Falcon*. Linzee's vessel had cannonaded Prescott's troops during the battle of Bunker Hill. Colonel Prescott's sword passed through his family and was eventually bequeathed to his grandson, William Hickling Prescott, one of the Society's stalwarts.

Linzee had married a Bostonian, Susanna Inman, during his American tour of duty. After resigning from the Royal Navy in 1792, he returned to the United States and established residence. His son, John Inman Linzee, gave his father's sword to William Hickling Prescott, who had married Linzee's niece, Susan Amory. Recognizing the symbolic value of the swords, Prescott placed the "two martial implements" in a crossed position and hung them in the library of his Jamaica Plain home; later, he moved them to the cornice of his library in his Beacon Street residence. In the words of George Ticknor, Prescott's closest friend: "The swords that had been worn by the soldier and the sailor on that memorable day came down as heirlooms in their respective families, until at last they met in the library of the man of letters, where, quietly crossed over his books, they often excited the notice alike of strangers and of friends."

In 1852, the British novelist William Makepeace Thackeray visited Prescott and was so taken by the crossed swords that he opened his work, *The Virginians*, published six years later, with these words: "On the library wall of one of the most famous writers of America, there hang two crossed swords, which his relatives wore in the great War of Independence. The one sword was gallantly drawn in the service of the King, the other was the weapon of a brave and honored republican soldier. The possessor of the harmless trophy has earned for himself a name alike honoured in his ancestors' country, and in his own, where genius such as his has always a peaceful welcome."[63]

At his death, Prescott bequeathed his grandfather's sword to the Massachusetts Historical Society "as a curiosity suitable to be preserved among their collections." He left Linzee's sword to his wife. Believing that the two swords should remain together as a symbol of British-American unity, Mrs. Prescott and her heirs donated Linzee's weapon to the Society. She sent both swords, a "singular trophy," to the Society in 1859. The Society arranged to have the swords attached to a tablet of

---

[63] *Witness to America's Past*, 87–88; M.H.S., *Procs.*, 4(1858–1860):258–266; George Ticknor, *Life of William Hickling Prescott* (Boston, 1864), 34, 53–54, appendix B, 461–463; Robert C. Winthrop to W.H. Gardiner, April 13, 1859, M.H.S. Recording Secretary, Records, 1858–1871 (M.H.S. Archives). William Makepeace Thackery, *The Virginians: A Tale of the Last Century* (Philadelphia, 1866).

black walnut. Where the weapons crossed there was a carved wreath of olive leaves. At the top of the tablet were placed two shields, "leaning against each other," bearing the Prescott and Linzee coats of arms. In the tablet below each sword were "suitable inscriptions"setting forth the history and circumstances of their donation to the Society.

It was now five o'clock and the prince had one final site to visit, the Boston Athenaeum, before his ceremonial duties ended for the day. Before leaving the Society, he signed his name in the visitor's register and urged the members of his official party to do likewise.

As the prince was preparing to board his train for Portland, Maine, on Saturday morning, Winthrop presented him with an autograph letter bearing George Washington's signature and, for good measure, a second document signed by Benjamin Franklin. If the prince believed he was receiving a gift from the Society, though, he was mistaken. The manuscripts, as the Society's records note, were "not, of course, from the archives of the Society." Then, as now, the Society was not in the habit of making gifts of its Washington and Franklin manuscripts, not even to British royalty.

In 1868, another distinguished person paid a visit to the Society: President-elect Ulysses S. Grant.[64] At 6:30 A.M. on December 2, Grant arrived in Boston "very quietly" after an all-night train ride from Washington. He took a carriage to the St. James Hotel, where he planned to rest. He was in Boston to meet privately with Republican party officials, but his presence soon became known, and word flashed through the city. A hospitality committee was hastily organized. This group met with Grant and invited him to participate in some sightseeing and social functions.

One of the programs the committee planned was a tour of the Society. On the "cold raw" morning of December 3, the hero of the Civil War, accompanied by ex-Gov. John H. Clifford and ex-Chief Justice George T. Bigelow, climbed the stairs to the Dowse Library. Winthrop, who had learned of Grant's impending visit "only a few minutes beforehand," greeted the group in his usual gracious manner. He invited Grant to sign the visitors' register. Because of the extreme cold, Grant's fingers were stiff and he had difficulty writing his name. Grant apologized and said

[64] On Grant's visit to Boston and the Society, see *Boston Daily Advertiser*, Dec. 3, 1868; M.H.S., *Procs.*, 10(1867–1869):369, 43(1909–1910):232.

that he "ought to have made his mark instead." Winthrop replied: "General, you have already made your mark, and it is not necessary to do it again." Grant's tour was perfunctory and brief. He was soon on his way to Cambridge and Harvard University.

In December 1871, another foreign visitor, the Grand Duke Alexis of Russia, accompanied by the Russian minister to the United States, a Russian admiral, and other dignitaries, paid a courtesy visit to the Society. The admiral presented a gift of several oak leaves together with a memorandum in the Russian language. It stated that "the enclosed (grew) from the acorn taken from the oak which overshadows the tomb of the immortal Washington, and presented as a token of high esteem by Americans to H.I.M., the Emperor of Russia." Unknown to the Russians, the acorn had been given to the emperor by the late George Sumner, a former member of the Society.[65] After leaving Boston the grand duke traveled across the nation, a trip highlighted by a buffalo hunt led by the ill-fated Gen. George Custer.

While the 1857 addition of the Dowse Library enhanced the quality of the Society's holdings, it also dramatically decreased the available shelf space. Society officials were acutely aware of the impact of the gift, but they were delighted to accept it. Nevertheless a number of the members began to complain that the Society should exercise greater discretion in its acquisition of materials. It should make certain that what was accepted was wholly relevant to the Society's mission.

In 1855, the standing committee had presented a "memorable Report" in which it called attention to "great quantities" of pamphlets requiring thorough analysis before "it can be known what is of sufficient value to retain, or what should be otherwise disposed of." The committee recommended that the Society "disburthen itself of much, at least, of this mass of cumbrous matter not immediately akin to our pursuits." It also questioned "how far it is desirable to embrace within our field of labor any considerable number of miscellaneous periodicals, when we know that many other societies and institutions amongst us make those branches special subjects of attention." The committee's recommendations and exhortations for more selective acquisitions and the removal of non-essential materials were ignored. There was no "careful discrimi-

---

[65] M.H.S., *Procs.*, 12(1871–1875):174.

nation in the matter of future accessions" and no "very thorough weeding."[66]

With each passing year after 1857, the storage situation progressively worsened.[67] In 1865, the standing committee, which was charged with the oversight and promotion of the interests of the Society and the general management of its affairs, informed the members: "The crying need is still for more room, as the shelves are now crowded; and it is difficult to see how the want is to be supplied." It expressed the hope that "the Society may at no distant day be provided with accommodations here or elsewhere more commodious and roomy, and, what is of greater consequence, more safe."[68]

The librarian was more to the point: "Our shelves are now all occupied, and little room remains in this building for farther acquisitions." He, too, looked forward to the Society's removal to a new site "before many years" where "there shall be ampler space."[69] In 1866, the librarian proposed redesigning the attic and "substituting a Mansard roof for the present one," thereby adding "another commodious story" for the uses of the library.[70] Lacking adequate funds, the Society did not act upon his proposal.

While recognizing the need for additional space, President Winthrop continued to cling to the notion that the Tremont Street site was an appropriate location for the Society because of its proximity to the historic King's Chapel burying ground. As he wrote to William H. Whitmore, a young lawyer and member of the Society, on July 6, 1866: "We have often meditated a change of locality for our Society; but if we can manage to keep the old site, overhanging the graves of the earliest settlers and rulers of City and State and Church, we may well be glad. The idea of sale, however, is frequently mooted, and perhaps we may be constrained to adopt it."[71]

[66] M.H.S., *Procs.*, 2d ser., 4(1887–1889):346–347.

[67] Librarian Nathaniel B. Shurtleff reported in 1863: "The shelf-room for books is very nearly occupied: therefore additional accommodations will soon be required for the increasing accessions to the library." M.H.S., *Procs.*, 7(1863–1864):22–23.

[68] M.H.S., *Procs.*, 8(1864–1865):259–260.

[69] M.H.S., *Procs.*, 8(1864–1865):266.

[70] M.H.S., *Procs.*, 9(1866–1867):184–185. He also pointed out that "nearly eight thousand pamphlets are heaped upon the floor" in one of the library rooms.

[71] Winthrop to Whitmore, July 6, 1866 (Robert C. Winthrop Letters to William H. Whitmore, 1862–1874, M.H.S.).

The Massachusetts Historical Society

The following year, Winthrop noticed an article in the *Boston Evening Transcript*, initialed by W.H.W., which called for the placement of a new street through the King's Chapel cemetery and the Society's quarters. Assuming that W.H.W. was Whitmore, recently elected to the city's Common Council, Winthrop wrote to him: "I observe your initials signed to an Article in this Evening's Transcript, proposing to run a Street through our Dowse Library; but I suppose there are other *W.H.W.*s beside yourself. Our old Society might, perhaps, make money out of such a proceeding, but I should be rather sorry to have the old graves of the First Settlers disturbed while I am gone."[72]

In 1867, the Society took one action that slightly eased the space problem in the crowded cabinet of curiosities. With the approval of the cabinet-keeper, it voted to deposit the artifacts relating to North American Indians in the newly organized Peabody Museum at Harvard University. The Society, however, retained ownership of its artifacts.[73] Even with the removal of these materials, the cabinet-keeper continued his chronic complaint of a lack of space in subsequent reports.

Despite this space shortage, the Society was extremely loath to part with any of its manuscript collections. Occasionally, battles over ownership took on the dimensions of full-scale warfare. One such incident revolved around the papers of Gov. Thomas Hutchinson, the historian and royal official of pre-Revolutionary fame, and took decades to resolve.

In 1819, Alden Bradford, the secretary to the Commonwealth and a member of the Society since 1793, donated some Hutchinson documents, which he had found in his office. The next year he gave an additional collection of Hutchinson papers "by permission of the Governor and Council." The Society eagerly accepted these documents, combined them with its own Hutchinson holdings, and bound the whole collection into three volumes.

Some years later, another secretary to the Commonwealth, John G. Palfrey, became convinced that his predecessor had erred, that his gifts to the Society were actually state property. He sought the return of the documents. The Society rejected his claim out of hand. Palfrey persisted. The Society refused to budge. The fact that Palfrey was a member of the

[72] Winthrop to Whitmore, May 25, 1867.
[73] M.H.S., *Procs.*, 9(1866–1867):450–451; 10(1867–1869):14–15.

Society may have made him feel uncomfortable, but it did not deter him from "doing his duty."[74]

In 1849, the Society decided to take the offensive. It appointed a committee to prepare a memorial to the General Court, challenging the state's claim and defending its right to retain custody of the papers. After reviewing the issue, the committee decided "that it is not expedient to address any memorial to the General Court, since, notwithstanding the repeated representations and requests of the Secretaries of the Commonwealth, the General Court has not indicated the slightest intention of setting up any such claim as they recommend; and, therefore, it would seem superfluous, if not obtrusive, to trouble them with a refutation of it."

The committee took the position that the "open and undisputed possession of these papers by the Society as their own for more than a quarter of a century constitutes a title which cannot be impeached." Added to this argument was the consideration that "the Society holds these papers . . . not for any pecuniary emolument to itself or its members, but on the implied trust that they shall be kept and preserved by it for the purpose of historical investigation." Finally, by invoking the statute of limitations argument, the committee concluded that it was "the duty of the Society to maintain its title to them. And if any claim to them should hereafter emanate from competent authority, they recommend that it be resisted on the ground above stated."

In 1867, the legislature became involved in the fray. The General Court directed the attorney general to begin proceedings against the Society for the recovery of the documents. This was an ominous development for the Society. Fearful of the state's repercussive power, the Society agreed to arbitration in 1870. It took three years before an arbitrator was found who was acceptable to both parties. Robert S. Rantoul, a Salem lawyer and representative, was appointed as the arbitrator.

The Society permitted Rantoul open access to its "archives and records." After the "fullest search," he uncovered a letter of transmittal from Bradford in which he had used the verb "deposited" rather than "presented." This considerably weakened, if not destroyed, the Society's

[74] He was a resident member from April 11, 1825 to June 28, 1838, when he resigned; was again a resident member from June 30, 1842 to Apr. 17, 1854, when he resigned again.

position. Rantoul ultimately decided for the Commonwealth. The Society conceded defeat and reluctantly returned the Hutchinson Papers.[75]

Following a different scenario, in 1869 the Society voluntarily returned a significant American Revolution document to the Boston Athenaeum. Not to do so would have been ungracious. In 1863, Josiah Quincy had donated to the Society Ezekiel Price's lengthy manuscript diary relating to the siege of Boston in 1775–1776.[76] It was one of "several valuable manuscripts" given by Quincy. In January 1869, a Mr. E. Price Greenleaf sent a letter to the Society in which he stated that Price's diary was actually the property of the Boston Athenaeum, that he himself had donated the document to that institution. "It had been lent to Mr. Quincy," and he apparently forgot to return it. Quincy had written upon the cover of the manuscript: "To be delivered to Price Greenleaf, if called for." Acknowledging Quincy's "inadvertence," the Society agreed to "restore" the diary to the Athenaeum.[77] The other manuscripts donated by Quincy ostensibly were his and the Society retained them.

The Quincy experience underscored the difficulty of maintaining control of a library collection in the nineteenth century. With collections stored haphazardly and largely untended in makeshift quarters, with constant reshuffling of materials, and lacking permanent, trained personnel, all of the Boston institutions which had libraries sustained losses of their holdings.

The impending expiration of the Suffolk Savings Bank lease on April 1, 1871, came to weigh heavily on the Society's leaders in the late 1860s. While they coveted the bank's space, they also recognized the importance of the rent they received. It was vital for survival. In the standing committee's annual report to the members in 1868, it called attention to the forthcoming termination of the lease and urged the Society to work strenuously to add to its funds so that it would not have to rely on rental income for financial stability. The Society could then occupy the entire

---

[75] M.H.S., *Procs.*, 1(1791–1835):283–287, 2(1835–1855):436–441; Stephen T. Riley, "Some Aspects of the Society's Manuscript Collection," 70(1950–1953):242–243. The Society apparently did not hold the negative decision against Rantoul, for he was elected to membership in 1908.

[76] The Society promptly published it in M.H.S., *Procs.*, 7(1863–1864):185–262.

[77] M.H.S., *Procs.*, 10(1867–1869):413, 414, 474.

building in 1871. If this could be done, the Society "would relieve itself of the embarrassments and annoyances which arise from the crowded condition of the shelves, walls, and cabinets."

The committee also made the provocative suggestion that the Society and the American Academy of Arts and Sciences "might wisely and to mutual advantage unite in providing a building for their joint occupancy." Both organizations had similar needs, the committee affirmed. Both required a "library room, a gallery, hall, and office, all of which might be disposed on a single story of a spacious fire-proof building, that they may well divide the expense of a site, foundation and roof."[78] The idea of linkage had been discussed informally in both organizations by those who were joint members. The proposal was "heartily welcomed" by the Academy but never moved past the point of earnest conversation in the Society. There were too many practical problems involved in such a joint venture.

The impending expiration of the bank's lease in less than two years led President Winthrop in June 1869 to recommend that the Society empower either the standing committee or a special committee to hire an architect to prepare plans and a cost estimate for enlarging the Tremont Street building and making it "absolutely fire-proof."[79]

The year 1870 was one of decision for the Society. In April, one year before the termination of the lease, the standing committee hired the architectural firm of Ryder and Harris and instructed it to prepare general plans for a new, five-story, fire-proof structure. The architects completed the assignment and projected a cost of $22,000. After enthusiastically endorsing the conception, the committee directed the architects to begin drawing up detailed specifications. It expressed the belief that the Society could raise the sum needed by means of a subscription.[80]

At the same time, the Suffolk Savings Bank notified the Society that it intended to construct a new headquarters across the street from its present location and, therefore, would not be renewing its lease. Knowing that the Society must have a tenant to make the project financially feasible, the standing committee entered into preliminary negotiations

[78] M.H.S., *Procs.*, 10(1867–1850):149–150.
[79] M.H.S., *Procs.*, 11(1869–1870):102.
[80] M.H.S., *Procs.*, 11(1869–1870):245. A committee "on the Society's Building," separate from the Standing Committee, was established at the June 1870 meeting (p. 326).

with officials of the City of Boston, who were acting as agents for Suffolk County, which was seeking quarters for the probate office and registry of deeds of Suffolk County.

In this atmosphere of uncertainty, Winthrop rose to address the members at the July 1871 meeting. A member since 1839 and president since 1855, he knew that the Society had reached another critical crossroad in its history. The lower floor of 30 Tremont Street had been vacant for over three months, and there was no longer rental income from the bank. The Society had been forced to take out a loan to meet operating expenses.

The Society had to make a decision on housing. A number of members were understandably apprehensive about embarking on a costly building program, and Winthrop inwardly shared their concern. But he knew that the time for action had arrived. He also knew that he must project an air of confidence and optimism. Above all, he must present a persuasive argument.

Winthrop began by stating that the Society had four options. First, it could retain the status quo: "We may remain just where we are, and just as we are." It could lease the lower floor on a long-term basis for the highest possible rent and go "along ourselves in the quiet occupation of our present apartments." Second, it could sell the entire building to the highest bidder and seek other quarters.[81] Third, it could lease the entire building on a long-term rent, allowing the lessee to improve the structure as it saw fit, with the Society reserving the right to accept or reject "any apartments which may be arranged by the lessee to suit us."

The fourth option offered the greatest challenge because of its profound financial implications, but this was the plan Winthrop favored: "We may remodel the Building ourselves, arranging apartments to suit ourselves, and providing other apartments which may be the subject of advantageous lease." He made a forceful appeal for its acceptance. He affirmed that it was the "most advantageous and economical plan for the City as well as for ourselves, saving the City from the great expense of erecting a new Building, and securing to both of us convenient and fire-proof accommodations." He underscored "two cardinal points": the

---

[81] In a letter to fellow member William H. Whitmore (June 15, 1871), Winthrop wrote: "I was sorry to seem so persistent in regard to our Building. I have, I confess, a very strong feeling that we ought not to part with our present premises, except at a price which nobody will give. It is the hallowed spot of our whole City, and we seem Providentially placed to guard the old grave yard." (Robert C. Winthrop Letters to William H. Whitmore, M.H.S.).

The Dowse Library and Gentlemen's History Club

Society must derive a rental income "or some substitute for rents" to meet its interest on a forthcoming loan and operating expenses; and it must have a fireproof building.

While Winthrop urged the members to approve this plan, he conceded that it was a compromise and not the ideal arrangement. The best possible plan had been introduced by the standing committee a year earlier, a joint facility with the American Academy: "We might . . . remain here safely and contentedly, at least until that dream of some of us shall be realized,—the dream of a noble edifice, in some fit locality, erected by private or public munificence, inscribed by some worthy name, and dedicated to the Arts and Sciences, as well as to History; where the American Academy and our own Society might have separate libraries, with a common hall; and where our respective labors might be carried on side by side."

Winthrop had definite ideas about the physical makeup of any new quarters for the Society and foresaw "a separate hall for meetings, hung with portraits of past Presidents of the Society and historical personages, said hall to have in connection with it, an ante-room and a commodious cloak-room." The "Dowse Library, or an exact reproduction of it in any new building, would continue to be used for informal gatherings of members, or for any historical work upon which they might be engaged,—its immediate proximity to books of reference, and to the desks of the Librarian, Editor, and Clerks, rendering it peculiarly convenient for this purpose." He also argued for "a very ample provision" in the new building for the society's cabinet of curiosities and a "General Library" of sufficient size "in order that it might not be necessary to send up stairs for ordinary works of reference, and that copyists and other persons might have room to discharge their duties under the eye of the clerks. He also favored retaining a Newspaper room, for bound volumes of newspapers, on the same floor with the Dowse and general Libraries."

The dream of a joint facility with the American Academy was not financially feasible at this time, the elder Winthrop stated, because "The University [Harvard] and the Museum of Science and of Art seem to be absorbing all the liberality of our community at present."[82]

---

[82] Winthrop's full address is printed in M.H.S., *Procs.*, 12(1871–1873):131–137; R.C. Winthrop, Jr., "Memoranda" in vol. 82 Winthrop Family Papers, M.H.S.

Spurred on by the horrific news of the great fire in Chicago, which destroyed the historical society and its collections among the many losses suffered by the city, the Society's building committee proposed a resolution: "that it is a duty of the Society, in view of its rich treasures, to render its building fire-proof; and that it be recommended to the Society, at its next meeting, to raise a sum not exceeding thirty-five thousand dollars to carry out the plan of the architect accepted by the committee." The resolution was quickly adopted.[83]

The second, and final, element of the project fell into place when, after protracted and difficult negotiations, the building committee worked out an agreement with the City of Boston whereby the probate office and registry of deeds of Suffolk County would occupy the lower two floors for fifteen years at an annual rental of $9,000 and the payment of taxes. The Society agreed to cover the cost of building a connection between the quarters of the registry of deeds and the adjoining county office to the rear of 30 Tremont Street.

Having completed the essential preliminaries, the Society moved to implement its plan. The first step was to remove the contents from 30 Tremont Street. The Boston Athenaeum offered "safe and free hospitality" for the books, manuscripts, portraits, and "other memorials of the past," an offer the Society accepted speedily and with appreciation.[84] The furniture and other non-library materials were carted to a storage facility on Cambridge Street, a short distance away. Both moves were carried out by special committees at a cost of $599.62. Demolition of the old building could now take place.

[83] M.H.S., *Procs.*, 12(1871–1873):160.
[84] M.H.S., *Procs.*, 12(1871–1873):216.

Chapter 5

Historical and Genealogical Tiff

IN THE LATE eighteenth and nine-
teenth centuries, a number of historical-cultural institutions were established in Boston and such neighboring communities as Worcester,
Salem, and Plymouth. Although some were similar in program and
general character, these organizations co-existed peacefully and enjoyed
surprisingly harmonious relations, possibly because there was an extensive intertwining of memberships and directorates. Calling attention to
this same remarkable system of integration in the twentieth century,
Walter M. Whitehill wrote: "It is reminiscent of the Soldier's Chorus in
Faust, where the same few soldiers march on and off the stage to create
the illusion of an army."[1]

Only on one occasion was there a serious altercation between two sec-
tors of this unique cultural complex. This occurred in the 1840s, when the
Society locked horns with the newly founded New England Historic Genealogical Society.[2] Robert C. Winthrop once referred to the dispute as
"our little Boston controversy."[3] The Genealogical Society had been
formed in 1845 by a "small and earnest coterie" of local antiquarians to
give specific emphasis to genealogy.[4] They were also interested in her-

---

[1] Whitehill, *Independent Historical Societies* (Boston, 1962), 33.

[2] For full details on the history of this organization, see John A. Schutz, *A Noble
Pursuit: The Sesquicentennial History of the New England Historic Genealogical Society,
1845–1995* (Boston, 1995).

[3] Robert C. Winthrop to Samuel F. Haven, Mar. 4, 1858 (American Antiquarian Society
Correspondence, 1850s-1890s, American Antiquarian Society).

[4] On the founding and early history of the New England Historic Genealogical Society,
see: William C. Hill, *A Century of Genealogical Progress: Being a History of the New*

aldry and antiquarianism and wished to fill a gap left by the Historical Society in these areas. Reflective of the organization's interest in antiquarian matters, at one of its early informal gatherings the host invited his colleagues "to see the ball which killed Gen. Joseph Warren, and to taste some apples borne that year on the tree planted by Peregrine White."[5] As Historical Society member George G. Wolkins sarcastically noted, these experiences were designed "probably to stimulate their appetites for matters historical."[6]

Five men were involved in the founding of the Genealogical Society: Charles Ewer, a bookseller and businessman, and the mainspring of the movement;[7] William Montague, a prominent merchant; John Wingate Thornton, a reputable lawyer; Samuel G. Drake, bookseller, publisher, and author; and Lemuel Shattuck, also a bookseller and publisher. Of the five, only Shattuck was a member of the Historical Society.[8]

After establishing their organization and drawing up a constitution in 1845, the five founders selected officers. Ewer became president and Drake, who was to become the prominent figure in the forthcoming brouhaha, became corresponding secretary. Their next step was to secure a charter from the legislature, and here they ran into a formidable barrier: the Historical Society.

The older body did not relish the thought of another group invading its territory. Robert C. Winthrop bluntly stated the case in a letter to an

---

England Historic Genealogical Society, 1845–1945 (Boston, 1945); Samuel G. Drake, "Origin of the New England Historic Genealogical Society," *NEHGR*, 9(1855):2–12; and George G. Wolkins, "The Prince Society," M.H.S., *Procs.*, 66(1936–1941):223–241.

[5] *NEHGR*, 9(1855):10.

[6] M.H.S., *Procs.*, 66(1936–1941):226.

[7] On Ewer, see Samuel H. Riddel, "Mr. Charles Ewer," in *Memorial Biographies of the New England Historic Genealogical Society*, 5 vols. (Boston, 1880–1894), 2:113–155. According to John A. Schutz, Ewer was unsuccessful in his business ventures, "in fact almost everything he touched turned to financial failure for him and gain for others." Schutz, *A Noble Pursuit*, 15.

[8] There is a prevailing view that the men who founded the Genealogical Society did so because they could not achieve membership in the Historical Society. See, for example, Wesley Frank Craven, *The Legend of the Founding Fathers* (New York, 1956), 116–117. John A. Schutz and David L. Greene believe that almost all of the founders, while annoyed with the Historical Society for overlooking them for membership, were deeply interested in genealogy, heraldry, and antiquarianism, subjects of no concern to the older body. See Greene, "Samuel G. Drake and the Early Years of The New England Historical and Genealogical Register, 1847–1861," *NEHGR*, 155(1991):203–233, esp. 211.

Historical and Genealogical Tiff

English friend: "It was originally founded in opposition to our old Society, & by persons disappointed at not getting admission to ours."[9] While not interested in genealogy as such, the Historical Society regarded the subject as perilously close to its own area of concentration, and its leaders decided to oppose the effort of the Ewer group to achieve a charter. Through some adroit lobbying, the Historical Society managed to have the application of Ewer's group referred to a legislative committee chaired by Charles F. Adams, an Historical Society stalwart of the first rank.

Although a staunch member, Adams did not favor the Society's restrictive membership policy. He disliked its elitist character. He deplored its development from "a modest, poor, obscure association" into a "pretentious, rich, greedy and showy one."[10] Nonetheless, Adams was personally opposed to the Genealogical Society's charter. He believed that it would duplicate the purpose of the Historical Society. Accordingly, Adams's committee denied the application. Ewer and his cohorts, particularly Drake, were outraged by the committee's decision. Drake branded Adams's pronouncement a "declaration of hostility."[11] The battle was now joined.

Undaunted by this defeat, Ewer's group resubmitted their application and worked assiduously to marshal legislative support. They also lobbied intensively for a review of their application by a committee not dominated by Historical Society members or subject to their influence. Ultimately, they were successful in these dual efforts and were awarded a charter in March 1845.[12]

[9] R.C. Winthrop to Richard Almack, Apr. 6, 1871 (Boston Public Library, Ms 2234[6]).

[10] Paul C. Nagel, " 'The Ice Age . . . Passed Away': Adams Family Meditations Upon Republican New England," in Conrad Edick Wright, ed., *Massachusetts and the New Nation* (Boston, 1992), 251–252.

[11] Drake, *Narrative Remarks*, 18–19. Schutz has branded the Society's attitude in this dispute as "arrogant." Siding with the Genealogical Society, he wrote: "Surely MHS in using its title could be easily distinguished by the public from the New England Historic Genealogical Society. But matters of prestige, rivalry, and exclusiveness separated the societies. NEHGS, in trying to find higher grounds, now took steps to locate the leadership and resources to challenge MHS as a scholarly society." Schutz, *A Noble Pursuit*, 27.

[12] Charles F. Adams attributed the legislature's turnabout to the Society's insistence upon retaining its "narrow and exclusive system" of membership. In 1878, the Genealogical Society requested Adams to write about his father, John Quincy Adams. He believed that this invitation indicated that the Society had forgiven him for steadfastly

The Massachusetts Historical Society

After receiving its charter, the Genealogical Society moved quickly to elect members. It, too, adhered to a policy of membership by election. But, unlike its competitor, the Genealogical Society had no numerical limit on membership. Nor did it conduct the process in a secretive manner and microscopically examine candidates. It openly solicited prospects, and, if a person were so inclined and willing to pay the $3 entrance fee and $2 annual dues, he was elected. Like the Historical Society, the new organization did not have a stated policy on the exclusion of women, but it considered only men as candidates, in keeping with the convention of the period.[13]

The Genealogical Society grew rapidly. By the end of 1845, after only nine months of operation, it had elected 53 resident members, 83 corresponding members, and 14 honorary members. Of the total 150 members, 27 or almost 20 percent were also members of the Historical Society. Thus, about one-third of the Historical Society's resident members, including such prominent figures as Edward Everett, George Bancroft, and Josiah Quincy, became members of the Genealogical Society. By the end of 1846, its second year of existence, the Genealogical Society's membership had soared to 593 resident and corresponding members and 33 honorary members.

After their bitter confrontation in 1845, both societies adopted a mutually tolerant attitude and, for the next dozen years, co-existed in a relatively peaceful manner. In 1850, Joseph Barlow Felt became the second president of the Genealogical Society, succeeding Charles Ewer, who had served nearly six terms. Felt had been a member of the society since its founding in 1845. He also was a member of the Historical Society, serving as its librarian in 1836–1837. Because of Felt's association with it, the Historical Society permitted the Genealogical Society to hold three board meetings in its Tremont Street quarters.[14]

In 1856, the Genealogical Society requested an exchange of publications with the Historical Society. The latter's standing committee voted

---

opposing its petition for a charter in 1845. See Nagel, "The Ice Age," 253.

[13] The Genealogical Society began admitting women into membership in 1898, after securing passage of a legislative act in 1897 giving it the authority to do so. Schutz, *A Noble Pursuit*, 62. In February 1898, the Society nominated 36 women and 29 accepted.

[14] Schutz, *A Noble Pursuit*, 20. Felt was a member of the M.H.S. from 1830 until 1869. Because of some internal strife, he resigned from the Genealogical Society in 1853.

Historical and Genealogical Tiff

"to accede to it under certain limitations, which, on inquiry, have been found to be satisfactory to the petitioners."[15] In this period, more Historical Society members joined the Genealogical Society, including such luminaries as Jared Sparks, John G. Palfrey, and President Robert C. Winthrop. The fact that so many Historical Society members were on the rolls of the Genealogical Society may have been responsible for the easing of tensions.

The era of detente ended abruptly in 1857, when another controversy erupted. One person was responsible for the uproar: the irrepressible Samuel G. Drake, who had harbored resentment against the Historical Society for a number of years because it had not selected him for membership.[16] Drake was, in Samuel Johnson's phrase, "a good hater."[17]

Drake was a self-made man. In the words of his memorialist, he "commenced his labors without the patronage of the rich or the smile of encouragement from the great." Born in rural Pittsfield, New Hampshire, the son of a farmer (and, later, storekeeper), Drake had only a smattering of formal education. His "aversion to schooling, when a little urchin, was peculiarly strong." Natively bright, young Drake developed a passion for old books, especially historical writings. While a teenager, he served as a schoolteacher. Later, he spent five years in New Jersey as a schoolmaster. Wherever he was, he continued to study on his own or with specialists. In this way, he became conversant in Latin, French, scientific subjects, and the law. All the while, his passion for rare books continued to grow. He eventually decided to settle in Boston.

In 1830, at the age of thirty-two, he realized a long-held ambition by opening an antiquarian bookstore in Cornhill. This was the first antiquarian bookstore in the nation. His store soon became a gathering place for many of the Boston literati. A number of Historical Society savants frequented Drake's establishment, including George Bancroft, William H. Prescott, Richard Hildreth, Jared Sparks, and Edward Everett.

Drake established the reputation of an accomplished bookman and

[15] M.H.S., *Procs.*, 3(1855–1858):94.

[16] On Drake's life and career, see John H. Sheppard, "Memoir of Samuel Gardner Drake, A.M.," *NEHGR*, 17(1863):197–211; Greene, "Samuel G. Drake," 211.

[17] Johnson was referring to his beloved friend, Dr. Richard Bathurst. Johnson said to Mrs. Henry Thrale: "Dear Bathurst was a man to my very heart's content: he hated a fool, and he hated a rogue, and he hated a Whig; he was a *very good hater*." Quoted in John Wain, *Samuel Johnson* (New York, 1974), 158.

antiquarian. He took immense pride in his achievements and was vehemently outspoken in his criticism of those who had benefited from wealthy parents, social privilege, and a Harvard education.

Drake provoked the problem with the Historical Society by altering the name of the Genealogical Society in 1857. When they planned their society in 1844–45, the five founders wrestled with the problem of an appropriate title. There was wide disagreement on this point. Ewer favored "The Genealogical and Heraldic Society" but the other founders disapproved of this title, possibly because it was thought undemocratic. Montague had argued for the inclusion of "Historical" in the title because, as he stated, "there was no really active historical society in the state," an obvious slap at the existing institution.[18] Drake favored "The Genealogical Society," although he insisted later, and maintained to his dying day, that his first and only choice was "The New England Historical and Genealogical Society."[19]

Thornton's choice was the "New England Historic, Genealogical Society," and since he drafted the charter, not bothering to circulate it among his colleagues before submitting it to the legislature, his view prevailed.[20] Drake was infuriated by Thornton's cavalier action. He also took umbrage when he learned that Thornton had not listed him as an incorporator.

At the Genealogical Society's annual meeting on January 7, 1857, under the prodding of Drake, the members unanimously voted to change the organization's name to "The New England Historical and Genealogical Society" and to make the president a committee of one to draft and submit an appropriate petition to the state legislature. In that same month, Drake assumed the editorial responsibilities for the eleventh volume of the Genealogical Society's quarterly. He also had been largely responsible for producing and financing the first ten volumes, for which reason he was called the "Father of the *Register*." In these early volumes, Drake had used the following format on the title page:

---

[18] Drake, *Narrative Remarks*, 12–13.

[19] See *NEHGR*, 9(1855):11.

[20] *Acts and Resolves of General Court*, 1845, Chapter 152 (approved March 18, 1845). Only three named incorporators: Ewer; J. Wingate Thornton; and Joseph Willard and "their associates and successors."

Historical and Genealogical Tiff

> The
> New England
> Historical and Genealogical Register,
> And
> Antiquarian Journal:
> Published Quarterly.
> Under the Direction of the
> New England Historic-Genealogical Society.

In setting up his title page for the January 1857 issue, however, Drake made a slight but significant change in the name of the institution, reflecting the vote at the annual meeting. "New England Historic-Genealogical Society" became "N. Eng. Historical and Genealogical Society." Thus, Drake was proclaiming to the Massachusetts Historical Society and the world that his organization had a new name.[21]

Because the legislature was nearing the end of its session, the Genealogical Society decided to postpone the submission of its petition.

The year 1858 loomed as a critical time in the relationship of the two organizations. Prior to the annual meeting of the Genealogical Society, President William Whiting, a respected lawyer, who had served five consecutive terms in that office, suddenly declined to stand for reelection. His letter of declination was printed in the *Boston Evening Transcript*.[22]

The nominating committee selected the sixty-year-old Drake as Whiting's successor.[23] He was elected. In his presidential address, Drake threw down the gauntlet to the Historical Society:

> For my part, I do not believe that any ten, even of our number, are quite smart enough to do as much as all of us together. Neither will any of you, gentlemen, believe that a few individuals associated together for historical purposes, however *smart* they may be, are yet quite sufficient to do all our historical and genealogical work for us. A small number may associate

[21] See Greene, "Samuel G. Drake."

[22] Jan. 9, 1858. Wolkins wrote that the tone of Whiting's letter indicated "that he knew trouble was brewing and "had no relish for the skirmish that was to follow." Wolkins, "Prince Society," 227.

[23] In his presidential address, Drake insisted that he did not seek the presidency. He was content to be a "common laborer in the historical field." *NEHGR*, 12(1858):97. The address is on 97–105.

themselves together and hedge themselves about, entrench themselves behind any amount of self-importance, and argue that they can take care of the history of us all. That doctrine may do among the monks of Spain, even in the nineteenth century, but it is ill-suited to the institutions of the *free* State of America. . . . This Society was formed, by its original members, in the full belief that the knowledge brought to light by it, should benefit everybody who desired such knowledge. There were, therefore, no limits allowed to be set as to the number who might incline to lend a hand in the undertaking; and hence, by enrolling their names, it might be known that they appreciated the objects of it, and were ready to encourage it with whatever additional advantage their names and services might give it. It was thought to be altogether too antiquated an idea to admit none into their ranks until they themselves were dead. . . . No, gentlemen; instead of here and there an individual laborer, a mighty army of antiquaries is necessary to rescue the perishing records of the past. . . . There is work enough for us all.[24]

The pugnacious president announced that he planned to file with the legislature the petition agreed upon in 1857 concerning the change of the Society's corporate name "in conformity with the name of its Periodical." Drake went on to contend that the "name *Historic-Genealogical* was never agreeable to the original members. They, with a single exception, contended that it did not express fully their objects. 'Historic Genealogy' covers but a small portion of the ground intended; whereas *History and Genealogy* was really what was considered to be comprehended by it."[25]

The Historical Society's response conformed to Sir Isaac Newton's third law of motion: "A force exerted in one direction produces a reaction of equal force in the opposite direction." On January 19, 1858, the standing committee of the Historical Society met "for the purpose of consulting as to the measures proper to be taken on account of a petition lately presented to the Legislature of Mass. by the Historic-Genealogical Society for the change of the name of said Society to that of New England Historical and Genealogical Society." One of the members moved, "after a long conversation," that the president be requested to prepare a "Remonstrance" to the legislature, "to be signed by all the members of the Society in case it should be found necessary to resist

[24] *NEHGR*, 12(1858):102–103.
[25] *NEHGR*, 12(1858):105.

before that body the application of the Historic-Genealogical Society."[26]

Later in January, a three-member committee of the Historical Society met with the committee on education of the senate and house, to which Drake's petition had been referred, and set forth its objections. The joint committee informed the Historical Society delegation that it planned no action on the petition for at least three weeks. This postponement provided President Winthrop, who was also a member of the Genealogical Society, with sufficient time to prepare the Society's remonstration. Winthrop drafted the document in February and, after being "examined and amended" by the secretary, it was circulated among the members for their endorsement.

Winthrop's memorial was carefully crafted. After providing the background on the founding, purpose, and early history of the Historical Society, the president challenged the Genealogical Society's right to adopt its proposed name:

> Within the last thirteen years, a society has been instituted and incorporated in the same city with our own,—Boston,—bearing the name of the Historic-Genealogical Society, for whose welfare and success the best wishes were entertained by us all. Believing it to be devoted to the interesting subject of genealogy, and only incidentally to history, and thus to occupy a field distinct from our own, many of our number have gladly become associated with it from time to time. Not would we presume to limit or restrict its operations or efforts to the particular sphere which its name has hitherto indicated.

However, Winthrop noted "with regret," the Genealogical Society petitioned "for leave to change its name, so as to make it approach much more nearly to the name which it has been our corporate privilege to bear for nearly threescore years and ten." Winthop then cited the act of incorporation of the Genealogical Society to show that "the founders of the society contemplated the subject of history as subordinate to that of genealogy." Winthrop felt that the "name hitherto employed expresses this subordination; while that which is proposed not only fails to designate it, but, on the other hand, gives history the precedence." He went on to catalogue confusions "both at the post-office and in the public mind" between the two organizations because of the similarity of names and suggested that "if any change of name is to be made, it may be one

---

[26] Records of the Standing Committee, Jan. 19, 1858 (M.H.S. Archives).

which will widen, and not narrow, the difference already existing." After carrying forth in this forceful manner over the course of several pages, Winthrop concluded his memorial in a gracious tone. "We trust that we shall not subject ourselves to any charge of discourtesy to an institution of so much more recent establishment, if we suggest that the adoption of a different name might not be inconsistent with their interests or their honor."[27]

A majority of the members, forty-four in all, signed it. Nearly half (20) of this group were also members of the Genealogical Society. The memorial was then sent to the legislature.[28]

Subsequently, Winthrop appointed a committee of three distinguished members to appear before the joint legislative committee and present the Historical Society's position: John H. Clifford and Emory Washburn, both former governors of the commonwealth, and the legendary Josiah Quincy, the eighty-six-year-old former president of Harvard and mayor of Boston, and the oldest living member of the Society.[29] The "Nestor of our fellowship," he had been elected a member in 1796, five years after its founding. Winthrop designated Washburn the main advocate for the Society and selected Quincy as the secondary speaker.

While this maneuvering was underway and both sides were preparing for the legislative hearing, the controversy spilled over into the public press. Writing under the pseudonym of "Sigma," Lucius Sargent, a member of both bodies, wrote a sprightly defense of the Historical Society, while blasting the opponent for proposing to change its name. Utilizing the imperial "we" in his prose, Sargent wrote that

[27] The memorial is in M.H.S., *Procs.*, 3(1855–1858):266–270. In a letter to Samuel F. Haven of the American Antiquarian Society, Winthrop wrote: "We have desired nothing but that the *names* of the two Societies might be kept so far separate, as to prevent confusion & misunderstanding. We feel, as you would feel, if a 'New England Antiquarian Society' were about to be established in the City of *Worcester*. It is the identity of the place & post-office, which renders so close an approximation of names inconvenient & objectionable. The attempt to represent us as desiring to monopolize the field of history is disingenuous & dishonest." Robert C. Winthrop to Samuel F. Haven, Mar. 4, 1858 (American Antiquarian Society Correspondence, 1850s-1890s, American Antiquarian Society).

[28] Schutz has written: "Apparently the MHS offered a compromise during the course of this confrontation and would have agreed to call the Society *The New England Genealogical and Historical Society*." (*A Noble Pursuit*, 27). He offers no evidence for this assertion.

[29] M.H.S., *Procs.*, 3(1855–1858):270.

Historical and Genealogical Tiff

We are not of Dr. Johnson's opinion that all change is an evil. The change of name, in matrimony, for instance, is frequently the forerunner of many blessings—we, by no means, intend to suggest, that matrimony is contemplated, between these two societies. But it is very well known that change of name, in relation to persons and things, to States and empires, and, to familiarize the idea, the local changes of names, in regard to streets, places, edifices, etc. within the compass of a single city, have eminently contributed to perplex the historian, in his researches. It is to be regretted, that a *historic* society should give any additional contenance to this mischievous practice.

Sargent utilized his position as member of both societies to claim an impartiality in his judgment that "the change proposed no possible, legitimate good, of any importance, and not a little contingent evil and inconvenience." Raising a concern about letters misdirected because of the similarity of names, Sargent added his own spin by darkly suggesting that some legacy might be accidentally waylaid by a confusion of names, or even worse, "perhaps, some historical fable, worthy of the treacherous and wilful pen of Babington Macaulay, may accidentally disfigure the pages of one of these societies, and the responsibility be erringly attached to the other." He concluded his argument with the wish for the Genealogical Society's "success in all things reasonable— but not in this effort to change its name. In one respect, it must necessarily outstrip the Massachusetts Historical Society, whose numbers are limited by law. An omnibus must ever be more popular, than a vehicle contrived to carry a limited number."

Two days later came the predictable reply, a spirited rejoinder of Sargent's article, penned anonymously by "A Member of the N.E.H. etc. Soc." It was probably authored by Francis Brinley, a lawyer and vice president of the Genealogical Society.[30] The "Member" decided that his best tactic was to take aim at "the objects and results of the two societies."

> The Massachusetts Historical in sixty-three years has published 33 volumes; we have issued 11 volumes in thirteen years. Nor is this all. Their issues are chiefly reprints—ours original documents. Our volumes also

---

[30] Because Brinley resigned from the Genealogical Society in 1859, he did not receive a printed memoir at his death. In 1848 and 1852, he served as commander of the Ancient and Honorable Artillery Company. The text of the letter is in the *Boston Evening Transcript*, Feb. 18, 1858.

contain much more printed matter than theirs, so that a mere enumeration does not do us justice. We have not confined our attention to genealogy, but have published proportionately as much historical matter as the other society. In fact, the line between historical matter as they interpret it, and genealogy, can hardly be seen.

The writer also willingly jumped upon Sigma's fear of misdirected legacies.

'I thank thee for the word!' Was it because we had no word 'historical' that the legacy left by a late member of our society, one interested much in its objects, was absorbed by the Massachusetts Historical Society, to which he *did not belong*, as it was left for such *historical* societies as his executors might select? Truly, if this little change is to benefit us in such a mode, we may well be strenuous for it.

In conclusion, he also could not let Sigma's analogy of public conveyance go without retort.

Mr. 'Sigma,' an omnibus may be more plebeian than a private carriage, and it may be less honor to belong to a large and democratic society than to a select and wealthy one; but the latter will no sooner succeed in hindering or demolishing the former, than (to revert to your simile) the Roxbury horse cars will obediently turn into the gutter, to let the private conveyance have the middle of the road.

As a close to the newspaper war, Sargent countered with one final salvo in which he professed to be "grieved and surprised, that our brother of the Historic-Genealogical Society should have worked himself up, so unnecessarily, into a nervous fever." Sargent, albeit still disguised as "Sigma," reiterated his objection to the change of name as a member of the genealogical society, "no less as a member of the Massachusetts Historical Society." By identifying himself with both societies simultaneously, Sargent skillfully interwove his "we's" and "they's" to produce an argument weighted in favor of the Historical Society by emphasizing the differences between the two organizations over their similarities. He was perhaps strongest on the sensitive point of exclusivity in membership.

When invited to become a member, I was not aware, that the Historic-Genealogical was a *democratic society*. If the proposition were to call our

Historical and Genealogical Tiff

society the *New England Democratic Historical and Genealogical Society*, possibly all objection might be withdrawn. The remark, made by us, was occasioned by a notice, in some journal, of the numbers, from time to time, and especially recently, elected members of this society. I read this notice with regret. No truth is more sure, than that the value of such membership becomes lessened, by its commonness. This proposition is so self-evident, that we shall not argue it. The practice may serve to raise a small revenue; but, infallibly, must lower the respectability of any historical society, by its too frequent employment. We have uttered, and repeat, our best wishes, for the welfare of this society.[31]

The Legislative Committee scheduled the hearing for February 1, 1859. The Genealogical Society's representatives appeared but not the remonstrants. Drake fumed that their "non-appearance was evidently intended for the annoyance of the new society, and the committee showed their subserviency by allowing the matter to be put off without any reason."[32] A new hearing was scheduled later in the month.

On the day of the hearing, in Drake's words, "the enemy appeared in force." The formidable trio of Clifford, Washburn, and Quincy arrived to do battle. The Genealogical Society was represented by Drake, Vice President Brinley, and William M. Cornell.

The Genealogical Society group spoke first. Brinley "made a fair statement respecting the importance of the change in name, showing that it was important to the society, and interfered with no one else." Cornell covered much the same ground in his presentation. In a more combative spirit, Drake argued "that the society had a right to a change of name, and that the committee had no right to refuse it; that gentlemen in any locality had a right to form a historical society and the legislature had no right to refuse them an act of incorporation."

Washburn and Quincy countered for the Historical Society. Washburn spoke for an hour, in Drake's works, "in a sort of laudation of the Massachusetts Historical Society, interspersed with here and there a supercillious compliment for the members of the new society." The venerable Quincy's comments were laced with sardonic humor. While the simple, straightforward name of Massachusetts Historical Society

---

[31] The complete texts of these letters are printed in Wolkins, "Prince Society," 232–239.
[32] Drake, *Narrative Remarks*, 35.

represented all the Puritan virtues of strength and simplicity, the other society

> called itself *The New-England Historic-Genealogical Society*,—a name long enough, one would suppose, to satisfy the taste or the appetite of any human being, or of any association of human beings, were they Spaniards or Frenchmen. After enjoying this name for twelve years without question or molestation, they suddenly find it is not long enough; and come to the Legislature of Massachusetts, almost with tears in their eyes, to lengthen it out by adding al to historic, so that they may be hereafter known as *The New-England Historical Genealogical Society*. Was ever a legislature called upon before to legislate upon a subject so small and so trivial? Nothing is wanted by these petitioners to make them perfectly happy and great, but the addition-*al* to their already sesquipedalian name. In other words, all they want is precisely the addition of that single element which now distinguishes that Society from ours. Unless there is some hidden hope or anticipated advantage concealed under this desired addition, the desire can have no other origin than idiosyncrasy, like that of the frog, who thought that, by a little swelling, he would grow into, or be mistaken for, something very great.[33]

However effective Quincy's speech may have been, it was irrelevant. Indeed, all of the presentations were for naught. They were not the crucial factor in the committee's decision. Drake had sealed his own fate by committing an egregious *faux pas*. He had failed to do his homework. A new law had been passed in Massachusetts in 1857 requiring every corporation in the commonwealth intending to apply for a change in its charter to publish a copy of its petition for four successive weeks in a paper printed in the county in which it had been founded.[34] Drake had failed to follow this procedure. Because of his non-compliance, the committee refused to act on the petition and "reported leave to withdraw."[35]

[33] Quincy's speech is printed in M.H.S., *Procs.*, 3(1855–1858):344–351. See also Robert A. McCaughy, *Josiah Quincy, 1772–1864: The Last Federalist* (Cambridge, Mass., 1974), 198–199. Drake did not find Quincy's remarks humorous. He wrote: "To oppose the grant required, the enemy brought Emory Washburn as chief advocate, and old Josiah Quincy for—one hardly knows what—except to say something at which those who came with him might laugh. The principal of these were one W. Brigham and Chandler Robbins. They showed their appreciation of the old man's stale jokes by grins and shrugs as boys are wont to do at those of a clown in a circus." Drake, *Narrative Remarks*, 36.

[34] *Acts and Resolves of the General Court*, 1857, Chapter 261, Section 5.

[35] *Boston Evening Transcript*, Feb. 19, 1858.

Historical and Genealogical Tiff

The Historical Society had won the Homeric battle of the titles.[36]

Drake was thrown into a swivet by the committee's failure to approve his petition. But rather than retreating in defeat, he took the offensive. After the hearing, he assembled seven of his inner circle, all "earnest antiquarians" and men of "congenial historical sympathies," and proposed the formation of another organization that would compete with the Historical Society in the publication of original manuscripts and rare books relating to American history. Not coincidentally, all seven men were also loyal members of the Genealogical Society.[37] And this time there would be no conflict over a name. He would call the new organization, "The Prince Society for Mutual Publication," in honor of Thomas Prince.[38] Drake held the organizational meeting on May 25, 1858, the anniversary of Prince's birth. A constitution was soon adopted and by mid-June the organization became operational, with Drake assuming the presidency.[39] The Historical Society offered no opposition to this group.

After the second encounter between the Historical and Genealogical societies, a calm fell upon Boston's cultural institutions. There was a return to the spirit of peaceful co-existence. In September 1859, the Historical Society received a communication from a committee of the "New-England Historic Genealogical Society," inviting its members to attend a celebration of the centennial anniversary of the capture of Quebec. Lorenzo Sabine was to speak at the program. The Historical Society voted to accept the invitation "and take pleasure in manifesting thereby, through the courtesy of a kindred Society, their interest in the

[36] Drake charged in his *Narrative Remarks* that the legislative committee had been "tampered with" by members of the Historical Society and the chairman "hoped to be *elevated* to a membership by reporting adversely to the petitioners" (p. 36).

[37] Schutz, *A Noble Pursuit*, 27.

[38] The organization shortened its name to Prince Society in 1873. For the early history of the Society, consult Wolkins, "Prince Society." According to David Greene, Drake patterned the Society after the Camden, Surtees, and Chetham societies, established British publishing organizations. Greene considers the founding of Drake's society as a significant development in American historical publishing.

[39] Drake retained the presidency until 1870. The society survived until 1944, when it dissolved and, in a strange bit of irony, turned over its books and residual funds ($1,345) to the Historical Society. The Society created an endowed fund and named it the Thomas Prince Fund; the income balance was to be used for publications. See M.H.S. Council Records, Feb. 10, 1944 (M.H.S. Archives).

great historical event which it is intended to commemorate." In a like manner, the Historical Society reported donations to its library by the Genealogical Society at its meetings of November 1859, and January and February 1860.[40]

Drake, however, failed to manifest this attitude of conciliation and benevolence. He remained an inactive volcano, still simmering with anti-Historical Society feelings. In 1874, one year before his death, the seventy-six-year-old bookseller had his final eruption. In a publication which he titled *Narrative Remarks, Expository Notes, and Historical Criticisms on the New England Historical and Genealogical Society, and Incidentally on the Massachusetts Historical Society*, he presented for posterity his side of the story of how the Genealogical Society came to be organized and the problems it had experienced with the Historical Society. His inclusion of "Historical" in the Genealogical Society's title indicated that he had not conceded on that point, despite his defeat at the legislative hearing.

Drake's work was pure invective. He bludgeoned the Historical Society on a number of counts. He branded it a closed and "secret" society, which refused to allow non-members to use its resources. He attacked it for its elitism and exclusionist policy on membership. He excoriated it for its opposition to the Genealogical Society. His chronicle of Historical Society misdeeds was voluminous. As Ahab was bedeviled by the great white whale, so, too, was Samuel G. Drake spiritually tortured by the Massachusetts Historical Society.

[40] M.H.S., *Procs.*, 4(1858–1860):373–374, 384, 424, 429.

Chapter 6

The Reoccupation
of Their Own Estate

WORKMEN GUTTED the building on Tremont Street and hauled away the debris in horse-drawn carts. Construction of the new facility began in April 1872.[1] To achieve the goal of a "perfectly fireproof" structure, the contractor made heavy use of iron and brick. The building committee provided details on the construction:

> To effect this necessary change, the whole interior of the old building was removed from the cellar to the roof, and built up anew; each story perfectly isolated by floors constructed with iron girders and brick arches. The north wall has been carried fifteen feet above the old structure, creating an additional room for the use of the Society, and forming a protection from fire on that side. The roof, like the floors, is of iron and brick, covered with copper and painted.
>
> The staircases are of iron: the vestibule is isolated from the main building by thick brick walls, connecting with it by iron doors, so that the protection from fire on the Tremont Street side is also believed to be complete. The connection with the old county building, by which the rooms of the Registry of Deeds and the Probate Office are united with our building, is by iron staircases and doors.[2]

The use of expensive materials made the cost of construction soar from a projected $22,000 to $65,000. The Society was forced to take out

---

[1] During the reconstruction, the Society held its meetings in the homes of members, in the room of the American Academy of Arts and Sciences in the Boston Athenaeum, and in its rented temporary quarters at 41 Tremont Street.

[2] On details of the reconstruction, see M.H.S., *Procs.*, 12(1871–1873):140, 160, 171, 212, 216, 232, 252, 385. The building committee rendered a comprehensive report on the reconstruction in April 1873. See ibid., 13(1873–1875):5–7.

a loan of $60,000, to be paid back in five years at an annual interest rate of 7 percent.[3]

If Winthrop was shocked by the appreciable increase in cost, he made no issue of it in his frequent reports to the membership. Instead he stressed the advantages of a fireproof building. He also expressed pleasure in the reconstructed Dowse Library, which was positioned on the third floor. This room was to continue serving as the Society's meeting hall and social center for the members. In size and design, it was a replica of the former Dowse library, although the committee in charge of furnishing the room had taken "a little license."[4]

While reconstruction was underway in 1872, Boston experienced a fire of major proportions which underscored for the members the value of a fireproof building. In the previous two centuries, Boston had suffered at least four major fires, but none as severe as the Great Fire of 1872.[5] This was on a scale of what New York City had undergone in 1835 and Chicago in 1871.

On the balmy, moonlit, Indian summer evening of November 9, shortly after 7 P.M., a fire broke out in the basement of a five-story granite building at the corner of Summer and Bedford streets, a few blocks from the Society's quarters. It was apparently caused by a spark from a steam engine used to power an elevator. The flames shot up the elevator shaft and burst into each floor, which contained highly flammable wool and cotton stuff. Soon, the entire building was a huge torch. Firebrands began falling on nearby buildings, which had wooden roofs covered in slate.[6]

With incredible speed, the blaze quickly raced out of control, "the devouring element leaping from roof to roof with such terrible energy." Buildings turned into live furnaces within five minutes. The residents of Worcester, 45 miles to the west, and Portland, Maine, 105 miles to the northeast, could see the red glow over the city.

[3] The Society did not pay off the mortgage until 1886. See R.C. Winthrop to C.C. Smith, July 18, 1886 (Charles C. Smith Papers, M.H.S.).

[4] M.H.S., Procs., 13(1873–1875):6–7.

[5] For an account of major fires in Boston in the colonial and early national periods, see M.H.S., Procs., 12(1871–1873):280–282.

[6] For accounts of the fire of 1872, see: "The Great Boston Fire, 1872, A Disaster With a Villain: Old Style Politics," special magazine publication of the Boston Globe, Nov. 12, 1972, ed. by John Harris; Howe, Boston, 364–371; Caroline Ticknor, ed., Dr. Holmes's Boston (Boston, 1915), 78–81; Harold Murdock, ed., Letters Written by a Gentleman in Boston to His Friend in Paris Describing the Great Fire (Boston, 1909).

The Reoccupation of Their Own Estate

For the next two days, the buildings burned like tinder, spewing volumes of black, acrid smoke laced with yellow flames and fiery debris.[7] As the voracious flames reached higher and higher, the heat pulverized the granite walls of the large commercial buildings. Huge sections of granite broke off from the facings and crashed into the street. Young Oliver Wendell Holmes, son of the "Autocrat" and future Supreme Court Justice, was surprised to see "great walls . . . tumble and yet one would hear no crash,—they came down as if they had fallen on a vast feather-bed."[8] The searing heat sent molten lead and zinc from the roofs pouring down twisted iron fire escapes. The fire raced to the waterfront, where it ignited piles of coal. The coal smoldered for over a week, laying a pall of black smoke over the city. While the inferno raged, looters roamed about, stealing what they could.

Before the flames from the main fire and subsequent sporadic blazes were finally extinguished seven days later, over sixty-five acres of central Boston were reduced to charred rubble. More than 760 buildings, many built of stone or brick, were leveled. Hundreds of businesses were destroyed, including seven banks and two newspapers. This section was the core of Boston's (and New England's) business and commercial district, featuring leather, shoe, dry goods, wool, and publishing firms. Property valued at more than half a billion dollars lay in ruins and thousands were thrown out of work. A contemporary annalist wrote that "the fire fiend, who had slowly but surely wormed himself through the commercial loins of our city, eating out the very vitals of our trade and our industries, was chained, and the pale moon came slowly up to throw its lambent rays into smoky clouds that rose from the vast domain of smouldering ruins."[9]

---

[7] On the evening of Nov. 11, while the burned district was still alive with flames, John Amory Lowell hosted a meeting of the Historical Society in his capacious home on Park Street (now the Union Club). The members were there to meet the English historian, James Anthony Froude, an honorary member of the Society, who had come to Boston to present an "anti-Irish talk . . . on the English in Ireland." Lowell's home was a short distance from the fire zone. Lowell had been urged to cancel the affair but, after consulting with President Robert C. Winthrop, decided to hold the meeting. In Edward Weeks's words, he "carried off the entertainment as if he had nothing but intellectual curiosity on his mind." Weeks, *The Lowells and Their Institute*, 85. See also, M.H.S., *Procs.*, 12(1871–1873):279–280.

[8] Ticknor, ed., *Dr. Holmes's Boston*, 78–79.

[9] Quoted in Howe, *Boston*, 369.

The Massachusetts Historical Society

Up to that time, this was the most widespread, most costly, and most damaging blaze in Boston's fire-filled history. Eleven regular or volunteer firemen were killed, seventeen firemen were injured, many seriously, and a number of citizens were injured or perished in the flames. The final death toll was over thirty. Because the fire began on a Saturday evening, and because the area contained few private residences (about sixty), the loss of life was minimal.

The district in which the Society was located escaped the "Great Conflagration" because of the firemen's action of blowing up a line of damaged buildings at the northern perimeter of the blaze. The fire did not spread beyond this point. If the new "fireproof" building, then under construction, had been completed and directly impacted by the blaze, it is doubtful that it could have survived such an inferno. Given the ferocious intensity of the fire storm, it seems certain that the building, as well as its contents, would have been heavily damaged by the intense heat and fast-moving flames.[10]

Whatever the possible outcome, the members showed no displeasure over the large cost overrun for the reconstruction. Like Winthrop, they viewed it as a justifiable expense. They may have looked upon the 1872 conflagration as a phenomenon, a once-in-a-lifetime occurrence.

It is of interest to note that the district in which the Tontine Crescent—and Society's former home—once stood was devastated by the fire. It was a charred wasteland, the center of the Burned District, as it was called. Bulfinch's stately creation and other elegant structures in this area, which had been the residence of the wealthy and fashionable of Boston for a quarter of a century, had been torn down in the mid-1850s, with the rapid commercial expansion of Boston. They were replaced by large warehouses and a number of imposing stores. These commercial structures had granite facades which were thought to be fireproof. Eight of these "palaces of trade" occupied the land on which the Tontine Crescent had been located.[11] Some of the warehouses contained the libraries, paintings, and art treasures belonging to Bostonians

[10] Maurice Reidy of Boston, a civil engineer with a broad knowledge of the historic buildings in the city, informed this writer that, in his judgment, the reconstructed Society with all of its safeguards against fire would not have survived the conflagration of 1872, if the flames had struck Tremont Street.

[11] *Boston Almanac for the Year 1859* (Boston, 1859), 56, *passim.*

who either were traveling abroad or storing their precious holdings.[12]

More than likely, the Society also would have placed its treasured possessions in one of these warehouses during the reconstruction of its quarters. Thus, had the Boston Athenaeum not extended its offer, it is certain that the Society's collection would have burned to ash. The members were mindful of this stroke of good fortune and grateful to the Athenaeum for its generosity.[13]

The city took custody of its two floors of the rehabilitated building on January 1, 1873. The Society's three floors were completed by mid-January but the library materials and furniture did not return until March. The Society opened its quarters in April.

With their reentry into the renovated building, the members foresaw the beginning of an "eventful epoch in the history of the Society." They were euphoric about their new quarters. Reflecting the buoyantly optimistic mood of the moment, the standing committee rendered a glowing report after one year of operation: "Our accommodations were never so ample, nor our surroundings so attractive to the eye."

All aspects of the program had shown dramatic improvement. Meetings were better attended. The members were presenting more "interesting communications" and publishing "valuable papers." The library was in a "better condition than at any previous period." There was ample shelf space for the books and the "number of volumes contributed have been threefold above the number received during any former year." In 1873, the library contained 21,000 books. In 1874, 1,269 books were added, as well as 3,747 pamphlets, 1,429 newspapers, 88 maps, and 73 volumes of manuscripts. More researchers than in past years were using the library for "reference and study." The various collections "have never before elicited so much attention, nor the rooms been so generally frequented." The committee stated "there are abundant reasons for congratulation, and every incentive to renewed effort."[14]

Despite his success with the building program, Winthrop did not regard his work at an end. He was not content with one hundred members. He desired more, at least fifty or one hundred more. In 1869, he again had

---

[12] Howe, *Boston*, 369–370.
[13] M.H.S., *Procs.*, 12(1871–1873):216, 13(1873–1875):12.
[14] M.H.S., *Procs.*, 13(1873–1875):264–265.

raised the issue of enlargement. The members appointed a special committee to study the question. Nothing came of the effort.[15]

In 1871, he renewed his request, arguing that the reconstruction and enlargement of the Society's headquarters, then underway, provided a rationale for an expansion in membership. He also asserted that the abundance of qualified candidates in the Boston area made the broadening of membership an expedient course of action.[16] The population of the city had grown considerably since the Society was founded, from less than 20,000 in 1790 to 250,526 in 1870.[17]

Early in 1872 a new scheme for increasing the Society's statute-limited membership was suggested. Removing some of the older members from the active list and placing them in an *emeriti* category would open up some spaces for new recruits, while still retaining the original members on the rolls. Winthrop, however, was not in favor of this scheme. He foresaw "many embarrassments in adopting the *Emeriti* system" and was "not sure that it would not be considered an evasion of Charter limitation." In any event "the application of such a rule would involve much delicacy. Old men do not like being laid on the shelf, even though it be an upper shelf." Winthrop thought "they would consider it disrespectful. And then to affix a title which implies 'services rendered' to names associated with inaction, would be of doubtful fitness."[18] The idea was abandoned.

The issue of expansion was formally introduced and debated at the annual meeting of 1872 but the forces of conservatism, or "Old Fogeyism," as George E. Ellis once described it, prevailed this time.[19] Winthrop conceded defeat but regarded it as a temporary setback. At the annual meeting of 1876, the Council informed the members that the issue was worthy of inquiry. Speaking for the Council but reflecting Winthrop's point of view, Robert M. Mason stated: "The claims of a

[15] M.H.S., *Procs.*, 14(1875–1876):319.

[16] M.H.S., *Procs.*, 12(1871–1873):137, 170.

[17] The growth of "Boston Proper" from 1800 to 1870 was enormous. The U.S. census figures show: 24,937 in 1800; 93,383 in 1840; 136,881 in 1850; and 177,840 in 1860.

[18] Winthrop to Whitmore, Feb. 21, 1872 (Robert C. Winthrop Letters to William H. Whitmore, 1862–1874, M.H.S.).

[19] M.H.S., *Procs.*, 12(1871–1873):216–217. George E. Ellis to Samuel Osgood, Domestic Corresponding Secretary of New-York Historical Society, Apr. 27, 1855 (New-York Historical Society manuscript collection).

growing and educated community call on us not too jealously to limit the advantages we enjoy, but rather extend our privileges by a judicious selection of new members."[20]

The special committee reported at the December 1876 meeting and recommended precisely what Winthrop had been urging, that the Society seek permission from the legislature to remove all restrictions on membership and allow the Society to handle this matter through its By-Laws. Because attendance was slight and "there seemed to be a difference of opinion," the members postponed action on the motion until the January meeting. They directed the recording secretary to notify members that the issue was to be discussed and acted upon at that time.[21]

The January 11, 1877, meeting drew forty members, who heatedly debated the question but did not resolve it, as expected. The group voted to hold a special meeting one week later and go at it again.[22]

The January 18 gathering was the climactic session in the twenty-year struggle to expand the membership beyond one hundred. There were now two contending forces within the Society. One, led by Winthrop, endorsed not only a more liberal policy in membership but also a more progressive program calling for greater outreach on the Society's part and increased participation in public affairs relating to historical issues.

Ellis was the nominal leader of the opposition, which was in the majority at the moment. He argued for the preservation of the past and a Society that resisted "the restive propensities and the eclectic eccentricities of our own times." He stood for the "old way," the small, insular club of patrician historians.

Forty-eight members were in attendance. They filled the Dowse Room and "overflowed into the library outside." Every prominent member was there. Charles F. Adams wrote that it was "the largest and most interesting meeting the Society has held since I have been a member; and I think also it was the largest and most interesting meeting which has been held within the memory of any living member." He called it "a turning-point in the history of the Society; for it was the final action

---

[20] M.H.S., *Procs.*, 14(1875–1876):319–320.
[21] M.H.S., *Procs.*, 14(1875–1876):327; 15(1876–1877):181.
[22] M.H.S., *Procs.*, 15(1876–1877):229.

taken by it on a proposition which looked to a complete change of policy in regard to its membership."

With Winthrop occupying the chair, the debate began. It persisted for hours. Because of the bitterness of the exchanges, the members agreed "that only a slight reference to the meeting should be printed, and that the carefully preserved arguments which had been read should not be preserved."

Fortunately for future historians, Charles F. Adams, wrote a "confidential" account of the meeting providing salient details on what transpired:

Mr. Winthrop occupied the chair. The debate opened with a motion, by Mr. Whitmore, that the further consideration of the proposition be indefinitely postponed. On this the discussion took place. Remarks in opposition to the proposed change were made by James Russell Lowell, who dwelt upon the exceptional position occupied by this Society, and upon the extreme inadvisability of breaking down the barriers and entering it among all similar organizations in the race for popularity. He believed in holding it high. Dr. Ellis spoke to the same effect; while our associate Mr. C.C. Smith followed in a carefully prepared paper. The spirit of the meeting was unmistakable; and it was also apparent not only that the Council was divided, but that a very considerable portion of those who gave their assent to the proposed change did so out of deference to Mr. Winthrop, and an unwillingness to oppose any policy in regard to the Society which met his approval.

The report and recommendation of the Committee were vigorously supported by Judge Hoar. Governor Washburn was not present. He died only a little more than two months later, and was already in failing health. In his absence, Judge Hoar took the broad ground, in opposition to Mr. Lowell, that an Historical Society was but the association of a number of persons interested in a common pursuit, and that, to further its purpose, it should be made as open to all as conditions permitted. His remarks bore that stamp of shrewd, aggressive sense and humor which characterized them always, whether delivered from the bench, at the bar, or from the floor. Mr. Winthrop closed the discussion with a carefully prepared paper, which he read from the chair. In it he argued the whole question, strongly advocating the proposed change on grounds of expediency, the allaying of invidious feelings and the removal of hostilities, the difficulties attending a limited selection, and, finally, financial exigencies. The vote was then taken, and was decisive of the feelings of the members of the Society. A number, out of deference to Mr. Winthrop, abstained from voting. Of those who did vote on the show of hands, thirty-one voted for indefinite postponement to eleven against it. The matter was thus finally disposed of. Since that time no proposition for a change in the membership of the Society has been considered.[23]

In 1897, Adams presented an extemporaneous address at the Society in which he reminisced about the 1877 meeting. Charles C. Smith, who heard Adams's talk, wrote later that he had "omitted to recall an amusing remark which he made in the course of his extemporaneous speech— that when he was elected he was a wholly unsuitable person for membership, and that he wished to keep out of the Society just such persons as he was." In his confidential report, Adams made no reference to his contribution to the debate. Nor did he refer to a "dramatic incident" that occurred when the vote was taken. Adams's father was seated behind the large table next to President Winthrop. The younger Adams sat near the door, directly opposite his father. "When the vote was called for, the father rose and voted in favor of an enlarged membership. When the nays were asked to rise and be counted, the son rose, and, facing his father, voted against it."[24]

The criteria for membership had long been a problem dogging the Society. In 1855, in a letter to the corresponding secretary of the New-York Historical Society, George E. Ellis addressed the question, stressing the importance of scholarly interest:

> The theory of the Society—one too that is more closely conformed to its practical working than are most theories—is that no person shall be chosen into it who has not proved his hearty interest in historical or antiquarian research by some contribution completed or in progress—or by some manifest token of his zeal for the cause. The seats occupied at our monthly meetings exhibit therefore a selected body of men, many of whom have been and are eminently distinguished for something more than social position, and some of whom bring the highest literary honors to dignify the little circle in which they are conspicuous.[25]

[23] Charles F. Adams, "Confidential Paper on Special Meeting of Jan. 18, 1877" (M.H.S. Archives). Adams presented this account to Librarian Samuel A. Green in 1895, and a portion of it was published in M.H.S., Procs., 2d ser., 10(1895–1896):318–320.

[24] M.H.S., Procs., 48(1914–1915):399–400.

[25] George E. Ellis to Samuel Osgood, Apr. 27, 1855 (New-York Historical Society manuscript collection).

Charles F. Adams noted that certain men had been "elected to membership for no apparent reason, except that their names were pressed by some friend, and a general feeling of kindliness and good nature prevented objection." Unlike Ellis, Adams did not believe that historical interest should be the determinant criterion in the election of members. He had a more progressive outlook. In his words:

> I see no reason why in filling our membership we should strictly limit ourselves to those who are interested, and much less to those who are directly engaged in pursuits of an historical nature. On the contrary, I see every reason why our ranks should be strengthened by the admission of any person in the Commonwealth who has attained eminence in any literary or associated field. In this respect my sympathies are entirely with the views which I remember were expressed by Mr. Winthrop, who wished to have the Society include in its membership all men of mark within the Commonwealth who have attained distinction in letters, as investigators, as scientific men, as professional men, or even who, through wealth and standing and inclination, occupy the position of a patron, or, as he expressed it, of a Maecenas. In my judgment the only thing we should distinctly avoid is degenerating into a mutual admiration society, or a mere coterie of antiquarians.[26]

The Society, Adams asserted, had shown a tendency to elect "figureheads and mummies." He favored a heterogeneous membership and took an active hand in recruiting candidates. As Edward Kirkland has written: "Apparently he accomplished something, for heretics, radicals, and even those abstractionists, the professors, now joined existing numbers who continued to think of the Society 'as a fortress' to hold against lesser breeds without the law."[27]

Robert C. Winthrop, Jr., shared Adams's displeasure with the system of nomination. He believed that "personal likes & dislikes entered too largely" in the process, and that "persons who had really a strong claim were often postponed to others who had little or none."[28]

Unlike his father, Winthrop believed that the Society should place a high value on the philanthropic potential of a candidate. As he wrote to

[26] Adams, "Confidential Paper, 1877"; for the printed version, see M.H.S., *Procs.*, 2nd ser., 10(1895–1896):325.

[27] Edward C. Kirkland, *Charles Francis Adams, Jr., 1835–1915: The Patrician at Bay* (Cambridge, Mass., 1965), 217.

[28] R.C. Winthrop, Jr., "Memoranda" in vol. 82, Winthrop Family Papers, M.H.S.

The Reoccupation of Their Own Estate

Charles C. Smith on June 17, 1885: "The next time an opportunity occurs for electing some one *not* a professed historian, I should like to suggest the name of Mr. T. Jefferson Coolidge, who is a man of real ability & exceptional liberality. He has given a couple of hundred thousand to Harvard & might some day prove our benefactor. If we can not find men who will *work*, let us, at least, choose men who can & will *give*."[29]

In 1892, the Society finally decided to deal with the persistently troublesome issue of criteria. A special committee, chaired by Charles F. Adams, studied the problem and delivered its report at the March meeting. It concluded, initially, that the membership should represent the entire Commonwealth. There was no such focus on geographic coverage in 1892. The committee discovered that seventy-six of the ninety-eight resident members lived within a ten-mile radius of the Society. Sixty-four of the ninety-eight were residents of either Boston or Cambridge. It recommended that "every county in the State should have at least one representative in the list of Resident Members."

The committee also observed that the selection of candidates had "not been made in pursuance of any consistent plan or on any wide general views either of the field or the material available. It has to a certain extent been matter of chance, or due to personal considerations; and in some cases to a natural unwillingness to give possible offence by opposing the evident desire of others." It, therefore, proposed two additional criteria: "that the eminence of candidates, either as historical students and writers, or as authorities in matters connected with history, be next considered; while, finally, the list should be filled by a careful selection from those who on general grounds, whether of high public office or of professional or social eminence, merit recognition, and in return would add value and dignity to membership in the Society."

The Council and members approved the committee's report. At the subsequent meeting, the Council stressed the importance of adhering to the criteria now in effect, and eliminating as far as possible the "personal or accidental element" in the selection of members. Hereafter, in October of each year, a sub-committee was to develop a list of ten candi-

[29] R.C. Winthrop, Jr., to C.C. Smith, June 17, 1885 (Charles C. Smith Papers, M.H.S.).

dates. When vacancies occurred, the council was to consider these men "in the order in which they stand."[30]

Time was to show that the effort to systematize the process of membership was a wasted exercise. New members continued to be selected in an unsystematic, serendipitous manner. Few, if any, Council members seriously considered the operative criteria when they nominated candidates.

No direct evidence exists on what transpired in the deliberations of the various nominating committees, but there are documents which provide an insight into the machinations of Council members when candidates were being considered. In February 1898, an opening developed and two men became leading candidates for the slot: the Reverend George A. Gordon and Andrew McFarland Davis. It was a hotly contested issue in the nominating committee and Council. Both men had a coterie of supporters.

President Adams strongly favored Davis. He found him "eminently fitted for membership by tastes and pursuits." Some members were opposed to him because "he was a member, and active, in the Colonial Society" [of Massachusetts], a newly founded and competitive historical organization. To Adams, this was "an objection so narrow and so little that it mortified me to hear it advanced."

The issue became filled with intrigue, as revealed in a letter from Robert C. Winthrop, Jr., to President Adams in which he recounted a meeting with fellow member, Henry W. Haynes:

> Haynes's prostate now gives him less trouble and he is able to sit in his library, where I communed with him yesterday aft., explaining the Davis imbroglio. He said that though, on general principles, he should be glad to have Gordon in the Society, yet he should not have voted for him in the Council *against Davis*, but would have supported you, as Thayer undoubtedly would have done had he been there. Thus, if there had been a full Council-meeting, the vote would have stood 6 to 5, instead of 6 to 2, which is encouraging. Haynes, like Lawrence Lowell, is fully in accord with your general policy. He does not expect to be able to attend the meeting on Thursday, but if there, would not take the responsibility of describing Gordon a man of pronounced historical tastes. He originally favored him on the ground that he is one of the most prominent clergymen in this neighborhood, a man of ability & personal popularity, Harvard Overseer,

[30] M.H.S., *Procs.*, 2nd ser., 7(1891–1892):332–335.

etc. I do not think it would be difficult to get together enough blackballs and abstentions to defeat Gordon, but I agree with you that this is not desirable. It is safer to elect him & try to be more careful next time.[31]

Adams suffered a rare defeat on this occasion. Gordon was the victor.[32]

When another opening developed in June, Adams asserted himself again on behalf of Davis and was successful in getting him nominated, but not without opposition: ". . . at the meeting of the Council, as the result of patient and persistent sub-soiling I secured the nomination of Andrew McFarland Davis; overcoming the equally persistent opposition of the narrow little clique represented by Dr. Green and C.C. Smith,— our librarian and treasurer. There's lots of human nature in man, and it gets illustration everywhere and all the time. I could write a volume, and not a wholly uninteresting volume either, on the ins-and-outs of that poor old Society,—the jealousies, the controversies, the intrigues which crop up and get growth in it."[33]

Having succeeded in getting Davis nominated, Adams now faced the problem of getting him elected. Again, it was no easy task. He had more work to do. As he wrote in his diary: "Finally in a reorganized Council, I last June got the necessary eight votes, and his [Davis's] name was reported. Then, feeling that the opposition was obdurate, I had to secure a full meeting to overcome the inevitable black-balls. This, through Goodwin and Goodell, I also did. We had 43 members present; Davis had to have 33 votes in his favor; he did have 35: Not much of a margin; but enough. And all petty narrowness,—contemptible local jealousies! That Society is little, and very droll. There's lots of human nature in it."[34]

The blackballing of Richard Henry Dana in 1897 was a particularly divisive event. The son and namesake of "Mast" Dana of *Two Years Before the Mast* fame, Dana appeared to be a certainty for election. He possessed all the necessary qualifications for membership. Also to his advantage was the fact that his father had been a revered member of the Society from 1858 to his death in 1882. The nominating committee submitted his name to the Council, which unanimously endorsed his can-

[31] Robert C. Winthrop, Jr., to Charles F. Adams, Feb. 6, 1898 (C.F. Adams Papers).

[32] M.H.S., *Procs.*, 2d ser., 12(1897–1899):138, 173.

[33] C.F. Adams, Memorabilia, June 10, 1898 (C.F. Adams Papers).

[34] C.F. Adams, Memorabilia, Oct. 14, 1898 (C.F. Adams Papers). For the election of Davis, see M.H.S., *Procs.*, 2d ser., 12(1897–1899):339.

didacy at the February meeting of the Society and announced his nomination to the members. Dana was to be elected at the March meeting.

At the March Council meeting, prior to the assemblage of the members, Vice President Justin Winsor, who was serving as temporary chairman in the absence of President Adams, inquired as to who should present Dana's name in nomination. This was a routine bit of business. At that point, Edward Lillie Pierce called for the floor.

The sixty-eight-year-old Pierce was a respected lawyer who came from sturdy Puritan stock. He had distinguished himself in the Civil War. Later, he had an active political career, serving a number of terms in the Massachusetts House of Representatives. At an early age, he became a disciple of Charles Sumner and, in later years, became his biographer, writing a three-volume "life and letters" study.

For many years, Pierce had coveted membership in the Society, but it did not happen until 1893, when he was sixty-four years of age. As his memoirist wrote:

> Longing for admittance to it [the M.H.S.] for many years and feeling keenly the lack of appreciation or the slight which prevented his election for so long a time, he accepted the membership when it came with gratitude. He counted it a great honor to belong to the Society, and believed too that duty went with honor. He was a diligent member.[35]

The diligent Pierce now deemed it his duty to oppose the candidacy of Dana. He stated that, because of business at the state house, he had been unable to attend the February Council meeting when it considered Dana's nomination. Had he been there, he would have opposed it. He admitted that, as a member of the nominating committee, he had approved of Dana's selection. Between the meeting of the nominating committee and the February gathering of the Council, however, Dana had participated in an event, which, in Pierce's judgment, disqualified him from membership in the Society.

What had Dana done that made him unworthy of membership? He had lent his support to the Irish in their protracted struggle against Great Britain. He "had spoken at a meeting in Faneuil Hall, called to protest against the policy of England, with whom we were at peace." Another Council member, Gamaliel Bradford, III, asserted that he also

[35] For Pierce's memoir, see M.H.S., *Procs.*, 2d ser., 18(1903–1904):363–369.

had attended the meeting "which was held in behalf of overtaxed Ireland, and was *not* directed against England." James B. Thayer also spoke up in defense of Dana. He "did not see that the matter concerned the Society at all."[36] Pierce reasserted his charge and said that he was unequivocally opposed to Dana's election.

The Council was now in a quandary. After heated discussion, the body concluded that it was too late to withdraw Dana's nomination because it had been "publicly announced" at the prior meeting. They would have to proceed with the election and bear the consequences of a floor fight.

When the Society meeting began, the Council called upon Charles C. Smith to read the report of the nominating committee, which documented Dana's "fitness" for membership, and the names of those who had endorsed his candidacy—which, of course, included Pierce. The latter took the floor and "repeated what he said to the Council, only more strongly, saying that he believed in having the names of those who had been associated with us, still continued on our rolls, but that he would *never* vote for any man to be a member who attacked a nation 'with whom we were at peace'."

The ballot was then taken. There were in attendance more than the twenty members needed for a quorum, but some did not vote so Dana "lacked a few votes necessary to three fourths, and *he was not elected.* This was a surprise to many, as a nomination from the Council is seldom rejected." In recounting the event to President Adams, then in Italy and who, as a member of the nominating committee, had favored Dana's candidacy, a thoroughly disgusted Edward Young wrote: "I am in doubt whether this black-balling should be placed upon our Records."[37]

An equally irate Robert C. Winthrop, Jr., registered a similar sentiment in a letter to the absent president. After reporting Dana's defeat, he wrote:

> The immediate cause of this slaughter was E.L. Pierce, who charged R.H.D. with having gone out of his way to preside at a *Home Rule meeting*, which

[36] Edward J. Young to C.F. Adams, Mar. 31, 1897; C.C. Smith to C.F. Adams, Mar. 12, 1897 (C.F. Adams Papers).

[37] Edward J. Young to C.F. Adams, Mar. 31, 1897. One "of the younger members" informed C.C. Smith that he voted against Dana because he was "not enough of an historical scholar." C.C. Smith to C.F. Adams, Mar, 12, 1897 (C.F. Adams Papers).

will hardly be a serious offence in your eyes, the house of Adams having been at daggers-drawn with the house of Brunswick for more than a century. I am not fond of Home Rulers myself, but it would never have occurred to me to object to him on this account, nor do I see why he might not have made a satisfactory member. I know him very slightly, but my father used to say that he made a useful Trustee of the Episcopal Theol. School at Cambridge. Gam Bradford and Professor Thayer tried to save him, but it was no go. I suspect occult reasons were at work. I remember that when I served on the Library Committee of the Athenaeum, a number of years ago, his name was brought up for a vacancy, when objections were made by several of the Committee, on the ground that he was not easy to get on with,—what the French call a *mauvais coucheur*. We sorely need some youngish men in the Society, who might be relied on to take an active interest in it,—some one after the fashion of G. Dexter (Deane's son-in-law), the most valuable young man, in his way, we ever took in. Such men seem to get rarer and rarer here in Boston.[38]

There is a postscript to this story. Dana was finally elected into membership on June 8, 1911. Because he had died on September 6, 1897, Pierce could no longer oppose Dana's candidacy.[39]

Aside from the regularly scheduled business meetings at its headquarters on Tremont Street, the Society occasionally held "social" meetings at the homes of members. Guests were sometimes invited to these gatherings. No formal business was conducted, but there were discussions of historical issues preceding drinks and dinner. Each spring, the Society also held a "strawberry festival" meeting at a member's home. These social gatherings of "The Saints" strengthened the clubby character of the organization.

A typical social meeting was held at the Cambridge home of Charles Deane on June 18, 1886, beginning at 5 P.M. The "business" consisted of a discussion by Deane of some correspondence of Dr. Joseph Priestly, the prominent English clergyman and chemist, with George Thacher of

[38] R.C. Winthrop, Jr., to C.F. Adams, Mar. 23, 1897 (C.F. Adams Papers).

[39] M.H.S., *Procs.*, 64(1930–1932):405. Samuel S. Shaw was another Bostonian who had to cool his heels for many years before he could secure membership in the Society. R.C. Winthrop, Jr., wrote to C.C. Smith on Mar. 15, 1903: "I am glad to perceive that Sam Shaw has been let in, even if it is only when he is nearly seventy. When he was about fifty I joined with others in trying to procure his election, but [Justin] Winsor was inexorable. . . ." (Charles C. Smith Papers, M.H.S.).

The Reoccupation of Their Own Estate

Maine for the years 1798, 1799, and 1800. Deane had been given these letters and was donating them to the Society. Others who owned Priestly letters supplemented Deane's remarks.[40]

Following this discussion, President Winthrop reminisced about past social meetings:

> We have had many social meetings elsewhere in former years; I hope we may have many more of them in future years. We have had them at Brookline; we have had them in Boston; and one of them was held at Nahant, under the auspices of the 'Ice-King,' as he was sometimes called,— our associate, the late Frederic Tudor,—when Prescott was able to drive over and join us from his villa on the Lynn shore, and when Sparks came down to give us the earliest account of the tour in Europe from which he had just returned.[41]

Winthrop considered "peculiarly notable" the meetings held in Cambridge, especially one held at Henry Wadsworth Longfellow's Brattle Street home, Craigie House, to commemorate Bunker Hill Day in 1858. Since Longfellow rarely invited groups to his historic home, this was a special affair and the members came in "unusual force."[42] And they probably arrived promptly at the appointed time, knowing that Longfellow was a stickler for punctuality. They did not wish to be "rebuked by a stony stare from the bluest and coldest eyes in New England."[43]

Mrs. Longfellow rendered an account of the gathering:

> . . . We had a very interesting meeting here on the 17th (Battle of Bunker Hill) of the Historical Society, and they were so pleased to come to this house on that day, that they came in unusual force, and had a great deal to say. Mr. Winthrop, Mr. Everett, Mr. Adams, etc. spoke of the associations of that time, and the former quoted Henry's lines in the poem on Charley, and they all seemed so full charged with reminiscences and facts that they could be hardly got to break up for supper. I wondered, too, they could resist the invitations of the birds to come into the garden, but they

---

[40] These letters were published in M.H.S., *Procs.*, 2d ser., 3(1886–1887):11–40.

[41] M.H.S., *Procs.*, 2d ser., 3(1886–1887):53. Henry W. Longfellow wrote in his journal on Aug. 11, 1858: "A misty morning, threatening disaster to the Meeting of the Hist. Soc. at Tudor's. But before noon it clears, and we have a pleasant gathering, records read, remarks made; walk in the garden, and an excellent dinner. Also a steroscopic view of the cottage taken; with the Hist. Soc. in groups on the lawn; done by Lloyd and Longheim. . . ." (Longfellow Papers, Houghton Library, Harvard University).

[42] M.H.S., *Procs.*, 2nd ser., 3(1886–1887):53.

[43] Lucius Beebe, *Boston and the Boston Legend* (New York, 1935), 105.

were listening to other more spiritual voices even. They refreshed themselves copiously with ice and strawberries and coffee and tea, and went off declaring, in all their annals, they had never had so interesting a meeting.[44]

David Sears hosted a social meeting at his home in 1859, when the "business" consisted of an informal memorial service for Washington Irving, an honorary member of the Society. Longfellow, Everett, and others who had known the celebrated Knickerbocker author delivered brief eulogies; Longfellow's and Everett's statements were published later in the *Proceedings*. In addition, the members presented a series of resolutions, praising Irving and his literary achievements.[45]

The Society also held meetings on occasion to commemorate significant historical events, such as on December 16, 1873, when the members assembled at the home of the Reverend Robert C. Waterston in Chester Square at 8 P.M. to celebrate the centennial of the "Boston Tea Party." Some of the members had attended a patriotic program at Faneuil Hall that afternoon "to take a commemorative cup of tea with the ladies of Boston, and to give brief expression to the feelings which the place and the day could not fail to excite in the hearts of all who were assembled there. Under this quiet domestic roof, we are privileged to indulge in calmer reflections on what occurred just a hundred years ago, and to contribute, as any of us may be able, in the most informal and colloquial manner, such historical statements or facts as may befit the sober records of our Society, and such contemporaneous accounts and traditions as may serve to illustrate the spirit or the conduct of those who took part in the memorable transactions of the 16th of December, 1773."

"Calmer reflections" included a lengthy introductory statement by Winthrop; a recounting of the events preceding the destruction of the tea and the act of violence itself by Richard Frothingham, which included the reading of a number of key documents from the Society's

[44] Fanny Longfellow to Mary Mackintosh, June 22, 1858, in Edward Wagenknecht, ed., *Mrs. Longfellow: Selected Letters and Journals of Fanny Appleton Longfellow (1817–1861)* (New York, 1956), 214. Longfellow recorded in his journal: "Historical Society in the afternoon; with much historical chatter and anecdote; letters read and books exhibited. . . . All very pleasant and very satisfactory." (Longfellow Papers, Houghton Library, Harvard University).

[45] M.H.S., *Procs.*, 4(1858–1860):393–424.

library; a communication from William Cullen Bryant, who was not able to attend the meeting; another lengthy disquisition on the Tea Party, which also involved the reading by Waterston of a number of documents owned by the Society; the circulation of a "large Silver Bowl" by Ellis, who informed the members that this artifact had been manufactured by Paul Revere and was intended to honor John Wilkes, the English radical politician, and, Ellis asserted, it doubtless had been used to hold powerful punch drunk by many a Boston rebel during the crises of the 1770s; a poetic offering by Oliver Wendell Holmes titled "A Ballad of the Boston Tea Party"; the reading of a letter from Samuel Adams to James Warren, dated January 10, 1774, a few weeks after the destruction of the tea, by Winslow Warren; a reading of verses by Ralph Waldo Emerson, which he had presented that afternoon at the Faneuil Hall program and was now repeating "by request"; a statement by Thomas C. Amory, in which he proposed that two Bostonians, heretofore unknown to the history books, be added to the rolls of those who had participated in the Tea Party: Amos Lincoln and James Swan; the reading of yet another communication, this one from an absent member, William T. Davis, with Winthrop performing the task; the reading of a letter, dated December 13, 1873, from Julius Dexter of Cincinnati, Ohio, by the recording secretary, in which Dexter explained the background of a 1778 engraving relating to the American Revolution, and announced that he was donating it to the Society.

The final item on the agenda was the reading of an extract from a letter written by Hannah Fayerweather Winthrop, wife of Professor John Winthrop, to Mercy Otis Warren of Plymouth, wife of Gen. James Warren, dated January 1, 1774, by Henry W. Torrey. This document reflected the prevailing opinion of the women rebels of Massachusetts during the Tea Party crisis:

Yonder, the destruction of the detestable weed, made so by cruel exaction, engages our attention. The virtuous and noble resolution of America's sons in defiance of threatened desolation and misery from arbitrary Despots demands our highest regard. May they yet be endowed with all that firmness necessary to carry them through all their difficulties till they come off conquerors. I was sorry to see the Protest from Plymouth. If we could see their connections and expectations affixed to their names, it would let us into the prime movement of their narrow hearts, and it would be no great task to trace the original influences. We hope to see a good account of the Tea cast away on the Cape. The Union of the Colonies, the firm and sedate resolution of the People, is an omen for good unto us. And be it known unto Britain, even American daughters are Politicians and Patriots, and will aid the good work with their female efforts.

"The meeting was now dissolved," the Society's scribe noted in the *Proceedings*.[46]

There were many memorable meetings in the Dowse Library between 1833 and 1895 but, for high drama, none was as memorable as that of February 10, 1881, which marked Ralph Waldo Emerson's final appearance before the Society. It was destined to be his second-to-last formal talk before any group. This was a meeting to remember, a painfully poignant yet exhilarating experience. The members in attendance knew that they would never hear another presentation in the Society from this magisterial figure, the sage of Concord.

Thomas Carlyle, the famous Scottish essayist and historian, had been elected a corresponding member in 1870, largely because of his strong personal interest in Benjamin Franklin and his English forebears, as expressed in his correspondence with Edward Everett, and his "grand biography" of Oliver Cromwell. Carlyle died on February 4, 1881. While in Washington on business, President Winthrop learned of his death and "felt that there was only one man in our Society, or perhaps anywhere on this side of the Atlantic, who could give authoritative and adequate expression to the views of his [Carlyle's] character and career which should follow such an announcement."[47] He promptly wrote Emerson, then seventy-seven years of age and in failing health, and urged him to appear at the February 10 meeting of the Society and present some pertinent remarks on his close friend after he, Winthrop, announced his death. It was customary for the president to make these remarks, after announcing the deaths of members. Later, a member would be appointed to prepare and present a formal memoir for the *Proceedings*. Whether Winthrop was aware of Emerson's rapid mental deterioration, which would prevent him from executing this type of assignment with any

[46] The complete program is described in M.H.S., *Procs.*, 13(1873–1875):151–215.
[47] M.H.S., *Procs.*, 18(1880–1881):323–324.

degree of competence, is unknown.[48] Emerson accepted the invitation.

Attired in his usual somber dark gray suit and accompanied by his "helpful daughter" Ellen, the feeble Emerson slowly climbed the stairs and reached the Dowse library on the appointed day.[49] A small table and two chairs, for Emerson and his daughter, were placed next to the large table where Winthrop sat.

George E. Ellis, who was there, described what transpired:

> . . . few of the members most constant in their attendance were aware what was to occur, and the regrets of many who might have been present are keen. Mr. Winthrop had, with his wonted felicity, introduced the theme and recognized the presence of Mr. Emerson. The scene which followed was a memorable one, never to be forgotten by those who felt what a privilege they enjoyed in taking the full impression of it, with all its vividness and suggestiveness, into heart and thought. In recalling it some may possibly have wished that the camera had been there to fix, for more elaborate art, the singularly suggestive and impressive elements of the scene. But anything like form, disposal, or preparatory effect would have marred the charm of its exquisite simplicity. The newspapers have, as fully as facts warrant, and much more so than a tender delicacy can approve, commented freely upon the character and degree of the disablement which the passage of years has visited upon Mr. Emerson. It is enough to say that such visitation as is upon him was manifested simply in enhancing the impression of his gentle, placid mien and tones, and, on this occasion, gave an added charm to his features and utterance. Some of the most impressive and memorable elements of the scene, will be most fondly cherished by the witnesses, do not allow of description or relation. . . . The manuscript, long since written but never put in print, was a loose one, and only parts of it were to be read by Mr. Emerson. Of the incommunicable features of the scene, very touching to its witnesses was his gentle reference and compliance as he looked to his daughter for direction as to the passages to be read, and to the connection of them. Some slight labial impediments caused an occasional halting in the delivery of elongated words, never favorites with Mr. Emerson. These served, in part, for those delays on words which are

[48] The full extent of Emerson's "mental mist" can be seen in Edward Bok's meeting with him on Nov. 22, 1881. See *The Americanization of Edward Bok: The Autobiography of a Dutch Boy Fifty Years After* (New York, 1921), 54–60.

[49] In Emerson's last years, his daughter frequently accompanied him when he came to Boston. She guided him to his destination and, since he was so forgetful, carried his books and papers in her case. See Mary Jane Regan, *Echoes From the Past: Reminiscences of the Boston Athenaeum* (Boston, 1927), 26. See also Paul Brooks, *The People of Concord: One Year in the Flowering of New England* (Chester, Conn., 1990), 31.

so familiar to his hearers as marking his pauses and emphasis. For the rest, he was helped in imitative utterances of them by the silent lips of his daughter. The apt and racy significance of the most pointed passages came forth in full force, and with the old incisiveness and humor. So hushed was the silence and so intent was the listening that those who were quick of hearing lost nothing of word or intonation. But even these, the more removed in their seats, one by one drew nearer in a closing circle around the reader. Their faces and inward workings of thought showed the profoundness of their interest as they waited for the interpretation of the great philosopher of England by the greatest philosopher of America.[50]

Emerson died on April 27, 1882, fifteen months after speaking at the Society.

[50] Emerson read from the original manuscript of an account he had written a third of a century earlier, shortly after meeting Carlyle in 1848. See W.C. Ford, "Mr. Emerson was Present," M.H.S., *Procs.*, 62(1928–1929):130–138. Emerson's address is printed in ibid., 18(1880–1881):324–328. Ellis's account is printed in *Scribner's Monthly Illustrated Magazine*, 22(May 1881):91n.

Chapter 7

The Century Mark

AS THE Massachusetts Historical Society neared the completion of its first century, there were many lasting landmarks of a fruitful tenure. The extraordinary collections gathered in the library and cabinet continued to expand and to entrance the members. Regular meetings brought together in Boston unequaled gatherings of intellectuals from the "Flowering of New England," to borrow Van Wyck Brooks's elegant phrase. Beyond local borders, however, perhaps the most lasting impact of the Society during these years was felt across the intellectual landscape of the nation through its publication program.

"Multiply the copies"—that is, publish the documentary sources of American history—was the dictum of Jeremy Belknap at the founding, and the Society took its direction from that command. With its development of an historical supplement to the *American Apollo* newspaper in 1792, the Society became the first organization in the world to publish Americana in a systematic manner. These offerings to the *Apollo* were combined as the first volume of the seminal *Collections* series, which marked the beginning of a publication program that has not been matched by any other historical society in the United States.

During its stay on Tremont Street, the Society accelerated its ambitious publication program. It added thirty-seven volumes to the *Collections* series, including such significant documentary works as: William Bradford's "Of Plimoth Plantation"; seven volumes of Winthrop Papers; three volumes of Samuel Sewall's classic diary, and two volumes of his letterbook; one volume of Mather Papers; three volumes of Jeremy Belknap Papers; two volumes of Jonathan Belcher Papers; two volumes of Trumbull Papers; and one volume of William Heath Papers.

The Massachusetts Historical Society

As a modern authority on historical societies has written: "The first thirty-four volumes of the *Collections of the Massachusetts Historical Society* are indispensable to American historians. Each contains some work of merit, and many are of superlative importance."[1] And further: "*Collections* published after 1820 and before 1860 contain much which is the basis of New England colonial history."[2] This series also circulated widely in Great Britain and key cities of continental Europe during the nineteenth century.

In 1859, the Society instituted another series, the *Proceedings*, which included the minutes of meetings, memoirs of deceased members, scholarly essays by members, and a variety of historical documents. When it left Tremont Street, the Society had published thirty-one volumes in this set.[3] Because corresponding members had access to the *Proceedings* and other copies were exchanged with various historical organizations, the publication had broad geographical distribution.

The Society also produced a number of special publications in this era, including catalogues of its library and cabinet, a catalogue of its paintings, a volume of lectures delivered by select members at the Lowell Institute in 1869, and a work on Washington's "Newburgh Address."

What is remarkable about this output in publication is that it was accomplished with volunteers on a shoestring budget. From four to six members pooled their editorial talents to produce a volume. While the Society was constantly faced with the prospect of having to delay publications because of a lack of money, it somehow managed to raise sufficient funds to sustain the program.

One endowed fund, largely dedicated to publications, was received through the largest bequest in the Society's early history in 1886, the John Langdon Sibley gift.[4] Sibley had served as assistant librarian and librarian of Harvard College from 1841 to 1877.[5] He earned a modest

---

[1] Dunlap, *American Historical Societies*, 97.

[2] Ibid., 97.

[3] Two retrospective volumes were published in 1879 and 1880 to cover the periods 1791–1835 and 1835–1855, respectively. They stand as volumes 1 and 2 of the first series of the *Proceedings*.

[4] The Society received the bequest following the death of Mrs. Sibley in 1902. It came in two installments in 1903 and 1904.

[5] For Sibley's biography, see: Clifford K. Shipton, "John Langdon Sibley, Librarian," *Harvard Library Bulletin*, 9(1955):236–261, and *Sibley's Harvard Graduates*, 4:6–10; and M.H.S., *Procs.*, 2d ser., 2(1885–1886):154–155, 487–507.

salary but lived frugally and invested wisely. As a result, he amassed an estate of more than $160,000. A member of the Society since 1846, he was a frequent visitor to the Tremont Street quarters while compiling information for his biographical sketches of graduates of Harvard College.[6] Plagued by cataracts, Sibley wore three pairs of spectacles, one over another, as he scanned source materials. When speaking, he would raise two pair to his forehead. His "dear wife" and "constant companion" sat next to him, knitting and sewing.[7] Sibley provided a life interest to his wife in his will "in token of her entire selflessness, and of her self-sacrificing devotedness to my comfort and happiness." Upon her death, the bulk of Sibley's estate reverted to the Society, the residuary legatee.[8]

Sibley set restrictions on the use of his money. The income of the fund had to be applied to the publication of the biographical sketches of Harvard's graduates; any residual income had to be used, initially, to purchase printed books, pamphlets, or manuscripts produced by graduates of Harvard or relating to such graduates and, secondly, for general purposes; one-fourth of the total income had to be added annually to the fund until January 22, 2202; the Society could "in its discretion, apply not exceeding one-half part of the said accumulated fund toward the erection of a new fire-proof building to be called by [Mr. Sibley's] name."

When the Society was preparing to vacate Tremont Street in 1898, it was operating with sixteen endowed funds and had benefited from "numerous gifts made . . . from time to time." This infusion of funds was largely responsible for the Society's "present prosperity and usefulness," in the words of Treasurer Charles C. Smith in 1898.[9]

From the time of its founding, the Society assumed the role of watchdog over historical properties in Boston. When someone threatened to desecrate or destroy a hallowed shrine, the Society rose to its defense. The near demise of King's Chapel in the 1870s can be cited as an example. When Harvey Parker built his Parker House Hotel on School Street in 1854, he discovered that the thoroughfare was too narrow for his plans for "a cabstand and also plenty of room for fine equipages to

[6] Sibley produced three volumes between 1873 and 1885.

[7] M.H.S., Procs., 61(1927–1928):100.

[8] For Sibley's will, see M.H.S., Procs., 2d ser., 2(1885–1886):168–170; an extract is printed in Sibley's Harvard Graduates, 4:9.

[9] M.H.S., Procs., 2d ser., 12(1897–1899):180.

bring important visitors to his door, and for carriages to carry Harvard students home; all this besides the ordinary traffic." To accommodate his dreams, he proposed moving King's Chapel some fifteen or twenty feet back into the graveyard. The opposition to such an iconoclastic plan "was spirited," with the Historical Society, "of course, taking a vigorous share therein." In the end, Parker was "finally obliged to abandon his villainous project."[10]

There was another manner in which the Society employed its expertise and extended its influence beyond the walls of Tremont Street. As the unofficial arbiter of historical values in Boston, the Society did not shirk from casting judgment on public projects that did not measure up to its standards of historical truth or significance. The Leif Ericson statue is a case in point.

At the May 1880 meeting of the Society, William Everett, youngest son of the illustrious orator, called to the attention of the members a "scheme which is assuming somewhat serious proportions; in which, if it is really judicious, the Historical Society ought to help; against which, if it is otherwise, it is our duty to protest." The scheme, Everett reported in words laced with sarcasm, was a proposal to erect a monument "to some person called the first discoverer of New England; not, however, John Cabot, or Sebastian Cabot, or Verrazzano, but an indefinite Northman, to whom, if I may be allowed a very bad pun, it is proposed to put up a *Leif* statue."

The Leif Ericson statue had been proposed by several Bostonians, whom Everett dismissed as "more enthusiastic than critical."[11] Chief among the current enthusiasts was Eben Norton Horsford of Cambridge, a Harvard chemist "of brilliance and distinction," who spent much of his leisure time studying and promoting the contention that Ericson and other Norsemen had explored and established settlements in New England.[12]

---

[10] M.H.S., *Proc.*, 60(1926–1927):164.

[11] The original movement for such a statue was begun by Ole Bull, the Norwegian violinist, assisted by a committee which included Henry W. Longfellow, James Russell Lowell, Charles W. Eliot, and Edward Everett Hale, all of whom were members of the Historical Society. After Bull's death in 1880, Horsford took the lead role in fundraising. Andrew Thurson, *History of the Leif Erikson Statue* (Scituate, Mass., 1989).

[12] See Wendell D. Garrett, "The Discovery of the Charles River by the Vikings According to the Book of Horsford," Cambridge Historical Society *Proceedings*, 40(1964–1966):94–109; *NEHGR*, 49(1895):85–87.

The skeptical Everett went on to discuss the murky history of the alleged American visits of the Norsemen, long a source of controversy among antiquarians and historians of the region, and a familiar story to the members. He concluded by urging the Society to prepare and submit a "proper statement" to the public of "the entirely unhistorical character of the events which it is proposed to commemorate in a form that ought to be reserved for real men, who did something for New England."

The highly respected antiquarian-historian Charles Deane heartily endorsed Everett's proposal. He shared Everett's qualms about the alleged Norse settlements in New England. "When I first critically examined the foundation of the stories," he stated, "and read the narratives themselves in the shape in which they have come down to us, I was deeply impressed with their unhistorical character. The narratives, if they can be called such, are mere traditions, orally repeated from generation to generation, and not committed to writing till two centuries or more after the events they pretend to relate took place."

Deane's judgments concluded the Society's discussion. The scribe noted: "The sentiment of the meeting appeared to be decidedly in favor of the views expressed by these members."[13]

The protest of the Society had little, if any, impact upon Horsford. He resolutely drummed his cause throughout the 1880s, and his persistence was finally rewarded in 1887. On October 29, a bronze figure of the Norseman, fashioned by Anne Whitney, was unveiled on Commonwealth Avenue, although for logistical reasons the ceremony was held in Faneuil Hall with Horsford delivering the main address, a lengthy oration of Edward Everett dimensions.[14]

At the November meeting of the Historical Society, William Everett brought up the question of supposed Norse explorations again, "and an interesting conversation followed, many members of the Society taking part in it."[15] As it was often inclined to do on such matters, the Society appointed a special committee to study the matter. In December, the committee rendered its report:

[13] For Everett's and Deane's statements, see M.H.S., *Proc.*, 18(1880–1881):79–81. Ironically, Everett's father had proposed a statue to honor Ericson in 1837. The son conceded this point in his remarks. See also, ibid., 2d ser., 7(1891–1892):73.

[14] Garrett, "Vikings' Discovery," 102–103.

[15] M.H.S. Council Records, Nov. 10, 1887 (M.H.S. Archives).

As regards the truth of the proposition that "Leif Ericson discovered America in the year 1000 A.D.," your Committee have reached the following conclusion: They think that there is the same sort of reason for believing in the existence of Leif Ericson that there is for believing in the existence of Agamemnon,—they are both traditions accepted by later writers; but that there is no more reason for regarding as true the details related about his discoveries than there is for accepting as historic truth the narratives contained in the Homeric poems. Your Committee believe not only that it is antecedently probable that the Norsemen discovered America in the early part of the eleventh century, but that this discovery is confirmed by the same sort of historical tradition, not strong enough to be called evidence, upon which our belief in many of the accepted facts of history rests; and that the date 1000 A.D., assumed for such discovery, is sufficiently near for all practical purposes,—much nearer the truth than is the traditional date given for the foundation of Rome.[16]

Even with the statue in place, the controversy roared on. In 1888, Horsford coupled his dedicatory address in Faneuil Hall with a number of "ponderous appendices" and published *Discovery of America By Northmen*, his first of what became a series of heavily detailed books on the Vinland question. In 1889, in volume one of his notable *Narrative and Critical History of America*, Justin Winsor, then serving as corresponding secretary of the society, derided Horsford's thesis and cast aspersions on his scholarship and historical methodology. He also underscored the Society's steadfast opposition to the erection of the Ericson statue: "The project, though ultimately carried out, was long delayed, and was discouraged by members of the Massachusetts Historical Society on the ground that no satisfactory evidence existed to show that any spot in New England had been reached by the Northmen."[17]

In a second work on the subject in 1889, Horsford lashed back at Winsor and also flayed the Society for regarding itself as the sole and official interpreter of New England's history, much as Samuel G. Drake had done in 1874:

It is quite true that members of the Massachusetts Historical Society discouraged the efforts of the immediate friends of Ole Bull here, and the two millions of Scandinavians of the West and the East who sympathized with him, in his patriotic wish to recognize in a monument, to be set up in

---

[16] M.H.S., *Procs.*, 2d ser., 4(1887–1889):42–44.
[17] page 98.

Boston, the services of Leif Ericson in the discovery of America. It is also true that they virtually caused the rejection by the city government of Boston of the offer by the late Mr. Thomas Appleton of $40,000 for the erection of a memorial in Scollay Square to the Discovery of America by Northmen.

It is also true that in the paragraphs cited there is, in carefully chosen terms, and in a tone of conscious infallibility better suited to an earlier day and another meridian, an intimation of the proper limit of geographical research, and of who may pursue it, in New England; and there is also an undertone of recognized authority,—all of which will find adequate appreciation. One may ask, Is Massachusetts a *preserve*?[18]

With the death of Horsford in 1893, the controversy subsided. Ericson joined the lonely legion of statues scattered about the city, little noticed, rarely mentioned.[19]

Meanwhile, the Society had become enmeshed in another bitter dispute involving an historical monument. In 1887, both houses of the state legislature, responding to pressure applied primarily by the black population of Boston, passed a resolution authorizing the governor and Council to erect a "suitable memorial or monument" to honor the five men killed in the "Boston Massacre" on March 5, 1770. The five were Crispus Attucks, assumed to have been black; Samuel Gray; Jonas Caldwell; Samuel Maverick; and Patrick Carr. The resolution authorized the state to spend up to $10,000 on this project, but until signed by the governor, it was not law.[20]

President Adams, firmly opposed to the resolution, introduced the issue as new business at the Society's meeting of May 12, 1887. He stated that the incident already had been commemorated with a bronze tablet on a building adjacent to the site and by a "radiated pavement" where the five had fallen. In his view, this was sufficient recognition of

[18] *The Problem of the Northmen* (Cambridge, Mass., 1889), 7–8.

[19] The statue, originally located on Charlesgate East near Massachusetts Avenue, was moved in 1917 to its present location on the Commonwealth Mall between Charlesgate East and Massachusetts Avenue. Due to its relocation and subsequent construction of highway ramps in the area, Ericson's statue no longer surveys the Charles River but rather "peers into nothing more poetic than a vast overpass that siphons automobiles from the Fenway to the Storrow Drive." Walter M. Whitehill, *Boston Statues* (Barre, Mass., 1970), 80.

[20] The resolution also called for placing "suitable headstones" on their graves "when their locations can be ascertained."

their martyrdom. He also noted that the Commonwealth "has never as yet raised any monumental memorial of a person or of an event in its history. . . . We may well pause upon that proposition."

Adams then presented a brief disquisition on the nature of Boston's opposition to the "oppressive measures" of the British government in the prerevolutionary period. Reflecting his inherent conservatism, he drew a sharp distinction between the "peaceful, earnest, patriotic protest and resistance by our wise and resolute popular leaders" and the riotous mob which had caused the destruction of private property and physically abused the British soldiers by pelting them with snowballs and clubs. When he concluded, the stage was set for a rousing discussion of the proposed memorial.

John D. Washburn remarked that, "assuming the voice of scholars to be unanimous in the declaration that these men were not acting in the character of patriots, but of rioters, and 'died as the fool dieth,' " the Society should focus upon the "parliamentary attitude" of the question. He was certain that a "thorough scholar in Massachusetts history" could have persuaded the house of representatives not to pass the resolution. But the deed was done, agreed to by both bodies of the General Court. What should the Society do now? Washburn suggested the passage of a resolution opposing the memorial and the appointment of a special committee, headed by the president, which would meet with the governor and urge him to veto the resolution, "provided that he, as a politician, was not more likely to be influenced by the negroes and the cheaper politicians than by the educated men."

Lucius R. Paige presented "another side of the question." He affirmed that Bostonians of the period had regarded the "slaughtered men" not as a "riotous mob" but as "perhaps misguided patriots, who had lost their lives in the cause of liberty." They had "rendered such funeral honors as had seldom been witnessed." He recalled that the incident had been commemorated annually after the Revolution, and orators at these public gatherings had never cast a "desparaging remark" against the five victims. He saw little distinction between the actions of Boston's citizens on March 5, 1770, and what transpired at Lexington Green and Cambridge five years later, or at Bunker Hill: "While we canonize the martyrs who perished at these later contests, and erect magnificent monuments in honor of them, it seems scarcely consistent to refuse recognition to the humble men whose death was followed by such important results."

The Century Mark

While against a resolution opposing the memorial, Paige agreed to vote in the affirmative, if a unanimous decision were in order.

Andrew P. Peabody expressed surprise that the event on March 5 could be regarded as anything but a riot "for which there was no justifiable motive." He stated that, over the years, he had heard many of the public orations commemorating the event and recalled that speakers always placed their stress upon British oppression. There was "no claim of patriotic purpose . . . for the men who were slain."

Abner C. Goodell, Jr., sided with Adams and other opponents of the memorial. In his view, "a monument to perpetuate the fame of rioters was preposterous." Prior to the meeting, he had spoken with the governor and leaders of both the senate and house of representatives and had strongly urged these men to schedule another public hearing before the governor signed the resolution. If his plea were heeded, it would provide the Society with an opportunity to present its case.

Charles Deane supplied the final word. He reaffirmed the majority view: "the attack on the soldiers was conducted by a mere mob, inspired by no elevated sentiments, and fatally bent on mischief . . . the martyr's crown is placed upon the brow of the vulgar ruffian."

When the discussion ended, the members followed Washburn's suggestion and appointed a committee, headed by the president, which was to present the Society's position to authorities at the state house. Adams begged off from serving on the committee because of political considerations, but he was certain that his thoughts on the proposed monument would be well known to state officials. Apparently, he intended to lobby behind the scenes. Edward Everett drew up the resolution opposing the monument, and it was approved.

At the June 9 meeting, Peabody, speaking for the committee, reported that his group had joined forces with the New England Historic Genealogical Society, which also opposed the "Attucks memorial," and made a "thorough statement" of their case to state house officials. "Their plea," however, "was unsuccessful, the colored people of Boston having used all the influence at their command to secure the building of the monument."[21] The Boston Massacre Monument, executed by Robert Kraus, was erected on Boston Common in 1888.[22]

In 1895, the Governor's Council passed a resolution calling for the

[21] M.H.S., *Procs.*, 2d ser., 3(1886–1887):313–318, 321.
[22] Whitehill, *Boston Statues*, 82.

erection of a monument in Boston to commemorate the site of the first town meeting held in the United States and of the first free public school. The resolution provided for an expenditure not exceeding $15,000. It also stated that the Boston city art commission must approve the design and the governor and Council must verify and approve the site of the monument. The Council appointed a special committee to implement its resolution.

The committee held public hearings and solicited advice from all interested parties. The predictable occurred. It received a "number of briefs which upon examination are found to contain mutually conflicting statements, involving varying interpretations of nearly every important word in the Resolve, and collectively making it evident that a just decision of the questions to be decided requires a most careful and critical examination of the historical and textual points at issue."

How was the issue to be resolved? Gov. Roger Wolcott (who was himself a member) requested the Historical Society to appoint a three-member committee of acknowledged "experts" on Boston's colonial history, consisting of Charles C. Smith, Samuel A. Green, and Professor Edward Channing, "to examine the whole mass of evidence submitted to the [special] Committee" and report its findings. The decision of the Society's committee was to be binding on all parties. This would be the final word on the issue.[23]

Another example of how the Society functioned as the community's watchdog against what the members conceived to be misguided patriotism, historical inaccuracy, or outright untruthfulness is offered by the Walter-Sharples portrait incident.[24] In 1886, a Maj. James Walter of England came to the United States with three portraits he was offering for sale. Two were of George Washington, one a full-face view and in military attire, and the second in profile. The third was a profile of Martha Washington. Walter claimed that the three paintings had been

---

[23] See Commonwealth of Mass. document, Feb. 28, 1895, signed by Governor Wolcott; and Commonwealth of Mass. document, Mar. 1, 1895, signed by E.F. Hamlin, executive clerk, both in Charles C. Smith Papers, M.H.S.

[24] The M.H.S. Archives contain an assortment of materials pertaining to this brouhaha throughout the period from 1882 to 1896. There are newspaper clippings from Boston, New York City, and Philadelphia; reports of the special M.H.S. committee; and correspondence of the major participants of the controversy.

executed by the English artist James Sharples, who came to the United States in 1794 and visited Washington at his home at Mount Vernon. He set his sights on two prospective purchasers. His prime potential customer was the United States Congress. He was hopeful that the government would buy the paintings for the nation as an expression of patriotism. A second possibility was a wealthy American or groups of Americans pooling their funds.

Ostensibly to assist in the marketing of the paintings, Walter published a book, *Memorials of Washington, and of Mary his Mother, and Martha his Wife*, in which he traced the background of the art works and included relevant correspondence of the principals and others, including letters by Washington, Ralph Waldo Emerson, Nathaniel Hawthorne, and Washington Irving. The book was designed to authenticate Walter's claim that these were the original Sharples art works.

Walter was anxious to secure the endorsement of the nation's oldest historical society. Such an approval was certain to strengthen the marketability of the paintings. Then, too, there was the possibility of a purchaser among that prestigious body. Walter arranged to have an acquaintance from Brooklyn, New York, send a letter of introduction to President George E. Ellis, requesting his cooperation in the Englishman's enterprise.[25]

The unsuspecting Ellis invited Walter to a Society meeting to display his artistic wares and inform the membership about them. The members listened attentively and politely to Walter's presentation. When he concluded, there was general discussion. The Society then appointed a four-man committee, chaired by Francis Parkman, to analyze the paintings and ascertain their "historical value."[26]

Parkman presented his committee's report in January 1897. More than likely, it was developed by Parkman alone and then endorsed by the other members of the committee. It was vintage Parkman, an exhaustive, incisive analysis of all relevant sources and issues.[27]

Parkman confirmed that Sharples had come to the United States

[25] Frederick A. Farley to George Ellis, Apr. 8, 1882 (M.H.S. Archives).

[26] M.H.S., *Procs.*, 2d ser., 3(1886–1887):136. Robert C. Winthrop, Jr., "never forgave Dr. E. for introducing that fellow at a meeting, and the recollection of it always stirs my bile." Winthrop to Adams, Dec. 11, 1897 (C.F. Adams Papers).

[27] Stewart Mitchell called it a "masterpiece." Mitchell, *Handbook*, 13.

"three, or possibly five years" before the death of Washington and had executed, chiefly in crayon, portraits of a number of prominent Americans, including George and Martha Washington. He had not completed all of these paintings. He returned to England with some unfinished works. The question that Parkman focused upon was: Were the three paintings presented by Walter the original Sharpless works, or were they spurious?

In keeping with his character as a meticulous researcher, Parkman began his critique by reviewing the corroborative evidence Walter had provided in his book. He discovered numerous factual errors, stylistic inconsistencies, and solecistic quirks. For example, a key Washington document in the book, which bore no date, was written in a style that, in Parkman's judgment, bore no resemblance to that of the Virginian:

> It bears, however, a striking resemblance to the very peculiar style of Major Walter, which is marked by frequent and conspicuous solecisms. One of these is his often repeated use of the verb *to name*, in the sense of *to mention*. Washington also is made to say: 'I have been solicited *to name*, that if Mr. Sharples thinks of returning to this country, a good opportunity would be offered to bring them [the pictures] out.' And again, a few lines below: 'My wife declines to join in asking your consent; I have undertaken simply *to name* it.' The letter begins with thanks for two jars of pickled tripe sent as a present by Cary; and the illustrious writer adds, 'Dental infirmity impels my caring for this necessary item in our domestic commissariat,'—a sentence eminently Walterian; as is also the injunction that Sharples shall be required to paint copies of his portraits 'in the best manner of his capability.'

Parkman also noted that Walter cited extracts from letters allegedly written by Sharples, which also bore a distinctive "Walterian style." If, as Walter himself admitted, "there are no journal or papers of Sharples in existence that we know of," where did the extracts originate? Even more damning, Parkman showed conclusively that Walter was a blatant plagiarist assigning to Robert Cary, Washington's agent in London, the "words almost identical" that Irish orator Charles Phillips used about 1814 at a dinner at Dina's Island, in the Lakes of Killarney.[28]

Moreover, Parkman was also troubled by the paintings themselves. He noted, for example, that when the three portraits had been exhibited

[28] John Howard Payne, a young American playwright, captured the words which were published in the 1837 edition of the *American Preceptor*, one of the country's leading school textbooks.

at the Museum of Fine Arts in 1882, curator Charles G. Loring observed that Washington's eyes were brown. It was a known fact that they were blue. Loring called this error to the attention of a number of people who saw the portraits. When the paintings returned to the United States in 1886, someone had changed the color to blue:

> When Major Walter was desired to explain this remarkable change, he replied that the blue came out in consequence of wiping the dirt from the picture and applying a coat of varnish. But we have it on the unimpeachable testimony of Mr. Loring that when the picture was in his keeping it was in excellent condition, with no dirt to be removed and no need of varnish. In the profile of Washington, as well as the full face, the eyes, which were brown in 1882, are blue in 1886. Curiously enough, Mr. Arthur Dexter observed, when the pictures were at the Art Museum, that while the eyes of Washington were brown instead of blue, those of his wife were blue instead of brown. Whether or not the three Washington portraits were based on drawings made from life by Sharples, this transposition of color betrays the hand of one who had forgotten or who never saw the essential features of his subject.

In concluding his withering criticism of Walter and the paintings, Parkman stated that he and his colleagues had begun their inquiry with the belief that the portraits "were what they were represented to be." On the basis of the evidence provided by Walter, however, they were forced to reject his assertion that these were the original Sharples works. While not stated directly, the implication was that Walter was an unprincipled opportunist and his paintings were fakes.[29]

The Society voted to print Parkman's report "in full in the daily newspapers," which was done. Walter did not receive the Society's endorsement. As Stewart Mitchell has written: "needless to say, Walter left Boston without palming off his portraits on any of its prosperous citizens."[30]

Parkman's report captured the attention of newspapers in New York, Philadelphia, and other major Eastern cities.[31] The Walter-Sharples is-

[29] For the complete text of Parkman's report, see M.H.S., *Procs.*, 2d ser., 3(1886–1887):179–187. See also 215–216, 277.

[30] Mitchell, *Handbook*, 13.

[31] After reading press accounts of Parkman's report, George H. Moore, librarian of the New York Public Library, congratulated Parkman and President Ellis for their "exposure of a humbug! whom I recognized years ago, when he managed to obtain an advertisement from the New York Historical Society, very much to my personal disgust at the time." Moore to Ellis, Jan. 18, 1887 and to Parkman, Jan. 15, 1887 (M.H.S. Archives).

sue developed into a *cause célèbre*. Most press reports sided with Parkman and branded Walter an "arrogant fraud," "a humbug," and the "Barnum of the so-called Sharples portraits."

The Englishman did not go down without a fight. He categorically rejected Parkman's report and characterized its statements as "libellous," although he never instituted legal action. After leaving Boston and returning to England, he directed several stern letters to the Society in subsequent years, "reaffirming genuineness" of the paintings. Charles F. Adams, Ellis's successor in the presidency, asked Abner C. Goodell, Jr., to review these letters and make a report. He did so at the May 1892 meeting. It was accepted and filed without comment. The Society washed its hands of the entrepreneurial Major Walter.[32]

The Society took note of its impending centennial in February 1890. The reason for this early attention was the issue of the founding date. The members were not certain what date they should select for the commemoration. They wrestled with the question: What was "the precise date of our nativity?" The choices were 1790, when the initial movement for founding took place; 1791, when the "eight faithful associates" held their "First Meeting" on January 24; or 1794, when the Society received its charter of incorporation. President Ellis set forth the options without indicating his own preference.[33]

At the March 1890 meeting, Ellis specified a date for the commemoration: January 24, 1791. Past President Robert C. Winthrop agreed with him. That settled the issue, for no one would dare disagree with Winthrop. However, because of the uncertainty of weather conditions in January, the members decided to leave the decision on the precise day of the observance in the hands of the Council.[34]

---

[32] M.H.S., *Procs.*, 2d ser., 7(1891–1892):349, 399. Walter renewed his claim of the authenticity of the paintings in 1897. An indignant Robert C. Winthrop, Jr., wrote Charles F. Adams on Dec. 11, 1897, that he "was taken utterly aback at the prospect of our discussing the claim of a man whom eleven years ago we had practically denounced as a forger. I now learn that you never saw or heard of Parkman's report & I dare say you were then too busy to cut the pages of that particular volume, but it passes my comprehension why [C.C.] Smith did not direct you to what was in print, instead of handing you to read a parcel of incidental material in manuscript." (C.F. Adams Papers).

[33] M.H.S., *Procs.*, 2d ser., 5(1889–1890):281–285.

[34] M.H.S., *Procs.*, 2d ser., 5(1889–1890):347–348.

The Century Mark

At the April meeting, the Council considered the issue but failed to resolve it. The governing body concluded that the program would be held "in the early part of the ensuing year" and requested "further time to consider as to the most convenient time and manner of commemoration."[35]

On January 8, 1891, Samuel A. Green, who had been appointed chairman of the centennial committee, announced that the "services" would be held at the Arlington Street Church on Saturday, January 24, beginning at noon. Thomas W. Higginson was to present the main address, while President Ellis, Winthrop, and the Reverend Lucius R. Paige, the oldest member, would contribute remarks.[36] The selection of the Arlington Street Church represented symbolic propriety since this Unitarian stronghold, renamed, was Belknap's Long Lane (and later, Federal Street) Church. A church was a proper venue for the program since its format was much like a religious service.

The weather was "remarkably mild and pleasant" on January 24 and a sizable audience attended the program. Sixty-five of the ninety-seven resident members were there. Five were in Europe and three were in public service in Washington. The others were either out of state or unable to attend because of "serious illnesses and other unavoidable causes."

While the members and guests were entering the church, the bells in the tower emitted "numerous familiar tunes." When the audience was seated, the church organist played a voluntary. Ellis opened the program with introductory remarks: "This centennial is to be simple and undemonstrative. We would commemorate our founders, and dignify their aims and work." The Reverend Mr. Paige followed with an extended prayer. Winthrop, who had been a member for fifty-two years, was called to the pulpit "to say a few words to us,—which is all that he has promised." His few words developed into a mini-lecture. The church choir then sang an anthem.

It was time for the main address. Higginson followed a well-worn path for historical commemorations. He retraced the history of the Society and, in a second section, reflected on the nature of history. It was an address certain to induce somnolence. The lengthy program con-

[35] M.H.S., *Procs.*, 2d ser., 5(1889–1890):430.
[36] M.H.S., *Procs.*, 2d ser., 6(1890–1891):175.

cluded with the audience singing the doxology and a benediction by the Reverend Alexander McKenzie.

While the non-members dispersed, the members walked to Winthrop's nearby home at 90 Marlborough Street and enjoyed a reception rich with food and drink and lively conversation.[37]

In late 1892, another historical organization was founded in Boston which promised to be a potential rival to the Society. It was organized "to commemorate the Founders of the Colonies of Plymouth and the Massachusetts Bay and their deeds" and was to be "composed exclusively of gentlemen whose ancestors were residents of the Colonies of Plymouth or the Massachusetts Bay." This society was the inspiration of Henry Herbert Edes, another quaint character in Boston's colorful history. Of iconoclastic bent, Edes projected himself as a "Gentleman of Old Boston," especially in his sartorial style. As a contemporary noted: "The high silk hat, the immaculate standing collar and white necktie, the correct cut-away coat, pearl gloves and cane were his habitual weekday attire. Needless to say, he was always accompanied by a chorus of small-boy hoots and jeers, which he seemed rather to like."[38]

A man of means and an enthusiastic antiquarian, Edes had hungered for membership in the Historical Society. He made the mistake, however, of crossing swords with Librarian Samuel Abott Green, one of the most cantankerous characters in Boston and a powerful force in the Society's internal doings. This doomed Edes to exclusion.[39]

Believing that he would never achieve his goal while Green was alive and in a position of authority, Edes founded his own organization. He decided to call it "The Massachusetts Society," an act tantamount to waving a red flag at a raging bull. At the January 1893 meeting of the Historical Society, a member reported on Edes's proposed organization and "expressed the opinion that great inconvenience and possible injury

[37] For a detailed account of the program, see M.H.S., *Procs.*, 2d ser., 6(1890–1891):268–283. For a summary account, see "One Hundred Years of Usefulness: The Massachusetts Historical Society," *Magazine of American History*, 25(1891):250–253.

[38] The Rev. Charles E. Park, quoted in *Handbook of the Colonial Society of Massachusetts* (Boston, 1992), 8.

[39] Edes and Green seem to have patched up their differences in later years since Edes was elected a resident member in 1911.

might result from the use of a title so nearly like that which was given to this Society more than a hundred years ago." It was the Genealogical Society imbroglio redux.

After receiving instructions from its officers, the Society voted: "That the Council be authorized to take such means as they shall think expedient to secure a change in the corporate name of the new organization."[40] The "means" involved an earnest conversation between member Solomon Lincoln and the founders of the new group. Lincoln apparently was a persuasive spokesman. At the February meeting, he reported that Edes and his colleagues "had applied to the proper authority for such a change in their corporate name as would prevent any inconveniences from the similarity of names of the two societies."[41]

The corporate name of the new organization was The Colonial Society of Massachusetts.[42] After receiving the charter, Edes and his colleagues began to recruit members. They had limited membership to one hundred resident and ten honorary. At the outset, the headquarters of the society was "in its editor's hat," as Walter M. Whitehill has written. Meetings were held initially in the homes of members and then in the hall of the American Academy of Arts and Sciences at the Boston Athenaeum. The formal program consisted of papers the members prepared and read on early Massachusetts history. The Colonial Society then gathered and published these writings. Edes had planned to develop a library but, lacking a headquarters, could not achieve this goal. The highlight of the Colonial Society's yearly program was its annual dinner, meticulously planned by Edes and consisting of an eleven-course meal with appropriate libations. One member recalled that "there was much typical after-dinner speaking, and toast-drinking, until many of us were reduced to a state of groaning repletion, both physical and men-

[40] M.H.S., *Procs.*, 2d ser., 8(1892–1894):59. See also, M.H.S. Council Records, Jan. 12, 1893 (M.H.S. Archives).

[41] M.H.S., *Procs.*, 2d ser., 8(1892–1894):90.

[42] For the early history of the Colonial Society, see Walter M. Whitehill's "Historical Sketch" in *Handbook of the Colonial Society of Massachusetts, 1892–1952* (Boston, 1953), 1–12; Whitehill, *Independent Historical Societies*, 31–33. For the recent history of the society, see the 1992 *Handbook of the Colonial Society*, which reprinted Whitehill's "Historical Sketch."

tal."[43] This tradition of gastronomic excess persisted through most of the twentieth century.[44]

The satisfaction resulting from the reconstruction of 30 Tremont Street persisted for only a decade. By the mid 1880s, order had given way to disorder. Once more, the librarian and other officers began to complain that the rooms were "very much crowded, the shelves filled to over-flowing, the natural accession of books far beyond its capacity to dispose of so that they can readily be made use of, and even the floor space so occupied that little or no working room is left." The library, located on the fourth floor, was "so choked with heterogeneous accretions that much of it is difficult of access."[45]

The lack of space for researchers was a particularly serious deficiency. "We occupy three floors of a spacious building," Robert C. Winthrop, Jr., asserted in the 1889 report of the Council, "but we enjoy no facilities for literary work." If a member wished to engage in research, he added, he "would naturally seek the spiral stairway which conducts to the floor above. But if in his innocence he does so, he emerges upon a disheart-ening scene of seemingly hopeless confusion and disorder which almost beggars description. I am careful to use this word 'seemingly,' because I have not the smallest doubt that the Librarian and his swift-footed assistants are familiar with the intricacies of this Gargantuan storeroom, and that for them little is here hid which cannot with some trouble be revealed. But it is no exaggeration to say that members who desire to find their own authorities and consult them on the spot are appalled by such surroundings. If they be persevering men who, indifferent to the soiling of their clothes, can thread their way through piles of books and mounds of dusty newspapers, they will eventually descry, in the inmost *penetralia* of these apartments, two small tables and two wooden chairs; but even this inadequate accommodation is half the time denied them,

[43] The Rev. Charles E. Park, quoted in *Handbook of the Colonial Society* (1992), 8.

[44] At various times in the twentieth century, both organizations sought to hold joint meetings and even considered a "possible consolidation" because of their common inter-ests and overlapping memberships. These efforts failed, however. See M.H.S., Council Records, Jan. 14, 1932; Dec. 26, 1940; Jan. 9, 1941; Feb. 13, 1941; Nov. 13, 1941 (M.H.S. Archives).

[45] These sentiments of despair are threaded into the reports of the Council, librarian, and cabinet keeper, which can be seen in the *Proceedings* for this period.

as the tables in question are frequently appropriated by the Society's copyists.''

The cabinet also had its share of problems. It was ''most inadequately provided for, and many of its interesting and valuable articles can neither be cared for nor properly exhibited for lack of room.'' The portrait collection was a case in point. With a few exceptions, these paintings were ''gradually driven out upon the damp, insecure walls of a public stairway, or banished to the obscurity of a rarely visited upper room, where, in order to provide shelf-room for public documents of questionable value, some of them have to be piled upon the floor.''[46]

In 1888, the Society revised its by-laws and established for the first time a standing committee to examine annually the state of the library and cabinet. This step was taken because many of the active members had become openly critical of the congestion and deterioration of library services. The complaints had been ''whispered for years.'' The committee was to report at the annual meeting of 1889.

Because of the space crisis, the annual meeting of 1889 took on a special significance. A report from the special committee was certain to spark verbal fireworks. Prior to this report, Robert C. Winthrop, Jr., the senior member at large of the Council, presented that body's annual review. Winthrop could not match his father as an orator, but he did possess a sharp tongue and never shrank from speaking his mind on an issue. None of his contemporaries ever accused him of being a bore.

Winthrop reviewed a range of conventional issues and then came to his final section, ''to a subject which is of the utmost importance to our well-being,'' the sad condition of the library and cabinet. He stated that he was not certain if the oversight committee ''is to-day ready with a report, nor am I at all aware how far they may be disposed to criticise a state of things which has long been a source of embarrassment and perplexity.'' Winthrop, however, *was* ready to present his views on this issue.

And speak out he did, in a most candid manner. He characterized the quarters as dingy, dirty, and dismal. After noting the poor physical state of the library and cabinet, he underscored a possible consequence of the untidy housing arrangement. Prospective donors, he warned, would not confer their ''important gifts of books and pictures, owing to a justifiable

---

[46] M.H.S., *Procs.*, 2d ser., 4(1887–1888):344–345.

fear that the crowded state of our rooms will prevent such objects from being worthily bestowed and from receiving proper care."

Who was to blame for the mess? Winthrop tactfully absolved the librarian and cabinet-keeper from responsibility: "These functionaries would like nothing better than to make our rooms as convenient and attractive as they ought to be; but they are handicapped by usages of the Society."

The culprit then was "usages"—that is, custom or tradition. From its inception, Winthrop asserted, the Society began the practice of accepting "nearly everything which any one chooses to send us, including books and pamphlets upon every conceivable subject, historical or otherwise, and wholly without regard to existing accommodations." Such a practice was proper for "great National, Municipal, or University Libraries," Winthrop stated, but not for a "small society, which is practically a sort of Literary Club, the object of which should be not so much to amass printed matter for posterity as to minister to the intellectual comfort of its living members and furnish them with agreeable facilities for historical research." In 1855, Winthrop reminded his listeners, the standing committee had strongly advised the Society to be discriminating in what it accepted and to weed out irrelevant materials, but its advice had been ignored. A storage crisis soon developed.

History was now repeating itself. So long as the Society refused to adopt and adhere strictly to well-defined accessions and deaccessioning policies, Winthrop said, it would always face a "similar problem." The time had arrived for draconian measures to be taken. The Society should have the courage to cast out "spurious relics and trivial gifts" from the cabinet; and eliminate from the library

> at least thirty per cent of the least appropriate of our bound volumes, and of at least sixty per cent of the most worthless of our unbound pamphlets and periodicals; if we had the nerve to set our faces sternly against the hoarding of miscellaneous matter, to discontinue our cumbrous clearinghouse for heterogeneous exchanges, and be hereafter as discriminating in what we receive inside this building as we try to be in our selection of members, maintaining only a comparatively select library of subjects akin to our pursuits.

If it had the resolution to take these steps, Winthrop affirmed, the Society could then remodel and rearrange its quarters and "make them for at least a generation to come one of the choicest and most convenient repositories of rare historical materials and valuable historical portraits in the country."

To strengthen his argument, Winthrop referred to a letter sent to him by a member, "one of the most eminent of our number," in which he wrote: "The Society is in the predicament of Sinbad the Sailor. An Old Man of the Sea has fastened himself upon its vitals, and is throttling it to death." The Society must break its "bad habits and bad customs." Winthrop concluded: "Some of you may be startled by the plainness of this criticism; others of you may, in part, deny its justice; but not one of you, who has the interest of the Society at heart, should fail to accord it some degree of careful and dispassionate consideration."[47]

The oversight committee did have a report, which it presented. Whereas Winthrop had appealed to the heart, the committee aimed for the head. It applied reason, not emotion. In restrained prose, the committee echoed Winthrop's criticism. Agreed: the rooms were cluttered and there was no work space for researchers. Agreed: it was imperative to develop accessioning and deaccessioning policies. In accessions, for example, the founding of numerous historical societies in the nation in the nineteenth century made it unnecessary for the Massachusetts organization "to collect, preserve, and communicate materials for a complete history of the country." The Society should restrict its geographical scope and "occupy a field more narrow than that contemplated by our founders." Massachusetts and New England were the logical areas of concentration.

As for deaccessioning materials, in this case the committee parted company with Winthrop. Whereas he had advocated a thorough housecleaning of the collections and a dramatic reduction, the committee recommended the elimination of only a small number of books. The paramount need, in its view, was physical reorganization of the holdings and the installation of more book stacks, not a massive discard.

[47] Winthrop's complete remarks are in M.H.S., *Procs.*, 2d ser., 4(1887–1889):337–348. President Samuel G. Drake of the New England Historic Genealogical Society had a different view on how to manage a library. In his presidential address of 1858, he stated: "Sooner than I would reject donations for the library, I would pack our apartment from floor to floor, and from wall to wall, until not even a mouse could find space to enter. . . ." *NEHGR*, 12(1858):101.

The committee presented a room-by-room analysis and offered practical, well-conceived suggestions for a more disciplined management of the Society's varied holdings. If its plan were implemented, the committee concluded, it "would provide not only for all our present books and pamphlets, but for all the probable accessions of the next ten or twenty years, beside furnishing adequate working room for students, whether members or not, and accessible quarters for the Cabinet."

The members may have found Winthrop's presentation more dynamic and entertaining but, after "careful and dispassionate consideration," they endorsed the committee's more conservative prescription. Subsequently, the committee consulted with an architect and was dismayed to learn that "many" of its proposals relating to stack installation were "impracticable" because the floor timbers would be subject "to a greater weight than they had been calculated to sustain."

The committee was forced to revise its plan. It proposed that the unbound newspapers "now cumbering on the floor" in the library on the fourth floor be bound and seven stacks be erected in this space. This improvement would have the secondary effect of providing room for researchers. The cabinet would be positioned in the large room on the fifth floor, and art works, then scattered in hallways and stored poorly in backrooms, would be hung on the walls. All but 2,000 to 3,200 books would be removed from this room. If these steps were taken, the committee believed that the Society's space needs would be met for the next ten years.[48]

The Society approved the revised plan at the June meeting and allocated a sum not to exceed $1,000 for its implementation. At the April 1890 annual meeting, the Council reported: "Our accommodations have been much improved during the year. . . ."[49] And so, another space crisis had been resolved—for the time being.

In 1893, Justin Winsor, an active member and corresponding secretary, had an idea: the Society should leave Boston and move to Cambridge; specifically, to the Yard at Harvard University. Acting on his own initiative, Winsor, who was Sibley's successor as the Harvard librarian, sent a letter to President Charles Eliot urging him to

---

[48] M.H.S., *Procs.*, 2d ser., 4(1887–1889):359–366, 382–383.
[49] M.H.S., *Procs.*, 2d ser., 5(1889–1890):439.

consider if the Corporation cannot invite the Society to build in Cambridge and practically add its resources to the department of historical research in the College. I marked in the plan which I submitted to the Corporation a second quadrangle, lying between that of the library and Quincy Street. I would suggest that the Massachusetts Historical Society be invited to build for their own occupancy a portion of that quadrangle, of a style approved by the College, and suffered to occupy it, subject to no ground rent and if at any time the College wishes to own the building, the College to be allowed to take it at cost, or at appraisal.[50]

There would be advantages to both institutions, continued Winsor. The Society would have a new building without having to purchase the land. Harvard would be affiliated with the "oldest, richest and best-known historical society in the country," whose record in publications was unmatched by any other historical society "in the world," and whose holdings, principally manuscripts, "could richly supplement those of the College Library, and practically be at the service of the staff of history, and the advanced students in that department."

If the Society and Harvard could persuade the American Academy of Arts and Sciences to participate in the venture, continued Winsor, the program would be further strengthened since that institution was "now almost an Annex of the College in its *personnel*, so far as *active* members are concerned."

The time was ripe for the Society's move to Cambridge, asserted Winsor. The twenty-year lease with the city for the lower two floors of 30 Tremont Street was to terminate that year, which would open up the possibility of the Society developing a more financially remunerative leasing arrangement with a new tenant, since the entire building would be vacant. Also, the Society's financial situation had improved considerably with a new gift of $40,000 from Robert C. Waterston, $10,000 of which was to be applied to a building fund. Then, too, the sizable bequest of John Langdon Sibley, who died in 1885, would devolve to the Society after the death of Mrs. Sibley, then an elderly lady. In 1885, his estate was valued at $161,169. Since Sibley's will allowed the Society to use up to half of his bequest for a fireproof building, it would be possible to

[50] Winsor to Eliot, Mar. 17, 1893 (Harvard University Archives). For scenes of Harvard Yard in the 1880s, see Moses King, *Harvard and Its Surroundings* (Cambridge, Mass., 1882), 4th edition.

transact a loan in anticipation of the money, wrote Winsor, and add it to the Waterston funds available for construction.

Winsor offered other reasons why a move to Harvard Yard was preferable to remaining in downtown Boston. There was so much noise and commotion along Tremont Street that it was no longer possible to have a "quiet meeting." There was also the "necessity of a climb to the rooms." The two flights of stairs had become an imposing physical barrier for the members, many of whom were well up in years and suffering from the common infirmities of old age.[51]

While a loyal member of the Society himself, Eliot was not of the mind that Harvard should build a new home for it, despite the obvious benefits which would accrue to the university. In his curt but polite reply, Eliot conveyed the corporation's response: "They could not see their way clear to appropriating land belonging to the University for this purpose, although they perceive that it would be a distinct advantage to the Historical Department if the Society's Library were within easy reach. They feared that they had no right to give the occupation of College land to the Society without rent."[52] Thus ended the effort to relocate in Cambridge.

Winsor's criticism of the Tremont Street site expressed a discontent shared by other Society leaders in the final years of the nineteenth century, most notably Winthrop and Charles F. Adams. Both men firmly believed that the Society should be housed in a "noble edifice" in a

[51] There were heavy iron doors at the entrance of 30 Tremont Street. There were also inner swing doors and a "long and tedious iron stairway running round an open well which extended to the top of the fifth floor." See M.H.S., *Procs.*, 61(1927–1928):98. "In making the ascent of the stairway," Samuel A. Green recalled in 1909, "I have counted the iron steps so often that their number, forty-nine, is now fixed indelibly in my memory." He also noted: "I remember on one occasion when Dr. [Oliver Wendell] Holmes came puffing into the [Dowse] Room, he suggested that the name of the Society be changed to the 'High-story-cal.' " Ibid., 42(1908–1909):175. Green remembered another unpleasant feature of the stairwell. Halfway up, there was a "blind closet without light, gas-jet or ventilation even, which was not objectionable to the eye, but at times in warm weather was decidedly so to the sensitive nerves of the nose." Ibid., 43(1909–1910):228. When Winthrop resigned the presidency in 1885, he alluded to the long climb up the stairs as one reason for his decision to retire. In a similar vein, Winslow Warren made note of the dreaded "two flights of stairs which may have shortened the lives of some of the older members." Ibid., 56(1922–1923):219–220.

[52] Eliot to Winsor, Apr. 3, 1893 (Harvard University Archives).

park-like physical setting with direct access from the street. Since the Society lacked the funds to achieve this ideal, Winthrop and Adams could do little more than dream. The death of President Ellis on December 20, 1894, however, set in motion a chain of events which eventuated in the achievement of Winthrop's and Adams's dream.[53]

Born in Boston on August 8, 1814, George E. Ellis was a "typical New Englander, tasting unmistakably of the natal soil."[54] Destined for the ministry from birth, he followed a well-trod educational path, which included college at Harvard. After completing his ministerial apprenticeship, he assumed the pulpit of a church in Charlestown, where he remained for thirty years. It was his only church.

Ellis abruptly resigned his ministry in 1869 and took up residence in Boston. He never returned to Charlestown, despite its closeness to his new home. Nor did he serve as a guest preacher at his former church, a common convention of the period. His total break with the past mystified his friends.

What had prompted Ellis's turn of mind? There is evidence that he grew disenchanted with traditional Congregationalism in his later years in Charlestown and embraced Unitarianism. He inserted a restriction in his will whereby Harvard, the residuary legatee of his estate, could not use any of his funds for the divinity school. Interestingly, he had served as a professor of divinity for a time.

Ellis seemed to have a stronger interest in history and literature than in theology. In this respect, he was very much like Jeremy Belknap. Worthington C. Ford described Ellis as a "sidetracked clergyman,"[55] a designation also applicable to Belknap. According to Charles F. Adams, "his predilections ran more strongly to certain somewhat limited fields of literature and literary expression than to theology or pastoral duties."[56] Ellis's close friend and clerical colleague the Reverend Octavius B. Frothingham said of him: "He was really more of an antiquarian than

[53] Winthrop also died in 1894.

[54] For biographical data on Ellis, see his memoir in M.H.S., *Procs.*, 2d ser., 10(1895–1896):207–255. See also 9(1894–1895):245–267.

[55] M.H.S., *Procs.*, 48(1914–1915):419.

[56] M.H.S., *Procs.*, 2d ser., 9(1894–1895):241. Adams did not hold Ellis in high regard, viewing him as somewhat of a bumbler who "discoursed discursively." See Kirkland, *Charles Francis Adams*, 216.

an historian. He was not an historian of the grand style by any means, but rather a chronicler, dealing in dates and figures and statistics. How such a man ever happened to become a clergyman was always a study to me."[57]

A few months after he moved to Boston, Ellis suffered two tragedies. First, his only child, a twenty-nine-year-old lawyer, died. Two months later, his second wife expired in Mt. Desert, Maine, where she had been spending the summer. These twin losses devastated Ellis. In 1870, he purchased a house at 110 Marlborough Street, within walking distance of the Society. "From that time," wrote his memorialist, "his life was solitary, devoted to literary and historical work."[58]

The Society, to which Ellis had been elected into membership in 1841 at the young age of twenty-seven, now became the center of his life. He threw himself into its activities. It was "his great interest and pride. . . ."[59] At Ellis's death, Charles Francis Adams stated: "From the beginning to the end, through the whole fifty-three years of his association with the Society, he was in every sense an active member, constant in attendance at meetings, evincing deep interest in the affairs and business of the organization, familiar with its collections, jealous of its prestige, working on its committees and contributing to its publications."[60] Ellis was the type of member Belknap had sought for the Society at its founding, wholly committed to its welfare. Showing their appreciation of Ellis's loyalty and contributions, the members elected him vice president in 1877, a position he held for eight years, and president in 1885, which he held until his death. In his final months, with the passing of Robert C. Winthrop, Ellis became the senior member or dean of the Society.

Ellis's ten-year administration was devoid of major achievements. His presidency was that of a caretaker. As a contemporary noted, the Society "moved along under his guidance quietly, respectably, and not inefficiently, on the lines marked down for it under the longer and more active administration of his predecessor,—lines which moreover wholly commended themselves to the judgment of Dr. Ellis, so that from them

---

[57] M.H.S., *Procs.*, 2d ser., 9(1894–1895):253.
[58] M.H.S., *Procs.*, 2d ser., 10(1895–1896):247.
[59] M.H.S., *Procs.*, 2d ser., 10(1895–1896):247; 56(1922–1923):227.
[60] M.H.S., *Procs.*, 2d ser., 9(1894–1895):245.

he saw no occasion to deviate." But Ellis did take one quiet action that had a profound effect upon the future of the Society. When he prepared his will a decade or so before his death, he bequeathed $30,000 and his home and contents to the Society. He also added these critical conditions in the tenth clause:

> To the members of the Massachusetts Historical Society—My esteemed associates and friends.
>
> I have devised and bequeathed to said Society in this my Will, the sum of thirty thousand dollars and also my present dwelling-house in Boston, in trust for perpetuity, for uses and purposes such as I will now indicate.
>
> Perhaps more in the future than at the present time it may be of service to the Society to have a place in this part of the City answering to some of the uses of a Club House confined strictly to members of the Society, where Committees may meet in the evening, and where individuals may at their leisure pursue investigations with such facilities as may here be afforded them.[61]
>
> My wish and expectation are that the bequest in money will yield sufficient annual income to insure, maintain, and repair the property without drawing upon the funds of the Society.
>
> The property of every kind herein devised and bequeathed to said Society is to be under the care, disposal, management, and regulation of the Council of the Society for the time being acting as a Committee. If they see fit they may allow any officer or member of the Society without a family to reside in the house free of rent, he meeting his own household charges; or an employee may be engaged at due compensation beyond the privilege of rent of assigned portions of the house. I am perfectly willing, indeed I much prefer, instead of myself dictating minute or even general conditions for the enjoyment and improvement of this trust by the Society, to leave all such matters to their discretion, good judgment, and appreciation of my single purpose to contribute to the welfare, prosperity, and useful resources of an honored fellowship in association with which for now nearly half a century I have found much good. The Society has my full allowance, and may infer my approbation if urgent or reasonable occasion should present itself to dispose of the real estate which is here bequeathed for the purpose of an equivalent that may be more convenient and eligible, but the real estate which I give the Society liberty to exchange for that which is bequeathed must not require in its purpose any portion of the above named sum of thirty thousand dollars, and any money or other things

---

[61] In later years, Worthington C. Ford described Ellis's plan of converting his home into a "social clubhouse" for the Society as a "somewhat grotesque idea." M.H.S., *Procs.*, 48(1914–1915):419.

received from the sale or exchange of, or insurance on, the property hereby devised or bequeathed to said Society, or anything substituted therefor, shall be used so far as practicable to rebuild, restore, or replace the property sold, exchanged, or insured.[62]

In informal conversations with President Winthrop in 1884, Ellis hinted of his testamentary intentions with respect to the Society. He was interested in hearing Winthrop's reaction. The president was elated to learn of the sizable monetary gift but, as his son informed the members in 1895, "felt aghast at a plan which he feared would inevitably lead us into pecuniary embarrassment; for not only would the Society derive no practical benefit from a fund the income of which was to be devoted to the maintenance of a dwelling-house in another part of the town, but this income was more than likely to prove insufficient for that purpose, thereby leading us into all sorts of incidental outlay."[63]

Winthrop reminded Ellis of the narrow financial means of the Society. He also called attention "to the very limited accommodations of 110 Marlborough Street,—a house which can never be made fire-proof, which is inconveniently arranged for literary gatherings, and which is built upon a lot of land so small that it can never be utilized as a site for that spacious edifice which it is our hope to be able one day to erect." As "delicately as he could," Winthrop implored Ellis to take another tack, "to bequeath to us an unrestricted fund, to be forever associated with the name of its donor; and he ventured to hint that the maintenance of the house might well be left to a relative of the testator with a suitable provision for that purpose."[64]

Ellis did not accept Winthrop's suggestions. He proceeded to fashion his will as he had planned, and upon his death the Society found itself in a quandary.

The Ellis issue was the principal order of business at the March 1895 meeting. Vice President Adams, who chaired the meeting, announced the news of Ellis's bequests, read the relevant sections of his will, and solicited the advice of the members. After lengthy and spirited discussion, the members concluded that the Society should not abide by Ellis's

[62] The sections of Ellis's will relevant to the Society are printed in M.H.S., *Procs.*, 2d ser., 10(1895–1896):1–3, 148–150.

[63] M.H.S., *Procs.*, 2d ser., 10(1895–1896):4.

[64] M.H.S., *Procs.*, 2d ser., 10(1895–1896):4.

wishes, that it would not be in the Society's best interests to accept his home and the cash gift under his conditions. But they were also aware that it was not in its best interest to reject these bequests. The members voted to appoint a special three-person committee, chaired by Vice President Adams, which would join the Council in evaluating all aspects of the issue and preparing recommendations for a course of action.[65]

Before reporting, the committee conducted an experiment. For several weeks, it kept Ellis's home open and staffed by his servants. Consistent with the late president's wishes, it was available daily to members as a clubhouse and to Society committees as an evening meeting site. The results were disappointing but predictable. Neither members nor committees used the facility. At the May meeting, the committee concluded "that the Society and its members have no use for an establishment of this character." To preserve it in this manner would be a "waste of Dr. Ellis's bequest." The committee was now convinced that the property should be sold and the proceeds used for a new home.[66]

[65] M.H.S., *Procs.*, 2d ser., 10(1895–1896):1–6.

[66] Adams presented the committee's report, which is printed in M.H.S., *Procs.*, 2d ser., 10(1895–1896):148–159.

Chapter 8

Adams in the President's Chair

JEREMY BELKNAP founded the Society; Robert C. Winthrop energized it; and Charles Francis Adams transformed it into a modern institution.[1] At the annual meeting on April 11, 1895, Adams was elected president, and his selection marked a major turning point in the history of the Society.[2] With the deaths of Winthrop and Ellis in 1894, Adams stood alone as the dominant figure of the

[1] Charles Francis Adams (1835–1915) was elected a member in 1875. He was the fourth Adams elected into membership, but he was the first of the family to take a leading role in the management of the Society. President John Adams (1735–1826), elected in 1800, took no part in Society affairs. President John Quincy Adams (1767–1848), elected in 1802, and his son, Ambassador Charles Francis Adams (1807–1886), elected in 1841, were moderately active members but not major figures. Ambassador Adams did serve as vice-president for twelve years and, during the frequent absences of President Robert C. Winthrop, acted as president pro tem at meetings. For an account of all of the Adamses' involvement with the Society, see Malcolm Freiberg, " 'Big things require time to mature': Adamses and the Massachusetts Historical Society," M.H.S., *Procs.*, 97(1985):81–102.

For further biographical data on Adams, see: *Charles Francis Adams, 1835–1915, An Autobiography* (Boston, 1916); M.H.S., *Procs.*, 48(1914–1915):383–423 (memoirs by his Society colleagues); Elliott Perkins, John A. Abbott, and Thomas B. Adams, "Three Views of Charles Francis Adams, II," ibid., 72(1957–1960):212–237 (written by his three grandsons); Francis Russell, *Adams: An American Dynasty* (New York, 1976), 282–296; and Edward C. Kirkland, *Charles Francis Adams, Jr., 1835–1915: The Patrician at Bay* (Cambridge, Mass., 1965). Adams's publications are listed in M.H.S., *Procs.*, 72(1957–1960): 238–293.

[2] M.H.S., *Procs.*, 2d ser., 10(1895–1896):137–138. Henry Cabot Lodge made this observation on Adams's elevation to the presidency: "He came to his new duties, as he had come to all the positions he had ever filled, with an abundance of fresh ideas and in the spirit of the reformer." Adams, *Autobiography*, xlvi.

organization.[3] Adams was well aware of the significance of the dual loss. The Society, he wrote, "then passed from the hands of the men of the first half of the century into the hands of the men of its second half. And, in the case of this nineteenth century of ours, that signifies much."[4] Nearly sixty years old, Adams was not elated by his new honor: "more work!—more details!," he grumbled.[5]

The day after assuming the presidency, writing in his private journal, Adams made this candid and revealing assessment of his personal position, the current status of the Society, and his plan to effect change:

> Yesterday I was chosen as President of the Massachusetts Historical Society to succeed Dr. Ellis; who became President of it exactly ten years ago, under the supposition that he would hold it for a year or two, but who hung along, lending no impulse whatever to the Society, until he dropped off by death.
>
> This is the oldest and most respected of all our Historical Societies, of the which the number is now beyond reckoning. To become its President, therefore, is something of an honor; though an honor of a class which does not very strongly appeal to me. It all depends, in such cases, on the person. In itself, now, it is nothing; a thing scarcely noticeable; but, if the holder, in one way or another, knows how to magnify and make much of the position, it can be made something considerable. And this in either, or both, of two ways, by building the Society up and, through its organization and prominence making of it a sort of French Academy the membership of which would be eagerly sought; or, secondly, by making of the Presidency a social honor, and causing oneself to be recognized as the head of a literary circle.
>
> To accomplish much in the first direction implies the command of a good deal of machinery, involving a large money endowment of the Society. A million dollars would be about the figure, allowing for both construction and maintenance. This seems large, but the Society has slowly accumulated, and now has, more than half the amount. With such an endowment, judiciously applied, and a membership strictly limited, the

[3] When Adams was elected vice president in 1890, he knew he was being groomed for the presidency. "My consent was not asked," he wrote, "nor did I think it a matter of sufficient importance to decline the position. I just drifted." Adams, *Autobiography*, 208.

[4] M.H.S., *Procs.*, 2d ser., 9(1894–1895):247. Adams also regarded the transition as a time of significant philosophical change: it was the "difference, historically speaking, between a generation which drew its cast of thought and modes of treatment from the teachings inspired by the Mosaic dispensation, and a generation which draws them from the methods and science of Darwin." Ibid., 2d ser., 10(1895–1896):573–574.

[5] Charles F. Adams, Memorabilia, Dec. 21, 1894 (C.F. Adams Papers).

position of the Society, in its way, would be unique. To be President of it then, would be something.

In the other, or social way, a good deal is possible by working in the lines upon which Mr. Winthrop was strong and Dr. Ellis wholly lacking. The President must entertain on behalf of the Society, give dinners and receptions, meet distinguished strangers, make the position felt. This is not difficult provided only the means are forth-coming.

I by no means sought this position. When, ten years ago the idea of my taking it was first suggested, I treated it as a joke. It was in no way in my line. Dr. Ellis was then chosen as matter of course; but, some five years later, I found myself suddenly made Vice President with the evident idea of putting me in the line of succession. I was then in the active swing of the Union Pacific management. I thought the matter over, and decided to let matters take their course. I did not mean to remain in active railroad work all my life; nothing need necessarily come of the new departure; possibly it might be worked into something agreeable for later life; in any event it could be avoided. So I let things drift; and they have drifted to yesterdays result. I am now in for it.

. . . Anyhow, I have now actively assumed a new burden, and something ought to be made of it. It is useless to assume these positions in a per-functory way, sort of small, honorary pedestals. It ought to be made something, or put aside. In this case it is my present intention to attempt the making of something of it; but I propose to go at it deliberately and in some well-considered plan. As it now stands, I hope to get a good deal of enjoyment and interest out of it, and to contribute very materially towards the building up of our literary organization which shall have some dignity and value; and not to be run on the democratic principle. In a word, I propose to take up Mr. Winthrop's work where he laid it down.[6]

Charles Francis Adams, like all of the prominent Adamses of the past, was a remarkable aggregate of experiences and talents. The grandson of John Quincy Adams and great-grandson of John Adams, he manifested all of the iconoclastic traits of his illustrious ancestors. Possessing a keen, active, and well-trained mind, he wore the mantle of leadership with a natural grace. He was a man of action. For most of his life, the bridge between thoughts and deeds was short, and he did not tarry in the crossing. He was to become the "maximum leader" of the Society, a position he would hold for the next twenty years.

While not as enigmatic as his brother Henry, Adams was nonetheless

[6] Charles F. Adams, Memorabilia, Apr. 12, 1895 (C.F. Adams Papers).

a "complex and many-sided personality."[7] His contemporaries regarded him as a rare character and they portrayed him in many different ways.

Although Gov. John D. Long thought that Adams was "inclined to give us rather long doses from the Adams' family record,"[8] Harvard President Charles W. Eliot found him "not naturally inclined to respect precedents, or to imitate in his own mental processes the methods of other men.[9] He was always independent, and sometimes recalcitrant. No wisdom of the ages, or of the multitude, necessarily commanded his respect." The same two men both agreed on the president's pugnacious manner, Eliot commenting that Adams "experienced in high degree the joy of combat, and the joy was not dependent on immediate or even ultimate victory." Long was equally direct, stating that Adams "was dogmatic and masterful—a fighter, for any position he took, who asked no odds and gave no quarter." Perhaps the result of being "the embodiment of mental and physical vigor," Adams was also "brusque and abrupt and outspoken, often not sparing a pungent word." "He was so strong in his conclusions, he pressed them so confidently, that, paradoxically as it may seem, the very intensity of his convictions often sooner or later led him, as an overloaded gun kicks backward, to question them and to go to the other extreme with equal earnestness."

While the Adams brusqueness struck some the wrong way,[10] Henry Cabot Lodge saw beneath this. "Under a manner somewhat brusque, sometimes abrupt, was concealed one of the kindest, most affectionate hearts that ever beat, and how tender his sympathy could be to those to whom it went out know well."

This intensity made Adams "as nearly independent in thought and act as the lot of humanity permits," as Moorfield Storey recorded, "prompt to say what he thought the situation demanded—to lead in

[7] After learning of Charles's death, Henry described his brother as "a man of action with strong love of power." Adams to Henry Cabot Lodge, [n.d.] 1915, in Harold Dean Cater, ed., *Henry Adams and His Friends* (Cambridge, Mass., 1947), 772.

[8] Margaret Long, ed., *The Journal of John D. Long* (Rindge, N.H., 1956), 283–284.

[9] For the appraisal of Adams presented below, I have drawn heavily from the multiple memoirs printed in the *Proceedings* after his death (see note 1). See also, Winslow Warren's evaluation in M.H.S., *Procs.*, 56(1922–1923):228.

[10] Gamaliel Bradford stated that "Charles was really superficial and commonplace. All that gave him significance was an aristocratic brutality in saying things that others keep quiet."

forming public opinion, but never fearing or even considering the consequences to himself."

The Society's editor, Worthington C. Ford, added that intellectually, "always questioning himself with conscientious thoroughness, he questioned others, while giving an opinion which was intended tentatively for acceptance. The expressed doubt clothed a certainty; yet he took suggestion and correction with good temper, never forgetting the amenities of difference, and inclining to treat the situation with a sense of humor. A positive manner and a speech vigorous and direct left no sting, even when giving correction. Impulsive and at times impatient, the resulting mood reverted to a questioning and calm discussion of conditions. He was thus ever a severe but reasonable and kindly critic, and when severe most helpful."

Perhaps the most perceptive appraisal came from James Ford Rhodes, who remarked that "No one but a many-sided man like Mr. Adams himself could do justice to his many and various activities. A true appreciation of him must come from a consolidation of a number of papers, each written by a man who knew him in a particular phase."

There was one point on which all of his colleagues, friend and foe, agreed: Adams had a genuine love of history. A reading of Macaulay at the age of thirteen ignited his passion for Clio. It intensified as he grew older.[11]

As the Society's new president, Adams tackled the question of the Ellis bequest as his first order of business. He presented the joint committee's report at the May meeting.[12] This was a significant gathering, another defining moment in the history of the Society. The report that Adams presented, and the consequences that flowed from its implementation, were to transform the Society into a completely different organization from that which functioned on Tremont Street.

Adams may have consulted with other members of the committee on the report, but there can be no question that he was its author and the formulator of its major conclusions. It was a masterful exegesis. Structured like a legal brief, it began with an analysis of the "intent of the

[11] For an incisive analysis of Adams as an historian, see Edward C. Kirkland, "Charles Francis Adams, Jr.: The Making of an Historian," M.H.S., *Procs.*, 75(1965):39–52.
[12] The report is in M.H.S., *Procs.*, 2d ser., 10(1895–1896):148–159.

testator." Adams obviously wished to provide a solid legal base for the committee's recommendations. He was intent upon proving that Ellis had merely suggested, not dictated, a course of action. After setting forth the clauses in the will pertaining to his bequests to the Society, the report zeroed in on those words and phrases in the critical tenth section that seemingly confirmed the committee's contention.

From his reading, Adams was certain that Ellis had vested the Council with discretionary authority. His conditions were not absolute; the Society did not have to retain his home as a clubhouse. One key phrase, in Adams's view, was: "to leave all such matters to the discretion, good judgment, and appreciation" of the Society. Ellis also had allowed for the sale of his property "if urgent or reasonable occasion should present itself," and the purchase of an "equivalent in real estate elsewhere at some more convenient and eligible point" could be effected. He had disallowed the use of the principal of his monetary bequest ($30,000) for a purchase but granted the use of interest income either to maintain or repair a new building.

Having taken the stance that Ellis had given the Society a free hand in the disposition of his home, Adams moved to the next logical issue: Should the Society remain at 30 Tremont Street, or seek a new home? Adams affirmed that the present quarters were no longer suitable. He listed the negative features of the property:

> the rooms ... are high above the street, and can be reached only by climbing long flights of stairs; the nearness of this building to the centre of business makes the site better adapted and more valuable for commercial than for literary purposes; while the reports of the Committees on the Library and the Cabinet, through a series of years, and especially those recently made, have dwelt with increasing emphasis upon the inadequacy of the space now occupied for the proper preservation, display, and convenient use of our accumulated possessions. Our pictures, stored away as if they were rubbish, are seen by no one. Our books and manuscripts are inconveniently placed, hard to be reached, and without adequate facilities for examination. Our curiosities are scattered, and the space allotted to them is totally inadequate.

Given these facts, Adams contended that the Society would need "more commodious quarters" in the near future. The sale of Ellis's property "for the purpose of an equivalent that may be more convenient and eligible" offered a golden opportunity for the Society.

A move to another location and the construction of a "proper fire-proof edifice," the report continued, was a costly enterprise, requiring a careful analysis of the current and future financial resources of the Society. There were three major elements to consider: purchasing land and erecting a building; maintaining the new facility; and planning for library and publications needs. The committee estimated the combined cost of purchasing land and construction at $250,000. The annual cost of maintaining the property was set at $10,000, which would require an endowment fund of $250,000, assuming a yield of 4 percent. The library and publication needs could be met with two endowment funds of $100,000, each of which would produce an annual return of $4,000. The estimated total cost for this program was $700,000.

Adams then reviewed the current financial resources, excluding the Ellis bequests but incorporating other gifts either in hand or to be acquired "at no very remote day." The building fund stood at $179,000, the maintenance fund at $99,700, the library fund at $6,000, and the publication fund at $60,000. These funds totalled $344,700. Thus, the Society was confronted by a deficit of $355,300. Factoring in the Ellis bequests, and considering only the purchase of land and construction, the two most essential elements, Adams reduced the shortfall to $170,000. He was certain that the Society could acquire this sum "within the next ten or fifteen years" through gifts and bequests.

Assured that the Society had sufficient resources to push ahead, continued Adams, he had begun to look at "desirable" real estate options. The members knew that Adams had had considerable experience in real estate ventures in Boston and environs and in many areas of the midwest and far west. They also knew that he had been remarkably successful in this activity, although he had suffered devastating losses in the panic of 1893.[13]

Adams was convinced "that the time is not remote when the centre of the residence portion of Boston will be in the immediate vicinity of the intersection of Commonwealth Avenue and Massachusetts Avenue." This was in the Back Bay section, formerly tide flats and marsh land but rapidly being filled in and developed. Between 1881 and 1885,

---

[13] On Adams's real estate ventures, see: Paul C. Nagel, *Descent From Glory: Four Generations of the John Adams Family* (New York, 1983), ch. 15; Russell, *Adams*, 291–294.

the accomplished landscape architect, Frederick Law Olmsted, working under the aegis of the Boston Park Commission, supervised the draining of the malodorous flats of the Muddy River and Stony Brook. From this stagnant and foul marsh arose the Fens, a beautiful link in Olmsted's "Emerald Necklace" of parks in Boston. Adams set his sights on property contiguous to the Fens.[14]

A principal requirement of the Society would be location on a central street-railway line so that visitors from all areas of the city could reach it easily. By the late 1880s, numerous horse-car lines began to traverse the Fenway-Kenmore area. Moreover, plans were developed for electric transit cars to begin operating on Huntington Avenue, Beacon Street, Massachusetts Avenue, and Boylston Street, which would provide rapid access to city center and neighbor communities; this system went into effect in 1897. Massachusetts Avenue between Boylston and Beacon streets had become the principal street-railway link between the business districts of Boston proper and Cambridge and Brookline. The proposed subway would also make the lower Back Bay area accessible from the north-side stations. For members living west of Boston Common or in Cambridge or Brookline, concluded Adams, "a Society building somewhere in the vicinity of the intersection of Massachusetts and Commonwealth Avenues would be, even at the present time, more convenient and accessible, besides infinitely better so far as air, light, and space are concerned, than the site we now occupy."[15]

In investigating potential sites in this area, Adams learned that real estate values were not only rising rapidly but "open spaces are being cut up to such an extent that the amount of land requisite for a proper building for the Society, looking ahead for a century, will soon be difficult, if not impossible, to obtain at any price within its means." The Society needed a "fire-proof building, two stories in height and standing by itself, with open grassed spaces between it and all adjacent buildings, with adequate room for the collections of the Society and its meetings." It needed 10,000 to 12,500 square feet for such a structure. Adams had noted several available sites with the requisite dimensions in the vicinity

[14] For the development of the Fens and Fenway district, see *The Fenway: Boston 200 Neighborhood History Series* (Boston, 1976).

[15] For the overall development of the Back Bay, see Walter M. Whitehill, *Boston: A Topographical History* (Cambridge, Mass., 1959), ch. 7.

of Boylston Street, Massachusetts Avenue, and Commonwealth Avenue. He was prepared to recommend one of these sites for purchase. Because of the tax situation and the rapid appreciation of prices, he called for prompt action.

The Society, Adams suggested, should sell Ellis's house and apply the funds to the purchase of the desirable location. He requested authorization from the membership to begin negotiations on the purchase. He also recommended that Ellis's bequest of $30,000 be set aside as an "accumulating fund" and a portion of its income be used to meet any mortgage interest on the land purchased until the building was constructed. Thereafter, the income of the entire fund could be used for the maintenance of "some room or rooms" in the new building. These would be called the Ellis Rooms and house his literary bequest to the Society and, in accordance with the late president's will, if desired, be used as a clubhouse, or place where "committees may meet in the evening, and where individuals may at their leisure pursue investigations with such facilities as may be afforded them." The members unanimously approved all of the report's recommendations, to the great satisfaction of Adams.

In presenting the committee's report, Adams had omitted some salient details. As Charles C. Smith noted in 1915, Adams alone had conducted the search for a new home at the outset. Not until he had concluded that the best location was in the lower Back Bay, in the Massachusetts Avenue-Boylston Street area, did he call upon the committee for its advice and seal of approval. Adams and the committee first visited a lot at the corner of Beacon Street and Massachusetts Avenue. Next, they inspected an open area at the corner of Commonwealth Avenue and Massachusetts Avenue. They cast a negative opinion on both of these sites.

The group then went to Boylston Street and the Fenway. Adams said to his colleagues: "Here, gentlemen, is what I think we want." The committee "at once fully and readily concurred."[16] They would not have dared to challenge or disapprove of Adams's choice.

After the March 1895 meeting, Adams promptly went to work. He arranged for the purchase of two lots on the corner of Boylston Street

---

[16] M.H.S., *Procs.*, 48(1914–1915):401–402.

and the Fenway. The lots contained 10,604 3/4 square feet and cost $53,500. Adams urged the members to inspect the site. He assured them that it had advantages "for the future needs of the Society, as respects location, convenience of access, light, air, outlook and quiet, which can hardly fail to be at once apparent."[17]

To make certain that the Society would have ample space for its new home, Adams personally bought the lot adjoining the Society's property; it fronted the Fenway and contained 3,000 square feet.[18] Adams had made a wise decision because the city subsequently required a set-back on Boylston Street. This meant that the Society's space was not large enough for its planned structure.[19] "It became necessary, therefore, to use my lot," Adams wrote. He did set forth one condition with his generous gift. He requested that "the Society will then at some future time, when its plans are matured, convey to me an appropriate equivalent of the land from its original purchase facing on Boylston Street."[20]

Adams also executed the sale of Ellis's home and arranged for the processing of his personal property in accordance with the instructions in his will.[21]

The energetic Adams next turned to the selection of an architect for the Fenway site and the preparation of preliminary plans for the new building. He chose Edmund March Wheelwright, just past forty years of age and a prominent architect in the city; the joint committee approved his action. It was a brilliant selection.

---

[17] M.H.S., *Procs.*, 2d ser., 10(1895–1896):295–296; 48(1914–1915):403; *Boston Herald*, Aug. 7, 1895.

[18] C.F. Adams to C.C. Smith, Apr. 25, 1896 (Charles C. Smith Papers, M.H.S.); M.H.S., *Procs.*, 2d ser., 15(1901–1902):35.

[19] On the set-back issue, see Edmund M. Wheelwright to Charles F. Adams, Feb. 21, 25, Mar. 5, 1896 (C.F. Adams Papers).

[20] C.F. Adams to C.C. Smith, Apr. 25, 1896 (Charles C. Smith Papers, M.H.S.). In 1901, the Society sold a portion of unoccupied land containing 2,622–4/10 square feet to in-demnify Adams for the lot conveyed by him to the Society in 1896. "The difference ($3,000) between the sum paid by the President ($15,000) and the amount received for the land sold ($12,000) was an absolute gift to the Society, and to this difference must be added the interest on $15,000 from the date of the original purchase up to the date of sale of the Boylston Street land, a period of nearly six years." See M.H.S., *Procs.*, 2d ser., 15(1901–1902):35.

[21] M.H.S., *Procs.*, 2d ser., 10(1895–1896):296.

The Massachusetts Historical Society

Born in Roxbury in 1854, Wheelwright was the descendant of distinguished Puritan forebears who had emigrated to Massachusetts Bay Colony in 1636.[22] He received his A.B. from Harvard in 1876 and then studied architecture at the Massachusetts Institute of Technology in 1876–1877. He worked in several highly respected architectural firms in Boston, New York City, and Albany until 1881, then took a year off and made the grand architectural tour of Europe, a common practice for young American architects of this era. Wheelwright studied a wide array of structures, from the storied monumental edifices to the vernacular. He returned to his Albany position but, in 1883, reestablished residence in Boston and went into private practice. Five years later, he took on Parkman B. Haven as a partner. The firm of Wheelwright and Haven soon established a reputation as one of Boston's premier architectural firms. Wheelwright designed a number of major structures in the Boston area, including Horticultural Hall, the New England Conservatory of Music, Boston City Hospital, and the Cambridge Bridge across the Charles River.

In 1891, newly-elected Mayor Nathan Matthews, Jr., who was a member of the Historical Society, appointed Wheelwright as the city architect of Boston.[23] Created in 1874, this job, while part-time, was an extremely important position. Previously, committees of several city departments had designed and arranged for the construction of public buildings. This system was rife with opportunity for abuse.

The first city architect, George A. Clough, was a conscientious, efficient administrator. Subsequent city architects, however, fell victim to venal municipal officials and predatory contractors. There was rampant fraud and corruption in building projects.

Highly principled and reform minded, Matthews was determined to eliminate the corruption and take the "Architect Department out of politics." His appointment of Wheelwright signaled the beginning of a new order. "An administrator, economist, and artist," and a man of

[22] For further biographical data on Wheelwright, see: Francis W. Chandler, ed., *Municipal Architecture in Boston From Designs by Edmund M. Wheelwright, City Architect, 1891 to 1895* (Boston, 1898), Part I, preface. The Wheelwright Family Papers in the M.H.S. include a biographical sketch by Barrett Wendell.

[23] On Wheelwright's career as city architect, see Chandler, ed., *Municipal Architecture*, introduction. This volume contains illustrations of Wheelwright's most important structures.

intense public spirit, Wheelwright resisted the blandishments and thwarted the efforts of both corrupt politicians and greedy contractors and performed an Herculean job in his brief tenure. He designed and constructed over eighty public buildings. They included many schools, fire and police stations, hospitals, athletic buildings, and subway entrances. His term was a veritable Periclean Age for Boston, and there was not a trace of scandal during his tenure.

Wheelwright was lauded by civic-minded Bostonians. Professor Charles Eliot Norton gave him high marks for the numerous schools he designed. "He has made the beauty of his buildings to reside in their proportions and in the lines and arrangement of their doors and windows," wrote Norton, "and he has had the strength to discard the superfluous ornament of detail which another man might have been tempted to add."

Another Bostonian wrote: "Not a little of the value of his work has been in showing that dignity and beauty may be obtained by simple and straightforward means without sacrifice of economy or the requirements of utility."[24]

After serving four successive one-year terms, Matthews left the mayoralty at the end of 1894. With his departure, Wheelwright's career as city architect also ended. Pressured by frustrated politicians and contractors to remove their nemesis, a compliant Mayor Edwin U. Curtis, the new executive, led a successful effort to abolish the position of city architect. While sorry to leave much unfinished business, Wheelwright was relieved to escape from the political pressures of his public position and return full time to his placid private practice, where all he had to deal with were contentious, complaining clients seeking bigger and better buildings at the lowest possible cost—clients like Charles F. Adams and the Massachusetts Historical Society.

Adams's progress on a new building was counterbalanced by a negative turn of affairs in the Tremont Street property. With the completion of the new county court house in nearby Pemberton Square in 1895, the probate office and registry of deeds of Suffolk County vacated their quarters of twenty-two years at Tremont Street, which they had

[24] Chandler, ed., *Municipal Architecture*, preface.

occupied as a tenant-at-will after the expiration of the fifteen-year lease, and moved into the massive granite facility. The city thereupon summarily terminated its relationship with the Society. This action provoked a financial crisis of major proportions. At stake was $9,000 of annual rental income. This was "a very considerable portion" of the Society's annual income, about 70 percent.

Alarmed by this sudden development and its financial implications, Adams met with Mayor Curtis and suggested that the city house one or more of its numerous agencies in the vacant space. Adams had approached his meeting with the mayor in a confident mood. He was certain that the city would leap at the opportunity to lease the site since it was fireproof and in close proximity to key municipal buildings, including city hall, the monumental second empire-style structure constructed in 1862–1865. Adams stressed the point that the entire complex could be connected by passageways, which would then provide the city with an "independent ingress and egress" to and from Tremont Street, a key arterial.

To Adams's surprise and dismay, the mayor showed no interest whatsoever in the property: "He would not even study the situation." Adams implored Curtis to reconsider and even offered him a reduced rental rate, but to no avail. "I tried in vain," the disappointed president later lamented.

After being rebuffed by the city, Adams consulted with real estate brokers about the possibility of leasing the space to a business firm. The brokers told Adams that the property was not suitable for commercial usage. As Adams later informed the members, "the rooms on the ground floor have merely an entrance from Tremont Street, and no outlook upon it; they are dark, ill-ventilated, and built and arranged in a way now no longer in vogue." Adams was coming to realize that "the building was a dead weight on our hands. It could be adapted to no useful purpose, and, indeed, no person or institution could be found who would pay any rent whatever for it."

The situation looked hopeless. Then, "by one of those mutations in city politics which are so common," as Adams phrased it, the Society's fortunes suddenly brightened. When Curtis, a Republican, had been elected in 1894, the Republican-dominated state legislature passed a measure increasing the Boston mayor's term to two years. The law was to take effect in 1895. They were certain that Curtis would win again that year. The Boston mayoralty was a large political plum to both major parties.

The Republicans had failed to take into account the masterful organizational abilities of Martin "Mahatma" Lomasney, the Irish Democratic party leader of Ward 8 and a kingpin in the city and state party structure. Lomasney and his Democratic cohorts "imported" Josiah Quincy of Quincy, arranged for his nomination, and placed him in opposition to Curtis in 1895.

It was a brilliant strategic move. The venerable Yankee had a distinguished political lineage and was a formidable candidate. His great-grandfather and namesake, President Josiah Quincy of Harvard University (1772–1864), had served as mayor of Boston for five years (1823–1828). His grandfather, another namesake (1802–1882), also had held the mayor's office (1846–1848). To the mortification of the Republicans, Quincy defeated Curtis and became the first beneficiary of the two-year term; he also was reelected to a second two-year term.[25]

From Adams's perspective, this political "mutation" was a providential act. He was certain he could do business with Quincy. There were at least three reasons for his optimism. First and foremost, he and the mayor were related. They were distant cousins and of the same patrician stock.

Secondly, Quincy had a strong familial association with the Society. His great-grandfather had been a resident member and mainstay of the Society for sixty-eight years. To that time, he held the record for length of membership. Further, the new mayor's father, Josiah Phillips Quincy (1829–1910), a distinguished lawyer and accomplished amateur historian, had been a resident member of the Society since 1865; he remained a member to his death in 1910. Had his father not been a member, there is strong reason to believe that the mayor himself would have been elected. Since the maximum number of members was one hundred at this time, the Society had adhered to an unwritten policy of restricting membership to one person from a family.[26]

In addition to the requisite social criterion, the newly-elected mayor

[25] On Lomasney and the mayoralty election, see Leslie G. Ainsley, *Boston Mahatma* (Boston, 1949), 79. On Quincy, see Geoffrey T. Blodgett, "Josiah Quincy, Brahmin Democrat," *New England Quarterly* 38(1965):435–453.

[26] On rare occasion, the Society made an exception and elected a second member of a family, as with the Winthrops and Adamses.

had another vital qualification for membership. He devoted considerable time to historical research. He was also fond of literary works and was a proud member of the Society of Colonial Wars.

After Quincy assumed office, Adams met with him and "renewed my negotiations." Not too surprisingly, Quincy looked with favor upon Adams's proposal. He agreed to a five-year lease, effective July 1, 1896, at the same rental price as in the past. He also endorsed the attached option whereby the city could purchase the entire building for the sum of $200,000 during the period of rental.

While gratified by the rental agreement, Adams was now wholly convinced that the most expedient course of action for the Society was to sell the Tremont site to the city. He knew that "the city was our one customer." If this were to be done, Adams reasoned, the sale would have to be made during the "safe period" of Quincy's tenure, which was an assured two years at this point. Given the vagaries of Boston politics, Adams knew full well that the next administration could display the same disinterest Curtis had shown.[27]

This was the situation when Adams rose to address the members at the annual meeting in 1896. "The weather could not have been better. . . . It was a bright bracing April day." He stated that he had intended to use this occasion, which marked the completion of his first year in office, for a "formal inaugural address." When elected president, he had briefly acknowledged the Society's action and stated that he would "take an early opportunity to present to the Society a carefully considered plan for the conduct of its future operations." He viewed the 1896 annual meeting as the proper time to deliver his plan. His intention, he said, was to review the history of the Society, summarize its accomplishments, and, "after considering present conditions and aspects of historical research, to outline a policy to be pursued with a view to maintaining the efficiency, increasing the usefulness, and systematizing the activity of the organization in the future."

"On the threshold of preparation" for the 1896 annual meeting, Adams informed the members, he concluded that the time was still not right for an address that projected his vision of the future. The Society faced "immediate and pressing" problems which must be "met, and in

[27] M.H.S. Council Records, June 30, 1886 (M.H.S. Archives). See also, Adams's personal letter to Quincy, Dec. 19, 1896 (Charles C. Smith Papers, M.H.S.).

some way disposed of." These related to "habitation, locality, and finance." He felt obliged to focus on these critical issues. He would postpone his major statement for four years, he stated, when the nineteenth century came to a close: "If any conceivable time is appropriate for a background glance, as well as for an effort to peer into the future, it is at the point where two centuries merge; and especially will this be the case when, so few years hence, and between the sunset of one day and another day's sunrise, the momentous nineteenth century ends, and the yet more momentous-to-be twentieth begins."

In projecting the topic of his presidential address four years hence, Adams was not displaying brashness. He knew, and the members seated before him knew, that he could retain the presidency as long as he wished to hold it.

Adams began by addressing the financial issue. His words underscored his stringent fiscal conservatism. Lacking a solid financial base, he affirmed, the Society would remain a frail institution. The Society's present fiscal foundation, Adams asserted, was weak. The institution's total accumulated endowment, including real estate and securities, was a mere $320,000. In the near future, the Society would receive an additional $160,000 from the Sibley and Waterston bequests. Adams's major source of concern was the unrestricted income from investments, which could be used for general operations, a meager sum of $1,500. This was not sufficient to sustain the program. Moreover, the loss of the annual $9,000 rental fee constituted a severe setback. Because of this loss, Adams said, the Society was "for the time being financially crippled."

Adams reviewed the key events which had transpired with respect to the impending move to the Fenway. The Society had voted to sell its Tremont Street building, resolved the thorny Ellis bequest issue, and arranged for the development of preliminary architectural plans for the Fenway structure. On the hoped-for sale of the Tremont Street site, Adams reported that his committee had made a vigorous effort to sell it to the city, after initially receiving a negative response. Mayor Quincy was now in favor of purchasing the property and had requested an appropriation to that end. "There the matter now rests," Adams stated. If the city did not buy the building, the Society would be in serious straits and have to consider other options, all of which were detrimental to the financial stability of the organization.

The Massachusetts Historical Society

Adams then turned to the estimates for the building and maintenance funds for the Fenway structure. These had been prepared in May 1895, before the land in the Fenway had been purchased and preliminary building plans drawn up. He had carefully reviewed the original figures "and with, I regret to say, the usual results. They do not seem to have been sufficiently liberal." He estimated the total cost of the Fenway site at $300,000, not $250,000.

How should the Society respond to this serious financial challenge? Adams suggested a strategy of undertaking the construction in phases. Initially, complete the basic structure so that the Society could use it for meetings and other essential purposes, but reserve the costly, non-functional features for the future: "Take, for instance, the entrance, the staircase, or the great hall of the proposed building. Each of these in the shape ultimately proposed is a costly ornamented structure of elaborate design, the supplying of which out of the resources of the Society would not, in my judgment, be justifiable." As the Society acquired more funds, it could undertake these improvements. "Indeed," the canny Adams asserted, ". . . pursuing this course holds out an inducement to liberality, whether posthumous or in advance of death."

If his suggestion were followed, Adams stated, the initial cost of the building could be reduced to $140,000. The Society could meet this financial obligation, especially if it sold the Tremont Street building for $200,000.

Adams foresaw greater difficulty in establishing an adequate maintenance fund. The new building would require an annual sum of $12,000 for upkeep. This figure was an absolute minimum. Adams computed all possible sources of income and projected an annual shortfall of $2,000 to $3,000. But this was not an insuperable problem to overcome, in his view.

In summarizing the Society's complex financial situation, Adams regarded the sale of the Tremont Street structure as the most critical factor in the equation. Everything hinged on this potential transaction. If there were no sale, the Society would face financial disaster.

Adams concluded with an examination of ways the Society's financial base could be strengthened. He offered no panacea. The Society must continue to rely on a "rigid economy, slow saving, and occasionally gifts and bequests." He did suggest a specific possibility for augmenting its financial resources. He encouraged his colleagues to become life members. This required a one-time payment of $150; life members were not obliged to pay annual dues. He offered Judge Ebenezer R. Hoar as an ideal model for the members. Hoar had assumed a life-membership "in a way characteristic of the man; for having paid his annual dues with regularity for over twenty years, in 1887, when he already felt that the end was not very remote, he called on the Treasurer, and stating that he did so for the benefit of the Society, he, a man making his final arrangements for this world, took out a life-membership."

The forthcoming year, Adams stated, would be a critical period in the Society's history. Major decisions would have to be made. On this basis, he recommended the continuance for one more year of the special committee appointed the previous October. This three-member body and the Council would comprise a "Joint Special Committee" and be "clothed with full power to decide and act . . . on all questions of finance or policy." The members "unanimously adopted" his recommendation.[28] In so doing, they were assuredly aware that they were providing their president with absolute authority to carry out all the changes he was seeking to effect. They knew his method of operation. Imperious in nature, Adams preferred to act independently and execute what needed to be done, and then have the committee ratify his actions. This was the Adams way.

There was one point about the new building that Adams did not mention in his address but which was known to most of the principal figures in the room. He was intending to pay "a large proportion of the total cost" of the structure. According to Robert C. Winthrop, Jr., Adams was especially interested in creating "a large hall for public meetings of the Society on special occasions, in distinction from its ordinary meetings, and desirous that this hall should be of an architecturally decorative character, he was prepared to pay for it, with the understanding it should be named the Adams Hall, and to cost about $75,000."[29]

If Adams's 1896 presidential address did not measure up to the major manifesto he had hoped to deliver, it was, nonetheless, a profoundly significant statement. He had set forth a plan of action which would have

[28] The report is in M.H.S., *Procs.*, 2d ser., 10(1895–1896):573–585.
[29] R.C. Winthrop, Jr., "Memoranda" in vol. 82, Winthrop Family Papers, M.H.S.

momentous consequences for the Society. Furthermore, he had affirmed his leadership in a most persuasive manner.

Adams had spoken with candor to the members, but he had not revealed his innermost thoughts. In the solitude of his study on the following day, he inscribed in his journal what he really believed was necessary for the future welfare of the Society:

> The meeting of the Historical Society was a very good one, and, I sincerely hope, the last which will be held in the old stone building next to the King's Chapel burying-ground on Tremont St. Nothing, I am persuaded, can be done with or for the Society so long as it continues in these quarters. It is a mere hodge-podge. Our library is neither good, nor available; our collection of objects of interest is out of sight and mind; our pictures are stowed away like lumber. The institution is, in fact, fossilized; and, to justify its existence, must undergo a thorough overhauling and revival.
>
> Yet it yesterday showed signs of vigor in a way. At the meeting just 32 members were present;—a fraction more than one third of the present active list,—and, altogether, there and at my house, I think that nearly fifty members must have put in an appearance. In the Dowse Library, those present just filled up the circle of chairs around the room, giving it a full appearance, without crowding. Those present made up a creditable representation of the existing Massachusetts order of literary men, but there is, I think, a distinct falling off in this respect. We have no-one to show of marked eminence or wide reputation, no-one who bears the stamp of fame. Justin Winsor, E.L. Pierce, J.F. Rhodes, and I do not fill the space in the public eye and mind formerly held by Holmes, Deane and Mr. Winthrop. William Everett is by no means his fathers equal, and Mr. Savage did a good deal better work in his day and line than any of our people are doing now.
>
> I was re-elected President, and, on delivering the vote, I did, what I did not do last year,—I read a paper. It was wholly devoted to the financial condition of the Society, and the question of its removal into new quarters; for, upon that issue, so far as I am concerned, everything hinges. In my judgment, it is perfectly useless now, to attempt to do anything for a Society like this without an abundance of money. The day of small things is gone. The Society has got to have a prominent, imposing habitation,—it must exhibit and make known its collections,—it must have its field days,—it must put on its ruffles and frills. It must, in a word, hold itself high. Heretofore, and under other conditions, it did its work through unpaid officials and in inadequate quarters. Charles Deane and Mr. Winthrop animated it with a certain spirit. In the future it cannot depend on this sort of support. It has outgrown that stage. It must have a building, a salaried curator and a staff

of officials. It must offer facilities for historical investigators and incite thereto; its activities must be broadened and quickened; its work systematized. It must be put at the head of all our Societies of the same character; and this is impossible without an adequate endowment. To securing that, my efforts must be directed. And to get money, it is necessary to make the need of money apparent. So, yesterday, I openly broke ground in this direction. The process must be,—our new home first; money next; reorganization last. It will, as I told the Society, call for five years of persistent effort; I did not tell the Society, that, to effect it, our present staff of officials must, during these five years, be replaced. They are fossils.[30]

Now invested with the authority to proceed, Adams vigorously pursued his plan to sell the Tremont Street property to the city. After "months of discussion and negotiation," the mayor agreed to buy the site for the stipulated sum of $200,000. However, he had one formidable difficulty: he did not have available funds for this purpose, the universal lament of all municipal officials. As Adams noted, ". . . Mayor Quincy sent for me, and frankly admitted that he could not command even the comparatively small sum of money necessary to the purchase. While, he said, all the members of the city government agreed that it should be made, yet every one of them, he also intimated, had some scheme of his own connected with his particular ward or district which in his mind had priority to it. His Honor, therefore, wished to know whether I could propose any plan under which the purchase could be made without the city in reality advancing any considerable sum of ready money towards it."[31]

The resourceful Adams could indeed propose an appropriate plan. On December 19, 1896, shortly before he was to depart for Europe for a six-month stay, he sent a confidential letter to the mayor in which he set forth his proposal stressing that "the transaction should be completed during your mayoralty." Adams bluntly noted that the major proponents of the plan were "large taxpayers of Boston," and to them the sale would "go far to putting a stop for a long time to the scheme of a new city hall." He proposed a sale of the property "at any time on a cash payment of $100,000, or $80,000, or $50,000, the remainder of the purchase money being represented by a mortgage placed upon the building before the sale, and the estate being sold subject to it." To ease the financial impact upon the city, Adams also offered that the individuals

[30] Charles F. Adams, Memorabilia, Apr. 9, 1896 (C.F. Adams Papers).
[31] M.H.S., Procs., 2d ser., 11(1896–1897):414.

"representing the Historical Society will also act in concert with the City Treasurer in securing the lowest rate of interest possible on the mortgage."[32]

Reassured by the knowledge that Adams would arrange for a short-term, low-interest loan for the bulk of the sale price, the mayor accepted his proposal in principle. He chose Adams's option of a $50,000 direct payment and a $150,000 mortgage. Then he began consultations with the aldermen, City Council, and other key municipal officials, who had to be persuaded that the purchase was a sound business deal. He was successful in this effort and was able to secure the necessary $50,000 through a $25,000 "loan appropriation" and the transfer of $25,000 from surplus revenue.[33]

Before Adams sailed for Europe, he designated Treasurer Charles C. Smith to complete the transaction with the city.[34] The Society approved Adams's action. The president also instructed Smith to keep him fully informed on this issue as well as on the plans for the new building on Boylston Street.

Smith, the "useful member," proved to be a conscientious, effective functionary and agent on the scene.[35] He skillfully conducted the negotiations with the city. On January 28, 1897, he informed Quincy that he could secure a mortgage on the building for $150,000 from the Massachusetts Hospital Life Insurance Company. The city had two options. The first provided repayment in five years with an annual interest rate of four per cent "with a gold clause." The city could repay the entire amount at one time providing thirty days' notice. The second option offered the same conditions "without the gold clause,—reserving to the city the right to pay not exceeding $25,000 on any interest day or giving 10 days' notice."[36]

---

[32] C.F. Adams to Josiah Quincy, Dec. 19, 1896 (Charles C. Smith Papers, M.H.S.).

[33] For details on this complex financial transaction, see Smith's letters to Adams, cited below.

[34] See Quincy to Smith, Jan. 26, 29, Apr. 22, 1897; Smith to Quincy, Jan. 27, 28, 30, Apr. 13, 1897 (Charles C. Smith Papers, M.H.S.).

[35] Elected a member in 1867, Smith became a major figure in the Society and served it in many capacities. He became the first salaried editor of publications in 1889 and was treasurer from 1877 to 1907. For Smith's biography, see M.H.S., *Procs.*, 51(1917–1918):345–352.

[36] C.C. Smith to C.F. Adams, Jan. 29, 1897 (C.F. Adams Papers).

Quincy selected "the latter proposition, namely, a mortgage of $150,000 payable in 5 years, with interest at four per cent per annum, without any gold clause, the city to have the right to pay not exceeding $25,000 on any interest day, on giving ten days notice." He added this significant qualification: "Of course you understand that the city does not assume the mortgage, but purchases the building subject to the mortgage arranged as above by you, you assigning to us your rights under the mortgage, as well as passing us your title to the property."

By mid-March 1897 Smith completed the complex transaction and the Society received its $200,000. As instructed, Smith sent a steady stream of reports to Adams.[37]

With the sale of its quarters, the Society became a homeless institution. The contract with the city called for a six-week, transitional period before the Society was to remove its contents and vacate the premises, but the mayor extended the deadline to "about May 1." When the deal was on the verge of completion, but before the final papers were executed, the Society appointed a three-member committee to find temporary quarters until the Fenway building was constructed.

In mid-February, the committee had arranged for the rental for two years of three unprepossessing rooms on the third floor of a large office building on the corner of Tremont and Beacon streets, diagonally across the street from the Society's former quarters.[38] The larger of the three rooms was to serve as a reference library, while the two smaller ones were to house Society publications and function as offices for those members preparing additional publications.

As a concession, the owner of the building permitted the Society free use of an adjoining room for its monthly meetings. This room was furnished and could seat fifty. The Society was to begin paying rent on April 1; the annual fee was $1,246, which included the heating cost.

After inspecting the site, Robert C. Winthrop, Jr., reported to Adams that the rooms were "a little dark as compared to the old ones, but *per contra*, we have the electric light." He was elated to discover that the

[37] C.C. Smith to C.F. Adams, Jan. 15, 29, Feb. 1, 12, 19, Mar. 9, 12, 26, 1897 (C.F. Adams Papers). See also, M.H.S., *Procs.*, 2d ser., 11(1896–1897):237–239, 268, 324.

[38] M.H.S., *Procs.*, 2d ser., 11(1896–1897):316; C.C. Smith to C.F. Adams, Feb. 19, 1897 (C.F. Adams Papers).

building had a "lift," which he hailed as "a great thing for old bones." "Altogether," he concluded, "it is a good arrangement."[39]

The committee appointed to locate temporary housing was also directed to supervise the move and storage of the Society's holdings. Cabinet-Keeper Samuel F. McCleary and Librarian Samuel A. Green were the key members of this committee, but McCleary had "principal charge" of the operation. McCleary rented space in the Metropolitan Storage Warehouse, a large facility in Cambridge, and, in short order, carted off the contents of the cabinet. He prodded Green to take similar prompt action with the library holdings, but the obstreperous librarian, who was not inclined to take direction from anyone, was reluctant to make a hasty departure from his beloved Tremont Street haunt. As Smith informed Adams, "our venerable senior member seems to cling to old associations, and to be in no hurry to leave. However, after the annual meeting . . . I think he will bestir himself."[40]

Even before the annual meeting, Green bestirred himself and began the laborious process of packing and moving. Robert C. Winthrop, Jr., notified Adams on March 23 that "Sam Green sits like Marius among the ruins of Carthage."[41] By the end of March, the quarters were nearly dismantled, with the exception of the Dowse library. This room was purposely left intact since it was to be the site of the annual meeting on April 8. This would be the last meeting of the Society at 30 Tremont Street after a residence of more than sixty-three years.

The final gathering was a powerfully nostalgic occasion and attracted an unusually large number of members.[42] In view of the historical import of the meeting, the governor of the Commonwealth, Roger Wolcott, and the chief justice of the Supreme Judicial Court, Walbridge A. Field, saw fit to attend. Both were members but rarely attended meetings because of their frenetic schedules. By custom, the annual meetings began at 11 A.M. and were followed by a lengthy luncheon in the home of a member. These were time-consuming affairs.

In addition to the customary business of an annual meeting—reports

---

[39] Winthrop to C.F. Adams, Mar. 23, 1897 (C.F. Adams Papers).

[40] C.C. Smith to C.F. Adams, Feb. 26, 1897 (C.F. Adams Papers).

[41] R.C. Winthrop, Jr., to C.F. Adams, Mar. 23, 1897 (C.F. Adams Papers).

[42] M.H.S., *Procs.*, 2d ser., 11(1896–1897):286–366. This is the full account of the meeting. See also, Edward J. Young to C.F. Adams, Apr. 9, 1897 (C.F. Adams Papers).

of officers, and the like—senior members Green and Smith delivered reminiscences to commemorate the occasion. Green focused upon the high quality of the membership, "the great and noble men who have sat around the table here, as they were wont to gather either by chance or for some special study." Society meetings, he continued, "have been dignified by the presence of members eminent in all the walks of life,—in literature, statecraft, the arts and sciences, the learned professions, business affairs, and in numerous other pursuits of a scholarly community."

Smith gave a brief account of the various quarters the Society had occupied since its founding and provided other historical data. Emphasizing the club-like character of the Society, he concluded with a "mystic chord of memory" sentiment:

> As we go hence, bearing our sheaves with us, we shall carry nothing more valued than the associations which cluster around this room. In the quiet and still air of delightful studies, here have been formed or cemented friendships, official and personal, which no differences of opinion or policy have ever ruffled. It was a pleasure never lightly to be esteemed that, however we might differ elsewhere on any subject, we could here work for common objects with Winthrop, Ellis, and Deane, with Chandler Robbins, Richard Frothingham, and George Dexter,—too early lost from our fellowship,—to name only a few of those no longer with us who were most closely identified with the purposes of the Society in the last thirty years. . . . Our founders would have rejoiced could they have seen in their day of small things this building and the literary and historical treasures crowded within its walls; and may we not confidently hope that our successors will look on results as large, or even larger? SIC VOS NON VOBIS, surrounding a hive of working bees, has been for more than sixty years the legend on our corporate seal, and for nearly forty years it has had a place on our walls. It was adopted only a few months after our predecessors held their first meeting on this spot; and as we gather here for the last time, the life which it symbolizes fills this room with gracious memories of those who have labored here. We may feel sure that it will be in the new century the inspiration of those who will then occupy the chairs we shall leave vacant.

After the meeting, the members walked up the stairs to the large room directly above the Dowse library. Formerly a library room, it had been emptied of its contents. Small tables had been set up and "an excellent collation was served."

The original plan had called for Thornton K. Lothrop to host the group in his home, but the sudden death of Lothrop's brother-in-law, Lewis Tappan of Milton, caused the change in venue. "It passed off very satisfactorily," Smith informed Adams, "and many members expressed themselves as much pleased with the arrangement."[43]

On April 16, the Society occupied its makeshift, interim quarters, and on the following day Smith delivered the keys for 30 Tremont Street to the city. The transition was now completed.[44]

[43] C.C. Smith to C.F. Adams, Apr. 9, 1897 (C.F. Adams Papers). Edward Young also rendered a positive assessment to the absentee president relaxing in Florence, Italy: "As it happened, it was a very pleasant occasion to be remembered in connection with our last meeting there." Young to Adams, Apr. 26, 1897; Smith to Quincy, Apr. 17, 1897; Quincy to Smith, Apr. 22, 1897 (Charles C. Smith Papers, M.H.S.).

[44] C.C. Smith to C.F. Adams, Apr. 26, 1897 (C.F. Adams Papers).

Chapter 9

The Return of
the Bradford Manuscript

WHILE THE SOCIETY was often preoc-
cupied with the mundane circumstances of housing its growing collections, it never lost sight of the principal goal established by Jeremy
Belknap of preserving historical resources for future generations. A key
example of this work, combining both archival and publication aspects,
is the story of the pivotal role the Society played in securing the return
of Gov. William Bradford's magisterial "History of Plymouth" from
England. Although the effort began in 1855, the action was not completed until 1897, and so the very institutional stability of the Historical
Society also played a role in the lengthy unfolding drama.

Bradford's journal, "the most precious relic of the kind in existence"
and one of the seminal writings of American history, described the
Pilgrims' life in England and Holland, their epic voyage across the Atlantic Ocean on the Mayflower, their storied landing at Plymouth in
1620, the formation of a government, and the first twenty-eight years of
the colony's existence.

The document itself had a fascinating history.[1] Governor Bradford
left the manuscript to his son William. The latter gave it to his son John.
In the seventeenth and eighteenth centuries, the Bradford family lent it
to some of the leading historians of New England, such as Nathaniel
Morton, William Hubbard, Cotton Mather, Samuel Sewall, Thomas

---

[1] For further details on the history of the Bradford manuscript, see M.H.S., *Procs.*,
3(1855–1858):19–23; 19(1881–1882):106–122; 2d ser., 7(1891–1892):53–54, 64–65, passim; Frederick H. Gillett, *George Frisbie Hoar* (Boston, 1934), ch. 13. I have relied heavily
on these sources in developing this account.

Prince, and Thomas Hutchinson, all of whom used it as a source in their writings. Prince, the historical collector *par excellence*, apparently requested and received permission from John Bradford to deposit it in his New England Library when he acquired physical custody of it in 1728. He later stored it with the rest of his "choice historical treasures" in the "steeple chamber" of the Old South Church. When he died in 1758, he willed this collection to the church. The Bradford work remained in the church tower until the 1770s.

From that point to its surprising discovery in the Fulham Palace library in 1855, the document was a lost treasure. It apparently was taken to London during the Revolution, although the exact year cannot be determined. There are two theories as to how it got there. Some authorities believe that Hutchinson borrowed it from Prince's library for research purposes and then packed it with his books and personal papers when he fled Boston in 1774. Others conjecture that it was purloined from Prince's collection in the Old South Church by a British soldier stationed there when the building was used as a riding school, and taken when the English evacuated Boston in March 1776. Lending credence to this second theory is the fact that Bradford's letterbook, which was also in the Prince library, was later found in Nova Scotia, apparently carried off by a loyalist or British soldier in 1776.

In any event, the document came to rest in the Fulham Palace library in the custody of the bishop of London, who had ecclesiastical jurisdiction over all American affairs before the Revolution. Why Fulham Palace? The bishop of London's chancellor suggested that it was deposited there because of the records attached to it of births, marriages, and deaths. Such vital statistics were always preserved in England by ecclesiastical authorities.

How long had the document been at Fulham Palace? According to the bishop of Oxford, "I should suppose for a very long period." It was stored with many uncatalogued manuscripts. While it had been seen and used by a few British antiquarians, no American historian knew of its location.

Early in 1855, while browsing in Burnham's Boston bookstore, as was his wont, John Wingate Thornton came upon the second edition of *A History of the Protestant Episcopal Church in America* (London, 1846) by Samuel Wilberforce, bishop of Oxford. In reading the work, he recognized passages similar to those contained in Prince's and Morton's writings, which the latter two had ascribed to Bradford's History. Wilberforce had cited as his source a "Ms. History of the Plantation of Plymouth, etc., in the Fulham Library." There were additional passages linked to the same source. This excited the avid antiquarian and aroused his curiosity. Could it be that Wilberforce's source was Bradford's long-lost manuscript? He believed it was.

Thornton made some notes on his discovery and gave them to his friend the Reverend John S. Barry of Roxbury, Massachusetts, an historian of modest talents, then writing the first volume of his history of Massachusetts. Barry also was excited and intrigued by the bishop of Oxford's citation. He met with Charles Deane, chairman of the Society's publishing committee, on February 17, 1855, and informed him of Thornton's discovery.[2] After reviewing the bishop of Oxford's book, Deane concurred in Thornton's and Barry's judgment and was anxious to secure a copy of the document for the *Collections*. He was then preparing selections for volume three of the fourth series, and Bradford's History would be a prize addition to the publication.

Deane took the baton from Barry.[3] On the same day he had met with the minister-historian, he wrote to the Reverend Joseph Hunter of London, vice president of the Society of Antiquaries of London and a corresponding member of the Society, with whom he had been exchanging information on historical matters. The English minister had a strong interest in the early history of the Pilgrims. Deane asked Hunter to examine the manuscript and, if it developed that it was Bradford's *History*, make a copy. He enclosed an original letter in Bradford's hand to help in the process of verification; Deane doubtless had secured this document from the Society's library. Wasting little time, he sent his communication to New York City, where it was placed on a steamer that left for England on February 21.

Hunter was a cooperative agent. Upon receiving Deane's letter, he sought the assistance of Bishop Wilberforce, since he was not personally acquainted with the Rt. Rev. Charles Blomfield, then the bishop of London. The bishop of Oxford consulted with his clerical counterpart in

---

[2] Barry also met separately with Nathaniel B. Shurtleff, another Society member.

[3] John A. Schutz asserts that "Thornton felt justly robbed of a share in the discovery and never forgave his former friend of theft." *A Noble Pursuit*, 7–8.

London and received assurances of complete cooperation. This cleared the way for Hunter. He wrote to the bishop of London, "explaining . . . what it was that the Massachusetts Historical Society had applied to me to perform for them (or rather what I was requested to do on behalf on the Society); namely to ascertain whether the Fulham manuscript were indeed Bradford's original in his own handwriting, and, more generally, what is the true nature and character of the manuscript."

Hunter further informed the bishop of his desire to secure an exact copy of the document. The bishop responded with his "accustomed promptitude" and brought the manuscript to his London home in St. James Square. He met with Hunter and told him that he "was at perfect liberty to take it home, and to make whatever extracts from it" he pleased, "or to copy the whole." The Society was free to publish any or all of the document.

Hunter made his examination, using the manuscript Deane had sent to him to verify the script. Hunter had "not the slightest doubt" that the manuscript was Bradford's *History*. The scripts of the manuscript and letter had a "sufficient degree of correspondence." Further, there was a letter from a member of the Bradford family written in 1705, which noted that the governor had given the manuscript to his son, Maj. William Bradford, who, in turn, gave it to his son, Maj. John Bradford. The clincher was a memorandum in Prince's handwriting, dated June 4, 1728, which stated that he had acquired the document from Maj. John Bradford.

The discovery of the document struck like a bombshell in the learned circles of Boston and environs. George Frisbie Hoar wrote: "I know of no incident like this in history unless it be the discovery in a chest in the castle of Edinburgh, where they had been lost for one hundred and eleven years, of the ancient regalia of Scotland, the crown of Bruce, the scepter and sword of State."

Hunter informed Deane that he would arrange for a "fair and exact" copy to be made. He knew a person who would execute it "in a scholar-like and business-like manner." He requested instructions from Deane on such technical, editorial matters as the use of contractions and orthography. Deane instructed Hunter to have an "exact copy" made "as soon as practicable" and informed him that the Society would reimburse him for his expenses. The copy was completed on July 10 and arrived in Boston on August 3, 1855.

The Return of the Bradford Manuscript

At the May 1856 meeting of the Society, Deane reported that the discovery of Bradford's document had caused an alteration of his committee's plans. The committee had published five hundred copies of a *Collections* volume, which contained the *History* and a memoir of the late Samuel Appleton, and five hundred copies of the *History* alone. Deane, who edited Bradford's account, noted that the cost of these two editions was $1,150; there was an additional charge of $257 for the copy made in London.

Acting upon a motion from Deane, the Society voted to provide complimentary copies of the scholarly landmark to the Fulham Palace library, the bishop of London, and the bishop of Oxford in appreciation for their cooperative efforts.[4] Later, the Society also sent a courtesy copy to Hunter. The Reverend Mr. Barry had received his payoff in November 1855, when the Society elected him a resident member.[5]

The Society did not remain satisfied with its publication of Bradford's *History*, the first such printing in American history. Now, it turned its attention to having the manuscript restored to Massachusetts, its rightful home. Some of the members, particularly Robert C. Winthrop, Justin Winsor, and Hoar, became obsessed by this issue. The question they faced was: How could it be achieved?

In 1858, an English minister lent his support to the Society's cause in an indirect manner. The Reverend John Waddington made an address, "An Evening with the Pilgrims," to a group in Southwark. He borrowed the Bradford manuscript and took it to the meeting. Showing it to his audience, he remarked: "So far as we know, not a person now living in the lands of the Pilgrims has ever seen this manuscript. It has been kept at Fulham among the papers of no use to the See. It is not in the catalogue of the library, and probably is not included in any inventory of the property. No one can tell how it came to Fulham." He urged that it be returned to the United States. If Waddington's words made an impact, it was confined to those in his audience. Nothing developed from his remarks.

In 1860, President Winthrop, learning of the impending visit of the Prince of Wales to the United States and Boston, conceived a scheme which, he hoped, would lead to the return of Bradford's *History*. Work-

---

[4] M.H.S., *Procs.*, 3(1855–1858):90–92, 98.
[5] M.H.S., *Procs.*, 3(1855–1858):44.

ing through an English friend, John Sinclair, archdeacon of Middlesex, Winthrop brought the question of returning the manuscript to Massachusetts to the attention of the bishop of London: "It was urged that the sanction of the Queen would be ample authority for the transfer, and that it would be a conciliatory act if the Prince of Wales were to take it across the Atlantic and present it to the people of Massachusetts." Sir Fitzroy Kelly, the attorney general of England, gave tacit approval to this plan, which had a powerful public relations value: "It would be an exceptionable act of grace on a most interesting occasion, and I heartily wish success in the application."

Archibald Tait, the new bishop of London, however, was not enamored with public relations. He took a legalistic position. "The difficulty," he informed Winthrop, "of alienating property of this kind could, I believe, only be got over by an Act of Parliament." With all of his British contacts, Winthrop could not secure this legislation. He was stymied.

During the Civil War, Winthrop and his colleagues were preoccupied by more pressing matters. After the war, they renewed their interest in the Bradford manuscript. Deane traveled to London in 1866 and made two visits to Fulham Palace. The first was to a garden party sponsored by the bishop of London. Because of this social event Deane only had time to glance at the Bradford manuscript. He arranged a second visit. On this occasion, he examined the document for four hours, "sitting in the same room with a number of young candidates for the ministry who had come to be examined by the Bishop." He made a number of exciting discoveries. He found in the volume a fly-leaf inscription in Prince's hand. He also uncovered two other volumes of manuscripts which had been taken from Prince's library; both contained Prince's book-plates. He also collated Bradford's *History* with the Society's printed version. A few weeks later, Samuel F. Haven, another member of the Historical Society, also visited the Fulham library and inspected the manuscript.

Early in 1869, the American government appointed John Lothrop Motley minister to the Court of St. James.[6] Prior to leaving for London, Motley met with Justin Winsor, then serving as librarian of the Boston Public Library. The library had acquired title to Thomas Prince's holdings from the Old South Church, and Winsor was intent upon restoring

---

[6] Motley had been a member of the Historical Society since 1856.

The Return of the Bradford Manuscript

Bradford's historical jewel to this collection. He laid out a strategic plan for Motley.

In the 1860s, an Englishman traveling in the United States had uncovered in the Library Company of Philadelphia, a repository founded by Benjamin Franklin, some "valuable and ancient" official Irish letterbooks dating from the reigns of Queen Elizabeth and King James I. Upon being informed of these documents, the proprietors of the library willingly and graciously returned them to the master of the rolls in London. Subsequently, the proprietors discovered and returned another significant document, belonging to the earlier set, which had been inadvertently overlooked. This 1614 document, signed by King James I, instructed Sir Arthur Chichester, the lord deputy of Ireland, to pacify the country and do all in his power to lessen the influence of the Catholic church, especially "those ffyer-brands the Jesuits," who were "the chiefe Corrupters of the Nobillitie and Gentrye."[7] Winsor believed that the English "could well reciprocate the courtesy and restore to the Prince Library, then in my custody, this Bradford manuscript."

Motley "eagerly seized the idea" and promised to exercise his influence with the appropriate English officials. When he reached London, he discussed the issue with the bishop of London and the law officer of the Crown. Both officials affirmed that an act of reciprocity was out of the question. What was needed was the passage of an act of Parliament.

Motley informed Winsor of this negative response and pointed out that such an act was not likely to pass under a government headed by Disraeli, then in power. Motley proposed a delay until the Disraeli government was replaced by the liberals, which appeared imminent. Before Disraeli left the scene, Motley did. He was recalled, and another hiatus developed.

Winsor was disappointed but not defeated. In October 1877, the librarian-scholar traveled to London and conferred with Canon Milman of St. Paul's Church. The canon advised him to make a direct appeal to the Rt. Rev. John Jackson, the new bishop of London, and composed a

---

[7] This manuscript was part of the Irish archives Henry Cox inherited from his grandfather, Sir Richard Cox, lord chancellor of Ireland, in 1703–1707. He gave it to the Philadelphia library in March 1799. See Edwin Wolf and Marie Elena Korey, eds., *Quarter of a Millennium: The Library Company of Philadelphia 1731–1981* (Philadelphia, 1981), 86–87.

letter of introduction.[8] Winsor made the short trip to Fulham Palace but the bishop was away. He left his letter of introduction and requested to see the Bradford volume. The bishop's steward took him "into the library, and, opening a cupboard in one of the cases, I saw the familiar binding of our Collections on a volume standing beside a parchment-bound book, which proved to be the Bradford manuscript." Winsor was deeply moved by the experience.

When Bishop Jackson returned, he wrote Winsor a gracious letter, expressing sorrow over his absence and inviting him to his office for a conference. Winsor was then preparing to leave London for home and could not honor his invitation. Aware of Winsor's purpose for seeing him, the bishop later wrote the Bostonian and underscored the reason why he could not give him the Bradford document.

> I have always regretted that I was not at home when you visited Fulham in 1877. I am not sure that it is sufficiently understood that the bishops of London are not the owners of the Bradford manuscript and many other documents of interest and value, and that they have no power of alien-ation. All these, like its library, the portraits and the furniture of the Chapel, belong to the See. The bishop for the time being is but the cus-todian; and if at his death any of the deposits were found missing, his representatives would be liable to be sued for damages.[9]

Winsor returned to London in 1891 and made another journey to Fulham Palace. He again failed to see the bishop[10] but had a second look at the manuscript. "When I noticed the tender care with which the precious memorial was treated," he wrote, "I came away with a growing conviction that it was unwise to attempt any further measures for its recovery."[11]

A decade earlier, when President James Garfield was assassinated and there was considerable sympathy for the United States in Great Britain, Benjamin Scott, the chamberlain of London, considered it an opportune time to recommend in the "public prints" the return of the Bradford manuscript "as a fitting evidence of that sympathy." At this time, the

---

[8] Jackson became the bishop of London in 1868 and served in that post until his death in 1885.

[9] M.H.S., *Procs.*, 2d ser., 6(1896–1897):302.

[10] Frederick Temple had succeeded Jackson in 1885 and served until 1897.

[11] Deane reached a similar conclusion. See M.H.S., *Procs.*, 2d ser., 7(1891–1892):53.

The Return of the Bradford Manuscript

British government had restored to France the will of Napoleon I, which had been on deposit at Canterbury. Subsequently, Parliament passed an act sustaining the action of the archbishop of Canterbury in making the transfer. Thus, there was precedent for an alienation of diocesan property, but Scott's appeal went for naught.

The issue finally reached its denouement in 1896. In that year, Society member Hoar, then a United States senator, decided to try his hand.[12] That previous December 21, Hoar had delivered at Plymouth the main oration at the celebration of the two hundred seventy-fifth anniversary of the landing of the Pilgrims "upon the rock." In preparation for this address, he had "read carefully, with renewed enthusiasm and delight, the noble and touching story as told by Governor Bradford." He doubtless used the volume published by the Society. "I declared then," wrote Hoar, "that this precious history ought to be in no other custody than that of their children."

At the October 16 meeting of the Society, Hoar announced to the members that he was going to England to renew the appeal to the bishop of London. Undeterred by a "slight paralysis in the face, which affected the muscles of the lower lid of one of my eyes, causing a constant irritation in the organ itself," he departed for England. "The desire to get it back," he wrote, "grew and grew during the voyage across the Atlantic." He laid plans to travel to Lincolnshire and Yorkshire where the three principal Pilgrim leaders, Bradford, William Brewster, and John Robinson, had resided and established their first church. He also intended to see Bradford's document, "which then seemed to me the most precious manuscript on earth unless we could recover one of the four Gospels as it came in the beginning from the pen of the Evangelist."

Arriving in London, he met with a friend, John Morley, the statesman and author, and sought his advice on how he should proceed. Morley, an honorary member of the Society, had no specific suggestion but pledged his help. Hoar also sought and received the support of American ambassador Thomas A. Bayard. Because of an emergency involving his traveling companion, Hoar had to make a hasty departure to the continent. This upset his plans to recover the Bradford document.

[12] For Hoar's involvement in this episode, see George F. Hoar, *Autobiography of Seventy Years*, 2 vols. (New York, 1903), 2:234–241; Gillett, *Hoar*, ch. 13; M.H.S., *Procs.*, 2d ser., 12(1897–1899):59–60.

The Massachusetts Historical Society

Hoar returned to London a few days before he was to leave for home. He decided to go to Fulham Palace, unannounced, confront Bishop Temple, and view the manuscript. The bishop was away. When he inquired about seeing the document, an attendant informed him that the library was a private repository and no one could examine its contents without securing permission from the bishop. Hoar was deeply disappointed.

Shortly before he was scheduled to depart for Massachusetts, Hoar dined with Moreton Frewen, "an accomplished English gentleman" who was well known in the United States and a gracious host to American visitors to London. As Hoar was leaving his home that evening, Frewen asked his guest if he could assist him in any way. Hoar inquired if Frewen knew Bishop Temple and explained his "great longing to see the Bradford Manuscript before I go home."

Frewen replied that he did not know the bishop but was acquainted with his nephew by marriage. He would do his best to arrange a letter of introduction for Hoar and a meeting with the bishop. Frewen worked out the arrangements in short order and the bishop notified Hoar that he would be pleased to meet with him and show him the "log of the Mayflower," as he called it.

When Hoar entered the bishop's chambers, he saw the cleric with the volume in hand. The bishop invited him to examine it. "I took the precious manuscript in my hands," Hoar later wrote, "and examined it with an almost religious reverence."

After glancing through the volume and reading the records on the flyleaf, Hoar said:

> My Lord, I am going to say something which you may think rather audacious. I think this book ought to go back to Massachusetts. Nobody knows how it got over here. Some people think it was carried off by Governor Hutchinson, the Tory Governor; other people think it was carried off by British soldiers when Boston was evacuated; but in either case the property would not have changed. Or, if you treat it as booty, in which last case, I suppose, by the law of nations ordinary property does change, no civilized nation in modern times applies that principle to the property of libraries and institutions of learning.

Bishop Temple replied: "I did not know you cared anything about it."
Hoar responded: "Why, if there were in existence in England a history of King Alfred's reign for thirty years, written by his own hand, it

would not be more precious in the eyes of Englishmen than this manuscript is to us."

The bishop then spoke words which must have aroused excitement in
Hoar:

> Well, I think myself that it ought to go back, and if it depended on me it
> would have gone back before this. But many of the Americans who have
> been here have been commercial people, and did not seem to care much
> about it except as a curiosity. I suppose I ought not to give it up on my own
> authority. It belongs to me in my official capacity, and not as private or
> personal property. I think I ought to consult the Archbishop of Canter-
> bury. And, indeed, I think I ought to speak to the Queen about it. We
> should not do such a thing behind Her Majesty's back.

"Very well," Hoar concluded, "when I go home I will have a proper
application made from some of our literary societies, and ask you to give
it consideration."

When Hoar returned home, he notified the Massachusetts Historical
Society, American Antiquarian Society, Pilgrim Society of Plymouth,
and the New England Society of New York of his plan to file a petition.
All of the societies formed committees to assist Hoar. The senator also
apprised Gov. Roger Wolcott of his plan.

Hoar developed the petition and dispatched it to Bayard, who delivered
it to the bishop.[13] Things moved quickly from that point. The consistory
court held a formal hearing on the petition on March 25, 1897, and voted
to return the manuscript not to the Commonwealth of Massachusetts or
the Boston Public Library but "to the keeping of the United States." The
chancellor of the court committed the book "to his Excellency, the American Ambassador, for safe transmission to the President and Senate of the
United States, upon such conditions and security as the Court may determine." Queen Victoria "gave the plan her cordial approval."

Precisely how the petition came to be approved is shrouded in mystery. Hoar knew that he had activated the process, but he never clearly
understood what had transpired subsequently in the higher councils of
the religious establishment. Possibly the approval was assisted by a
fortuitous changing of the ecclesiastical guard at a critical time and the
placement of sympathetic officials in key positions. Bishop Temple was
elevated to the prestigious station of archbishop of Canterbury, the

[13] A printed copy of Hoar's petition, dated Nov. 18, 1896, is in the M.H.S. Archives.

primate of all England. His successor as bishop of London was the Reverend Dr. Mandell Creighton, who had served as delegate of Emmanuel College, John Harvard's college, to Harvard University's two hundred fiftieth anniversary in 1886. He had received an honorary degree from Harvard and been a guest of President Eliot, a member of the Society. He had hosted Eliot when he later visited England. Bishop Creighton was also an honorary member of the Massachusetts Historical Society!

The decision of the consistory court was bittersweet news for Justin Winsor, now serving as librarian of Harvard University. He welcomed the return of the manuscript to the United States but not to the federal government in Washington. While no longer the librarian of the Boston Public Library, he believed that the document should be restored to the Prince collection. Another "fit place of deposit" was the registry of deeds at Plymouth because all of the original Plymouth Colony records were stored there. He knew "from personal experience how poor a place the Library of Congress was, when one wanted to find a document."[14]

Winsor's fears proved to be unwarranted. Hoar also was vehemently opposed to housing the volume in Washington. However, he did not favor depositing it in the Boston Public Library, either. He regarded it as Massachusetts property. Therefore, the commonwealth should retain legal title to it.

And so it came to pass. An arrangement was worked out between Bayard and Hoar, and the English ecclesiastical officials, whereby the bishop of London delivered the document to Bayard, now no longer ambassador, and he, in turn, placed it in the hands of Governor Wolcott when he returned to Boston.

Wolcott appeared at the Society's May 13 meeting and conveyed the happy news to his overjoyed fellow members. Thus, after more than forty years of effort, the struggle came to an end. After an absence of about 125 years, Bradford's "precious memorial" returned to Massachusetts.

On May 26, 1897, the delegates to the General Court and an assembly of citizens, which included many members of the Society, gathered in the state house and, in an emotional ceremony, Bayard formally pre-

---

[14] See Edward Young to C.F. Adams, Apr. 9, 1897 (C.F. Adams Papers).

sented the treasured document to the governor. Bayard, Wolcott, and Hoar delivered addresses which were suffused with sentiments of ancestral self-congratulations. Wolcott expressed the spirit of the occasion in these words:

> ... the story of the departure of this precious work from our shores may never in every detail be revealed; but the story of its return will be read of all men, and will become a part of the history of the Commonwealth. There are places and objects so intimately associated with the world's greatest men or with mighty deeds that the soul of him who gazes upon them is lost in a sense of reverent awe, as it listens to the voice that speaks from the past, in words like those which came from the burning bush, "Put off they shoes from off thy feet, for the place whereon thou standest is holy ground."
>
> The story here told is one of triumphant achievement, and not of defeat. As the official representative of the Commonwealth, I receive it, sir, at your hands. I pledge the faith of the Commonwealth that for all time it shall be guarded in accordance with the terms of the decree under which it is delivered into her possession as one of her chiefest treasures. I express the thanks of the Commonwealth for the priceless gift, and I venture to prophecy that for countless years to come and to untold thousands these mute pages shall eloquently speak of high resolve, great suffering and heroic endurance made possible by an absolute faith in the over-ruling providence of Almighty God.

The bishop of London had given the governor the authority to deposit the document either at the state house or with the Massachusetts Historical Society. Hoar advised the governor to place it in the state house. He explained his reasoning, as follows: "It seemed to him and to me that the Commonwealth, which is made up of the Colony which Bradford founded, and of which he was Governor, blended with that founded by the Puritans under Winthrop, was the fitting custodian of the manuscript which contains the original record of the life in Leyden of the founders of Plymouth, of the voyage across the sea, and of the first thirty years of the Colony here." Administrative responsibility for the manuscript was conferred upon the state library.

The document was placed on permanent exhibition in Bulfinch's beautiful building. Some years later, Hoar, the hero of the restoration, remarked that Bradford's *History* was "open at the page which contains the compact made on board the *Mayflower*, the first written constitution in history. Many visitors gaze upon it every year. Few of them look upon it without a trembling of the lip and a gathering of mist in the eye."

In the summer of 1897, learning that President Charles F. Adams was traveling to Europe and planned to visit England, Governor Wolcott entrusted him with the engrossed copy of the state legislature resolve, thanking Bishop Creighton for his cooperation in the return of Bradford's manuscript. On October 4, Adams met the bishop at Fulham Palace and presented the parchment to him. It was an exceptionally pleasant meeting for Adams since Creighton had been a corresponding member for a decade.

At the December 1897 meeting of the Society, Adams announced the death of honorary member James Hammond Trumbull of Connecticut that past August. Trumbull's death created an opening in the honorary member category; the maximum number of honorary members was ten. Adams reported that he had been instructed by the Council to transfer Creighton's name from the corresponding to the honorary list: "It is to the Bishop of London that we owe the return of the Bradford Manuscript, for had he been even passive in the matter no action would have been taken." Adams concluded: "through his resourceful intervention after more than a century of loss, her Book of Genesis was restored to Massachusetts."[15]

---

[15] M.H.S., *Procs.*, 2d ser., 12(1897–1899):59–60. The Society published a two-volume edition of Bradford's *History of Plymouth Plantation, 1620–1647* in 1912. A prefatory note provides information on the four editions produced in earlier years.

Chapter 10

The Move
to Boylston Street

WHILE THE SOCIETY was in the process of negotiating the sale of its Tremont Street quarters and acquiring and setting up its temporary home in the Tremont Building, Wheelwright began to draft preliminary plans for the Boylston Street structure. Periodically, he sent these "purely tentative and experimental" drawings to a general building committee, established in October 1895 with fourteen members including the president, Council, and three members-at-large. Since these were only fragmentary plans, the committee did not hold a formal meeting to review them.

In January 1897, however, Wheelwright forwarded a complete set of plans that differed from the segments sent earlier. He did not submit cost estimates.[1] Despite the continued absence of President Adams in Europe, this time the committee felt obliged to review the architect's offering, and its judgment was "not altogether favorable." The members found "great fault" with Wheelwright's design on two general counts. First, they were alarmed by the grandeur and scale of the building. They regarded it as too imposing and likely to be prohibitive in cost. They were doubtful that the Society would have sufficient funds to construct the edifice, much less furnish and operate it.[2]

The committee also took exception to the design of some key ele-

---

[1] Wheelwright enclosed a bill for $1,500. The Council "expressed much surprise" at this charge since it had paid him a $1,500 advance earlier. It sent the bill to Adams in Italy for his approval.

[2] C.C. Smith to C.F. Adams, Feb. 19, 1897; and R.C. Winthrop, Jr., to C.F. Adams, Feb. 19, 1897 (C.F. Adams Papers).

ments of the building, particularly the "monumental stairway" dominating the interior of the structure. It affirmed that Wheelwright, while "a man of undoubted talent, seemed to look at the whole matter from an ornamental and architectural point of view, with little regard to the convenience or requirements of the Society."[3] In Treasurer Charles C. Smith's judgment, "convenience had been sacrificed to architectural effect."[4] Function had become subservient to form, a familiar refrain in client-architect relations.

Robert C. Winthrop, Jr., one of the three at-large committee members and a powerfully influential figure in the Society, was the most vocal critic of Wheelwright's design. While believing that "all architects are more or less disappointing," Winthrop had a particularly low opinion of Wheelwright.[5] As he informed Adams on March 22, 1899, Winthrop

> contracted a prejudice against him at the very outset, when he pressed upon me (and probably upon others) the desirability of decorating the new building with the emblazoned escutcheons of early New England families! Whatever misfortunes may be in store for the Mass. Hist. Soc. I devoutly trust we may never fall victims to the genealogical & heraldic craze which pervades the country with increasing severity. Not only did the proposal seem to me a *Snobbish* one, but on drawing Wheelwright out a little, I thought I discovered that he knows little of the period outside of his own family and was ignorant that the descent of many of the most distinguished of the fathers of N.E. can not be traced back with any certainty, and that the right of their descendants to armorial bearing is, to say the least, problematical.[6]

[3] R.C. Winthrop, Jr., "Memoranda," in vol. 82, Winthrop Papers, M.H.S.

[4] C.C. Smith to C.F. Adams, Feb. 19, 1897 (C.F. Adams Papers).

[5] Winthrop to C.F. Adams, Mar. 23, 1897 (C.F. Adams Papers). Winthrop adhered to Ambrose Bierce's definition of an architect: "One who drafts a plan of your house, and plans a draft of your money." Ambrose Bierce, *The Enlarged Devil's Dictionary*, comp. and ed. Ernest J. Hopkins (Garden City, N.Y., 1967), 16. At the completion of the Boylston Street building, the Society decided to make alterations in some of the rooms. This required the services of an architect. Adams asked Winthrop to chair a special committee to oversee the project. Winthrop agreed to take on the job but wished to select Clipston Sturgis as the architect, not Wheelwright. In a direct slap at Wheelwright, Winthrop wrote that Sturgis was "neither conceited, obstinate, nor extravagant." Winthrop to Adams, Mar. 17, 1899 (C.F. Adams Papers).

[6] Winthrop to Adams, Mar. 22, 1899 (C.F. Adams Papers). On Aug. 16, Winthrop wrote to T. Frank Waters: "In the case of the Mass. Hist. Soc. I was one of those who succeeded in defeating a wish of the architect to introduce heraldry decoration into our new building

The Move to Boylston Street

Winthrop was convinced that, in designing the interior, Wheelwright "considered his own reputation rather than our comfort."[7] He underscored one "radical defect" of the architect's overall design: the "utter separation of the working force" of the Society. All of the units—publications, library, and the cabinet—were physically separated. Winthrop firmly believed that they should be "within easy distance of one another *on the same floor*."[8]

In a lengthy letter to Adams, Winthrop detailed the negative features of Wheelwright's conception. The Dowse library was double the size of the two earlier Dowse libraries on Tremont Street: "Many of us regard it as a *point of honor* to reproduce the old room, as well as a matter of sentiment." The general library room, which was to be named the "Ellis Library," should be designed as a portrait gallery and meeting hall. It should not be used to house Ellis's books, which, unlike Dowse's collection, were "neither rare nor curious." Moreover, the Society already had discarded many of these works since they were duplicates. The proposed newspaper room was far too small for the Society's holdings. The catalogue room had sufficient space but had a "very inconvenient shape." The editor's room was badly positioned; it was far removed from the librarian and the clerks. The cabinet-keeper's room was not carefully thought out and should be located in another area.

Winthrop was particularly displeased by Wheelwright's excessive use of "curves" in his design. In Winthrop's judgment, "rectangular rooms are much more convenient for the purposes of a learned Society." The architect had proposed semi-circular halls and a grand stairway, two

---

on the Fenway, tho' I daresay some members would have liked it." Miscellaneous Mss. "W," American Antiquarian Society.

In early 1899, there was a movement afoot to nominate Wheelwright for membership in the Society. Adams was among those who favored his candidacy. Winthrop was vehemently opposed to his nomination. He apparently persuaded Adams to hold off from presenting his name in nomination "until another year." Adams relented and said that it could be put off "for a long time to come." Winthrop to Adams, Mar. 17, 22, 1899 (C.F. Adams Papers). Wheelwright never did achieve membership.

[7] Winthrop to Adams, Mar. 17, 1899 (C.F. Adams Papers).

[8] Winthrop to Adams, Jan. 31, 1897 (C.F. Adams Papers). Not too surprisingly, Winthrop's ideas on the interior design of a new Society headquarters mirrored those of his late father.

wholly circular rooms, two with semi-circular ends, and a semi-circular catalogue room.[9]

When Adams was in the process of selling the Tremont Street property and laying plans for a new structure, Winthrop communicated his views on its interior design to the president. Adams had assured Winthrop that he was in "hearty sympathy" with his thoughts, but "he wished to provide, in addition, a large hall for public meetings of the Society on special occasions, in distinction from its ordinary monthly meetings, and desirous that this hall should be of an architecturally decorative character, he was prepared to pay for it, with the understanding it should be named the Adams Hall, and to cost about $75,000."

Because of a sudden reversal in his financial affairs, Adams could not carry out his plan for the room honoring his family. As Winthrop wrote: "As ill luck would have it, an unexpected and very serious shrinkage of investments defeated the generous purposes of President Adams."[10]

Winthrop informed Adams that the committee did not wish to make any binding decisions until he returned from Europe. At that time, the Society should appoint a five-member subcommittee, including Adams, and invest it with the authority to administer the project. He had no confidence in the general committee, regarding it as "unwieldy."

In Winthrop's opinion, the close involvement of Adams in the affairs of the Society was critical at this juncture. "The main thing is for you to preside over our destinies until we are fairly established in our new home, early in the next century, and as much longer as you may be willing to serve. Without you we should go to pieces."

Winthrop also believed that the Society must exercise fiscal responsibility since its funds were limited: "The gist of the whole matter is this. If you or any other benefactor of the Society, saw fit to make us a present of a building, we should not look a gift-horse in the mouth. We should gratefully accept it and try to make the best of it. If, however, we are to build with our own money, we must be governed by considerations of prudence and utility."[11]

When confronted with the committee's criticisms, and especially Winthrop's, Wheelwright agreed to review the project and revise his

[9] Winthrop to Adams, Feb. 19, 1897 (C.F. Adams Papers).
[10] R.C. Winthrop, Jr., "Memoranda," in vol. 82, Winthrop Papers, M.H.S.
[11] Winthrop to Adams, Feb. 19, 1897 (C.F. Adams Papers).

plans. He accepted most of the proposed changes but was adamant on retaining the "curves." He deemed this design necessary due to the "very peculiar shape" of the lot.

Writing from Italy, Adams authorized Wheelwright to continue his work but also instructed him to consider the critical comments of the general committee. On April 8, the architect notified the Society that he could produce a building, with the third story "left in the rough," at a price of $146,634. Smith reported to Adams on April 9 that he was confident the committee could reduce the cost below Wheelwright's new figure "and require a larger part of the building to be finished for the price they will be willing to appropriate." He was also certain that it could persuade Wheelwright to reduce the size of the Dowse library.[12]

Smith proved to be overly optimistic. The committee met in late April and wrestled with the revised plans. It remained concerned about the projected cost. After a lengthy discussion, it decided to postpone action and await the return of Adams the following month.

When Adams returned in late May, there was an immediate burst of activity. The Society appointed the sub-committee Winthrop had recommended, but it consisted of three, not five, members. Adams was the key figure. The committee was given the authority to approve contracts and supervise construction.[13]

Wheelwright "prepared and perfected" a new set of plans, calling for an expenditure of $117,310. This was below the maximum figure of $120,000 set by Adams's committee. Acting on the sub-committee's recommendation, the Society approved Wheelwright's revised plan. All contracts were drawn up and signed by July 8, 1897.[14] Construction could now begin. The long-held dream was on the verge of realization.

[12] C.C. Smith to C.F. Adams, Apr. 9, 1897 (C.F. Adams Papers).

[13] Winthrop had presented the motion for the sub-committee on July 8, 1897. "In offering this motion," wrote Winthrop, "I explained that while the Sub-Committee would obviously be allowed much latitude in matters of detail, yet if disagreement arose or materials changes in the plans should seem desirable, such questions should be referred back to the General Committee. In point of fact, nothing was ever referred back with the exception of the ten years' lease to the American Academy, nor was any meeting of the General Committee summoned after July 1897." R.C. Winthrop, Jr., "Memoranda," in vol. 82, Winthrop Papers, M.H.S.

[14] M.H.S. Council Records, July 8, 1897 (M.H.S. Archives); M.H.S., Procs., 2d ser., 11(1896–1897):450.

The Massachusetts Historical Society

When the Society gathered for the December meeting in its makeshift quarters, the members gazed upon an unusually pensive, somber, and contrite Adams. He bemoaned the exchange of their Tremont Street quarters "with its cheerful afternoon outlook, towards the western sky, over the King's Chapel burying-ground" for temporary lodgings which were "distinctly unaesthetic, and in no way suggestive of literature and research." At the last meeting in the old building, Adams confessed that

> if while on that occasion I mechanically went through the form of presiding, the room seemed to be peopled with ghostly shades of the past,—Winthrop and Deane and Frothingham, Holmes, Lowell, Parkman, Ellis, and Hoar,—gazing down upon me with fixed and stony eyes, which seemed to say,—"Why hast thou done this thing?" And it was true,—I, even I, had done it! Conscience does make cowards of us all; and so, in my case, too, the native hue of resolution was then and there sicklied o'er with the pale cast of thought, and, in hesitation and doubt, I asked myself,—After all, was it wise, was it necessary? And so, at once, instinctively, involuntarily, I found myself thrown on the defensive, and in apologetic tone carefully explaining to the Society why and wherefore all this had to be thus. In my own eyes a degenerate descendant,—on that dreary day amid these more dreary surroundings, another Esau, I seemed to have sold the Society's inestimable birthright for what in comparison with it was a mere mess of pottage.[15]

On a more positive note, Adams went on to review the developments that had taken place from the sale of the Tremont Street quarters to the present, and reported on the ongoing construction of the new building. There was conspicuous progress. The walls were "rapidly rising." They were complete to the windows of the third floor. If the weather held up, the contractor was hopeful of completing the outer walls and having the building "covered in" by the turn of the year.

Adams reaffirmed his long-held view that the "location and outlook" of the new structure were "the best that Boston affords." He was also confident that the building would be an architectural success. Within a period of months, he stated, "the Society will find itself fairly domiciled in its future abiding-place." Its "homeless wandering" was nearing an end.[16]

Because of Adams's displeasure with the temporary site, there were no more meetings at the Tremont Building. All but one of the subse-

[15] M.H.S., *Procs.*, 2d ser., 12(1897–1899):56–57.
[16] M.H.S., *Procs.*, 2d ser., 12(1897–1899):55–59.

quent gatherings were held in the Boston Athenaeum in the room rented by the American Academy for the Arts and Sciences; William S. Appleton hosted a meeting in his spacious Beacon Street home.

Not even the Academy's quarters could elevate Adams's spirits. After attending the October 1898 meeting there, he wrote in his journal:

> Yesterday was held the October meeting of the Historical Society,—in that dreary, sunless tomb of the American Academy, on Beacon St., in the Athenaeum Building. I can't endure these Historical Society meetings as now held; they depress me,—take the life out of me. With my love of sunshine and cheerfulness, these sombre holes chill and dishearten. So it was yesterday. It was rather an important meeting for me, but I felt my whole force ooze out as I went into that shadow of autumnal New England.[17]

The American Academy officials shared Adams's distaste for their "dreary sunless tomb." They were also anxious to locate in a different site. They selected the Society's proposed new home on Boylston Street. Committees from both organizations entered into negotiations late in 1897 and, in early 1898, concluded an agreement whereby the Historical Society agreed to lease for ten years "suitable rooms" on the third floor for the Academy's library and reading rooms, and to allow it the use of Ellis Hall for meetings. The rental price agreed upon was equivalent to the fee the Academy had been paying the Athenaeum.[18]

Adams's hopes for a rigid construction schedule did not materialize. The walls and roof were not completed by January 1898. A subcontractor made a mistake and sent machine-cut instead of hand-cut stone, which caused a delay. Also, "variable" weather in December made it impossible to lay brick further impeding the project.[19]

There was steady progress, however, through the remainder of the year. By the end of 1898, the building had begun to take shape. It was "of excellent proportions, sober, dignified, and simple,—a building altogether suitable in appearance to the serious character of the Societies

[17] C.F. Adams, Memorabilia, Oct. 14, 1898 (C.F. Adams Papers). A modern commentator, the noted poet David McCord, described the Boston Athenaeum in these words: "No other Boston institution has anything like its unique, endearing and enduring atmosphere. It combines the best elements of the Bodleian, Monticello, the frigate *Constitution*, a greenhouse, and an old New England sitting-room." Quoted in *Change and Continuity: A Pictorial History of the Boston Athenaeum* (Boston, 1976), preface, 5.

[18] M.H.S. Council Records, Mar. 10, 1898 (M.H.S. Archives).

[19] M.H.S., *Procs.*, 2d ser., 12(1897–1899):174.

that are to occupy it." It stood majestically alone, overlooking the Muddy River and acres of vacant building lots.

This physical isolation concerned Adams. He was fearful that the architectural splendor of the structure would be diminished if adjoining buildings, soon to be constructed, were of inferior design and quality. In 1902, they were constructed, and the results were pleasing to Adams. He wrote to Wheelwright:

> I am impelled to enquire whether you have recently been down to look at the Historical Society building, and its architectural effect, now that the edifices on both sides of it have been completed. If not, I pray you to do so.
>
> In my judgment, the result is one of the happiest undesigned architectural effects to be seen in Boston, or, indeed, anywhere else. When I saw the building on Boylston Road going up, I trembled for the results, feeling, in a certain degree, responsible. The front wall is now completed, and the balustrade put on. The result quite surpasses any expectation I should have dared to entertain. The fact is, the buildings on either side, contrary to what I feared, prove a frame, as it were, and an almost perfect foil to our building. Neither of them is so good in architecture; but they are sufficiently harmonious, and their defects set out the severe simplicity of the Historical Society Building.
>
> I feel greatly relieved, and, I may say, quite enthusiastic on the subject.[20]

[20] Charles F. Adams to Edmund M. Wheelwright, June 6, 1902 (Wheelwright Family Papers, M.H.S.). The next-door neighbor on The Fenway was the Boston Medical Library; its building was completed in 1901. The abutting neighbor on Boylston Street was the Carlton Hotel, which was designed as a luxury hotel. Lyman H. Butterfield has described its architectural style as "Back Bay rococo." It had 200 rooms with 100 bath rooms; suites of one, two, and three rooms, each of which had a bath and "long distance telephone"; a barber shop; a "gentlemen's den and smoking room, the last two furnished in the heavy Dutch style"; a ladies' and gentlemen's writing room; a billiard room and ping pong room. In 1913, the hotel acquired a new and "admittedly improbable" name, The Fritz-Carlton; its proprietress was Mina F. Fritz. As Butterfield wrote: "It survived thus through the '20s, splendidly indifferent to but not readily confused with The Ritz-Carlton downtown (built in 1926), and achieved notoriety among undergraduates in the Boston area as a place where something called gin could be bought with no questions asked." The hotel became The Bostonian in 1943 and, in 1965–1966, was purchased and rehabilitated as the Berklee School (now College) of Music. See: *Boston Sunday Journal*, May 4, 1902; Lyman H. Butterfield, "Worthington Chauncey Ford, Editor," M.H.S., *Procs.*, 83(1971): 53, n.15. Other monumental structures soon appeared in the Fenway: Horticultural Hall and the New England Conservatory of Music in 1901; Simmons College in 1902; and the Isabella Stewart Gardner Museum in 1903. Symphony Hall had been built in 1897.

The Move to Boylston Street

Confident that the structure would soon be fully operational, Adams arranged to have the Society extend an invitation to the American Historical Association, which was to hold its annual meeting in Boston in December 1899, to schedule some of its sessions at its property.[21] Adams also intended to host a luncheon at the Society for the delegates, an invitation motivated by his desire to show off the new facility to the leading historians in the nation. For him, the building was a physical reaffirmation of the Society's singular status as the nation's premier historical society.

Adams also had an ulterior motive in extending the invitation. He was intent upon achieving the presidency of the fledgling professional association, then but fourteen years old.[22] His brother Henry had held the presidency in 1893–1894.

In anticipation of the opening of the building in early 1899, Adams began work on his presidential address for the Society in early 1898. Because of the special nature of the occasion—the completion of a monumental structure by the nation's oldest historical society—Adams contemplated a major address, which would have a national orientation and stand as a seminal statement for the times. He chose the topic: "Historians and Historical Societies." He completed a "rough draft" in April and "laid it aside. I have not read it over, and have no idea whether it is good enough to go, or must be recast;—but that is out of the way, for the present—fairly off my mind."[23] Then he returned to writing the biography of his father.

March 9, 1899, was a banner day in the history of the Society. The members held their first meeting in the new building. Because the Dowse Library was the only room fully completed, the meeting was held there, although the original plan called for Society meetings to be held in Ellis Hall.

There was an "unusually large attendance of members." Workers were still on the scene, scurrying about, performing their various duties. Adams and other Society officials were seething with anger because of

---

[21] M.H.S. Council Records, Dec. 12, 1898 (M.H.S. Archives).

[22] For the founding and early history of the A.H.A., see: J. Franklin Jameson, "The American Historical Association, 1884–1909," *American Historical Review* 15(1909):1–20; Herbert B. Adams, "The New Historical Movement," *Nation*, 34(Sept. 18, 1884):240.

[23] C.F. Adams, Memorabilia, Apr. 4, 1898 (C.F. Adams Papers).

the failure of the architects and contractor to complete construction by the time of the meeting.[24]

Even with the building in an unfinished state, the event provoked extensive newspaper coverage. One Boston paper featured articles on the new building for an entire week. Journalistic hyperbole ran rampant.[25] Bold headlines in the *Boston Herald* proclaimed: "Members of the Massachusetts Historical Society Have Added an Ornament to Boston." A feature article read, in part: "There stands today at the corner of Boylston street and the Fenway one of the most beautiful of modern buildings. In its ownership, in the purpose to which it is dedicated and in its style of architecture it is unique. For it belongs to the Massachusetts Historical Society, is dedicated to the preservation of historical material, local and national, and in its exterior appearance is one of the most ornate clubhouses in the whole country." And further, in as strange a metaphor as can be imagined: "The place will be known as one of the surest storage batteries of historic knowledge in the city."

The reporter called attention to the Society's penchant for avoiding notoriety and maintaining a low public profile: "It is not a society that seeks public commendation for what it does. On the contrary, it seeks rather to escape it."

In profiling Librarian Green, the reporter stressed a similar theme and contrasted the styles of historians and journalists:

> Few men have so exact a knowledge of the value of true historical material as Dr. Green. Yet, few men having such a knowledge are so infrequently heard from as he. His work is of immense value. . . . Any one who looks for information for popular use at the society's rooms will very likely be informed that "we have always kept out of the newspapers." There is deemed to be an inconsistency between the historian's work of research and the up-to-date toil of the newspaperman.[26]

Adams presided at the meeting but made no address. He was saving himself for the annual meeting in April. That would be his day to shine.

[24] M.H.S., *Procs.*, 2d ser., 13(1899–1900):63.

[25] In addition to the local newspaper coverage, the New England edition of *The Youth's Companion* (July 27, 1899) ran a photograph of the new building on its cover, and *American Architect and Building News* (Aug. 12, 1899) featured coverage of the edifice with heliotype images of the interior and exterior.

[26] *Boston Herald*, Mar. 9, 1899.

The Move to Boylston Street

The business of the afternoon was of a routine nature. Green presented the main offering, a prosaic historical account of the Back Bay.[27]

As the date of the annual meeting approached, the Society began to take on the appearance of a functional organization. While not all of the interior was finished, the rooms required for the day's activities were "in practical readiness for service."[28] The critical room was Ellis Hall, the site of Adams's address. It had been completed. The library materials, which had "slumbered undisturbed" for two years in a storage warehouse in nearby Cambridge, were now in place on Boylston Street. The portraits and busts also had been returned to the Society and many were now positioned in the building.[29] All was in readiness for the grand event.

Some weeks before the annual meeting, Adams and other Society officers drew up an extensive list of dignitaries from throughout the United States and invited them to the Ellis Hall program. The list included the vice president of the United States; the secretaries of State, Navy, Treasury, and War; the United States ambassador to Great Britain; presidents of a number of major universities and historical societies; and leading historians and literati.[30]

The annual meeting was a two-stage affair. On a pleasant spring day, the members assembled at noon in the Dowse Library for the business session.[31] It was a routine meeting with the officers presenting their customary reports. In his report of the Council, senior member-at-large

[27] M.H.S., *Procs.*, 2d ser., 13(1899–1900):1–4.

[28] M.H.S., *Procs.*, 61(1927–1928):102.

[29] M.H.S., *Procs.*, 2d ser., 14(1900–1901):145; 13(1899–1900):79.

[30] Scrapbook: "Dedication—New Building—April, 1899" (M.H.S. Archives), which contains the responses to invitations for the opening reception. None of the major political figures accepted the invitations.

[31] The Dowse library was the meeting site because Ellis Hall "was to be used for ceremonies and inauguration." Someone, most likely Adams, summarily decided that the Dowse library would thereafter serve as the permanent meeting site. Winthrop "accidentally" learned of this decision at the end of April and was angered by it: "To my enquiry why a decision of such importance had been arrived at without consultation with the General Building Committee and a subsequent reference to the Society at large, I received an unsatisfactory and, it seemed to me, an evasive answer. . . . If the adoption of the new Dowse Library as a hall for meetings instead of a convenient place for consultation and work, had been made after full and free discussion, I should have had no cause of complaint, but under the circumstances I felt that the change had been effected in an arbitrary and occult manner." R.C. Winthrop, Jr., "Memoranda," in vol. 82, Winthrop Papers, M.H.S.

Charles R. Codman showered accolades upon all who had contributed to developing the building. His most lavish praise was reserved for Adams, who had selected the site and arranged for the purchase of the land and sale of the Tremont Street building.

At the conclusion of the meeting, the members descended to the first floor, treading cautiously down the uncompleted grand stairway. A crowd of fashionably dressed members and invited guests, including numerous women, were milling about the lobby, conversing and admiring the architectural features. Some people were already seated in "large and beautiful" Ellis Hall. When Adams rose to deliver his address, every seat was occupied. Some people were standing. There were about one hundred fifty in the room.

The president's address was a typical Adams performance, learned and lengthy, characteristic of the major pronouncements of his father, grandfather, great-grandfather, and other notable members of this distinguished clan. Adams ranged across the historical landscape of western civilization in the eighteenth and nineteenth centuries. He alluded to the writings of such Olympian figures as Burke, Gibbon, Hume, Robertson, Voltaire, Montesquieu, Darwin, Stephens, Macauley, and others. He placed historical writing in the United States and the history of the Society against the backdrop of European intellectual developments.

Adams's main thesis was that earlier historians dealt with large themes and painted with broad strokes. They were "great generalizers" and brilliant conceptualizers. In the twentieth century, historians—and historical societies, as well—would be forced to focus on monographic studies:

> The monograph will be the basis; in fact, I cannot but consider the monograph as the foundation and corner-stone of the historical edifice of the future. I have already alluded to the bewildering multiplicity of topics and phases with which the modern historian must deal, and deal as a master. He must be a specialist in everything; and to no man is it given to combine even a dozen specialties, and be a great generalizer besides. The work calls indeed for mental aptitudes rarely if ever found in a highly developed form in one and the same organization. He who aspires to be a general historian, or to write history on a large plan, can by no possibility cover all the minutiae and infinite details of his theme. If he would avoid error, he must accept the work of others, often differently organized from himself, almost always distinctively trained. On this point, I fancy, appeal might with confidence be made to any historical investigator who has ever written a

monograph in which he attempted an exhaustive study of an historical incident, it matter not what.

The principle of reduction also would apply to collecting. Echoing sentiments earlier expressed by President Winthrop, Adams asserted:

> The day of indiscriminate, unsystematic accumulation is . . . past; no receptacle will suffice for it, no power of assimilation is equal to the work of ordering and digesting it. It only remains for us, as for others, selecting our field, to labor in it intelligently as well as strenuously, so as in it to attain and hold a position of recognized superiority. If we would not fail in our mission, we must then make this building a place where the investigator in certain specific branches of history will be more likely than elsewhere to find what he wants and to find it readily.[32]

The audience listened in "rapt attention." One ardent admirer later described Adams's "oratorical production" as "really a *poem* as well as a philosophical discourse."[33] A sympathetic reporter wrote: "There has seldom, of late years, been a finer instance of intelligent and scholarly discussion of an important topic than that we find in it."[34]

Following Adams's presentation, the members and guests wandered about the building, examining the rooms. Later, a luncheon was served "on the personal invitation of the President."

Adams was exhilarated by the experience. He had completed another major building block in his effort to reconstitute the Society.[35] The Society had had its field day. It had "put on its ruffles and frills." It had held itself high.

As in the case of the March meeting, the annual meeting also inspired a barrage of newspaper articles. Every aspect of the affair, including the business meeting, was covered in fine detail. The coverage was not restricted to Boston papers. Newspapers throughout the state reported the event.

---

[32] M.H.S., *Procs.*, 2d ser., 13(1899–1900):81–119.

[33] A.C. Goodell to C.F. Adams, Apr. 15, 1899 (C.F. Adams Papers).

[34] *Springfield Republican*, Apr. 14, 1899. After the annual meeting, Adams mailed copies of his address to friends and associates across the nation. He received many perfunctory congratulatory responses. A modern commentator described the speech as "one of the few really pompous addresses of his career" (Kirkland, *Adams*, 219).

[35] The total cost of the building was $195,044.83, including $53,500 for the purchase of the land and the balance covering all construction costs. See M.H.S., *Procs.*, 2d ser., 14(1900–1901):255.

The *Springfield Republican* also provided a detailed picture of the structure's distinctive architectural features:

> It is a handsome, substantial and appropriate building of the Georgian renaissance style, of three stories. It is built of Sayre-Fisher brick, with Indiana limestone trimmings. The visitor enters by a very dark oak door to the entrance hall or vestibule, which is finished in Amherst sandstone and from which rises the staircase directly opposite the door, having a bronze rail. The woodwork is in American oak, stained dark to resemble the genuine dark English oak. The Ellis room and the committee room on the first floor are treated in rich Georgian renaissance style, with pilasters, heavy architrave and cornice. They have a heavy paneling on which will be hung portraits of past presidents of the Society.... The second and third-story halls are finished in Vermont marble, green and white. The floors of the first floor hall are laid in slabs of Vermont marble, in patterns, while the floors of the second and third are of mosaic laid between stripes of Vermont marble. The general library, which serves as a lobby to the Dowse library, is fitted with the old mahogany bookcase which was used in the old building on Tremont Street. The Dowse library is fitted with black walnut cases which have been extended from their size in the old building. Above the committee room on the first floor is the librarian's room, and both of these are elliptical rooms. Both are panelled in oak, and in both will be hung portraits of worthies of the colonies in the 17th century. On the third floor in the same section is a room which is to be used as a reading-room for the American academy. In the future it will be a lobby to the large hall in the third story. That large hall will now be used for the storage of books, pending the construction of the library stack.... On the left of the entrance on the first floor is the cabinet room, in which will be displayed autographs, pictures and relics.... Immediately above this room is the future Waterston room for the bequest which is eventually coming to the society, but will now be used temporarily for newspapers. Above this, on the third floor, in the same section, is a stack in three tiers which will be used by the American academy for the time being, which will have quarters for five years in the third story.[36]

---

[36] "Dedication of New Building" (Scrapbook, M.H.S. Archives). According to Thomas B. Adams, "one minor deficiency was discovered on the day of the dedication of the new house. A man was sent to bring up some champagne from the cellar and returned to report there were no stairs. The first toast had to be postponed till a search party could find its way out the front door, down the steps, and clear 'round the building to the outside ground-level entrance and back again" (*Here We Have Lived: The Houses of the Massachusetts Historical Society* [Boston, 1967], foreword).

The Move to Boylston Street

The curmudgeonly Robert C. Winthrop, Jr., did not attend the annual meeting and opening of the new building, much to the surprise of Adams and other members. On the following day, he wrote his longtime friend and occasional nemesis, Adams, in his inimitable, pungent style, and explained the reasons for his absence:

> Between ourselves, however, I never had the smallest intention of attending the Celebration,—not from diminished interest in the Society or lessened regard for you,—but merely because, as one of the older members, I should have been rather expected to palaver invited guests and even be introduced to strangers, the sort of thing I hate, in my old age.
>
> Nor did the prospect of female attendance allure me, as I fancied it would chiefly consist of "cultured and patriotic" types with which I am not in sympathy. I still enjoy jabbering to physically-seductive young women,—provided they have never read a page of Darwin and would not understand it if they had,—but, alas, such triflers have long since ceased to be willing to prattle to me. So I stayed at home, deciphered with labor an early Colonial MS and endeavored to approximate its date. Every man to his hobbies.

Winthrop commended Adams for his "scholarly and effective" address. "I rejoice," he wrote, "you said what you did about indiscriminate accumulation." This was one of Winthrop's favorite themes: "What the Society needs in its new building, in my judgment, is to be able to say to the community we have wall-space enough for valuable historical portraits, besides those we have already, and we have shelving and lock-ups for rare books, manuscripts and relics, if people are willing to give them to us; but we are not a dust-bin or a rubbish-dump."[37]

In his address, Adams made no reference to a plan he had discussed informally with certain members who were close friends—that is, to replace the librarian and cabinet-keeper with a "highly-paid editorial maid-of-all work."[38] Winthrop was one of his confidants but was stead-

[37] R.C. Winthrop, Jr., to C.F. Adams, Apr. 14, 1899 (C.F. Adams Papers). Thereafter, Winthrop rarely attended a Society meeting. In addition to disliking the building, he "found its quarters so remote that for me to go there partook of the nature of a special expedition and I have since gone there only at long intervals, preferring to work in my own house." R.C. Winthrop, Jr., "Memoranda," in vol. 82, Winthrop Papers, M.H.S. Adams and Winthrop had a complex personal relationship. At times, they crossed swords and were bitter adversaries. See, for example, Nagel, "The Ice Age," 272–274.

[38] When cabinet keeper Samuel F. McCleary left his position in 1898, Adams wrote to him: "I am . . . sorry that you have decided to withdraw at just this time. I do not hesitate to say that I am anxious about the future of the Society. It has now developed to such a

fastly opposed to this scheme and voiced his objection. While he could see the value of such an employee, Winthrop believed that she should be subordinate to the librarian and cabinet-keeper. Both of these officers should be retained, he asserted. They were essential to the overall welfare of the Society. He cited a list of learned men who had held these positions in his period of membership and noted that they had strengthened the organization considerably through their daily personal contacts with members. This type of sociability would disappear if a paid "maid-of-all work" replaced these key officers. The atmosphere of the Society would become formal, cold, and business-like. Members would stop coming.

Winthrop then projected his nostalgic vision of the Tremont Street Society, with its warm and friendly club-like character: "The strong point of the Mass. Hist. Soc. used to be that it was a sort of Literary Club, whose members tried to be well acquainted, and, as a rule, liked coming together. I shall be sorry to see this otherwise, tho the sociability is no longer what it was & there has not been an evening-meeting at the house of a member for at least ten years."[39]

Given his vision of the Society, it was perhaps wise of Winthrop not to have attended the festivities on April 13. He would not have been at home there. He longed for "the good old days." The Society he remembered, however, no longer existed. It was part of Boston's history.

Now secure in its new home, the Society could once again turn its attentions to the collections. The library had grown at a rapid pace during the Tremont Street years. Books, manuscripts, pamphlets, maps, newspapers—the materials came in a constant flow. At every meeting, the librarian reported additions to the collections. Almost all of these

---

degree that I see clearly a reorganization of its machinery is only a question of time. We have got to give up the system of relying on volunteer and uncompensated services, and have recourse to permanent, salaried officials." Adams to McCleary, Mar. 17, 1898 (C.F. Adams Papers).

[39] R.C. Winthrop, Jr., to C.F. Adams, Apr. 14, 1899. Winthrop had cautioned Adams against proposing a reorganization of the staff and replacing volunteers with paid personnel. "I can not help thinking that, whether your re-organization projects are wise or unwise, practicable or impracticable, it is a mistake to ventilate them in advance in a way to run the risk of offending men who have for years voluntarily rendered important services to the Society." R.C. Winthrop, Jr., to C.F. Adams, Mar. 14, 1898 (C.F. Adams Papers).

acquisitions were gifts, especially manuscripts.[40] In 1898, Charles C. Smith noted that "in only two instances, almost too unimportant in amount to be mentioned, has the Society, so far as I know, bought any manuscripts." Member Jared Sparks, in an uncharitable gesture that would have infuriated Belknap, offered to sell to the Society the papers of Francis Bernard, a colonial governor of Massachusetts, for $600. The Society declined his offer.

In a more creative attempt to augment the library shortly after leaving its Tremont Street quarters, the Society issued a circular, urging school children to hunt for historical materials and to donate any finds to the Society. The circular, however, produced little more than the following satiric response in one of the local weekly newspapers.

I am lead into this doddering mood through catching sight of a circular issued more or less recently by the Massachusetts Historical Society. This circular, signed by Professor Hart, Senator Hoar, and other distinguished members, invites all school children to start on a still hunt for original materials. It hints darkly at the possibility of rich finds in garrets. The Society says to ingenuous youth that it "does not pay money for manuscripts, but is glad to receive them as gifts," and in the most delicate way possible indicates that it will accept, without trying to bite, from any child, files of newspapers earlier than 1800; letters written at the time of the Revolution or even of the Civil War; letters, books, diaries, journals, and other helpful trifles. The Society, anxious to preserve the innocence of childhood, does not betray the fact that there are wicked men, and women too, abroad, who, meeting a little helpless child on his way to Professor Hart, bearing a twine bag filled with colonial manuscripts, would have the temerity to offer a fat and comforting sum. Not thus our worthy Society, which has long since learned the precious truth that it is more blessed to receive than to give. But what inducement is offered to the infant who may have industriously explored his father's garret and hair trunks? Simply this, that he "will be doing something toward preserving the memory of his own ancestors and of the present generation." As if any motive could be higher for the mind of youth than this, and as if, moreover, fresh

---

[40] The annual reports of the librarian, printed in the *Proceedings*, are the best source for tracing the growth of the library. Also of value are: Samuel A. Green's account of the formation and growth of the library in M.H.S., *Procs.*, 2d ser., 8(1892–1894):312–344; Michael J. Walsh, "Some of the Treasures of the Massachusetts Historical Society," ibid., 70(1950–1953):248–262; Stephen T. Riley, "Some Aspects of the Society's Manuscript Collections," ibid., 240–247; Louis L. Tucker, "From Belknap to Riley: Building the Collection of the Massachusetts Historical Society," *Witness to America's Past*, 15–23.

impulse were needed for the preserving of memories beyond what is now rendered without surcease by the Daughters of the Revolution, who claim any ancestor to whom they may happen to take a fancy.[41]

As noted previously, the early librarians failed to exercise discretion in their collecting, which resulted in a chronic storage problem. In its 1893 report to the members, the committee on the library, alarmed by the rapid accumulation of low-grade material and the shrinking storage space, had urged that the library be "maintained and developed in what we may venture to call a spirit of historical chastity. The cells of our famous beehive should be found filled, if not with the best of honey only at any rate with honey."[42] The metaphor may have been mixed but the message was clear. In 1894, the same committee made this acerbic comment on the librarian's excessively liberal policy on accessions: "The main growth of the Library has always been through donations, and in accepting gifts the Librarian has never been actuated by any churlish spirit of refusal."[43]

In 1897, as the Society was preparing to vacate the Tremont Street quarters, Librarian Green reported the addition of 3,986 items for the year. It included: 1,196 books; 2,481 pamphlets; 90 broadsides; 88 volumes of manuscripts; and 39 maps. This was a normal annual increase for this period. The overall statistics for the library were: more than 40,000 volumes, including files of unbound newspapers, bound manuscripts, and the Dowse Collection; over 90,000 pamphlets; almost 4,000 broadsides.[44] In 1850, the library had held only 6,000 books and several thousand pamphlets.

The acquisition of the personal papers of prominent historical figures was particularly impressive during the 1833–1897 era. For example, the Society acquired the papers of: James Otis; Timothy Pickering; William Heath; Thomas Hollis; William Pepperrell; Jeremy Belknap; Israel Williams; and Francis Parkman, including the vast collection of transcripts of the foreign documents he had collected for his major writings. The Society also acquired numerous documents pertaining to the lives of

---

[41] *Time and the Hour*, Apr. 8, 1899.

[42] M.H.S., *Procs.*, 2d ser., 8(1892–1894):198–200.

[43] M.H.S., *Procs.*, 2d ser., 9(1894–1895):38. If the Society moved in the near future, continued the report, it should consider a program of "weedings out."

[44] M.H.S., *Procs.*, 2d ser., 11(1896–1897):331–332.

ordinary citizens—soldiers, clergymen, businessmen, adventurers—although little value was placed upon these types of materials at the time.

Perhaps the most significant single document acquired during this period was George Washington's "Newburgh Address," which he delivered at the New Windsor Cantonment on March 15, 1783, near the end of the American Revolution. The officers were in a rebellious mood at this time because of the failure of Congress to pay their salaries and assure them of retirement pay and other well-deserved benefits. In a dramatic encounter with his restless officers, Washington exhorted them to remain loyal and obedient, to "continue to have an unshaken confidence in the justice of Congress and their Country." The "Newburgh Address" is a seminal document in American history because it reaffirmed the principle of the subservience of military authority to civilian control. In the American system, political leadership retained transcendent powers.

There is a prevailing view in writings about the Society that its library was "closed" to outsiders during these years, its use restricted solely to members and a small group of their friends. A few, well-publicized incidents have contributed to this view. In 1868, for example, the historian Henry Dawson, a corresponding member of the Society from New York, sought a key document, a British orderly book, for his meticulously researched examination of the Battle of Bunker Hill. Dawson was appalled when he learned that the holdings were not open to all serious scholars. He vented his spleen in a footnote to his article decrying the fact that "the Massachusetts Historical Society . . . has seen fit to adopt and adhere to Rules which remove from the use of working students of American history every such authority which falls into its hands." He protested the practices of the Historical Society which "greedily absorbs important materials for history and as studiously withholds them from those who have occasion to use them, *even for historical purposes*, except under such restrictions and after such delays as, in nine cases out of ten, render the information which they contain of no practical use whatever."[45]

An outburst like this is counterbalanced, however, by numerous references in librarians' reports of non-members using the library for

---

[45] Henry B. Dawson, "Bunker's Hill," *Historical Magazine*, 2d ser., 3(1868):338.

research purposes.[46] These reports project a spirit of cooperation with outsiders. In his report for 1862, for example, Librarian Nathaniel B. Shurtleff wrote: "The Librarian is gratified in stating, that persons engaged in historical writings have made frequent visits to the Society's rooms, where they have made use of the valuable material to be found on our shelves and in our cabinets; and many, after availing themselves of the benefits which the library affords, have sent to the Society printed copies of their works."[47] This hardly sounds like a "closed" library.

There is further evidence that the Society welcomed visitors to its quarters after it had moved to Tremont Street. Having considerable wall space available, the librarian hung many paintings in the room that housed items from the cabinet. These began to attract visitors, and the Society warmly welcomed them. In 1838, because "the Hall has been much visited for the purpose" of viewing the portraits, Librarian Thaddeus M. Harris developed for the *Collections* series a catalogue of these art works. The catalogue listed forty-four portraits and was divided into seven categories: discoverers; Winslow family; governors and lieutenant governors; generals; distinguished laymen; clergymen; and aged women. Almost all of the portraits were painted in the eighteenth century; a few dated from the seventeenth century. The bulk of these works were of New England's most eminent worthies: Gov. John Winthrop; Gov. Thomas Hutchinson; Increase Mather; Thomas Prince; Charles Chauncy; Peter Faneuil; Gov. Edward Winslow; Gov. John Endicott; Oliver Wolcott; and Jeremy Belknap. Some were of figures with international reputations: Christopher Columbus; Sebastian Cabot; Americus Vespucius; George Washington; Marquis de LaFayette; and Dean George Berkeley.

The aged women category contained only two paintings, but they were of a special character. They portrayed two remarkable and durable ladies of Boston's past. Anne Pollard, who died in 1725 at the age of 105, was shown as she appeared at age 103. A descriptive note pointed out that "she left of her offspring 130"; and that she was on the first boat

[46] Article 15 of the new by-laws instituted in 1873 stated that "persons not members of the Society, engaged in historical pursuits, shall be allowed to consult the manuscripts . . . provided an application in writing, stating the object of the inquiry, be first made to the Librarian." M.H.S., *Procs.*, 13(1873–1875):147. This was a continuation of a policy which was contained in the by-laws from the founding of the Society. See, for example, ibid., 2(1835–1855):520–521.

[47] M.H.S., *Procs.*, 6(1862–1863):14–15.

that crossed the Charles River and landed at what is now Boston, and she was "the first that jumped ashore." She described Boston as "very uneven, abounding in small hollows and swamps, covered with blueberry and other bushes."

A second portrait featured Mrs. Mary Davis as she appeared at age 117! The biographical note presented these fascinating, if not astonishing, facts: "She had three husbands, by whom she had nine children. She had fifteen grand-children; 215 great grand children; 800 great grand children's children. At 104 years she could do a good day's work at shelling corn; at 110 she sat at her spinning wheel."[48]

A more powerful piece of evidence that the Society welcomed outsiders into its quarters is a manuscript "visitors' register" in the institution's archives. The register covers the years 1859–1899. The bulk of the registrants were from Boston and environs. The remainder were from other areas of the northeast, the nation, and from all corners of the world: Canada; Europe (London, Cambridge); Near East (Constantinople); Far East (Japan, Australia, New Zealand).

There was a surprisingly large number of female visitors. On some days, as many as eight to ten women entered the male bastion. Many of these were not Massachusetts residents. The register does not indicate if these visitors were researchers or merely museum viewers.[49] More than likely, they were the latter, viewers of the portraits and cabinet holdings.[50]

One constant problem was Librarian Green, who developed a reputation as a "growling Cerberus" during his incredible fifty-year tenure (1868–1918).[51] During his administration the library did become increasingly restrictive in public access. Green did not welcome non-members to the library with enthusiasm. Indeed, he did everything in his power to deter them from using the library, which he regarded as the

---

[48] M.H.S., *Colls.*, 3d ser., 7(1838):285–291. Bentley, *Diary*, 2:283, from which the Davis description was copied by the *Collections*, gives the more plausible number of 45 grandchildren.

[49] There is specific evidence on women researchers in the library in the 1890s. See M.H.S. Council Records, Nov. 12, 1891, Jan. 12, 1893, Feb. 13, 1896 (M.H.S. Archives).

[50] For additional evidence of use of the library by non-members, see: M.H.S., *Procs.*, 6(1862–1863):14, 10(1867–1869):3; *Boston Daily Evening Transcript*, Apr. 16, 1852.

[51] This fitting characterization was coined by Walter M. Whitehill in *Independent Historical Societies*, 21.

private preserve of the members. However, he did not interfere with visitors who simply came to view the portraits or gaze at the holdings of the cabinet.

Because Green was such a powerful personality and formidable force in the Society, few members dared to challenge him openly. Not even Presidents Winthrop, Ellis, and Adams were willing to engage him in open combat. Beginning in the 1890s, however, select members began to voice mild criticism against his restrictive policy. The report of the Council in 1893, prepared by the senior retiring member, Edward J. Lowell, contained the first sign of dissatisfaction. Since he was conveniently away in Europe, Lowell did not have to gaze upon Green's glaring countenance. Abbott Lawrence Lowell, who read his report, had to face the imperial librarian.

After emphasizing the historical importance of the Society's vast manuscript holdings, Lowell underscored the need to make these materials available to "the members of the Society *and other persons.*" His next words doubtless made Green bristle:

> I say *other persons*, as well as members of the Society, for no policy could be more short-sighted than to refuse to scholars who are not members here the use of our unpublished, and for the most part unpublishable, manuscripts. We are, in a sense, trustees for the scholars of the country. While it is our duty to see to the careful preservation of our possessions, while we must surround their use with such precautions as may insure their safety, our policy as to the manuscripts in our hands should be thoroughly generous. This only will secure the continued reception by us of valuable manuscripts. The rooms of this Society are not now only the possible place of deposit for family papers and historical material. Testators and donors can find other repositories, and will do so, if we do not let our light shine before men. Let us make this the safest, and at the same time the most useful place. Let us imitate the liberality of the men in charge of best-managed public archives of Europe; and being known to give generously, we shall receive freely. Thus shall we best collect materials, thus best preserve them. The motto over our door may remind us that it is not for ourselves, but for others, that our labors are performed.[52]

Until the mid-nineteenth century, the library was open infrequently and on an irregular schedule. In 1809, the bylaws called for the librarian "to attend at the Library, or to procure some member to attend in his stead, on the afternoon of each Thursday, at three o'clock P.M., for the

---

[52] M.H.S., *Procs.*, 2d ser., 8(1892–1894):183–184.

accommodation of the members." Few people, members or otherwise, used the library when it was located at the Tontine Crescent.

Beginning in 1839, the Society had accumulated sufficient funds to hire an assistant, the brother of a member, to open the library on a part-time, but regular, schedule. When the Society's finances declined in 1843, the assistant was released and the schedule again became irregular.

This arrangement persisted until 1853, when a new regulation directed the librarian or a substitute to be at the library daily "at the regular hours appointed for keeping it open." The directive did not achieve the desired result. A year later, the officers once more authorized the employment of an assistant "to keep the library open according to the By-Laws of the Society, and to proceed at once to the preparation of a complete and systematic catalogue of the Library, Cabinet, and pictures." Dr. John Appleton was hired on December 4, 1854. Thereafter, the library remained open on a regular basis and the Society's quarters became a more active facility.[53]

The American Historical Association met in Boston and Cambridge in late December 1899.[54] These two cities, wrote an Association representative, "furnished unquestionably a most admirable local environment for the meetings of a national historical organization."[55] "Even the weather, that 'last infirmity' of New England celebrations, was propitious and constant."[56] Two hundred delegates were in attendance and "several hundred persons showed by their presence their interest in the general work." It was the "largest and most enthusiastic gathering" in the association's young history; this was its fifteenth annual meeting.

At the time, the membership of the association consisted of a small

[53] For the early history of the library, see Green's account in M.H.S., *Procs.*, 2d ser., 8(1892–1894):312–344.

[54] For a summary of the meeting, see *American Historical Review*, 5(1899–1900):423–439; American Historical Association, *Annual Report* (1899), 1:9–12. The M.H.S. program is listed on p. 35.

[55] *American Historical Review*, 5(1899–1900):423. The association's annual report later described the meeting as "the largest and most enthusiastic in the association's history." About 200 attended and "several hundred persons showed by their presence their interest in the general work." American Historical Association, *Annual Report* (1899), 1:4.

[56] *American Historical Review*, 5(1899–1900):423.

body of newly trained and certified (that is, holders of doctoral degrees) professional or "scientific" historians and a larger group of "amateur" historians and representatives of historical societies and agencies.[57] Charles Francis Adams was a charter member of the association; he also had subscribed to a life membership in 1884.

The young professional historians represented a new breed of scholar. Trained in the "scientific" techniques of the German historical tradition, they were at odds with the "literary" historians of the nineteenth century. As David Van Tassel has written: "The critical younger generation summed up its major attack in the epithet 'literary historians.' As literary artists the great mid-century historians received the respect of the newcomers, but history was no longer to be considered a branch of literature; it was a science whose practitioners marshaled and classified data and published monographs modeled after the laboratory report of the natural scientist."[58]

Adams, who was a disciple of the new historical school, had invited the association to hold its opening session on December 27 in the Society's "handsome new building." He also offered to sponsor a luncheon for the delegates and their guests. Not all of the Society members approved of his action. Professor Barrett Wendell of Harvard was a forceful dissenter. He listed his concerns in a letter to the president:

[57] There is no authoritative figure for holders of doctoral degrees in history for this time. J. Franklin Jameson, who called this group "that noble army of doctors," wrote in 1909 that there were 7,000 graduate students in the United States, of whom about 300 were in history. In 1884, he noted, there were only 30 studying in history. See *American Historical Review*, 15(1909–1910):3.

[58] David D. Van Tassel, *Recording America's Past: An Interpretation of the Development of Historical Studies in America, 1607–1884* (Chicago, 1960), 173. Chapter 19, pp. 171–179, provides an excellent summary on the rise of "scientific history" and demise of "literary historians." See also: John Higham, *History: Professional Scholarship in America* (Baltimore, 1986), 3–23; W. Stull Holt, ed., *Historical Scholarship in the United States, 1876–1901* (Baltimore, 1938); Michael Kraus, *The Writing of American History* (Norman, Oklahoma, 1953), ch. 8. Some "literary" historians grew contemptuous of their "scientific" brethren. Theodore Roosevelt was one of these. He wrote: "After a while, it dawned on me that all of the conscientious, industrious, painstaking little pedants, who would have been useful in a rather small way if they had understood their own limitations, had become because of their conceit distinctly noxious. They solemnly believed that if there were only enough of them, and that if they only collected enough facts of all kinds and sorts, there would cease to be any need hereafter for great writers, great thinkers." Quoted in Howard K. Beale, "The Professional Historian: His Theory and His Practice," *Pacific Historical Review*, 22(1953):228.

The Move to Boylston Street

Has it occurred to you that the proposed invitation to the American Historical Association would involve the official reception by the Historical Society of a considerable number of women? I make the suggestion, with diffidence, that this is a rather serious departure from our traditions. Mr. [James F.] Rhodes and Professor [Albert B.] Hart are among the personal friends for whom my regard is warm. I greatly hesitate in any way to oppose a plan they bring forward. Nor do I feel at all sure that the plan is not a good one. Perhaps our traditions of dignity are a little akin to the literary ones which would preserve the "dignity of history." At the same time I cannot forget the astonishment with which I attended the meeting of the American Historical Association at Washington, I think in December, '92. Your brother Brooks and I read papers then. Our audience impressed both of us as of such quality that we felt no further interest in the organization; nor did the personality of Professor [Herbert Baxter] Adams, of Johns Hopkins, serve to counteract this impression. I resigned at once; and I think your brother did likewise.

All of which may be snobbery. We live in an age too democratic to preserve even the gracious side of scholarship. What is more, some of our best scholars actively participate in the work of the American Association. The truth is that there is no standard of admission there whatever. And we cannot entertain the association without receiving women, negroes, etc. I remind myself of the charge said to have been preferred by the Holy Office against Paul Veronese—that he introduced in his painting a table whereat our blessed Lord was seated with "dwarfs, buffoons, Germans, and other indecencies."[59]

Showing no fear of "women, negroes, etc.," Adams followed through on his plan. The association held its opening session in the Society's quarters, and the delegates were treated to a tasteful luncheon. After this pleasant repast, there was a "Public Session of the Church History Section." The program was "moderately well attended, although the absence of academic teachers of church history from the meetings was more marked than usual."[60] With Moses Coit Tyler, a respected historian from Cornell University and a corresponding member of the Society, serving as chairman, a panel of two ministers and an academic historian presented papers. A professor and a third minister led a brief discussion of the papers.

The division of participants between "amateurs" and "professionals" was the inspiration of Herbert Baxter Adams, director of historical stud-

[59] Wendell to Adams, Nov. 13, 1898 (C.F. Adams Papers).
[60] *American Historical Review*, 5(1899–1900):427–428.

ies at The Johns Hopkins University in the 1880s and 1890s and the chief architect of the American Historical Association.[61] A New Englander, Adams had attended Phillips Exeter Academy, Amherst College, and the University of Heidelberg, where he absorbed German historical values. He did more than anyone else to germanize historical values in the United States.

While Professor Adams personally maintained an attitude of superiority towards amateur historians, he realized "the importance of corporate influences, of associations of men and money." He became intent upon fostering a union of professors and patricians. He took special care to involve the non-professionals in the American Historical Association and thereby make it a broadly national organization. A man of acute political sensitivity, he recognized the value of inclusiveness. Largely through his influence, prominent patrician historians were selected for the presidency of the American Historical Association.[62]

Some of Professor Adams's professional colleagues took umbrage over this, but his influence was dominant. He was well aware of the friction that had developed between the two principal constituencies of the association. There was growing discontent among the non-academic members who charged that the association was run "in the interest of college professors only and to give those of us who are not of that clan the cold shoulder." They began voicing threats of leaving the association and forming their own organization.[63] Herbert Adams sought to mollify the dissidents by balancing the "boys and the patriarchs" on some of the panels.

Later in the afternoon, five standing committees of the association held their annual business meetings in various rooms of the Society.[64]

On the following morning, in the study of South Congregational Church, Charles F. Adams presented a paper titled "A Plea for Military History" in the "Public Session on Fields of Historical Study." He was one of two non-academic participants on the seven-person panel. The

[61] Adams served as the secretary of the Association for its first 16 years.

[62] Of the first 16 presidents, only 2, Andrew Dickson White and Charles Kendall Adams, were professional historians. They were also university presidents.

[63] J. Franklin Jameson, "History of Historical Societies," *Seventy-Fifth Anniversary Report of the Georgia Historical Society* (Atlanta, 1914), 31–51.

[64] On the M.H.S. meetings, see American Historical Association, *Annual Report* (1899), 1:9–12. The M.H.S. program is on p. 35.

other was a woman from New York City, Mrs. Robert Abbe. The remaining five were professional historians.

The compiler of the program for the *American Historical Review* described Adams's presentation as a "brilliant paper."[65] Adams began by quoting "at some length" from his address at the opening of the Boylston Street building. He repeated some of his main themes from that speech.[66] At one point, he directed criticism at one of the Society's icons, the legendary Francis Parkman. In the words of the association's compiler: "Speaking of the battle of Quebec upon the basis of recent examination of the ground, he [Adams] showed how misleading was in some respects the account of it given by a civilian historian like Parkman, and how largely such writers, from want of professional training or technical knowledge, missed the really perplexing questions respecting a battle; in this case, for instance, why Montcalm fought at all."[67]

At the annual business meeting of the association, acting upon the recommendation of the nominating committee, which was heavily influenced by Herbert Baxter Adams, the delegates elected Adams second vice president. That placed him on the Council and in line of succession for the presidency.[68] Thus, Adams had accomplished both of his objectives. After the delegates had left Boston, Professor Albert B. Hart of Harvard University and an academic pillar of the Society, extended congratulations to Adams and added: "It is a special cause for congratulation that the Massachusetts Historical Society, mother of them all, should, through its president, have shown such a kind and well appreciated hospitality."[69] Adams gave but he also got something in return.

---

[65] A précis of his paper is in *American Historical Review*, 5(1899–1900):429.

[66] American Historical Association, *Annual Report* (1899), 1:36.

[67] *American Historical Review*, 5(1899–1900):429.

[68] Albert B. Hart to C.F. Adams, Jan. 1, 1900 (C.F. Adams Papers). Adams became the 16th president in 1901. Fourteen of the first 16 presidents were either resident or corresponding members of the M.H.S. Only Charles K. Adams and Edward Eggleston were not.

[69] Hart to Adams, Jan. 1, 1900 (C.F. Adams Papers).

Chapter 11

Adams Begins His Reforms

"MR. ADAMS," Worthington C. Ford wrote in 1915, "brought an historical instinct, but what was more necessary to the Society, an intellectual energy, united with a prescient sense of what problems the Society must face. In 1895 the hour had struck for making radical changes in the circumstances of the club; the conditions forced the changes, and the proper man was there to control the situation. He rejected entirely the idea of a social club; he insisted upon the serious purposes of the Society; he took the office of President seriously, as affected by responsibilities of leadership."[1]

Notwithstanding his "historical instinct," "intellectual energy," and "prescient sense" of future problems, Adams did not have an easy time in implementing his master plan for the Society. In fact, he never fully achieved his goal. After successfully completing the initial phase, "our new home first," he turned to the second step, "money next." In this instance, he could not take direct action. The future financial well-being of the Society hinged largely upon major gifts by members and these were likely to come only through bequests. "Waiting for dead-men's shoes," he called it.[2] In the interim, the Society was destined to exist as a marginal operation.

The brightest prospect for an imminent major gift was Samuel Abbott Green, known to be wealthy and kinless.[3] He had had an active associ-

---

[1] M.H.S., *Procs.*, 48(1914–1915):420.

[2] C.F. Adams, Memorabilia, Apr. 29, 1901 (C.F. Adams Papers).

[3] For further details on Green's biography, see: M.H.S., *Procs.*, 52(1918–1919):45–55, 54(1920–1921):236–242; *Boston Evening Transcript*, Dec. 5, 1918.

ation with the Society since becoming its librarian in 1868; he had been elected a member in 1860 at the age of thirty. He also had served as vice president since 1895.

"This extraordinary man, a kind of latter-day Falstaff in bulk, appetites, and cheery raffishness,"[4] was a native of Groton, Massachusetts, and a graduate of Lawrence Academy, Harvard College, and Harvard Medical School.[5] Most of Green's early adult life was spent in medical work. When the Civil War began, he volunteered for service, announcing at his farewell dinner that: "This war has come at just the right time for me." The first physician to join the Union forces for a full term of three years, he served with distinction as a surgeon and medical administrator.

After the war, he maintained a private practice in the seamy section of Boston where he lived. He later served as superintendent of "that sterling charity," the Boston Dispensary, from 1865 to 1872, and as city physician of Boston from 1871 to 1882. He was a Harvard overseer and trustee of Lawrence Academy for many years and performed a variety of civic good works in Boston.

Green's professional life underwent a dramatic transition in the late 1870s. Since he was independently wealthy, he began to devote less time to his medical career and more to his bookish and historical interests, and civic and cultural activities. From 1877 to 1878, he was the librarian of the Boston Public Library, as interim successor to Justin Winsor.

In 1881, Frederick Octavius Prince, a "Yankee Democrat" who had served five successive one-year terms as mayor of Boston, decided to retire from active political life. The Democrats selected Albert Palmer of Roxbury as their nominee. A graduate of Dartmouth College, Palmer had served as a teacher at the Boston Latin School and as a state legislator, and was treasurer of the Jamaica Pond Ice Company.[6] An accomplished speaker and political operator, Palmer appeared to be a shoo-in for the position.

---

[4] Butterfield, "Ford, Editor," 52.

[5] Green's father also had been a doctor and was the first "house-officer" of the Massachusetts General Hospital when it opened in 1821.

[6] A former student remembered Palmer as a highly nervous teacher who had a tendency "when irritated to pull his black beard apart and stuff the ends into his mouth." M.H.S., Procs., 42(1918–1919):50.

In a surprise move, the Republicans nominated Dr. Green as their candidate. Like all Boston mayoralty elections, this was a hotly contested campaign. Supported by a coalition of reform-minded citizens (goo-goos), temperance advocates, and a bloc of Irish voters, Green won by the narrow margin of 523 votes. He served only one term. In the following year, Palmer gained revenge defeating Green by a majority of 2,187 votes. This ended Green's political career.[7]

Green resided on Harrison Avenue in Boston's South End, one of the poorest sections of the city. It was inhabited by "God's poor, the devil's poor, and the poor devil." He was a sensitive, compassionate neighbor and maintained a close interest in the personal lives of his fellow citizens. "He doctored them, advised and assisted them, and soon earned their confidence, affection, and admiration."[8] In the late nineteenth century, newly arrived Armenians, Italians, Chinese, and other immigrants settled in Green's neighborhood. Criminal elements, from prostitutes to robbers, also could be found there. It was a dangerous community, especially at night. Green even fraternized with his lawless neighbors, in some cases establishing permanent friendships.[9] He developed an "uncanny knowledge" of Boston's underworld. Some of the more respectable citizens of means moved away, but not Green. He remained with the "plain people of the city."[10]

Green achieved a folkloric reputation in Boston as a humanitarian and defender of the poor, oppressed, and downtrodden. "Like a philosopher of olden times much of his life was centered among the poor and unfortunate." Many stories circulated about his deeds as a good Samaritan. For example, an elderly, indigent lady who sold apples at a stand at the United States courthouse, then at the corner of Temple Place and Tremont Street, had been ordered off the premises by federal officials. She appealed to Green for assistance, pleading that this was the source of her livelihood. He remonstrated in her behalf to the assistant United States treasurer, the United States district attorney, and the United States

---

[7] On Green's political career and these two mayoralty campaigns, see John T. Galvin, "Samuel Abbott Green: Mayor of Boston, 1882, His Life and Times," 3–11 (manuscript in M.H.S.).

[8] M.H.S., *Procs.*, 54(1920–1921):239.

[9] M.H.S., *Procs.*, 54(1920–1921):238–239.

[10] M.H.S., *Procs.*, 45(1911–1912):541–542.

marshal and secured their written approvals for the continuance of her apple stand. He mailed these approvals, with a petition and personal letter, to the secretary of the Treasury in Washington. The secretary rescinded the order, and the lady was permitted to sell apples again.[11]

At one time, Boston experienced a severe outbreak of smallpox. Those poor citizens afflicted by the disease were herded into the Marcella Street Home for treatment. Green, then city physician, went to the site and spent countless hours ministering to their needs. He became an heroic figure to these people.[12]

There seemed to be no limit to Green's samaritan deeds. He even sought to reform "ladies of the night." Charles K. Bolton, a former librarian of the Boston Athenaeum, told one such tale:

> Some gossip today about the earlier days of Dr. S.A. Green when he lived on Harrison Avenue. He knew all the keepers of bad houses, understood them and had a certain kind of regard for some of them. One old dame used to send to him every inmate of her house who seemed capable of a better life and he would get the girl a place. At a Harvard commencement an attractive woman bowed and after a moment he [Green] recalled her as a girl whom he had saved from that house. When a Harvard man had wanted to marry her she went to Dr. Green for help, saying that the truth must be told. The Dr. went to the young man, told the story and he had married her. She whispered to the Doctor: "This is my husband's mother; she does not know my history, so be careful what you say." Dr. Green at once gave her his two tickets to the commencement exercises. He must have done enduring good in those days.[13]

Green also manifested kindness towards children, especially the wayward youngsters of his own squalid neighborhood. His memoirist stressed this aspect of his character:

> He loved all children, but I think he preferred the semi-barbarous ones. Every night in the spring and summer and when the weather permitted a crowd of young urchins collected before his door and waited for him to come out and talk to them. If he happened to be late, some of them would crawl up and knock on his window and call out, 'Say Doc, aren't you coming out tonight?' And almost every night the Doctor came out onto his

[11] *Boston Evening Transcript*, Dec. 5, 1918.

[12] M.H.S., *Procs.*, 52(1918–1919):49.

[13] C.K. Bolton, *Journal*, Jan. 7, 1918 (Charles Knowles Bolton Papers, M.H.S.). Hereafter Bolton, *Journal*.

doorsteps. He told stories to the children, advised and corrected them, and listened to their stories and answered their questions. They wanted to know among other things whether he had been at the battle of Bunker Hill and was a friend of George Washington. The Doctor always admitted that he thoroughly enjoyed these conferences.[14]

The man of good deeds also had a distinct style for ending a discussion. While serving as mayor, he was confronted by a truculent old lady from South Boston who "sought audience of the Doctor to complain of water in her cellar which had seeped in and drowned her hens. Even in those benighted days keeping hens in a cellar was contrary to the city's ordinances. Loud was the good woman's keening, and there was no stopping her. At last the Doctor, who could be brutal on occasion, ended the matter by saying: 'But why don't you keep ducks?' "[15]

The officers and many members of the Society were fairly confident that Green, a lifelong bachelor, would become their Samaritan and leave a liberal bequest. After all, the Society had been his "personal 'abiding place' " for many years. It was his home away from home.

Moreover, it was Green, who, as co-executor of John Langdon Sibley's estate, had persuaded his close friend and librarian of Harvard to structure his will so that the Society would receive the bulk of his holdings upon the death of his wife.[16] Green and Sibley had been friends for years. When Sibley had come to the Society to do research on his biographical sketches of Harvard graduates, Green displayed "great vigilance" and assisted him in every possible way. He also had visited Sibley at his home in Cambridge every Sunday afternoon to consult further with him on his project.[17] If he had worked so diligently to influence Sibley to assist the Society, surely he planned to do likewise with his own estate.

This certainly was the thinking of Adams. In April 1911, after receiving word from Treasurer Lord that the Society was in a weak financial condition and faced the prospect of a "deficit in the annual income," Adams replied: "Moreover, as you know, financially we have

---

[14] M.H.S., *Procs.*, 54(1920–1921):239–240.
[15] *Harvard Alumni Bulletin*, March 1919, p. 328.
[16] For Sibley's will, see M.H.S., *Procs.*, 2d ser., 16(1902):20–23.
[17] M.H.S., *Procs.*, 61(1927–1928):100. Sibley left his estate to the Historical Society because President Charles W. Eliot had no interest in his project.

'expectations.' Whether they will materialize or not remains to be seen. Nevertheless, I feel confidence in our star. The Doctor has, as you know, in this respect been a good friend. It was he who directed the Sibley bequests our way. Why should not the future in this matter be a repetition of the past?"[18] That Green never confided in Adams or any other member of the Society about the disposition of his estate should have given the president and his colleagues pause to wonder.[19]

If Adams viewed Green as a future financial savior of the Society, he also regarded him currently as its greatest liability. The "everlasting and inescapable Big Medicine Man," as Adams once derisively described Green, was the personification of the Society's clubby character. He symbolized what Adams disliked about the Society. Adams sarcastically referred to this condition as "Greenism," defined by Lyman H. Butterfield as the "somnolent, puttering, proprietary, un- and even anti-professional management" of the Society.[20]

Adams had a different conception of the Society. He envisioned it as an active center of historical scholarship. He regarded the library as the key element in his scheme. First and foremost, it must be open to all responsible researchers. Membership must not be the sole criterion for usage. Secondly, it must be staffed by trained personnel and administered in a professional manner.

Adams had conceived a plan for administering the library and it was a change "of the most radical and far-reaching character." He was determined "to end, once [and] for all, root and branch, the old regime." He intended to "put the Library, and practically the entire working organization, so to speak, in charge of a Commission." His plan called for the appointment of a special, three-member body, consisting of the editor, librarian, and recording secretary. Green, as librarian, would be the nominal head of the group.

The major reform was to be the introduction of a "corps of educated female assistants, who would do the work as it is now done in every well

[18] Arthur Lord to C.F. Adams, Apr. 8, 1911 (C.F. Adams Papers); C.F. Adams to A. Lord, Apr. 10, 1911 (Editorial Correspondence, M.H.S. Archives).

[19] Since Green was seventy years old in 1900, and not in the best of health, Adams was of the belief that his imminent demise was all but certain. Green, himself, was surprised that he had survived to 1900. He thought that he was on the verge of death seven years earlier. See M.H.S., *Procs.*, 43(1909–1910):223–227.

[20] M.H.S., *Procs.*, 83(1971):50.

organized Library and Society throughout the Country." The commission would develop the principles of operation and "introduce their changes and reforms gradually, and in the ways which experience showed in our case were most likely to accomplish the ends in view."[21]

With his intention of introducing a "corps of educated female assistants," Adams gave evidence that he had become a disciple of Melvil Dewey, who revolutionized the library profession in the United States in 1883 by hiring six Wellesley College graduates to work in his Columbia University library.[22] The "Wellesley Half Dozen" constituted "the world's first class in library science" and their hiring by Dewey paved the way for the introduction of women into the library profession. When Dewey introduced this innovation, "Columbia College was almost as hermetically sealed to women as is a monastery, and the advent of a group of young college women, appearing in the sacred precincts, must indeed have give occasion for dire forebodings."[23]

Since Adams did not reveal his plan in a formal document, it is doubtful that Green was fully aware of it. He did know that Adams wished to make drastic systemic changes, and he was unalterably opposed to this notion. Dr. Green was bound and determined to preserve the Society as a private club. He did not favor opening the library to outsiders or replacing the librarian and cabinet-keeper by salaried, professional personnel, male or female.

The increasingly "vast and indolent" Green was a large obstruction for Adams. As president, Adams could direct the affairs of the governing board strictly, but within the Fenway building the imperious "growling Cerberus" reigned supreme. He bestrode the institution. This was his domain. He was a daily, commanding presence there. He had his special

---

[21] C.F. Adams to Edward Stanwood, Aug. 27, 1912 (C.F. Adams Papers).

[22] Adams also had witnessed the introduction of paid women librarians at the Boston Athenaeum. This reform did not come easily. The Athenaeum Trustees proposed the use of women library assistants in the 1850s but were opposed by Librarian Charles Folsom (1847–1856), who felt that the "narrow galleries and steep staircases should 'cause a decent female to shrink' and, also, their presence would occasion frequent embarrassment to modest men." Folsom was also afflicted with the traditional chauvinistic prejudices of his age: "Nor is it desirable that a modest young woman should have anything to do with the corrupter portions of the polite literature. A considerable portion of a general library should be to her a closed book." The reform took place after Folsom retired in 1856. See: *Change and Continuity: A Pictorial History of the Boston Athenaeum* (Boston, 1976), 8; *The Influence and History of the Boston Athenaeum* (Boston, 1907), 41–42.

[23] Fremont Rider, *Melvil Dewey* (Chicago, 1944), 79; see also, 78–82.

desk and chair and spent all of his time at that station. In his later years, when he was sickly, he rarely left his "large armchair," one of the original Windsor chairs purchased by the Society in 1791. Green's "shabby little desk" always contained a "mountain high" stack of "never-to-be-answered memoranda."[24] Surrounding his desk and chair were piles of manuscripts and pamphlets, many of which dealt with the antiquities of Groton, his favorite subject.[25] He was enamored of it. He constantly read, talked, and wrote about the history of his home town.[26] Worthington C. Ford wrote: "I do not think that Dr. Green has read a novel in his life in which the scene was not laid in Groton."[27] One of Green's friends stated, "when not interested in what one said, he simply changed the subject and could always fall back on Groton."[28]

By the early 1900s the Society had hired three young men to assist Green in the library.[29] None had had formal training in this field. The high-handed and extremely cantankerous Green regarded these attendants as his personal servants rather than Society employees. He was constantly shouting orders at them from his desk. Petrified by Green, they promptly responded to his every need and whim. The man who loved slum children and was kind to down-and-outers was a virtual dictator within the confines of the Society.

When Worthington C. Ford began his employment as editor of pub-

[24] *Harvard Graduates' Magazine*, 27(1918–1919):330. Warren Wheeler described Dr. Green's desk as "a small 2½' x 3' tip-top, containing a variety of clippings and miscellaneous objects." M.H.S., *Procs.*, 78(1966):40.

[25] Ford considered the accumulation of combustible matter in and about the librarian's desk and in "dust heaps and loose accumulations," which were "scattered all over the building" a serious fire hazard. Frederick Jackson Turner, as a member of the library committee, suggested that "automatic sprinkling pipes" be run into the building from the cellar. Ford hypothesized that "the chief advantage would be that some night the pipes might work automatically, and so wash out all the Doctor's accumulations—that alone would be worth a handsome sum to the Society." W.C. Ford to C.F. Adams, Apr. 7, 1911 (C.F. Adams Papers)

[26] According to Ford, there were piles of Green's articles on Groton throughout the Society. W.C. Ford to C.F. Adams, Feb. 14, 1911 (C.F. Adams Papers).

[27] W.C. Ford to Grenville H. Norcross, Jan. 1, 1916 (Editorial Correspondence. M.H.S. Archives).

[28] M.H.S., *Procs.*, 52(1918–1919):51.

[29] The three were Julius H. Tuttle, Alfred B. Page, and Charles Stearns. Warren Wheeler was added in 1913. As the foursome all lived in Dedham, Wheeler referred to them as the "Dedham Dynasty." Warren Gage Wheeler, "Fifty Years on Boylston Street," M.H.S., *Procs.*, 78(1966):44.

lications in 1909, he was shocked by Green's tyrannical treatment of the attendants. As he informed Adams: "My picture of the quietude of the Society rooms equals the reality. It is a perfect condition for study and uninterrupted work; with an occasional realization that there is in the ante-chamber a Turkish pasha with three 'slaveys' doing God knows what. I have never seen so complete a state of subjection! Conditions in early New England were liberty rampant by comparison."[30]

Green did not totally bar non-members from entering his fiefdom, but neither did he welcome them graciously or provide a full measure of service.[31] He regarded them as interlopers. One example of the "intolerant and exclusive spirit" which could be found at the Historical Society was soon made public through a "letter to the Editor" in the *Boston Evening Transcript*. In early September, 1910, E. C. McKnight, a visitor from the Pittsburgh suburb of Sewickley, made a pilgrimage to Boston and the Society for the express purpose of seeing the manuscripts of Samuel Sewall's and Cotton Mather's diaries.[32] The visitor

> found the Society open. At least the door was open. There was nothing of the slightest interest visible, and evidently no welcome for chance visitors, none of the well-arranged and plainly-labelled relics, none of the obliging and intelligent attendants, that we naturally associate with an historical society. I asked to see Sewall's diary and Cotton Mather's, and was

[30] W.C. Ford to C.F. Adams, Jan. 7, 1909. A month later, Ford wrote to Adams: "It is needless to say that things remain unchanged in this Constantinopolitan empire; only, the *young* Turk party gains in force daily. It constitutes a tyranny without a shadow of benevolent assimilation, and offers a field for very interesting study. I cannot but wonder at the patience of those desiring better things." Ford to Adams, Feb. 5, 1909 (C.F. Adams Papers)

[31] Prof. Albert B. Hart wrote of Green: "It is not creditable to the Society that our splendid collection should be so little accessible, or that the atmosphere should be so repellant to those who have a right to expect cordiality and aid in using the books. Dr. Green practically never gives anybody any help—at least I have never been able to get out of him any useful information. . . . I recognize Dr. Green's long interest in the Society, which however has abundantly honored him, and would continue to do so if he were Vice President only. Why cannot the Society take this opportunity to make a librarian who will actually foster the library, fill up gaps, exchange extraneous material, open the doors, draw investigators, give effect to that side of our property and historical interests? Hart to C.F. Adams, Mar. 10, 1911 (C.F. Adams Papers).

[32] Ford believed that the letter in the newspaper was "manifestly the product of a woman," but the gender of E.C. McKnight cannot be confirmed. See Ford to Adams, Sept. 13, 1910; and Adams's response on Sept. 14, 1910 (both in C.F. Adams Papers).

promptly refused. When I inquired if there were no manuscripts that I could see, the clerk called my attention to two crossed swords high up above a door. Whose they were or what they looked like, I do not know. But to be offered a cold, cruel sword when you want a glimpse of a most passionate and appealing diary—that 'is just being tortured.' Stung by the disappointment, I ventured to plead my cause. The clerk yielded a little bit. 'If there was any special passage.' Any one! There were a hundred. The place where he tells how he courted—in the most Scriptural and decorous manner—the charming Abagail, how on the wedding day he arrived at her father's house too early for the ceremony, and beguiled his impatience by meditating on the marriage at Cana of Galilee, 'fetching one observation and one supplication out of every verse,' that saddest and most touching passage where he tells how he kissed her 'most lovely hand' and gave her up forever, his description of the 'calamity of the spreading measles,' his account of the insane tormentings of his third wife, that most 'ungentle womanly gentlewoman,' his tragic and heartrending lament for Increase, his wayward son, or his very trenchant statement that the Corporation of Harvard College would never elect him president and would always do the most foolish thing possible. I longed to see them one and all. But while I hesitated, trying to remember a date or some dry, statistical fact, reluctant to appear so foolishly sentimental. . . .

The Librarian appeared and I was passed on to him. I can't help wishing that he would let me 'redd up' his desk. I have always maintained that the appearance of one's desk is a very good index of the state of one's mind. No one could be very open to impressions with such a litter of papers filling and overflowing every pigeon-hole. That probably accounts for the very unresponsive manner, against which my appeals dashed helplessly. I did not ask to examine the diary, not even to touch it, only to look at it from a distance, through a glass, with my hands tied behind me, if necessary. Maddened by the thought that I was in the same building with the precious manuscript and yet not able to look at it, I ventured one last plea. 'I have come all the way from Pittsburgh'—Alas, that argument was a fatal one. You could almost hear the Librarian say: 'Odi profanum vulgus et arceo,' as he turned his back on me and began opening his mail. I retired discomfited, but not convinced that I was in the wrong.[33]

With apparent glee, the *Philadelphia Inquirer* printed an article, heavily boosterish in tone, that lambasted the Society for its restrictive policy and elitist character. Under the headline "Boston Turns Down a Pennsylvanian," the article satirized the traveler who "went unannounced, even without letters of introduction. How he expected under

[33] *Boston Evening Transcript*, Dec. 12, 1910.

these circumstances to pry off the lid of Boston culture to the slightest extent is more than we can imagine, but it shows the temerity and even innocence of the man" to attempt to see the great Puritan diaries in the "umbrageous recesses of the noiseless halls of the Massachusetts Historical Society." The Society was an "ancient and sacrosanct institution which none but the one hundred members of the society (and few of them) ever think of entering," and it would be "sacrilege for the outsider to attempt" a visit. Nonetheless, the

> bold, ignorant man from Pittsburg went up the steps without the fear of the intellectual Brahmins before his eyes, and he got his rebuke in strictly Bostonian fashion. He asked an aged attendant for permission to see the manuscript, and that functionary almost swooned. It was unprecedented, it was impossible. Finally he managed to force himself past this man and reached the secretary, who was even more aghast at the proposition. It was simply unthinkable. Even a request to look at the manuscript under glass so shocked the custodian that he was obliged to turn his back and continue his correspondence lest he give way to his feelings. And so the visitor came out without attaining the object of his visit.

However, even the Philadelphia newspapers knew that the fault did not lie with the president of the Society. "We are glad to learn that Charles Francis Adams, president of the society, was not in Boston at the time. It would have produced consequences scarcely less than fatal. We think that a lot of Massachusetts alleged history deserves to be embalmed forever in the tomb of the Historical Society."

The *Evening Transcript* reprinted the article in its September 21 edition. Curiously, six days earlier, the paper had published a letter to the editor from a resident of Brunswick, Maine, praising Green for his helpful service to library patrons. "Whatever may be the rules of the Massachusetts Historical Society with reference to visitors, surely 'Odi profanum vulgus et arceo' is not applicable to its librarian. The writer is but one of many that have found in him a generous, painstaking and self-sacrificing helper of literary workers who had no claim upon his time nor upon the organization he serves."

Another similar incident occurred in 1912. Ford's sister came to Boston from New York City on a "bibliographical errand." While there she visited the Society and Ford "placed her in the Dowse Library, and Mr. Tuttle [the assistant librarian] gave her all the material she wanted. She knew nothing about the internal situation and she knew nothing of certain views, necessarily strong, which I share with others on the opportunities for reform." In the evening she complained to her brother about "that old man." She said that he was "so ugly and cross to the other men that she felt tempted to go out and ask him to be gentler in his manner and not treat them so like dogs! . . . She wanted to know who he was. This, as I say, was an unbiased picture of what goes on there; but I succeeded in convincing her that she was extremely fortunate in being in the Dowse room and in not having to ask his permission to see the collections. It would be amusing if it were not so tragic."[34]

A young Harvard scholar also felt the effects of Green's imperial rule, as well as the sting of his acerbic tongue, in "about 1906 or 1907." Samuel Eliot Morison, a scion of one of Boston's best-known families and destined to become a renowned American historian, entered the library for the first time to conduct research on Harrison Gray Otis, his distinguished ancestor. He failed to check in with the librarian, a cardinal error. He withdrew a drawer of cards from the catalogue and was leafing through the entries, at which point "Dr. Green roared at me: 'Get the hell off that catalogue! That's for members only!'" That experience remained indelibly engraved in Morison's memory for the rest of his life.[35]

In 1905, Allan Forbes, an energetic young officer of the State Street Trust Company, entered the Society and had a similar experience. His bank had just opened a branch office nearby at the corner of Massachusetts Avenue and Boylston Street and he was scouring the neighborhood for new customers. Green wasted little time with Forbes. He summarily ejected him from the building. "The recollection of this initial rebuff," Walter M. Whitehill wrote in his memoir of Forbes, "always amused him during his subsequent service as the Society's treasurer from 1921 to 1928 and from 1951 to 1955."[36]

In addition to being overbearing to his attendants and rude and surly

[34] W.C. Ford to C.F. Adams, Jan. 24, 1912 (C.F. Adams Papers).

[35] Morison recounted this incident in an address before the Society at the Spring Reception, June 6, 1975; there is a tape of his talk in the M.H.S. Archives. Morison was a member of the Society from 1914 to his death in 1976.

[36] M.H.S., *Procs.*, 71(1953–1957):414; Whitehill, *Independent Historical Societies*, 20. Forbes served as president of the bank from 1911 to 1950, then became chairman of the board. He was a member of the Society from 1921 to his death in 1955.

to researchers who were not members, Green had other shortcomings as a library administrator. He was inefficient and did not perform his assigned functions promptly or conscientiously. He did little cataloguing and rarely acknowledged gifts. On one occasion he did acknowledge the receipt of a book, but the donor could not have been pleased by Green's caustic comment: "This book fills a gap long needed."[37]

Nor did Green keep the library in a tidy condition. Piles of books, manuscripts, pamphlets, and other materials were strewn about in all of the library rooms. Much of this mess was Green's own historical output. He used the library as a storage area for offprints of his prodigious publications, many of which dealt with the history of Groton. Only occasionally were new topics introduced, such as in 1911 when he produced an article on piracy. Never missing an opportunity to bash Green for the physical woes of the library, Ford informed Charles F. Adams:

> The Dr. awaits the proofs of his piracy article, and it will appear as a separate. As nearly the whole number of these separates is stacked on the lower range of our stacks, we have cause to 'view with alarm' his continued output. Fortunately the essays are small in bulk, and he sees the increasing number of titles in much the same light that Cotton Mather saw his increasingly large number of titles. But Mather circulated his. There are about two tons of the Dr's imprints now here—a library in themselves.[38]

In 1889, Robert C. Winthrop, Jr., informed fellow member Charles C. Smith that Green's poor management of the library would dissuade donors from giving books and similar materials:

> It was impossible for me to go into detail without offending S.A.G., but Dr. Deane & Everett furnished me with particulars of valuable books found either on the floor, or in a dirty, uncared for, or practically inaccessible condition, when miscellaneous pamphlets and pub. docs. of no value were safely stowed on shelves. Dr. D[eane] expressly authorized me to state that the Society was in danger of losing, if it had not already lost, important legacies of books or pictures, from dissatisfaction with the existing state of things.[39]

In a similar vein, in 1909, Ford appealed to the house committee "to move against the accumulation of matter which is piled under the, so

---

[37] M.H.S., *Procs.*, 52(1918–1919):51. The source of this information was Robert Grant, who had been Green's secretary when he was mayor.

[38] Ford to Adams, Feb. 14, 1911 (C.F. Adams Papers).

[39] R.C. Winthrop, Jr., to C.C. Smith, July 28, 1889 (Charles C. Smith Papers, M.H.S.)

called, students' table in the Doctor's room, on the ground, that a student was entitled to a place for his leg, no matter what was done with his head." In its response, the committee admitted the validity of Ford's plea "but does not wish to antagonize the possessor of the Society."[40]

Some of Green's detractors accused him of "promiscuous collecting." They asserted that he did not exercise discrimination in his acquisition of materials. He took everything that was offered. After reading a newspaper account about "our excellent friend" celebrating his seventieth birthday, Robert C. Winthrop, Jr., informed Adams on March 18, 1900: "The much needed weeding of printed matter belonging to the M.H.S. would thus seem appreciably nearer, tho' you & I may not live to witness it. Indeed, I incline to think rubbish on the increase."

Winthrop went on to note that when his father had moved to Pemberton Square more than half a century ago, he discovered that his next-door neighbor was

> an unattractive old party named Mark Healey, whose daughter Caroline had married a Unitarian minister named Dall & was then, and for long afterward, an authoress in a small way, with an ambition to regenerate her sex, combined with a propensity to 'interview' men of note. Availing herself of her propinquity, she from time to time plied my father with all sorts of questions & at great length, causing him to exclaim 'This lady's name ought not to be Dall, but Dull.' Imagine my surprise to discover on p. 310 of the recently issued Serial that last November the Society accepted the following gift from this now venerable person:
>
> 'Three trunks containing type-written material; seven quarto volumes of MSS, 12 printed volumes, 5 pamphlets, & three other volumes of MSS' *the whole apparently autobiographical!*
>
> No wonder the new building is already too small for our purposes, and the joke of the matter is that as I hear whispered, the lady had vainly offered this cumbrous material to other institutions, who respectfully declined to house it.[41]

Adams began to vent his spleen against Green and Smith when the Boylston Street building became operational, but only in private con-

[40] W.C. Ford to C.F. Adams, Aug. 2, 1909 (C.F. Adams Papers).

[41] R.C. Winthrop, Jr., to C.F. Adams, Mar. 18, 1900 (C.F. Adams Papers). Winthrop was short-sighted in this case. The Caroline Dall Papers have become one of the Society's prize holdings in the late 20th century with the rise of the women's studies movement. A selected edition of her journals is now being prepared by Prof. Helen Deese for publication in the *Collections* series.

versations and correspondence with close friends, or in his journal. In his personal relationships with these two senior officials, he remained cordial and deferential. He was especially respectful of Green since he did not wish to antagonize him and jeopardize a possible bequest.

An incident developed in June 1900 which provoked Adams to unburden in his journal his antipathy toward Smith, initially, and, then, both of his adversaries. At the June meeting, Adams had recommended Worthington C. Ford for membership as ''a man who would really be greatly useful, learned in American history, up in library methods . . . an attendant at our meetings, a contributor to our Proceedings.'' Ford was then a resident of Boston and head of the newly established department of documents and statistics at the Boston Public Library. Smith openly opposed his nomination. Adams was furious. He wrote in his journal:

> Immediately the voice of C.C. Smith is heard in objection,—Ford had, in his edition of Washington's writings, used Sparks's notes without acknowledgement,—a most discreditable proceeding, &c. &c. And so it goes!—the old, hide-bound traditional element, which would fill the Society with respectable names, and deplete it of working force and utility. It has always been so, and I fear I shall not be able to wrench it out of the rut. Certainly I can do absolutely nothing as long as Sam Green and Smith remain,—men who have wholly outlived their usefulness, and now linger along only to obstruct. Both of them I sincerely regard. They have the interests of the Society deeply at heart; they, and they alone, connect us with its traditions; but they have done their work, such as it was, and now they go lumbering along, blocking my way. And they do it very effectively. Both are now over 70 years old; but they show no signs of being other than they for years have been; and I must wait,—the head of a lifeless concern until nature removes this obstacle—or me. I am ashamed of myself and my position; but I have thought the whole thing over, and see no escape. I might, it is true, resign, and let things take their course. Not impossibly that would be wisest and best; but I hate to sever my connections with what I see under other conditions could easily be made a living historical force. But I feel under the restraint of the situation. I do not like to feel myself responsible for it. It is a dead-alive affair. It must remain so for two lives in being.[42]

Smith's opposition to Ford proved futile. He was a solitary dissenter. Not even Green supported him on this issue. Adams easily secured Ford's election. When the corn and black beans were counted, only one black bean was in the ballot box, presumably Smith's vote.

[42] C.F. Adams, Memorabilia, June 15, 1900 (C.F. Adams Papers).

Adams Begins His Reforms

Adams's dark mood persisted in 1901. After the annual meeting in April, he contemplated resigning the presidency. He reconsidered and decided to stay on for a seventh term. He described his quandary in his journal in a characteristically frank prose style:

Of the Historical Society, I do not know what to say. The Annual Meeting (April 11th) presented no new features. We had a full meeting—over 40—in the Fenway building. The day was pleasant enough, and everything passed off without a hitch. The old officers were re-elected as of course, I among them as President, for the seventh time. I notified the committee that I was tired of the position, and that my resignation was always in their hands; but added that, from my knowledge of the intimate affairs of the Society, I apprehended that my pressing the matter at this time might be embarrassing, and I therefore did not do so. It was intimated to me in reply that my so doing would be most embarrassing; and so things took the usual course. I gave the usual entertainment in the Ellis room,—of which about 125 partook. The new Waterston room[43] was thrown open for the first time, and was much appreciated. I think it is a creditable piece of work. My guests seemed to enjoy themselves, and were cordially as well as politely expressive of the fact.

At the same time . . . this is getting to be an old and unprofitable story, as well as, both in time and responsibility, a very considerable tax. In mere money, it has cost me $1500 during the last year,—interest on the lot, now sold, $15,000 @ 5% = $750, reception $425, gifts to Library etc. $200 = $1400;—and I have constantly to provide intellectual instruments. But the trouble is that the thing is eminently unsatisfactory. The organization is worn out, and circumstances prevent any effort at renewal. That process, to be successful, implies at least three funerals, and a large increase of endowment. The waiting for dead-men's shoes is proverbially tiresome. I find it so in this case. Nothing can be done to cause that Society to justify its continued being until its Librarian, its Editor, and Mrs. Sibley pass away; and even then, modern requirements are such that it will require $200,000 of additional endowment. Can it get such a sum? I linger along in hopes. Dr. Green is very well to do; for that reason, I humor him—and wait, as well as serve. But it is a very considerable tax.[44]

The death of Mrs. Sibley in 1902 brought some measure of comfort to Adams, as well as to the Society. The latter received a twofold finan-

---

[43] This room housed the collection willed to the Society by Robert C. Waterston, which was received in November 1899, after the death of his widow. See *Catalogue of the Library and Collection of Autograph Letters, Papers, and Documents Bequeathed to the Massachusetts Historical Society by The Rev. Robert C. Waterston* (Boston, 1906). The room is now (1995) the director's office.

[44] C.F. Adams, Memorabilia, Apr. 29, 1901 (C.F. Adams Papers).

cial windfall. Sibley's bequest yielded a whopping $282,723.65. His estate had increased considerably during the final years of Mrs. Sibley's life because of compounded interest. To that time, it was the largest gift by far received by the Society. Despite the restrictions imposed by Sibley in the use of these funds, it was a most welcome gift. Through the influence of Dr. Green, her sole executor, Mrs. Sibley bequeathed an additional $22,509 to the Society.[45] Her gift was unrestricted. Both legacies were paid in two installments in 1903 and 1904.

The Sibley bequests provided only temporary pleasure for Adams. The basic problem of "Greenism" persisted. The "Big Medicine Man" and Smith continued to be hindrances at every step. His frustration had reached the breaking point. Every year he threatened to resign the presidency but, on reflection, decided to stay in office, awaiting and longing for the death of Green and the retirement or removal in some other way of Smith.

In 1905 Adams conceived a new strategy. He decided to resign as president, thereby opening the way for Green to succeed him. He believed that, once ensconced as president, Green was certain to "leave a big legacy to the Society." The honor of the presidency would be the clincher. How could he possibly do otherwise? And he certainly could not live much longer. In Adams's blunt words:

> Green is now 75 and not at all a good life,—very fat and tremulous, he eats enormously and takes no exercise. He is rich and kinless; he may go any day. We ought to get a large legacy from him; and I need it for the successful reorganization of the Society on that new basis I have long had in mind. So I proposed to make way for Green, and, in so doing, thought to make sure of the legacy.[46]

Following Green's death, Adams planned to reclaim the presidency and move swiftly to phase three, reorganization. Adams enlarged upon his secret scheme in his January 1, 1905, journal entry:

> As to the Historical Society, after long deliberation I concluded not to accept another election to the presidency at this time. I did so against very active remonstrance; but, thinking it all over, the balance of considerations seemed to favor my so doing. I held this position anyhow simply because there was no satisfactory successor in sight; and, in it, there was, and is, as at present

[45] C.F. Adams credited Green for both Sibley bequests. See Adams to Arthur Lord, Jan. 12, 1914 (C.F. Adams Papers).

[46] C.F. Adams, Memorabilia, May 27, 1905 (C.F. Adams Papers).

circumstances, nothing for me to do. I simply staid, and did the work, to prevent the necessity of choosing Sam Green as my successor,—a thing difficult to avoid doing, but what no one wanted to do. The fact is the Society moves in a rut, and, under present conditions, cannot be got out of it. All has been done which can be done, until a complete reorganization can be effected. I have been its president ten full years; and, during these years, everything preliminary to a complete reorganization has been completed,—and it is a good deal. The Society has been moved from Tremont St., and established in permanence on the Fenway. Its old estate has been disposed of on perfectly satisfactory terms. That much I did. It has then,—which I did not do except in part,—been put on a firm financial footing, and in position to do good and systematic work in future. It can be made a factor in historical accomplishment of real value; but, first, a complete change of systems is necessary. To even approach such work, it must be freed from the survivors of the old regime,—Sam Green and C.C. Smith. Both old men,—74 to 76,—they are absolutely wedded to the ancient ways, and no effectual change is possible, while they are there. To get rid of them is simply out of the question,—courtesy and consideration block the way; so they ride the Society like two old men of the Sea. As for Sam Green,—Vice President and Librarian,—he is simply impossible. Without the [illeg.] conception of a librarian's functions, he is as set as a vice; and, to do anything while he is there, is hopeless. A thoroughly good fellow and, in his way, a learned man, he is an incubus. Old and Falstaffian, he is now physically inert, and, withal, mean to a degree. Rich, he spends nothing; nor has he anyone to leave his property to. So, as respects him,—tired of standing in his way, and waiting for him to give me a chance to do something—I have changed my tactics! I will make room for him, and angle for a legacy! He may delay reorganization,—that he will do anyhow; but, if he can be induced to make the Society his heir, he will, by so doing, render reorganization not only possible but complete, once he is out of the way. If he becomes President, he is very likely to leave a big legacy to the Society. So, I make room for him! It is an uncertain game; but this seems to me a prudent card to play in it. We may get nothing; for he is an odd fish, and keeps his own counsel: but, at any rate, we lose nothing. He has got, as Vice President, to preside anyhow in my absence, and I shall now be absent most of the time; and if on the spot, I can do nothing. So what is the advantage to come from my just hanging along, waiting for him and Smith to drop away. I sometimes question whether I shall not go first—and what then? As to Smith, he has lost all his virility and grip. He is quite unfit for work, and absolutely inaccessible to new ideas. But he is there, and there he must remain until he drops away! There is no place for new wine in these old bottle. Why, then, should I hang about, awaiting their collapse?

So I have declined to continue in the presidency; with the understanding that I am quite ready to return to it whenever the work of reorganization can be taken in hand. Until then, let the old regime rule! At this immediate prospect the Society makes a very wry face; but what of it? It may welcome me back the more cordially. I will say at once, I would like to reorganize it. I know, also, how to do it. I have thought it all out; and could put my plan in operation at once. But absolutely nothing can be done while Smith and Green are where they now are,—and their exit will not be hastened by my continuance in position. So, I have concluded to withdraw, and bide my time. Will they, or I, go first?[47]

Adams followed through on his intention to resign the presidency. Before leaving for an extended trip to Egypt, he notified William R. Thayer, chairman of the nominating committee, that he did not wish to be renominated for the office. The committee was placed in a quandary and did not wish to exclude Adams without consulting the membership, so it arranged for the printing of ballots without listing a candidate for the presidency.

When the members assembled for the annual meeting, the predictable occurred. Charles E. Norton rose and, after lauding Adams for his sterling service to the Society, moved that his resignation not be accepted and that the nominating committee insert his name on the ballot. The members unanimously adopted the motion. When Adams returned from Africa, he wrote in his journal that "I found myself re-elected; and there was nothing for me to do but accept the situation. Without a single word of explanation, I did so."[48]

In June 1907, a development occurred that had to raise Adams's spirits a few notches. One of his two principal obstructionists, Smith, resigned as editor of publications, a position he had occupied for eighteen years. Restraining his sense of joy, Adams made the announcement to the members. At that same meeting, Adams effected a minor reform that had been on his mind for some time. Acting upon his recommendation, the Society voted to abolish all assessments for members. This included entrance fees and annual dues. Hereafter, all membership became honorary.[49]

Why did Adams advance this policy? He provided no written rationale for his action, but it would appear that he believed the abolition of dues would motivate members to become more generous in their phi-

[47] C.F. Adams, Memorabilia, Jan. 1, 1905 (C.F. Adams Papers).
[48] C.F. Adams, Memorabilia, May 27, 1905 (C.F. Adams Papers).
[49] M.H.S., Procs., 3d ser., 1(1907–1908):95–97, 413.

lanthropy. Experience had revealed to him that few members contributed anything beyond their annual dues, a trifling sum of $10.

Lyman H. Butterfield perceptively observed that the new policy was intended to "elevate the qualifications of members and to inspire their stronger allegiance" but had the "counter-effect of making the drones more dronish since nothing whatever seemed to be expected of them."[50] Only a handful of the one hundred resident members, possibly twenty-five to thirty, showed an active interest in the Society. The remainder were shadow members who contributed little to the program, financially or otherwise. Time was to show that Adams had grossly miscalculated when he eliminated all assessments.

Throughout the nineteenth century, and beyond, membership was a controversial and divisive issue at the Society. It could bring members' blood to a boiling point—and frequently did. The issue revolved around two interrelated questions. Who should be invited into membership? How many resident members should the Society have?

An explanation of the elective process is in order. Any member could nominate a candidate. He need only inscribe his name in a membership book. When vacancies occurred, and they occurred infrequently, the nominating committee screened these names and selected candidates. It then presented the names to the Council for review. The Council had the authority to reject these candidates.

Most of the battles erupted around these two processes. When the nominating committee deliberated and when the Council was making its review, there was intense lobbying among the members of these two bodies and by members at large, who were pleading the cause of preferred candidates. There was also an abundance of intrigue.

What role did the president of the Society play in the election of members? The best answer to this question was provided by Worthington C. Ford in a letter to President Henry Cabot Lodge on January 12, 1918. Lodge was uncertain as to his function in the process and seemed to believe that his influence would be slight. Ford provided him with some historical perspective:

> You are quite too modest in saying that the President's opinion on membership has little weight. The feeling has always been, from the days of

[50] M.H.S., *Procs.*, 83(1971):51.

Mr. Winthrop, that it is only right he should be consulted, because his presence and administration are made more pleasant and useful by a consciousness that the members are with him and enjoy his friendship. Mr. Savage often acted as executioner, and Mr. Winthrop did not hesitate to express his dislike to a proposed member. Dr. Ellis was indifferent, being a clergyman and therefore without a soul. Mr. Adams rarely interfered, but he was very careful about the names to be proposed. So now anyone whom you would like to have as a member requires only a mention from you and his name will be considered at an early date.[51]

In theory, the members were supposed to abide by a code of secrecy when considering candidates. In practice, the word usually leaked out and prospective candidates became aware of their status. In his fifty-year reminiscence, Green confessed about his own election back in 1860 to his colleagues, assuredly to their amusement:

Of course I was not supposed to know anything about the nomination, but as a matter of fact I did know that it had been made. One day in November as I was going into the Athenaeum, I met in the large hall a prominent member of the Historical Society just as he was coming out of the building, and he greeted me cordially. We stopped for a moment or two to exchange the time of day, as the saying is, when he told me confidentially that I had been nominated for membership, at the same time adding that I must not mention the fact to a living body. I knew perfectly well when the next meeting would be held, and I awaited the result with fear and anxiety. The second Thursday in December passed, and several more days, and no official notification came from the Corresponding Secretary; and I felt sure that I had been rejected, perhaps on account of my youth, as I should have been the youngest member in the Society. A few more days passed, when one evening I was calling at the house of a kinsman, a member of the Society; and with some hesitation I mentioned the subject to him and told him my inference that I had been blackballed at the December meeting. He at once relieved my disturbed mind by saying that on account of a severe snowstorm on that day and the small attendance of members there had been no balloting. He said that there were not persons enough present to secure an election, and furthermore in all probability that it would be brought about at the January meeting, which turned out to be true.[52]

[51] Ford to Lodge, Jan. 12, 1918 (Ford-Lodge Correspondence).

[52] M.H.S., *Procs.*, 43(1909–1910):227-233. The members also were to maintain absolute secrecy in the process of voting. At a much later date, Walter Whitehill observed that the "absolute secrecy of the vote is open to question. I have heard a teller, observing a bean on its way to the hole, remark in a stentorian whisper: 'You're putting in a black ball,' at

Adams Begins His Reforms

Once the Council had settled upon its nominees, as a general rule, the process was virtually at an end. The Council presented the names of "the Elect" at a stated meeting and secured the endorsement of the members. This was usually a perfunctory exercise. The recording secretary then notified all members by mail of the nominations, and the election occurred at the subsequent meeting. Before the vote could be cast, it was necessary to have a quorum of twenty members, three-fourths of whom had to vote in the affirmative.

When the ballot boxes were passed, almost all of the members selected the corn kernels, but it was not unusual to find one or two black beans in the container. After Worthington C. Ford was elected a member in November 1900, James Ford Rhodes wrote to him: "Mr. Adams was the prime mover in the matter. . . . At his request I took charge of your candidacy in the Council. . . . The meeting was unusually large, 37 being present, but there was only one black ball. It is a saying in the Society, No one can get in without at least two black balls."[53]

Rarely did a member or members challenge the standing order and mount an active campaign to blackball a candidate approved by the nominating committee and Council. This was considered unseemly behavior.

The question of who was to be invited into membership should logically be centered upon the factor of criteria for selection. What guidelines did the nominating committee and Council follow when they made their choices? The fact is that there were no prescribed criteria. The founding fathers had not established any, nor did the governing officials who followed them.

Yet, despite having no written set of criteria, there were certainly unstated standards well known to the Society's founders and their successors. These did not have to be spelled out on paper. Initially, membership would be restricted to white males. There was no mention of sex or race in the charter of 1794, but this is not surprising given the *zeitgeist* of the time. Other factors considered when evaluating candidates included: interest in history, family background, social eminence, occupation, education, financial status, political and religious views, mo-

---

which the elderly voter, whose eyes were not of the keenest, retrieved his vote with a grateful: 'I didn't intend to.' " Whitehill, *Independent Historical Societies*, 34.

[53] Quoted in M.H.S., *Procs.*, 83(1971):64.

rality, and cultivation. The founding fathers and their immediate successors were patricians and members of Boston's intellectual elite, and they sought similar types to join their ranks. Holmes the Autocrat aptly described this element as "the sifted few."[54]

For founder Belknap, a prospective member had to fulfill two criteria in particular: he had to have a deep-seated interest in the Society and its mission; and he had to be willing to devote time, energy, and financial resources to the organization. Belknap preferred "doers" to "joiners." Shortly after the founding of the Society, when additional members were being considered, Belknap exhorted the Society to select only those men disposed to "become active workers in that field; in order that it should not be tempted to elect members for the sake of bestowing upon them *a feather*, and become pursy and heavy by numbers, without proportionate activity, and power of progress."[55]

John Eliot, a fellow founder who vibrated in tune with Belknap on every aspect of the Society, echoed his sentiment in a letter to Benjamin Trumbull of Connecticut on December 11, 1790: "We have added five Members, and mean to increase our number still, tho' never to exceed 25. . . . By making the number extensive, or very *honourable*, it may be less useful. By *honourable* . . . I mean such members as are chosen into other Societies merely to do honor unto the institution, or to receive honor from it. Every person shall be under obligations to assist in the business of the Society."[56] Belknap and Eliot projected the ideal. Only a few new members, however, met their standards.

Throughout the early history of the Society, and certainly during the period of its Tremont Street residence, there was little turnover of officers. Once elected, an officer could claim a life occupancy of the position. A severe health problem, a total lack of interest, or death—these were the only factors which would lead an officer to leave his post. To be voted out of office by a dissatisfied membership was unheard of. Once the nominating committee had prepared a slate, the "election" had ended.

The Society's "system" was candidly stated by Andrew McF. Davis, senior member-at-large, in his report of the Council in 1904:

[54] Quoted in Jack Beatty, *The Rascal King: The Life and Times of James Michael Curley, 1874–1958* (Reading, Mass., 1992), 10.

[55] Josiah Quincy, elected a member of the Society in 1797, quoting Belknap at a March 1858 meeting of the Society. M.H.S., *Procs.*, 3(1855–1858):346.

[56] John Eliot to Benjamin Trumbull, Dec. 11, 1790 (Abiel Holmes Papers, M.H.S.).

Adams Begins His Reforms

The various officers of this Society are required by our by-laws to be elected annually, and with the exception of a provision in the case of Councillors whereby rotation in the Council is secured, it is evident that, notwithstanding the prescribed brevity of the term of their office, it was contemplated by those who drafted the instrument that such persons as should secure election to the permanent offices of this Society should practically hold them through successive re-elections—if not for the remainder of their respective lives, at least as long as the service should prove agreeable to them. These expectations have been practically realized, and year by year the Nominating Committee has had thrown upon it the simple duty of selecting the names of two candidates for the Council. Election to office in this Society is not an absolute guarantee against ill health or death; hence once in a while there will be some vacancy, from one of these causes, in the list of permanent officers; but it seldom happens, as is the case this year, that the Nominating Committee has thrust upon it the important service of presenting simultaneously the names of candidates to fill two vacancies in the staff of the Society.[57]

Charles C. Smith formally submitted his resignation as editor at the June 1907 meeting. In doing so, he delivered a "farewell address," aimed directly at President Adams, to whom he addressed his letter. He stated his "strong conviction" that his successor should be a member of the Society and not a rank outsider on salary:

> It seems to me from a very long experience, both before and after I became editor, that the responsibility of selecting from the mass of manuscripts in our archives such as are suitable for publication, and of editing the proceedings at our stated meetings, should only be intrusted, under the control of the Society and the Council, to one who is a Resident Member, and never to one who is not identified with it by membership, and whose chief interest in the office will be in his salary and in making for himself a personal reputation. Under the changed conditions since the Society was organized it is no longer possible for any member to give to our publishing the care and thought which are needful for bringing out the volumes without some pecuniary compensation. But that should be his last thought. He should be, or should be immediately made, one of our own number, and should always keep in mind our time-honored motto: *Sic vos non vobis.* I cannot think it either dignified or for our interest to go outside of our membership for an editor.[58]

---

[57] M.H.S., *Procs.*, 2d ser., 18(1903–1904):270.

[58] Smith's letter (dated June 1, 1907) in included in M.H.S. Council Records, June 13, 1907 (M.H.S. Archives).

The Massachusetts Historical Society

Adams was not of a mind to heed Smith's advice. Smith's resignation induced him to move ahead on his long-standing plan to reorganize the staff. Since he could not dislodge Green, he knew that his effort would constitute only a partial reorganization, but some progress was better than none. His objective was to appoint a salaried "curator." He sought an academic of considerable stature who would become "practically the general executive officer of the Society having charge in a general way of its building, its library, its editorial work, its records, etc. etc." He was prepared to pay a "very handsome salary; whatever salary, indeed, is necessary to obtain the services of such an official, for he must be a very competent man."[59]

In August, Adams wrote to Ford, soliciting his "advice and assistance in connection with a most important crisis" in the Society's affairs—that is, Smith's resignation. Ford was now residing in Washington, having left his position at the Boston Public Library in 1902 and assumed the more prestigious job of chief of the division of manuscripts in the Library of Congress. After providing his job description, Adams solicited the names of qualified candidates. He mentioned Professor Edward G. Bourne of Yale, a distinguished scholar, as the type of person he had in mind.[60]

After noting that Adams had placed the requirements of the position "so high as to leave little choice among possible candidates," Ford submitted the names of seven prospects. Heading the list were Adams's paradigm, Bourne, and Frederick Jackson Turner of the University of Wisconsin, a rising star in the academic firmament.[61] Ford suggested Professor John S. Bassett of Smith College as another strong possibility. He also recommended Reuben Gold Thwaites, George Parker Winship, and J. Franklin Jameson as "pre-eminent of their kind," although he expressed doubt that any of these men would be attracted by the job. They were already well situated.

Adams had had the foresight to send a copy of his letter to Ford to Jameson, then head of the department of historical research of the Car-

---

[59] C.F. Adams to W.C. Ford, Aug. 10, 1907 (C.F. Adams Papers).

[60] C.F. Adams to W.C. Ford, Aug. 10, 1907 (C.F. Adams Papers).

[61] There is little likelihood that Turner would have accepted an offer from the Society. He was then being wooed by almost every major university in the United States. See Ray A. Billington, "Frederick Jackson Turner Comes to Harvard," M.H.S., Procs., 74(1962): 51–83.

negie Institution of Washington. It was another case of his prescient sense. Jameson also had a broad knowledge of major academic historians in the United States, although, as a leading "scientific" historian, he had a withering contempt for historical societies, in general, and "amateur" historians, in particular. He characterized the latter, and this would include such gifted "literary historians" as Parkman and Prescott, as "*quasi* historians."[62]

Sublimating his prejudices, Jameson provided a thoughtful response to Adams's request for candidates. Perhaps he may have regarded the Massachusetts society in a different light because he had been a corresponding member since 1898 and was fully aware of its long history as a center for serious scholarship. Initially, he asserted that Adams's job description was flawed. In his judgment, one person could not handle so many responsibilities: "No one could do *all* these things well, and the saddling of a scholarly editor with administrative details would hamper his effectiveness in the primary task."

After this exchange of correspondence, Adams and Jameson conferred in person in Washington. Jameson apparently persuaded Adams to limit the position to that of a "director of research and publication," whose basic assignment would be to edit the *Proceedings* but whose "special and higher obligation" would be to produce definitive editions of the two

---

[62] A student of Herbert Baxter Adams, Jameson was the first person to receive a doctorate in American history at The Johns Hopkins University (1892). He later was elected president of the American Historical Association. Jameson believed that historical societies were provincial beyond redemption and their collections "are to us the poke bonnets and spinning wheels of old garrets." "History of Historical Societies," 31–51. In 1887, Jameson predicted "that the local antiquaries, the professional literary men, and the men of wealth and leisure devoted to study, will no doubt continue to write historical books. But an increasing portion of the annual product now comes from the teachers of history in the universities and colleges, and the signs are that the immediate future belongs to the professional class" (Jameson, *The History of Historical Writing in America* [Boston, 1891], 158–159). He also wrote that a student should complete his historical work so "that he may be duly enrolled in that noble army of doctors who are now instructing and converting New England" (Jameson to H.B. Adams, Apr. 30, 1890, quoted in Van Tassel, *Recording America's Past*, 173. See his discussion on clash between scientific and amateur history: ch. 19, esp. 171–179). Henry Adams shared Jameson's conviction. In the last days of 1884, after reading an advance copy of *Montcalm and Wolfe*, Adams wrote Parkman of his admiration for the book. But he predicted that "before long a new school of history . . . will leave us antiquated." Adams to Parkman, Dec. 21, 1884, in Harold Dean Cater, ed., *Henry Adams and His Friends* (Boston, 1947), 134.

historical landmarks, William Bradford's *History* and John Winthrop's *Journal*. As for his top candidate for the position, Jameson was convinced that "unquestionably Ford is the best man." His second choice was Turner.

Adams called upon James Ford Rhodes of Harvard, a vice president of the Society, as an unofficial advisor. The two men deliberated on this issue for nearly a year before they arrived at a decision. Ford was also their choice. A scholar of international reputation, he was then fifty years of age, in the prime of his life.

While beginning negotiations with Ford, Adams remained mindful of Green's possible reaction to such an appointment. He knew that he was "treading on somewhat delicate ground." On July 20, 1908, he wrote to Rhodes:

> I have been a little perplext as to the happiest course to pursue with our senior Vice President. Situated as he is, and holding the position he does at the Society building, he certainly would have a right to feel ignored were an arrangement reached with Mr. Ford without his knowledge. He might, and probably would, feel that he ought to have been consulted.
>
> On the other hand, the situation, so far as he is concerned has possibilities of grave consideration.[63]

After "full reflection," Adams decided to inform Green of his negotiations with Ford. What he told him is not known.[64]

Adams offered the job to Ford, contingent upon the approval of the Council.[65] He also informed him that he was free to set his own salary, a most unusual, if not extraordinary, action. After reflecting upon his circumstances, Ford agreed to take the job. He also set a figure for his annual salary: $5,000. This was "perfectly agreeable" to Adams although it was four thousand more than Smith's stipend.[66]

What prompted Ford to leave his secure position in a major, high-

---

[63] C.F. Adams to J.F. Rhodes, July 20, 1908 (C.F. Adams Papers).

[64] Adams sent Rhodes a copy of his letter to Dr. Green, but the letter is not in his correspondence. Rhodes replied that Green favored the appointment of Ford. See C.F. Adams to J.F. Rhodes, July 20, 1908; and Rhodes to Adams, July 25, 1908 (C.F. Adams Papers).

[65] He also asked Ford to serve as a consultant to the Adams Manuscript Trust, which managed the Adams Family Papers. See Chapter 15 for a discussion of the Adams Papers.

[66] James B. Wilbur to Arthur Lord, Dec. 5, 1924 (Editorial Correspondence, M.H.S. Archives).

visibility, cultural-educational institution in the nation's capital and take employment with a small, financially impoverished historical society in Boston? Was it the appreciable increase in salary? Ford's papers provide no answers to this intriguing question. Butterfield has offered the most plausible explanation for his decision: "Ford was attracted here in the first place by his understanding of the Society's distinguished record and high potential in advancing historical knowledge. Respect for Charles Francis Adams as an able, working historian himself was the main source of Ford's attachment to Adams and of his confidence in the arrangements made for his own appointment as Editor."[67]

Adams knew that he would incur opposition in the Council on Ford's salary. He also anticipated criticism from some of the members, including Smith, although they would not be voting upon the appointment. Ford's salary was higher than the average salary of a full professor of history at that time.[68] It was double the salary he was receiving from the Library of Congress.

Adams recommended Ford's appointment at the October Council meeting. He also cited Ford's proposed salary. As he expected, there was considerable discussion on the issue. As he knew, his recommendation was approved. He was "empowered to arrange with Mr. Ford to enter upon his duties at the beginning of the next calendar year."[69]

At the subsequent Society meeting, Adams did not announce Ford's appointment since he had not confirmed the arrangement with him. He merely stated that, because it was a significant appointment, "those having the matter in charge . . . have deemed it best to move slowly, and with the utmost circumspection." He was, however, "glad now to announce that a selection has practically been reached," and he felt certain that an "official announcement" would be made at the November meeting of the Society.

After receiving Ford's written acceptance, Adams announced his appointment at the November meeting.[70] Ford was to be "responsible for the proper editing of all volumes, whether of Collections or Proceedings,

---

[67] M.H.S., *Procs.*, 2d ser., 18(1903–1904):270.

[68] Francis R. Hart to James Wilbur, Dec. 11, 1924 (Editorial Correspondence, M.H.S. Archives).

[69] M.H.S. Council Records, Oct. 8, 1908 (M.H.S. Archives).

[70] M.H.S. Council Records, Nov. 12, 1908 (M.H.S. Archives).

the supervision of the Society's copyists, and the adequate preparation of all material intended for the press." He would begin in early January, 1909.[71]

"Mr. Ford goes to Boston" ran as a headline in the *Washington Evening Star*. Working from a press release issued by the Library of Congress and presumably drafted by Ford, the newspaper reported that Ford "has just been elected to the most important salaried office in the Massachusetts Historical Society and one of the most important of its kind in the United States. It is nominally that of an editor, but with functions and authority much beyond the implication of that term."[72]

In his public statements, Adams gave the impression that Ford was to occupy the same role in the Society as Smith had, that his duties would largely encompass editorial matters. Thus, in theory, he would be one member of a *duumvirate*, a co-equal with Green in the table of organization. It was obvious that Adams had Green's sensibilities in mind when he made such pronouncements. It soon became evident, however, that Adams actually hired Ford as a *de facto* chief executive officer, in keeping with what he had written him on August 10, 1907.

Ford was to become more than a "Prince of Editors."[73] He was to become Adams's agent on the scene and his duties would transcend editing. They also would include: formulating the Council agendas and organizing all aspects of these meetings; planning the programs for the meetings, including the selection of speakers; communicating materials from the Society's collections; preparing the manuscripts of speakers and memoirists, and the "remarks and communications," for the publisher of the *Proceedings*, and then reading the proofs; consulting with and advising the nominating committee in drawing up annual slates; writing the Council's reports to the membership, which were presented at the annual meeting; and handling acquisitions for the library and cabinet.

Adams also expected Ford to achieve his broader mission of creating an "open" library that was in harmony with the new spirit of the time.

---

[71] Ford began his new job on Jan. 4, 1909, and his appointment was confirmed by the members at the Jan. 14 Society meeting. M.H.S., *Procs.*, 42(1908–1909):68.

[72] *Washington Evening Star*, Nov. 17, 1908. See also, M.H.S., *Procs.*, 83(1971):50.

[73] In 1949, Samuel F. Bemis dedicated his biography of John Quincy Adams "To the memory of Worthington Chauncey Ford, Friend, and Prince of Editors."

"The long age of the amateur historian had ended," in the words of David Van Tassel.[74] The new age of the professional historian had begun. Greenism was passé.

In his report of the Council in April 1909, senior member-at-large Nathaniel Paine stated that Ford's acceptance of his position "marks the beginning of a new era in the history of our Society." The statement was trite but true.[75]

[74] Van Tassel, *Recording America's Past*, 179. For another informative account of the stresses and strains between the amateur and academic historians in this transitional era, see David J. Russo, *Keepers of Our Past: Local Historical Writing in the United States, 1820s-1930s* (New York, 1988), ch. 12.

[75] M.H.S., *Procs.*, 42(1908–1909):237.

Chapter 12

Greenism Must Go

WORTHINGTON C. FORD was descended from a long line of distinguished ancestors, and so it was no surprise that he became enamored with books and learning and American history.[1] One of his forebears was Charles Chauncy, the second president of Harvard College. His great-grandfather was Noah Webster, the eminent lexicographer. His grandfather William Chauncey Fowler published works of philology and genealogy.

Ford's parents also were bookish and highly refined. His father, a successful Brooklyn lawyer and businessman, was an avid bibliophile and collector of historical manuscripts. He amassed a considerable library on history, political economy, and Americana. His book and pamphlet collection grew to 100,000 works and his manuscripts numbered about 60,000. According to Alan Nevins, it was "one of the finest private libraries in America."[2]

Worthington's mother, the daughter of an Amherst College professor, was a poet and essayist and produced several publications. Two of her children, Worthington and Paul, became habitués of the father's library at an early age. This became their playroom, their favorite retreat. Both youngsters had lively and curious minds and a ravenous appetite for books. They became passionate devotees of American history, particularly for the period of the American Revolution.

Paul, an intellectual prodigy, took up the practice of printing genea-

[1] The best biographical account of Ford is Lyman H. Butterfield, "Worthington Chauncey Ford, Editor," M.H.S., Procs., 83(1971):46–82. See also: Stewart Mitchell's brief but perceptive memoir, "Worthington Chauncey Ford," ibid., 69(1947–1950):407–411; Clarence S. Brigham's memoir of Ford in A.A.S., Procs., 51, pt. 1(1941):10–14.

[2] Dictionary of American Biography, 6:518. The New York Public Library acquired this collection.

logical and bibliographical works on a hand press given to him by his father. Worthington and the father assisted him in this enterprise. Between 1876 and 1899, the Fords issued about eighty titles under the imprint of "Brooklyn, N.Y.: Historical Printing Club." According to Lyman H. Butterfield, some of these publications "remain tools and sources indispensable to the historian today."[3] After a relatively brief but remarkably productive career as an author, journalist, historical editor, and biographer, Paul was murdered in 1920, at the age of thirty-seven, by his younger brother Malcolm, who then committed suicide.[4]

Worthington was destined to a long life of scholarly achievement. He attended Brooklyn Polytechnic Institute and Columbia University, where he won honors in classics and specialized in history and economics. He left Columbia after his junior year because of an acute hearing disorder and never completed his degree. He worked as a cashier at an insurance company for three years and had short stints as a journalist at the *New York Evening Post* and *New York Herald*. In his free time, he became an author of civics books. In 1885, through political contacts with the Cleveland administration, he obtained the position of chief of the bureau of statistics in the Department of State.

During his stay at the Department of State, Ford discovered a collection of historical documents amassed by that agency in the nineteenth century. The cache included papers of such luminaries as Washington, Jefferson, Hamilton, Franklin, Madison, and Monroe. The Library of Congress had manifested little, if any, interest in collecting historical manuscripts, preferring to concentrate on books. The Department of State had assumed this responsibility by default, but it had not paid much attention, or committed many resources, to the management and preservation of these valuable documents.

Disturbed by the inaccessibility of these materials to scholars and by their deteriorating condition, Ford attempted to mount a massive publication program. Like Belknap, he was intent upon "multiplying the

[3] M.H.S., *Procs.*, 83(1971):56 n.24.

[4] Malcolm, once known as "the best all-round athlete in the United States," had been disinherited and was in serious financial straits. For the background of this tragic domestic crime, see M.H.S., *Procs.*, 83(1971):57.

copies" as a means of preserving and disseminating historical information. Acting in the role of a behind-the-scenes catalyst, he solicited and gained the support of historians and historical organizations throughout the United States. This effort provided a vital grass-roots character to his proposal. He next secured the cooperation of the Cleveland administration, which directed an appeal to Congress for funds. The money did not materialize, however, and Ford's valiant effort failed.

Ford then turned for support to a commercial publisher, the G.P. Putnam's Sons firm of New York City, and succeeded in producing a number of volumes of documentary works based upon State Department holdings. Ford himself produced a fourteen-volume edition of *The Writings of George Washington*. His brother Paul also was a principal agent in this editorial project.

When Cleveland was defeated in the election of 1888, Ford joined the ranks of the unemployed. During Cleveland's second term, he returned to government service, becoming head of the bureau of statistics in the Treasury Department. When McKinley won the presidential election of 1896, Ford again lost his job.

Ford went to Boston in 1898 to head the department of documents and statistics at the Boston Public Library. He became intrigued by the library's large collection of historical documents and soon took on the extracurricular assignment of publishing these primary sources on an annual basis.[5]

During his residence in Boston, Ford was elected a member of the Society. His sponsor was President Adams, who had come to know him during his years of government service in Washington. Adams had been impressed by his scholarly acumen and "colossal capacity for work."[6] The two men also held similar political convictions; both, for example, were vehemently opposed to McKinley's expansionist policies. They became close friends in Boston and collaborators on an historical project, a study of John Quincy Adams's career. Charles F. Adams displayed his trust in Ford by permitting him to use a portion of the treasured Adams family documents at his place of employment, the Boston Public Library; the Adams Papers were then housed in the family's ancestral

---

[5] The series was titled *Historical Manuscripts in the Public Library of the City of Boston*.

[6] M.H.S., *Procs.*, 69(1947–1950):410–411.

home in Quincy.[7] The two men contemplated other joint scholarly ventures involving the Adams Papers, but these did not materialize because Ford returned to Washington in 1902 to become chief of the division of manuscripts in the Library of Congress.

Ford spent the next six years at the Library of Congress. He had a successful tenure there. Full of vim and push, he more than doubled the library's manuscript holdings by acquiring private gifts and by having documents transferred from federal agencies, like the Department of State. When he left the Library of Congress to join the Society's staff, he was fifty-one years of age and at the height of his intellectual powers and career.

While negotiating with Ford about the Society position, Adams thoroughly briefed him on the "Green problem." He stressed that Green would remain the librarian as long as he wished to serve, and that both he and Ford would have to kowtow to him. But he raised the hope that Green would not live too much longer. Time was on their side. Ford agreed to abide by the status quo and suffer Green gladly. As Adams informed Vice President Rhodes:

> As respects our senior Vice-President and the delicacy of the situation so far as he enters into it, when in Washington I did express myself to Mr. Ford on that head with all possible clearness.
>
> I thought it well to have no misapprehension. I, therefore, told Mr. Ford that one of his most important functions, after accepting the editorship, would be to ingratiate himself with the senior Vice-President, treating him with superabundant deference. In this I understood him to concur fully. I also explained to Mr. Ford that, as the world was not made in a day, so also the Massachusetts Historical Society could boast of over a century of accumulated experience and traditions; and, while the measures of rehabilitation and change now contemplated, by me at least, were very comprehensive, yet it would unquestionably take time to effect them. The field had first got to be carefully surveyed, and a policy matured. In this also Mr. Ford quite concurred.
>
> I told him, therefore, that, if he should decide to accept the position, I should expect him to take things very much as he found them, and give

[7] Initially, Adams lent Ford a volume of John Quincy Adams's correspondence. Ford then requested five more volumes, writing: "I have tasted blood, and am now ravenous for flesh; and you must be the sufferer." Ford returned all the volumes within fourteen months. Ford to C.F. Adams, June 15, 1901, Jan. 15, Sept. 1, 1902 (C.F. Adams Papers).

one or two years,—which probably would cover all that remained of the senior Vice-President's activities,—to familiarizing himself with the situation, the collections, and especially the composition of the Society. The first thing I personally should expect of him would be to take hold of the Winthrop and the Bradford histories, and map out his work in connection with these two publications, amassing material, etc. The editing of the *Proceedings*, I told him, could safely be left in the hands of Mr. Tuttle, as Assistant Editor, and he need give himself very little concern about them, except in a supervisory way. He would, however, find ample occupation in familiarizing himself with our collection of manuscripts and our publications; mapping out his work, so far as the Winthrop and Bradford histories were concerned; looking into our library and pamphlets; and, especially, in getting ready to take hold of things in an intelligent as well as a comprehensive way whenever the active connection of the senior Vice-President with the Society should terminate. The field would then be free for a reorganized Society, and the plan of work hereafter to be pursued would by that time have been matured. To this preliminary preparation I thought he could well devote one, if not two, years. He would then be ready to take up editorial work in a large way, and press it to a speedy and satisfactory conclusion.[8]

Green was no stranger to Ford. During his tenure at the Boston Public Library, Ford came to know the gruff Grotonite. He saw him at Society meetings and, since he was also a librarian and lover of books and manuscripts, spent more than a passing moment in Green's domain. It was evident to Ford that Green was an inefficient library administrator and a detriment to the Society.

Shortly after Ford's election to membership, Adams had appointed him to the three-member oversight committee whose function it was to inspect the library and cabinet and report at the 1901 annual meeting.[9] The conscientious Ford made an intensive examination of both facilities. In his report, he muted his criticism of Green's failings so as not to embarrass him before the membership and, possibly, incur the wrath of the hyper-sensitive librarian.

Ford's final words, however, while delicately phrased and not directly naming Green, underscored one of his glaring defects: He hindered

[8] C.F. Adams to J.F. Rhodes, July 16, 1908 (C.F. Adams Papers).

[9] Ford, William Everett, and Andrew McF. Davis were appointed to the committee although only Ford and Davis signed the report. M.H.S., *Procs.*, 2d ser., 15(1901–1902):2, 50.

non-members from using the rich manuscript resources. For although "among workers in history the Society deservedly stands high," that reputation remained only "until some unfortunate seeks to use some of the manuscript material stored in its cases." Recognizing the need for special rules to "assure the safety of these precious and unique records," Ford, however, implicitly charged Green with managing a "closed" library. The Society, Ford affirmed, "has a trust to perform, and one to be used for the public benefit." He cited the examples of the United States Department of State and the Historical Society of Pennsylvania, "both of which were forbidding monopolizers of their stores, and both have found their interest in offering freely the use of their riches to all who may show reasonable credentials." This type of openness would undoubtedly redound to the eventual benefit of the Society, for, as Ford asserted, "generous treatment invites generous treatment, and there are many even in this State who would prefer to place their collections where the student and even the public may have almost free access to and the use of them, to depositing them in a place to which even the worthy experience difficulty in gaining entrance."[10]

"Shut not your doors to me proud libraries," Walt Whitman once proclaimed. Ford fervently agreed with the poet's assertion.

When he began employment at the Society and observed Green on a daily basis, Ford grasped the full dimensions of the librarian's inadequacies. He gained first-hand knowledge of his incompetence, slovenliness, and boorish behavior toward library patrons and his young male attendants. He was appalled by Green's imperious demeanor and lack of managerial skills. Since his office was on the third floor and Green held forth on the second floor, Ford could avoid constant physical contact with the librarian, but his editorial work made it necessary for him to enter Green's lair frequently.

Ford's patience soon wore thin. He became increasingly disenchanted with Green and often registered his discontent, *sub rosa*, to Adams, who spent the winter months in his Washington home and functioned as an absentee president.[11] Among other complaints, Ford castigated Green

[10] M.H.S., *Procs.*, 2d ser., 15(1901–1902):49–50.

[11] Over the years, Adams developed an intense dislike of "provincial" Boston, especially in the winter months. When he moved to his new home, "Birnham Wood," in South Lincoln, he wrote: "I have summered and wintered it, tried it drunk or sober, there's

for wasting the researchers' valuable time with incessant chatter about his Civil War experiences and "Groton families." "As an encourager of concentration the Librarian is open to criticism . . . but as an extinguisher of budding questions and a questioner, he is masterly. The resonances of a Napoleon or a Wellington in encountering distasteful situations were not equal to those developed in a lifetime spent in devising means of how not to do it."[12]

In the following month, Ford noticed Green and his staff hard at work tidying up the library, "cleaning decks preparatory to the visit of the Library Committee. This is a formality which is quite charming at times, as it discloses packages of unacknowledged or unidentified material, which have been courteously given to the Society—and consigned to a dust heap."[13]

The library oversight committee, chaired by Professor Frederick Jackson Turner of Harvard University, took its responsibilities seriously and made many suggestions for improving the facility, much as Ford had done in 1901, but it was all for naught. Ford knew that the committee was wasting its energy. He sought to convey the "facts of life" about Green to Turner, newly arrived on the scene from the University of Wisconsin, "that the Dr. was the very Devil on reform, and no committee had ever been able to keep up with him." The committee "went through the ordeal with proper solemnity, and never smiled when they bowed themselves out," but Ford could barely contain his annoyance. "I

---

nothing in it—save Boston" (Russell, *Adams*, 294). He wrote in his *Autobiography*: "Socially . . . the trouble with Boston is that there is no current of fresh outside life everlastingly flowing in and passing out. It is so to speak stationery—a world, a Boston world, unto itself . . . it tends to stagnate. . . . The winter climate of Boston is distinctly Arctic, and society life, from sympathy, perhaps, seems then to pass through a long period of cold storage" (pp. 204–205). Adams did make an effort to attend the Society's annual meetings, which took place in April. In his first eighteen years as president, he missed only five annual meetings. See M.H.S., *Procs.*, 46(1912–1913):382.

[12] W.C. Ford to C.F. Adams, Apr. 26, 1911 (C.F. Adams Papers).

[13] Ford to Adams, Apr. 3, 1911. In 1912, Ford noted that Green "is bringing a wagonload of books from Dr. Hall's library, which will be stacked in the telephone room. Inasmuch as the last lot which came to this Society in like manner has remained untouched for seven years, his operation gives one a disquieting sense of permanency. I shall suggest to the House Committee that it establish a rule that storage facilities shall be paid for. Ford to Adams, Mar. 18, 1912 (both in C.F. Adams Papers).

feel like getting out on the house-top and shouting out of school."[14]

Following the incident involving the visitor from western Pennsylvania, whom Green had refused permission to glance at Samuel Sewall's and Cotton Mather's diaries, Ford strongly urged President Adams that the Council confer *emeritus* status upon the librarian, thereby forcing his removal.

> In favor of such a move could be urged his increasing age, and his increasing inability to attend to the many functions which should apply to his office. You will know better than I whether he would feel and resent such a step; but, as I have said many times, no one can appreciate what goes on here who is not within the inner circle. Much is done 'around' him, but I am more and more amused by the atmosphere of conspiracy which pervades such evasions. Does this offer any solution to this problem?[15]

Adams sympathized with Ford but insisted that patience was the best policy. Green's days on earth were numbered. They must await his demise. "Time alone," he wrote

> in my judgment will bring about the change desired, unless recourse is had to other measures of a most decided and vigorous character. For these I am not prepared. In other words I should have no faith in half-way measures; it would in my opinion be a case of all, or nothing. The Doctor could not, I fancy, follow the example set by Mr. Smith, and nothing less than that would solve the difficulty. . . .
>
> The only other alternative would be for some move on the side of our "Big Medicine" friend. Perhaps this might be brought about by indirection. It is, however, a result not easily accomplished inasmuch as it would involve the adoption by him of the course pursued by Mr. Smith. That is, he would have to take himself and all his affairs from the Society's building, and come over only occasionally, exactly as Mr. Smith does—interfering with the library as little as Mr. Smith now interferes with the editorial work.
>
> I fairly admit I do not see my way to accomplish this result. It would have to be done by indirection, and in that path I do not know how to make the first step.[16]

[14] W.C. Ford to C.F. Adams, Apr. 6, 1911 (C.F. Adams Papers).

[15] W.C. Ford to C.F. Adams, Sept. 13, 1910 (C.F. Adams Papers). As far as Ford was concerned, there would be no progress until the "mountain of obstruction" was gone: "I sometimes feel that in the three years I have been here, we have been marking time only and that any real progress must await that miracle which you have been awaiting for so many years." W.C. Ford to C. F. Adams, Mar. 12, 1912 (C.F. Adams Papers).

[16] C.F. Adams to W.C. Ford, Sept. 14, 1910 (C.F. Adams Papers).

Earlier that year, Green had reached his fiftieth year of membership. He was now the "Dean of the Society." When a member achieved this milestone, it was customary for his colleagues to pay tribute to him in the course of a Society meeting. In his role as presiding officer, Adams was obliged to acknowledge Green's half-century of service to the Society. Following tradition, Green delivered his reminiscences on his long association with the organization.[17] All was sweetness and good cheer on this memorable occasion. Charles K. Bolton noted in his diary that Green "looked rather feeble and his clothes for the first time seemed to hang from his shoulders. But he was very optimistic, and closed with the remark that the liver rather than reason made pessimists."[18]

The ceremony for Green inspired Adams to concoct a new plan, which, he hoped, would rid the Society of its incubus.[19] He tested his proposal on Arthur Lord, then serving as treasurer of the Society. If Green agreed to retire as librarian, wrote Adams, the Society would take the initiative to secure a doctorate of laws degree for him from Harvard University. Such an award would represent the capstone of his career, marking the termination of his lengthy service to the Society and his alma mater. That would be the proper time for him to step aside. With Green removed from the scene, "the working organization [of the Society] would then pass easily and naturally into the hands of Mr. Ford. Thus the Society would in no way suffer, and the Doctor would get his reward." For the plan to materialize, Green would have "to start the ball a-rolling" with his resignation.[20]

The question was: Who was going to approach Green with the proposal? Adams did not volunteer for the assignment. Ford, too, did not have the stomach for it. He passed the buck to Arthur Hall, whom he hoped to involve as a co-conspirator. Hall responded that "Mr. Adams's scheme seems to me an excellent one." Hall agreed to "sound him [Green] on the matter before taking any steps about it." He added: "Of course it will look to him at first like a broad hint for his retirement, but

[17] M.H.S., *Procs.*, 43(1909–1910):222–233.

[18] Bolton, Journal, Jan. 16, 1910. Green's actual words were: "Happy is the man who lives in sympathy with the surrounding events; and his views of life depend as much on the condition of his liver as on his reason."

[19] Other Society leaders also were thinking of ways to remove Green from his positions of authority. See, for example, Albert B. Hart to C.F. Adams, Mar. 10, 1911 (C.F. Adams Papers).

[20] Adams to Lord, Sept. 16, 1910 (Editorial Correspondence, M.H.S. Archives).

I believe he can be made to see that it is all in good part and for his best interests."[21]

It is not known if Hall did approach Green. It is known that Green did not receive an honorary degree from Harvard, and he continued as librarian.[22]

On March 27, 1912, an unexpected development occurred. The Society learned that Green had been struck by an express wagon, thrown to the ground, and taken to City Hospital. After taking x-rays, the physicians learned that the ball-and-socket joint of the hip was contused but not broken. Ford promptly relayed the news to Adams in Washington.

On the following day, Ford informed Adams that a "curious fact has developed that there was no horse in the case; that was the Dr.'s delusion. He just fell. . . ." Green refused to acknowledge that he had fallen, insisting that he had been struck by a horse-driven wagon. The attending doctor notified Ford that Green would be hospitalized "for some weeks."[23]

On the next day, Ford learned that Green "now talks of presiding" at the April annual meeting. He had not missed an annual meeting since 1865 and, as first vice president, served as chairman when Adams was absent. Ford notified Adams of Green's intention and added:

Was there ever a man his equal? In a previous incarnation he must have been a cat, for by actual count he has parted with seven lives, and still has some to his credit. Meanwhile he is basking in the limelight of publicity, and his reportorial following visit him as one would pay respect to a potentate, recording every word that drops from his lips. His rabbit's foot must be of the proper kind, possessed of all possible virtue in shielding its possessor from harm.

Ford was hopeful that Green would remain in the hospital until after the meeting, "for he can eat, sleep, and smoke to his content and at his ease. But he may insist upon coming."[24]

For the next week, the reports from the hospital were positive. Green seemed to be recovering, although his doctor did provide a cautionary

[21] Hall to Lord, Oct. 23, 1910 (Editorial Correspondence, M.H.S. Archives).

[22] The only honors Green received were an LL.D. degree from the University of Nashville in 1896 and a Decoration of Merit from Venezuela, possibly because of his services as a military surgeon. *Harvard Graduates' Magazine*, 27(1918–1919):328.

[23] Ford to Adams, Mar. 28, 1912. This and subsequent Ford to Adams correspondence on the Green situation are all from C.F. Adams Papers.

[24] Ford to Adams, Mar. 29, 1912.

note: "... when a man of his years is once on his back no one can foresee what complication may arise; that outwardly everything may be all right and progressing satisfactorily but the unexpected may happen. ... there is this uncertainty."[25]

The doctor seemed to be a prophet. Green suddenly took a turn for the worse. By April 5, it appeared that Ford's and Adams's fervent wish was about to materialize. Green was on the verge of death. Ford provided Adams with detailed accounts of Green's rapid decline:

> The reports from the hospital are very unfavorable. He passed a bad night, and had a sinking spell which frightened his attendants. This morning he seemed better, but this afternoon the word is again unfavorable, and the end cannot be distant. We will not telegraph you of it should it come, as there is no reason for your changing your plans in any particular. Everything here runs smoothly and will do so after the event. We are marking time.[26]

On the late afternoon of April 8, however, Green suddenly began to show signs of improvement. His doctor even spoke of a recovery. Ford relayed the unwelcome news to Adams in a hurried postscript to his near-daily letter: "P.M. The Doctor is getting better than he has been, is giving orders and has resumed smoking! Dr. McCallum is very hopeful and every thing points to a recovery."[27] On the next day, the report of his recovery, like the earlier report of his imminent death, appeared to be exaggerated. While Green was exhibiting his usual feistiness, he was still showing the signs of a seriously ill person.

The annual meeting took place on April 11, and Green's remarkable attendance record of forty-six consecutive appearances came to an end. Gov. John D. Long, who served as the presiding officer, opened the meeting with a florid tribute to Green and concluded with an expression of hope for his "speedy restoration to health."[28]

A few days later, the reports from the hospital took a negative turn, once again raising Ford's hopes that the cat had finally used up all of his lives. He informed Adams on April 13 that Dr. McCallum "expects an end at any time." Two days later, Ford began to set plans for reporting Green's death at the May Society meeting.

[25] Ford to Adams, Apr. 1, 1912.
[26] Ford to Adams, Apr. 5, 1912.
[27] Ford to Adams, Apr. 8, 1912.
[28] M.H.S., *Procs.*, 45(1911–1912):542.

Greenism Must Go

The Doctor is distinctly failing. He could hardly endorse a check this morning, because of inability to hold a pen. . . . It is now thought that he cannot outlive the week. This makes it probable that at the next meeting due attention be given to him. Would it not be well to give some consideration to the speakers? I think that Professor Channing would be the most fit among the younger men, as he has always been something of a pet of the Doctor's and sympathised thoroughly with his policy of accumulation. . . . Physically he now seems more comfortable, but the weakness grows rapidly.[29]

Nearly every day health bulletins shuttled from Ford in Boston to Adams at his home in Washington. Ford's tone ranged from hopefully expectant of Green's imminent demise to exasperation that the process was taking so long, "even the doctors are surprised by him holding on as he does."[30] But by the beginning of May, Ford was barely able to contain his annoyance:

As to the Doctor, he is worse today than he was yesterday, and yesterday was a bad day. Still, Dr. McCallum says he may hold on some time longer, though the chances are against it. He may snuff out at any hour. He is passing as he has lived—with great deliberation and without regard to others—self-centred to the last.[31]

However, "further failing" Green was "listless, weak, and of wandering mind at night," and his case became grimmer and grimmer, although even Ford was forced to admit that it was "certainly a remarkable case of smouldering vitality."[32] By May 10 the end appeared imminent—again.

The Doctor's condition was weaker today, and his mind less assured. He wept while talking to Mr. Tuttle, and every effort seemed to unhinge him. He realizes that his mind is going, spoke of it, and cried like a child. We only hope for his early release.[33]

While Green was seemingly on his deathbed, Adams received a "strictly confidential" and assuredly unsettling letter from Edward Stan-

[29] Ford to Adams, Apr. 15, 1912. "Young" Professor Channing was 56-year-old Edward Channing of Harvard.

[30] Ford to Adams, Apr. 24, 1912.

[31] Ford to Adams, May 1, 1912.

[32] Ford to Adams, May 3 & 6, 1912.

[33] Ford to Adams, May 10, 1912.

wood, the Society's recording secretary. Stanwood noted that Green's death would elevate Ford into a position of supreme authority and, in his judgment, this was not a desirable development. He characterized Ford as a latent autocrat, a potential replica of Green. "Is it not well, when we take a new departure, and eliminate the feature of a too great control by one man, to see to it that we do not begin another era in which the same feature will be introduced?" Although he was on good personal terms with Ford, Stanwood, "with regret, but with a feeling that loyalty to the Society requires it," presented his case against the editor as a potential leader.

> Mr. Ford has filled many positions, and has filled them well. But he has never been able to keep on good terms with those with whom he was associated. In the Bureau of Statistics at Washington, in the Boston Public Library, and in the Library of Congress the story was always the same. He has a way of seeking to get all things into his own hands, and that has been resented by his associates.

Stanwood went on to detail Ford's faults as he saw them, especially that since "he has been Editor he has ignored the Committee on Publication altogether. He even ceased sending me the proofs of Proceedings until I asked him why. I know that one member of one of the Committees on a volume of Collections remarked that he did not like to have his name appended to work that he had not been permitted to see." Stanwood continued:

> These are reasons why, it seems to me, we should be very careful about entrusting too much independent power to him at the outset. Whatever power we give him he will increase, I think. It is solely with a view to avoid a repetition of the administration that is just closing that I write these words of caution. In his work as Editor he is all we could wish, but do we desire that he or any one shall become something like a dictator? . . . It was with such thoughts as these in my mind that I did what I did the other evening, when I opposed your suggestion that Mr. Tuttle and the library should be put under him absolutely. It seems to me that the evil—if there be an evil—can be avoided by putting the library under the control of a permanent committee of the Council, Mr. Ford to be one of the members of the committee, but not to have power over the Librarian independently of the committee. That method of control is in vogue in every important library. No man should be allowed to decide what books should and what should not be purchased.[34]

[34] Stanwood to Adams, May 14, 1912 (C.F. Adams Papers).

Greenism Must Go

While Adams may not have concurred with Stanwood's judgment of Ford, he did agree to develop an administrative structure that would curb or neutralize the editor's authority.[35] This may have mollified Stanwood for the moment, but the question of a post-Green era was still premature.

It was now mid-May and "Old Imperishable" was still alive—although barely. Charles K. Bolton made this interesting reference to him in his journal on May 16:

> Dr. Sam Green, ex-mayor, is slowly dying. He asked to be placed in the children's ward at the City hospital so that the boys and girls might be with him when he got better. He now says that he is losing his mind. Mr. Tuttle read to him a list of old Groton cradles in which he had been interested. Weak as he was he said: "You have forgotten the cradle in which Amos Lawrence was rocked in 1783."

Two weeks later, Ford wrote to Adams that "Dr. Nichols believes that he [Dr. Green] cannot hold out another month." Dr. Nichols apparently had only a slight acquaintance with Samuel Abbott Green. Ford remained optimistic that Green's end was near.[36] His belief represented "the triumph of hope over experience," in Samuel Johnson's celebrated phrase.

Ford's optimism was shattered on June 8. On that day, an unknown person provided Green with a glass of champagne, which he drank. Almost immediately, he showed signs of dramatic improvement. Everyone was incredulous. Within days, Green's doctor began to speak of a complete recovery. Ford relayed the shocking and miraculous news to Adams:

> The champagne worked a miracle. From the first taste the improvement set in, and he is now practically out of danger, and a removal to Groton is in view. It was Mumm's, something to be noted. The Dr. owes it to that estimable wine manufacturer to send a recommendation as will attract attention. My only conjecture on the matter is that no library beyond the gates is yet prepared for our librarian.[37]

The death vigil was over. Defying all odds, Green had survived. He left the hospital and returned to his ancestral home in his beloved

[35] Adams to Stanwood, May 23, Aug. 27, 1912 (C.F. Adams Papers).
[36] Ford to Adams, May 29, 1912.
[37] Ford to Adams, June 8, 1912.

The Massachusetts Historical Society

Groton to recuperate. He experienced discomfort on some days but, with the passage of time, grew stronger. By mid-July, he was taking daily automobile rides into the neighboring countryside and setting plans for a trip to New York City in November, with "nurse and Mr. Tuttle as body guard," to attend the meeting of the Peabody Trustees "for the uplifting of the colored race."[38]

Ford now began to contemplate his future at the Society with Green back at his librarian's position. It was not a pleasant prospect. As he informed Adams on July 31:

> Mr. Tuttle made his weekly pilgrimage to Groton yesterday, and sat at the feet of Mumbo Jumbo. The improvement continued, and the talk is now of what he is to do when he comes back here. Thus far nothing very radical is in prospect, for he proposes "to look over my papers," something which he has been doing, or going to do, for half a century—or more. Still I have some goose-flesh when I think of his return. It is so unnecessary, and it is the unnecessary things of life that consume us.[39]

The improbable Green saga reached a climax on September 4, 1912. Green returned to the Fenway, to his newly rented apartment, next door to the Society. A dispirited Ford chronicled the dramatic and incredulous scene in a letter to Adams:

> At 11.18 A.M. today Horace came breathless to me to ask me to look out of the window. The street had three autos in sight, but in one I recognized a pair of shoulders and a hat. It was HE, Old Imperishable, come to his new residence, with Doctor, Nurse, bag, baggage, chauffeur and incidentals. The machine soon started down town, as I supposed to keep some engagement with a reporter or photographer, but, as I learned, to get an 'invalid's chair.' The main thing, however, is that he is here, and proposes to come to his desk tomorrow. With this hegira a new cycle begins, and Tuttle has not had a chance to sneeze today, as he prepared the house, aided in carrying him out the four steps of the hotel, and has been with him til Miss Warren tucked him into his afternoon sleep. There is something uncanny about it, for we are dealing with a man who died—any doctor will say that he has no reason to doubt that he died. . . . I shall try to worm out of the

---

[38] Green attended this meeting. M.H.S., *Procs.*, 47(1913–1914):130. Tuttle traveled to Groton on occasion to assist Green, which led Ford to comment to Adams: "Personally, I feel that the Doctor owes him a good remembrance in his will but I have my doubts as to whether gratitude will take that form in that particular instance." Ford to Adams, June 28, 1912.

[39] Ford to Adams, July 31, 1912.

Dr. exactly what passed between him and St. Peter. It savors of the methods of a Congressional Conference Committee.[40]

Although despairing, Ford resigned himself to the prevailing situation, busied himself in his editorial projects and voluminous correspondence, while drinking countless cups of tea, and became a wry observer of doings in the library. He reported to Adams on November 22: "The Dr. has just climbed the marble stairs with nearly as great deliberation as he is climbing the golden stairs. The journey is shorter, and once at his desk all work ceases for his satellites. He has in mind another Groton volume!"[41] On December 2, he wrote: "The Doctor remains as usual, and gains in capacity for mischief daily."[42]

The return of the "Venerable Librarian" to the Society marked a restoration of the *status quo* prior to his illness. Greenism was once again the prevailing mood. Both Ford and Adams were at wit's end. Adams informed William R. Thayer that Green "will not listen to any suggestion of voluntary retirement. Nevertheless, I think it is quite clear that, between now and next April, some scheme should be settled upon under which the Society can enter a new phase of existence. I am getting to be thoroughly ashamed of existing conditions."[43]

Adams, now seventy-seven years of age, wondered if he would live long enough to achieve his reforms. Green appeared to be indestructible. "Judging by observation and experience," Adams had written to Edward Stanwood on August 27, 1912, "I should say it was not unsafe to predict that our friend [Green] will live until the Day of Judgment, when it will be necessary to put him to a violent death! I have neither hope nor expectation that such will prove the case either with you or with me."[44]

Green's incompetence may have frustrated and angered Ford, but it did not make him apoplectic—until October 1912. He discovered "by mere accident" that Green kept "some ten thousand" catalogue cards on the Civil War collection plus the catalogues for the Waterston and Dowse libraries apart from the general catalogue. This fact, compounded with the

[40] Ford to Adams, Sept. 4, 1912.
[41] Ford to Adams, Nov. 22, 1912.
[42] Ford to Adams, Dec. 2, 1912.
[43] C.F. Adams to W.R. Thayer, Oct. 4, 1912 (C.F. Adams Papers).
[44] C.F. Adams to E. Stanwood, Aug. 27, 1912 (C.F. Adams Papers).

knowledge that during four years of working in the collections neither the librarian nor his assistants "ever intimated . . . that one of the important series could not be found there and must be sought in another place," sent Ford beyond the pale. "If it took me four years to discover this fact, how long would it take a poor wretch of an investigator who comes in to the Library casually or for a week, to learn that he is depending upon a rotten foundation? I confess I lost my temper, because I could see no defence either for retaining the cards in a separate compartment or for keeping them so well concealed from one whose needs were almost daily made visible. I compliment you upon your powers of observation, for you must have felt this was so, and you may enroll me under the banner that 'Greenism must go.' I see no hope for the Society, if his methods are to be perpetuated, even in a moderate degree."[45]

Having vented his anger, Ford recovered his composure and returned to his normal state of frustration and helplessness. The months moved on and the situation at the Society remained stagnant. Green refused to retire or die. Ford continued to register his discontent to Adams in his stream of correspondence, and the latter continued to console Ford, urging him to be patient.

The forthcoming annual meeting of the American Historical Association in Boston and Cambridge during the week between Christmas and the New Year of 1913 deflected Ford's attention from his tribulation with Green to the business at hand. As in 1900, the Society offered its building to the Association for two sessions on Saturday, December 28. Adams, a former president of the Association, also agreed to sponsor a luncheon-reception for the delegates, Society members, and invited guests on that same day; he had done the same in 1900. Ford agreed to present a paper at the afternoon program, the ninth annual conference of historical societies. He was also heavily involved in making arrangements for the two meetings.

The luncheon-reception nearly ended in fiasco because of a lack of planning. As of December 24, no arrangements whatsoever had been set for the affair. Ford had expected Adams to take primary responsibility for this costly social function since he was underwriting it. But

[45] Ford to Adams, Oct. 19, 1912.

Adams, in residence in Washington, became absorbed in other matters and remained "strangely and altogether oblivious of my obligations."

While offering to sponsor the luncheon-reception, he had no intention of attending the affair or any of the meetings, not as long as Theodore Roosevelt occupied the presidency of the Association. He detested the "damn cowboy," as Mark Hanna derisively referred to Roosevelt. "I look forward to it [the A.H.A. annual meeting] with no considerable satisfaction," wrote Adams, "as I look upon the President of the Association as a sciolist in history and a fraud in politics."[46] He intended to stay put in Washington.

As a result of Adams's inattention, no caterer had been selected and no invitations sent, not even to the members of the Society. The only written announcement of the reception was a notation in the Association's printed program. "So far as I can see," Adams informed Vice President Rhodes on December 24, "you and I, 'the Doctor' and the officials of the Society and of the Association will have it all to ourselves."

Adams advised Rhodes to convene hastily "the ever capable and resourceful Ford and the ever willing and active Tuttle and the everlasting and inescapable 'Big Medicine Man' into council,—omitting the last, if you prefer to do so,—and then do whatever is yet possible to be done." He had sent a telegram to Evans, the caterer, directing him to contact Rhodes, Ford, *et al.*, at once and determine the menu.

Adams assumed responsibility for the failure in arrangements and supplicated mercy. "Things with me, I fear," he acknowledged to Rhodes, "are getting to a very bad pass. Unhappily, in this respect unlike our Friend, 'the Doctor,' I am only too painfully conscious of the fact. I am the victim of an incurable disease,—to wit, old age! Senility will out!"[47]

On the appointed day, however, all went well at the Society, thanks to Ford's organizational talents and industriousness. The two sessions and luncheon-reception were well attended and went off without any problems. Ford also acquitted himself in the meeting sponsored by the conference of historical societies. His paper, dealing with institutional changes in the Massachusetts Historical Society from its founding to his

[46] Quoted in Kirkland, *Adams*, 219.
[47] Adams to Rhodes, Dec. 24, 1912 (M.H.S. Archives).

period, was described by the compiler of the association's program as "exceedingly suggestive."[48] Once again, the Society had put its best foot forward for the national historical body and increased its reputation as a major learned society. Ford also strengthened his position as a potential president of the association, an honor he achieved in 1917.[49]

In early 1913, because of his weak physical condition and advanced age, Green reduced his schedule, appearing at the Society "only every few days." When he did not come in, his attendants carted materials to his apartment. When he decided to come, it became necessary for the custodian and one of the library staff to assist him from his adjoining quarters in the Fritz-Carlton Hotel to the Society and up the staircase to his chair and desk.[50] Once there, he rarely moved. The library attendants ministered to his personal needs, bringing to his desk a quart of milk and his newspaper.[51]

As in the past, Green continued to abuse his staff. One rainy day, he instructed Charles Stearns to deliver a package for him. "He asked Mr. Stearns if he had an umbrella. 'No, Doctor,' said Mr. Stearns. 'Have you a raincoat?' 'No, Doctor.' 'Have you any rubbers?' 'No, Doctor.' 'Well, Charles, I'm afraid you will get wet!'" On another occasion, he sent Stearns to the post office to mail a package. When he returned, Green inquired about the postage charge. "It was half a cent more than the Doctor had estimated. The Doctor insisted that he return and get back the overpayment. What would you have done in that case? Exactly! Charles Stearns paid the half cent himself, and the Doctor was satisfied."[52]

[48] American Historical Association, *Annual Report* (1912). The account of the Boston meeting is on pp. 27–47.

[49] Ford's A.H.A. presidential address was an astounding performance. "He did what no president of the Association had ever done before or has ever done since: he delivered every word of it without a note of any kind, apparently extemporaneously." *American Historical Review*, 46(1940–1941):1013. Ford's address was published in ibid., 23(1918): 273–286.

[50] According to William C. Endicott, "during the last years of his incumbency, he [Green] was carried up and down the stairs every morning and every evening on the shoulders of Horace Fuller." Endicott to James D. Phillips, May 20, 1936 (Endicott Family Papers, M.H.S.).

[51] Wheeler, "Fifty Years," 48. Green stayed at the Fritz-Carlton only temporarily, and from 1914 was listed in the city directories as boarding at the nearby Hotel Canterbury, 14 Charlesgate West.

[52] Wheeler, "Fifty Years," 48.

Greenism Must Go

Ford continued to pour out his resentment of Green in regular letters to the often-absent President Adams. Their correspondence began to take on a predictable, ritualistic character. Ford would set forth his litany of woe, and Adams, evermore considerate of Green's feelings than was the editor, would reply with a defensive response—as illustrated by this typical letter of February 6, 1913:

I note what you say of our friend, the Doctor, his condition, and the course which had best be pursued as respects the organization, if organization it could fairly be called. You know perfectly well just how I feel on this subject, without any occasion for repetition. I am thoroughly mortified. I recognize the fact that the Society is at least thirty years behind the times. Its position is discreditable to me, and to all concerned in its management. We have done nothing since we constructed the new building, at which time we moved the old organization into it; and it has been a case of old wine in new bottles from that time to this,—some fifteen years.

You also know why this has been thus. It has not been because of any lack of appreciation on my part.

On the other hand, I have a keener appreciation apparently, than you or most others of the infinite service Dr. Green has been to the Society. With historical societies, as with everything else, the chief essential is to get them on a satisfactory financial basis; and having done so, to keep them there. It is most dangerous for them to assume obligations beyond their capacity to carry out.

We owe it exclusively to Dr. Green that the Society is now on a tolerably satisfactory financial basis. It was he, as I have repeatedly said in my correspondence with you, who steered the Sibley bequests into its Treasury. But for his so doing, our Society would be back where it was at the time I became President,—that is, it would be hobbling along on an insufficient income, eked out by small annual payments on the part of the members, and the admission fees. If there has been one thing a source of satisfaction to me of late, it has been the doing away, in our case, with annual fees and admissions. Our Society is not a social club.

All this we owe to Dr. Green; and, in return, it is incumbent upon us to pay all possible consideration to him and his feelings. This it is which causes me to be so very tender-handed, calling down on myself no little criticism on the part of many of our members. You, however, at least understand the situation.

Were it not a trifling matter, my position would be awkward, and almost painful. I am perfectly conscious of the position in which you find yourself as respects the Society and its activities. Up to the present time, I have possessed my soul in patience, and awaited the apparently inevitable course of events. As you know, last April I felt assured that the time had come. Instead of that, the period of what might be called 'purgatory' has been merely stretched out. How much longer this will continue defies all forecast. It is, however, up to us to decide, under these circumstances, what course shall be pursued. I am perfectly willing to conform to your advice as respects the question of details,—the succession to Page, which immediately presents itself.[53] I should try, however, to do so in such a manner as would cause to our unfortunate friend, the Doctor, the least possible occasion for feeling himself superannuated or overruled. That he should withdraw from his position and relieve us from embarrassment goes without saying. Nevertheless, he does not so see it. In this respect he and I differ. It would be a source of infinite relief to me to get out of the position I now hold in the Society, were my successor in sight. Meanwhile, were I so to do at the coming annual meeting, no one knows better than yourself the complications which would be caused. For myself,—I do not hesitate to say I am tired. At the age which I have reached my father had gone all to pieces, and his father was on the verge of his final collapse. I myself would be simply rejoiced could I get out of all kinds of harness. The position of our friend, the Doctor, is one of the obstacles in the way of my so doing.[54]

In March 1913, Green requested the Council to authorize the employment of another "boy" who would assist him on the Sibley Harvard graduates project. Concerned about the financial consequences, Adams and other key officials debated the advisability of this addition. Finally, fearful that Green would take umbrage and not leave the Society a gift in his will, they acceded to his request. " 'Animated by a lively sense of favors to come,' the Council granted the request without a dissenting vote," a colleague reported to Ford, then in London on a research trip. "We have cheerfully and gladly yielded to the Doctor's importunities and that there is now installed at the office an unnecessary employe[e] at $12.00 per week."[55]

The new "boy," twenty-one-year-old Warren Wheeler, began employment in April, with the stipulation that his appointment "does not

[53] Alfred Baylies Page, who died on Aug. 9, 1912, had been a library assistant at the Society for twenty-nine years. As Dr. Green's report for 1913 noted: "This is the first death in the Library staff during a period of more than threescore years." M.H.S., *Procs.*, 46(1912–1913):395.

[54] C.F. Adams to W.C. Ford, Feb. 6, 1913 (C.F. Adams Papers).

[55] C.F. Adams to Arthur Lord, Mar. 16, 1913; James F. Rhodes to Arthur Lord, Mar. 19, 1913; [C.F. Adams?] to W.C. Ford, May 12, 1913 (Editorial Correspondence, M.H.S. Archives).

necessarily involve a life tenure." He remained at the Society for the next fifty-three years, retiring in 1966![56]

Wheeler quickly learned that his responsibilities transcended library duties. In the summer of 1914, the *Boston Post* sponsored a campaign to purchase three elephants for the City of Boston. Funds were solicited from school children, a favorite tactic of that era. The campaign was successful and the elephants, Molly, Waddy, and Tony, were purchased. On June 6, a special program was held in Fenway Park to present the elephants to the City. A capacity audience was there to hear addresses by Gov. David I. Walsh and the charismatic mayor of Boston, James Michael Curley.

Because Green was a former mayor and a prominent personality in Boston, the committee invited him as an honored guest. Since he was unable to walk to Fenway Park, nearly a half-mile from his hotel, Green commandeered his young library assistant, Wheeler, and the Society's custodian and had them push his wheel chair to and from the ceremony. Wheeler wrote: "It was a memorable day for Dr. Green, and he often recalled it in his later years."[57]

In December 1913, the sickly eighty-two-year-old Green finally came to the realization that he could no longer fulfill the responsibilities of the two offices he held. He decided to relinquish his vice president's position.[58] He conveyed the news to Adams through an intermediary, library assistant Julius Tuttle.

While he would have preferred to see Green vacate the library position, Adams leapt at the opportunity presented to him. Half a loaf was better than none. In correspondence with Green, he approved of his decision, underscoring his need for a "physically active" vice president who could vigorously conduct the business of the Society during Adams's frequent absences. He advised Green to submit his resignation at the January Society meeting. He assured Green that he was welcome to remain as librarian, but, should he wish to move into emeritus status, he could always occupy his favorite chair and desk. In presenting these choices, it was obvious that Adams was hoping that Green

---

[56] Wheeler, "Fifty Years," 39.

[57] Wheeler, "Fifty Years," 47.

[58] M.H.S., *Procs.*, 47(1913–1914):129.

would accept his second option, that is, become *Librarian Emeritus*. That would eliminate his *bête noire* from the active management of the library.

Green did not snap at the bait. He submitted his formal resignation as vice president, as requested, but, in a cover letter to Adams, expressed a desire to retain his position as librarian, "if the Society is so inclined." He wrote: "I should like to come to the Library as often as I can to occupy my accustomed chair and desk, and do a little work here. It will be a source of great satisfaction to me to continue my official connection with the society in this way."[59]

With Green's possible bequest in mind, Adams felt obliged to accede to the doctor's request. Assuredly with a heavy heart, he informed Green: "You will occupy your special chair and your familiar desk, in its accustomed locality, just as long as you feel disposed to do so. No one, I think, has the most remote thought of disturbing you."[60] The "I think" was a curious inclusion.

On December 29, 1914, a few months before the 1915 annual meeting, Adams notified senior Vice President James F. Rhodes that he was coming to Boston and desired an appointment "at your house some afternoon about dusk, when we can discuss matters in the undisturbed quiet of your library." Initially, the "matters" involved Adams's decision not to run for reelection—which may not have surprised Rhodes since he had heard this refrain for at least the past ten years. He would be eighty years old in May, wrote Adams, and "it is high time I went." As of April, he would have completed twenty years as president. He was now too old and tired to execute his planned reforms. He was prepared to concede defeat. Green had won the war and "outlived my period of activity."

Not that Adams regarded his presidency as a total failure. If he had

[59] S.A. Green to C.F. Adams, Dec. 15, 1913 (C.F. Adams Papers). See also, Adams to Green, Dec. 13, 1913.

[60] C.F. Adams to S.A. Green, Dec. 18, 1913 (Editorial Correspondence, M.H.S. Archives). A minor flap developed among the Society hierarchy as to how they should phrase their acceptance of Green's resignation. This led an exasperated Adams to write to Lord: "As we advance in the vale of years. . . I find that nothing contributes more . . . to the gaiety of old age than a philosophical contemplation of the process known as manufacturing mountains out of molehills, and studying the art of brewing a tempest in a teapot." Adams to Lord, Jan. 20, 1914 (C.F. Adams Papers).

not accomplished all of his objectives, wrote Adams, he nonetheless felt that progress had been made during his tenure and the Society was changing for the better. He noted that Ford had begun to settle in and take charge. As Adams phrased it, Ford "practically runs the machine. I merely serve as a species of *ex deus machina.*"

Adams next turned to the issue of his successor. He urged Professor James Ford Rhodes to assume the presidency. He considered him the logical successor. He was also of the proper age: sixty-six years. He sought to assure the distinguished historian that the duties of the position were neither onerous nor time-consuming since Ford handled much of the organizational details. His principal function would be presiding at the meetings.

If Rhodes was determined not to take the job, Adams speculated that possibly Ford could serve as both president and editor of publications. But Adams, mindful of Stanwood's prior admonition, was aware that such an arrangement might be opposed by the members since it concentrated total power in one person.

Adams also knew that Ford's acute hearing problem would hinder him severely as a presiding officer. Because of his deafness, Ford rarely engaged in such a common social experience as dining out with friends. He informed Adams in 1910 that his only suitable dinner companions would be Stentor and Thersites, "with music by a steam calliope." At another time, he wrote: "My world is such a silent one that I am partially reconciled to be deprived of talk."[61] Stewart Mitchell speculated that Ford's massive output as an editor was due to his deafness: "His industry was prodigious, partly, perhaps, because the failure of hearing shut him off from many of the pleasures with which other men amuse themselves, or waste their time."[62]

In January 1915, Adams and Rhodes had their meeting in Boston, but at the Harvard Club, not in the historian's library. The charade was renewed. Rhodes adamantly refused to accept the presidency. He in-

[61] Quoted in M.H.S., *Procs.*, 83(1971):77.

[62] M.H.S., *Procs.*, 69(1947–1950):407. In his final years at the Society, Ford began to use a "mechanical device" to improve his hearing. Francis R. Hart reported in 1924 that the device had helped his hearing and "really made him a much more intimate member of the after-dinner conference and that when he has become accustomed to some of its reverberations he will get considerable comfort out of it." Hart to James Wilbur, Dec. 11, 1924 (Editorial Correspondence, M.H.S. Archives).

sisted that Adams retain the position. In a subsequent meeting, a group of Society power brokers, consisting of Rhodes, Long, Norcross, and Lord, met with Adams and implored him to stay on. His leaving, they stated, would be "undesirable and just now inopportune." Once more, Adams yielded to their wishes, allowing himself to be "over-persuaded." The charade was at an end.

Adams, however, did not serve a twenty-first term. On March 20, 1915, less than a month before the annual meeting, he died in his sleep at his Washington home. "My brother Charles and I had a race for our graves," his brother Henry wrote to Elizabeth Cameron, "and he won. An attack of grippe fell suddenly on his heart, and carried him off in a moment."[63]

Because of the death of Adams, the annual meeting on April 8 took on a special significance. It "was the largest meeting in the history of the Society." At the outset, a number of members rose and extemporaneously paid glowing tributes to their deceased president. The members voted to sponsor a formal memorial service for him in a local church and designated his close friend, United States Sen. Henry Cabot Lodge, to present a "memorial address," subject to the approval of the Adams family.[64]

The election of a new president was the major business at hand. Replacing Adams was no easy assignment. Following Adams's death, the nominating committee began considering candidates. The two top prospects were Gov. John Davis Long and, once again, Rhodes. Long declined to be considered for the nomination, while Rhodes continued to disclaim interest in the position. The nominating committee and Council con-

[63] H. Adams to E. Cameron, Mar. 26, 1915 (Henry Brooks Adams [1838–1918] Papers, M.H.S.). Charles Adams was a morose, embittered man in his final months of life. His last diary entry contained but two words: "heartsick" and "homesick." His funeral was held in the First Church in Quincy. His tombstone read: "He left to his descendants an honorable name worthy of those which had before him shone in the annals of the state. For an account of his final days, see Nagel, *Descent From Glory*, 371–373.

[64] James F. Rhodes to Henry Adams, Apr. 13, 1915 (Henry Brooks Adams [1838–1918] Papers, M.H.S.). The family did approve the choice of Lodge, and the service took place on Nov. 17 at Boston's First Church. Fifty-six members, slightly more than half of the total membership, attended. Following Lodge's eulogy, the audience sang "the not inappropriate hymn," as Paul Nagel has written, "Give ear, ye children, to my law." Henry Adams did not attend this service but later wrote Lodge and thanked him for his address. He added: "As you know, I loved Charles." See Nagel, *Descent From Glory*, 373.

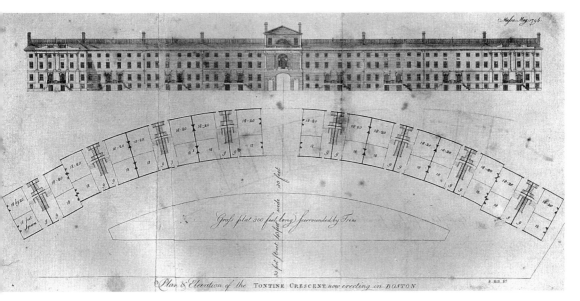

"Plan & Elevation of the Tontine Crescent, now erecting in Boston." From the *Massachusetts Magazine,* 1794. The M.H.S. was given use of the "upper chamber" above the arch.

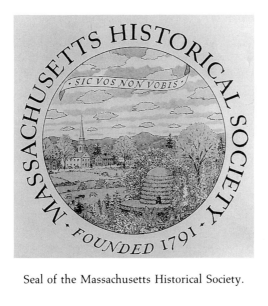

Seal of the Massachusetts Historical Society.

Jeremy Belknap (1744–1798). Portrait by
Henry Sargent, 1798.

James Sullivan (1744–1808), first president of
the M.H.S. Portrait by Gilbert Stuart, 1807.

James Savage (1784–1873), fifth president of the
M.H.S. Miniature by Richard Morell Staigg, 1849.

Frances Manwaring Caulkins (1795–1869), historian of
New London, Conn., the first female MHS member.

Members of the M.H.S., May 17, 1855, taken in commemoration of the presidency of James Savage. From the salt print by John Adams Whipple.

Seated, left-right: Charles Francis Adams; Rev. Joseph Barlow Felt; Nathan Appleton; Rev. William Jenks; John Chipman Gray; Jared Sparks; Josiah Quincy; James Savage; Lemuel Shaw; Edward Everett; William Hickling Prescott; Daniel Appleton White; David Sears; Abbott Lawrence;

Rev. George Washington Blagden; George Ticknor. Standing, left-right: Rev.
Chandler Robbins; Charles Deane; Richard Frothingham; Nathaniel Bradstreet Shurtleff; Joseph Willard; Rev. William Parsons Lunt; Rev. Samuel
Kirkland Lothrop; Rev. George Edward Ellis; George Stillman Hillard; Robert Charles Winthrop.

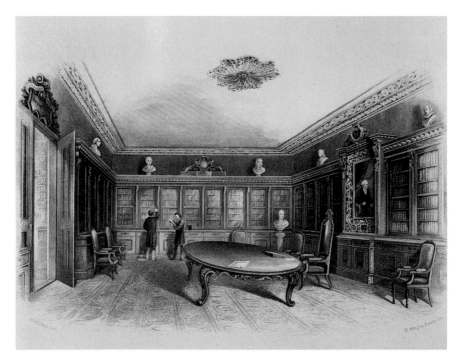

Engraving of the Dowse Library.

Edward Everett (1794–1865). Portrait by
Gilbert Stuart, 1820, formerly owned by
Thomas Dowse.

Thomas Dowse (1772–1856). Portrait by Moses
Wight, commissioned by the M.H.S., 1856.

Members of the M.H.S., June 10, 1869, meeting at the Brookline home of
Robert C. Winthrop. Photo by J. W. Black.

William G. Brooks; Charles Deane; Francis Parkman; Robert C. Water-
ston; Charles C. Smith; Lucius R. Paige; James Walker; Henry G. Denny;
Nathaniel B. Shurtleff; Jacob Bigelow; William Latham; Emory Washburn;
William S. Bartlet; William Newell; Robert M. Mason; John H. Clifford;
John C. Gray; Jeffries Wyman; Frederic H. Hedge; Benjamin F. Thomas;

Samuel A. Green; Robert C. Winthrop; Samuel F. Haven; Henry W. Torrey; John J. Babson; John Langdon Sibley; George E. Ellis; George B. Emerson; Lorenzo Sabine; Erastus B. Bigelow; George T. Davis; Thomas Aspinwall; Stephen Salisbury; Nicholas Hoppin; Oliver Wendell Holmes; Chandler Robbins; Thomas C. Amory; Seth Ames; Francis Bowen; Richard Frothingham; Samuel K. Lothrop; Ellis Ames; Joel Parker; James M. Robbins; Theophilus Parsons; Leverett Saltonstall.

John Langdon Sibley (1804–1885). Portrait by
Frederic Porter Vinton, 1879.

Robert C. Winthrop (1809–1894), sixth president
of the M.H.S. Portrait by David Huntington, 1885.

George E. Ellis (1814–1894), seventh president of
the M.H.S. Portrait by Frederic Porter Vinton,
1880.

Tremont Street headquarters of the M.H.S., before renovations.

Tremont Street headquarters of the M.H.S., April 4, 1899. Photo by William H. Drew.

1154 Boylston Street headquarters of the M.H.S., 1899. Photo by H. H. Sidman. Reproduced in the *American Architect and Building News*, August 19, 1989.

Worthington C. Ford (1858–1941). Portrait by Hermann
Hanatschek, 1927.

Charles Francis Adams (1835–1915), 1913, eighth president of
the M.H.S. Photo by Elliott & Fry, London.

Henry Cabot Lodge (1850–1924), 1920,
ninth president of the M.H.S.

Samuel Abbott Green (1830–1918), October 4, 1915.

William Crowninshield Endicott (1860–1936),
twelfth president of the M.H.S. Portrait by
John Singer Sargent, 1907.

M.H.S. staff on the Society's roof, watching the flight of the dirigible
Hindenburg, October 9, 1936.

Left-right: Warren Wheeler; Stephen Riley; Stewart Mitchell; Allyn B.
Forbes; Marjorie M. Bruce; —— Baker; unidentified; Phyllis Murphy;
Persis Koch.

150th Anniversary dinner, April 14, 1941, at the Algonquin Club, Boston.
Photo by Thomas A. Slater.

Seated, left to right: Joseph Warren; Frederic Jesup Stimson; Thomas God-
dard Frothingham; Albert Bushnell Hart; Abbott Lawrence Lowell; Henry
Lefavour; William Lawrence; Dixon Ryan Fox; Roger Bigelow Merriman;
Clarence Saunders Brigham; Harlow Shapley (president of the American
Academy of Arts and Sciences); George Parker Winship; Frank Washburn
Grinnell; Samuel Atkins Eliot. Standing, left to right: Henry Bradford Wash-
burn; Thomas Winthrop Streeter; Lawrence Counselman Wroth; George
Gregerson Wolkins; Bliss Perry; Gaspar Griswold Bacon; Mark Antony De-
Wolfe Howe; David Cheever; Henry Rouse Viets; James Phinney Baxter, 3d;
Stewart Mitchell; Allen Forbes; Hermann Frederick Clarke, James Melville

Hunnewell; Charles Eliot Goodspeed; Howard Corning; Clifford Kenyon
Shipton; Allen French; Philip Putnam Chase; Roland Gray; James Duncan
Phillips; Edward Kennard Rand; Henry Lee Shattuck; Arthur Meier Schles-
inger; William Vail Kellen; Albert Francis Bigelow; Arthur Stanwood Pier;
Fred Norris Robinson; Lawrence Waters Jenkins; Boylston Adams Beal;
Keyes DeWitt Metcalf; Herbert Brown Ames; William Scott Ferguson;
Paul Herman Buck; Milton Edward Lord; Theodore Clarke Smith; Sidney
Bradshaw Fay; Gardner Weld Allen; Franklin Delano Putnam; Augustus
Peabody Loring, Jr.; Allyn Bailey Forbes; William Leonard Langer; Fred
Tarbell Field; Henry Wilder Foote; Fitz-Henry Smith; Zechariah Chafee,
Jr.; Perry Miller; Henry Adams; Stephen Willard Phillips.

Allyn B. Forbes (1897–1947).

Stewart Mitchell (1892–1957). Photo by Bachrach.

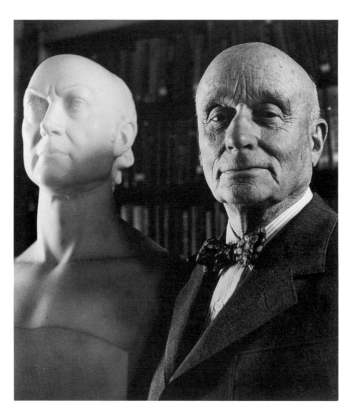

John Adams (1875–1964), sixteenth president of the M.H.S., 1953,
with a bust of Pres. John Quincy Adams. Photo by Thomas B.
Hollyman.

Henry Adams (1875–1951).

Ellis Hall as the M.H.S. reading room.

Esther Forbes (1891–1967), Pulitzer Prize winning member of the MHS.

Unloading the Papers of George Frisbie Hoar, November 1961. Photo by George M. Cushing.

Left-right: Stephen T. Riley; Wendell D. Garrett; John D. Cushing; Lyman H. Butterfield; Malcolm Freiberg; Warren G. Wheeler.

Henry Lee Shattuck (1879–1971).

Stephen T. Riley, 1973. Photo by George M. Cushing.

Four presidents of the Historical Society, 1990. Photo by Roger Farrington.

Left-right: James Barr Ames; Thomas Boylston Adams; F. Douglas Cochrane; Henry Lee.

M.H.S. Council, in the Director's Office, 1990. Photo by Roger Farrington.

Seated, left to right: Caleb Loring, Jr.; David R. Godine; Henry Lee; Kathryn Preyer; Lilian Handlin; Leo Beranek. Standing, left to right: John W. Adams; Helen Spaulding; William Bentinck-Smith; Thomas McCraw; John Lowell; Oliver F. Ames; Charles F. Adams; Theodore Chase; Louis L. Tucker.

"The American Revolution," exhibition segment from "Witness to America's Past" at the Museum of Fine Arts, Boston, 1991. Displayed on the wall are Copley's portrait of John Hancock, the Prescott-Linzee crossed swords, and the Boze portrait of Lafayette.

vened in joint session and finally selected Henry Cabot Lodge to succeed Adams. He accepted the nomination.

The sixty-four-year-old Lodge had impeccable credentials for the presidency but was not a shoo-in for election. In the course of his lengthy career in the United States House of Representatives (1888–1893) and United States Senate (1893–1924), he had tussled with many prominent Bostonians, some of whom were fellow members of the Society. One of these was Grenville Norcross, a "mild member of the Edes wolf-pack," who vehemently opposed Lodge's nomination.[65] President Charles Eliot of Harvard also was not in favor of Lodge. He castigated Lodge as a "skillful boss," "a compromiser on moral questions," "an opportunist politician," and "not an historian at all."[66]

As the senior vice president, Rhodes had the responsibility of presiding as chairman of the annual meeting. Fully aware of the opposition to Lodge by a small but vociferous minority, he did not relish the assignment. From a personal standpoint, the Harvard scholar abhorred this type of wrangling. He was also fearful of its divisive effect upon the Society. He did not wish to have the institution become a cauldron of conflict.

Rhodes was particularly concerned about the opposition of Eliot and Moorfield Storey, two formidable protagonists who were forceful speakers and wielded considerable influence. He wished that these two would confine their opposition "to the ballot box." If the election proceeded quietly, Rhodes projected only four to five anti-Lodge votes. But if Eliot and Storey insisted upon voicing their opinions, Rhodes expressed anxiety "about the temper of the meeting and the result."[67]

Some weeks before the meeting, Rhodes had contacted known and prominent pro-Lodge supporters, urging them to attend and plan to speak in the senator's behalf should Eliot and Storey mount an attack. But he was not entirely successful in this effort. "We are not well off for

---

[65] Bolton, Journal, Mar. 31, 1915.

[66] Eliot to J.F. Rhodes, Apr. 5, 7, 1915 (James Ford Rhodes Papers, M.H.S.). Lodge wrote of Eliot: "Eliot has opposed and fought me diligently for forty years." Lodge Memorandum, Apr. 11, 1924 (Henry Cabot Lodge [1850–1924] Papers, M.H.S.).

[67] Rhodes to Arthur Lord, Apr. 7, 1915; [W.C. Ford?] to Rhodes, Apr. 6, 1915 (Editorial Correspondence, M.H.S. Archives).

speakers to cope with Eliot and Storey," he lamented to Vice President Arthur Lord on the day before the meeting.

Rhodes was in a quandary. He did not wish to "rush the ballot." If Eliot and Storey asked for the floor, he must grant their requests. Why? Because Charles F. Adams would have done so. If Adams were alive, wrote Rhodes, he would insist upon "free discussion." The spirit of Adams pervaded the Society. "At five o'clock tomorrow afternoon," Rhodes informed Lord, "the Society will regret Mr. Adams more than ever."

The meeting was a tense session. Eliot and Storey, as anticipated, refused to remain silent and implored their colleagues to reject Lodge's nomination. His candidacy seemed to be in peril. At that point Governor Long entered the fray, like the United States cavalry rushing to the rescue of a besieged band of pioneers.

Long delivered a reasoned defense of Lodge. While not personally enamored of the senator, he acknowledged his administrative talents and commendable record as an author of numerous historical works. He was fully worthy of the honor. Charles K. Bolton, who was in attendance, recorded in his diary that Long "made a fine defence, saying that altho Lodge always hit him [Long] on the head when opportunity offered and even fought his appt. as Secretary of the Navy, he thought Lodge measured up to the position."[68]

Long neutralized the opposition and saved the day for Lodge. When Rhodes opened the ballot box and peered in, he was pleased to see an abundance of kernels of corn and only a few black beans. The crisis was over. Lodge became Adams's successor.[69]

Like Adams, Lodge also functioned as an absentee president. His senatorial duties prevented him from attending many Society meetings. Lodge's absenteeism led to a sticky problem over a membership issue in January 1916. An opening developed in the resident membership. After considering two candidates proposed by the nominating committee, the Council settled upon Albert E. Pillsbury.[70] He appeared to be an excellent choice. He had impressive credentials.

Descended from an old New England family, Pillsbury was a graduate

[68] Bolton, Journal, Mar. 31, 1915.

[69] For Lodge's acceptance, see Lodge to Rhodes, Apr. 3, 1915 (Editorial Correspondence, M.H.S. Archives).

[70] For Pillsbury's biography, see: *The National Cyclopaedia of American Biography*, 11:182–183; *Harvard Class Report of 1871: 50th Anniversary Report*, 134–135.

of Lawrence Academy and had attended Harvard but did not complete his degree. He read law with his uncle in Illinois, then returned to Boston and was admitted to the Massachusetts bar in 1871. He developed a flourishing law practice and, like many successful attorneys of this (and any other) era, gravitated into politics and public service. He served multiple terms in the Massachusetts lower house and Senate. He was president of the Senate in 1895 and 1896. In 1893, after serving three years as attorney general of the Commonwealth, he sought the Republican nomination for the governorship but was defeated in the primary by Frederic T. Greenhalge, who then won the coveted position.

Pillsbury belonged to many benevolent, professional, and historical groups, was a popular lecturer at civic programs, and published *Lincoln and Slavery*, an historical work. In recognition of his many achievements, Harvard awarded him an honorary degree in 1891. His candidacy was also strengthened by the fact that the late Charles F. Adams had been one of his ardent supporters.

Following the council meeting, Vice President Rhodes, presiding in Lodge's absence, reported his nomination. The members were to vote upon Pillsbury at the February 10 meeting. To this point, everything went along smoothly. It appeared to be a *pro forma* piece of business.

However, when Lodge heard of Pillsbury's nomination from Ford, he fell into a state of acute distress.[71] The Council's action, he informed Ford, "creates for me a most unpleasant situation." Lodge despised Pillsbury with an Old Testament intensity. Pillsbury felt the same about the senator.

The source of their mutual dislike was the gubernatorial campaign of 1893. Rather than support his classmate, Lodge had favored Frederic T. Greenhalge, who ultimately won the contest. "Since that time," Lodge informed Ford, "Mr. Pillsbury has pursued me with a virulent hostility, attacking me whenever he could find opportunity."

What particularly galled Lodge was how Pillsbury carried "political enmity into private life." For example, he pilloried Lodge at their Harvard class meetings, and, as Lodge reported, "made himself so disagreeable that I was obliged to submit in silence to offensive remarks, or resent them, and I did not care to do either, as at my age I have an

---

[71] The Pillsbury issue provoked a small mountain of correspondence, now housed in the Henry Cabot Lodge (1850–1924) Papers, M.H.S. I have used these documents in reconstructing the events of this heated dispute.

objection to descending to personal wrangles." Lodge stopped attending these gatherings, "as did others who thought that Mr. Pillsbury made the meetings unpleasant."

Lodge was determined to block his candidacy. If Pillsbury were elected, he notified Ford, he would resign not only his presidency but his membership as well; he had been a member for forty years. He could not tolerate such an unbearable situation.

Lodge urged Ford to find a way to withdraw Pillsbury's nomination. He noted that there was precedent for such an action in the United States Senate as well as in the Society. He affirmed that Council recommendations were not irrevocable.[72]

Since neither Ford nor any member of the council had been aware of the two men's mutual hostility when they were considering Pillsbury's nomination, they were taken completely by surprise by Lodge's bitter reaction. They now knew that they faced a major public relations problem. Above all, they did not wish to see the incident escalate and become newsworthy for the local press. Lodge, in particular, did not want this type of publicity.

Lodge seized the initiative and began a correspondence campaign to quash Pillsbury's nomination. He fired off "personal and confidential" letters to every member of the Council. He implored them to withdraw Pillsbury's name. If they permitted this nomination to reach the floor for a vote at the February meeting, he informed his colleagues that he would attend the meeting and wage a personal campaign to blackball his nemesis. He informed J. D. Henley Luce that he would pack the meeting with all of his close friends. This was a scenario no one wished to see unfold, for it would polarize the Society and could have devastating repercussions.

Lodge's persuasive correspondence was sufficient to achieve the desired effect. Almost to a man, the Council agreed to correct the "mischief." Ford, Rhodes, and other leading Council members devised a proper strategy. At the February Council meeting, the members voted to withdraw Pillsbury's nomination. Immediately after the meeting, Rhodes sent a postal telegram to Lodge: "Council unanimously with-

[72] Lodge to Ford, Jan. 15, 1916.

draws nomination considered unnecessary report action to meeting."[73] At the Society meeting, Rhodes announced the council's decision, merely adding that "opposition has developed in certain quarters."

With President Lodge generally absent in Washington, Ford became the mainspring of the Society during Lodge's term of office, conducting all of the vital business of the Society. As Lyman Butterfield has written, "this quiet, efficient, and tireless man bestrode the Massachusetts Historical Society." After the monthly meetings, he reported to Lodge with "absolute fidelity" and kept him fully apprised of all Society business. Green's authority had waned perceptibly. Lacking physical stamina, the old librarian was a mere shadow of his former self. Time had taken its toll. He was fading, finally.

The "period of what might be called 'purgatory,'" in Charles F. Adams's phrase,[74] came to a close on December 5, 1918, when Green's many lives ran out and he died. His passing marked the end of an era. He had been a member of the Society for nearly fifty-nine years, a record surpassed only by Josiah Quincy and James Savage.[75] He had been librarian for nearly fifty-one years, the longest tenure held by any officer.

Ford, the final survivor of the triumvirate, reported "Old Imperishable's" death to Lodge. He described it as a "blessed relief for himself and for the Society."[76] At the December meeting, Vice President Winslow Warren announced Green's death and there followed the usual laudatory comments by select members. For Ford, this traditional exercise was a time for celebration rather than a time for mourning.[77]

Six years earlier, when Green appeared to be on the verge of death, Adams had prepared a memorandum outlining the Society's program following his funeral. He had listed a number of speakers who were to cover facets of Green's varied career. Ford informed Lodge that he had

[73] Feb. 10, 1916.

[74] C.F. Adams to W.C. Ford, Feb. 6, 1913 (C.F. Adams Papers).

[75] Quincy was a member for nearly sixty-eight years and Savage for more than sixty-two years.

[76] W.C. Ford to H.C. Lodge, Dec. 5, 1918 (Ford-Lodge Correspondence). The letter is printed in M.H.S., Procs., 69(1947–1950):409.

[77] M.H.S., Procs., 52(1918–1919):45–55.

devised a memorial program based upon Adams's model but with a few notable alterations, one of which was his own participation. He intended to serve

> as a sort of Devil's advocate, telling some truths which may appear harsh. But I hate to see such a mass of selfishness handed down to posterity as a great man. The Society has lost so heavily by his incumbency that a million dollars cannot make good. But what is printed will naturally be 'on the soft pedal,' for we cannot wash our dirty linen in public. Mr. Adams would have touched off a portrait in high lights and had a liking for the man though thoroughly disliking him as a librarian.[78]

On the appointed day, however, Ford had a change of heart and decided not to present his candid revelations.

Ford's reference to a possible million-dollar gift from Green was made before his will was known. Subsequently, it was revealed that the venerable librarian had left nary a cent to the Society. Green had committed the ultimate insult to the Society. He willed half a million dollars, the bulk of his estate, to Lawrence Academy—of Groton, naturally.[79]

The Society's officers, as well as members, were astounded and outraged by Green's action.[80] (One can only imagine Charles F. Adams's response, had he been alive!) Voicing restraint, Lodge informed Ford on December 7, 1918: "I confess . . . that his attitude towards the Society, his announced refusal to give the Society anything after the way in which he used it and lived in its rooms, leaves on my mind a most unpleasant impression. There is a lack of gratitude about it under the

---

[78] W.C. Ford to H.C. Lodge, Dec. 5, 1918 (Ford-Lodge Correspondence).

[79] W.C. Ford to S. Mitchell, Nov. 11, 1936 (Mitchell Papers, Boston Athenaeum). Green was chairman of the Academy's board of trustees at his death. Harvard also had great expectations for a sizable bequest but also came up empty. Warren Wheeler, who had signed the codicil as a witness, surmised that "his nurse may have had some influence here." M.H.S., *Procs.*, 78(1966):49.

[80] William C. Endicott wrote in 1936 that Green "was allowed to do very much as he pleased, for it was well known that he had money, but when he died it was discovered that not one penny of several hundred thousand dollars had been left to the Society. For fifty years, then, Dr. Green had got an office free of rent and secretarial services without charge for himself, while he wrote his *History of Groton* and, in the meantime, saved the money which he left to the Lawrence Academy. Was this good policy on the part of the Society"? Endicott to James D. Phillips, May 20, 1936 (Endicott Family Papers, M.H.S.).

circumstances which is not pleasant."[81] A week later, in another letter to Ford, Lodge's judgment was more tart. He wrote that Green's "treatment of the Society after the way in which he had used it was positively indecent."[82]

Ford's anger with Green for failing to provide the Society with a generous bequest was tempered by his joy over his physical removal from the scene. The "Big Medicine Man" was finally gone. "Everything is running smoothly," he exulted to Lodge on December 23, 1918, "and one can hardly express in words the relief in no longer having the incubus of Dr. Green weighing upon the Society. He had so thoroughly cowed the working force that they dared make no change lest he should take it into his head to revisit the rooms and notice the change. Even now they seem to expect a call from him, or at least a protest in some form."[83]

Following Green's death, Ford began a systematic examination of his overladen "shabby little desk." What he discovered fully confirmed his suspicions about Green's failure to fulfill his responsibilities as librarian:

'Diggings' (no other term will be appropriate) in the accumulations of Dr. Green develop a number of very curious facts. We find papers which were given to him as long as forty years ago for the Society which were never turned over to it, papers of value and many of historical interest. But we have also found that years ago there was given to the Society the Gosnold memorial at Cuttyhunk, a tower situated on an island in one of the lakes. The transfer never seems to have been completed. Cuttyhunk is some distance from Groton and the two names are not at all alike, hence the Doctor took no interest in the matter. We are now seeing if our title is good, and if we are really a custodian of the tower.

And then Ford made his final assessment of Dr. Samuel Abbott Green:

This is only one of a number of questions buried in the inertia of our late Librarian. In fact I could hardly name two more expert librarians of the old school than Sibley and Green, with possibly a third in Little of the Astor, New York. They each represented a masterly inactivity, fruitful to those who came after but very trying during their incumbency. I thought at one

[81] H.C. Lodge to W.C. Ford, Dec. 7, 1918 (Ford-Lodge Correspondence).
[82] H.C. Lodge to W.C. Ford, Dec. 14, 1918 (Ford-Lodge Correspondence).
[83] W.C. Ford to H.C. Lodge, Dec. 23, 1918 (Ford-Lodge Correspondence).

time the truth might come out about the Doctor, but I believe now it would be impossible to tell the truth or even to get a part of it. It would vie in interest and extent with the "Thousand and One Nights."[84]

Green's death now paved the way for Ford to implement, finally, his and Charles F. Adams's long-held vision of an open library.[85]

---

[84] Ford to Lodge, Jan. 13, 1919. The letter is printed in M.H.S., *Procs.*, 69(1947–1950): 410. In 1934, from his home near Paris, Ford provided Stewart Mitchell this appraisal: "Dr. Green *was* a blot on the Society, or rather a devastating influence. He had but one real interest—Groton, Massachusetts—and he sacrificed the Society to that. He did not buy books and his gifts to college libraries were composed of material given to the M.H.S. which he thought had no place there. It would be a holy show to describe the librarian and the library as they were when I took office, and his death did not end the ignorant hostility to development. It would take a volume to describe it and would not be worth the labor." W.C. Ford to S. Mitchell, Nov. 11, 1934 (Mitchell Papers, Boston Athenaeum).

[85] Following Green's death, the Council appointed Julius Tuttle librarian and made him a salaried employee. He was the first librarian to be paid for his services.

Chapter 13

The Most Prolific Editor

BY THE 1890s, the winds of change had begun to stir in the Society. The Council's report of 1893 had reflected a spirit of nascent reform. It had recommended a "thoroughly generous" policy of accessibility to the manuscript collection, but did so on the rationale of expediency. If the Society did not open its library to a broader constituency, stated the report, prospective donors might place their gifts elsewhere. The warning was explicit. "The rooms of this Society are not now the only possible place of deposit for family papers and historical materials. Testators and donors can find other repositories and will do so, if we do not let our light shine before men."[1]

At the annual meeting of 1900, as the Society began its new life on Boylston Street, William S. Appleton asserted that the organization should also make a greater effort to augment its museum holdings and strengthen this aspect of its program. He noted that the Bostonian Society and Genealogical Society were acquiring items which rightfully belonged in the Historical Society. The problem, in his judgment, was that the Historical Society was too reclusive. It made no effort to inform the public of its needs or seek to involve the citizenry in its program.

Appleton offered a twofold solution. Initially, the Society should advertise its museum in Boston's newspapers. His second proposal involved using one of the "two excellent young men" from Green's staff as a guide in the museum "at certain hours of certain days." He could "accompany visitors over the building, showing our beautiful new rooms and the interesting contents of other less beautiful rooms." He concluded by offering a motion: "That the Council be requested to

---

[1] M.H.S., *Procs.*, 2d ser., 8(1892–1894):183–184.

consider the question of making this building and its contents better known to the world."[2]

Not all the members shared Appleton's view that the museum was a potential major tourist attraction, or that the Society should seek to develop such a facility. Worthington C. Ford, then a new member, was one of these. In a report he prepared on the library and cabinet for the 1901 annual meeting, Ford made highly critical judgments about the contents of the cabinet. He affirmed that the cabinet contained many items which did not relate to the Society's main areas of interest. "What satisfies an idle curiosity," he asserted, "what is possessed of no historical import and is affected with a merely sentimental character, should justify on some ground its presence in our collections." Ford proposed that the bulk of the Society's artifacts be deposited in the Bostonian Society because "its rooms are central, its collections are well housed, and its quarters are thronged by the very people who would be most interested in a lock of hair, the buckle of a shoe, the belt of some general, or similar object of personal use."[3]

Ford shared Appleton's enthusiasm for bringing more of the public into the Society's quarters, but his focus was upon serious historical researchers for the library, not wide-eyed tourists eager to gape at historical bric-a-brac. William R. Thayer, the senior member-at-large of the Council, spoke Ford's language in his report at the 1905 meeting:

> A society like this should be a granary to which investigators may come freely, fill their sacks, and go hence to feed many minds. There is always the danger that instead of a granary, there may be a mausoleum, in which the most precious materials has a magnificent but unavailing preservation.

---

[2] M.H.S., *Procs.*, 2d ser., 14(1900–1901):147–148.

[3] M.H.S., *Procs.*, 2d ser., 15(1901–1902):46–50. In 1902 the Society began advertising in the "Strangers' Directory" of the *Boston Evening Transcript* that it was "open to the public," both the library and museum. The library was open daily and the cabinet from 2:00 to 5:00 P.M. on Wednesdays—"Free." See, for example, the *Transcript*, Mar. 4, 1902. The Society was primarily interested in bringing visitors into the museum. Few came. In April 1915 Tuttle informed the Library Committee that the average weekly attendance was six. The committee made three recommendations to increase attendance: open the museum on Saturday from 9:00 to noon, and close at 5:00 on Wednesday, except in mid-winter; invite teachers of history and their students by appointment; and post a sign, "such as shall not injure the dignity of our portals," listing the hours when the museum was open. M.H.S., *Procs.*, 48(1914–1915):380–381.

The Most Prolific Editor

The Massachusetts Historical Society is venerable from its age. It had, through good fortune which is not likely to be repeated, many of the most illustrious makers of American literature and writers of history among its active members during the nineteenth century. It has now a fine house for its printed and manuscript stores. But it cannot hope to retain its primacy simply by sitting still. It must be the first, not only in age and illustrious membership and in precious historical possessions, but in fruitful service. Not only to collect, but to share and spread, must be the aim of our Society.[4]

Share and spread—this was also Ford's creed. He was a disciple of Belknap. In April 1910, one year after he became an employee of the Society, Ford wrote the report of the Council for the annual meeting; it was read by Melville M. Bigelow. He concluded this document with a paragraph that was a manifesto of the open library to which he, like Charles F. Adams, was committed with every fiber of his being:

It is generally admitted that the relations of the Society, not only to the outside public but to the scholars, are far from what they should be, and demand a radical improvement. To accumulate and bury was never the intention of the founders of this Society. To collect and to hold rigidly for the use of the Society would be a suicidal act. The book or the manuscript which enters the doors of this Society has been lost to investigators, on the double plea that it was a private society, and that its collections should be held for the use of its members or its own publications. The Society has lost by cultivating such an impression, and, by what is probably an unconscious narrowness of policy, permitting that impression to become general.[5]

In 1912, Ford presented a paper before the American Historical Association then meeting in Boston. The meeting site was the Society, and Ford's subject was, fittingly, "The Massachusetts Historical Society." Ford traced the history of the Society from its founding to his period of employment. Near the end of his presentation, he reaffirmed his vision of the Society as an open institution or, as Stewart Mitchell would later phrase it, "a national institute for research."[6] The Society, Ford stated, "seeks not to accumulate but to advance the study and use of mate-

---

[4] M.H.S., *Procs.*, 2d ser., 19(1905):204.

[5] M.H.S., *Procs.*, 43(1909–1910):463–464.

[6] M.H.S., *Procs.*, 70(1950–1953):329. Mitchell also used the phrase: "a great free national research society." Ibid., p. 302.

rial—to serve as an active influence, not as a burial place of accumulation. Here the earnest investigator should be welcome, for what is here is intended to be used."

Ford underscored his point by relating an exchange he had had with a researcher:

Last month a gentleman came in, a stranger, and with the air of proper timidity which marks those who ask in the expectation of being denied. His question was, "What are the restrictions and what the privileges in making researches here?" My reply was, "There are no restrictions and there are all privileges." I saw him blink, as if I had tapped him lightly between the eyes; but he soon caught my meaning, explained his wants, and in 10 minutes had the pleasure of making some unexpectedly rich discoveries of materials on his subject.[7]

Ford's proclamations for an open library remained in the realm of rhetoric until Green finally departed in late 1918. Only then was Ford able to institute his new policy. Only then could Fordism supplant Greenism.

Beginning in 1919, the Society underwent a dramatic transformation. Researchers were welcomed with enthusiasm and started coming in increasing numbers. Ford was now firmly in charge of the Society. His values permeated the institution.

Green's successor, the mild-mannered Julius Tuttle, was a benign force in the library. To his credit, he also welcomed the rush of researchers. He spent his day busily servicing their needs and relishing their presence, as evidenced by his annual reports.

Within five years of the introduction of the new order, the Society began to experience serious problems, but they were not related to Ford's reforms. These were familiar problems, generic difficulties. The Boylston Street building, the monumental structure, had run out of work and storage space, like all of the earlier Society quarters.

In truth, the "curious building" had never been a practical facility. As director Stewart Mitchell affirmed in 1950, "what the Society needed for a home was not a handsome clubhouse of marble and quartered oak, but the kind of building which would now be called 'functional.' "[8] Even Adams, who was responsible for the structure, "acknowledged

---

[7] American Historical Association, *Annual Report* (1912), 221.
[8] M.H.S., *Procs.*, 69(1947–1950):474; 70(1950–1953):301.

that he hardly ever entered the present building without seeing something more about it which displeased him." Shortly after the building was opened, Adams had written to Robert C. Winthrop, Jr.: "My position at the head of the Society is one of increasing embarrassment. I suppose I am held responsible for the course things have taken, but I never go through the rooms without seeing much that is repugnant to me. Correction will undoubtedly come in time, but we are so hampered by vested interests that I do not yet see my way clear to effective action."[9]

The edifice had many conspicuous failings, as Clarence S. Brigham pointed out in 1935 in his report of the Council. The meeting-room was "makeshift" with deplorable ventilation. The entire building was "curiously designed" and not appropriate for a library; despite elaborate "panels of oak and slabs of marble," the offices were simply "corridors." Many members found "its spacious halls and splendid stairways a babel of echoes and a cave of the winds." Ellis Hall in particular was marred by defective acoustics, making it useless for "purposes of assembly." The "most handsome, if not the most rare, books" were housed in the dingy cellar. Finally, the stockroom was a "labyrinth of dust, darkness, and congestion."[10]

Lack of storage space was the most serious defect. After less than twenty-five years of service, Wheelwright's architectural masterpiece could no longer accommodate the needs of the fast-expanding Society. It was filled to capacity and its floors were "groaning from the overweight of necessary accessions."[11]

In 1919, the Society embarked on an effort to add an annex to Wheelwright's building. President Lodge appointed a committee to raise funds for a "stack building" that was to be "absolutely fireproof." The need for a fireproof stack area was imperative because a number of the Society's major manuscript collections, including the Winthrop, Parkman, and Sibley papers, were being stored on wooden shelves or in wooden cases.[12] A few of the members opposed Lodge's action because they felt

[9] C.F. Adams to R.C. Winthrop, Jr., June 19, 1899 (R.C. Winthrop, Jr., Memoranda, vol. 82 of the Winthrop Papers, M.H.S.).

[10] M.H.S., *Procs.*, 63(1932–1936):407.

[11] M.H.S., *Procs.*, 55(1921–1922):293. See also, ibid., 54(1920–1921):247.

[12] M.H.S., *Procs.*, 53(1919–1920):145–146.

certain that the Society could not raise a large sum of money. This lack of confidence did not augur well for the campaign.

Lodge became exasperated by this negative attitude. As he informed Ford, after hearing of the opposition: "If we can't get it, that will end it; but we ought at least to make the attempt."[13]

Lodge's committee did not help matters any when it decided to run a low-level fund drive, limiting itself to an appeal by mail. In 1920, the committee reported that it was "not the plan . . . to conduct an active campaign for this purpose, but merely to give an opportunity for friends, whether members of the Society or not, to assist us in protecting our collection."[14] The admission of a half-hearted attempt to raise funds preordained the campaign to failure.

In 1921, Ford sent a form letter to a select list of wealthy Bostonians, appealing for donations. He stressed the central feature of the proposed annex, an "Historic Hall" containing alcoves filled with memorabilia pertaining to New England's prominent families and storied past. They would contain "not only books and papers but also medals, busts, and flags or banners commemorating individuals or events." There also would be representations of historic Boston institutions, such as the Old South Church, King's Chapel, and some of the old Massachusetts guilds; and events, such as the battles of Lexington and Bunker Hill, and "such families as are represented by the name of Revere and Adams." The Society also would exhibit specimens from its Civil War holdings, one of the largest collections in the nation.[15]

To the prospective donors Ford offered placing their names "in some fitting manner by tablet or other memorial to this desirable work."[16] Despite this blatant appeal to familial and patriotic pride, the response was negative.

With his time and energy consumed by activities in the United States Senate, Lodge limited his involvement in the "campaign" to a few personal fund-raising letters, presumably drafted by Ford. In one such

[13] H.C. Lodge to W.C. Ford, May 10, 1919 (Ford-Lodge Correspondence).

[14] M.H.S., *Procs.*, 53(1919–1920):145–146.

[15] The turnabout from Ford's 1901 opinion that the museum collections should be disbanded seems to result from a pragmatic view of fund raising possibilities.

[16] A copy of the form letter, dated Feb. 9, 1921, is in the Ford-Lodge Correspondence.

letter, designed specifically for wealthy Bostonians who were not members, he made a strong appeal for public support, asserting that the Society performed a vital service for the general citizenry. Its "very large" collections of books, manuscripts, and pamphlets, he asserted, were "really for the benefit of the public and historical students and inquirers." Lodge honed in on the imperative need for a fireproof addition. A "destructive fire," he warned would be a "public calamity" since the materials were irreplaceable. The Society's membership, he concluded, could not meet these financial obligations. It was comprised of "scholars and students, and with very few exception" the members were not rich men. Thus, he was obliged to turn to the public for assistance.[17]

Given the lack of personal involvement by its absentee president and the failure of the membership to respond to his and the committee's appeals for contributions, the drive was doomed to fizzle. The report of the Council in 1923 bluntly acknowledged the failure: "With public functions to perform no aid had come from the public, directly or indirectly, and on private contributions expansion in the future depends."[18]

In his subsequent annual reports to the Council, Ford continued to hammer away at the stale old themes of a non-functional building bursting at the seams and the need for an addition. He also stressed that the problems of the library had been compounded by the new policy of "admitting freely any investigator of honest intent." There was "too little space" for tables for readers, and no alcoves "in which quiet may be had and books reserved for the student."[19] An "urgent need of enlarged accommodations," an old staple, again became the standard theme of annual reports—for years to come.

The far-sighted Ford was solely responsible for conceiving and implementing the pioneering and large-scale "Photostat Americana"

[17] H.C. Lodge to J. Collins Warren, Jan. 15, 1921 (Ford-Lodge Correspondence).

[18] M.H.S., *Procs.*, 56(1922–1923):285. Reflecting on this campaign while in France in 1936, Ford wrote: "We did try in the '20's to raise a building fund, and look at the result! We did not adopt the method of the N.E. Gen. Socy.—a plaque in a hall way—nor that of the Antiq. Socy.—a professional money raiser—so we failed." W.C. Ford to S. Mitchell, Nov. 11, 1936 (Mitchell Papers, Boston Athenaeum).

[19] M.H.S., *Procs.*, 52(1923–1924):312–313.

project, which the Society sponsored between 1915 and 1943.[20] This program corresponded to Belknap's effort to "multiply the copies," to reproduce rare manuscripts and imprints. Whereas Belknap had used the medium of the newspaper, Ford employed the photostat machine.

Ford first saw a photostat machine while serving on a visiting committee of the John Carter Brown Library in Providence, Rhode Island. He was deeply impressed by the newfangled contraption and quickly foresaw its application to the Society's program. For twenty years, he had been seeking a means of cheaply reproducing the *Boston News-Letter*, one of colonial America's most significant newspapers and a prime source for scholars of early American history. The photostat seemed to offer the solution to his problem.

In 1914, he urged the Council to purchase a machine and embark on a program of reproduction. The Council approved his request, authorizing the purchase of a "machine of medium size." Ford acquired one and promptly went to work.

The New-York Historical Society owned an "almost unique" file of the *Boston News-Letter*. Ford requested its loan and the New York society graciously complied. Ford and a Society employee operated the machine each morning for two hours. They completed a negative copy of the newspaper and "indulged in other experiments."

Experience soon proved to Ford that the Society's machine was too small to be cost effective. It could print a single page of moderate size, but it would have been more cost effective if it could reproduce two pages of text on a single page. Ford became convinced that the Society needed a higher quality machine. Cost, however, prevented such a purchase. It required several hundred dollars, a sizable barrier in those days.

Then, fortuitously, the Commonwealth of Massachusetts came to the rescue. The Commonwealth had agreed to participate in an exhibition of manuscripts at the California Exposition and required reproductions for which they placed an order with the Society. The Society made a suf-

---

[20] The best sources for this subject are: Worthington C. Ford, "Ten Years of the Photostat," M.H.S., *Procs.*, 58(1924–1925):288–316, and "The Society's Photostat, 1925–1929," 62(1928–1929):87–110. See also, Massachusetts Historical Society, *Handbook of the Publications and Photostats, 1792–1935* (Boston, 1937), 111–144. Wilberforce Eames, the noted bibliographer who was a close friend of Ford and collaborator in numerous scholarly projects, assisted him in the "Photostat Americana" program.

ficient profit from this venture to buy a new and larger machine receiving "full allowance" for its old one.

After some months of experimentation with the new instrument, Ford concluded that the Society should operate its photostat program on a formal business basis, using a professional operator. In 1916, he received authorization from the Council to hire Robert H. Pearman of Washington, D.C., a professional photographer with thirty-two years of experience. From that point on, the enterprise proved to be a success, both from a business and professional standpoint. In the first two years of continuous operation, the cost of operating the machine was about $45,000. The Society took in receipts amounting to $46,000.

Ford's first major project was to reproduce the *Boston News Letter* from its inception in 1704 to its disappearance in 1775. By the time he retired in 1929, he had printed all known issues of the journal through the year 1769. The Society distributed twenty-three sets across the country, making the paper available to numerous students. Ford was pleased by the success of the project. "The result has fully justified the undertaking," he wrote, "for it has placed at the command of the searcher a body of contemporary record, hitherto available in widely separated libraries, and of a nature that could not be found in any other form." This effort was an example of Fordism *par excellence*.

Ford's greatest single achievement in the realm of reproduction was his two-part "Photostat Americana" series. In the first phase, Ford reproduced 261 publications of rare books, newspapers, maps, and broadsides in the collections of major repositories in the United States and Europe. The second series consisted of 169 numbers, which brought the full list of titles to 430. In the opinion of Lyman H. Butterfield, these two series "enriched beyond measure not only its [the Society's] own holdings but those of research libraries throughout the country."[21]

Ford's contribution to the Society transcended his individual achievement of administering the photostat program. As Butterfield has writ-

[21] Butterfield, "Ford, Editor," 68. These series involved the cooperation of ten other American research libraries, all of which contributed items to be duplicated and received copies of the reproduced material: the New-York Historical Society; the State Historical Society of Wisconsin; the American Antiquarian Society; the Library of Congress; the New York Public Library; the John Carter Brown Library; the William L. Clements Library; the Henry E. Huntington Library; and the Newberry Library.

ten: "Ford brought to the Society a knowledge of history and its resources, of historians, and of methods for promoting historical scholarship that were national and international in outlook rather than
parochial."[22]

Ford was the central figure in the deaccessioning of two major documentary collections: the papers of Gov. Jonathan Trumbull of Connecticut and the letterbooks of John Hancock while he served as president of
the Continental Congress. Both collections were public papers, and Ford
firmly believed that they belonged at their point of origin. He worked
from the idealistic principle that every historical document, public and
private, should be placed "where it will have its highest utility. I would
not come to Massachusetts to write the history of Georgia any more
than I would go to Georgia to write the history of Massachusetts. The-
oretically all that is needed for Georgia history should be in Georgia, and
what is wanted here should be here."[23]

Ford was fully aware that many collections of public documents, in
particular, had been "looted or have been scattered by want of care." He
held to the conviction that these materials should return to their source.
"If I have here a volume known to be of State records or a manuscript
known to have come from a State archive," he wrote, "why not return
it for a like courtesy from the receiving State?"

The Trumbull Papers had long been a source of controversy between
the State of Connecticut and the Society. In 1771 the Connecticut General Assembly had instructed Gov. Jonathan Trumbull to "collect all
publick letters and papers which may hereafter in any way affect the
interest of this Colony and have the same bound together, that they
may be preserved." The assembly was becoming increasingly concerned
about the loss and destruction of vital historical documents pertaining to
Connecticut.

Trumbull took this charge seriously and amassed a large corpus of
materials, including agents' letters, 1742–1773; council of safety's pa-

---

[22] Butterfield, "Ford, Editor," 68. The full dimensions of Ford's singular achievement
can be seen in the Society's *Proceedings* of 1924–1925 and 1928–1929 in which are listed
the items reproduced during Ford's era and his personal reports on this remarkable project
(See 58[1924–1925]:297–316; and 62[1928–1929]:91–110).

[23] American Historical Association, *Annual Report* (1912), 223.

pers, 1775–1782; council orders, 1743–1775; Gov. Joseph Talcott's papers, 1724–1741; Gov. Jonathan Law's papers, 1741–1750; and Gov. Thomas Fitch's papers, 1754–1766. This was the richest extant collection on the political history of eighteenth-century Connecticut. When he left office, Trumbull moved this collection to his home in Lebanon. He regarded it as his private property in keeping with the convention of that era. Upon his death in 1785, it became part of his personal estate.[24]

In April 1794, the heirs of the late governor, through his son David, offered his papers to the Massachusetts Historical Society. As David wrote to Jeremy Belknap: "Had the Massachusetts Historical Society existed during his Life, there is no doubt but He would have chosen to give them to an Institution whose Patriotic Views they would so directly subserve in preference to a Collegiate or other Library, where they probably would soon become 'Food for Worms.'"

Belknap, the collector extraordinaire, traveled to Lebanon in 1794 and selected much of Trumbull's holdings for the Society. After arranging for their shipment to Boston, he processed and bound these documents in twenty-three large volumes.[25]

In 1845, the Connecticut state legislature made a strong effort to secure the return of Trumbull's papers. Taking the position that these were public documents and the property of the State of Connecticut, it threatened legal action. The Society categorically rejected Connecticut's claim and refused to return the papers.[26] No legal action ensued.

For the next sixty-five years, the collection quietly reposed in the Society, rarely consulted by researchers. At the Council meeting of October 14, 1920, Ford "raised the question of the continued possession by the Society of the Trumbull Papers." He urged that the documents be returned to Hartford, where a new state library had been completed. The Council appointed a four-man committee to review the issue. Ford and President Lodge were among the four.[27]

---

[24] On the early history of the Trumbull Papers, see: M.H.S., *Colls.*, 5th ser., 9:vii–xiv, Editorial Note; M.H.S., *Procs.*, 2(1835–1855):330–333, 343–346, 357–359; Christopher P. Bickford, "Public Records and the Private Historical Society: A Connecticut Example," *Government Publications Review*, 8A(1981):311–315; Tucker, *Clio's Consort*, 111–114.

[25] One volume was lost in a fire in 1825.

[26] The key documents can be seen in M.H.S., *Procs.*, 2(1835–1855):330–333, 357–359.

[27] M.H.S. Council Records, Oct. 14, 1920 (M.H.S. Archives).

The committee adopted Ford's view, and the recommendation for return was approved by the Council and membership.[28] News of the decision "fell like a bomb shell" in Hartford. The Connecticut authorities were ecstatic.[29] On September 17, 1921, 126 years after leaving Connecticut, the documents returned to the Nutmeg State.

There was a two-part program in Hartford to commemorate the event. First, an appreciative Gov. Everett J. Lake hosted a lavish luncheon at a private club for the three Society representatives in attendance: Lodge, Ford, and Arthur Lord. The formal transfer took place in an elaborate ceremony in Memorial Hall. The governor's colorfully costumed Foot Guard escorted the official party and dignitaries into the meeting site. In his address to the large gathering, Lodge made it clear that Ford had inspired the transfer: "It is pleasant to know that the members of the Massachusetts Historical Society were of one opinion in desiring their return, but it is also fitting to say that the thought, the intent, the necessary effort, the appreciation of the larger meanings of the action were due, as is apt to be the case, to one man, Mr. Worthington C. Ford of the Massachusetts Historical Society, editor, scholar, historian, a man of letters and learning, to whom we are all indebted."[30]

At a meeting of the Council in 1924, Ford called attention to the Society's ownership of six volumes of John Hancock's letterbooks, which covered the period when the rebel leader had served as president of the Continental Congress. Regarding these documents as private property, Hancock had retained possession of them when he returned to Boston. Citing the return of the Trumbull Papers as precedent, Ford asserted that these were also public documents and should be given to the Library of Congress to complete its collection of Continental Congress letter-

---

[28] M.H.S. Council Records, Jan. 12, 1921 (M.H.S. Archives).

[29] See Gov. Everett J. Lake to W.C. Ford, May 4, 1921; Ford to H.C. Lodge, May 6, 1921; Arthur Lord to Lodge, May 14, 1921; Lodge to Lord, May 16, 1921; Julius H. Tuttle to Lodge, Sept. 8, 1921 (Ford-Lodge Correspondence).

[30] For detailed accounts of the Trumbull Papers episode, see: M.H.S., *Procs.*, 54(1920–1921):353–357, 55(1921–1922):30–40. The Henry Cabot Lodge (1850–1924) Papers, M.H.S., contain a copy of the January 1923 resolution of the Connecticut General Assembly, thanking the Society for its generosity, and a letter from state librarian George S. Godard to Julius H. Tuttle (Apr. 4, 1923), acknowledging receipt of the catalogue cards for the Trumbull Papers.

books. Having worked there, Ford was well aware of this significant gap in its holdings.

The Council appointed a three-man committee to review the issue. Ford was designated one of these, and his will prevailed. At the May meeting, Ford, speaking for the committee, recommended that the letterbooks be donated to the Library of Congress. The Council accepted the recommendation and the members later approved it. In his annual report, Charles Moore, chief of the Library of Congress manuscript division, praised the Society for its voluntary action of returning the Hancock documents as well as the Trumbull Papers: "That the Massachusetts Historical Society of its own motion has established for itself a policy of distribution so enlightened must win for that institution the additional regard and esteem of historical scholars." To which Ford responded: "We accept the compliment, but firm in our belief that the distribution was fully justified, we also hoped and still hope to influence other institutions to recognize in the same manner the proper claims of origin and localizing of public records."[31] It was a high-minded thought, but no other historical organization emulated the "enlightened" action of the Boston society.

Ford, however, did not respond so positively to requests from private organizations for Society materials. "You have something in your collection we want." So wrote Miss Laura E. Wilkes, president of the Afro-American Historical Society of Washington, D.C., in 1915. What Wilkes wanted was one of the Society's prize artifacts, the flag presented by John Hancock to the "Bucks" of the American Revolution, a Black military unit that fought against the British. Wilkes affirmed that her organization planned to do "for the colored people just what you have done for Mass. We also intend to tell the stories we collect to our children, much the same way American History is told in the Old South Meeting House to Boston school children." She conceded that "we have no rooms as yet but will have soon" and "we are responsible folks." The flag, she asserted, "can stimulate and make proud no one but us, colored people, any way and so belongs to us."

[31] M.H.S., *Procs.*, 58(1924–1925):250. For further information on the transfer of the Hancock letterbooks, see: M.H.S. Council Records, Apr. 10, May 8, Oct. 9, 1924 (M.H.S. Archives).

Should a "colored" historical organization ever incorporate in Massachusetts, she added, her group would willingly return the banner. "Please put yourself in our place, when you reply," she concluded.[32] Ford's reply is unrecorded, but the banner remained in Boston.

Ford was involved in a rousing brouhaha in 1920, which seemed to run counter to his pronounced liberal attitude on the free transmission and unfettered use of historical information. His problem arose at the "famous" October meeting of the Society, which began on an ominous note when Charles P. Bowditch, responding to an article on the prominent political personality, James G. Blaine, by fellow-member Gamaliel Bradford, "let forth a torrent of abuse." This did not set well with President Lodge, one of Blaine's political allies. Although visibly angered by Bowditch's remarks, Lodge had to exercise discretion since he was chairing the meeting. He "restricted himself to whispers," and when no one replied, "there was a terrible hush."

At this point, Ford rose and, ostensibly to ease the tension that had developed, reported the acquisition of the Woodman family papers. He would have been well advised to stop with his announcement. But he proceeded to read one of the letters, from Charles Sumner to Horatio Woodman, in which Sumner "blackguarded his own divorced wife and the Hooper family in general."[33] Ford, unwittingly, had stepped into a social hornet's nest. He had committed an unpardonable sin in Boston, making public comment on the delicate private affairs of Yankee patrician families. "The air was blue with tension," reported Charles K. Bolton, who was in attendance, "and then Dr. Sturgis Bigelow with a white face and trembling voice rose to defend the Hoopers as well as to excoriate Sumner (and Ford)."[34]

[32] Laura E. Wilkes to Secretary of the M.H.S., Mar. 13, 1915 (Editorial Correspondence, M.H.S. Archives).

[33] The letter in question is probably one dated Feb. 17, 1868, in which Sumner writes: "Genl. Burt tells me that her late husband, with whom he became intimate at New Orleans, told him, that he did not wish to return home; that the misconduct of his wife made him wish to stay away. So she began early. He communicated this to Dr. Howe before my marriage thinking & hoping it might reach me. It never did." Woodman Papers, M.H.S. Sumner's marital history is treated in David Donald, *Charles Sumner & the Rights of Man* (New York, 1970), esp. ch. 7.

[34] Bolton, Journal, Oct. 21, 1920.

Ford's action compounded Lodge's displeasure and also aroused the ire of others, aside from Bigelow. As Lodge later wrote to Recording Secretary William R. Thayer:

> He ought not to have read the letter. It was unfortunate that he did not know more about Boston relations for in that case he never would have brought it forward. Dr. Bigelow was Sturgis Hooper's first cousin. He was also very much attached to Mrs. Mason, who was the first Mrs. Sturgis Hooper and then Mrs. Sumner. She took her maiden name of Mason after the divorce. The letter, which contained a story that was familiar at the time and for which there was no authority but hearsay, troubled him very much indeed and Mr. Rhodes and I, after the meeting, told Mr. Ford that we thought it would be as well to destroy it.[35]

Ford was not only prepared to follow through on Lodge's and Rhodes's recommendation, he fully agreed with them. Thayer, when he learned of their decision, became irate. Whatever his position on the contents of the letter, he vehemently opposed the destruction of sensitive documents by the Society. He met with Ford, objected to the proposed action, and demanded an explanation. Ford responded that, as "Editor or Keeper of the Manuscripts," he had the right to destroy any letter or document donated to the Society, if he regarded it as "indecent or undesirable" and unfit to print. He stated that he had followed the same practice while employed at the Library of Congress.[36]

Ford's response only increased Thayer's outrage, and in a letter to Lodge, Thayer strenuously objected to the practice of destroying con-

---

[35] H.C. Lodge to William R. Thayer, Dec. 2, 1920 (Ford-Lodge Correspondence). Two days after the meeting, Moorfield Storey, "who once lived with Sumner for two years," told Charles K. Bolton that Sumner "was the social leader of Washington when Mrs. Sturgis Hooper determined to marry him and set up a salon. He was engrossed in his work, irregular at meals, and gave her that liberty which led her to fall in love with an Austrian diplomat. She followed him to Europe and was brought back by old Sam Hooper." Bolton, Journal, Oct. 22, 1920.

[36] Ford's position should be contrasted with that of Charles Francis Adams, who wrote Ford: "My family seems to be somewhat peculiar. We welcome all kinds of historical material, and savage criticism rolls from us like water from the back of a duck. I welcome all which enters, for what it is worth, into the grand historical result. It is all evidence, and it is for the jury of posterity to pass upon the character and reliability of the witness. The one mission we have to accomplish is not to suppress the facts." Adams to Ford, Jan. 15, 1912 (C.F. Adams Papers).

troversial documents: "that anybody, Ford, or you, or I, or any coterie of members, shall be allowed to destroy what they don't like, is certainly monstrous." He reminded Lodge that "Mrs. Kitty O'Shea's letters might be of great historical importance, *if* from them the historical student could learn the facts of her *liason* with Parnell, which not only shattered his career, but dislocated the course of the Irish movement."

Thayer warned Lodge that the public would provide the Society with "very few more gifts of family or other papers" if it permitted "such mutilation." His wife and her sister, he noted, had many papers of their distinguished ancestor, Dr. Benjamin Waterhouse, including his journal and twenty pieces of correspondence with Thomas Jefferson. They intended to donate these documents to the Society "but I shall dissuade them from doing so, *if* the Ford plan is continued." Thayer added that he also had a "good many papers of my own, including some letters of [Theodore] Roosevelt, which I expect to bequeath to the M.H.S. but I shall find some other destination."

Thayer recommended as an alternate policy that all gifts containing "questionable or delicate matters" be reviewed by three persons, the president, editor, and recording secretary and, "if not approved, placed in an 'inferno', where they could not be consulted without special arrangement, and where they would be safe from printing." If the matter was not resolved to his satisfaction, Thayer threatened to bring the issue before the Council to have Ford's policy changed.

Having directed Ford to destroy the letter, Lodge now found himself in an untenable position. He fully recognized that Thayer's remonstrance related to an issue of fundamental importance to the Society. The willful destruction of historical documents was no trivial matter and had profound implications for the library and publications program. Above all, he did not wish to see the issue brought before the Council, where it would assuredly escalate into a bruising battle that would destroy the cohesiveness of the governing body.

In a thoughtful response, Lodge sought to mollify Thayer, assuring him that "it is entirely understood by Mr. Ford and everyone that there is no authority anywhere to destroy papers in the possession of the Society. . . . Not only has no officer of the Society any authority to destroy papers deposited or bequeathed to the Society, but I do not think the Council or the Society itself has that power. Papers of that sort, of which we have a good many, are, it appears to me, in the nature of a trust. The Society has absolute authority to decide on publication or whether certain letters should be shown to the public, but they certainly have no power, in view of the papers being the nature of a trust, to destroy any of them."

Lodge also informed Thayer that he and Dr. Bigelow had visited Ford at the Society, discussed the central issue, and all had concluded that no official could destroy a document given to the institution. The three men thereupon sealed up the controversial Sumner letter, "which was so objected to in an envelope and put it away in the case where other papers are kept, and endorsed on the outside that it was not to be opened for fifty years." Lodge concluded that "the matter has been settled and settled correctly and in just the way you suggest, and now it seems to me it would be better to let it sleep."[37]

Echoes of Edward Stanwood's 1912 warning about the arbitrary and controlling aspects of Ford's character must have begun resounding in the thoughts of Council members after this incident.[38] However, Ford still had powerful advocates among the membership. In the mid-1920s, when he was nearing sixty-five years of age, some key members of the Society, who were also close friends of the editor, became concerned about his modest salary and lack of a pension. Ford was living in straitened circumstances. Corresponding member Albert J. Beveridge, United States senator from Indiana and a well-known historian who had spent considerable time at the Society while researching his *Life of John Marshall*, strongly urged Vice President Arthur Lord to find the means to increase Ford's salary so as to alleviate his financial hardship and assure his continued employment at the Society. Wrote Beveridge: "If ever we lose him, all of us will realize that an

[37] The events of this incident can be traced in the following letters: Thayer to Lodge, Nov. 30, 1920; Lodge to Thayer, Dec. 2, 1920; Thayer to Lodge, Dec. 4, 17, 1920; Lodge to Thayer, Dec. 23, 1920; Lodge to Ford, Dec. 23, 1920; Ford to Lodge, Jan. 3, 1921 (Ford-Lodge Correspondence).

[38] See Chapter 12.

element has gone from our lives that never can be replaced; and in the world of scholarship, there will be a vacant place that never can be filled."[39]

Unfortunately, the final years of Ford's notable career at the Society were further marred by an episode concerning the publication of the Winthrop Papers. In 1920 the Winthrops had established a fund to publish a comprehensive edition of the family's collection of manuscripts, which they had donated to the Society over a period of years. Without seeking the authorization or approval of the Council, Ford entered into a "gentleman's agreement" with representatives of the Winthrop family whereby he promised that, if the Winthrops contributed "$10,000 or more," the Society would publish a volume of their papers every other year, the expense to be divided between the Winthrop Fund and the Society.[40]

Because he was involved in a number of other editorial projects, Ford did not complete his editing and publish the first volume until 1925. Subsequently, some scholars pointed out, in letters to the Society and reviews in professional journals, that Ford's volume contained errors in translation of documents reproduced in facsimile. They also noted other glaring defects: the lack of a stated and consistent editorial policy; the omission of key documents; and a paucity of annotation.[41]

The Society's officers, who took enormous pride in their publications, were severely stung by this criticism. They stopped distribution of the volume and considered various remedies, from issuing a pamphlet listing errata to inserting new signatures into a revised edition. William C.

[39] Beveridge to Lord, Dec. 11, 1924. Beveridge admitted that his "admiration for Ford is vitalized and vivified by affection." Warren Wheeler recalled that Beveridge and Ford conferred often when the senator researched at the Society. "His oratorical voice still echoes in my memory as he and Mr. Ford conferred on the third floor, where he worked." Wheeler, "Fifty Years," 45. Francis R. Hart also expressed concern over Ford's weak financial condition. See Hart to James Wilbur, Dec. 11, 1924. Treasurer Allan Forbes recommended to Vice President Lord on Dec. 17, 1924, that Ford's salary be increased by $1,500 (all from Editorial Correspondence, M.H.S. Archives).

[40] Later, when this information surfaced, Society officials, including President Endicott, were slightly more than irritated. "Mr. Ford certainly had no authority under any circumstances to commit the Society to this policy." William C. Endicott to Grenville Lindall Winthrop, Feb. 9, 1935 (Endicott Family Papers, M.H.S.).

[41] See, for example, *American Historical Review*, 32(1927):328–330.

Endicott, the Society's new president, appointed a special committee, headed by Samuel Eliot Morison, to review the issue and make recommendations for a new policy governing publications. Distressed and embarrassed by the criticism, Ford assumed full responsibility for the mess and, in a letter to the *American Historical Review*, absolved the publication committee, whose names appeared in the front matter of the volume, of all blame.[42]

In 1928, Morison's committee recommended the recall and destruction of all copies of the first volume of the *Winthrop Papers* distributed to that time and the development of a revised edition. It also recommended new procedures for future publications. Hereafter, the publication committee was to supervise closely the manuscripts prepared by the editor. No manuscript was to go to the printer until it had been approved by the committee and the Council. Another prerequisite for publication was adequate funding. The Council approved these recommendations. By doing so, it severely curtailed Ford's authority.[43]

In a candid letter to President Endicott, Morison expressed the belief that Ford's days of usefulness at the Society were nearing an end. Because of his forceful personality and propensity to work as a solitary agent, he would not accept the new policy, Morison asserted. "It will be very difficult to make a useful instrument of Ford in the future," wrote the Harvard professor. "He is exceedingly stubborn and I fear will do all in his power to defeat the new policy. One cannot force a man to consult experts if he does not think the advice of experts desirable or advisable, as Ford apparently does not. Still, we cannot make Ford resign, and will have to make the best of him if he stays." He added, as an afterthought, "Ford has his 70th birthday on February 16."[44]

Ford, himself, realized that the end was at hand. In December 1928, he confided to Charles K. Bolton at a private luncheon that, since William C. Endicott had assumed the presidency of the Society in 1927 and now that his two close friends, Samuel Eliot Morison and Francis Russell Hart, were soon to leave the Council, he knew he would be "fired" and

---

[42] *American Historical Review*, 32(1927):675.

[43] The Winthrop Papers issue can be followed in the M.H.S. Council Records and the special committee's report; see also M.H.S., *Procs.*, 61(1927–1928):130. The revised volume was published in 1929.

[44] Morison to Endicott, Jan. 28, 1928 (Endicott Family Papers, M.H.S.).

so decided to retire.[45] In a lengthy letter to President Endicott from Hart on December 12, 1928, it is manifestly apparent that the Winthrop publication incident was the key factor in Ford's forced retirement. There is also a sharp reference to "past causes of friction."[46]

On December 13, the sixty-nine-year-old Ford submitted his resignation as editor, effective June 20, 1929, after twenty years with the Society. The Council accepted it with official regret. Samuel Eliot Morison presented a motion of thanks, praising Ford for his many contributions to the Society and offering "hearty wishes for his future welfare and happiness." The motion was approved.[47] As the Society had no formal pension plan, the Council also voted Ford an "honorarium" of $3,000 a year for life as of July 1, 1929.[48] At Ford's final appearance at a Society meeting, William V. Kellen, officiating in the absence of the president and vice presidents, reviewed the editor's illustrious career at Boylston Street.[49]

Ford's retirement ended the most productive era of publications in the history of the Society. He had edited about fifty volumes of Society publications in these two decades. In Lyman Butterfield's authoritative judgment, his output was an "awesome record, probably unequaled in either quantity or quality by any other learned institution at any time."[50] He edited twenty volumes of *Proceedings*, each of which contained one or more contributions he had prepared. He also edited ten volumes of *Collections*, including *Cotton Mather's Diary* (1911–1912), the *Copley-Pelham Letters* (1914), the *Warren-Adams Letters* (1917–1925), and a *Bibliography of Massachusetts Broadsides, Ballads, etc.* (1922), which he personally prepared. In addition, he produced ten vol-

[45] Bolton, Journal, Dec. 21, 1928.

[46] Hart to Endicott, Dec. 12, 1928 (M.H.S. Archives). It is obvious from this fascinating letter that Ford's retirement was a carefully orchestrated event. The stated reason for Ford's leaving was his desire to "go on with the Lincoln work," that is, the completion of Albert J. Beveridge's biography of Abraham Lincoln.

[47] Charles Bolton, who attended this Council meeting, reported that he and another member made a "little speech" praising the editor," but Endicott, Hart and Morison had it all cut and dried." Bolton, Journal, Dec. 13, 1928.

[48] M.H.S. Council Records, Dec. 13, 1928 (M.H.S. Archives).

[49] M.H.S., *Procs.*, 62(1928–1929):160–161.

[50] Butterfield, "Ford, Editor," 69–70.

umes of the *Journals* of the Massachusetts provincial House of Representatives (1919–1929). He also was responsible for a number of special publications, including a superb two-volume edition of William Bradford's *History of Plymouth Plantation, 1620–1647* (1912),[51] Charles Francis Adams's *Autobiography* (1916), and the first regularly published edition of Henry Adams's celebrated and controversial *The Education of Henry Adams: An Autobiography* (1918).[52] And these were only his Society publications. Ford was simultaneously engaged in a myriad of non-Society editorial projects.[53] There was ample reason for his election as president of the American Historical Association in 1917.

Ford was a remarkably productive and faithful employee of the Society, but, according to Stewart Mitchell, he was also a "strange combination of contradictions." "He could be courteous, helpful, and even amiable, but there were occasions when he was tactless and arbitrary. He would not suffer fools gladly, for he wilfully forgot, or perhaps he had never learned, that the 'more part of mankind is foolish.' He was furiously intolerant of frauds, and, in particular, of arrogance which aspired to intellectual eminence."[54] Butterfield called attention to Ford's minor failings as an editor but attributed them to his desire "to do too much too fast." He fell victim to his industriousness.[55]

[51] Mitchell called this work "the noblest monument to Mr. Ford as a scholar." M.H.S., *Procs.*, 69(1947–1950):408.

[52] Some Bostonians and Cantabrigians found Adams's book something less than brilliant. President Charles Eliot of Harvard was led to comment: "An overrated man and a much overrated book." Quoted in M.H.S., *Procs.*, 69(1947–1950):408. This "overrated" book has been producing many thousands of dollars in royalties for the Society from its first printing to this writing.

[53] Butterfield, "Ford, Editor," 70–71. Somehow, Ford also found time to teach a course sponsored by the Harvard history department. It was a practicum on the use, arrangement, editing, and printing of manuscripts through the year 1800. It also focused upon elementary English, French, and Spanish paleography of the sixteenth and seventeenth centuries. Ford held the class at the Society once a week; it was a two-hour session. He offered it one semester each year. See Samuel E. Morison to Stewart Mitchell, Jan. 24, 1933 (Mitchell Papers, Boston Athenaeum).

[54] M.H.S., *Procs.*, 69(1956):409.

[55] Butterfield, "Ford, Editor," 78–79. Samuel E. Morison informed Stewart Mitchell that Ford "played a final joke" on the Publication Committee when he left the Society, "sending to press a whole mess of Gordon letters without proper editing, or introduction." Morison to Mitchell, Aug. 14, 1929 (Mitchell Papers, Boston Athenaeum).

The Massachusetts Historical Society

Whatever his personal shortcomings and infrequent gaffes as an editor, Ford made a massive contribution to the Society—and American historical scholarship—that can be matched only by that of the illustrious founder, Belknap. This "proud, aloof, and yet selfless and deeply dedicated scholar" singularly made the Massachusetts Historical Society a dynamic center of historical scholarship, the leading institution of its type in the nation. "Allowing for certain clogs he was aware of," Butterfield has written, "he wanted the Society always to be at its best and to do its best, which he knew was very good indeed, as good in its chosen field of activity as the world could offer."[56]

One month after Ford's resignation took effect, the Library of Congress appointed him to succeed Samuel F. Bemis as director of its "Project A" program. This involved the library's effort to copy material pertaining to American history in European governmental archives and private repositories. For Ford, this was the Photostat Americana project writ large. Designed to service a growing legion of American scholars who lacked the financial resources to conduct research in Europe, the project was funded by John D. Rockefeller, Jr., and became a boon to historical scholarship. Ford also received the imposing title "European Representative of the Library" because his job involved public relations activities with learned institutions and similar organizations in Europe.[57] From his farm in Le Vésinet, near Paris, Ford supervised the work of teams of technicians producing photostatic and microphotographic reproductions of documents. He was eminently successful in this complicated enterprise. The enormous collection of "Foreign Reproductions" in the Library of Congress's division of manuscripts bears witness to his effective management of "Project A."

When the program came to an end because of budgetary cutbacks, Ford remained in France. He came back to the United States for a brief period in 1937 to complete the second volume of *The Letters of Henry Adams*, a project in which he had been engaged for over a decade. He then returned to his farm.

When the Germans invaded France in the summer of 1940 and were approaching Paris, Ford hastily packed two suitcases and fled to the

[56] Butterfield, "Ford, Editor," 76, 79.
[57] Butterfield, "Ford, Editor," 74.

south, to the unoccupied zone. In February 1941, he decided to return to his native land. He was now eighty-three years old and in frail health but gritty in his determination to reach the United States. He traveled through Spain and Portugal and reached Lisbon, where he boarded the American Export Line's *Excalibur* for the final leg of his arduous journey. After a week on the high seas, "the most prolific editor in American historiography" died on March 7, 1941.[58]

[58] *American Historical Review*, 46(1940–1941):1013. Ford wrote, edited, and compiled 259 separate titles (articles, books, and reports) and this "does not pretend to be complete." Butterfield, "Ford, Editor," 46n.1. See also the unsigned tribute to Ford by Samuel F. Bemis in *American Historical Review*, 46(1941):1012–1014, and James T. Adams's tribute in *Saturday Review of Literature*, April 1941, p. 10.

Chapter 14

The Arrival of Mitchell and Forbes

FOLLOWING FORD'S retirement, the Council considered a number of candidates for his position. It first offered the job to Mark Howe, then assistant editor at the *Youth's Companion*, but discounted him because he "wanted more salary even than Ford."[1] It then appointed Robert Stewart Mitchell,[2] a Harvard doctoral candidate who had an independent income and no need for a large salary.

Mitchell was born November 25, 1892, in Cincinnati, Ohio.[3] As a youth, he manifested a love of literature, especially poetry, and displayed a talent for creative writing. He was an exceedingly bright student and had an "extraordinarily retentive memory." He attended Harvard University, taking an A.B. (*cum laude*) in 1915 and an A.M. in 1916.[4]

John Dos Passos first met Mitchell when both were students at Harvard and involved with the *Harvard Monthly*; Mitchell served on the board of editors of the journal and was editor-in-chief from July 1915 to

---

[1] Samuel E. Morison to Grenville Norcross, Boston, Feb. 11, 1929 (Mitchell Papers, Boston Athenaeum). Mark Antony DeWolfe Howe was a member of the Society and widely known as a biographer and editor. For a memoir, see M.H.S., *Procs.*, 72(1957–1960): 403–408.

[2] Mitchell preferred to be called by his middle name and legally dropped "Robert" in 1939.

[3] For further biographical data on Mitchell, see: *New England Quarterly*, 30(1957):513–514; M.H.S., *Procs.*, 72(1957–1960):361–363; A.A.S., *Procs.*, 68(1938):13–14.

[4] Mitchell's coterie of literati at Harvard produced an anthology of poems entitled *Eight Harvard Poets: E. Estlin Cummings, S. Foster Damon, J.R. Dos Passos, Robert Hillyer, R.S. Mitchell, William A. Norris, Dudley Poore, Cuthbert Wright* (New York, 1917).

The Arrival of Mitchell and Forbes

June 1916. "It was the capaciousness of his mind that struck me," Dos Passos recalled in 1957.

> We called him the Great Auk in those days. He was a little older than the rest of us and a great deal better read. He laid down the law to us in that half-comic, half-pompous way he had. Already he had acquired a massive knowledge of everything that had been written in English, and a quite unique collection of information about American politics. It wasn't only that he could tell you the names of all the vice-presidents back to 1790, but he could give you an aloof and amusing account of the political trends that had placed them where they were.[5]

In late 1916, Mitchell became an instructor of English composition at the University of Wisconsin. It was a disillusioning experience. He soured on public educational institutions when one of his students, who should have failed his course, received a passing grade through the intercession with the administration of his father, a politician. Mitchell left Madison in disgust in 1917 and returned to Cincinnati.

From 1917 to 1919, Mitchell served in the United States Army in France as a field artilleryman. He returned to Cambridge, Massachusetts, after the war ended. In late 1919, two of his Harvard classmates bought the controlling interest in *The Dial* and determined to make it one of the nation's leading literary journals. They hired Mitchell as managing editor. The young littérateur helped to transform that journal into a literary magazine of distinction, in the judgment of Dos Passos, but he remained only one year in that position.[6] He preferred to work on his own writing and in 1921 published a book of verse, *Poems*.

Assisted financially by his wealthy, widowed "aunt,"[7] Mrs. Georgine

[5] *New England Quarterly*, 30(1957):513.

[6] *New England Quarterly*, 30(1957):513n.

[7] Although Mitchell referred to Mrs. Thomas as his aunt, she was actually the sister of Mitchell's father's first wife and therefore, the aunt of Mitchell's half-brother. The half-brother had introduced Mitchell to Mrs. Thomas, who took an immediate liking to him and soon placed him under her financial wing. For a detailed description of their relationship, see Stewart Mitchell to Sydney G. Soons, July 10, 1940 (Mitchell Papers, Boston Athenaeum). Dos Passos described Mrs. Thomas in these words: "Saw the Auk [Stewart Mitchell] in Stamford & the delightfullest aunt, who plays Bach raptly and with charm—pensez—speaks with a French accent and is full of the old regime—The Chopin, Liszt (?) old age—you know the time I mean—Also she's an occultist and has the tiniest little feet I ever saw on mortal—She ought to be a marquise." Townsend Ludington, ed., *The Fourteenth Chronicle: Letters and Diaries of John Dos Passos* (Boston, 1973), 43.

Holmes Thomas, Mitchell spent the next two years traveling and studying in Europe at the University of Montpelier and Jesus College, Cambridge University. Returning to the United States, he settled in New York City with Mrs. Thomas and, for two years, indulged his intellectual appetite by studying French and Greek.

In 1925, Mitchell returned to Harvard to begin a doctoral program in American history. He prolonged his degree by taking on other assignments.[8] He served as a tutor of history at Harvard for a time and as managing editor of the *New England Quarterly*, the historical-literary journal founded by Samuel Eliot Morison.[9]

While a graduate student, Mitchell effected a Faustian arrangement with Mrs. Thomas, a decision that shaped the rest of his life.[10] In the words of Clifford K. Shipton, who was also a graduate student at Harvard during Mitchell's attendance there, "Mrs. Thomas offered to settle a life income on him if he would forego marriage and be her social companion. So he moved out of our graduate-school world and became for our children an out-of-season Santa Claus who used to come in a big chauffeur-driven limousine."[11] Thereafter, finances were never a problem for Mitchell.

Stewart Mitchell became editor of publications on October 1, 1929, serving first on a part-time basis because of his graduate school com-

[8] He received his doctorate in 1933 and published his dissertation, a biography of New York Gov. Horatio Seymour, in 1938. Allan Nevins described this book as "a truly definitive biography." Melvin Landsberg, ed., *John Dos Passos' Correspondence with Arthur K. McComb; or "Learn to Sing the Carmagnole* (Niwot, Col., 1991), 244n.

[9] "As Managing Editor of the *Quarterly*, Mr. Mitchell set the high editorial standards which have been the model and the despair of his successors. His rigorous editing ruffled a small minority of contributors, earned the gratitude of the large majority, and rejoiced the hearts of all readers. He warred to the knife on pedantry, refusing to profane his pages with a single *ibid.* or *op. cit.*" *New England Quarterly*, 30(1957):513.

[10] According to Melvin Landsberg, Mitchell "became far closer to her [Mrs. Thomas] than to anyone in his family, enjoying with her a happiness that he had not known with his mother. He traveled with Mrs. Thomas and for long periods dwelt with her in Gloucester, in a large house with servants. Mrs. Thomas's largess enabled Mitchell to live luxuriously. However the relationship did not foster social independence or economic self-reliance in him. Dos Passos in a letter to Poore once, perhaps merely in a moment's anger, called her a vampire." Landsberg, ed., *Dos Passos' Correspondence*, 244–245.

[11] A.A.S., *Procs.*, 2d ser., 68(1958):14.

mitments, and then, a year later, giving his full time to the Society.[12] On the surface, he appeared to be an ideal successor to Ford. He was learned and eloquent. Then, too, he shared Ford's values about the Society. Progressive in outlook, he viewed it as a national research center for the study of American history, not an insular private club for a small group of Boston intellectuals. He believed that its library should be open to all serious researchers.

Mitchell functioned very much as Ford had. His chief responsibility was editing. As Malcolm Freiberg, the successor to Mitchell, has noted, he was an accomplished historical editor: "His training in English literature and in European and American history fitted him for the role, and his naturally keen memory and sharp eye, coupled with a sure ear for words and an occasionally brilliant wit, permitted him to excel."[13] While a talented editor with high standards, he was not overly productive. As Shipton has written: "The output of his years in office was pitifully small because he worked only when the spirit moved him."[14]

Mitchell also handled a wide range of administrative duties and implemented decisions made by the Council. Unlike Ford, he did not take an active hand in the management of the library, leaving these functions to Julius Tuttle.

In 1934, Allyn B. Forbes joined the staff as librarian, Tuttle having retired after fifty-six years of faithful service.[15] A native of Taunton,

[12] M.H.S., *Procs.*, 63(1929–1930):170. After the first three months, Samuel E. Morison wrote to President Endicott: "Mitchell is a little dubious about his acceptability in the Society. The Publication Committee are very well pleased with his work so far. . . . He has cleaned up the horrible mess left by Ford, and done quite a lot besides. He proves a neat and accurate worker." Morison to Endicott, Jan. 20, 1930 (Endicott Family Papers, M.H.S.).

[13] M.H.S., *Procs.*, 72(1957–1960):362. Shipton wrote that Mitchell was fortunate to have a "dual personality in office," Marjorie Bruce, a superb editorial assistant. She provided strong backup to Mitchell. A.A.S., *Procs.*, 2d ser., 68(1958):14. Miss Bruce had earlier worked as Mitchell's private secretary, and when she came to the Society he continued to pay the greater part of her salary.

[14] A.A.S., *Procs.*, 2d ser., 68(1958):14. The Harvard History Department offered him the opportunity to teach Ford's old course, History 46, in 1933, but Mitchell declined, stating that he was overburdened with work and "if I add anything more, nothing will be done well." Stewart Mitchell to Samuel Eliot Morison, Jan. 28, 1933 (Mitchell Papers, Boston Athenaeum).

[15] See Council's resolution of thanks to Tuttle: M.H.S., *Procs.*, 65(1932–1936):328. Writing from Paris to Stewart Mitchell, W. C. Ford expressed pleasure over Tuttle's retirement: "The retirement of the Librarian is good news. He was a product of Dr. Green

Massachusetts, Forbes received an A.B. from Amherst College (1919) and for the next five years taught at Deerfield Academy. He moved to Cambridge in 1925 and began work at Harvard on an A.M., which he received in 1927. For the next three years, he served as a tutor of history at Harvard. Like Mitchell, Forbes also became involved in peripheral activities. He was appointed editor of the Colonial Society of Massachusetts in 1931 and chosen for the board of the *New England Quarterly* in 1933.

When Forbes assumed his new duties at the Society, he was aware that, in his words, "beginnings are fraught with difficulties. The task of succeeding Mr. Tuttle as Librarian of this Society is enough to give any one pause." Tuttle had an "intimate knowledge of the vast resources of this library, which made it possible for him to meet at a moment's notice the almost incredible variety of demands which are daily made upon an institution of this character." Forbes bared his soul to one of the members, confessing his fright and stressing his inadequacies. "I asked him what he thought was the first thing for me to do. The answer was immediate: 'Learn everything that is in Mr. Tuttle's mind.' "[16]

Forbes proved to be an industrious and effective librarian. He rolled up his sleeves and went to work. There was much to be done. According to Stewart Mitchell, he cleaned out and catalogued "the accumulations of years."[17]

$$* \qquad * \qquad *$$

---

and Dr. Green exercised for half a century a control that was harmful." Ford to Mitchell, Apr. 6, 1934 (Mitchell Papers, Boston Athenaeum). Walter M. Whitehill wrote that Mitchell and Forbes "reined as joint consuls, without too clear definition of authority." Whitehill, *Independent Historical Societies*, 36.

[16] M.H.S., *Procs.*, 63(1932–1936):424. In the Council's resolution of thanks to Tuttle, it was stated that "his brain is still the best catalog of the manuscripts the Society possesses." Ibid., 65(1932–1936):328. According to President Endicott, Tuttle was not an effective librarian in his final years: "Good as was his health, Mr. Tuttle was becoming dangerously forgetful. Two of the most valuable items in the possession of the Society were last seen in his hands about two years ago—just where the old gentleman tucked them away in the building will probably not be discovered for years. Now, would it have been wiser to continue Mr. Tuttle in his post until he died—or simply dismiss him"? Endicott to James D. Phillips, May 20, 1936 (Endicott Family Papers, M.H.S.).

[17] Mitchell to W.C. Ford, Oct. 16, 1934 (Mitchell Papers, Boston Athenaeum). After praising Tuttle, Mitchell could not resist the opportunity to scourge the late librarian Samuel A. Green: "Sometimes I am tempted to wonder if the very widely known Dr. Green ever did anything *as Librarian*."

The Arrival of Mitchell and Forbes

In 1939, after a decade on the job, Mitchell resigned his position with the Society. It was not a voluntary action. Mitchell wrote to President Henry Lefavour on November 8, 1939: "Dr. Robbins tells me that he has written you to the effect that he feels I must resign my position as editor of publications of the Society at once. I think he is right, for, in addition to an illness of three weeks, I have lately suffered a personal misfortune which has caused me much trouble."[18] Apparently, Robbins and other Society officials had become concerned by Mitchell's excessive drinking, which was having an effect upon his performance as an editor.

Mitchell's personal life may have been another factor in their request that he submit his resignation. The "personal misfortune" cited by Mitchell was a relationship, well known among Mitchell's friends and associates. As Melvin Landsberg explained: "Mitchell's private life was unfortunate. Aggressively homosexual, he was strongly attached to a young man named Richard Cowan. . . . when Cowan committed suicide in 1939, Mitchell was overwhelmed with grief."[19]

Following his resignation, Mitchell took up residence in Mrs. Thomas's spacious North Shore home in Gloucester, where he planned to pursue his personal studies and writing. Mrs. Thomas died in 1940, at age ninety-one and bequeathed to Mitchell the income of a half-million dollar trust fund so that he could continue his literary work. Mitchell revealed to a friend that he received $57,000 a year from Mrs. Thomas's estate.[20]

In June 1940, the American Historical Association offered Mitchell the position of executive secretary. He accepted the job and made plans to take a furnished house in Alexandria, Virginia, and begin his new assignment in December. But the Association withdrew the offer, ostensibly because the western members objected to the appointment of a "Harvard man."[21]

After Mitchell's departure, the Council decided to restructure the administrative organization. At the April 1940 meeting, acting upon the recommendation of the publication committee, it combined the positions

[18] Mitchell to Lefavour, Nov. 8, 1939 (Mitchell Papers, Boston Athenaeum).
[19] Landsberg, ed., *Dos Passos' Correspondence*, 245.
[20] Landsberg, ed., *Dos Passos' Correspondence*, 245, 310 n.39.
[21] Mitchell to Henry M. Atkins, June 13, 1940, and Mitchell to Sydney G. Soons, June 29, 1940 (Mitchell Papers, Boston Athenaeum).

of editor and librarian to create a "single officer who shall be called the director." It appointed Allyn Forbes to this position.[22]

While no major achievements took place during Forbes's eight-year tenure as director, the Society operated in an efficient manner and all was serene. Forbes was the essence of stability. Mitchell, who was fond of Forbes, painted this perceptive portrait of his character and personal habits:

> He was always prompt to arrive and just as prompt to leave: unlike Rabelais, he liked to live by clocks and bells. He thoroughly disapproved of natural indolence.
>
> Forbes was amazingly industrious. Every waking hour was appropriated for some designated duty. Whitman's lovable line, 'I loafe, and invite my soul,' would have had no charm or meaning for him. His favorite task was cataloguing manuscripts, an occupation most amusing to one who would not look once at letters from William Shakespeare to his so-called collaborators, Francis Bacon and the Earl of Oxford. He was demanding, and his capacity for intellectual indignation was colossal. He could not suffer fools gladly; so his abrupt manner often offended certain persons with whom he came in contact, both socially and professionally. He was quietly generous with his money, but he practised some of the peculiar economies of prosperous people. He spent dollars, but sometimes he pinched pennies.
>
> Silly after-dinner speeches were his pet aversion. I remember being at his side one evening at a 'high-class' dinner when a distinguished scholar made a fool of himself for the better part of one hour, in the course of which Forbes's resentment became noticeable, if not noisy. Whenever he became bored at the Club of Odd Volumes, he quietly fell asleep. He liked to ride horseback and play bridge and his piano, and was a faithful member of the audience of the Boston Symphony Orchestra, to which he left a neat sum of money. In preparing manuscripts of Members of the Society for the press, he was always ruthless, and he was always right. Because he could not merely smile at frauds, snobs, and toadies, and leave well enough alone, he was always tumbling off the tightrope of tact.[23]

A competent, conscientious administrator, Forbes performed his assigned duties in a workmanlike manner and earned the respect of the staff, the members, and the Council. Stephen T. Riley called him "an unsung hero."[24]

---

[22] Council also voted that the Director's salary "be advanced as soon as practicable to five thousand dollars . . . a year." Council Records, Apr. 11, 1940 (M.H.S. Archives).

[23] M.H.S., *Procs.*, 70(1950–1953):267–268.

[24] *Stephen Thomas Riley: The Years of Stewardship* (Boston, 1976), 75; hereafter Riley, *Years of Stewardship*.

The Arrival of Mitchell and Forbes

Forbes assumed the directorship almost one year before the outbreak of World War II. When the Americans entered the conflict, Forbes and the Council became terrified at the thought of German bombs raining down upon 1154 Boylston Street and destroying one of the greatest collections of Americana in the world.[25] Less than one week after the Japanese bombed Pearl Harbor, Forbes and his colleagues huddled in the Society and gave serious thought to moving their prize holdings, such as the best paintings, the manuscripts, and rare books, away from Boston to a safe haven. While they did not reach a final decision on the manuscripts and rare books, the Council members directed Forbes and Cabinet-Keeper Henry Wilder Foote to select and move the paintings "with the least possible delay." They also invested Forbes with full power to make decisions on relocating the manuscripts and rare books.[26]

By January 1942, Forbes and Foote had selected nineteen paintings and shipped them to the Phillips Academy Chapel in Andover, where they were stored in the basement. Their selection included: four paintings by John Singleton Copley; four by John Smibert; three by Gilbert Stuart; one by Thomas Sully; and one by John Trumbull.[27]

Forbes pondered the removal of the remainder of the Society's treasures. After long and careful consideration, he decided against "immediate evacuation." If these materials were transferred out of Boston, he concluded, there would be no reason to keep the Society open. It would have to close its doors for the remainder of the war, which could be a lengthy hiatus, perhaps many years. Forbes did locate a suitable depository for storage, if sudden removal were necessary, and stockpiled containers in the Society for the shipment of manuscripts and rare books. Wrote Forbes: ". . . knowing that we are ready at a moment's notice to evacuate the library's most important collections, we are resolved, so far as is possible in view of the limitations imposed by the shrinkage in num-

[25] M.H.S., *Procs.*, 67(1941–1944):589–590.

[26] M.H.S. Council Records, Dec. 11, 1941 (M.H.S. Archives).

[27] Bartlett H. Hayes, Jr., to Allyn Forbes, Dec. 13, 1941; Anne P. Peabody to Allyn Forbes, Jan. 23, 1942; M.H.S. Council Records, Jan. 8, 1942 (all from M.H.S. Archives). Eleanor Bates wrote to Riley on Dec. 19, 1944: "There is a special atmosphere about this mausoleum early in the morning. The very furniture seems somnolent, and you half expect to hear one to the pictures snore. Of course our best snorers are still stored 'out in the country', but the stairway walls have a few likely specimens left." Peter Drummey, ed., " 'As If I Never Was Away': The Letters of Eleanor Bates to Stephen T. Riley, 1944–1945," M.H.S., *Procs.*, 104(1992):168.

bers, to make the work of the library go on as usual."[28] Forbes gave passing thought to microfilming the manuscripts and rare books, but the immensity of such a project, both in time and cost, made it an unrealistic option.

Forbes furnished the Society's quarters with "essential equipment" in the event of an air raid. Also, two of the staff members had taken an "intensive air raid wardens' course" and were prepared to respond, should the bombs drop.

While Forbes did not wish to see any bombs fall upon Boston, he did welcome the aura of fear that gripped the city. He believed that the Society stood to acquire valuable historical materials because of the threat of air raids. As he wrote in 1943: "In these days when talk of bombs is on everyone's lips and attic storerooms are being excavated, vast quantities of this material are coming to light, and owners of family archives are becoming conscious as never before of the responsibility for the preservation of such sources of history. The opportunity for a library such as this to profit from this turn of events is obvious, and I bespeak the cooperation of every member of the Society in enabling us to capitalize on the good which ill winds may blow our way."[29]

The constant need for storage space led the Society to join with seven other Boston-area institutions in June 1941, just prior to American entry into the war, and establish the New England Deposit Library.[30] This was the first cooperative library storage program in the United States. Inspired and conceived by Harvard University Librarian Keyes DeWitt Metcalf, who was also a member of the Society, this facility, an inexpensive, functional, six-story building, was constructed between August

---

[28] M.H.S., *Procs.*, 67(1941–1944):640.

[29] M.H.S., *Procs.*, 67(1941–1944):641.

[30] The other institutions were: the Massachusetts State Library; Boston Public Library; the Boston Athenaeum; Boston College; Boston University; Harvard University; and the Massachusetts Institute of Technology. For the founding and history of the Deposit Library, see: Keyes D. Metcalf, *My Harvard Library Years, 1937–1955: A Sequel to Random Recollections of an Anachronism* (Cambridge, Mass., 1988), 56–66, "The New England Deposit Library," *Library Quarterly*, 12(1942):622–628, and "The New England Deposit Library After Thirteen Years," *Harvard Library Bulletin*, 8(1954):312–322; Andrew D. Osborn, "The New England Deposit Library," *College Research Library*, 5(1954): 21–28; Francis X. Doherty, "The New England Deposit Library: History and Development," *Library Quarterly*, 18(1948):245–254, and "The New England Deposit Library: Organization and Administration," ibid., 19(1949):1–18.

The Arrival of Mitchell and Forbes

1941 and February 1942 in the Allston section of Boston on land donated by Harvard University.[31] The Deposit Library was officially opened on March 2, 1942. It was designed to house little-used, non-valuable materials. Each library was assessed a rental fee based upon the amount of space it occupied.

The building was filled immediately. In addition to the incorporating institutions, there were a number of temporary, war-time tenants, including the Victory Book Campaign, the Red Cross, the Department of the Navy, and several area museums.

The Deposit Library did not provide the ultimate solution for the Society's chronic storage problem. The M.H.S. occupied only a small section of the facility. Because of the rare value of its holdings, the Society was reluctant to house them in a structure that was not fireproof and did not have rigid security.

The most controversial issue of Forbes's directorship was the Bernard Faÿ affair.[32] In April 1943, at the height of World War II, Forbes and two prominent Harvard University professors, Arthur M. Schlesinger, Sr., and Kenneth B. Murdock, met with Stewart Mitchell and made a request.[33] They had assembled evidence that Bernard Faÿ, a well-known French historian and corresponding member of the Society, was "openly and widely" collaborating with the Germans, now in control of France, and should, therefore, be expelled from the Boston organization. Schlesinger was the catalyst for the meeting.

Faÿ had taken his A.B. and doctorate at the University of Paris but in the interim came to Harvard for his master's degree. This established his American connection. At the outset of his academic career, he became a specialist in Franco-American relations and began to publish in this field. One of his books was a best-selling biography of Benjamin Franklin.[34]

---

[31] Harvard also lent the corporation $225,000, the cost of the building, at a reduced interest rate of 2½ percent on a 30-year mortgage.

[32] There is a bulky file of materials on the Faÿ episode in the Mitchell Records, M.H.S. Archives (hereafter Faÿ File). It contains documents, correspondence, and newspaper clippings. A key manuscript is Stewart Mitchell's "The Case of Bernard Faÿ," which he prepared on Dec. 16, 1946. Mitchell summarized the key developments in the episode from the bringing of charges against Faÿ to his expulsion as a corresponding member.

[33] Mitchell had continued an active association with the Society and had completed a term on the Council earlier this same month.

[34] *Benjamin Franklin: The Apostle of Modern Times* (Boston, 1929).

Because of his knowledge of Franco-American affairs and his publications bearing upon the history of the United States, Faÿ received invitations from a number of prestigious American universities to serve as a visiting professor. He readily accepted and taught at Columbia University, Northwestern University, the University of Iowa, and Harvard University.

Schlesinger had encountered Faÿ from time to time in Cambridge on his many lecture tours in the United States. He was one of the few American scholars who held a low opinion of Faÿ's *magnum opus*, the biography of Franklin. He regarded it as "shallow and ill-informed." At one of their social encounters in Cambridge, Faÿ asked Schlesinger what his opinion was of his Franklin biography. Schlesinger related: "Upon my replying that some of his crucial interpretations lacked adequate supporting evidence, he had heatedly retorted, 'Be assured, Schlesinger, that the historians of the next fifty years will prove beyond doubt everything I have said.' This novel doctrine of future verification naturally left me unmoved."[35]

Forbes and the Harvard professors asked Mitchell if he would prepare a statement calling for Faÿ's expulsion and present it to the Council and Society.[36] Mitchell agreed to consider their request but insisted upon reviewing all of the available evidence before going through with the "ugly business." Subsequently, after assessing the documents supplied by Forbes and his colleagues, and after conducting an intensive personal investigation, he agreed to become "Lord High Prosecutor,"[37] but with reluctance. He did not relish the "dirty work" involved in the affair and was concerned that he would be called a "witch-hunter by liberals and denounced by those persons whose loyalty to the United States was doubtful."

Mitchell was also troubled by another point. He had come to know Faÿ slightly when he was teaching at Harvard. He had seen him socially on several occasions at the homes of mutual friends and had developed a dislike of him. Nonetheless, as a member of the Council, he had voted

---

[35] Arthur M. Schlesinger, *In Retrospect: The History of a Historian* (New York, 1963), 144.

[36] Ironically, Faÿ had served with distinction with the French army in World War I, receiving the *Croix de Guerre* for exceptional bravery at Verdun in 1917 and the *Medaille de Léopold* for his service in Belgium. He was lamed in the war.

[37] This was Allyn Forbes's phrase. Forbes to Mitchell, June 16, 1943 (Faÿ File).

for Faÿ's nomination for membership; and as a member of the Society, he also had voted in the affirmative at the regular meeting on April 13, 1933. Faÿ's sponsor at that meeting was Samuel Eliot Morison, who had proposed him for membership.[38]

Mitchell also recognized that expulsion from the Society was a serious matter and not to be taken lightly. In the long history of the organization, only three members (two corresponding and one resident) had been expelled. In Mitchell's words: "All tradition was against expulsion of any member, and I fully realized that, if I were to ask for the expulsion of M. Faÿ, and the Council of the Society, or the Society itself, should vote to refuse my request, I should be subjected to grave personal embarrassment."[39]

During the summer and autumn of 1943, Mitchell made "careful and lengthy enquiries, both by conversation and correspondence," about the charges Forbes and his compatriots had made against Faÿ. One of the most salient documents he saw was a statement, dated May 12, 1943, from Morison, by then a lieutenant commander in the United States Navy. He had had a change of heart about Faÿ. In a letter to Augustus P. Loring, Jr., concerning the possible expulsion Morison wrote that "I should certainly vote for it if I were there." He went on to detail a report from a mutual friend "about a luncheon he attended in Paris early in 1940 where Faÿ and a notorious French Fascist talked pure pro-Hitler stuff. Faÿ's case is particularly reprehensible as he has used his knowledge of the U.S. and his contacts here to give himself prestige in France, and then sells out to the Nazis. In fact, he was already preparing the French defeat when I was in France in 1938."[40]

Mitchell became convinced that the "ineffable" Faÿ was an active collaborator with the Germans, not a "victim of circumstances," and

[38] Unlike his Harvard colleague, Schlesinger, Morison had been profoundly impressed by Faÿ's biography of Franklin. He gave it a rave review. He began: "Superlatives alone are appropriate for Faÿ's *Franklin*. It is at once the best biography that has ever appeared of the greatest Bostonian (pace, Philadelphia!), and the most masterly and interesting biography of an American that I have read for years. M. Faÿ's knowledge of the subject is only equalled by his intelligence and humor." And further: "No one but a Frenchman could have written so profoundly and beautifully of an eighteenth-century figure, and no Frenchman but Faÿ, with his knowledge of America, could have written so understandingly and humorously of Franklin." *New England Quarterly*, 3(1930):368.

[39] Mitchell, "Case of Bernard Faÿ," 2 (Faÿ File).

[40] Morison to Loring, May 12, 1943 (extract attached to Forbes to Mitchell, June 16, 1943. Faÿ File).

should be expelled.[41] At the December meeting of the Society, he presented his proposal and recommended that the Society vote on the matter three months hence, at the March 9, 1944, meeting. This would afford sufficient time for every interested member to become fully acquainted with all of the facts in the case.

As Mitchell anticipated, his proposal caused an "uproar." There were "murmurs of disapproval" by a few members who affirmed that Faÿ was being denied due process and being victimized by "hearsay evidence." They likened it to a kangaroo court. Leading the dissenters was George Parker Winship, one of Mitchell's longtime adversaries.

Mitchell prevailed. The Council voted that he should prepare and present his case to that body at the earliest possible time. On the following day, in a letter to Forbes, Mitchell reflected upon the Council meeting and Winship's "impertinent protest":

> What an odious ass Winship is! Strange that the one and only member of the Society for whom I feel contempt should turn up at that meeting and behave himself completely in character. His objection that if the Society were to expel Faÿ it ought also to expel certain other members was flippant and gratuitous. . . .
>
> I wonder if Winship has ever been told that I call him "the bearded worm"? I am willing to wager that he will not have the guts to show up at the meeting next March and openly oppose the expulsion of Faÿ— *unless* he learns in advance that the Society is going to reject my proposal.[42]

For the next three months, Mitchell proceeded to "collect all the additional evidence on which I could lay my hands." One of the items he acquired was the August 24, 1942, edition of *Life* magazine, which contained an article on French traitors. The article featured a "Black List" of thirty-nine French collaborators condemned by the underground. Some were targeted for assassination and others were to be tried for treason by the courts when France achieved its freedom. Faÿ was on the list.[43]

[41] Mitchell to Arthur M. Schlesinger, Sr., Apr. 25, 1943 (Faÿ File).

[42] Mitchell to Forbes, Dec. 10, 1943 (Faÿ File). Mitchell wrote that, in 1928, Winship had been demoted from curator of the Widener Collection to "some post in the Treasure Room—the kind of position which Harvard always finds for its dolts and lugs."

[43] Maurice Chevalier, the entertainer, and the writers Marcel Pagnol and Louis-Ferdinand Céline were also on the list.

The Arrival of Mitchell and Forbes

Arthur Schlesinger, Jr., then with the office of strategic services, provided additional corroborative evidence of Faÿ's traitorous behavior. Schlesinger concluded with these forceful words:

> Let me add that it is the considered judgment of all the French experts in the Office of Strategic Services that Bernard Faÿ is one of the most ardent and the most vindictive of pro-Nazi Frenchmen. His statements in contempt of democracy and in admiration of Nazi-Germany cannot, of course, be documented, often as they have been heard by persons of character and responsibility. Bernard Faÿ has played a cagey game—but he seems to have guessed wrong at last. He is on our black list of the underground here in Washington, and is marked to be tried for treason if he does not meet death before then.[44]

Mitchell appeared before the Council at its meeting in February 1944, although he was not a member of the board at this time. It was a tense session. After presenting his evidence against Faÿ, he informed the group that he refused to include any information on his sexual morals, regarding it as irrelevant. If the Council insisted upon including this information, stated Mitchell, he would withdraw from the affair. The Council accepted his position. After lengthy discussion, the Council voted to defer its decision on Faÿ until the March meeting.

At the March meeting, Mitchell repeated his charges, then withdrew from the room so that the Council members "might be free to vote without my knowing *how* they voted." Nine of the ten present voted that Faÿ be "dropped."

At the subsequent meeting of the Society, President Albert F. Bigelow reported the vote of the Council and called upon Mitchell to summarize the charges against Faÿ. Following Mitchell's presentation, Professor Zechariah Chafee, Jr., of the Harvard Law School, rose and opposed Mitchell's motion. He contended that the dismissal reflected wartime hysteria. He offered an amendment, calling for a postponement of a decision until after the war. The members rejected Chafee's motion.[45]

[44] A. M. Schlesinger, Jr., to A. M. Schlesinger, Sr., Feb. 23, 1944 (Faÿ File). Schlesinger, Sr., sent a copy of his son's letter to Mitchell.

[45] Mitchell later wrote a gracious letter to Chafee, commending him for his action: "Strange as it may seem, I am glad that someone spoke up for him." Chafee responded with an equally gracious reply: "The Historical Society needs a little excitement now and then and among us all we succeeded in loosening things up a bit. In future, I hope that we shall be more careful when we take in corresponding members." Mitchell to Chafee, Mar.

After a "prolonged debate," the members voted to expel Faÿ but stipulated that "no publicity should be given to this action, that no notice of it should be sent to M. Faÿ, and that in preparing for publication the next list of members to the Society the Director should merely omit M. Faÿ's name." Twenty-six dropped kernels of corn (affirmative) into the box, and six deposited black beans (negative).[46]

In June 1944, after British and American forces had recaptured Paris, French authorities arrested Faÿ. When Mitchell learned of his arrest, he wrote to a correspondent: "The wretched creature was a lifelong climber; but instead of the band-wagon, he got on the garbage-wagon at last. I await his ultimate fate with interest."[47]

Faÿ remained incarcerated for seventeen months while awaiting his trial. While in prison, he prepared a lengthy defense of his conduct. He fervently insisted that he was a loyal Frenchman and not a collaborator, stating "most emphatically that at no time did I take a pro-german stand nor make any speech to advise 'collaboration' with the occupying authorities. At no time did I say a thing that could hurt American interests. On the contrary all my efforts had one aim: to counteract the German action and influence as much as it was in my power."[48]

Shortly after the Historical Society had taken its action, Mitchell spoke with Clarence S. Brigham and asked what the American Antiquarian Society planned to do about Faÿ. Brigham replied that his Council had refused to take any action "in view of the absence of positive legal proof as to his collaboration with the Nazis." This did not sit well with Mitchell: "I scoffed at him, and he flushed with resentment."

The French government brought Faÿ to trial in Paris on November 25, 1946. It charged him with only one crime, that he had blacklisted 60,000 French freemasons for the Germans, of whom 989 went to internment camps, where 549 died.

13, 1944; Chafee to Mitchell, June 21, 1944 (Faÿ File).

[46] When Mitchell compiled the *Handbook of the Massachusetts Historical Society* in 1948, he included Faÿ with the list of members but noted that he had been "dropped" on March 9, 1944. He also included the other three members removed from the Society (William Blount, Edmund Randolph, and Samuel Turrell), but he cited them as "expelled."

[47] See Shepard Pond to Mitchell, Aug. 29, 1944; Mitchell to Pond, Sept. 3, 1944 (Faÿ File).

[48] Bernard Faÿ, "On my activities from September 1939 to 1944" (typescript copy in Faÿ file).

The Arrival of Mitchell and Forbes

Mitchell followed the progress of the trial with keen interest. He had decided that, if Faÿ were acquitted, he would resign immediately as a member of the Society. The "high purge court" found him guilty and sentenced him to prison for life at hard labor. The prosecution had pressed for the death penalty.

After Faÿ's conviction, the American Antiquarian Society "quietly dropped" his name from its rolls—which provoked Mitchell to comment: "Thus, law, if not courage, was satisfied—in Worcester. Nothing fails like failure."[49]

In late 1955, the Harvard office of alumni records directed an inquiry to Mitchell, requesting information on Faÿ. Mitchell replied on November 7 that Faÿ had been expelled from the Society and "tried in the courts of the Fourth Republic and sentenced to life imprisonment as a collaborationist." He added: "A year or two ago, he escaped from the chapel of the prison and has not been seen or heard of since."[50]

Writing in 1963, Arthur M. Schlesinger, Sr., looked back upon Faÿ's dismissal "with self-reproach." He regretted not siding with Chafee when he opposed Faÿ's expulsion, "and I probably would have but for my low estimate of Faÿ as an historian, which, of course, was not the question at issue."[51]

The Society limped along during the war years. It was "merely marking time."[52] There was not a single new programmatic initiative in these years.

There was a marked decline of visiting researchers and a rapid increase of local genealogical investigators. Forbes noted in 1946: "At our low point during the war, it looked at times as though we might turn into a genealogist's hunting ground."[53]

The Society lost two key personnel to military service, depleting an already undermanned staff. Assistant Librarian Stephen T. Riley, who was fast becoming an indispensable employee, reported for in-

---

[49] Mitchell, "The Case of Bernard Faÿ," 4 (Faÿ File).

[50] Mitchell to Harvard Alumni Records, Nov. 7, 1955 (Faÿ File).

[51] Schlesinger, *In Retrospect*, 144.

[52] M.H.S., *Procs.*, 68(1944–1947):476.

[53] M.H.S., *Procs.*, 68(1944–1947):512–513. He added: "It is good to have the historians out in force again."

duction into the army in 1942; "his absence, even though it should be only a brief one, cannot but cripple the Society's activities at every point."[54] Photostat operator Carl E. Olsen enlisted in the navy in the fall of 1943. Neither employee was replaced. In another cost-cutting measure, the Society terminated the photostat program, which was admittedly outmoded at this point, microfilming now coming into vogue.

An oil shortage in Boston in the winter of 1943–1944 forced the Society to close its doors on Saturdays from Christmas to the middle of March. On weekdays, the heat was turned off at 3 P.M., "or earlier," making it necessary to close the building and send the staff home. The fireplace in the Dowse library provided a measure of warmth for that large room and the adjoining reading room, but it did not afford sufficient heat for the Society meetings.[55] These were held at other sites in Boston, like the Club of Odd Volumes.

Surprisingly, there was a slight increase in attendance at Society meetings during the first year of the war, from "31.6 to 33.3," "giving valid evidence that, whatever our shortcomings, we are not completely moribund."[56] During the second year, however, attendance declined, from "33.3 to 28.375."[57]

The end of the war brought understandable joy to 1154 Boylston Street. On May 8, 1945, V-E Day, which marked the surrender of Germany, the staff gathered in the library and listened on the radio to President Harry S Truman's and Prime Minister Winston Churchill's proclamations and King George VI's address in the afternoon. Assistant Editor Eleanor Bates noted "that the seven of us on the staff had never before been gathered in one room for any purpose whatever. It took the end of the war to do it!"[58]

The war had ended, but the Council had no illusions about the perilous state of the Society. It was a weak institution, barely holding on:

[54] M.H.S., *Procs.*, 67(1941–1944):589.

[55] On the Society's monthly meeting days, no visitors or researchers were permitted to enter the building. It read: "Closed Today Except To Members." This led Thomas Boylston Adams to write: "To the stranger, 1154 Boylston Street, outside and inside, from solemn door to echoing halls and inaccessible shelves, was desolate as the great pyramid of Cheops." Riley, *Years of Stewardship*, vii-viii.

[56] M.H.S., *Procs.*, 67(1941–1944):591.

[57] M.H.S., *Procs.*, 67(1941–1944):626.

[58] Drummey, ed., "Bates-Riley Correspondence," 189.

The Arrival of Mitchell and Forbes

"We are no richer now than we were then [1941]."[59] Moreover, the building was no longer adequate to serve the Society's needs: "Now that restrictions on new building are on the point of being raised, the Council will feel free to consider seriously any opportunity that may arise for disposing of the present structure." The Council set forth two realistic options, either build a new wing on land adjoining the present building, or abandon Boylston Street and erect a building on another site.[60]

On January 21, 1947, Forbes suffered a massive heart attack and died. A week later, Mitchell spent an afternoon and evening with Arthur M. Schlesinger, Sr., at the Harvard scholar's home in Cambridge.[61] The two men naturally discussed the topic of Forbes's successor. They developed a list of seven prime candidates: Walter M. Whitehill, director of the Boston Athenaeum; Clifford K. Shipton, librarian of the American Antiquarian Society; Ernest S. Dodge, director of the Peabody Museum in Salem; William G. Roelker of the Rhode Island Historical Society; James Gore King of Cambridge; Charles G. Foster of Worcester; Herbert R. Brown, professor of English at Bowdoin College and managing editor of *The New England Quarterly*; and a Mr. Bowdoin.[62] They concluded that, if their advice were solicited by the Society's search committee, chaired by Augustus P. Loring, Jr., they would recommend Brown for the position.

Three days later, Loring called Mitchell and inquired if he would permit him to propose his name to the Council as a candidate for the directorship. Mitchell would not give him an immediate answer. He subsequently met with Loring and informed him that, while interested, he was not yearning for the job. He urged Loring to consider the candidates he and Schlesinger had discussed. If, however, the Council was intent upon offering him the position, he would accept it, provided certain conditions were agreed upon.

The conditions were these. If his nomination provoked "any opposition *whatever*" in the Council, his name was to be withdrawn "*at once.*"

---

[59] M.H.S., *Procs.*, 68(1944–1947):494.

[60] M.H.S., *Procs.*, 68(1944–1947):495.

[61] Schlesinger was the chairman of the Society's important committee of publication and Mitchell served on the committee. They frequently met to discuss Society affairs.

[62] Mitchell Records, M.H.S. Archives.

He would be willing to serve on an interim basis until the Council located and appointed a permanent director. If he were selected, Stephen T. Riley had to be elevated into the librarian's position. Finally, while Forbes's annual salary had been $6,500 he would insist upon a figure of $5,000, with the "bulk" of the difference to be added to Riley's salary and a portion ($520) added to his secretary's salary.

Following his meeting with Loring, Mitchell wrote to Clarence S. Brigham, a member of the Society's Council, and listed the conditions he had set forth to Loring. He instructed Brigham to read "*aloud* to them carefully, *from the first word to the last*" what he had written.

The search committee settled upon Mitchell as its choice. At the February meeting of the Council, it presented his name. The Council approved the recommendation and agreed to abide by Mitchell's conditions.[63] On March 25, Mitchell wrote to Charles Warren: "I took the office from a sense of duty, rather than desire, for my decision means postponing certain of my own work with which I had planned to go forward as soon as I had finished the *New Letters of Abigail Adams* for the American Antiquarian Society. Mr. Forbes was a dear friend, and an excellent Director; but I shall do the best I can until I find a suitable successor."[64]

---

[63] M.H.S. Council Records, Feb. 13, 1947 (M.H.S. Archives). See, also, S. Mitchell to A.P. Loring, Jr., Feb. 1, 1947; S. Mitchell to C.S. Brigham, Jan. 30, 1947 (Mitchell Records, M.H.S. Archives).

[64] Mitchell to Warren, Mar. 25, 1947 (Mitchell Papers, Boston Athenaeum).

Chapter 15

Mitchell as Director

UPON BECOMING director in 1947, Stewart Mitchell "quietly determined to do three things": improve the physical condition of the building; "break open" the resident membership; and strengthen the financial base of the Society. When he achieved these goals, he informed the Council, he "would bow himself out of duty and return to the prudent and pleasant life of minding his own business."[1] He made a few modest gains in these three areas but, overall, his tenure was not a period of marked progress and it ended on a flat note.

Mitchell had little liking for the Society's headquarters. His major criticism was that it was not functional. Although "the 1897 building of quartered oak, marble, columns, and tesselated floors" looked attractive, Mitchell complained that "every time I have to contend with its architectural eccentricities, I am tempted to dig up the remains of the father of the late John Brooks Wheelwright and knock his bones together."[2]

While Mitchell could not alter the design of the structure, he was in a position to improve its dingy, unkempt appearance. After decades of benign neglect, the building was a sight not to behold, "more the tomb

---

[1] M.H.S., *Procs.*, 69(1947–1950):482.

[2] Mitchell to e.e. cummings, June 21, 1954 (Mitchell Papers, Boston Athenaeum). In his report of the Council in 1935, Clarence S. Brigham listed the defects of the building, noting in particular: "The whole building was curiously designed without any proper provision whatever for the shelving of books; its panels of oak and slabs of marble are elaborate, and its offices are corridors. Many members find its spacious halls and splendid stairways a babel of echoes and a cave of the winds. The defective acoustics of Ellis Hall make that part of the building useless for purposes of assembly. The photographer works in a cellar, and there, of necessity, repose some of the most handsome, if not the most rare, books in the possession of the Society. The stock-room is a labyrinth of dust, darkness, and congestion." M.H.S., *Procs.*, 65(1932–1936):407.

of history than a cradle of research."[3] One member of the Council stated that he had actually been afraid to enter the Society in his younger years, so dark and fearful was its appearance.[4] When Stephen T. Riley joined the staff in the mid-1930s, he was appalled by the scrubby look of the interior. "Few women came to the building then," he wrote, "to lift their noses at the dust, the torn and dirty shades, the wretched heating and lighting conditions, the overcrowded book stacks, and other obvious evidence of male housekeeping."[5]

Shortly after being appointed director, Mitchell informed Treasurer Augustus Peabody Loring that he ought to take the Council on a tour of the building "and let them see for themselves the shocking conditions, particularly in regard to the shelving of certain books. At some places, the shelves have fallen down, and the books are lying on the floor. No report to the Council will do any good—the members of the Council should *see* conditions for *themselves.*"[6]

The physical deterioration of the quarters, in addition to the perilous state of the Society's finances, led some vociferous members to call for a return to "our natural neighborhood on Beacon Hill—near the Archives of the Commonwealth, the New England Historic Genealogical Society, and the Boston Athenaeum, the neighborhood we left in 1897 in the popular, if unlucky, drift toward the Fenway."[7] This subject was discussed on occasion in Council meetings. In 1935, for example, no less a person than President William Crowninshield Endicott recommended a move to Beacon Hill "or its vicinity," observing that "such a change of site would serve both the work of the Society and the convenience of members from Boston and Cambridge."[8]

The Council took no action on these calls for removal at this time, but by 1950, perhaps the lowest point in the Society's history, some of the members were again strongly advocating a return to Beacon Hill. Mitchell decided to address the issue in his report of the Council at the annual

[3] Thomas Boylston Adams in Riley, *Years of Stewardship,* vii. Adams also described the museum as "a clutter of dusty showcases jammed with the tatters and old shoes of time."

[4] Lyman H. Butterfield, "Bostonians and Their Neighbors as Pack Rats," *American Archivist,* 24(1961):156.

[5] Riley, *Years of Stewardship,* 103.

[6] Mitchell to Loring, July 7, 1947 (Mitchell Records, M.H.S. Archives).

[7] M.H.S., *Procs.,* 70(1950–1953):301.

[8] M.H.S. Council Records, Mar. 14, 1935 (M.H.S. Archives).

meeting that year. He, for one, did not favor a return to Beacon Hill. Like Charles Francis Adams of a previous generation, Mitchell held that the future of the Society was in the Fenway, and he was able to convince the Council of the wisdom of remaining there.[9]

If they were to remain, though, Mitchell knew that attention had to be directed at improving the facility. In one area, a staff member had already decided to take matters into her own hands, although the approach she chose would set a later generation's conservator's teeth on edge. In 1945, Augusta Bruce Hitchcock gave the portrait collection "a soap-and-water scrubbing," as humorously described by Eleanor Bates to Stephen Riley, then overseas in military service:

> You will be glad to know that all the Ellis Hall worthies on the walls down there have been sartorially spruced up for Easter. Mrs. Hitchcock got some preserving varnish, which she applied after giving each picture a thorough soap-and-water scrubbing. As a result, the Winthrops are all perked up, and so is Redford Webster, in the hall over the Ellis Hall lintel. In fact, Redford is so vitalized that he now lurches slightly to one side, hanging sword-of-Damocles-like over anyone who ventures through the doorway. Rev. John Clark (the one who looks just like Mr. Wheeler, so that we always call him the Rev. Warren Wheeler) is so resplendent that he almost leaps out of his century and out of his square clerical collar. The Feather Store and the State House scene show a lot of new features; and Mrs. Hitchcock was delighted to discover that old Governor Winthrop used raspberry colored lipstick, Stephen Winthrop was discovered to have lots of lace on him. Mrs. Hitchcock for some time thought he was a lady, until she looked at the plaque. Fitz-John Winthrop's armor shines like a morning star (the very armor which is molding away inside one of the glass cases in Ellis Hall). Mrs. Hitchcock is contemplating varnishing Henry Adams in the flesh,[10] and if that proves successful, she may tackle each one of us. Perhaps if you come back in time she may paint you a nice suit of civilian clothes or else refurbish your uniform, whichever you prefer.[11]

In a move to brighten up the building as well as attract more visitors to the Society, exclusive of library patrons, Mitchell renovated the mor-

---

[9] M.H.S., *Procs.*, 70(1950–1953):301. Mitchell wrote: "The Second World War put an end to that hope, and your Council was persuaded by your Director to 'cast down its bucket' where it was. How much fresh water will come up from the Muddy River remains to be seen."

[10] Adams was a trustee and custodian of the Adams Family Papers. See below.

[11] Drummey, ed., "Bates-Riley Correspondence," 181–182.

ibund "dreary Old Museum."[12] This facility had been housed in a ground-floor room[13] and was a clutter of dusty historical artifacts characteristic of many historical societies of the period. Its six large wooden cases with glass tops and fronts contained "a miscellaneous collection of curios and relics." Together with some of the better paintings of the Society, the museum crowded together "a collection of John Brown pikes, old Civil War rifles, and an eight-foot trunk of a tree from the battlefield of Gettysburg" along with old cradles and chairs, the remarkable Indian weathervane from the old Province House, and other bits and pieces from the Society's "Cabinet of Curiosities."[14]

Mitchell's staff moved the contents of the museum across the lobby to the much-larger Ellis Hall and filled the vacant room with modern steel stacks for the volumes of five prize collections, the private libraries of Henry Adams, Francis Russell Hart, Kingsmill Marrs, Robert Cassie Waterston, and Curtis Guild, Jr. After deaccessioning a number of unwanted items and setting aside others for the "inevitable process of judicious defecation," Mitchell established his "New Museum" with scrubbed walls, freshly painted ceiling, and "twenty steel exhibition cases" arranged "in such a way as to show to Members and the public much of the most interesting and precious property in our possession." Mitchell proudly announced to the Council that "for the first time, if memory serves, Ellis Hall presents an appearance which is not repellent."[15]

After thanking the three women employees who had organized the cases in the new facility, Mitchell stated to the members: "The only thanks which these ladies ask of you is that some time some of you may visit our New Museum—without having to be asked to do so!"[16] The facility was to remain open five days a week, but time was to show that the effort was a failure.

Mitchell's physical improvements, while small in scope, ranged throughout the building. Shortly after becoming director, he became

[12] M.H.S., *Procs.*, 69(1947–1950):475.

[13] The library of Henry Adams, of *Education* fame, is now housed in this room.

[14] Wheeler, "Fifty Years," 42. For an entertaining discussion of the general subject, see Walter M. Whitehill, ed., *Five Episodes in the Evolution of American Museums: A Cabinet of Curiosities* (Charlottesville, 1967).

[15] M.H.S., *Procs.*, 69(1947–1950):475–476.

[16] M.H.S., *Procs.*, 69(1947–1950):476.

aware of the "disgusting condition" of the women's locker room and adjoining toilet. These were used by female members of the staff and visiting female researchers. A staff member informed Mitchell that the Society "had the reputation of providing the filthiest quarters known to female scholars in the country." Mitchell inspected the site, ostensibly to survey the windows for new shades, and discovered that the criticism was warranted. He promptly arranged for a major cleanup, including washing and painting the walls. He requested a $100 check from Treasurer Loring to pay for the work and added: "Later on, I will send you my check for one hundred dollars, for which you can send me one of the regular receipts."[17]

This is an example of what was perhaps Mitchell's most significant contribution to the Society, his generous financial support. As Malcolm Freiberg has noted, "Generosity was, in short, one of Stewart Mitchell's great virtues."[18] He was a frequent "anonymous donor" to general appeals, and he personally underwrote the cost of a few of the Society's employees. It is known that Mitchell provided four-fifths of the salary of Marjorie Bruce, his private secretary, who also served as his editorial assistant.[19] In 1954 Mitchell was certainly the "anonymous donor" who paid the $1,800 a year for hiring an editorial assistant, Richard R. Beatty, Jr.[20]

Mitchell also purchased costly, vital materials for the library. In 1953, for example, "with his usual generosity," he bought an expensive, fifty-

---

[17] Mitchell to Loring, July 7, 1947 (Mitchell Records, M.H.S. Archives).

[18] M.H.S., *Procs.*, 72(1957–1960):362. Mitchell also was generous to his friends, frequently lending them money. John Dos Passos requested a loan of $300 in 1940 and informed Mitchell that he hoped "fervently to stop borrowing." Ludington, ed., *The Fourteenth Chronicle*, 530.

[19] Mitchell to Albert F. Bigelow, Oct. 20, 1947 (M.H.S. Archives).

[20] M.H.S., *Procs.*, 71(1953–1957):461. In 1954, an "anonymous donor," more than likely Mitchell, gave the Society $3,000 to pay the annual salary of a manuscript cataloguer. The following year, the cataloguer was retained and his salary increased to $3,500. The deal was "privately arranged." See M.H.S. Council Minutes, Apr. 10, 1952; Apr. 9, 1953. See also Mitchell to Allan Forbes, Dec. 8, 1953; and Mitchell's lists of staff salaries for June 30, 1953, to June 30, 1954; Jan. 1, 1955; Apr. 1, 1955; May 15, 1957 (Mitchell Papers, M.H.S. Archives). Librarian Allyn Forbes also paid his secretary and assistant "out of his own pocket." William C. Endicott to James D. Phillips, May 20, 1936 (Endicott Family Papers, M.H.S.).

six volume, extra-illustrated edition of the Yale *Chronicles of America*.[21]

Mitchell's most significant financial contribution was a gift that came from another source. He persuaded his aunt, Mrs. Thomas, to include a bequest of $50,000 to the Society in her will, this sum "to be held by said Society and invested by it and the income therefrom accumulated until the total fund, both principal and income, shall have a value of $100,000, and thereafter . . . to use the income therefrom for the purposes of the Society. This fund shall be known as the Stewart Mitchell Fund."[22]

On the program side, Mitchell was responsible for beginning the Society's newsletter, the *Miscellany*, to be "published occasionally," as the masthead would declare.[23] The first issue appeared in 1955 and featured an article by the librarian, Stephen Riley, on a recently acquired letter from the twenty-one-year-old George Washington to Gov. Robert Dinwiddie of Virginia, and included a facsimile of the document. Future issues highlighted items from the collections and provided a new venue for Jeremy Belknap's old dictum of "multiply the copies."

Mitchell also claimed credit for instituting two new programs, an annual dinner and an annual spring reception and exhibition, although John Adams attributed them to "the group who have been so active in the M.H.S."[24] Mitchell described the annual dinner as "something of an innovation after one hundred and sixty years of nothing but 'a feast of reason and a flow of soul.' "[25] He firmly believed that this social pro-

---

[21] Riley, *Years of Stewardship*, 29.

[22] Mrs. Thomas died in 1940. For creation of the fund, see M.H.S. Council Records, Dec. 1940 (M.H.S. Archives). The fund reached $100,000 in 1955. See M.H.S., *Procs.*, 71 (1953–1957):504.

[23] M.H.S. Council Records, Jan. 13, 1955 (M.H.S. Archives). In recommending the publication of the newsletter, Thomas B. Adams reported that he had discussed with Lyman Butterfield, Walter M. Whitehill, and Mitchell.

[24] Adams cited Walter M. Whitehill, Edward P. Hamilton, Chauncey C. Nash, Henry L. Seaver, "and others." During Charles F. Adams's presidency, there was a social affair known as "The President's Lunch." Seaver frequently bore the expense of this gathering. See John Adams, "Random Sketches over Eighty Years," Part II, in Editorial Correspondence, *Proceedings* 72(1957–1960), M.H.S. Archives.

[25] M.H.S., *Procs.*, 70(1950–1953):307. In his 1951 report to the Council, Mitchell stated that he "had to plead for years" for the Society to sponsor an annual dinner program. Ibid., 329. Through W.C. Ford's initiative, the Society had held a dinner program in 1919. It was so successful that Ford proposed to President Lodge that it be held annually on the Wednesday before the second Thursday in November. Ford conceived it as a combined business meeting and social affair. "More can be accomplished in two hours of leisurely

gram strengthened the interest and involvement of the members in the
Society and hoped it would stimulate their philanthropic instincts. He
had been dismayed by the lack of interest displayed by many members,
as reflected by the low attendance at meetings. The usual attendance was
twenty-eight to thirty-two, less than one-third of the total membership.

The annual dinners were restricted to members and attracted fifty to
sixty.[26] When the Council adopted the program, it debated the question
of how to pay for it. The committee on meetings and the Council decided
that the Society should not assume the full cost of the dinners since it
was incurring deficits annually. Mitchell argued persuasively that the
members should not pay the entire cost themselves. With the consent of
the treasurer, a compromise was struck, "but for this year only." Sixteen resident members, "who prefer to remain anonymous," established
an annual dinner fund of $730 to pay for these affairs.[27]

Mitchell's purpose in initiating the spring receptions, which were
under the sponsorship of the wives of the officers and featured an exhibition and lavish social fête, was to underscore the point that the
Society was not a restrictive organization and welcomed outsiders. His
guest list included many non-members. As he wrote in his report of the
Council in 1956: "One aspect of our relations with the public is still
discouraging: time after time your Director hears expressions of surprise
from persons learning from him that the building of the Society is open
for use to people who are not Members. The Spring Reception was
initiated in 1952 for the express purpose of trying to correct this lamen-
table state of mind."[28] These affairs were surprisingly well attended.

---

intercourse," wrote Ford, "than can be done in four or five meetings of the Council under
pressure." Ford to Lodge, Jan. 13, 1919 (Ford-Lodge Correspondence). The program did
not take hold because of Senator Lodge's busy schedule in Washington. His attendance
would have been essential for the program to be a success.

[26] M.H.S., *Procs.*, 70(1950–1953):362; M.H.S. Council Records, Oct. 13, 1949 (M.H.S.
Archives). The dinners were held at various sites. The first one was held in 1950 at the
Club of Odd Volumes on Beacon Hill. United States Sen. Leverett Saltonstall, a member,
was the speaker.

[27] M.H.S., *Procs.*, 70(1950–1953):307.

[28] M.H.S., *Procs.*, 71(1953–1957):504. After the first reception, Mitchell wrote: "The
party went off successfully and the 225 guests consumed six gallons of Peabody Punch
besides martini cocktails." Stewart Mitchell to Neal O'Hara, May 18, 1954 (Mitchell
Papers, Boston Athenaeum).

The 1956 reception, for example, attracted 222 guests and in 1957 there were 252 attendees.[29]

Despite the influx of non-members into the library and the attendance of many non-members at spring receptions, the Society could not divest itself of its long-standing reputation as an elitist, exclusive institution. This was primarily because of its continuing restrictive membership policy. Resident membership was limited to one hundred, and the unwritten rule was that members should be white, Anglo-Saxon, Protestant men with a long Massachusetts heritage. There was even an elitist bias reflected in the Society's selection of academic members. With rare exception, the only academics considered were senior professors at Harvard University. No scholars from the other colleges and universities of Greater Boston, or other parts of the state, were deemed qualified. Many learned, historically-minded men in Greater Boston craved membership, but few achieved it because of the small prescribed limit. Only when a member resigned or died did an opening occur. During the Forbes-Mitchell era, there were many years when there were less than five resignations and deaths of resident members.[30]

Mitchell was no populist or democratic reformer, far from it. Not once in his pronouncements to the Council or Society did he espouse the principle of open membership. But he did favor increasing the limit on resident membership. He "preferred 150 or 200" but knew that there would be severe opposition to such a dramatic increase. He therefore lowered his goal to one hundred twenty-five.[31] Mitchell was motivated by two considerations. Initially, twenty-five new members offered the possibility of additional financial support, and the Society, then incurring annual deficits and in severe financial straits, needed all the help it could get. Secondly, he believed that the addition might increase attendance at Society meetings and bring more vitality to these staid programs. In the 1930s, the average attendance had dropped below twenty and it was often difficult to transact business requiring a vote because of a lack of a twenty-member quorum.[32] During Mitchell's directorship,

[29] M.H.S., *Procs.*, 71(1953–1957):508; 72(1957–1960):416.
[30] From 1791 to 1912, a period of 112 years, the Society elected only 475 resident members, or about 4 a year. American Historical Association, *Annual Report* (1912), 218.
[31] Mitchell to Samuel E. Morison, Mar. 15, 1949 (Mitchell Records, M.H.S. Archives).
[32] M.H.S., *Procs.*, 70(1950–1953):329.

the average attendance increased to thirty, still a low percentage of participation.[33]

Mitchell presented his plan for expansion to the Council in early 1949 and began to lobby for its approval. As he anticipated, the opposition was formidable. Even some of his close friends were not in favor of an increase: "one has gone so far as to accuse me of acting like Caracalla."[34] A few Council members were willing to increase the membership to one hundred five but that was their absolute limit.[35] The debate finally came to a head at the March 1949 Council meeting. After a "tense and almost stormy meeting," the governing body approved an increase of twenty-five and set plans to submit the proposal to the members at the April meeting of the Society.[36] "I finally had my way," Mitchell informed Samuel E. Morison. "If I had asked for a Resident Membership of 200 or for admission of women, *at the present time*, I should have got nowhere."[37] Mitchell and some of the Council members were still not certain that the members would approve the increase. There was stern opposition, but the measure passed.[38]

Mitchell also functioned as a self-appointed, one-man recruiting committee. He took an active role in the selection of candidates for membership and operated in a highly irregular fashion. There was a well-established process for reviewing and selecting candidates, but Mitchell frequently ignored it. When he found a likely prospect, he approached that person directly, asked him if he wished to become a member and,

[33] In 1935, Mitchell compiled a remarkable set of statistics on attendance at meetings from 1900 to the early 1930s. He also developed statistics on the age of members at election; the number of college graduates among the membership and the colleges they attended (Endicott Family Papers, M.H.S.).

[34] The Roman emperor Caracalla granted Roman citizenship to everyone in the empire in order to increase the number of taxpayers.

[35] S. Mitchell to S.E. Morison, Mar. 15, 1949 (Mitchell Records, M.H.S. Archives).

[36] Mitchell personally claimed responsibility for increasing the membership to 125 "over the opposition of certain snobs and dodos in the Society, one or two of whom have, I am happy to say, died since that time." Mitchell to George C. Homans, Mar. 7, 1952 (Mitchell Records, M.H.S. Archives).

[37] S. Mitchell to S.E. Morison, Mar. 15, 1949 (Mitchell Records, M.H.S. Archives). Mitchell also wrote that he was "drawing up a list of twenty-five citizens of Greater Boston who would make good Resident Members." Resident membership was increased to 150 in 1957, shortly after Mitchell resigned. M.H.S. Council Records, Apr. 11, 1957 (M.H.S. Archives).

[38] M.H.S., *Procs.*, 69(1947–1950):471–472, 478.

if the answer was in the affirmative, proceeded to lobby aggressively for his nomination and election. For example, in 1949, he informed Samuel E. Morison that he was personally responsible for the election of staff members Stephen T. Riley and Warren Wheeler "in direct contradiction to one of the creditable traditions of this Society, which is, I am sometimes tempted to think, a cross between a spoiled brat and a snob."[39] Because Mitchell was such a forceful personality and because only about one-third of the members attended Society meetings and took an active interest in its internal affairs, he was usually successful in such efforts.

As the membership increased so, too, did the library continue to expand. Historical materials of all types, from single manuscripts and books to discrete collections, flowed into the Society's library throughout the Forbes-Mitchell era. As always, almost all of these acquisitions were gifts. Rarely did the impoverished Society purchase an item.[40]

The Society acquired some notable collections in this period. In 1938, for example, Francis Russell Hart, a past president of the Society, bequeathed his outstanding book collection relating to the Caribbean and South America, regions he had written about and in which he had had extensive business dealings. In 1940, the Paine family donated the papers of Robert Treat Paine, a leading lawyer of his era and a signer of the Declaration of Independence. In 1956, the Society acquired title to the Paul Revere Papers, a collection that had been on deposit for many years. That same year, there were also significant additions made to the Francis Parkman Papers, including a remarkable book of drawings of Indian life on the Great Plains.[41]

Without question, the most important acquisition was the Adams Papers, which were donated during Mitchell's directorship.[42] Possessing

[39] Mitchell to Morison, Dec. 1, 1949 (M.H.S. Archives).

[40] These gifts were reported at every Society meeting and are recorded in *Proceedings*.

[41] Riley, *Years of Stewardship*, 46–47.

[42] On the history of the Adams Papers, see: Lyman H. Butterfield, "The Papers of the Adams Family: Some Account of Their History," M.H.S., *Procs.*, 71(1953–1957):328–356; Walter M. Whitehill, "The Adams Papers: The Records of Two Centuries of a Harvard Family," *Harvard Alumni Bulletin*, 57(1954):117–119, 123–124; Lyman H. Butterfield, "The Adams Papers," *Daedalus* 86(1955):62–71; *Life Magazine*, Oct. 25, 1954, pp. 39–41, July 2, 1956, pp. 66–76.

a keen sense of history and knowing he was a main actor in the formation of the American republic, John Adams, the "Atlas of the American Revolution," began preserving his personal writings in 1776. As he wrote: "I have some very solemn notions on the sanctity of history. I pretend to nothing more than to furnish materials to serve history."[43]

This was the beginning of the Adams family archives, a massive epistolary legacy. Succeeding members of this preeminent dynastic family, including John Quincy Adams and his son Charles Francis, added to John's base. As Lyman H. Butterfield has noted, the Adamses were "tireless scribblers" and a number of them also kept daily journals.[44] Thomas Boylston Adams, great-great-great-grandson of John Adams, informed a reporter in 1961: "My family throws up an occasional savage, who cares nothing for writing, but most of us can scarcely stop; it *amuses* us to set things down, and always has. In the old days, the house at Quincy would be full of Adamses from cellar to attic, all writing."[45]

Not all of the Adamses shared the family's passion to save their correspondence. The curmudgeonly Henry Adams was convinced that members of his family had written far too much. "Thanks entirely to our family-habit of writing," he informed his brother Brooks in 1900, "we exist in the public mind only as a typical expression of disagreeable qualities. Our dogmatism is certainly odious, but it was not extravagant till we made it a record."[46] Henry was determined not to contribute to this archive. He destroyed his diaries, saying "I mean to leave no record."[47]

In the early and middle years of the nineteenth century, the Adamses

---

[43] Lyman H. Butterfield described Adams as "self-important, pugnacious, beset by self-doubts but mulishly stubborn, vain, jealous, suspicious almost to the point of paranoia," and, at the same time, "affectionate, sociable, incurably playful, passionately devoted to the welfare of his country, and as courageous a public servant as his country ever had." Quoted in *The New Yorker*, Oct. 14, 1961, p. 45.

[44] Butterfield, "Papers of Adams Family," 333.

[45] Quoted in *The New Yorker*, Oct. 1961, p. 45.

[46] H. Adams to B. Adams, Mar. 4, 1900, quoted in Harold Dean Cater, ed., *Henry Adams and His Friends* (Boston, 1947), 487.

[47] See Nagel, *Descent From Glory*, 282; Butterfield, "Papers of Adams Family," 338. Charles Francis Adams and Brooks Adams also destroyed large portions of their personal papers. Charles F. Adams, Jr., willed his "manuscript papers" to the Society. He directed that his father's diary be destroyed, but this did not occur. Memo to will, Aug. 20, 1900 (Adams Papers, M.H.S.).

kept the family papers in the venerable "Old House," as they referred to their ancestral home in Quincy. In 1869–1870, Charles Francis Adams, the elder, at the request of his father, John Quincy, constructed the Stone Library in the adjoining garden and placed the papers there. Made of Quincy granite, this handsome little structure was designed as a fireproof facility.[48]

By the twentieth century, with additions having been made by newer generations of Adamses, the collection grew to massive dimensions and family members became concerned about its preservation. They also fretted about the future of other material possessions representing the family's patrimony to the nation: the birthplaces of John and John Quincy, the two presidents; and the Old House, including the Stone Library.

The papers, however, were their immediate and primary concern. This was a special treasure, the collective memory not only of the family but of the nation. In Professor Samuel F. Bemis's words: "The Adams manuscripts are the most important of all family records preserved in the United States."[49] Butterfield made a similar judgment: "Of its kind, the collection known as the Adams Papers is beyond price and without peer. No such assemblage of historical records touching so many aspects of American life over so long a period has ever been created and kept together by any other family in this country."[50] While filled with many instances of personal tragedy, the history of this family was, nonetheless, as Ambassador Charles Francis Adams (1807–1886) expressed it, with pardonable pride, of "extraordinary brilliancy."

In 1902, still fearful of the "danger of fire and the certainty of damp," Charles Francis Adams, Jr., arranged to have the collection transferred to the Society's new home on Boylston Street for "safe keeping"; Adams was then serving as president.[51] The materials were stored in locked cabinets in a small chamber adjoining Ellis Hall. Only the Adams family retained the key to this room and the cabinets. The area was off limits to the Society's staff, trustees, and members.

To administer the collection in a proper manner, Charles Francis

---

[48] The architect was Edward Clarke Cabot, who designed the Boston Athenaeum.

[49] M.H.S., *Procs.*, 73(1961):135.

[50] Butterfield, "Papers of Adams Family," 353.

[51] C.F. Adams, Memorabilia, 2731–2733 (C.F. Adams Papers).

Adams conceived the idea of the Adams Manuscript Trust in 1905.[52] The family approved the concept and designated Charles and his two historian brothers, Henry and Brooks, and their nephew, yet another Charles Francis Adams, as the trustees. These four were given absolute control of the papers during the fifty-year duration of the trust. The Society had no jurisdiction whatsoever and merely served as a repository.

While there were four trustees, the Society's president, Charles Francis Adams, was the dominant figure, while the others, although interested, were inclined to take a "let Charles do it" attitude. This arrangement worked to the advantage of Worthington C. Ford, who maintained a close professional and personal relationship with President Adams. When Ford joined the Society's staff in 1909, he came to regard himself as a surrogate trustee and the "custodian of the Adams mss. by appointment." The official trustees, especially President Adams, were inclined to allow the strong-minded editor to manage the collection and make decisions as to its use by researchers. Ford wrote to J. Franklin Jameson in 1910 that he "would be unwilling to turn anyone loose among the papers, who did not possess my complete confidence and who was not engaged in a work which needed my sympathy."[53]

Because the young scholar Samuel Eliot Morison possessed Ford's complete confidence and was engaged in a study that needed his sympathy, the biography of his noted ancestor Harrison Gray Otis, he gained access to the Adams Papers.[54] Ford extended this privilege only to a handful. In general, he adhered to the family's dictum that the papers were off limits to researchers. Entombed in the Society, they were to rest in peace.

[52] The Trust is discussed in detail in Malcolm Freiberg, "The Adams Manuscript Trust, 1905–1955," presented at the Adams National Historic Site, Sept. 21, 1994 (in M.H.S., *Procs.*, 106[1994]). It was first called a declaration of trust. The trustees also had responsibility for the three historic Adams houses in Quincy and the Stone Library. See also, Lyman H. Butterfield, ed., *Diary and Autobiography of John Adams* (Cambridge, Mass., 1961), 1:xxx-xxxi.

[53] Ford to Jameson, Apr. 18, 1910 (Editorial Correspondence, M.H.S. Archives).

[54] Morison wrote "The *Adams MSS.*, undoubtedly the most valuable family archives in the United States, were opened to me, through the intercession of Mr. Worthington C. Ford, by the Adams heirs: an act of singular graciousness to the descendant and biographer of their grandfather's ancient enemy." *The Life and Letters of Harrison Gray Otis, Federalist, 1765–1848*, 2 vols. (Boston, 1913), 2:313.

Why did the Adamses adopt this policy of exclusion? Brooks Adams provided the answer in letters to Charles in 1907 and 1908. "Our ancestors, especially John Adams, have suffered enough from indiscreet publication, and breach of private confidence," wrote Brooks. "I do not care to further diminish what credit we have by continuing to print, or to permit to have printed, documents which may sell some publication, but which injure us. I am clear that if I have any duty further in this world, it is to try to the best of my power to save the family reputation for the next generation." He added: "If we wished the public to inspect our private affairs we should put our family papers in some library." A stranger "has nothing whatever to do" with the private life of the Adamses, he asserted, and "as for giving him a fishing license I should as soon think of it as letting him inspect my own correspondence or bank account."[55]

Writing in 1961, Professor Samuel F. Bemis noted that the family was "particularly sensitive to a new school of writers seeking sensational copy to debunk great men by a display of their petty human qualities. Such exhibitionists were prone to exploit human weakness rather than strength of character."[56]

With the subsequent death of Charles Francis Adams, Jr., in 1915, Henry Adams in 1918, and Brooks Adams in 1927, the family appointed Henry Adams II (1875–1951) of Concord, the bachelor son of Charles Francis, Jr., as trustee to serve with his cousin Charles Francis Adams (1866–1954) of Boston, the remaining original trustee. Henry Adams quickly took on the role of "vigilator of the collection," the guardian of the family history and heritage. He was deaf as a stone and the image of his famous great-grandfather, John Quincy Adams. He was a resolute trustee and curating the collection became his life's work.[57]

This change of administrators led to the termination of Ford's active involvement with the papers and reduced him to the status of a bystander.[58] Henry Adams now made all decisions on how the collection was to be managed. He firmly believed that researchers should not be permitted to use the papers and did not want to set a precedent for doing

[55] Brooks Adams to Charles F. Adams, Sept. 20, 1908; Jan. 30, Feb. 1, 1907 (C.F. Adams Papers).

[56] M.H.S., *Procs.*, 73(1961):142.

[57] Freiberg, "Adams Manuscript Trust, 1905–1955."

[58] Butterfield, "Papers of Adams Family," 350.

so. "No one has had access to them since my father's time," he confided to his diary when Professor Bemis first requested to use the papers. "Must refuse or let any one in."[59] Adams later asked Bemis: "What do the historians think of our policy of keeping these papers closed?" Bemis candidly replied: "They don't think much of it; they contrast it with unrestricted access to the papers of Washington, Jefferson, Hamilton, Madison, Monroe, and those of many another great American, long since open to scholars, in the Library of Congress, and elsewhere."[60]

Not even the highly respected scholar Clifford K. Shipton, the compiler of *Sibley's Harvard Graduates*, one of the Society's major scholarly publications, could use these valuable documents, which would have been a prime source for him. The family rejected his petition in 1935. Stung by this decision, Shipton conferred with Samuel E. Morison, chairman of the Society's publications committee, and sought his support. Not anxious to cross swords with the Adams family, Morison "respectfully suggested that the Council take no further action." That ended the issue.[61]

Henry Adams appeared almost daily at the Society, opened the double-locked heavy oak door of the Adams room, entered his treasure house, put on his black alpaca coat, and busied himself arranging the documents and reading letters of inquiry from scholars. If these researchers demonstrated evidence of being serious and made their requests in a polite, deferential manner, Adams was most accommodating.[62] If the tone of their letters was aggressive or uncivil, he ignored their requests. Those researchers requesting copies of letters or other documents were provided only with copies received by the Adamses, not with items written by them.[63]

The accomplished biographer Catherine Drinker Bowen had her own

[59] Quoted in Freiberg, "Adams Manuscript Trust," 18.

[60] M.H.S., *Procs.*, 73(1961):144.

[61] M.H.S. Council Records, Apr. 11, May 9, 1935 (M.H.S. Archives).

[62] Adams was extremely helpful to a scholar from Cornell University, sending him on interlibrary loan the complete manuscript of John Quincy Adams's metrical translation from the German of the poetical romance by Christoph Martin Wieland entitled *Oberon*. He also provided considerable assistance to Bernhard Knollenberg, Yale University librarian. See Henry Adams, Diary, Oct. 14, 1939, and Apr. 15, 1942; Henry Adams to Knollenberg, Nov. 4, 1941 (Henry Adams [1875–1951] Papers, M.H.S.).

[63] Adams became exasperated by the volume of these requests. He once remarked to Samuel F. Bemis: "I wish Hitler would drop one of his bombs right in the middle of all this!" M.H.S., *Procs.*, 73(1961):144.

difficulties with Adams, but she was determined to gain access to the documents. Early in her career as a writer, Bowen came to understand that it was important to gain the confidence and friendship of the librarians who managed the research collections she wished to consult. It was far better to have them as allies than as enemies. Bowen therefore purchased a large notebook and began listing the names of the librarians she encountered and inserting a "brief and useful characterization." Her entry for the Massachusetts Historical Society read as follows:

> Mrs. Hitchcock, the nice one who knows Mr. Henry Adams. When he comes in the basement she will notify me upstairs. Says better not let him catch me downstairs near the Adams Papers. Says he takes off his hearing aid to make it harder. Says don't be put down by this. Says just yell.

While preparing her study of John Adams during the American Revolution, she sent numerous letters to Henry Adams by mail and messenger. His replies were something less than helpful. He finally directed Bowen to reduce her inquiries to eight specific questions. She did so, "carefully worded and typed." They dealt with issues relating to John Adams's student days at Harvard between 1751 and 1755. She had this document delivered to Adams's office in downtown Boston. She also requested a personal meeting with him at the Society. It was, as she phrased it, "a last chance and I knew it."

Bowen traveled to Boston from her home in Philadelphia and pursued her research in the Society's library. She was there for a week, but Adams was not to be seen in his familiar post in the Adams Room. Then, one morning, he arrived at the Society. Mrs. Hitchcock, the "nice one," promptly notified Bowen that Adams was on the elevator en route to the second floor. Bowen described what followed:

> The second floor of the Massachusetts Historical Society is a succession of handsome, open rooms that echo, with lofty doorways and marble floors. I stood perhaps ten steps from the elevator. Mr. Adams got out, took a startled look at me and snatched a hearing button from each ear. My instinct was for retreat but I advanced, and there in the open room gave tongue for a full half-hour. Mr. Adams had my list; I had a carbon. We stood and I shouted. Finally Mr. Adams seized me by the elbow. "Mrs. Bowen," he said, "I don't want to block your work. I don't want to be the cause of destroying your chapters, as you say I will. But you cannot have this material. It has never been printed. You know very well it has never been printed. *How do you know it is in the Adams papers?*"
> I told Mr. Adams I did not know, but that I had studied his ancestor for

a long time, and such studies permitted one to infer that John Adams might have mentioned these matters in his *Autobiography*. I said that inference was the business of a biographer.

Mr. Adams's voice rose to a pitch of real distress. "Mrs. Bowen," he said, "I wish I had never laid *eyes* on you."

Something in the desperate pronunciation of the noun softened me; plainly, Mr. Adams's suffering was worse than mine. I gave up and we parted in a mutual rush. Downstairs in the little retiring room I threw myself on the couch; the sound of my voice still rang in my ears. The entire Historical Society had been apprised of my work, hopes, ambitions; right now I desired nothing so much as dignified anonymity. A Japanese girl was standing by the mirror, arranging her hair. "Excuse me," she said, "but are you writing a life of John Adams?"

I told the young woman she must know that, by now. Everyone in the building must know it.

She smiled politely, but her next words startled me. "What was the old gentleman afraid of?" she said.

I went home to Philadelphia and fidgeted. How could I complete my chapter without that material? I was genuinely worried, in a condition of frustration, and I could not proceed. At the end of three weeks, on the day before Christmas, an envelope came in the mail, postmarked Boston. Inside, typed laboriously by Mr. Adams, was everything I had asked for. Plainly, he had entered that sacred room, had found what I wanted, taken it down, and copied it line for line. What alchemy melted his New England heart I do not know. I know only that a surge of relief and joy came over me; I can feel it now, some ten years afterward.[64]

Young academics, in particular, tended to be impatient and came to regard Henry Adams as an unreasonable, crotchety curator and a formidable impediment to scholarship. Viewing him as another "growling Cerberus," they were constantly invoking "rights" and demanding access to the papers. Their intemperate statements caused Adams to disregard their requests for information.

Professor Bemis, by contrast, received Adams's full cooperation. After some initial reluctance concerning any entry in the family papers, Henry took a shine to the Yale professor when he came to the Society to begin research on what became a two-volume biography of John Quincy Adams.[65] A warm and sympathetic man and accomplished storyteller, Be-

[64] C.D. Bowen, *Adventures of a Biographer* (Boston, 1959), 143–144.

[65] The titles of this magisterial study were *John Quincy Adams and the Foundations of American Foreign Policy* (New York, 1949) and *John Quincy Adams and the Union* (New York, 1956). Bemis was awarded the Pulitzer Prize in 1950 for the first volume.

mis had qualities that appealed to Adams, for he was "without pretense, direct, a relentless clarity of mind, unaffected, honesty of purpose, the force of a New England conscience."[66]

Bemis's work station was in a corner of Ellis Hall, then a museum and adjacent to the Adams room. He communicated with Adams almost daily, requesting information. Adams responded to his requests with undue haste, copying passages from diaries and letters from the documents. As their relationship ripened into a warm friendship, Bemis wrote that Adams "would leave the key with me, finally leave the door open so I could go in and get whatever I needed, provided I would lock up and put the key in an agreed place when I went out for lunch. Now what do you think of that, for a fellow hailing from what Cotton Mather called 'the wrong side of the hedge'?"[67]

Bemis provided a graphic description of his relationship with Adams and the old man's daily doings:

> I can still picture Henry Adams II coming in from Concord of a frosty winter morning, his pale blue eyes running from the cold, rubbing his hands briskly, unlocking the door, opening the window of the inner Adams sanctum and unbolting the iron fireproof and thiefproof shutters one high story up from the ground alleyway. Sometimes he would speak to me, sometimes not. I soon came to feel that this made no difference in his inner friendliness and developing interest in my work and concern for its success. Then he would bring out the volume or volumes of manuscripts for which I was waiting. While I was reading, he would be busy on some concern of his own, answering inquiries, copying passages for scholars, studying Civil War documents for himself, or perhaps wandering around among earlier Adams manuscripts. Sometimes he would get so absorbed in these old family letters that he would almost talk to their authors, certainly to himself: 'Confound it! [At least so I remember his words at this distance of time.] Abigail shouldn't have said that!' or 'the old man should have known better.' When I once referred to the 'old man,' Henry Adams quickly reacted: 'In the family we can call him that, but other people

---

[66] For a biographical sketch of Bemis, see M.H.S., *Procs.*, 85(1973):117–129. Thomas B. Adams wrote in 1961 that "because of his sincerity, because of the honesty of his purpose, [Bemis] gained the complete confidence of my uncle Henry Adams, then the active Trustee of the papers. Never was confidence more completely justified." Ibid., 73(1961):134.

[67] M.H.S., *Procs.*, 73(1961):143. Mather's reference was to Yale College, which he despised with a passion. Bemis may have taught at Yale, but he took a doctorate in history at Harvard, where he studied with Edward Channing and Frederick J. Turner.

shouldn't.' He didn't seem to mind, however, when I spoke of the 'Old Man Eloquent.'[68]

By 1950, with the date of the trust's termination drawing near, the Adamses began to give serious thought to a permanent home for the collection. They considered at least two possibilities. One called for returning the papers to the Stone Library, enlarging that facility, and placing them in the custody of the National Park Service, which now owned and managed the Old House as a national historic site. This seemed to be an ideal solution to their problem. A second plan was to donate the collection to Harvard University, the academic home of many of the male Adamses, beginning with the patriarch, John. Both proposals, however, never passed beyond the point of conversation.[69]

When Henry Adams died in 1951, his nephew, Thomas Boylston Adams, and the latter's young cousin, John Quincy Adams, became the active trustees. The irrepressible Tom Adams was the mainspring of this duumvirate. He had a different idea for the disposition of the papers. He had decided to give them to the Historical Society as an unrestricted gift. His decision was "much influenced by my father and by what I knew of my Uncle Harry's wishes in the matter."[70] His cousin concurred with the decision.

Assisted by Walter Muir Whitehill, the two trustees assembled a

[68] M.H.S., *Procs.*, 73(1961):143. "Old Man Eloquent" was the appellation given to John Quincy Adams.

[69] According to Thomas B. Adams: "At some time in the past Cousin Charlie Adams had suggested that possibly Harvard might be interested. However in discussion within the family we all agreed that Harvard had much more important things to do than editing of a collection of family papers. Even the Houghton Library would be inappropriate because their interests covered the whole spectrum of English literature." Adams to Malcolm Freiberg, June 1, 1992. In 1937 J. Franklin Jameson of the Library of Congress informally suggested to Worthington C. Ford that the Adams Papers "ought to be" in Washington. Ford unadvisedly showed the letter to Henry Adams who, when he was formally approached by Jameson, quashed the idea with the dismissive: "I am sorry to say the possibility of removing the Adams Correspondence to Washington does not appeal to me." On this point, see: J.F. Jameson to W.C. Ford, Feb. 9, 1937; Henry Adams to W.C. Ford, Mar. 11, 1937; J.F. Jameson to Henry Adams, Mar. 17, 1937; Henry Adams to J.F. Jameson, Mar. 22, 1937 (Henry Adams [1875–1951] Papers, M.H.S.).

[70] Adams to Freiberg, June 1, 1992. Thomas Boylston Adams's father was then president of the Society.

panel of distinguished scholars, including Julian Boyd, editor of the Thomas Jefferson Papers, and Lyman H. Butterfield, director of the Institute of Early American History and Culture, and representatives of cultural institutions from Greater Boston.[71] The group met in the Stone Library in Quincy on a beautiful August day in 1952. The setting itself was profoundly historical. They sat around a baize-covered table on which Charles F. Adams had edited his father's memoirs and Henry Adams had completed his monumental *History of the United States.* The scent of roses drifted in from the adjoining garden. Some of these bushes had been brought back from London by Abigail Adams in 1788.

The guests had been led to believe that they had been brought together to offer advice on the future of the collection. They were due for a surprise. Tom Adams opened the meeting with his bombshell announcement. As Lyman Butterfield later noted, when Adams "rose to tell us why we were there, it was at once apparent to my colleagues and me that all we were doing was breaking in an open door. The Trustees had already made up their minds."[72] The scholars and institutional representatives listened in rapt attention to the momentous announcement. They emphatically endorsed the plan revealed by Adams. Not one was annoyed by Adams's failure to solicit their advice.

Events moved quickly following Adams's announcement. The entire collection was microfilmed. The Historical Society administered the filming and made positive prints available at cost to all libraries wishing to subscribe.[73] Further, the Harvard University Press agreed to publish a comprehensive letterpress edition of the papers over its Belknap Press imprint, and Time, Inc., agreed to furnish editorial funds to the Society in return for the right to serialize selections from the edited copy in *Life*

[71] The representatives were affiliated with the Historical Society, American Antiquarian Society, Boston Athenaeum, American Council of Learned Societies, National Park Service, Institute of Early American History and Culture, and several universities. Freiberg, "Adams Manuscript Trust."

[72] "History of Adams Papers," M.H.S., *Procs.*, 71(1953–1957):352. Butterfield went to the meeting "prepared to argue a case." He was then serving as director of the Institute of Early American History and Culture.

[73] The filming began in 1952. It was produced by the Micropublication Laboratory of the Massachusetts Institute of Technology, then under the management of Peter Scott, a top authority in this field. The set required 608 reels and ran to 24,464 feet of 35-mm film. It was an enormous project. See M.H.S., *Procs.*, 73(1961):145.

magazine. An Adams Papers editorial staff was established at the Society in late 1954.

The final chapter in this phase of the history of the Adams archives occurred in April 1956. The trustees sent a one-page document to the Society in which they assigned, transferred, and conveyed to the Boston institution "all manuscripts, letters, letter-books, documents, public and private, diaries and other material belonging to the said Trust and now located on the premises of the said Society at 1154 Boylston Street, Boston, Massachusetts." They also assigned the literary rights to the Society.

The trustees attached but one condition to the gift. The Society was obliged to honor and implement the agreements made by the trust in 1954 and 1955 with Time, Inc., and the president and fellows of Harvard College relative to publication of the papers by the Harvard University Press. The president of the Society, John Adams, father of Thomas Boylston and twin brother of the late Henry, agreed to honor these obligations and signed his acceptance.[74] The Adams Papers were now the property of the Massachusetts Historical Society.

In the history of the United States, there had never been a more significant collection of historical materials donated to a repository, public or private. While others were involved in the decision, one person can be particularly credited for this singular achievement: Thomas Boylston Adams.[75]

In November 1954, newly appointed editor-in-chief of the Adams Papers editorial project, Lyman H. Butterfield, took up quarters in the Society.[76] Butterfield was well qualified for his new assignment. As his close friend and professional colleague Marc Friedlaender stated at his memorial service: "Never were man and his work more happily met."[77]

Born in western New York State on August 8, 1909, the son of a high

[74] All of these actions were recorded in the M.H.S. Council Records in 1954. On Oct. 14, the Council appointed a three-person administrative board to deal with matters of policy and funding issues.

[75] Because of his close relationship to Thomas B. Adams and behind-the-scenes lobbying, Stephen T. Riley also deserves some of the credit for the acquisition of the Adams Papers.

[76] The Adams Administrative Board hired Butterfield and also appointed an editorial advisory committee for the project.

[77] *Lyman Henry Butterfield: Commemorations of His Life* (Boston, 1982), 2.

school teacher and principal, Butterfield took his collegiate training at Harvard College, receiving an A.B. (*summa cum laude*) in 1930. He remained at Harvard for graduate study in English and was awarded an A.M. in 1934. Disenchanted by the rigid graduate school process, he left Harvard before completing his doctoral dissertation to teach English at Franklin and Marshall College. In time, he grew tired of academia, noting that among his younger colleagues there were "rather more neurotic personalities" than scholars.[78]

In 1946, Julian P. Boyd, then librarian of Princeton University, was preparing to launch the papers of Thomas Jefferson editorial project. He was to be its editor-in-chief and invited Butterfield to join him as an assistant editor. Butterfield accepted the offer and spent five years with the Jefferson Papers, participating in the editing and publication of five volumes. In 1951, he was appointed director of the Institute of Early American History and Culture at Williamsburg, Virginia. In 1954, he returned to Boston to direct the Adams Papers project.

The Adams staff grew to four full-time editors by 1956. Eleanor Bates joined the program in 1955, and Marilyn B. M. Johnson and Leonard Faber came aboard in 1956.

The project was considerably strengthened in 1965 with the addition of Marc Friedlaender, a Georgian by background, who had taken an A.B. degree from Princeton, spent two years at Harvard Law School, and acquired a doctorate in English at the University of Chicago. After a successful teaching career at Tulane University, the Women's College of the University of North Carolina at Greensboro, and Vassar College, he entered the publishing field, joining the newly-formed Athenaeum Press in New York City. In 1965, he became an editor at the Adams Papers. The "kind, gentle, warm, witty, honorable" Friedlaender spent ten productive years on Butterfield's staff. He officially retired in 1975 but continued to edit and advise other Adams Papers' editors for seventeen more years, until his death on Thanksgiving Day in 1992.[79]

* * *

[78] Butterfield never took the doctorate, holding the degree in low repute. Friedlaender stated: "He closed his door to such as placed too great value upon 'Doctor' as title." *Butterfield Commemorations*, 1, 3.

[79] For further biographical information on Friedlaender, see M.H.S., *Procs.*, 104(1992): 206–209.

Mitchell as Director

The Forbes-Mitchell years saw a rapid increase of "guest-historians"[80] as graduate history programs began to expand in American universities. The library was now wide open. Annual visitation rose from an average of 1,000 in the late 1930s to over 1,500 by mid-century. Few of these researchers were members. In 1950, for example, there were 1,528 library patrons, of whom only 114 were members.[81]

Requests for information by mail and telephone also took a quantum leap. Mitchell was not keen on providing information to telephone patrons. "The telephone is a necessity and an almost constant nuisance," he wrote. "We now have to protect ourselves from impertinent persons who call up to elicit answers for quiz programs on the radio and contests in the newspapers. We never provide the information asked for, but merely refusing to do so takes precious time from the duties of the staff."[82]

The Society's staff during the Forbes-Mitchell years consisted of less than ten full-time employees. In addition to a director, librarian, and editor of publications, there were three to four library assistants, one editorial assistant, and one to two custodians.[83] The library was always short-handed. It had a pressing need for at least one full-time cataloguer of manuscripts and books.

Despite Mitchell's aversion to telephone requests, the fact was that any serious researcher could enter the library and conduct inquiries

[80] Julius Tuttle's phrase. M.H.S., *Procs.*, 64(1930–1932):462–463.

[81] M.H.S., *Procs.*, 70(1950–1953):301–302.

[82] M.H.S., *Procs.*, 69(1947–1950):460. Malcolm Freiberg related this incident. The Society received a phone call from a "sophisticated nuisance of a magazine in New York." The caller wished to know which Adamses had served as presidents of the United States and the Massachusetts Historical Society. None had, Freiberg wrote, "but Mitchell invented two on the spur of the moment. What about so-and-so? 'Not he!' improvised Mitchell with a roar into an instrument carefully held a yard away, 'he chose not to stand for the Presidency of the United States in order to become President of the Massachusetts Historical Society.' Down went the telephone on its cradle, and back came Stewart Mitchell to our dangling conversation wearing a sheepish grin." M.H.S., *Procs.*, 72(1957–1960): 362.

[83] Mitchell had bad luck with custodians during his tenure as director. As he reported in 1957: "The janitor on duty when your Director took office lost his mind in this building, here, before our very faces, and had to be locked up until he died; his very good successor died of a heart attack overnight; his brother and successor suddenly developed a strange illness and had to be relieved; the present janitor lost his wife and sole companion last June and is now desperately ill." M.H.S., *Procs.*, 72(1957–1960):417.

without any impediments. The library was now an institution open to all serious students of American history. This aspect of Charles Francis Adams's and Worthington C. Ford's dream was now a reality.

Most of the Forbes-Mitchell era, certainly from the early 1930s to the mid-1950s, was marked by critical financial problems. A line from Juvenal's *Satires* well describes the Society's plight: "Here we all live in a state of ambitious poverty." In 1950 the Society was on the verge of insolvency and dissolution. The end seemed to be at hand.

The Society had begun to experience acute financial distress during the depression. In the late 1920s and early 1930s, the market value of its small portfolio declined precipitously and, of even greater consequence, the annual income dipped dramatically.

Concerned about the Society's serious financial plight, Francis R. Hart, the corresponding secretary and a banker by trade, conceived a "little confidential plan" in 1930 to raise essential operating funds. He proposed to President Endicott "that a few of us, without any action by the Society at all—privately—raise enough money to give to the Society about $2,000 to $2,500 additional income per year for the next five years." During this period, Hart asserted, the Society should make a serious effort to increase its endowment by $100,000 and achieve "permanent relief."[84] Endicott, who was preparing to embark on an extended trip to Europe, agreed to discuss the plan with Hart, but his first reaction was "that the Society ought to live within its means and . . . raising subscriptions from the friends of the Society is a poor plan.[85]

Because of the time constraint, their meeting did not take place, and Endicott sailed for Europe. Without authorization, Hart proceeded on his plan, working closely with the Finance Committee.[86] He drew up a list of members of means, twenty-one in all, and solicited their participation.[87] The response was "highly satisfactory," and the checks began to flow in.

When Endicott returned to Boston in June 1931, Hart wrote a mock

[84] Hart to Endicott, Sept. 25, 1930 (Endicott Family Papers, M.H.S.).

[85] Endicott to Hart, Sept. 26, 1930 (Endicott Family Papers, M.H.S.).

[86] Hart to Henry Lefavour, Jan. 23, 1931; Hart to Allan Forbes, Feb. 10, 1931; Hart to Harvey Cushing, Feb. 27, 1931 (Endicott Family Papers, M.H.S.).

[87] Hart enclosed the list in his letter to Cushing, cited above.

confession of his "wickedness," and appealed for "absolution."[88] There is no record of Endicott's response, but thanks to Hart's initiative, the yearly infusion of funds "helped the Treasurer through a long period of stress and strain."[89] But it was merely a stop gap. No steps were taken to mount a campaign to augment the endowment.

Despite Hart's heroics, the situation remained precarious. In 1934, Samuel Eliot Morison sounded a "warning bell in the night" with these forceful words:

> The present prolonged crisis has accentuated conditions long existing in the Society. Our funds, facilities, and equipment are inadequate to do the work reasonably expected of the oldest historical society in America; or even properly to care for the treasures already in our hands. As long as the Society is organized like an eighteenth-century academy, we can not expect financial support from the public, but must look mainly to our own members. Membership is rightly considered an honor and a privilege; it also implies duties and obligations.[90]

In the preceding year, the Society was forced to cut 10 percent from its staff's already meager salaries; the treasurer reported that the employees "graciously accepted reduced compensation."[91] The 10 percent reduction remained in effect until April 1936, when a cost-of-living adjustment was made.[92]

In 1939, the Society was presented with an opportunity to acquire a gift of $100,000, but there were strings attached. Charles Hammond Gibson of 137 Beacon Street offered to leave his home to the Society, together with $100,000, on the condition that the house be preserved intact as a museum of nineteenth-century interiors. After "careful discussion," the Council voted to decline the offer "with thanks."[93]

The financial fortunes of the Society took a dramatic turn for the worse during the years of World War II (1941–1945). The Society received few gifts in this period when Bostonians, including the members, were preoccupied with more weighty issues. The Council gave

[88] Hart to Endicott, June 13, 1931 (Endicott Family Papers, M.H.S.).

[89] M.H.S., *Procs.*, 65(1932–1936):402.

[90] M.H.S., *Procs.*, 65(1932–1936):310.

[91] M.H.S., *Procs.*, 65(1932–1936):97, 307, 405.

[92] M.H.S., *Procs.*, 65(1932–1936):547.

[93] M.H.S. Council Records, Feb. 9, 1939 (M.H.S. Archives). The Gibson House was later organized as a private museum and still operates in that fashion.

consideration to an appeal to the members for contributions. It also considered an appeal to the descendants and families of former members who had shown an interest in the Society. But apathy prevailed. When all was said and done, no action was taken. The Society's financial woes increased.

Annual deficits became a chronic condition. They persisted throughout the 1930s and 1940s into the early 1950s. In one six-year span, 1945–1950, the deficit totaled nearly $30,000.[94] Throughout these years, the Society's records are filled with doleful wails of imminent financial disaster. Cassandras abounded, led by Mitchell and Treasurer Augustus P. Loring, Jr., who asserted in 1946 that "unless the Society devises some way of raising more additional funds there will always be a deficit."[95] Two years later, Mitchell regretfully reported to the Society about the continuing deficits and announced that "this cannot go on indefinitely; however, no accessions to endowment in sight are likely to provide the income with which to meet this deficit."[96] By 1949 the situation had reached a point of requiring even stronger language. "We are rapidly reaching the end of our rope. This Society is living beyond its means. It has been doing so, and blithely, as far as can be determined, for many dangerous years. The easy method of surviving is to pass the hat for annual deficits. The *hard* way—and, of course, the *right* way—is to add to our capital funds."[97]

In 1950 the treasurer reiterated his warning. "As I have said again and again, I don't see how it is possible to live within our income unless we receive voluntary contributions, as the deficit is eating steadily into our funds."[98] And Stewart Mitchell charted a path with "just three ways to escape from this dream world of impending doom."

> The first way would be to cut our staff to a skeleton crew, and then close the building, and the services of the Society, to the public. A second would be to increase our income from endowments; . . . A third means—and the most evident—would be to add to our endowment by an appeal, first to

[94] For 1945: $ 1,009.40; 1946: $494.59; 1947: $5,214.26; 1948: $8,928.23; 1949: $8,763.20.

[95] M.H.S., *Procs.*, 68(1944–1947):511–512.

[96] M.H.S., *Procs.*, 69(1947–1950):460–461.

[97] M.H.S., *Procs.*, 69(1947–1950):482.

[98] M.H.S., *Procs.*, 70(1950–1953):298. The deficit for fiscal year 1949–1950 was $12,524.

Members of the Society, and then to the public. . . . At the very best, then, the financial state of this Society is such as would have taxed the ingenuity of Alexander Hamilton.[99]

In the first year of Mitchell's directorship, some of the members openly asserted that the root of the Society's persistent financial problem was administrative mismanagement, a direct slap at both Forbes and Mitchell. These critics charged that the Society was "living beyond its means," that is, the staff was too large and too costly.[100]

Mitchell took umbrage at this criticism. "I must say," he wrote to Treasurer Loring, "that it tries the patience of a saint to put up with the ugly gossip that the staff of the Society is costing more and more, when such statements are simply *not* true." Mitchell conceded that the Society was "living beyond its means," but, in his judgment, that was not the fault of the finance committee, the officers, or the staff. The repeated annual deficits were "the result of the time in which we live."[101]

Outraged by the criticism, Mitchell dug up the vouchers for the Society's payroll for May 1929, just prior to his joining the staff as editor, and for November 1947. He sent these documents to President Albert F. Bigelow, pointing out that there were ten employees in May 1929 and only eight in November 1947. He excluded his private secretary from the 1947 list since he was paying four-fifths of her salary. "I want you to keep these two payrolls," he wrote, "so that you can confront complainers with them."[102]

After a few years as director, Mitchell lost his enthusiasm for the job he had never actively sought. "The duties of this office," he complained to his brother Jethro in 1948, "are constant and confining. I mind everybody's business but my own, have chronic indigestion, and pay half

---

[99] M.H.S., *Procs.*, 70(1950–1953):303–304.

[100] S. Mitchell to A. Loring, Oct. 20, 1947; Mitchell to Albert F. Bigelow, Oct. 20, 1947 (Mitchell Records, M.H.S. Archives).

[101] Mitchell to Loring, Oct. 20, 1947 (Mitchell Records, M.H.S. Archives).

[102] Mitchell to Bigelow, Oct. 20, 1947. In a tactful response, Loring absolved Mitchell of blame for the deficits: "Of course, everybody understands that it is no case of mismanagement," he wrote. "As you say, it is simply the result of the times in which we live. The increased cost of everything, including salaries, with the income not increasing proportionately, just makes it impossible to make ends meet, unless you get a big increase in endowments or contributions." Loring to Mitchell, Oct. 21, 1947 (Mitchell Records, M.H.S. Archives).

my salary in one lump as a tax to the federal government."[103] Mitchell's negativism extended to the bleak future of the Society. He wrote to George G. Wolkins: "I often become much discouraged with the prospect of the future of the Society—more frequently now than before. I remember Forbes saying to me, privately, and more than once: 'Most of our Members, Stewart, do nothing but complain.' "[104]

Of course, Mitchell himself was not above offering his own share of complaints. Once he wrote to a friend: "I spend so much time and worry on this institution that I call it, in moments of petulance, 'the Mitchell Historical Society.' I draw a salary of $28 a month, just as a token of respect, and I shudder to think what will happen to the Society when I drop dead."[105]

The Society's response to this implicit fiscal crisis was tepid. There were the usual perfunctory annual appeals to the members, which produced the usual disappointing results. In 1933, in a rare display of aggressiveness, the Council had voted to assess each member the sum of $10 "in view of the present financial condition of the Society." If every member had paid this assessment, only $1,000 would have been added to the capital funds, hardly a sufficient sum to ease the financial distress the Society was then experiencing.

In 1946, the Council made one of its standard annual appeals. The response was predictable. The puny sum of $3,800 was raised, of which Treasurer Loring contributed $1,000. The Council was "particularly impressed by the frequency with which this appeal elicited the suggestion that the members should be required to pay annual dues." While acknowledging that such an assessment would not solve the Society's fiscal dilemma, the Council felt that "it could easily, however, prove to be an important step in educating the members in their responsibility for the Society's financial welfare."[106] The Council, however, did not vote to impose dues.

Loring gave thought to issuing another appeal in 1947, but he was not overly optimistic about achieving success, admitting "how much we will get, I don't know. After all, I heard from nearly everybody to whom we

[103] S. Mitchell to J. Mitchell, Jan. 27, 1948 (Mitchell Papers, Boston Athenaeum).
[104] Mitchell to Wolkins, Feb. 13, 1950 (Mitchell Papers, Boston Athenaeum).
[105] Mitchell to Fay Ingalls, Aug. 4, 1955 (Mitchell Papers, Boston Athenaeum).
[106] M.H.S., Procs., 68(1944–1947):508.

sent the appeal [in 1946], and everybody had a good excuse for not giving or for giving very little."[107]

This negative attitude underscored the basic problem—a lack of forceful leadership. The presidents during this period of crisis, William Crowninshield Endicott (1927–1936), Francis Russell Hart (1937–1938), Henry Lefavour (1938–1942),[108] and Bigelow (1942–1950), were earnest, pleasant, well-intentioned men, who were fond of the Society but were not bold, dynamic leaders.[109] They were not from the mold of Robert C. Winthrop or Charles Francis Adams.[110]

John Adams, who assumed the presidency in 1950, *was* of this mold.[111] Indeed, he was the son of Charles Francis Adams. An ardent sailor, like his father, he was determined to steer the Society away from the shoals of financial disaster.

Born in Quincy, Massachusetts, on July 17, 1875, in the Victorian house on President's Hill built by his father, John Adams began his education in a private school in that South Shore community. Because

[107] Loring to Mitchell, Oct. 21, 1947. Mitchell firmly believed that there should be an annual appeal. In a letter to Treasurer Loring, he compared the Society's reluctance to ask for money to the aggressive attitude of the American Antiquarian Society in Worcester: "Is it *right* for the American Antiquarian Society to ask for annual contributions to meet its deficit and *wrong* for the Massachusetts Historical Society to 'go and do likewise' "? Mitchell to Loring, Oct. 20, 1947. Bigelow responded: "The American Antiquarian Society does ask for annual contributions to use for their book purchases, etc., but the difference between the American Antiquarian and the Massachusetts Historical Society is that they have a lot of rich people like Lille and people who live outside of Worcester who are willing to chip in a lot of money. . . . They have a number of Worcester gentlemen who are taken not for any special scholastic capabilities but a liberal pocketbook." Bigelow to Mitchell, Oct. 21, 1947 (all in Mitchell Records, M.H.S. Archives).

[108] Lefavour was first president of Simmons College, serving from 1903 to 1933.

[109] According to Charles K. Bolton, there was a strong movement to place Samuel Eliot Morison in the presidency in 1938, but his Harvard colleague Roger B. Merriman "kept him out of office." Bolton, Journal, Oct. 19, 1938.

[110] This was Stewart Mitchell's appraisal of the Society's presidents: "Since Mr. Adams died in 1915 we have been unlucky. Senator Lodge was nearly always absent; Arthur Lord lived one day after his election; and Professor George Foote Moore resigned after a tenure of two years. Mr. Endicott held office for nine years, during seven of which I had to be editor and try to do much of his work as well. Mr. Hart died after nine months, and Mr. Lefavour took the office, under protest, as a stop-gap." Stewart Mitchell to Albert F. Bigelow, Apr. 4, 1942 (Mitchell Papers, Boston Athenaeum).

[111] For further biographical data on Adams, see Stephen T. Riley's insightful memoir in M.H.S., *Procs.*, 76(1964):160–165.

he was a slow reader, his father took a personal hand in his schooling and required the lad to read to him every evening while he shaved. The son was pleased to report that "this method worked and soon I became an insatiable reader." After attending Endicott Peabody's school in Groton, Adams entered Harvard in 1894 and graduated in 1898.

Adams went to work for his father and became involved in his speculative real estate affairs in the West. When these ventures subsequently fizzled out, he settled in Kansas City, Missouri, where his father had taken up residence, and joined the United Zinc and Chemical Company in nearby Argentine, Kansas. He eventually worked his way up to the presidency of this firm. His business career in the mid-West mirrored that of his father's, as uneven and unsettling as a ride on a roller coaster. He had "a succession of disappointments, and defeats, over a stretch of twenty-five years." Nearing retirement, Adams returned to Massachusetts, settling in Lincoln, where he managed his late father's shrinking estate.

Adams was elected a member of the Society in 1945 at the age of sixty-nine. He accepted membership with hesitation because he recalled with bitterness that, after his father's death in 1915

> when I was having a desperate struggle to put his affairs in order and to save the family property, this Society brought to my notice that he had guaranteed a certain investment; it had gone bad, and requested us to make it good. Twenty-five thousand dollars it was, and we did make it good, but with great inconvenience, not to say risk. Not unnaturally this left me with no great enthusiasm for the M.H.S., nor any wish to become a member.[112]

John Adams later learned from a member of the membership committee that when his name came up there were objections "that there were already enough Adams members—and they didn't want any more. So the dislike was mutual."[113]

[112] The investment involved bonds relating to Henry Adams's firm, the United Zinc and Chemical Company, and the exact figure was $25,779.17. In 1909 Charles F. Adams advised the Society to purchase the bonds and agreed to take them and the stock which went with them as a bonus off the hands of the Society at the price paid by the organization, if the investments went sour. See: John Adams, "Random Sketches Over Eighty Years," Part II, Editorial Correspondence, M.H.S., *Procs.*, vol. 72(1957–1960); C.F. Adams to Arthur Lord, Jan. 9, 1909; Mar. 14 and July 8, 1913; Arthur Lord to John Adams, Jan. 29, 1916; Mary Ogden Adams to Arthur Lord, Feb. 14, 1916; Arthur Lord to M.O. Adams, Feb. 21, 1916 (C.F. Adams Papers).

[113] Adams, "Random Sketches," 24–25. John's uncle Brooks Adams also had a difficult time achieving membership, possibly because of the over-loading of Adamses. Upon hear-

Two years after achieving membership, Adams was elected to the Council. Again, he reluctantly accepted. He served on the Council from 1947 to 1950, during which he became acutely aware of the Society's critical financial condition and "the personalities of those who were running it." "Like everything else in this world," he wrote, "this Society though it cannot live by bread alone, yet it cannot live without bread, and the bread was getting scarce and rapidly scarcer, and very few were giving much thought to it. So it was quite a problem, for not only was the lack of income serious, but the M.H.S. itself seemed sunk in lethargy."[114]

While Adams was serving on the Council, the governing body frequently discussed the Society's weak financial situation. At one meeting, President Bigelow affirmed that "an additional $300,000 of capital was needed, but remarked gloomily he didn't know where it was to come from, and the treasurer said the members would not give."[115]

Chauncy C. Nash, one of the councilors, urged the body to establish a permanent endowment fund. He was convinced that the members would contribute to such a fund rather than provide support for current expenses. Adams favored Nash's idea, believing that this was the proper course of action. The Council ignored Nash's suggestion.

As conditions worsened, the Council and a few other leading members met in emergency session at the Union Club, an exclusive men's club on Beacon Hill composed mainly of businessmen and lawyers. Wrote Adams: "We all sat around the table and got nowhere. Toward the end I tentatively advanced Nash's idea and was I sat upon! It was painful and I felt like a small boy who had been spanked. So that was that." No other proposals emerged from the meeting.

While suffering a crushing rebuff, Adams did not lose the confidence of his colleagues. They apparently saw traces of the father in the son for they tapped him for the presidency in 1950, despite his advanced age of

---

ing of his election, Brooks wrote to a friend: "The poor old dully Historical Society here, of which Charles is the President, actually, the other day, discovered that I am alive and elected me. After all these years—it was too funny. Harvard College will discover me next—who knows!" He wrote to his brother Henry: "After fifteen years they suddenly discovered me. So I decorously accepted, my sins forgiven." See Brooks Adams to Mary C. Jones, May 26, 1902; Brooks Adams to Henry Adams, Apr. 20, 1902 (Brooks Adams Papers, M.H.S.).

[114] Adams, "Random Sketches," 25.
[115] Adams, "Random Sketches," 28–29.

seventy-five. Like his father, Adams was reluctant to accept the position. He was filled with apprehension. As his son, Thomas Boylston, wrote: "He had spent his life pulling broken wagons out of the mud and he did not especially relish the prospect of pulling one more."[116]

John Adams had this to say when notified that he had been elected president:

> to my great alarm I was told I was picked to be president. I can honestly say I did all I could to dodge it. The words of the old song about describe it.
> > First she said she wouldn't.
> > Then she said she couldn't.
> > Then she answered, Well I'll see.
> Only I wasn't coy about it, but much in earnest.
> Yet it couldn't be helped and I went into the job with no great hope. As I said to my wife, most of my life had been passed in hard struggles, in some I had been successful, in some failed, and it was just too bad in my old age to lead one more forlorn hope and to end with another failure marked against me.[117]

Adams knew that he had taken charge of an institution on the verge of collapse. He wrote

> Briefly the situation was this—here was an institution that had once been quite well off, in easy circumstances, let us say, but it had not adapted itself to changing times—to the falling dollars and to increasing costs all along the line—and what was more alarming, seemed old and decrepid, its members taking little interest and the meetings so dull they were something to avoid—meetings at which those who came sat around and listened to the reading of a paper, then a few questions possibly but no discussion, after which they went out, had a glass of wine and that was the end of it.[118]

Despite his pessimism—and advanced age—the stern old Yankee began his new assignment with a burst of energy. He set one major objective, to build a solid financial base for the Society. Upon taking office, he informed the members that their small body alone could not provide sufficient funds to reverse the trend of annual deficits. The public also must contribute. While he did not define the "public," there

[116] Riley, *Years of Stewardship*, viii.
[117] Adams, "Random Sketches," 26.
[118] Adams, "Random Sketches," 27.

is no doubt that he was referring to the learned, financially successful element of Greater Boston, not to the masses.

Boston's newspapers picked up on Adams's theme. The *Herald* headline for October 6, 1950, was "Historical Group To Ask Aid of Public." The *Daily Globe* headline read "Historical Society Makes First Public Appeal For Funds."[119] The next day, the *Globe* also contributed an editorial, titled "To the aid of history," which pled the Society's case for public support. "Without additional endowment to provide more income and halt an annual deficit of $12,000, the Society may be forced to close its doors," the newspaper declaimed. Serving as a "research center for American and European scholars and a shrine of Americana," the historical society was truly worthy of public assistance. The editorial was insistent that "A people proud of their history will not stand idly by and let such an institution fall."[120]

Adams's strategy was to resurrect Nash's plan and establish an endowment fund with the income to be unrestricted. He issued his first appeal to resident members and a select list of "movers and shakers" in Greater Boston in 1950. The response was encouraging. Each year thereafter he renewed his appeal in thoughtful, personal letters and acknowledged every response. "As the Fund mounted, so did John Adams' delight, for some of the best-intentioned Members had not been optimistic. The credit belonged to John Adams. . . . His warm, direct letters won new friends for the Society and moved many Members to an activity that they had not shown before. He was hard to resist."[121]

Adams's effort began to bear financial fruit by 1952. The market value of the Society's portfolio rose to $1,385,818.[122] More importantly, it was generating sufficient income to cover operating expenses. Mitchell proudly announced to the members at the annual meeting: "The Society is no longer running a deficit."[123] From that date, there was slight but progressive improvement in the Society's finances. By October 1957,

[119] Oct. 6, 1950. The headline was in error, as there had been other appeals for public support.

[120] Boston *Daily Globe*, Oct. 7, 1950. The annual deficit was not always $12,000. That was a one-year high in fiscal year 1949–1950.

[121] M.H.S., *Procs.*, 76(1964):166. In 1965, the Council voted to name the endowment the John Adams Memorial Fund.

[122] M.H.S., *Procs.*, 70(1950–1953):360.

[123] M.H.S., *Procs.*, 70(1950–1953):361.

when John Adams retired as president, the fund had passed $100,000. The fear of dissolution was at an end. Adams was the savior of the Society.

Adams's presidency was successful beyond the financial factor. He also strengthened the Society's internal operation. He was an active president. As Mitchell wrote: "He has made his office one of the first responsibilities of his life."[124] Adams, with his "winter-apple face creased with a smile or grin according to his mood, his figure dressed in a brown suit, blue shirt, and bow tie," visited the Society weekly, meeting individually with Director Mitchell and Librarian Riley "to explore the problems and difficulties of our daily duties, to keep in touch with every part of our business, and to offer friendly suggestions and advice."[125] Riley fondly remembered these weekly sessions with Adams, "a half-hour to catch up on the doings of the week."

> We would often talk about recent manuscript acquisitions. Sometimes I would read him selections from letters that interested me. While I think he was often amused by my enthusiasms, he was always an appreciative listener. The sentiment expressed, if gay, would draw his hearty laugh; if serious, might lead to very instructive comments on men and affairs.[126]

Riley further noted that Adams's "close attention to Society affairs encouraged not only the Members but the Staff as well. At last the Society was headed by a man who was really interested in it, would listen to suggestions, and would rap knuckles when necessary."

Adams's leadership also reinvigorated the Council and made it a more effective governing body. Council meetings suddenly became "great fun" because Adams "encouraged discussion and preferred people who would speak their minds even if their ideas were diametrically opposed to his. On more than one occasion he was outvoted on an issue and had to content himself with having his negative vote recorded in the minutes. Before long, Council members were looking forward to the meetings, and it took a compelling reason not to have them present. This

---

[124] M.H.S., *Procs.*, 71(1953–1957):441. On Aug. 4, 1955, Mitchell informed Mrs. Fay Ingalls: "Just now, I have the best President with whom I have served—John Adams." (Mitchell Papers, Boston Athenaeum). Stephen T. Riley, who also had the opportunity to work with many officers over the years, echoed this sentiment, calling John Adams "certainly one of the Society's best Presidents" M.H.S., *Procs.*, 76(1964):194.

[125] M.H.S., *Procs.*, 71(1953–1957):440–441.

[126] M.H.S., *Procs.*, 76(1964):160.

interest was gradually carried over to the regular Society meetings, which John Adams first thought pretty dull affairs.

Since assuming membership in 1945, Mr. Adams had found most of these sessions full of "dreary drivel," an opinion shared by many of his colleagues.[127] Indeed, dullness had become the hallmark of the programs since the Society had left the club-like atmosphere of the Tremont Street quarters and moved to Boylston Street.[128]

Complaints about meetings of the Society were many and longstanding.[129] Worthington C. Ford's reports to President Lodge had frequently contained a reference to the boring nature of the papers and the somnolent effect their reading had upon the members, many of whom were of an advanced age. After one such session, he reported: "On the whole

[127] Adams to James F. Rhodes, Oct. 9, 1914, printed in Mitchell, "The Society 'Beats' Adams, 1914" M.H.S., *Procs.*, 70(1950–1953):146–147.

[128] The New-York Historical Society experienced similar problems dating back to the mid-nineteenth century. George Templeton Strong noted in his diary on May 3, 1858: "The lectures and 'papers' it generates so abundantly I set down as equal to zero; an estimate more charitable than accurate, for they are properly affected with a negative sign, as gaseous secretions of vanity and dilettantism." Quoted in Whitehill, *Independent Historical Societies*, 49–50. See also, 47.

[129] Some challenged the competence of the speakers. Ford, for example, recalled "when that rather strongly marked character, Franklin B. Sanborn, rose and announced as his subject, 'The Metathesis and the Metabolism of the Slavery Question.' the announcement was enough. The few who could follow the speaker concluded that Mr. Sanborn did not know what he was talking about, and they were so far correct that the paper never appeared in print." Ford, "Historical Societies," *Miss. Valley Historical Review*, 16(1929): 314. Lengthy papers were another source of irritation, especially to Ford. As he wrote to Lodge on Dec. 17, 1917: "Mr. Bigelow took twice the allotted time and as I am told, had just reached the important part of his paper when the presiding officer asked him to finish the reading in January as there was another member who had something to say. . . . It is amazing to me that a person accustomed to speaking (as a university professor is) can so miscalculate his time and his matter." Ford to Lodge, Dec. 17, 1917 (Ford-Lodge Correspondence). See also: Mitchell's humorous article "The Society 'Beats' Charles Francis Adams, 1914," 144–147; and Professor Albert B. Hart's similar experience in 1911, Ford to Adams, Apr. 4, 1911 (C.F. Adams Papers).

Long-time Society member Gamaliel Bradford wrote to Alfred C. Potter in 1931: "I see that you were elected to the Massachusetts Historical Society and I to the [American] Academy [of Arts and Sciences] on the same day," "both very august assemblies and both intolerably dull. . . . I had far rather read an old play with you and Hooker over a glass of lemonade and whiskey than go to any of their meetings." Van Wyck Brooks, ed., *The Letters of Gamaliel Bradford, 1918–1931* (Boston, 1934), 362.

it was a tame meeting and the sleepers were undisturbed."[130] And further: "I think I told you that at the last meeting a good proportion of the congregation slept."[131] Only occasionally was there an exception, such as on January 12, 1918, when the "orator of the day," Charles G. Washburn, "gave an informal talk, which was witty, *of thirty minutes*, and suggestive of the material with which he was dealing. He left his audience still interested and alert. I did not notice any sleeper except the Chairman."[132]

Lyman H. Butterfield, who later attended many such meetings himself, noted that during this period: "The members tended to doze, partly because many of them were old and found only the obituary tributes interesting;[133] partly because some members were much too loquacious during (and beyond) the period regularly set aside for 'communications and remarks'[134]; and partly as [W.C.] Ford ruefully observed, because the heating plant paid no attention to the weather signals, so that on

[130] Ford to Lodge, Oct. 13, 1920 (Ford-Lodge Correspondence).

[131] Ford to Lodge, Feb. 1, 1924 (Ford-Lodge Correspondence).

[132] Ford to Lodge, Jan. 12, 1918 (Ford-Lodge Correspondence).

[133] Every deceased member was memorialized, which led to the Society becoming known as the "Obituary Society." See Ford to C.F. Adams, Jan. 16, 1914 (C.F. Adams Papers). "If I had known that the entire meeting, or a large portion of it, was to be taken up in the deliveries of obituaries," Charles Warren complained to Secretary Henry W. Cunningham, "I should not have arranged to come on from Washington for last Friday's meeting." Warren to Cunningham, Oct. 16, 1926 (M.H.S. Archives). Charles Bolton went to a meeting to read a paper, but "the whole time was taken up with Eliot and Bigelow eulogies. Everyone bored. Dr Walcott aged 88 talked 55 minutes (Ford limited him to 20). . . . The Lord keep me in the sunny B.A. [Boston Athenaeum]." Bolton, Journal, Oct. 14, 1926.

[134] There was a classic example of this problem in 1915. Ford wrote to Lodge" "It was an old problem which was presented yesterday, old in more respects than one. Mr. Adams gave the matter up in despair, preferring to let the meeting be as yesterday but admitting that no man could empty the room more rapidly than Mr. [Franklin S.] Sanborn. When Mr. Adams had given up the problem I sent out, with the notice, what I enclose; and purposely put Mr. Sanborn yesterday in the section of the day, that he might be under the ten minute limitation, but I think you were wise in not enforcing it. He is a dangerous man when aroused, because he has no idea of what is due to another. It is nearly a year since he has undertaken to read any paper, and I think he intended to take advantage of your coming to the position as a man not knowing what the Society has suffered from his loquacity. On the whole he was moderate yesterday, rising only three times, but you noticed the effect on the audience . . . I merely make this statement in order that you may know that measures have been taken in the past to suppress what became a veritable menace to the Society, for no program could be prepared or speaker provided but faced the probability of Mr. Sanborn's rising and monopolizing the whole hour." Ford to Lodge, June 11, 1915 (Ford-Lodge Correspondence).

warm spring afternoons speakers found themselves addressing solid ranks of sleepers."[135] Walter M. Whitehill, another veteran of Society meetings, often observed members asleep during the reading of a paper. "Even during the best papers," he reported, "some member . . . is certain to be asleep, thanks to a combination of afternoon sun and comfortable chairs." In the course of one of his own addresses, Whitehill "quoted John Brown of Osawatomie's four-letter opinion of Wendell Phillips, [and] I was diverted to observe the speed with which the sleepers awoke.[136]

Long-time member Roger Wolcott developed his own technique to avoid the usual dull papers read after the business session. As he informed Charles K. Bolton, " 'I always leave *before* the speaker turns toward the audience.' So he [Wolcott] tapped my shoulder and slipped out as Sam Eliot rose to tell us about his grandparents. They were 'cultivated and well-bred people' he told us several times with his booming voice."[137]

In sum, Adams's attempts to liven up Society meetings were also gradually successful, "although he thought he could have accomplished more had it not been for his increasing deafness."[138]

Despite these successes on behalf of the Society, Adams had more work ahead of him. He regarded the staff as an area of weakness, with the exception of Librarian Riley. He held a particularly low opinion of Stewart Mitchell. He believed that Mitchell was an "extravagant administrator" and lacked essential personal qualities to lead the Society effectively.

> Stewart Mitchell was a curious person. A brilliant man and gifted with an extraordinary memory, yet he had never had to earn a dollar and had been the care of an old aunt. In a way, he was like a child, and to make matters worse he was breaking down in mind and body—faster and faster as the

---

[135] Butterfield, "Ford, Editor," 51–52.

[136] Whitehill, *Independent Historical Societies*, 47n. That the papers were too long was a common lament of the members. A frustrated Ford wrote to Lodge: "There is always complaint of too long papers and too limited subjects. Yet the same men will go to the Colonial Society and sit through long studies, microscopic in interest, and express themselves as pleased!" Ford to Lodge, June 12, 1924 (Ford-Lodge Correspondence).

[137] Bolton, Journal, Feb. 9, 1939.

[138] M.H.S., *Procs.*, 76(1964):167.

years went on. He did not have his organization well in hand—in fact he couldn't, constituted as he was.[139]

By the mid-1950s, Adams observed that Mitchell's physical condition was rapidly deteriorating and urged him to retire. Nearing sixty-five years of age, and not in the best of health, Mitchell collapsed at the annual meeting in October 1956 and had to be helped to his chair, and then to his room. Adams "saw him early the following week and told him the time had come, that he was no longer strong enough to do his work, that I would resign at the end of the year, and he must go then. He was much upset, but it had to be."[140]

At the following annual meeting in 1957 Mitchell did submit his resignation as director.[141] Afterwards, Mitchell, writing in the third person, informed the members that, "at his own request, he has been left off all committees, but he will always give the Society all the help he can for which it may ask. He will take care to offer no advice."[142] A few months after resigning, he died.[143]

How should history assess this curious character who dominated the Society for seventeen years? The fundamental fact about Mitchell is that he was beset by "serious personal failings." In carefully measured words, Shipton wrote that, "after the death of Mrs. Thomas he developed serious personal failings which were a trial to his friends, who never ceased to regard him with exasperated affection."[144]

One of these failings, which had a profound negative effect upon his administrative duties, was his excessive consumption of alcohol. A lead-

[139] Adams, "Random Sketches."

[140] Adams, "Random Sketches."

[141] Mitchell announced his resignation on Apr. 11, 1957. It was to take effect on Oct. 10, 1957. M.H.S. Council Records, Apr. 11, 1957 (M.H.S. Archives). In a letter to e.e. cummings (July 15, 1957), Mitchell wrote: "I am retiring, at my own request, as Director of the Massachusetts Historical Society on October 10." (Mitchell Papers, Boston Athenaeum).

[142] M.H.S., *Procs.*, 72(1957–1960):415.

[143] According to John Dos Passos, Mitchell's life took a turn for the worse after Richard Cowan's death and in 1940, when Mrs. Thomas died, at the age of ninety-one, and bequeathed to him the income of a half-million dollar trust fund. "Despite the income, his life deteriorated badly. He had other young men, on whom he spent much money, and he became notorious as a rake and alcoholic. On November 3, 1957, he died in a fit of delirium tremens." Landsberg, *John Dos Passos' Correspondence*, 245.

[144] A.A.S., *Procs.*, 2d ser., 68(1958):14.

ing Society official, who knew Mitchell well, has described him as "very pleasant and good-natured when sober. Unfortunately he was very seldom sober."[145]

Malcolm Freiberg, Mitchell's successor as editor of publications, portrayed him as a "bundle of contradictions": "Sober, he was a delight: kind, thoughtful of others, elegant in manner and appearance, in short, a Genuine Presence. Drunk, he was a boor: elegant only in appearance, rude of manner, full of bathos, immersed in self-pity, in short, a Jekyll and Hyde personality."

Freiberg recalled a dinner party Mitchell sponsored in a private dining room of the fashionable Ritz-Carlton Hotel for the Society's new management team following his retirement. Present were newly-elected President Thomas Boylston Adams, newly-appointed director Riley, Freiberg, Lyman H. Butterfield, Clifford K. Shipton, and their wives. "Our host was roaring drunk," wrote Freiberg, "and delivered a monologue that focussed on himself and his numerous problems. We all felt at once both sorry for the man and repelled by him."

Freiberg concluded: "One may never know who the obscene demons were that perched on his shoulders whispering the opposite advice into his ears that made him such a bundle of contradictions. But one surely knows that Stewart Mitchell squandered his very real talents. The result—an empty life—was a tragedy that should never have happened."

After Mitchell's death, it fell to Freiberg, who prepared the *Proceedings*, to find a memoirist for him. Acting upon the advice of the Council, he approached a number of members who were likely candidates for the assignment. They all declined, "politely but firmly." Wrote a frustrated Freiberg: "This, I thought, was ridiculous: as former Society director, he *had* to be memorialized, and if no one else would do so, I would. And I did, my memoir being cast in the best *de-mortuis-nil-nisi-bonum* tradition. I liked the man and said so then; I was repelled by him but did not say so then."[146]

In sum, Stewart Mitchell was a tormented soul, a man of powerful intellect and many latent talents, who never fulfilled his promise. Retired Society employees who worked for Mitchell instinctively refer to him as "poor Stewart" when they mention his name.

---

[145] Letter to author, Aug. 25, 1993. The writer has requested anonymity.
[146] Letter to the author, Aug. 3, 1993.

Chapter 16

The Arrival of Riley

ON SEPTEMBER 22, 1961, at a formal ceremony in Ellis Hall marking the first publication by the Harvard University Press in the Adams Papers series, the four-volume *Diary and Autobiography of John Adams*, President Thomas Boylston Adams called upon Director Stephen T. Riley to rise and be recognized for his contribution to that stellar achievement. Riley was not to be seen in the room, which was filled to capacity. Adams repeated his name, but the director remained among the missing. The quick-witted Adams then remarked: "I am sorry that Mr. Riley cannot be found. I suppose he is down in the cellar holding up some corner of the building."[1]

The striking image of Riley positioned in the basement, his legs stretched wide and arms fully extended, like Atlas holding up the heavens, was an apt symbolic portrayal of his importance to the Society. From the moment he began employment in September 1934, this remarkable "keeper of the past" was a powerful pillar of support. He was destined to join Jeremy Belknap, Robert C. Winthrop, Charles F. Adams, Worthington C. Ford, John Adams, and Thomas Boylston Adams in the pantheon of illustrious leaders of the institution.

Given his background, it is incredible to believe that Riley became the chief executive officer of one of Boston's most important and exclusive Yankee institutions. He was not cut from the same social, ethnic, or financial cloth as Allyn Forbes and Stewart Mitchell. He came from humble origins, did not attend Harvard, and, most significantly, was an Irish Catholic. His was the quintessential American success story.

Born in the industrial city of Worcester, Massachusetts, on December

---

[1] M.H.S., *Procs.*, 73(1961):123. Riley was in a distant part of the building, answering a telephone call.

The Arrival of Riley

29, 1908, Riley was one of eight children.[2] His parents had emigrated from Ireland in the late nineteenth century. His father was a crew foreman for the city of Worcester. Both parents had received a minimal education in Ireland, no more than grade school. While not learned, bookish people, they were determined to provide an education for their children so they could grasp the opportunity America offered.[3]

An intelligent, disciplined, purposeful youngster, Riley breezed through grade school and high school, then entered Clark University in Worcester. After completing his first year, he was awarded a scholarship. He earned his A.B. in three and one-half years, graduating *magna cum laude*; he was elected to Phi Beta Kappa. He took his A.M. in 1932. He stayed on at Clark for a doctorate in American history, completing all but his dissertation and oral examinations.[4] Throughout his years at Clark, he worked at the Worcester Public Library after school hours.

Finding it necessary to secure full-time employment, he applied for the position of assistant librarian at the Society. The salary was low, but it was the height of the Depression and jobs were scarce. Because of Riley's library experience and a glowing recommendation from one of his professors at Clark, Ray Billington,[5] Allyn Forbes hired the young man from Worcester. It was perhaps the most important decision Forbes made at the Society. Riley thought he would remain "a year or so" and then move on. Forty-two years later, when he reached the age of retirement, he was still there, but as its chief executive officer.[6]

From the outset, Riley was a success. The man and the institution were a perfect match. In his colleague Malcolm Freiberg's judgment:

---

[2] Mrs. Stephen T. Riley provided biographical information to the author.

[3] Five of the Riley children received college educations. One of Stephen's brothers earned a doctorate, and another completed a master's degree.

[4] The topic he selected for his dissertation required considerable research in Pennsylvania, but he lacked the financial resources to pursue this study. In 1949, while employed at the Society, he took on a new topic that could be researched in Boston. He completed his dissertation and passed his oral examinations in 1953.

[5] Billington later taught at Northwestern University and became one of the nation's leading scholars of western American history.

[6] Until 1991, Riley had an office at the Society, where he worked on various projects, especially his longstanding plan to publish the papers of Robert Treat Paine. The two volumes that he co-edited with Edward W. Hanson for that series were issued in 1992, shortly after Riley was admitted to a nursing home.

"the Massachusetts Historical Society and Steve Riley were meant for each other."[7] Conscientious, energetic, endowed with a sunny disposition, polite and helpful to researchers, he impressed all who came in contact with him. When Riley received his orders for induction into the army in early 1942, Director Forbes paid this tribute to him in his report to the members: "To him has been due no small measure of the success attending the recent merger of the offices of Librarian and Editor in that of Director, and his absence, even though it should be only a brief one, cannot but cripple the Society's activities at every point."[8]

When Riley returned from military service in 1945 and renewed his employment, he picked up where he had left off. An ecstatic Forbes wrote: "Without a moment's loss of time, as though military service were the ideal tonic for a library worker, he took over again all the activities that had formerly been his responsibility and then found it possible to assume charge of additional ones."[9] Years later, Riley recalled Forbes saying to him: "It was as if I had never been away."[10]

Riley served as assistant librarian until 1947. After the death of Allyn Forbes in January of that year, the new director, Stewart Mitchell, made it a condition of his acceptance that Riley be raised to the position of librarian with an increased salary.[11] Although the members of the Council readily agreed to a new salary of $4,000 a year, they discovered that the by-laws adopted in 1942 prevented separating the positions of librarian and editor from that of director. However, by-law changes to accommodate the new situation were quickly drafted and were approved by the membership meeting on May 8, when the Council appointed Stephen Riley "Librarian of the Society."[12]

Riley had had a compatible working relationship with Forbes, but he had a difficult time during Mitchell's directorship because of the latter's propensity for alcohol. As an authoritative source informed this writer,

---

[7] Letter to the author from Freiberg, Aug. 16, 1993.

[8] M.H.S., *Procs.*, 67(1941–1944):589.

[9] M.H.S., *Procs.*, 68(1944–1947):512.

[10] Drummey, ed., "Bates-Riley Correspondence," 148.

[11] Stewart Mitchell to Clarence S. Brigham, Jan. 30, 1947 (Mitchell Records, M.H.S. Archives).

[12] M.H.S. Council Records, Feb. 13, Mar. 13, Apr. 10, May 8, 1947 (M.H.S. Archives).

The Arrival of Riley

"Stephen Riley worked hard to help and protect Mitchell, and I am sure suffered intensely while he made this effort."[13]

After becoming president in 1950, John Adams discovered Riley "only by degrees" but eventually realized that he was the mainstay of the staff. "His title was librarian and that he certainly was, but also he it was who handled all the routine, and looked after all the daily details and chores, as well as the duties of librarian." As Mitchell's physical condition deteriorated, Adams began to view Riley as the director's successor: "I long had Stephen Riley in mind, watching him and helping him develop as I could."[14] Riley's background, while known to the Yankee from Lincoln, was of no consequence to him. He judged Riley solely on merit.

In 1955, the New-York Historical Society contacted Riley and offered him the librarian's position at a salary considerably higher than he was then receiving. Since he was now married, Riley gave serious consideration to the "handsome offer."[15] Founded in 1804, the New York City society had the largest endowment of any private historical society in the nation and was a highly regarded cultural/educational institution.[16]

Riley informed Adams of the offer. The latter was deeply concerned over his possible loss. This would upset his plan to have Riley replace Mitchell. Adams wrote:

> Had he told Mitchell? I asked—No, only me—What was he going to do? He didn't know, but he liked his job and his wife liked her life here, yet wouldn't stand in his way. So I left him to think it over, and I did the same.
> We met again in a day or two and I had my answer, but what was his?

[13] Thomas B. Adams to author, Aug. 25, 1993. Riley often informed the author of his trials and tribulations with Mitchell.

[14] Adams, "Random Sketches," 31–32, 34. In a letter to the author (Aug. 25, 1993), Thomas B. Adams wrote: "I do know that when I first began to hear about the Historical Society and how it was doing he [John Adams] spoke very often of Steve Riley. They became great friends. It was a friendship that saved the Historical Society. . . . They were the two rebuilders of the Society. Without them it would have crumbled into dust."

[15] He had married Alice Riehle on July 2, 1949.

[16] See: R.W.G. Vail, *Knickerbocker Birthday: A Sesqui-Centennial History of the New-York Historical Society, 1804–1954* (New York, 1954); Whitehill, *Independent Historical Societies*, 38–64. The New York society went into financial decline in the 1970s and 1980s and neared the point of dissolution. At this writing (1994), it remains in a perilous financial condition and is barely surviving.

His was that having talked it over with Alice, his wife, he had decided to stay—and then it was up to me.

Adams reviewed the Society's finances and concluded "that with luck there would be a surplus of $4,000 that year." He now knew what to do. Adams would increase Riley's salary by $4,000 and stay on as president until Riley was appointed director.[17] From that time, Adams "dealt mainly with Riley. He was actually in charge and everything went better." When Mitchell resigned, the way was cleared for Riley's appointment as director. It came at the annual meeting on October 10, 1957. At the same time Malcolm Freiberg was appointed as the Society's editor, and Thomas Boylston Adams was elected to succeed his father as president.[18]

Riley provided the Society with a rich legacy, one aspect of which was the physical transformation and enlargement of the Boylston Street quarters. When he joined the staff in 1934, he quickly saw that a number of key rooms were not being used in the most efficient manner. He also noticed that the building had an "air of decayed gentility." Its rooms were "dark, dismal, and dirty."[19] After more than three decades of intensive use, and a minimum of maintenance, the building looked heavily worn. No longer an architectural jewel, it created an impression of institutional impoverishment. It was a tired building. Mitchell had made some cosmetic improvements, but their effect was minimal.

Riley decided to make the quarters more functional and, at the same time, beautify the interior. He set forth his overall plan in the director's report of 1959: "We need a larger reading room, better exhibition space, and better facilities for Members and visitors." He targeted three rooms for renovation.[20]

Riley began with Ellis Hall, the large room on the first floor, which housed Mitchell's "New Museum." This facility had been a colossal failure from its inception. Mitchell's optimistic hopes for a vibrant,

[17] Adams, "Random Sketches," 34–35; M.H.S. Council Records, Oct. 13, 1955 (M.H.S. Archives).
[18] M.H.S. Council Records, Oct. 10, 1957 (M.H.S. Archives).
[19] Riley, *Years of Stewardship*, 62, 75.
[20] Riley, *Years of Stewardship*, 62.

well-attended museum program did not materialize. Bostonians stayed away in droves: ". . . it is a rare day indeed that sees a visitor."[21]

At Riley's suggestion, the Council appointed a special museum assessment committee, chaired by the director's close friend and confidant, Edward P. Hamilton.[22] Taking its direction from Riley, the committee concluded that the museum should be dismantled: "Since there is a minimum of interest shown in the Museum, since it has little if any direct value to the Society's major purpose, and since it occupies a great deal more space than is justified while at the same time the Society urgently requires more space, we recommend that the Museum be discontinued as a separate entity occupying a room by itself." Further, Ellis Hall should be converted into a reading room.

The report also recommended that "a considerable part" of the museum collection be given or loaned to institutions in the area better suited to utilize such materials. It called for the retention of the portraits and such significant artifacts as George Washington's military gorget, Shem Drowne's Indian weathervane, and the pen used by Abraham Lincoln to sign the Emancipation Proclamation. The committee subsequently reconsidered this issue and decided to retain all of the articles "for the present." They were to be used in rotating exhibitions, which were to be installed in the old reading room on the second floor. This would be phase two of Riley's plan. Phase three called for the renovation of the room in which the special libraries had been housed in earlier years. Henry Adams's library and the maps and atlases were destined for this space.

The Council approved the committee's recommendations and authorized an architectural study of the three rooms.[23] The study was soon developed, and in 1960, "after months of dust and confusion," the first phase was completed with a refurbished, well-lighted Ellis Hall ready for researchers. In October, the annual meeting was held, as usual, in the second-floor Dowse Library, adjacent to the old reading room. After

[21] M.H.S. Council Records, Apr. 9, 1959 (M.H.S. Archives).

[22] Hamilton spent his winters at the Society, where he researched and wrote books on the French and Indian War era. From late spring to early fall, he served as director of the Fort Ticonderoga Museum in Ticonderoga, New York.

[23] The report is in M.H.S. Council Records, May 14, 1959 (M.H.S. Archives). See also, M.H.S., *Procs.*, 72(1957–1960):460–461.

reporting to the members at the annual meeting that Ellis Hall on the ground level was now in use as a reading room, President Thomas Boylston Adams, "with the relish of a soldier nailing an Indian scalp to a town gate, . . . hung the sign 'Closed Today Except To Members' on the frame of Thomas Dowse's portrait and expressed his satisfaction that we had seen the last of that particular nuisance, for henceforth scholars could work freely in the building on meeting days."[24]

Riley was nostalgic over leaving the old reading room in which he had labored for close to a quarter of a century. In this small, crowded, and cluttered room, which could "comfortably" seat only eight, years of research had been conducted by some of the nation's most prominent historians, "many first as fledgling scholars whose skinny posteriors squirmed uneasily on our hard chairs, later as veterans with more physical and mental ballast." The list represented a who's who of American scholars: "Channing, Hart, Turner, Rhodes, Bassett, Beveridge, Bemis, Fox, Jameson, the Adamses, Andrews, Morison, Merk, the Schlesingers, Nevins, Freeman, Morse, Commager would merely start the litany."[25] Riley had assisted almost all of these Promethean figures, as attested in the acknowledgment pages of their copious writings.

Phase two came in 1961 with the creation of the Peter Oliver exhibition room in the old reading room. All of the library furniture was removed, an antique rug was added, and custom-made, wooden exhibition and print storage cases were installed along the perimeter of the room. Members of the Oliver family were the major contributors to the tasteful renovation. On October 27, 1961, the Society officially dedicated the room with an exhibition and reception.[26] The final phase, the development of the Adams Room, was begun and completed in 1962.

Riley also made a major change in the heating system. He described the improvement: "The old system, tampered with through the years by enthusiastic but uninformed workers, had reached a state in which it managed to conduct most of the heat through the building and out

[24] M.H.S., *Procs.*, 72(1957–1960):486–487.

[25] Riley, *Years of Stewardship*, 63.

[26] The Society's print collection was housed in drawers built into the base of the exhibition cases. James Lawrence, Jr., an architect with sensitive aesthetic taste and a member of the Society, planned the alterations for Ellis Hall and the Oliver Room. He refused to take a fee for his own time in planning and supervising the projects. M.H.S., *Procs.*, 72(1957–1960):487.

through the vents on the roof without entering some of the rooms, yet at the same time distributing dust with complete impartiality."[27] The new system corrected these deficiencies and was designed so that air conditioning could be installed in the future.

Riley derived a bonus from his improvements. One member, Henry Latimer Seaver, a former professor of fine arts at the Massachusetts Institute of Technology, was so impressed with the physical changes that he offered to pay for the conversion of a basement coal bin into a two-level stack that would eventually accommodate 25,000 volumes. Riley was elated by the offer, since the Society was always in need of storage space. In his usual, far-sighted manner, he already had worked out the general plan for the conversion so the improvement was made in short order in 1963.[28] Thus, in a period of three years, Riley had made a major overhaul of the Society's interior.

In his annual appeal letter to the members in November 1963, President Thomas Boylston Adams exulted over the progress that had been made.

> In November 1959, we set out to make over the form and face of the Society's building. Today we have a building as useful as the most modern, more beautiful than much that is new. The portraits are seen in glory, the halls welcome the visitor, the Oliver Room displays our treasures, the scholars work under near perfect conditions. Out of the general sight, the heating system has been made over, the electric wiring renewed. Even the coal bin has been made into a clean, white, bright stack. The last bill has been paid. The job is done.[29]

But not for Riley. There was still work to be done, and he had even a bigger change in mind. The final link in his chain of physical improvement was a "functional stack building," which would serve primarily as a storage area for library materials and, secondarily, provide additional office space. He knew precisely where such an addition could be built, in an open area at the rear of 1154 Boylston Street, then used as a parking lot. At this juncture, the plan was merely a vision, a glint in his eye. He knew it would be a costly enterprise and require a massive fund-raising effort, and he also knew that the Society had an abysmal record at raising

---

[27] Riley, *Years of Stewardship*, 68.
[28] Librarian John D. Cushing prepared the detailed plan.
[29] M.H.S. Archives.

money. But Riley was a visionary as well as an enthusiastic achiever. After completing the initial renovations, he informed the members in 1962: "If we [the staff] look pale from plaster dust and turn green at the sound of a carpenter's drill, you will now know why. But we shall gladly go through it all again when you give us the word to start the Annex."[30]

Another option for additional space suddenly developed in 1963 when the Boston Medical Library, which was located at 8 The Fenway and shared a common wall with the Historical Society, announced that it was vacating its spacious quarters in 1965 and offered the building for sale at a price of $125,000. During the late spring and summer of 1963, Riley and a coterie of Society officials walked next door and made a number of intensive inspections of the structure. It was a tempting proposition. They finally decided not to purchase the property. "It was the general feeling of our inspecting Members," wrote Riley, "that the Boston Medical Library building was not suited to our needs and would be too expensive for us to maintain. It seemed preferable to all that we construct at some future date a functional stack wing as an annex to our present building."[31] Towards this end, the Council in April 1964 requested the Turner Construction Company to outline a tentative plan for building the proposed "new stack in the present back yard."[32]

In his annual report to the members for 1963, Riley had asserted that the existing building could accommodate ten more years of growth, provided that the Society did not acquire any more "blockbuster collections" of manuscripts (like the George Frisbie Hoar and Adams family papers).[33] Another cause for concern to Riley was the growing disposition of old Massachusetts institutions, such as churches, patriotic societies, and charitable organizations, to deposit their archival records in the Society. While he welcomed these acquisitions, he lacked the space to house them.

In his report to the annual meeting the following year, Riley had to reduce the figure for the approaching need of additional storage from ten

---

[30] Riley, *Years of Stewardship*, 71.

[31] M.H.S., *Procs.*, 75(1963):134. Years later, when the Society again had a serious storage problem, Riley told this writer that they had made an egregious mistake by not purchasing this building.

[32] M.H.S. Council Records, Apr. 9, 1964 (M.H.S. Archives).

[33] M.H.S., *Procs.*, 75(1963):134.

to five years noting parenthetically that "in a library such as ours, usable space disappears faster than a successful missile."[34] The reason for the sudden disappearance of five years worth of storage space was Riley's hyper-aggressive collecting of manuscripts.[35] The documents were pouring in at a rapid rate. Riley listed some of his newest acquisitions and their relative sizes. The Allen French Papers occupied 40 archival boxes, 22 albums, 15 bundles, and numerous bound volumes; the Francis Blake Papers ran to 132 volumes; the Bowditch, Goldsbury, Hassam, and White land title records took up 221 volumes; and Andrew Oliver was depositing Oliver family papers "at a rate that will soon make the collection one of our largest and most important."

Riley foresaw no abatement in collecting. On the contrary, it was certain to intensify. Two weeks earlier, he reported, he had examined two massive collections which would be coming in "a relatively short time." The Society must assume its responsibilities: "We must house these collections properly; we must describe them properly; and we must make them available to a wider audience through publication by microfilm, letterpress and other means."

Riley also reported that the preliminary plans for the building addition had been completed. He invited the members to examine them "and advise us how to transform them into reality"—that is, answer the question: where can the Society get the funds to build the wing?[36]

In his concluding remarks, after reminiscing about the changes he had witnessed in his thirty years of employment, Riley set forth his vision of the Society of the future. The addition headed his list of goals, all of which had costly price tags attached to them: "I hope that I may see the day when we have our annex so that we can properly care for the great treasures in our custody." And he expressed the hope that a "benevolent angel like the one who has visited many of our sister institutions will

---

[34] M.H.S., *Procs.*, 76(1964):192.

[35] See Chapter 17 for a discussion of Riley, the collector.

[36] The Council established a Library Addition Fund in October 1963 with an initial gift of $1,000 from an anonymous donor. "It was the informal opinion of the Council, however, that there should be no great publicizing of this new fund at the present time, that it would be expedient to wait until the need for an addition had become more generally apparent, particularly as members have in recent years been very generous in contributing to the current alterations of the building, which have put it in excellent shape for the present." M.H.S. Council Records, Oct. 10, 1963 (M.H.S. Archives).

call on us. He is long overdue."[37] Riley had been seeking that elusive "benevolent angel" since he became director in 1957.

In November 1964, President Adams appointed a six-member commission to assess the past accomplishments of the Society and project its needs for the future. The commission's conclusions on future needs, the most significant part of the report, mirrored Riley's position exactly. The Society needed a new wing, an enlarged staff, and a substantial increase in endowment. It projected a cost of $4,325,000 for these three components.[38]

In January 1966, the Society took a major step to implement its long-range plan. Acting upon Riley's recommendation, it purchased a four-story apartment complex, which faced on Hemenway Street and backed up against the public alley running along the rear of the Society's quarters. The structure consisted of six buildings, joined together, which contained twenty-four rental units. The price was $325,000.[39]

The principal defect of the building was its poor physical condition. Since its construction in 1889, it had had a succession of owners, who exploited the property for rental income but were negligent in maintaining the building. However, since the Society intended to level the structure in the near future, it was not unduly concerned about its deteriorated state. The Hemenway Street property was seen as the hope of the future, a further possible expansion beyond the proposed new wing.

Constantly prodded by its dynamic director, the Council finally made the decision in 1968 to build an addition to the existing structure, provided that the details could be worked out and the funding secured. It appointed a number of committees to accomplish the objective, chief of which was the campaign steering committee, chaired by James Barr Ames, a prominent Boston attorney. This body had the responsibility of organizing and directing the fund campaign. The next step was to hire an architectural firm to draft preliminary plans. The Council authorized this action and entered into a contract with the old-line Boston firm of Shepley, Bulfinch, Richardson and Abbott.[40]

[37] Riley, *Years of Stewardship*, 74–76.
[38] *Confidential Report from the Council to the Members, August 1966.* Copy in M.H.S. Archives.
[39] M.H.S. Council Records, Jan. 13, Feb. 10, 1966 (M.H.S. Archives).
[40] M.H.S. Council Records, Oct. 13, 1966 (M.H.S. Archives).

The Arrival of Riley

One of the first strategies devised by the Council was to deaccession and sell some of the Society's less relevant holdings. Riley was vehemently opposed to this move on principle but was forced to draw up a list of items, which would yield about $2,000,000 for the fund drive. When he submitted it, the Council renewed the debate about the advisability of deaccessioning. The issue provoked "considerable and lively discussion" at the meeting of March 14, 1968. The motion was soundly defeated, 8 to 2, much to Riley's satisfaction.[41] A watered-down motion was hurriedly drawn up and passed, permitting the Society to sell select items.

Riley recommended the sale of a large portion of the Society's outstanding coin collection, specifically duplicates and non-American coins. From its founding, the Society had acquired many coins, mostly by gift or bequest, such as the collections of William Sumner Appleton and the Adams family. However, Riley knew that these items were now little used by scholars and had moved the coins in 1965 to a bank vault in central Boston because of the fear of theft and the lack of a proper facility for exhibiting them. He now recommended the sale of such duplicates, and the Council approved.[42] The first sale was held at Stack's auction house in New York City on October 23–24, 1970, and the Society netted about $92,000.[43]

Ames's committee divided the fund campaign into two stages. The goal of the first stage was $2,500,000. One million dollars was allocated for construction of the new wing, and $1,500,000 was to be set aside as an endowment, the income from which would be used to maintain the structure and support "the broader and richer program that it will make possible."

The second stage called for an additional $2,500,000. Of this sum, $2,100,000 was to be used to build an annex on the site of the Hemenway Apartments, and $400,000 would be placed into an endowment fund, the income to be used for maintenance.[44]

---

[41] M.H.S. Council Records, Mar. 14, 1968 (M.H.S. Archives).

[42] M.H.S. Council Records, Jan. 12, May 11, 1967; May 14, 1970 (M.H.S. Archives).

[43] Subsequently, Stack's held three more auctions. The Society netted $307,889.40 from the four sales. Riley, *Years of Stewardship*, 96–97, 100; M.H.S., *Procs.*, 88(1976):157.

[44] An architectural sketch of the proposed annex appears as the final illustration in *Here We Have Lived: The Houses of the Massachusetts Historical Society* (Boston, 1967).

In 1969, the Council instructed the architects to develop working drawings of the addition. Its final decision to begin construction was still contingent upon the assurance of funding. This was a busy and exciting year for Riley. He organized and attended numerous meetings of the various committees. He spent considerable time with the building committee, reviewing and refining detailed plans of the substantial, six-story structure.

Riley was also involved in a myriad of activities relating to fund raising. To help raise public awareness of the Society, he organized and supervised the installation of a major exhibition featuring the greatest treasures of the Society.[45] And he took an active role in soliciting funds for the campaign. He developed a fuller appreciation of Shakespeare's line in MacBeth: "Methought I heard a voice cry 'Sleep no more!' "

While well-organized, the fund drive did not take off with a rush. At the outset, returns were small and slow in coming. The campaign began to falter, and there was a growing fear that it would not reach the designated goal. By April 1970, the plans for the building addition were in place. All that was now needed was a formal vote by the Council to proceed with the construction.

There was hesitation, however, by the governing body because of the slow pace of the fund drive. Some Council members were apprehensive. As Riley noted, "faced with worsening business conditions, the Council had to determine whether to proceed with the building plans or wait for more propitious times."[46]

At that critical juncture, Riley's long-awaited "benevolent angel" appeared. Henry Lee Shattuck, the "last Brahmin" and a resident member since 1935, stepped forth and offered a gift of $300,000 if it were matched by a stated time. Shattuck, who had a "long and affectionate concern" for the Society and was particularly fond of Riley, already had made an initial gift of $250,000 when the campaign began.[47]

[45] See *Collecting for Clio: An Exhibition of Representative Materials From the Holdings of the Massachusetts Historical Society* (Boston, 1969).

[46] Riley, *Years of Stewardship*, 92.

[47] Shattuck gave more than money to the Society. As indicated in Riley's reports, he also donated his rare book collection, some manuscripts, and "many of his valuable prints." Riley described his donations in 1970 as "one of the greatest gifts to come to our library in many years." Riley, *Years of Stewardship*, 95. In Thomas B. Adams's judgment, Shattuck "most certainly would not have made his great benefaction to the Society had

The Arrival of Riley

Encouraged by Shattuck's generosity, the Council voted to begin construction.[48] If this body anticipated more largess from him, it was not to be disappointed. On April 27, 1970, at 3:06 P.M., Riley and a small number of members and staff met at the rear of the Society and watched the driving of the first steel pile. The new wing was underway. Riley's dream was moving toward reality.

Just as John Adams had rescued the Society from insolvency in the 1950s, so did Harry Shattuck come to the rescue now. An appreciative Council designated him an honorary member and honorary chairman of the campaign steering committee, and named the new wing for him. Shattuck's challenge gift was matched by July 1970, in no small measure due to his personal solicitations. As Henry Lee has written: "When it became apparent that the Society must have a new building to house its expanding collections, indeed to survive as a viable research institution, he gave much of his time and energy to the task. During his last two years he worked tirelessly to solicit contributions (especially from foundations), afforded invaluable advice, and made an initial gift of $250,000."[49]

The new wing began to rise, but construction worked a severe hardship upon Riley and his small staff, who were determined to keep the Society open for researchers. "The coming of the tradesmen," Riley wrote, "brought about a marked disruption of our well-ordered life. Like locusts they swarmed through the building, ripping out walls and floors, making way for new lighting, heating, and air-conditioning, and filling the air with a fine plaster dust which we could not escape inhaling. The staffs no longer worry about immortality: we shall be preserved in plaster long before we are carted away to our final resting places." The Society did remain open, although there was limited service because some materials were not accessible. There was no heat during construction, leading one senior staff member to recall "early days spent in the

---

not he approved of the work done by Steve Riley and my father." Letter to author, Aug. 25, 1993. For biographical information on this unusual and remarkable man, see: John T. Galvin, *The Gentleman Mr. Shattuck* (Boston, 1996); and Henry Lee's perceptive memoir in M.H.S., *Procs.*, 83(1971):168–174.

[48] M.H.S. Council Records, Apr. 9, 1970 (M.H.S. Archives).

[49] M.H.S., *Procs.*, 83(1971):172.

British Museum reading room, where he had to wear his overcoat to keep warm."[50]

President Adams provided a graphic description of life in the Society during "the noisy, dusty, and always uncomfortable time of construction."

> The staff has carried tons of books up and down stairs. There has been no elevator for months. They have gone without heat in winter when the pipes were shut off and borne with heat in hot weather when the new heating system has been on trial. And they have gone right on serving the needs of research scholars with calm good humor.[51]

Because of two strikes, there were delays in construction, and the new wing was not completed until the end of 1971. Riley commented: "Toward the end it became debatable whether the Staff or the Addition would be finished first. Thankfully, the Staff survived."[52] The campaign goal for the first stage had been reached earlier, no small thanks to Shattuck, although the Society's greatest benefactor in its history had died on February 2, 1971, before completion of the wing bearing his name. He bequeathed the Society another gift of $300,000, which closed out the fund drive. And there was more to come. He made the Society a residuary legatee of his estate. In time, this yielded an additional $1,500,000 to the endowment.[53] Shattuck also willed to the Society John Singleton Copley's prize portrait of John Hancock, a painting Riley had long coveted.[54] Little wonder that Riley described Shattuck as the "first citizen of Boston. His greatest gift to the Society was his belief in it."[55]

The Society honored Shattuck, his twin brother, George, another

[50] Riley, *Years of Stewardship*, 93. The air conditioning and humidity control systems were extended to the 1897 Wheelwright building.

[51] Appeal letter to members, Dec. 14, 1971 (M.H.S. Archives).

[52] Riley, *Years of Stewardship*, 103.

[53] Ever the practical Yankee, Shattuck specified that this gift "is to be held as a permanent fund and the income only to be used for salaries, maintenance and other operating expenses, but not for the purchase of expensive books, manuscripts or other items." Riley, *Years of Stewardship*, 100.

[54] Riley frequently told this writer and others of meeting with Shattuck on one occasion in his spacious, treasure-laden Brookline home and requesting the Hancock portrait for the Society. Shattuck listened intently but made no response, in keeping with his usual taciturn demeanor.

[55] Riley, *Years of Stewardship*, 100.

generous benefactor, and their forebears at its 1971 spring reception with an exhibition and publication on their family.[56] The program attracted a large, colorfully attired crowd. The *Boston Globe* reported that "there were miniskirts, long blonde tresses and even pantsuits at the Massachusetts Historical Society's spring reception yesterday, along with sedate silk prints and proper straw hats. There were mod mustaches and bold plaid trousers, mingling amiably with classic Cambridge tailoring and uncompromising crew cuts."[57]

The Shattuck wing was opened for viewing to those who attended the spring exhibition and reception on June 1, 1972. The average attendance for this annual fete was about 250, but on this day over 700 members, fellows of the library, and friends came and meandered through the expanded quarters. Elated by the huge turnout, Riley wrote: "They were particularly impressed by the skillful blending of the old and new buildings, finding it difficult to tell where the old ended and the new began."[58]

What Riley failed to mention was that he had placed his own aesthetic stamp upon the enlarged structure. The walls in every room of the old and new buildings exhibited, in a most tasteful manner, the finest art works owned by the Society. Positioned at every significant focal point were statuary, antique furniture, and the most visually attractive artifacts in the collection.[59] It was unique decor for a research library. The building was, in essence, a museum of early American history.

From the first days of his employment in 1934, Riley had become aware of the lowly state of the library. This facility was a far cry from the Worcester Public Library in which he had worked while a student at Clark University. There was a semblance of professionalism at the Worcester institution. Not so at the Society. Because of the small staff, Riley was obliged to perform a plenitude of assignments, some of which

---

[56] *Pro Bono Publico: The Shattucks of Boston* (Boston, 1971).

[57] *Boston Globe*, May 5, 1971.

[58] Riley, *Years of Stewardship*, 103.

[59] Over the years, the Society had acquired some stunning artifacts and antique furniture. See Patricia E. Kane, "Furniture Owned by the Massachusetts Historical Society," *The Magazine Antiques*, (May 1976), 960–969. For a glimpse at some of the Society's prize artifacts, see *Witness to America's Past: Two Centuries of Collecting by the Massachusetts Historical Society* (Boston, 1991).

did not pertain to the library. If he had a formal job description, it was a meaningless document.

Riley noticed that some vital functions, like cataloging and conservation, were being neglected because of a lack of staff, which, in turn, was due to financial constraints. These limitations had been a perennial problem from the founding of the Society. The reports of the librarians since the 1790s had been an unremitting litany of woes, classic jeremiads.

Upon becoming director, Riley addressed this issue. He regarded the library as the heart of the institution. If it withered, the Society also would decline. If the Society was to prosper, the library must be strengthened. Moreover, Riley had a passionate love affair with libraries.

Riley convened his library committee and undertook a full review of the facility, from storage space to cataloging to conservation. From their deliberations came a comprehensive report, one part of which recommended the creation of an endowed library fund. This money was to be used solely for library needs. The Council approved the Library Fund in 1958, commencing with a $1,000 gift from Henry L. Seaver.[60]

To augment the fund, Riley resorted to the conventional technique of written and personal appeals to members and friends. President Adams also participated in this process. The results were not entirely positive. The Society did receive gifts, but they were small and infrequent. But it was a start, and the fund began to mount. At the annual meeting of 1958, Riley reported that it contained $3,500.[61]

In 1967, James Barr Ames proposed to the Council, of which he was a member, the formation of a support group for the library to be called the "Fellows of the Library of the Massachusetts Historical Society."[62] President Thomas B. Adams and Riley enthusiastically endorsed the proposal, and the Council readily approved it. Ames, Adams, and Riley viewed the fellows, first and foremost, as a vehicle for raising needed funds for the library. The fellows were to be assessed annual dues of

[60] M.H.S. Council Records, Feb. 13, 1958 (M.H.S. Archives).

[61] M.H.S., *Procs.*, 72(1957–1960):445. In 1962, acting upon the advice of a consultant, Riley withdrew the non-New England Civil War books from the collection and sold them to Rice University. The funds received were added to the principal of the 1958 Library Fund to create a new fund with the same name. Ibid., 74(1962):116. See Appendix III.

[62] M.H.S. Council Records, May 11, 1967 (M.H.S. Archives).

$100; a husband and wife were provided a joint membership. The dues were to be consigned to the library fund.[63]

Riley was pleased by the Council's action: "Up to now the library has struggled along with completely inadequate funds for acquisition, furnishings, and all the other tools that a library must have. Now members and friends can form a group that will support every activity of the library and consequently of the Society."[64]

A number of Boston's other cultural institutions, including some libraries, had already established similar bodies of "friends" as a means of securing additional funds, using it as a tactic to broaden their constituency. Ames, Adams, and Riley were of the same mind. They wished to bring more Greater Bostonians into the Society to extend the ring of supporters. In so doing, they were following in the footsteps of Charles Francis Adams, Worthington C. Ford, and Stewart Mitchell. Like them, they were inclusive, not exclusive.

Since there was a ceiling of one hundred fifty resident members, a number of people interested in the Society were not able to make an affiliation with it. Now they could. The fellows were permitted to attend all of the Society's social functions and regular meetings. Their only restriction was the lack of a vote at business meetings.

When the Council established the fellows program, it directed that all applicants were to be "elected" by the governing body. While a perfunctory exercise, this was designed to provide a measure of control over the program. There is no record of a prospective fellow's application being rejected, and in a short time, the Council quietly abandoned the practice.

The recruitment of fellows proved to be a pleasant surprise to Riley. At his urging, a number of resident members signed on, providing a base. At this time, resident members were not being assessed dues, so, for many of them, this was the only financial obligation they incurred. Riley also appealed to many of his personal friends and professional associates; their response was generally positive. It was not easy to say "no" to this persuasive personality. At the outset, Riley was doubtful that "more than 50" would become fellows because of the relatively

[63] A fellow could pay his dues "in kind," that is, by donating materials valued at $100 or more to the library.

[64] Riley, *Years of Stewardship*, 92.

high dues. To his joy, over 170 accepted the Society's invitation. This assured the library fund over $17,000 in annual income.[65]

On October 30, 1969, the Society inaugurated the fellows of the library program with a formal dinner in the executive dining room of the New England Merchants National Bank atop the nearby Prudential Tower. Over 170 fellows and their spouses and guests were in attendance. Joining the fellows as honored guests were retired United States Sen. Leverett Saltonstall, United States Sen. Edward M. Kennedy, Henry Lee Shattuck, and Sir Frank C. Francis, director emeritus of the British Museum.[66] After dinner, the group boarded busses and made the short trip to the Society, where they were to hear brief talks by Shattuck, Saltonstall, and Kennedy, and a major address by Francis. They were then to preview the special exhibition of historical treasures prepared for the kickoff of the capital campaign for the new wing. The dinner for the fellows had been coordinated with the fund drive.

When the group arrived at the entrance to the Society, they were confronted by a large, unruly crowd of anti-Senator Kennedy protesters. They had gathered there to express their displeasure over his actions at Chappaquiddick Island, in July, when he had driven his Oldsmobile off Dike Bridge into the water, leading to the death of his passenger, Mary Jo Kopechne. It was a "scene of tumult." In Adams's words: "It was one of the moments of political passion in that passionate period. Mounted police were cavorting and rearing. Crowds of reporters were pushing and yelling. Senators Saltonstall and Kennedy, thanks to the diligence of the staff, entered the sanctuary safely."[67]

Upon entering the building, each fellow received a specially printed and numbered edition of the exhibition catalogue, entitled *Collecting for Clio*, as a keepsake. The exhibition was open to the general public on the following day.[68]

---

[65] Riley, *Years of Stewardship*, 96. By 1991, the fellows numbered over 280 and contributed close to $30,000 annually to the Library Fund.

[66] Saltonstall, Kennedy, and Shattuck were resident members and Francis was a corresponding member.

[67] A horde of reporters and television crews met Kennedy when he arrived at Logan Airport in Boston at 5 P.M. (*Boston Globe*, Oct. 31, 1969). The senator made a brief statement on the Chappaquiddick issue and hastily departed, the reporters in hot pursuit. The reporters hounded him for the remainder of his stay in Boston.

[68] Despite the fact that there was no admission fee, surprisingly few visitors came to the Society to view the exhibition. Riley was deeply disappointed by the low attendance.

The Arrival of Riley

President Adams presided at the formal program preceding the viewing of the exhibition. He greeted the group, which had a large contingent of women, and drew raucous laughter when he stated: "This is a glorious occasion. I've just figured it out. It's now 178 years since we were founded, and finally ladies have been admitted to equal status. This is an epochal moment for the Society." While the statement was made in jest, Adams and Riley were determined to change the all-male character of the organization. They intended to bring women into resident membership as they had into the fellows of the library.

Following Adams's introductory comments, the speakers held forth. Shattuck, "the Society's Uncle Harry," opened "with remarks straightforward and effective, as had been his whole career of more than 90 years." Senator Saltonstall, the "parfait gentil knight," followed, stressing his warm affection for the Society, which housed his family's and his personal papers. Senator Kennedy "spoke earnestly of the duty of historians to help government avoid future mistakes by laying bare mistakes of the past." He called for the creation of a "Council of Historians," which would serve as an advisory body to the government and insure that the government had access to "the full spectrum of historical scholarship."[69]

Standing with his back to the portraits of "high-bosomed, 18th-century ladies in low-cut evening gowns," Sir Frank C. Francis delivered the main address. "It was a night to remember," President Adams later wrote. "Politics and scholarship met together with a bang and the echo of their cheers resounded up and down Boylston Street."[70] The echo of the jeers of the anti-Kennedy detractors, who were clustered outside, also resounded up and down Boylston Street.

One year later, the list of fellows rose to 190 and Riley asserted that he was "working to increase that number." The library was already benefitting from the infusion of funds from fellows' dues. Riley reported: "Thus far contributions have been used to buy books and manuscripts, acquire expensive bibliographies, purchase a microfilm reader, and hire two young ladies for the summer months to work on pressing library projects."[71] The library had now entered a new and higher phase of development.

[69] *Boston Globe*, Oct. 31, 1969.

[70] M.H.S., *Procs.*, 100(1988):147–148.

[71] Riley, *Years of Stewardship*, 96.

Chapter 17

Watchdog and Manuscript Hound Extraordinary

AFTER BECOMING director, Riley continued to function as librarian. As administrative responsibilities began to consume more of his time, he concluded that he could not carry out all of his library assignments. He needed an assistant. He found that person, John D. Cushing, and hired him in 1960.

A native of Hampton, New Hampshire, Cushing attended the University of New Hampshire and was awarded an A.B. in 1949 and an A.M. in 1950. From 1950 to 1954, he taught history and government at Norwich University, a military school in Vermont. In 1954, he moved to Worcester and enrolled in the doctoral program in history at Clark University.

For his dissertation, Cushing undertook a study of the public career of William Cushing, associate justice of the United States Supreme Court from 1789 to 1810.[1] Since many of the Judge's manuscripts were at the Society, Cushing made frequent trips to Boston. Riley, who made a conscious effort to fraternize with researchers, became well acquainted with Cushing.[2] Because of their mutual relationship with Clark University and its history department, the two developed a warm friendship.

In 1958, Cushing had joined the staff of Old Sturbridge Village, an outdoor history museum, as a research assistant, while continuing to

---

[1] The two Cushings were not related.

[2] Riley made it a point to know the researchers, especially those who came for extended periods. His first action was to invite the researcher to lunch. When this writer, then a graduate student at the University of Washington, entered the Society in the mid-1950s, Riley promptly introduced himself and, a few days later, invited me to lunch at an elegant French restaurant. As I later learned, this was no contrived public relations gambit. This was the essence of the man.

work on his doctorate. He received the degree in 1959. The following year Riley offered him the position of assistant librarian and, to his "great joy," Cushing accepted.[3]

Three years later, in October 1963, Riley relinquished the librarian's title and elevated Cushing into the position. He invested him with the responsibilities of managing the library and acquiring all printed material, while Riley retained the responsibility of acquiring manuscripts, an activity he passionately enjoyed.

An industrious, "quiet, self-contained person," Cushing proved to be an invaluable helpmate to Riley.[4] Cushing's father had been a building contractor, and the son had acquired a wide range of skills relating to construction, from carpentry to plumbing to electricity. Cushing played a major role in planning and implementing Riley's physical improvements, including the Shattuck wing. He was singularly responsible for planning and developing the Society's paper conservation laboratory in 1972. There had been a preservation program at the Society since the late nineteenth century, but it was a minor effort and not highly organized. Cushing desired a well-equipped laboratory staffed by a professional conservation specialist. After consulting with Harold Tribolet, manager of the highly reputed Extra Bindery of the Lakeside Press in Chicago, Cushing developed the facility he envisioned.[5]

While the Shattuck wing was being completed, Riley and the Council turned their attention to the Hemenway Apartments, which the Society had purchased in 1966 for future expansion. Because of the poor physical condition of the building, the Society decided to evict the tenants, demolish it, and use the space for parking until acquiring the financial means to construct a new annex. In the interim, the entire area would be "screened by an adequate fence or wall of presentable appearance."[6]

---

[3] Riley wrote in 1987 that when he hired Cushing "a happy triumvirate was formed [Riley, Cushing, Freiberg] that worked closely together until our retirement years arrived." M.H.S., *Procs.*, 99(1987):170.

[4] In addition to his duties as librarian, Cushing was an active scholar. He specialized in early American legal history and published widely in this field. He also served as a member of the board of editors of the *New England Quarterly* and its book review editor from 1966 to 1982. See Stephen T. Riley's memoir of Cushing in M.H.S., *Procs.*, 99(1987):168–174.

[5] M.H.S., *Procs.*, 99(1987):172.

[6] M.H.S. Council Records, Dec. 9, 1971 (M.H.S. Archives).

The Massachusetts Historical Society

The Society hired a firm from Quincy to level the building. The firm applied to the city and received a demolition permit. The Society then applied to the Boston Redevelopment Authority (BRA), the city agency responsible for urban planning and new construction, for a zoning variance. The Society informed the BRA that the property was to serve as a temporary parking lot and an addition would be constructed in "about ten years."

While hopeful that the BRA would grant the variance, Riley was mindful of a meeting he had had with officials of that agency in March 1970 at which he had spelled out the Society's plan. They were "anxious that the Society not demolish any of its buildings on Hemenway Street, if that can be avoided."[7] It, therefore, could not have come as a complete surprise to Riley and the Council when the BRA rejected their application.[8]

While denying the variance, the BRA offered to survey the apartment complex for code violations. Under the circumstances, the Society decided to accept the offer since it "did not wish to be in the position of a slum landlord." At the same time, it did not want to enter into an arrangement whereby the property would be alienated for a long period.[9] It was still intent upon demolition as soon as possible.

The BRA survey uncovered numerous violations, some of them major. The roof, for example, leaked and needed to be replaced. To correct all of the problems would cost the Society, according to preliminary estimates, the enormous sum of $750,000.[10] Realizing that it would never recover an adequate return on this investment, the Council again voted to demolish the structure and made a second appeal to the BRA.

This time the Society was successful. A BRA official decided "that he did not see how the city could object to the Society's proposed demolition of its apartment buildings in view of their condition and the cost of

[7] M.H.S. Council Records, Mar. 12, 1970 (M.H.S. Archives).

[8] M.H.S. Council Records, Oct. 17, 1971 (M.H.S. Archives). Joseph Berlandi, the Fenway area project director for the BRA, told a newspaper reporter that he had repeatedly warned the Society that his agency would oppose its attempt to secure a zoning variance, that it had earmarked Hemenway Street for rehabilitation. *Boston Ledger*, Jan. 5, 1973. A reporter from *The Real Paper* found the BRA's position to be hypocritical. This agency, he wrote, "had been known to tear down whole neighborhoods and replace them with parking lots." Jan. 10, 1973.

[9] M.H.S. Council Records, Oct. 17, 1971 (M.H.S. Archives).

[10] *The Real Paper*, Jan. 10, 1973.

putting them in presentable condition."[11] Heartened by this decision, the Society moved swiftly to remove all tenants from the building by the end of the year. Demolition would then follow.

The Society sent the tenants their notices in October 1972, and the process of removal began.[12] A number of tenants were in arrears in their rental payments but the Society decided to absorb this loss, which came to about $9,000.[13] By December, "there were about one sticky tenant in each building."[14] At the end of the year, there was only one tenant left, Dennis Doyle, who refused to move as a matter of principle. The Society made a "token stop" in its plans for demolition, awaiting his departure. To hasten it, the Society ordered the gas company to shut off his supply.[15] With the exception of the obstinate Doyle, all was proceeding smoothly at this juncture.

Then the problems began. One of the evicted tenants was David Scondras, a bright young lawyer and social activist who had developed a strong interest in Boston's housing problems, especially in the Fenway district. He was an avid advocate of "affordable housing" and unalterably opposed to commercial development or the expansion of non-profit institutions, be they medical, religious, cultural, or educational. Scondras enlisted the support of a number of Back Bay community groups and initiated legal action against the Society. He appealed to the Boston housing court to issue a temporary injunction to stay the demolition of the apartment complex. After weighing the arguments of both parties, Judge Paul Garrity issued a restraining order. He also decreed that those tenants who had been evicted, like Scondras, were free to return to their apartments.

Buoyed by this victory, Scondras and his cohorts embarked upon a media campaign designed to preserve the apartments as residential stock. They portrayed the Society as a heartless, elitist institution intent upon ousting infirm, indigent senior citizens from their low-cost homes.[16] They conveniently disregarded the fact that the bulk of the Hemenway Apartments residents were college students, not senior citizens.

[11] M.H.S. Council Records, Feb. 10, 1972 (M.H.S. Archives).
[12] M.H.S. Council Records, Oct. 12, 1972 (M.H.S. Archives).
[13] M.H.S. Council Records, Nov. 9, 1972 (M.H.S. Archives).
[14] M.H.S. Council Records, Dec. 12, 1972 (M.H.S. Archives).
[15] *The Real Paper*, Jan. 10, 1973.
[16] *Boston Globe*, Jan. 3, 1973.

Scondras and his group also organized and staged a demonstration in front of the Society during the noon hour on January 2, 1973. About thirty students and senior citizens paraded in front of the Boylston Street quarters chanting anti-Society slogans. They carried signs reading:

"Dear Liberals Please Wake Up"
"History or Shelter?"
"Save Our Housing"
"Who Wants to Park There?"
"From 9 to 5, No Parking in My Bedroom"
"Why Are These Buildings Empty?"

Joining the protestors were newly-elected State Representatives Melvin King and Barney Frank and State Senator Jack Bachman, whose sign read: "No More Luxury Housing."[17] Receiving word that a demonstration was to take place on January 2, Society officials "locked its doors for the day to both the public and the press."

Scondras notified the media of the demonstration and they came in force. The noisy pickets attracted television crews and radio and newspaper reporters. The Society suddenly found itself featured on television and radio newscasts and in newspaper accounts.

Fearful that the protestors might become violent and inflict physical damage against its headquarters, the Council took the precaution of hiring and positioning security guards at the building from closing time until it opened in the morning, and twenty-four hours on weekends. This was an additional financial strain on an already tight budget. During this period, a rash of suspicious fires broke out in the Fenway district, not far from the Society. This development heightened the fears of Society officials.[18] The Council thereby authorized the expenditure of $3,000 to $4,000 to install protective doors leading to the stacks on four of its floors and a rolled screen on the first and second floors, which was

[17] A developer had proposed to the Society that the apartments be considerably upgraded. Scondras told a *Boston Herald-American* (Jan. 3, 1973) reporter that the Society "will tear the buildings down first, present the city with a pile of rubble and then say 'let us build a parking lot'."

[18] An intensive investigation by authorities revealed that the fires had been set by an arson ring for insurance purposes. Scondras was credited with solving these crimes. His investigative work led to the arrest of the arsonists, who were later convicted and sent to prison.

to be pulled down and secured every evening when the building closed.[19] These were tense times for the staff.

But no violence occurred. The Scondras faction confined its campaign to a war of words. The director of the Boston Center for Older Americans and fourteen other leaders of community organizations sent a stern letter to the Society in which they asserted their determination to oppose the plan for demolition. The community leaders also stressed their exclusion from Society activities, thereby underscoring, in a subtle manner, the institution's elitist character: "We are aware of your basic sincerity in existing as a public good; yet sincerity is not what we want. We want our homes." They also enclosed a copy of the restraining order prohibiting the Society from demolishing the structure. They sent a copy of their letter to the community newspaper, which readily printed it.

Negative publicity soon began to take its toll. A reporter from *The Real Paper*, a liberal weekly, visited President Thomas B. Adams in his State Street office, which he described as "a stark clutter of ancient Victorian office furniture that could have been the setting for Melville's 'Bartleby the Scrivener,'" and found the president "a little confused by all the adverse publicity." Adams told the reporter: "We tried to handle this thing decently. . . . We've even been considering a little urban park for the area . . . along with the parking lot, though."

The reporter continued:

> The decision to tear down the building had been made in a vacuum. Adams, the soul of propriety, had obviously been unaware of the symbolism of the act: the outrage of a tax-exempt institution pulling down an apartment building in a time when apartments are scarce was bad enough, but to replace it with a parking lot! . . . When the pickets and TV cameras drove the irony home last week, he seemed ready for some sort of compromise.[20]

Adams was ready to cut his losses. The Society was in a no-win situation. It was being severely pressured to preserve a near-slum dwelling for low-cost housing but, before offering rentals, must renovate the building. Adams's numerous meetings with city officials, neighborhood groups, and other activists, in which he and Riley had explained their future plans and pled for understanding and cooperation, had failed to succeed. Scondras and his allies would not yield.

[19] M.H.S. Council Records, Jan. 11, 1973 (M.H.S. Archives).
[20] *The Real Paper*, Jan. 10, 1973.

The Society offered to lease the apartments to any responsible person or organization for a nominal rent for a period of fifteen years on condition that the person or organization pay the taxes and assume the cost of renovation. One organization, the Boston Center for Older Americans, appeared to be a serious prospect to utilize the building. It was unable to secure the necessary financing for rehabilitation, however, and their plans fell by the wayside.[21]

Shocked by the original estimate for renovation, the Society called in other construction analysts and discovered that the building could be made suitable for habitation and meet code at a cost far less than that projected earlier. One outside appraiser conveyed the more palatable news that "between $185,000 to $200,000 was needed to do the minimum rehabilitation."[22] Whatever developed, the Society was determined to hold title to the property "under any circumstances." This land was vital for future expansion.

Early in 1973, the Society received the news that the "injunction forbidding the demolition of the property had been removed without prejudice."[23] While the report was welcomed, it was a Pyrrhic victory. The Society now had a legal right to level the building, but the opposition by neighborhood groups had grown so intense that it hesitated to exercise this option. There was a constant drumbeat of criticism being directed against the Society.

By August 1973, the Society knew that it had lost the battle. It conceded defeat, agreeing to renovate the building and continuing to operate it as low-cost housing. In the lease arrangements with tenants, however, it inserted a seventeen-year time limit into the contract.[24] Thus, in 1990, it would have the legal right to terminate the use of the building as a rental property.

The estimated cost of the renovation was $213,000. Playing the role of a good neighbor and anxious to facilitate the expansion of low-cost housing in the Fenway district, the First Church of Christ, Scientist

[21] M.H.S. Council Records, Feb. 8, Mar. 8, 1973 (M.H.S. Archives).

[22] M.H.S. Council Records, Mar. 8, 1973 (M.H.S. Archives).

[23] M.H.S. Council Records, Mar. 8, 1973 (M.H.S. Archives).

[24] In addition to approving the lease, the Council also approved a Management Agreement with Edwin D. Abrams, Inc., and a Construction Contract with Sidney L. Kumins, Inc. M.H.S. Council Records, Aug. 24, 1973 (M.H.S. Archives).

agreed to lend the Society $50,000 at a modest 5 percent annual interest rate.[25] The renovation was completed by December 1973, and tenants began to occupy the apartments. By March 1974, all but three of the units were filled. On March 14, Mayor Kevin White came to the Society and addressed more than eighty neighborhood residents, praising both groups for their resolution of the vexing problem.[26] The apartments were completely occupied by October.[27] The controversial Hemenway Apartment issue was at an end, for the time being.

Riley made innumerable contributions to the Society, but his most enduring achievement was his acquisition of historical manuscripts. This was his "true love."[28] He was, as his colleagues referred to him, "a manuscript hound extraordinary," one of a kind.[29] John Cushing may have mixed his metaphors in his description, but he was entirely accurate when he called Riley "that great vacuum cleaner of the collecting world, whose keen senses almost seemed to detect the odor of 17th- and 18th-century papers being opened anywhere within a 50- or 100-mile radius of Boston."[30] As a compulsive collector of manuscripts, Riley conceded that he had "sticky fingers."[31] If he was not the most acquisitive and successful institutional collector of manuscripts in the history of the United States, he was certainly near the top of the list. In the judgment of his colleagues, "where institutional collecting has been concerned, Steve Riley wrote the book."[32] He deserves to be ranked with Jeremy Belknap and Lyman Copeland Draper of the State Historical Society of Wisconsin in this activity.[33]

One can gain a partial insight into the volume and scope of Riley's

[25] M.H.S. Council Records, Aug. 24, 1973 (M.H.S. Archives); Riley, *Years of Stewardship*, 111.

[26] M.H.S. Council Records, Feb. 14, Mar. 14, 1974 (M.H.S. Archives).

[27] M.H.S. Council Records, Oct. 10, 1974 (M.H.S. Archives).

[28] Riley, *Years of Stewardship*, 110.

[29] Riley, *Years of Stewardship*, xi.

[30] M.H.S., *Procs.*, 89(1977):219.

[31] Riley, *Years of Stewardship*, 121.

[32] Riley, *Years of Stewardship*, xi.

[33] On Draper as a collector, see: William B. Hesseltine, *Pioneer's Mission: The Story of Lyman Copeland Draper* (Madison, Wisc., 1954); Larry Gara, "Lyman Copeland Draper," in Clifford L. Lord, ed., *Keepers of the Past* (Chapel Hill, 1965), 40–52.

acquisitions by reading his published annual reports as librarian and director, which cover only the years 1951 to 1976.[34] He continued to collect when he was director, so powerful was the compulsion. His reports contain a staggering list of accessions. While the Society had accumulated a massive corpus of manuscripts before Riley began his employment, it had one of the nation's largest and most important collections when he retired. In 1954, the compilers of the *Harvard Guide to American History*, six distinguished historians from Harvard University, wrote: "The Massachusetts Historical Society ... houses the most important collection of American manuscripts outside the Library of Congress."[35] That statement of high praise was, in part, a tribute to the collecting of Riley.

Riley was the reincarnation of Belknap. He had a ferret's nose for manuscripts. Once he had the scent, he jumped the leash, his eyes bright with battle. He was an unrelenting pursuer of his quarry. Malcolm Freiberg has written that "adding to the Society's collection was a joy [for Riley]. He could outwait the most tenacious collector, in the end making a donor *want* to give an assemblage of materials to the Society, knowing that Steve Riley would faithfully see to their maintenance and availability to scholars."[36]

If it took years to achieve his objective, he was prepared to wait. In the late 1920s, the Lodge family placed on deposit in the Society the papers of United States Sen. Henry Cabot Lodge, one of the dominant political figures of his age. It was an appropriate decision by the family, since the Society owned the papers of their ancestors dating back to their arrival in New England in the early seventeenth century. However, Riley was troubled by the fact that Senator Lodge's papers were only "on deposit" and not a gift. The family could withdraw the documents at its pleasure and place them elsewhere. Riley feared their loss. He knew he was in a competitive business. Many other research institutions would have accepted them at a moment's notice.

For years, Riley persistently but discreetly pursued this matter with Ambassador Henry Cabot Lodge, the senator's grandson and longtime

[34] These have been brought together in Riley, *Years of Stewardship*.

[35] Oscar Handlin et al., *Harvard Guide to American History* (Cambridge, Mass., 1954), 59.

[36] Letter to the author, Aug. 16, 1993.

member of the Society. Whenever their paths crossed, he tactfully and subtly raised the issue. Riley wrote in 1969: "I am certain that at times I reminded Ambassador Lodge of Francis Thompson's poem 'The Hound of Heaven,' for I did indeed pursue him down the years 'with unhurrying chase and unperturbed pace.'" On September 19, 1969, he made his "kill." The ambassador signed the deed of gift to the Society. The acquisition, Riley wrote, "gave me the greatest personal satisfaction."[37]

At an earlier date, Ambassador Lodge had placed on deposit in the Society the papers of his father, George Cabot Lodge, a poet. There were also his own papers to consider since he, too, had had a long and remarkable political and diplomatic career. For the time, the ambassador was storing these documents in his home in Beverly. Riley had more work to do.[38]

Riley racked up successes every year he served as librarian and director, but he had a banner year in 1956. As he wrote in his 1957 annual report: "After reporting last year the acquisition of the Adams Papers, the Paul Revere Papers, and certain Francis Parkman Papers, your librarian felt like some one who had won the Pulitzer Prize at the age of sixteen. What else was there to live for?"[39]

The most significant addition to the library in 1957 was a collection of Thomas Jefferson letters, 282 all told, dating from 1775 to 1827 and consisting of his correspondence with business agents and overseers, and letters between the sage of Monticello, his daughters, and their respective husbands. In this case, Riley played no active role in the acquisition, which came one month after he was appointed director, but he was deeply excited by the gift. Thomas Jefferson Coolidge III of Boston, who made the donation, was merely continuing a tradition of philanthropy instituted by his grandfather at the close of the nineteenth century.

The Coolidge-Jefferson connection began in 1825 when Joseph Coolidge married Jefferson's granddaughter, Eleonora Wayles Randolph. The son of this union, aptly named Thomas Jefferson Coolidge,

[37] Riley, *Years of Stewardship*, 89.

[38] Riley secured the bulk of Ambassador Lodge's papers as a gift before he retired. This writer was involved in additional acquisitions, including Lodge's significant Vietnam War journal and a remarkable collection of correspondence between his grandfather and Theodore Roosevelt.

[39] Riley, *Years of Stewardship*, 51.

purchased over 9,000 of his great-grandfather's manuscripts from the Randolph family, who had inherited them, and, in 1898, donated them to the Society, of which he was a resident member. The Society was about to move into its new home on Boylston Street, and Coolidge deemed it a proper repository for the collection. In conferring the gift, he stated that his action should be viewed "as a sign that all party feeling had long ceased to exist, and that the two States of Virginia and Massachusetts, where Jefferson's blood had intermingled, treasured alike his memory."[40]

Coolidge's remarkable gift consisted of approximately 8,800 pieces of correspondence, of which 3,280 were letters written by Jefferson and 4,360 letters received by him. It also included his garden book, 1766–1824; his farm book, 1773–1824; annotated almanacs from 1771 to 1776; account books for 1783–1790; manuscript expense accounts from 1804 to 1825; notes on the weather spanning the years 1802–1816; plans of American forts in 1765; law treatises from 1778 to 1788; legal papers for the period 1770–1772; and the catalogue of his personal library. Here was a treasure trove of incalculable historical value. And this was only the beginning.

Coolidge's son, Thomas Jefferson Coolidge, Jr., visited Monticello in 1911 and discovered a large number of Jefferson's original architectural drawings of his home. These documents were owned by two of Jefferson's great-great-granddaughters. Coolidge purchased many of the more significant drawings and, emulating his father, carted them off to Boston and donated them to the Society, of which he was also a member. He continued to collect additional Jefferson materials in subsequent years and in 1937 made a second gift to the Society. This donation included three volumes of "Acts of the Virginia Assembly," 1764–1765 and 1770–1772, two of which were believed to be Jefferson's personal copies; correspondence between Jefferson and his business agents; correspondence between his daughters, Martha and Maria, and their husbands; and over 200 architectural drawings. Thus, over a period of sixty years, in four separate gifts, the Coolidge family made the Massachusetts Historical Society a major repository of Jefferson holdings, much to the consternation of Virginians.

[40] M.H.S., *Procs.*, 2d ser., 12(1897–1899):264–265.

Watchdog and Manuscript Hound Extraordinary

Riley not only had a passion for collecting manuscripts, he also thoroughly enjoyed reading them. As a professional historian, he knew the value of these raw materials. They yielded insights into historical events that no secondary works could match. He spent a considerable amount of his spare time perusing documents. Again, the testimony of his colleague, Malcolm Freiberg: "He savored most of all those days when, incoming correspondence and outgoing obligations early dispensed with, he could sit at his work table, assess a recently received manuscript, and make sense of it in context."[41]

In many of his annual reports to the members, Riley quoted at length from either historically significant or intrinsically interesting documents he had acquired in the course of the year. Riley's values as a collector of manuscripts, as well as a human being, were suggested by the document he selected to end a talk he had prepared for a meeting of the Society in May 1952. The presentation was titled "Some Aspects of the Society's Manuscript Collection" and complemented an exhibition of documents then on display in Ellis Hall, then still the museum area. Riley urged his audience to view this "humble document," which contained the signatures of thirty-nine "relatively obscure" people from Salem, Massachusetts, who had had the courage to defend Rebecca Nurse, during the celebrated witchcraft craze of the seventeenth century. Nurse had been accused of being a witch.

> We whos nams Are heareunto subscribed being desiered by Goodman Nurse to declare what we knewe concerning his wiues conversation for time past: we cane testyfie to all whom it may concerne that we haue knowne her for many years and Acording to our obseruation her Life and conuersation was Acording to her profession and we neuer had Any cause or grounds to suspect her of Any such thing as she is nowe Acused of.

Riley concluded that "this is one of the truly great documents of Massachusetts history."[42]

Almost all of Riley's special acquisitions, such as manuscripts and rare books, were gifts. As he wrote in 1951, "there is no sweeter word than 'gift' to a Librarian with a small book fund."[43] Like every other area of

[41] Letter to author, Aug. 16, 1993.

[42] Riley, *Years of Stewardship*, 12. Despite this statement of support, Rebecca Nurse was convicted and executed.

[43] Riley, *Years of Stewardship*, 15.

the Society, the financial condition of the organization also improved markedly during Riley's tenure. When he was appointed director, the market value of the portfolio was nearly $2,320,000. When he retired at the end of 1976, it was close to $7,800,000, an increase of over $5.5 million.

While Riley, John Adams, and Thomas Boylston Adams deserve some of the credit for the strengthening of the endowment because of their success in fund raising, John B. Paine, Jr., who served as treasurer from 1957 to 1970, deserves the bulk of it. Paine was a remarkably astute fiscal manager. After beginning his career as a stock analyst for a bank and brokerage firm, he went into business for himself in 1932, "first as an investment adviser and then as investment attorney for a small group of clients." By 1937, he refused to take on new accounts because he had "all the business he wanted." Paine's efforts in behalf of the Society were free of charge, but, as Riley indicated, "he worked extremely hard to bring its finances into shape." A man of broad-gauged interests and a direct descendant of Robert Treat Paine, a signer of the Declaration of Independence, Paine had a special affection for the Society. He had been elected a resident member in 1954 and served on its Council from 1955 to 1970. He was a generous contributor to the Society's various fund drives, and he also became one of Riley's closest friends.[44]

As treasurer, Paine completely restructured the Society's portfolio. This resulted in a rapid increase of its market value and income return. After Paine had delivered his annual report in 1960, in his "deep, rich voice," President Adams good-naturedly reprimanded him "for not having more clearly underlined the remarkable nature of his performance in increasing the Society's income by more than 40% in the past three years."[45]

While Paine's talents brought benefits to the portfolio, Riley's innate fiscal conservatism helped considerably in keeping the balance sheet of the annual operating budget healthy. As an administrator, Riley was a

[44] For biographical information on Paine, see Riley's memoir in M.H.S., *Procs.*, 88(1976):117–120.

[45] M.H.S., *Procs.*, 88(1976):118. Adams stated to the members at the 1958 annual meeting: "For the first time in many years, perhaps in a generation, the Massachusetts Historical Society finds itself really solvent. This is due much to the efforts of Mr. Paine, who has done a remarkable job of investing the funds and bringing up the income return." Ibid., 72(1957–1960):449.

classic penny-pincher, spending only on essentials. He managed his lean budget with a shrewd, exact, and scrupulous eye. "Whatever you have, spend less," Dr. Samuel Johnson once advised Boswell. Deeply scarred by the Great Depression, Riley also adhered to this conservative fiscal theory. The Society benefited from his parsimonious administrative style. The old New England adage, "waste not, want not," was more than a quaint aphorism to him.[46]

The cost of publications was a constant drain on the Society's financial resources, but Riley was willing to bear it. He was proud of the Society's distinguished record as a publisher, especially its documentary output, which dated from 1792 and the first volume of the *Collections*. Like Jeremy Belknap and Worthington C. Ford, he was firmly committed to the principle of "multiplying the copies." He favored microfilm as well as letterpress publications.

It pleased Riley greatly when he received the type of letter sent to him in 1955 by Professor Merrill Jensen, the well-known early American historian, who requested permission to reproduce some Society manuscripts in a volume of American colonial documents, which he created for the series *English Historical Documents*, an Oxford University Press publication. "When I came to sorting out the documents according to sources in which I found them," wrote Jensen, "I discovered that the Massachusetts Historical Society wins by many lengths! It is not flattery but a simple statement of fact that the Massachusetts Historical Society has published more of what I consider to be the basic documents for early American history than any other society in the country."[47]

One key to a strong program of publication was a first-rate editor. Even before the Council officially appointed him director, Riley turned his attention to filling this vital position. The person he sought was a prom-

---

[46] When not saving money, Riley was out raising funds. He was an aggressive fundraiser, always on the search for new prospects. On Jan. 9, 1958, for example, he informed the Council that the Bostonian Hotel, which adjoined the Society, was being converted into an apartment-hotel for ladies over sixty years of age. The new tenants would have to pay an "admission fee" of $6,000 and a monthly charge of $150 and upwards. Riley regarded this affluent group of ladies as prime prospects for monetary donations. Some Council members shared the director's judgment and "made facetious suggestions about the possibility of contracting for gifts from future tenants of the hotel if, indeed, they had any funds left after paying their rent." M.H.S. Council Records, Jan. 9, 1958 (M.H.S. Archives).

[47] Quoted in Whitehill, *Independent Historical Societies*, ix-x.

ising young scholar, Malcolm Freiberg, whom he had known for many years. Riley first met Freiberg when he came to the Society as a graduate student to do research on his dissertation, a biography of Gov. Thomas Hutchinson.[48] Even then, he was impressed by Freiberg's meticulousness and disciplined work habits, essential qualities for an editor.

Freiberg had received an A.B. in American literature from Middlebury College in 1941. He was awarded an A.M. in 1947 and a Ph.D. in American Civilization in 1951 from Brown University. After receiving his degree, he taught at Hampton Institute [now University] from 1950 to 1951; at Brown University from 1951 to 1953; and at The Pennsylvania State University from 1953 to 1957. Riley extended the offer, Freiberg accepted, and the Council appointed him to the position on October 10, 1957.[49]

Riley made another major appointment to his editorial staff in September 1969 when he hired Marjorie Gutheim as the assistant editor. A graduate of Radcliffe College (1937), she also held a master of teaching degree from the Harvard School of Education (1938), and a Ph.D. in American history from Columbia University (1955), where she had studied under Allan Nevins, one of the nation's preeminent historians. From 1945 to 1969 Gutheim had taught at Mt. Vernon Seminary in Washington, D.C.; she also served as the dean from 1962 to 1969. A prodigious worker and meticulous editor, Gutheim proved to be a valuable assistant to Freiberg and made a major contribution to the publication program.

Having a high-quality, professional staff to process manuscripts was only one essential for a successful publications program. A second paramount need was money, lots of it. As Belknap and every successive Society official eager to publish historical tracts discovered, this was a costly enterprise. Riley was well aware of the problem long before he became director. He had observed Forbes and Mitchell wringing their hands over a lack of funds to go to press.[50] In May 1945, while he was

[48] M.H.S., *Procs.*, 99(1987):170.

[49] M.H.S. Council Records, Oct. 10, 1957 (M.H.S. Archives). This was the same day that the Council made official Riley's appointment as director.

[50] See, for example, Mitchell's 1949 report to the Council, in which he lamented the lack of funds to publish a volume of *Proceedings*, and other vital works. "The gap between income and cost of publication grows wider year by year. The cost of printing is rising by leaps and bounds." M.H.S., *Procs.*, 69(1947–1950):479–482.

in military service, Assistant Editor Eleanor Bates informed him of a bit of Society business that was all-too-familiar to him:

> The chief news in the Editorial Department is that the current members of the Winthrop family have come forward with a check to cover the cost of Volume V of the *Winthrop Papers*, which is virtually ready for press but which was being held up (for three or four years, as we feared) while funds accumulated sufficient to pay for publication. Mr. Forbes may well feel triumphant, not only for having survived as Editor of Volumes III and IV, but for having done a piece of work which won the approval of the Winthrops and elicited cold cash as a symbol thereof! Unfortunately, few outsiders can appreciate the nature of the triumph.[51]

Riley had no surplus of funds available when a manuscript was ready to be converted into a publication. In 1964, he expressed the hope that he would see the day when there were adequate funds for publications "so that we need not worry about the next printer's bill."[52] Over the years, a few individuals and old-line families had established endowment funds which yielded income for publications. But these funds were not heavily capitalized and did not generate a great deal of income. The Winthrops had established two such funds and it was still necessary for the family to make an additional gift to produce a volume of documents.[53]

Two publication funds were well endowed. John Langdon Sibley had bequeathed ample funds for the continuation of the monumental *Sibley's Harvard Graduates* series, and William Bradford Homer Dowse had provided sufficient money for the reprinting of the *Journals of the House of Representatives of Massachusetts (1715–1780)*. *Sibley's Harvard Graduates* became one of the Society's most significant and successful publications. Sibley produced the first three volumes of the series and Clifford Kenyon Shipton, the "American Plutarch," authored fourteen more before his death in December 1973.[54]

[51] Drummey, ed., "Bates-Riley Correspondence," 190. The Winthrops provided $5,500 for the publication.

[52] Riley, *Years of Stewardship*, 76.

[53] In 1957, Riley persuaded Treasurer John B. Paine, Jr., and other members of the Paine family to establish a fund to finance the printing of select documents from the Robert Treat Paine papers as part of the *Collections* series. M.H.S., *Procs.*, 72 (1957–1960):443.

[54] For information on Sibley's contribution see: Samuel E. Morison's introduction to the fourth volume of *Sibley's Harvard Graduates*; Rene Bryant, *American Heritage*, 9, pt. 4(1958):28–33, 106–107; C.K. Shipton, *Harvard Library Bulletin*, 9(1955):236–261. For

In Riley's view, there was but one solution to the chronic problem of underfunding, the creation of a well-endowed publication fund. As in the case of the library fund, this reserve would be limited to that single purpose. Riley had no difficulty persuading the Council to establish the fund in 1965. He decided not to use the income from this fund until it had accumulated a principal of $100,000. For the remainder of his tenure, he strove to build up the fund through gifts, the sale of duplicates, and publishers' permission fees for reproducing iconographic materials belonging to the Society. He reached the $100,000 goal in 1975, just prior to his retirement.[55]

In 1964, a federal agency, the National Historical Publications Commission (NHPC), which was a sub-unit of the National Archives, offered to subsidize the micropublication of select manuscript collections. This was a pilot project for the agency. It had conducted a survey of manuscripts of national importance outside of federal depositories and discovered that, of 5,536 cubic feet in the United States, the Massachusetts Historical Society was the largest holder with 364 cubic feet.[56] Because of the extent and quality of the Boston society's holdings, and because of its demonstrated willingness to "multiply the copies" and make them available to scholars, the NHPC selected it as the first in the nation to receive a grant; the sum was $30,000.

Riley favored the Society's involvement, but he was aware that the Council was apprehensive about accepting governmental grants because of a possible loss of its independence. Riley assured the Council that its fears were groundless and the Society and the historical profession stood

---

biographical information on the incredibly productive Shipton, see Harley Holden's memoir in *The Harvard Librarian*, 10(1973–1974):1–3; and Stephen T. Riley's moving memoir in M.H.S., *Procs.*, 85(1973):130–135. Riley and Shipton were close friends. "We went to so many [historical] conventions together," wrote Riley, "that we were often referred to as the Smith brothers." Shipton explained his distinctive methodology in developing the biographical sketches in his introduction to *New England Life in the 18th Century* (Cambridge, Mass., 1963), xv-xxvii.

[55] Riley, *Years of Stewardship*, 119.

[56] Behind the Society were: Yale University, 344 cubic feet; Historical Society of Pennsylvania, 263 cubic feet; Clements Library, 250 cubic feet; Harvard University's Houghton Library, 244 cubic feet; New York Public Library, 200 cubic feet; New-York Historical Society, 170 cubic feet; University of North Carolina, 152 cubic feet; New York State Library, 150 cubic feet; and Cornell University Library, 124 cubic feet. M.H.S. Council Records, Dec. 10, 1964 (M.H.S. Archives).

to benefit from an association with the governmental agency. He was successful in this effort and, in 1965, the NHPC awarded the grant.[57] These were the first public funds the Society had ever received. In 1966 the NHPC awarded the Society a second grant for additional filming.[58]

Women members! For many years these two words constituted an oxymoron to members of the Society. These men were in full accord with John Adams's assertion that "History is not the Province of the Ladies."[59] The first woman to cross the gender barrier was Frances Manwaring Caulkins, but she was a corresponding member (1849–1869) and, living in Connecticut, never appeared at a meeting in the Tremont Street clubhouse and so represented no threat to the all-male bastion.[60] Through the remainder of the nineteenth century and well into the twentieth, there was no further reference in the official records to electing women into membership, corresponding or resident. Not even such progressive and seemingly enlightened leaders as Charles F. Adams or Worthington C. Ford raised the issue. Both were intent upon increasing the resident membership, but only with males.

The issue finally arose at the Council meeting of February 10, 1949, when the "question of admitting women to membership was also discussed" but was quietly laid to rest.[61] By the late 1950s, however, the winds of change began to stir in the United States and the admission of women members was no longer a subject of ribald humor. Riley and Adams became aware of the new *zeitgeist* and gave serious thought to removing the gender barrier.[62] In 1958, Adams arranged to have one of

[57] M.H.S. Council Records, Dec. 10, 1964 (M.H.S. Archives).

[58] Riley, *Years of Stewardship*, 79, 81–82.

[59] John Adams to Elbridge Gerry, Apr. 17, 1813, Warren-Adams Letters, 2:380, M.H.S., *Colls.*, vol. 73; letterbook copy, Adams Papers, M.H.S. Adams was commenting on Mercy Otis Warren and her *History*.

[60] By contrast, the Boston Athenaeum, another fusty Yankee institution, began to admit women as members in 1829. An Athenaeum promotional document justified the admission of women in these words: "whatever raises the character of men has a favorable influence upon the other sex." See *Change and Continuity: A Pictorial History of the Boston Athenaeum* (Boston, 1976), 6.

[61] M.H.S. Council Records, Feb. 10, 1949 (M.H.S. Archives).

[62] Adams informed this writer that his close friend Judge Charles E. Wyzanski, Jr., constantly badgered him to elect women members, urging him to "get to it!" Adams admitted being heavily influenced by Wyzanski's prodding. Interview on Oct. 20, 1993.

his colleagues on the Council, Charles P. Curtis, introduce the subject of women membership at the April meeting. Adams cautioned Curtis on moving carefully and slowly on this potentially explosive issue:

> I do not think the matter should be discussed on the floor of the Society until it has been discussed in the Council. I know that outside of the Council there is some rather strong opposition to the idea and I think the matter should be handled with care. It would be my suggestion that we discuss the matter somewhat informally in the Council and after a meeting or two if there is a strong feeling in the Council, then the matter can be brought next year before the membership.[63]

Curtis raised the issue at the April 10, 1958, Council meeting but it "generated rather more heat than light during an extended discussion."[64]

While the subject was beginning to reach a high degree of seriousness, there were still occasions when the members lapsed back to their old chauvinistic ways. At the Council meeting of February 12, 1959, for example, in an apparent effort to inject some levity into the somber proceedings, Director Riley circulated an advertisement he had received in the mail for some pornographic postcards and then inquired, facetiously, if he should pursue the matter. The recording secretary, the waggish Walter M. Whitehill, wrote: "It was suggested that the naked lady displayed on the sample was undoubtedly being proposed for membership. Mr. Curtis spoke warmly in favor of her election."[65]

In 1965, Thomas B. Adams introduced the topic of women members at a meeting of the resources commission, a special body he had appointed to study the future direction of the Society. The secretary *pro tem* failed to sense the historical importance of the issue and merely recorded: "The President then brought up the question of admitting women members to the Society and there was considerable discussion of the matter." The historian longs to know the content of that "considerable discussion." In its report to the Society, the resources commission did not make a mention of electing women members.

Adams and Riley made their first assault against the barrier in 1966. They succeeded in electing two women as corresponding members:

[63] Thomas B. Adams to Charles P. Curtis, Mar. 25, 1958 (M.H.S. Archives).
[64] M.H.S. Council Records, Apr. 10, 1958 (M.H.S. Archives).
[65] M.H.S. Council Records, Feb. 12, 1959 (M.H.S. Archives).

Watchdog and Manuscript Hound Extraordinary

Cicely Veronica Wedgwood of England, an accomplished historian of the seventeenth century, biographer, and friend of Adams; and Ola Elizabeth Winslow, a highly-regarded professor of American literature who had taught at Wellesley College and other major academic institutions and whose biography of Jonathan Edwards had been awarded the Pulitzer Prize in 1941. The door was now partially open.

The following year, Riley exerted his influence upon the membership committee and secured the election of the first woman resident member, Esther Forbes. This historic "first" took place at the Society meeting of February 9, 1967, one hundred and seventy-six years after the founding of the organization. This was a major breakthrough of the once-impenetrable gender barrier.

Forbes was an appropriate choice for the role of pioneer. She had won the 1943 Pulitzer Prize in history for her highly-acclaimed biography, *Paul Revere and the World He Lived In*. A native and resident of Worcester, she was a longtime friend of Riley. She had spent considerable time at the Society while researching her biography; the Paul Revere Papers were there. As an author, she was a stickler for detail and authenticity. Riley once found her perched on a stepladder in the Society's reading room, peering intently through her thick glasses at John Vanderspriet's 1688 portrait of Increase Mather. When she climbed down, Riley asked her what she was doing. "I wanted to know the color of his eyes, Stephen," she replied, "and, damn it, I can't be sure."[66] Unfortunately, Forbes's membership was of brief duration, six months, as she died on August 12, 1967.

In 1969, Lyman Butterfield, editor of *The Adams Papers* and a strong proponent for removing the gender barrier to membership, nominated Caroline Robbins, an accomplished academic scholar who specialized in colonial American history and frequently conducted research at the Society. She was elected in 1970.

Four more women were elected to membership in 1972, each one co-sponsored by Adams, Riley, or Butterfield, together with a growing number of like-minded men.[67] The new corresponding members were

---

[66] M.H.S., *Procs.*, 79(1967):205. Riley's memoir of Forbes is on 204–205. Forbes was known for her quick wit. Someone once inquired about her progress on a book she was writing. Forbes's response was: "It's something like putting an octopus to bed."

[67] M.H.S. Nomination Book (M.H.S. Archives).

Barbara Wertheim Tuchman, the prolific author-historian who wrote a spate of best-selling books, from *The Guns of August* (1962) to *Stillwell and the American Experience in China* (1971), both of which were awarded the Pulitzer Prize for history; and Elizabeth Hamer Kegan, a leading library and archival administrator and top executive at the Library of Congress. The resident members were Amelia Forbes Emerson of Concord, who was linked to a host of prominent literati of the past, including Ralph Waldo Emerson; and Louisa Dresser Campbell, an accomplished art historian at the Worcester Art Museum and a close personal friend of Riley.

Six other women achieved membership during the Adams-Riley era. In 1973, Cecelia Marie Kenyon, of Smith College, was elected a resident member and Mina Kirstein Curtiss, of Bethel, Connecticut, a corresponding member. In 1975, Kathryn Lee Conway Preyer, of Wellesley College; Winifred Virginia Collins, the Society's reference librarian; and Kathryn Buhler, an expert on early American silver, were elected resident members, and in 1976 Nina Fletcher Little, the American folk art specialist, became a corresponding member. The tally for the Adams-Riley era was seven resident members and six corresponding members. This opened the door for the election of numerous other women members.

Both Riley and Adams were determined to make the Society a more vibrant institution for the members and their spouses and its growing legion of friends, male and female. Both believed that lively social and educational programs held within the Society's quarters would strengthen these people's interest in the organization and make them more responsive to solicitations for funds. For these reasons, in 1963 they instituted the "Evening Gatherings." There were to be three of these annually. They were to be black-tie programs and feature lectures in Ellis Hall by prominent speakers, preferably Society members; exhibitions in the Oliver Room and adjoining areas of the second floor, complementing the speakers' topics and drawn from the varied holdings of the Society; and a post-lecture reception in the Dowse Library.[68]

The first gala was scheduled for December 6, 1963. The speaker was to be Arthur M. Schlesinger, one of the nation's most prominent his-

[68] Speakers were almost always drawn from the membership because the Society did not provide honoraria.

torians and special assistant to President John F. Kennedy. Both Schlesinger and Kennedy were members of the Society.[69]

When the invitations were in the mail, tragedy struck. President Kennedy was assassinated in Dallas, Texas, on November 22, 1963. Adams and Riley promptly convened to consider cancelling the program. A Democrat in political conviction, Adams revered Kennedy. Riley was also a strong supporter of the president. The two officials decided to "hold it as planned, disregarding our private feelings." As Adams informed the audience at the Society: "It does give us an opportunity to speak out publicly concerning him. In modern times no chief executive has so enthusiastically encouraged the study of history. One must return to the age of John Adams and Thomas Jefferson to find Presidents who sought to learn so much from the past, who believed so passionately that the study of history is a national duty."

The program attracted a capacity audience of resident members, invited friends, "and their ladies." Ellis Hall, a library room by day, "on this evening [was] transformed into a great assembly room made brilliant with illumination, conversation, and multi-hued evening dress." In place of his announced address, a somber Schlesinger delivered a "sensitive and perceptive" eulogy of Kennedy.[70] Adams followed with a brief disquisition on "Of Plimoth Plantation," "deftly touching on certain events and personalities in that colony more than three centuries ago with wit and imagination."

---

[69] While President Kennedy was not an active member, he valued his association with the Society. On May 9, 1961, he wrote to Thomas B. Adams: "I have learned with greatest pleasure that the Massachusetts Historical Society has proposed my name for resident membership. This is of course a high distinction, and I should be delighted to accept membership if the Society acts favorably at its May meeting. It brings me special pleasure that my name is under consideration on an occasion when you will hear a paper delivered by Professor Morison, whose writings have given me the greatest satisfaction since my school days." (M.H.S. Archives).

On Oct. 8, 1964, after the Society established an award in memory of the late president, Jacqueline Kennedy sent a telegram to Thomas B. Adams: "I would like on behalf of the Kennedy family to express our deep appreciation to the membership of the Massachusetts Historical Society for its decision to award a John F. Kennedy Medal for Distinguished Service to the cause of history. My husband was very proud of his membership in the Society. I do not believe that any recognition could have pleased him more." (M.H.S. Archives).

[70] Schlesinger's remarks are published in M.H.S., *Procs.*, 75(1963):113–117.

After the speeches, Adams and the guests moved up the grand staircase to the second floor to view an exhibition on Plymouth Colony and "to partake of refreshments in the Dowse Library." The program lasted until midnight. It was both a solemn and socially invigorating evening.[71]

It was also an evening of near-disaster for Director Riley, his wife, and Treasurer Paine. While returning home on that "clear, wonderful night," they were involved in a serious automobile accident. Paine, the driver, was nearly killed, suffering multiple injuries. Riley's head smashed against the windshield, and he spent three days in the hospital. Alice Riley was badly injured and remained in the hospital for two weeks.[72]

At the Society meeting the following week, Adams commented on the success of the gala and reported a donation of $25 "from a delighted Member present at the first evening affair to be used only for potables at the second evening affair," scheduled for January 24, 1964.[73] On a more serious note, he stated that members Lyman H. Butterfield and Samuel E. Morison "had donated their payments received for testimonials written in memory of the late President Kennedy as the nucleus of a John F. Kennedy Fund."[74]

In January 1964, the second evening gathering drew another capacity audience. Ellis Hall "glittered with illumination, floral decorations, and brilliant evening garb." Professor Bernard Bailyn, the eminent historian from Harvard University, discussed "Pamphlets of the American Revolution: The Literature of Rebellion." Speaking "informally and with a sure touch," Bailyn explored the role of colonial American pamphlet literature, pointing out its contributions and its drawbacks." He also read excerpts from the pamphlets. The guests then moved to the second floor to view an exhibition of colonial American pamphlets and share a collation and potation. The three-hour program was, "like its predecessor, a distinct success."[75]

---

[71] M.H.S., *Procs.*, 75(1963):144–145.

[72] Telephone interview with Mrs. Stephen T. Riley, Mar. 11, 1994.

[73] The donor, William B. Osgood, inserted a note with his gift in which he specified that it be used for "nothing but liquor." M.H.S. Council Records, Dec. 12, 1963 (M.H.S. Archives).

[74] Their combined donation was $450. M.H.S. Council Records, Dec. 12, 1963 (M.H.S. Archives).

[75] M.H.S., *Procs.*, 76(1964):173–174.

Watchdog and Manuscript Hound Extraordinary

The final evening gathering of the year took place before another full house on April 24, 1964. The speaker was Clifford K. Shipton, the Society's Sibley editor, who spoke with wit and humor on "John L. Sibley and His Consequences." An exhibition on Sibley and Harvard College and a reception concluded the evening.[76]

Adams and Riley were elated by the success of these programs. They had added a new dimension to the life of the Society and brought many new people into its orbit. They were particularly pleased by the inclusion of women at these and all other Society social affairs. Riley wrote in 1971: "the presence of the ladies has enlivened our evening gatherings and added a new touch to our Annual Dinner, which the Fellows attended for the first time last year."[77] Malcolm Freiberg, editor of publications, correctly predicted that the evening gathering series "seemed well on its way to becoming a welcome tradition." The program prospered for the remainder of Riley's directorship and to this writing, thirty-three years later.[78]

In the 1970s, largely because of President Adams's wishes, the Society began to hold its annual dinner within its quarters, rather than at neighboring sites. This was in keeping with Adams's conviction that, as in the case of evening gatherings, members, fellows of the library, and friends would develop a stronger interest in the Society if they visited the building frequently. Ellis Hall and the adjoining library room in the Shattuck wing were transformed into a large restaurant. All the library furniture was removed and fifteen to twenty circular tables, each seating eight to ten, were spread about. The tables were adorned with glistening white cloths and candles and flowers. The lights were dimmed in both rooms. It was an elegant physical setting for a formal dinner party. Food and beverages were provided by a caterer who used the basement as a staging area and temporary kitchen.

There were two drawbacks to these affairs. Initially, the program disrupted library activities. Researchers were not able to use this vital facility for most of the day. Secondly, the areas in which the party was held, including the basement, sustained excessive wear and tear, affect-

---

[76] M.H.S., *Procs.*, 76(1964):181.

[77] Riley, *Years of Stewardship*, 102.

[78] The only change has been the relaxation in the dress code. Black tie became optional in the early 1980s, and business attire became standard within the decade.

ing the overall physical condition of the building. Riley was concerned about these factors but did not raise an objection.[79]

While Riley deserves the bulk of the credit for the successes achieved during his directorship, it would be improper to slight the contributions of President Thomas Boylston Adams. He was an active consort of Riley and was in office for over eighteen years, from 1957 to 1976, the third longest presidency in the Society's history. Riley's directorship and Adams's term were almost coterminous. The two men enjoyed and respected each other and worked in close harmony.

Charismatic in personality and iconoclastic in temperament, Adams was a larger-than-life figure.[80] Like his grandfather and father, he was a hands-on leader. He was involved in all aspects of the Society's program without being intrusive. Riley remained firmly in charge of operations. Because of his brilliance as a speaker, Adams was an effective spokesman for the organization at social and public functions.

Adams was particularly active in the fund-raising effort for the Shattuck annex, sharing Riley's enthusiasm for the project. Riley noted: "Perhaps no one in the history of the Society has written so many appealing and charming letters pointing out to members and friends our continuing contributions to history and our current needs—and with such good returns. He is our present-day Lord Chesterfield."[81] In recognition of Adams's good works in behalf of the Society and his contributions to American historical scholarship, the organization awarded him its highest honor in 1975, the John Fitzgerald Kennedy Medal for service to history.[82]

[79] Dinner programs in the Society came to an end shortly after Riley's tenure. Thereafter, they were held in the nearby Harvard Club.

[80] Adams's iconoclasm was reflected by his early and passionate opposition to the Vietnam War, despite the fact that his son was then engaged in the conflict as a helicopter pilot. For his outspoken antiwar activities, which included an unsuccessful run for the United States Senate in 1966, he was placed on John Dean's "enemies list" of the Nixon White House; "partly fortuitous, because of alphabetical precedence," his was the first name on the list. Adams regarded his inclusion on the list as "the greatest honor I ever received." Harvard Class of 1933, *50th Anniversary Report*, 7.

[81] Riley, *Years of Stewardship*, 99.

[82] Adams was the third recipient of the award. Samuel Eliot Morison was the first, receiving it in 1968 and Dumas Malone, the biographer of Thomas Jefferson, was second (1972).

Watchdog and Manuscript Hound Extraordinary

*   *   *

During Adams's presidency, Lyman Butterfield and his staff industriously continued their editorial work on the Adams Papers within an unorthodox administrative arrangement. Since it owned the Adams Papers and was providing Butterfield's staff with a full range of support services, the Society regarded the project as an integral part of its overall program. In reality, however, Butterfield's group functioned as an independent unit. It operated on its own funds and was administered by a special board appointed by the Council. Riley had no direct authority over the project or the staff of four. While he had no direct administrative jurisdiction over this unit, Riley considered the enterprise an integral part of the Society's program. In point of fact, the project had no separate corporate existence. Every grant it received from federal or private agencies, for example, was made payable to the Society, and its employees, in a legal sense, were members of the Society's staff.

This was a complicated and awkward administrative structure, which could have resulted in problems affecting both the project and the Society in a detrimental way. For this arrangement to work effectively, Riley and Butterfield had to maintain a harmonious relationship. Both men were strong-minded and held powerful convictions on a wide range of issues, from politics to intellectual matters. In personality, they were polar opposites. Riley was the essence of congeniality. With his sunny disposition and hail-fellow-well-met personality, he mingled easily with people and had a sharp sense of public relations. Butterfield, on the other hand, was "reticent, reserved, intensely private."[83] After meeting him for the first time, Phyllis L. Levin, the biographer of Abigail Adams, described him as a "slight man with puzzled eyes and a distant cordiality."[84]

The two men also had different work habits. Riley worked hard, but he could relax on occasion and relished social affairs. He also took time off for lunch. Not so with Butterfield. Often he was so engrossed in his editing that he would forget to stop for lunch. One of his concerned staff members "developed the practice of bringing him vegetable juice in the late afternoon, knowing that more likely than not he would

---

[83] This was the description of Butterfield's son, Fox, who also stated: "When he was angry, my father did not raise his voice; instead he retreated into silence." *Butterfield Commemorations*, 12.

[84] Levin, *Abigail Adams: A Biography* (New York, 1987), 489.

be working late. His eyes would twinkle as he obediently accepted nourishment.''[85]

Despite their many differences, Riley and Butterfield worked well together. Their staffs engaged in a number of cooperative enterprises, from microfilming the Adams Papers to preparing and mounting exhibitions.

A principal reason for their successful relationship was Riley's wholehearted support of the editorial project. A longtime advocate of documentary publications, he believed in the project implicitly. He also knew that whatever success the Adams Papers program achieved would redound to the Society. Every positive review of a volume of Adams Papers—and they almost always received rave reviews—was also a feather in the Society's cap. The first major review the Adams Papers received was written by President John F. Kennedy for the *American Historical Review*, the foremost journal of the historical profession in the United States. He reviewed the four-volume *Diary and Autobiography of John Adams* and gave it high marks, declaring them ''the auspicious herald of a major feat in American historical citation.''[86]

The Society also received its share of kudos when the television series ''The Adams Chronicles'' aired in 1976 to commemorate the bicentennial of the American Revolution. Consisting of thirteen episodes and produced by WNET of New York City, with funding provided by the National Endowment for the Humanities, the Andrew W. Mellon Foun-

[85] *Butterfield Commemorations*, 6. Noticing that his staff began to take a mid-morning coffee break, which he never did, Butterfield distributed a memorandum stating that, in the future, there would be a staff meeting with coffee each morning. Ibid.

[86] *American Historical Review*, 68(1962–1963):478–480. In October 1961, *The Washington Post* celebrated the publication of the four-volume *Diary and Autobiography of John Adams* by sponsoring a Book Luncheon at the Statler-Hilton Hotel in Washington. J. Russell Wiggins, editor of the *Post* and a member of the Society, inspired the program. President Kennedy attended the affair as a special guest and received a set of the volumes for his personal library at Hyannis. Kennedy spoke to the group, prefacing his remarks with this statement: ''First of all, I want to say to Mr. [Thomas Boylston] Adams that it is a pleasure to live in your family's old house and we hope that you will come by and see us.'' Further reflecting his sense of humor, he said: ''I have no doubt that Lyman Butterfield and Thomas Adams are breathing heavy sighs of relief—four volumes out and only eighty-eight or a hundred to go. Obviously the worst is over.'' *The Adams Papers* (Cambridge, Mass., 1962).

dation, and the Atlantic Richfield Company, the series was viewed by millions and was showered with critical acclaim, including the prestigious George Foster Peabody Award for Broadcasting Excellence for 1977. The Adams editorial staff made an important contribution to the program, offering advice both on the script and on the sets.[87] It also had a large hand in the publication of the companion volume to the television series, *The Adams Chronicles*, published by Little, Brown and Co. Also in honor of the bicentennial, the project published *The Book of Abigail and John*, a collection of over 200 letters between the famous duo. Designed as a trade book, it became one of Harvard University Press's most successful publishing ventures, selling over 25,000 copies in cloth and 10,000 more in paperback.

Butterfield served as editor-in-chief until 1975 when ill health forced him to retire. In his twenty-plus years of service, holding forth in the same office that Ford had used during his brilliant career at the Society, he produced twenty "stout" volumes of *Adams Papers* and achieved the reputation of one of America's most productive and accomplished historian-editors. He died in Boston on April 25, 1982.[88]

In the course of his lengthy career as librarian and director of an historical society, Riley (as well as many of his professional colleagues) had witnessed a growing mutual distrust and alienation between manuscript curators and archivists and academic historians. In general, academic historians tended to look down their noses at the staff of historical and archival agencies, including their directors, regarding them as an inferior breed of professional. A caste separation had developed between scholars (i.e., college and university teachers) and those skilled in library, archival, and editorial techniques.

Riley came to believe that the way to reduce the tension between these two antagonistic branches of Clio's domain was to bring history graduate students into historical societies and similar agencies, expose them to the holdings of these repositories, and teach them how to use their resources. His hope was that such an experience would offer the

---

[87] It need be underscored that Butterfield, a stickler for historical accuracy, severely objected to the dramatic license taken by the script writers and producers of this popular television series.

[88] Memoirs of Lyman Butterfield appear in M.H.S., *Procs.*, 94(1982):99–114.

students a fresh awareness of what manuscript curators and archivists did and serve as a basis for enhanced cooperation.

While working in these settings, students also would acquire worthwhile knowledge about the agency. They would learn how it was organized, what functions it performed, and what constituencies it served. Such training, Riley believed, would not only improve the students' research methodology but also develop in them a more respectful attitude toward manuscript curators, archivists, editors, and their institutions.[89]

Acting on this idealistic belief, Riley effected an agreement with Boston University's American and New England Studies Department in 1972 whereby the two institutions offered, one semester a year, the "Massachusetts Historical Society Seminar." A select number of Boston University's graduate students, eight to ten, were permitted to enroll in the seminar, which was held at the Society and conducted by a team of its senior staff members. The Society personnel were appointed adjunct professors in the Boston University graduate school and received a small stipend from the university for their services.[90]

In the course of a semester the students performed a variety of nontraditional research assignments, from processing manuscript collections to editing documents to assembling exhibitions and preparing catalogues. "We trust by this method," wrote Riley, "we can instruct others in the various techniques we have acquired in our years at the Society and do something toward removing any differences that may exist between the two branches."

The seminar persisted for the remainder of Riley's tenure and was later offered in alternate years. In 1982, Boston University terminated the program because of fiscal constraints. Because it was a short-lived experiment and impacted only a small number of students, the seminar had only a minimal impact upon the larger problem.

A few months before he retired, Riley received word from the National Endowment for the Humanities that two grant applications submitted by the Society early in 1976 had been approved. The grants totaled

[89] Riley's thoughts on these issues were provoked by an article he read in the *American Archivist* by Herman Kahn. See M.H.S., *Procs.*, 83(1971):194, 84(1972):143.

[90] M.H.S., *Procs.*, 84(1972):143–144.

nearly $500,000. One was a matching grant of $390,000, requiring the Society to raise one-half of this sum ($195,000).[91]

The first grant dealt with micropublication. The Society was given funds for three years to film at least eighteen of its most frequently used manuscript collections and provide them with introductions and finding aids. The grant called for the hiring of three people: a conservator, who would repair and restore the collections selected for filming; a cataloguer of manuscripts; and a camera operator.

The matching grant, which was also for a three-year period, provided funds for a full range of library services and included subventions for maintenance costs and the salaries of four new employees: a conservator, who would work on rare books; a cataloguer of pamphlet literature; and two manuscript cataloguers, who would process manuscripts, prints, drawings, and photographs.

For many years Riley had yearned for additional staff members to provide needed services for the library. He had inserted his lamentation into a number of reports while serving as librarian and director. Throughout his forty-two-year career, the staff at the Society had remained static, numbering about ten to twelve full-time employees; there were thirteen in 1976. Only about six of these were library employees. Now, as he prepared to leave the Society, he had laid the foundation for the addition of seven new library employees for the next three years. As Librarian John D. Cushing noted, it was "probably the largest single infusion of new blood in 185 years."[92]

There was still one unfinished piece of business on Riley's agenda and it was conducted after he had retired. Just prior to his retirement, Riley and this writer had had a brief conversation with John Sawyer, chief executive officer of the Andrew Mellon Foundation, at a social function in Boston. Riley underscored the many needs of the Society and its limited financial resources. His words apparently caught Sawyer's ear. He instructed us to contact him soon and arrange a meeting in his New York City office. The meeting took place in February 1977.

In a persuasive fund-raising presentation, Riley convinced Sawyer

---

[91] This was an experimental grant. Only three independent research libraries in the nation received this type of award.

[92] M.H.S., *Procs.*, 88(1976):160.

that the Mellon Foundation should provide assistance to the Society. The upshot of the meeting was the subsequent awarding of a $400,000 grant. Of this sum, $100,000 was to be applied to the National Endowment for the Humanities' matching grant, and the remaining $300,000 was to be placed in the Society's endowment fund.[93] The Mellon grant was the cap-stone of Riley's fund-raising career.

When Riley retired, the Council, his staff, members of the Society, and professional colleagues showered him with accolades for his personal achievements and outstanding contributions to the Society and American historical scholarship. In his farewell address to the members on November 12, 1976, he remained as self-effacing as ever, heaping praise upon others for the achievements made during his tenure. "Mine has been a happy life here, thanks to you," he stated. "I have never wanted to work anywhere else, perhaps because of the generally pervasive good-will which has surrounded me here."[94] His audience knew that it was he who had created the "pervasive goodwill."[95]

Of all the tributes paid to Riley, perhaps the most meaningful and insightful were the sentiments expressed by his close friend and colleague Thomas B. Adams in the preface to a commemorative publication containing Riley's reports as librarian and director. Adams reminisced about Riley's relationship with his father and himself when they served as presidents.

> The new President [John Adams] found himself falling into a habit. After each visit with the Director [Stewart Mitchell] he stopped for a minute—then for an hour—to talk with the Librarian. This quiet man knew where everything was, he knew everybody. His tact was unlimited. He never said an unkind word. When unkind words were said in his presence, he softened them by a bit of humor if they were applied to others, if to himself he did not hear. He was deeply serious. He was also amused by life and he taught others to share the comedy. He was a profound scholar, but his

---

[93] M.H.S. Council Records, Apr. 14, 1977 (M.H.S. Archives).

[94] M.H.S., *Procs.*, 88(1976):158.

[95] In 1981, Riley's *alma mater*, Clark University, conferred upon him the degree of Doctor of Humane Letters, *honoris causa*. The citation noted that his lifelong professional task had been "to seek out and make accessible the research materials vital to the historian's craft." Riley was deeply touched by this honor, Clark being one of his four major "loves." The other three were: his wife; the Historical Society; and sweet desserts.

scholarship was most often at the service of others. Generations of historians, famous or unknown, served by him so faithfully, were falling hopelessly in his debt.

When John's son became President he had really very little to do. Riley was appointed Director, a recognition overdue but never coveted. The new Director advised the new President in everything, told him what to do and then did it. But the new President did not know this. Only in retrospect is it obvious. For Riley had some of the good qualities of Benjamin Franklin and some of those of Thomas Jefferson. Perhaps he was a reincarnation, always urbane, always good-humored, persuading people to do sensible things, sometimes wise things, and always persuading them that the ideas were theirs, the acts the product of their energy.

The collections of the Society have grown vastly during the Riley years. He has attracted people and their historical possessions as a magnet. When it was time to put up a new building to house the increased possessions, the means were found because the loyal following was there, believers in the honesty of purpose, beneficiaries of the goodwill and good management of Stephen Riley. He lives in the midst of his monument. As long as men search the past for paths into the future, or perhaps are satisfied merely to find their way into the present, his name will be repeated with respect and affection.[96]

[96] Riley, *Years of Stewardship*, viii-ix. The commemorative booklet, a "happy conspiracy," was a collaborative effort, but the catalyst for the project was Malcolm Freiberg, its appointed chairman. In the author's years in Boston, 1977 to the present (1995), he has met hundreds, if not thousands, of people who knew Riley, many very well. Not one has ever uttered a negative comment about him, either as a person or as an official of the Society. He was universally admired and respected.

Chapter 18

On to the Bicentennial

IN JULY 1976, as Stephen Riley prepared for retirement, the Society's Council, acting upon the recommendation of a search committee, appointed Louis Leonard Tucker of Delmar, New York, as his successor. He was to assume office on January 1, 1977.[1] In making its selection, the Council broke precedent with tradition, as Tucker was the first director not a resident of Massachusetts at the time of appointment.

While not a resident or native of the Bay State, Tucker was a son of New England, having been born and raised in northeastern Connecticut, and a student of its history. He also had a special interest in Boston. As a youngster, he had a passion for baseball in general and the Boston Braves in particular. His all-consuming ambition was to become the second baseman of the Boston team, the replacement for his idol, Sebastian "Sibby" Sisti. As a teenager, he had a brief stint in the minor leagues in hot and humid North Carolina, where he endured a thousand bumpy bus rides and dozens of squalid hotels, but his interest in professional baseball soon waned, and he abandoned the "field of dreams."

Following Horace Greeley's advice, the young man went west, to the state of Washington, to seek his fortune.[2] He began his collegiate schooling there. After a year at Olympic College in Bremerton, he transferred to the University of Washington at Seattle, where he took an A.B., A.M., and Ph.D. In graduate school, he studied early American history,

---

[1] Riley remained on duty until Dec. 31, 1976.

[2] Tucker first went west in 1946, courtesy of the United States Army. Inducted at Fort Devens, Massachusetts, he was shipped to Fort Lewis, Washington, where he spent his entire eighteen-month term of enlistment. After being discharged, he returned to the East for a brief stay, then went west again.

with a geographical concentration on New England, principally Connecticut and Massachusetts. After receiving his doctorate in 1957, he taught at the Davis campus of the University of California.

Tucker's professional path then veered sharply to the East. In 1958, the Institute of Early American History and Culture in Williamsburg, Virginia, awarded him a three-year, post-doctoral fellowship. His duties also included a limited amount of teaching at the College of William and Mary. Seemingly destined for a teaching career in higher education, Tucker abruptly changed direction and entered the field of historical administration upon completion of his fellowship. In 1960, he became director of the Historical and Philosophical Society of Ohio, one of the oldest such institutions in the mid-west.[3] He also was an adjunct instructor of history at the University of Cincinnati, where the society was then located. In 1966, he was appointed state historian of New York and assistant commissioner for state history in the New York State Education Department. While in Albany, he also served as executive director of the New York State American Revolution Bicentennial Commission from 1969 through 1976.

From his days in Cincinnati, Tucker became an active participant in national historical society doings. He was elected president of the American Association for State and Local History in 1972, serving in that capacity until 1974. He was forty-nine years of age when he became director of the Boston society.

While familiar with the reputation and resources of the nation's first historical society and a frequent user of its publications as a graduate student, Tucker did not enter the Boston institution until the summer of 1956, when he conducted research there on his doctoral dissertation.[4] He met Riley for the first time then and in later years frequently encoun-

[3] The Society was founded in 1831. See Dunlap, *American Historical Societies*, 194–195. Tucker was responsible for changing the Society's name to the Cincinnati Historical Society in 1963, a process that provoked considerable controversy among its members. See Tucker, "Clio Comes to the Northwest," The Cincinnati Historical Society, *Bulletin*, 38(1980):221–232; Tucker, "The Cincinnati Historical Society, 1844–1849," Historical and Philosophical Society of Ohio, *Bulletin*, 21(1963):212–214; Tucker, "What's in a Name," Ibid., 21(1963):139–140.

[4] His topic was Thomas Clap, the first president of Yale; the dissertation was later published as *Puritan Protagonist: President Thomas Clap of Yale College* (Chapel Hill, 1962).

tered the affable director at national meetings of historians and historical societies. The two developed a cordial professional relationship.

On January 1, 1977, Tucker assumed control of a strong organization. Riley had left him a rich legacy, not the least of which was a sudden expansion of the staff thanks to the two major grants awarded to the Society in late 1976. Throughout Riley's nineteen-year directorship, the staff consisted of twelve to thirteen full-time employees. In Tucker's first months, the staff suddenly swelled to twenty.

The seven additions were assured of employment for only three years, the term of both categorical grants. Tucker's first objective was to develop sufficient financial resources so that the Society could retain "five, and possibly six," of the additions. These employees were desperately needed for the backlog of decades of library projects and the multi-faceted activities of the Society. The endowment, about $7,800,000 at the close of 1976, could not provide sufficient income to assure the continued employment of the newcomers. Almost 20 percent of this income had to be diverted to special funds and could not be used for general operating expenses.

Tucker was also concerned about the low pay scale of the Society's employees.[5] Their salaries were far below the norm, comparing especially unfavorably with those of major libraries in Greater Boston. Thus, salary increases also became a prime priority.

With these concerns in mind, Tucker stressed a familiar theme in his first annual report to the members, the critical need for greater financial resources. He appealed to the members for a stronger financial commitment, much as Belknap had done at the founding and many others in later days, and affirmed his intention to enlarge the list of fellows of the library so as to increase the funding for this vital facility. He also called for a more aggressive campaign of fund raising from federal agencies. The Society had been reluctant to apply for this type of assistance in the

---

[5] When Tucker became director, Riley often expressed to him deep dismay about the low salaries but explained that the Society lacked the financial resources to increase them. In 1974, in a tribute to Riley, the Council established a special fund in his name and voted "to credit $5,000 and $2,500 thereafter annually" to it as long as he was director. Riley designated the income from his fund to staff salaries and building maintenance. M.H.S. Council Records, Nov. 15, 1974 (M.H.S. Archives).

past, fearing that it would result in governmental meddling in its internal affairs. Experience had shown, he stated, that these fears were unfounded. He also asserted that, through its affiliation with the Independent Research Libraries Association, a consortium of the nation's fifteen most important private libraries, the Society was in a favorable position to secure grants from major private foundations.

Tucker concluded with a "more weighty consideration" for the future, the development of an addition that would permit the Society to display its historical treasures and offer a limited educational program to the general public. Such a structure, he reminded the members, constituted the final link of Riley's master plan. The Hemenway Apartments problem had aborted the former director's grand scheme. Reflecting upon his first year in office, Tucker likened his situation to George Bernard Shaw's definition of marriage: "An arrangement that provides the maximum of temptation with the maximum of opportunity."[6]

In his private musings about the future, Tucker set three long-range goals for his tenure. He would seek to create the facility Riley had envisioned. If this could not be achieved, however, he would strive to increase the Society's endowment to $30,000,000. This would provide a solid financial base for his successor, who assuredly also would attempt to realize Riley's vision. His third objective was to establish endowed chairs for the three principal administrative positions: director; librarian; and editor of publications. He harbored the hope that Jeremy Belknap's name would be attached to the endowed fund for the director or librarian and Worthington C. Ford's name to the endowment for the editorship.

With respect to the Society's agenda, Tucker planned for a slow but steady expansion of existing activities, building upon the sturdy foundation Riley had fashioned. He also projected some new initiatives, if adequate funding could be developed: fellowships for graduate students and professional scholars; an annual series of public lectures; an occasional academic conference; and an expanded publication program. Some years down the road, Tucker looked forward to the creation of a new division in the table of organization: a Center for the Study of New England History, which would serve as an umbrella for many of these activities.

The Adams Papers editorial project did not enter into Tucker's long-

[6] M.H.S., *Procs.*, 89(1977):207–215.

range thinking. He had been cautioned by Riley when he arrived to "let sleeping dogs lie," that is, allow the project to function as it had from its inception. The work plan of the five-member Adams Papers staff, "this small army of editors," was consistent from year to year and not likely to change for decades. Every eighteen months, the team produced two volumes of edited documents, which were then published and marketed by the Harvard University Press. "If only we could edit as fast as the Adamses could write," Editor-in-Chief Richard A. Ryerson would later lament.[7]

One of Riley's strengths as an administrator had been his ability to select high-quality personnel for his staff. He had displayed this talent in his choice of Malcolm Freiberg and John Cushing as division heads. Tucker realized that the success of his administration would hinge largely upon finding suitable replacements for these two accomplished employees, both of whom were in the winter of their careers.

In 1984, after twenty-seven years of dedicated service, Freiberg announced his retirement, and Tucker was faced with his first major appointment. His goal was to find a person who would regard the editor's position as a long-term job, much as Ford and Freiberg had, rather than a brief stepping stone to other employment opportunities. After a national search, which produced twenty-six well-qualified candidates, he selected thirty-four-year-old Conrad E. Wright for the position. He was to begin his duties on January 1, 1985.

Wright's arrival in Boston represented a return to his native soil. The son of C. Conrad Wright, a highly respected Harvard Divinity School professor of American church history, Wright was born in Boston and grew up in Cambridge. He took an A.B. at Harvard and an A.M. and Ph.D. at Brown University, where he specialized in early New England history. While completing his doctorate, Wright applied for teaching and administrative positions. He received an offer from the Institute of Early American History and Culture to become executive assistant to the director and accepted it. His career path was now set in the direction of historical administration. After three years in Williamsburg, he became assistant director of the New-York Historical Society. Two years later, he began his assignment in Boston. He had come full circle.

[7] M.H.S., *Procs.*, 95(1983):187.

On to the Bicentennial

In 1987, the second major anchor of the staff, Cushing, decided to retire. Like Freiberg, he, too, had rendered twenty-seven years of faithful service. His health deteriorating for a number of years, Cushing nonetheless applied himself diligently to his assigned tasks. But, in 1987, he knew the end was near—for both his career and his life.

Each morning, Cushing customarily dropped into Tucker's office when he arrived, usually well before 9 A.M., the official opening time. They would exchange thoughts on current library and personnel issues for ten to fifteen minutes. When they concluded their business, Cushing would rise and say: "Well, back to the rock pile."

On the morning of June 11, 1987, Cushing and Tucker had their usual get-together. When the librarian left for his office, Tucker wrote out a personal memo:

> John just informed me that his doctor told him that he has only a few months of life left, six at the most. He relayed this information in a calm, matter-of-fact tone, as though he were reporting the acquisition of a rare book or commenting on a minor library problem.
>
> He said he would retire on August 31 ("if I can make it") and requested that there be no ceremony or gift to mark his departure. He asked me to keep the matter of his health problems confidential and urged me to give consideration to appointing Peter Drummey as his successor. I assured him that I would honor his requests. He thanked me and said he would spend his remaining months cleaning up unfinished business and briefing Peter thoroughly so that there would be a smooth transition. He intended to complete his long-delayed project of placing in one area the books listed in the Society's first printed catalogue (1796). And he would intensify his efforts to secure some manuscript collections he had been "bird dogging" for years.
>
> As he discussed these matters, he frequently chuckled. When he had finished his business, he rose and said: "Well, back to the rock pile."

Cushing ended his career on August 31 without a ceremonial farewell, in keeping with his wishes. A genuine "profile in courage," he died on September 17.

Even before Cushing had indicated his preference of Drummey as his successor, Tucker had marked him as the heir to the throne. A native of Massachusetts, Drummey had taken an A.B. in history from Columbia University and a M.S. in library science from the same school. Committed to a career in librarianship, he worked as a cataloguer at the Fraunces Tavern Museum in lower Manhattan, New York City, then moved to Boston, where he became curator of manuscripts at the New

England Historic Genealogical Society. Recruited by Cushing, he joined the Historical Society's staff in 1978 as a manuscript cataloguer and steadily moved up the ranks to assistant librarian and associate librarian. As Cushing's understudy, he was a mainstay of the library staff, a prodigiously productive employee, with unbounded energy and an encyclopedic knowledge of the history of Boston and environs, the Commonwealth of Massachusetts, New England, and the United States.

After selecting his two division heads, Tucker delegated to them the authority to hire all employees for their respective units. Riley had followed a similar policy in the main.[8] Both Cushing and Freiberg had demonstrated a discerning eye in their selections, choosing such well-qualified and industrious personnel as Robert V. Sparks (senior assistant librarian), Drummey, Anne E. Bentley (conservator), Ross E. Urquhart (curator of graphic arts), Mary E. Cogswell (associate librarian), Katherine H. Griffin (assistant librarian), Catherine S. Craven (supervisor of the reading room), and Marjorie F. Gutheim (associate editor).

Both Drummey and Wright were equally discriminating in their selections. Drummey added to the library staff such efficient personnel as Brenda M. Lawson (curator of manuscripts), Heath C. Steele (curator of photographs), and Virginia H. Smith (reference librarian). Wright hired Edward W. Hanson (associate editor), who had served as editor of publications at the New England Historic Genealogical Society; and Donald Yacovone (assistant editor), formerly of the *Black Abolitionist Papers Project*.

Researchers at the Society frequently acknowledged in their publications the high degree of professionalism and courtesy of the Society's staff. These personnel helped to perpetuate the Society's reputation as a researcher's paradise, a reputation established during Riley's long tenure as librarian and director.

The financial state of the Society steadily improved from 1977 to 1991. No longer was it an organization living on the "knife edge of starva-

---

[8] Riley did appoint Winifred Collins as reference librarian. In time, she achieved a legendary reputation as a servant of scholars. Her pertinacity in searching for information, coupled with her warm personality, endeared her to all library patrons (See *M.H.S. Miscellany*, no. 59 [Fall 1994]). He also appointed two excellent custodians, Edwin Bligh and Julius Prince, and an extraordinarily capable library assistant, Aimée Bligh. The Blighs and Prince gave many years of high-quality service to the Society.

tion." The endowment markedly increased with the passage of time, as shown by its balance at the close of the fiscal year on June 30:

1976:	$ 7,475,517
1980:	9,627,566
1985:	14,885,912
1989:	24,680,844
1991:	28,321,747.[9]

There were a number of reasons for the progressive growth of the endowment. The principal factor was an astute investment policy developed and implemented by Treasurers F. Murray Forbes, Jr., John Lowell, and Arthur Hodges, and the finance committee, and approved by the Council. Heavily influenced by the incessant pleading and cajoling of Vice President Andrew Oliver, the Society tied its financial destiny to the stock market, committing over 70 percent of its capital to equities. It derived the benefits of the rapid surge of the market during the presidencies of Ronald Reagan and George Bush, the "trickle down" era.

Not even the dramatic slump on October 19, 1987 ("Meltdown Monday") deterred the Society from maintaining its concentration on equities. On that fateful day, the market experienced a cataclysmic decline. In the blink of an eye, the market value of the Society's portfolio decreased by more than 20 percent, from an all-time high of $23,330,000 to $18,400,000. Fortunately, with the rapid rebound of the market, the Society's financial fortunes quickly improved.[10]

There were also other reasons for the financial well-being of the Society. Its three presidents during this period, James Barr Ames (1975–1978), F. Douglas Cochrane (1978–1987), and Henry Lee (1987–) provided strong leadership, exploiting every opportunity for financial improvement. They were complemented by a vigilant Council which eschewed deficit budgets and displayed a New England tendency to measure one's cloth before choosing a pattern. In sum, the governors of the Society exercised prudent management. A number of members and friends bequeathed gifts, and federal agencies and private foundations, most notably the Andrew W. Mellon Foundation, made major grants.

Another positive financial development was the re-institution of an-

---

[9] These statistics were extracted from the annual financial statements and provided by Bacall and Coniff, Certified Public Accountants.

[10] M.H.S. Council Records, Dec. 10, 1987 (M.H.S. Archives).

nual dues in 1989 for resident members, a proposal initiated by the director, approved by the Council after considerable discussion, and ratified by the members.[11] The Society had imposed dues from 1791 to 1907, when President Charles F. Adams prevailed upon the Council and membership to abolish them. The Council set the dues level at $100, and the new policy took effect on July 1, 1989.[12] This action produced an annual income of over $20,000, which could be used as the Council directed.

The Council was wary of instituting annual dues, fearing mass resignations, but only three of approximately 210 resident members left the fold. One dropped out because of old age and acute health problems. The two others, senior professors of history at Harvard University, resigned in protest, although one later had a change of heart, paid his dues, and renewed his membership.

The financial situation was destined to improve further after the annual meeting in 1991. In 1887, a resident member, who insisted upon absolute anonymity, established a special fund with a gift of $1,000. A year later, he donated an additional $250. He set only one condition, that the income from his two gifts be added to the principal until the annual meeting in 1991. The Council aptly designated these gifts as the Anonymous Fund. As mighty oaks grow from little acorns, so, too, did the Anonymous Fund greatly increase in size in the course of a century. By 1991 the original sum of $1,250 had expanded to the whopping figure of $982,023![13]

In the fall of 1982, the National Endowment for the Humanities, a federal agency, awarded the Society a $100,000 "special initiative" matching grant. The grant was part of a $5.3 million comprehensive award conferred upon thirteen members of the Independent Research Libraries Association by the Endowment. President Ronald Reagan announced the gift at an impressive ceremony in the Oval Office of the White House, attended by the chairman of the Endowment, William J. Bennett, and the

[11] M.H.S. Council Records, Oct. 13, 1988, Jan. 12, April 13, 1989; M.H.S. Meeting Minutes, Apr. 13, 1989 (M.H.S. Archives).

[12] M.H.S., *Procs.*, 101(1989):135.

[13] The anonymous donor was George Bigelow Chase, a fact revealed in 1992 at a Council meeting with the dramatic opening of documents sealed in wax, which had been housed in a Boston bank vault since 1887. For an account of this fascinating story, see M.H.S. *Miscellany*, no. 52(Autumn 1992).

chief executive officers of the libraries. To receive its award the Society had to raise $300,000 from private sources by July 1985.

Tucker viewed this grant as a golden opportunity to establish an endowed chair for the Society's librarian, one of his principal objectives when he became director. The sum of $400,000 would serve as a base. He made this recommendation to the Council and suggested that the chair by named for Director Emeritus Riley.[14] The Council unanimously endorsed his proposals. The match was subsequently achieved, primarily because hundreds of members and friends of the Society held Riley in high esteem. They were only too glad to contribute to this campaign. In time, other funds were added to the endowment, increasing its principal. Cushing became the first holder of the chair.

The Society launched a public lecture series in the spring of 1980. Lacking a suitable auditorium for such functions, the Society joined forces with the Boston Public Library, which had a meeting hall with a seating capacity of 375. The Lowell Institute, a local philanthropic organization dating back to the early nineteenth century, agreed to fund the lectures. Promoting public educational programs was the prime purpose of the foundation. John Lowell, the sole trustee of the Institute, then served as treasurer of the Society and was deeply interested in public education.

In selecting its speakers, the Society drew upon some of the nation's most influential academicians, writers, and public figures. The first speaker of the series was the renowned historian Henry Steele Commager, a longtime member of the Society. His lecture commemorated the bicentennial of the birth of William Ellery Channing, the celebrated Unitarian leader. The lecture drew an overflow audience with a number of attendees actually sitting on the stage adjacent to Commager. The second lecture, presented in the fall, featured another Olympian figure among American historians, Oscar Handlin of Harvard University, who spoke on "Completing the Revolution: The Boston of 1780." The Society complemented these lectures with exhibitions of relevant source materials in the public library's Boston Room and a post-lecture reception.[15]

[14] M.H.S. Council Records, Dec. 9, 1982 (M.H.S. Archives).

[15] Because of logistical and security problems, the Society and Public Library eliminated the exhibitions and receptions in later years.

In succeeding years, a host of distinguished speakers participated in the series. The list included: President A. Bartlett Giamatti of Yale University; Arthur Miller, the playwright; Tom Wicker, Harrison Salisbury, and Anthony Lewis of *The New York Times*; Bernard Bailyn of Harvard University; Associate Supreme Court Justice Harry A. Blackmun; Frances Fitzgerald, the Vietnam War correspondent; David McCullough, author and television personality; and Hodding Carter, the well-known television journalist. Through this type of outreach, the Society enhanced its reputation as an educational institution.

While there were no major additions to the physical plant from 1977 to 1991, there were three notable cosmetic improvements to the property. The first was in the Dowse Library, which over a period of years had developed an increasingly seedy appearance because of excessive use. The situation called for a renovation, and that occurred in 1980. The ceiling was painted, the floor refinished, and a number of other minor improvements effected. The most dramatic improvement was the addition of an antique chandelier for the classic Victorian room. After a long search, Robert G. Neiley, an accomplished architectural historian from Cambridge who served as consultant for the renovation, discovered an appropriate Victorian-era chandelier in Philadelphia, which fit the library with extraordinary felicity.

In 1982, the Society undertook a project to refurbish its front and side yards. The general appearance of this pivotal area of the Fenway had deteriorated over a period of years and become an eye sore. It was a sad setting for the handsome Wheelwright structure. Cracked sidewalk sections were replaced, the curbstones realigned, an attractive iron fence installed, new privet hedges and flowering trees added, and a sparse lawn replaced by a verdant covering of pachysandra.[16] These improvements enhanced the beauty of the building, which had been designated a National Historic Landmark by the Department of the Interior in 1966.[17]

In 1985, the marble in the main lobby, stairway, and second-floor lobby of the Wheelwright building received a thorough scrubbing, the first such cleaning since the structure was erected. Eighty-five years of

[16] M.H.S., *Procs.*, 94(1982):127.
[17] M.H.S., *Procs.*, 78(1966):174.

accumulated grime was removed and the intrinsic beauty of the marble reappeared.[18]

Certain that there would be a fund drive for the Society's bicentennial observance, Tucker knew the time had come to increase the base of support, much as Mitchell had done during his tenure. To expect to be successful in a major fund drive with 175 resident members, most of whom were academics, was wishful thinking. At the annual meeting of 1983, he called for the increase in resident membership from 175 to 200.[19] This goal was achieved in 1985, and two years later the figure was enlarged to 250.[20] Tucker would have preferred raising the limit to 300, or possibly 400, but he recognized that such a quantum leap was not in keeping with tradition. Slight increments represented standard operating procedure at the Society.

The Council and membership approved both proposals without a ripple of dissent. Whereas such proposals had provoked a firestorm of protest and bitter internecine warfare in earlier years, they now failed to evoke any opposition.

This lack of interest in internal affairs provided graphic evidence of the total disintegration of the "old boys' history club" of the past. Only a small number of the resident members, some twenty-five to thirty, were active participants in the Society's regular endeavors—that is, users of the library or regular attendees at business meetings or social affairs. Most paid their annual dues and were rarely to be seen on the premises. Two long-time members sheepishly confessed to this writer that they not only had never attended a meeting or social function, but did not know where the Society was located!

The apathy of the bulk of members was an issue of deep concern to Tucker and the Council, as it had been for prior administrations. It was a frequent topic of conversation at informal gatherings and membership and Council meetings, but the problem was enigmatic and defied solution.

Periodically, there was talk of scrapping the elective system and adopt-

[18] M.H.S., *Procs.*, 97(1985):168.
[19] M.H.S., *Procs.*, 95(1983):178.
[20] M.H.S. Meeting Records, Jan. 10, 1985, May 14, 1987 (M.H.S. Archives). There was no change in corresponding membership, the number remaining at 150.

ing a policy of open membership. This system was in effect in every historical organization in the nation, with the exception of the Society, the American Antiquarian Society, and the Colonial Society of Massachusetts. But talk was never translated into action, and the old system remained in place at the bicentennial.

Like "old man river," the Adams Papers project continued to flow along its established course. Robert J. Taylor, an experienced editor and well-respected historian and formerly chairman of the history department at Tufts University, had succeeded Lyman Butterfield as editor-in-chief in 1975.[21] Together with his staff, Taylor produced two volumes of edited documents every eighteen months.

All was proceeding smoothly until 1979, when Taylor was in his third year as editor-in-chief and the project began to experience its first financial problems. The National Historical Publications and Records Commission (NHPRC), the federal agency that annually provided a substantial subsidy, began to fund all of the five Founding Fathers editorial projects out of Congressional appropriations.[22] Suddenly, the fear arose that this support could shrivel up or disappear altogether. Such a development also became a source of concern to the Society since it could provide only partial funding for the Adams Papers. Full funding would have worked a severe hardship on its financial resources.

Responding to the uncertainty of future federal support, the Adams Papers joined the other four Founding Fathers projects in seeking a major grant from the Andrew W. Mellon Foundation. This led the projects' sponsoring institutions—the Historical Society, Yale University (Franklin Papers), Princeton University (Jefferson Papers), the American Philosophical Society (Franklin Papers), and the University of Virginia (Washington and Madison Papers)—in 1979 to form the Founding Fathers Papers, Inc., a corporation chartered under the laws of the State of New Jersey, to raise funds cooperatively. This body embarked upon a fund-raising campaign. Subsequently, the corporation received major grants from the Andrew W. Mellon Foundation, the Pew Memorial Trust, and the Culpeper Foundation. These grants provided

---

[21] M.H.S. Council Records, Mar. 7, 1975 (M.H.S. Archives).

[22] Previously known as the National Historical Publications Commission, this agency changed its name in 1974.

secure funding until the early 1990s, and the crisis was averted for the time being.

After overseeing the editing of eight volumes of Adams documents, Taylor retired to Martha's Vineyard in 1983. He was succeeded by Richard A. Ryerson, who held an A.B. from Harvard College, an M.A.T. from the Harvard Graduate School of Education, and an A.M. and Ph.D. in history from The Johns Hopkins University. After teaching at Hebron Academy and the University of Texas, Ryerson turned to historical editing, joining the William Penn Papers staff at the University of Pennsylvania in 1979. Like Butterfield and Taylor, Ryerson was also an accomplished historian and skillful editor. The diligent work of the Adams Papers staff, including Senior Associate Editor Gregg L. Lint, Associate Editor Celeste Walker, and Assistant Editor Joanna M. Revelas, ensured that the unending river of Adams volumes would continue to flow under Ryerson's able direction.

The Society's bicentennial began to loom large in Tucker's thoughts in the early 1980s, a decade before the event. He knew that 1991 would be a significant milestone in the history of the organization, a time for a major celebration. A one-day, subdued, ceremonial observance, marked by long, turgid speeches followed by a sumptuous meal, as occurred at the 50th, 100th, 150th, and 175th anniversaries, was not in order for the bicentennial. The words expressed by President Charles F. Adams in 1896, as the Society prepared to move into its new home on Boylston Street, were also relevant for the bicentennial: "It must exhibit and make known its collections,—it must have its field days,—it must put on its ruffles and frills. It must, in a word, hold itself high."[23]

Having directed New York State's program for the bicentennial of the American Revolution, Tucker clearly understood the importance of a long lead time for planning a sizable commemoration; the planning for that event began in 1968. He underscored the point in his annual reports to the membership in 1980 and 1981 in which he linked the Society's bicentennial with a capital campaign to increase the endowment. A bicentennial is a propitious time for a major fund drive, he asserted in 1980, and recommended a $10,000,000 goal.[24] The gasps from the audience were audible.

[23] Charles F. Adams, Memorabilia, Apr. 9, 1896 (C.F. Adams Papers).
[24] M.H.S., *Procs.*, 92(1980):175.

The Massachusetts Historical Society

President F. Douglas Cochrane, a lawyer by profession and a strong advocate of methodical planning for all Society undertakings, heeded the director's words and appointed a special committee in 1982, consisting of Council members Paul C. Reardon and Theodore Chase, to assist him in formulating suitable goals for the commemoration.[25]

Directly linked with plans for the bicentennial celebrations was the need for long-term planning for the Society's development during its third century. Between 1982 and 1984, four intensive round-table seminars were held in which advice and suggestions were solicited and specific programs and activities proposed and discussed. The junior professional members of the staff attended the first colloquium. The second session brought together senior staff members and those retirees who continued to maintain offices in the Society where they pursued research and writing projects; Director Emeritus Riley was one of these.[26] Seven administrative heads of comparable institutions in Greater Boston, all of whom were resident members of the Society, attended the third seminar. Key members of the Council attended all three sessions.

The fourth colloquium, held in April 1984, was especially noteworthy. It was designed as a "self-study." Assisted by funding from the National Endowment for the Humanities, the Society invited eight cultural and academic figures of national reputation to Boston to examine its four principal functions: library; publications; public education; and membership.[27] All were familiar with the Society and historical societies in general. Specifically, they were requested to project a course of action for the Society as it prepared to enter its third century of institutional

[25] M.H.S. Council Records, June 15, 1982 (M.H.S. Archives).

[26] The practice of providing retired professional staff members with free office space and other perquisites, such as parking and supplies, began at the end of Riley's directorship. It grew in scope during Tucker's tenure with the retirement of a number of senior members of the staff. The Society derived many benefits from this arrangement.

[27] The eight were: Dr. William T. Alderson, director of the Margaret Strong Museum, Rochester, New York; Dr. Richard D. Brown, professor of history, University of Connecticut; Wendell Garrett, editor and publisher of the *Magazine Antiques*; John Knowlton of the Manuscripts Division, Library of Congress; Daniel Porter, director of the New York State Historical Association; Dr. James M. Smith, director of the Henry Francis du Pont Winterthur Museum; Thomas Vaughan, director of the Oregon Historical Society; and Don Wilson, director of the Gerald R. Ford Library and Museum.

life. Society officials exhorted the visitors to be candid in their appraisals; weaknesses as well as strengths were to be pinpointed.

In the final analysis, there was remarkable consistency between the thinking of the consultants and that of the participants in the earlier colloquia. The central points on which they agreed were that the Society should continue to function as a learned society, but it must be an active, not a passive institution; it must continue to strive for greater outreach; it must provide a wider range of services for the scholarly community and that element of the general public in sympathy with its programs and purposes; and it must develop plans to make its remarkable holdings better known to the citizens of Greater Boston.

Based upon these suggestions, the Society in 1990 formulated its official bicentennial program and blueprint for the future. It was the most ambitious anniversary commemoration the Society had ever conceived. It consisted of five elements: a capital campaign; public exhibitions; celebratory events, including receptions and dinners; a series of special events; and a series of publications.

The first and most important component was a $5,100,000 Bicentennial Fund campaign, tailored to long-range needs. The figure was about one half of what Tucker had proposed in 1980 but, after considering a host of factors, the Council deemed it a more realistic goal. Through this fund, the Society sought to establish four endowment funds. The Society allocated $2,100,000 for a Center for the Study of New England History, which would administer research projects, special publications, scholarly conferences, seminars for graduate students and high school social studies teachers, and predoctoral and postdoctoral research fellowships. It committed $1,000,000 to library development, with the income to be used for the purchase of rare books and other source materials as well as for conservation of the collections. It set aside $1,500,000 to provide partial endowment for one or two senior positions. Finally, it provided for an endowed fund of $500,000, the income to be used for basic maintenance and capital improvements of the Society's headquarters.[28]

As part of its public programming, the Society mounted three exhibitions to display its diverse holdings during the bicentennial. The first,

---

[28] M.H.S., *Procs.*, 102(1990):177.

titled "A Common Wealth: The People's History Secured, 1630–1991,"was shown at the Bank of Boston's gallery in its corporate head-quarters from December 14, 1990, to February 6, 1991. The bank underwrote the cost of the show, which was open to the public. There was a second exhibition at the Society in conjunction with its annual spring reception in 1991. The title chosen was: "Honey from the Hive: Treasures of the Massachusetts Historical Society."

The third exhibition, "Witness to America's Past," was the Society's major public offering for the commemoration. It was held at the Museum of Fine Arts, Boston, from April 12 to July 13, 1991, and featured over 160 of the finest items in the collection, from documents to prints and paint-ings to artifacts. Jonathan Fairbanks, Katharine Lane Weems Curator of American Decorative Arts and Sculpture at the museum and a member of the Society, was the coordinator of the show, utilizing the services of staff members from both institutions. Anne E. Bentley, the Society's con-servator, served as Fairbanks's principal liaison and arranged for the se-lection and preparation of all materials used in the exhibition. Fidelity Investments, through the Fidelity Foundation, covered the expenses of this venture. The hard-dollar cost was over $250,000. This included the publication of an exhibition catalogue, *Witness to America's Past: Two Centuries of Collecting by the Massachusetts Historical Society*. De-signed to be of lasting value beyond the time limits of the exhibition, the catalogue, edited by Edward W. Hanson, was a fully illustrated introduc-tion to the Society's collections of books and manuscripts, as well as art and artifacts. The surge of attendance at the exhibition elated Society and museum officials. Over 260,000 people visited the display, which received rave reviews in the local media outlets.[29]

A third element of the commemoration was a set of four celebratory events. The first was a bicentennial birthday reception at the Bank of Boston exhibition site on the actual day of the founding, January 24. There was symbolic propriety in the bank's good works since its eighteenth-century predecessor, the Massachusetts Bank, gave the So-ciety its first quarters, free of charge, when it was founded. There was also a gala reception to mark the opening of the Society's exhibition at the Museum of Fine Arts. Skinner, Inc., the well-known auction house, sponsored this affair.

[29] See, for example, the *Boston Globe*, Apr. 26, 1991.

On to the Bicentennial

The bicentennial banquet, held at the American Academy of Arts and Sciences in Cambridge on May 17, continued the celebrations.[30] One of the high points of the evening was the presentation of the Society's John Fitzgerald Kennedy award to Professor Oscar Handlin by United States Sen. Edward M. Kennedy, honoring Handlin for his massive contributions to American historical scholarship. He was only the fourth recipient of the award, the others being Samuel Eliot Morison (1968), Dumas Malone (1972), and Thomas Boylston Adams (1975).[31]

The Society's annual dinner at the Harvard Club in Boston on October 16 was the climactic event of the bicentennial year. It featured Arthur M. Schlesinger, the distinguished historian and long-time member of the Society, as the evening's speaker.[32] After the dinner, President Henry Lee announced that the Council had established the Jeremy Belknap Award, designed to honor those who had made extraordinary contributions to the Society. To the surprise of no one, he conferred the first Belknap Award to Director Emeritus Stephen T. Riley who had suffered a serious illness and unfortunately could not be in attendance.[33]

There was also a series of special events in the course of the bicentennial year. The Bank of Boston and the Society co-sponsored a public lecture at the bank's auditorium on January 23 featuring Thomas Boylston Adams and State Senate President William Bulger, one of the most colorful political leaders in Massachusetts and a member of the Society. This event, which attracted a capacity audience, complemented the exhibition at the bank.

A public lecture series took place at the Museum of Fine Arts as an educational adjunct to the Society's exhibition. On April 24, a professional actor and actress associated with the Poets' Theatre of Cambridge read from documents drawn from the display. Susan Montgomery of Boston University presented four lectures at the Museum, titled "Bostonians Observed," in April and May. On May 15, Michael Kammen, a Pulitzer Prize-winning historian from Cornell University, gave a lecture: "Rethinking History: Changing Perceptions." On May 18, Michael

---

[30] This event is discussed in the preface of this volume.

[31] M.H.S., *Procs.*, 103(1991):198.

[32] His remarks, "History: Text vs. Context," are published in M.H.S., *Procs.*, 103(1991): 1–8.

[33] M.H.S., *Procs.*, 103(1991):199.

Robbins, a former president of the Society of Antiquaries of London, the organization that provided the model for the Historical Society at its founding, spoke on "The Past in the Present." Both Kammen and Robbins were corresponding members of the Society, and Robbins's presence gave the celebration an international dimension.

The Independent Research Libraries Association and the International Group of Publishing Libraries each held meetings in Boston during the year and were hosted by the Society to receptions, dinners, and private viewings of the exhibition.

The final element in this variegated program was a series of publications. These ranged from a catalogue of the Society's portrait collection; to the catalogue of the exhibition at the Museum; to a volume comprising the papers given at a conference on New England and the early republic; to a monograph on Jeremy Belknap and the founding of the Society.[34]

Because of a lot of hard work by the staff and Council, all went smoothly in 1991. Each event went off as scheduled without a glitch. The Society had exhibited and made known its collections, had its field days, put on its ruffles and frills, and held itself high.

As 1991 came to a close and the bicentennial celebration receded into memory, Tucker reflected not only upon the memorable events of the year but also on the changes the Society had experienced since his arrival in 1977. While occupying the same physical quarters and fulfilling the same general purpose of the past, the Society was a far different organization from the one he had inherited from Riley. Some of the changes had been profound, some subtle.

The most visible change was the increase in staff. There were now about twenty-five full-time employees, plus a number of part-timers and student assistants, and a few volunteers. Principally because of the additional personnel, annual expenditures for general operations, ex-

[34] The Society's bicentennial publications are: *Portraits in the Massachusetts Historical Society*, by Andrew Oliver, Ann Millspaugh Huff, and Edward W. Hanson (Boston, 1988); *Clio's Consort: Jeremy Belknap and the Founding of the Massachusetts Historical Society*, by Louis Leonard Tucker (Boston, 1990); *Witness to America's Past: Two Centuries of Collecting by the Massachusetts Historical Society* (Boston, 1991); *Massachusetts and the New Nation*, based upon the 1990 conference, edited by Conrad Edick Wright (Boston, 1992); the forthcoming annotated catalogue of the Society's library in 1796, edited by the late John D. Cushing; and the present volume.

cluding the Adams Papers editorial project, also had increased substantially, from $281,953 in 1976 to close to $1,000,000 in 1991.

The administrative system had been totally revamped. During Riley's era, all business matters, from the processing and payment of bills to maintaining financial records, had been handled by a unit of the State Street Bank and Trust Co., the custodian of the Society's endowment. The Society paid a modest fee for this service. Riley was forced to use this system through expediency since he could not afford to hire a person to do this time-consuming work. He could barely find funds for a part-time secretary to handle his correspondence, filing, and other routine office tasks.

The arrangement with the bank was unwieldy and inefficient. Riley did not have immediate access to information on expenditures or the current status of line items in the operating budget. He had to await periodic reports from the bank. Then, too, the opportunity for error was rife in this type of fragmentary system, and the bank made numerous errors.

Because of these factors, in addition to the elaborate accounting requirements associated with the administration of the federal grants the Society received in 1976, Tucker terminated the arrangement with the bank in 1978 and centralized all business activities, exclusive of the payroll, within the director's office. With the increase in the Society's finances, he was able to hire a full-time administrative assistant, part of whose assignment it was to handle business affairs and maintain financial records. This involved the processing of bills and invoices, preparing dues statements for members and Fellows of the Library, maintaining the records of these two constituencies, and recording contributions and other forms of receivable payments.

The new system resulted in a much more efficient administrative operation. With the passage of time and the introduction of word processors and computers, record-keeping became even more efficient, and financial information was more readily accessible.[35] Jennifer Hall, who served as administrative assistant beginning in 1990, developed a num-

---

[35] During the 1980s, the Society made the transition from the era of manual typewriters, tape recorders, and simple photocopy machines to the age of high-tech word processors, computer terminals, laser printers, a facsimile machine, a sophisticated telephone system, pagers, and other technological equipment.

ber of sophisticated record-keeping systems with the new high-tech equipment.

There were also significant changes in the library between 1977 and 1991. These were initiated by Peter Drummey, the first professional librarian to direct this key unit. Prior to Tucker's tenure, only one employee in the history of the Society had formal training as a librarian.[36] Until that time, library personnel learned their duties as "apprentices" or worked in other libraries where they received hands-on experience. The full extent of Riley's library training, prior to his arrival at the Society, was as a part-time student employee of the Worcester Public Library. Cushing, likewise, had no formal schooling in librarianship and learned "on the job."

The presence of "amateur" librarians accounted for eccentricities throughout the collection, such as the development of an idiosyncratic catalogue at the Society, which baffled and frustrated countless researchers over the years. One of Drummey's primary goals, when he became librarian, was to professionalize his staff to counteract some of the legacies left behind by well-intended predecessors. When openings occurred, he sought and hired employees who had formal library training.

Prior to Drummey's appointment, there had been another peculiar tradition at the Society that male employees catalogued manuscripts and female employees catalogued books.[37] The tradition came to an abrupt end when Drummey became librarian. The gender factor was removed from cataloguing.

Drummey was also responsible for developing an inventory of the library's holdings. When he came to the Society in 1978, there was no shelf list for the library. Many hundreds of thousands of books and documents were described in the card indexes, but there was no overview of the collection, no consistent, detailed descriptions. Drummey and his staff undertook this Herculean and necessary task.

The inventory was closely related to the process of automation, which took hold at the Society in 1979 when it joined OCLC, a computerized,

---

[36] Margaret Hu, who was employed during Riley's directorship.

[37] The only exception to this tradition was Priscilla Ritter, a part-time employee, who did process manuscripts.

national, shared cataloguing system. From 1979 to 1991, the library reported the bulk of its manuscript holdings and descriptions of thousands of books and pamphlets to an on-line data base through the OCLC network.[38] As a result, information on the Society's holdings became available to a wide number of researchers in the United States and around the world.

Drummey thrived as a "hands-on" librarian. While others on his staff held the title of reference librarian, Drummey often performed this function himself and derived great personal satisfaction from assisting scholars. Unlike his predecessor, who preferred to remain closeted in his office working at his desk, the gregarious Drummey was a visible presence in the library, constantly consulting with researchers, discussing their projects, and offering suggestions on manuscript collections and reference books they should examine. A voracious reader, the polymathic Drummey had an extensive bibliographical knowledge of regional and national history.

There was seemingly no limit to Drummey's passion for providing assistance to his patrons. In 1991, a researcher in the state of Washington inquired about the *Columbia*, the first American ship to circumnavigate the globe. Drummey reported to a Society meeting that "on a sweltering Saturday in July I found myself searching the banks of the North River in Norwell [Massachusetts] to find a lost historical marker commemorating the launching site of the *Columbia*. This mission was on behalf of yet another researcher from the West Coast who was more than a little confused by Massachusetts local geography. The Briggs Shipyard site turned out to be located in a Norwell resident's backyard, and the very perplexed, but accommodating, present inhabitant kindly assisted a researcher 3,000 miles away in Washington in verifying the location, rather than having your librarian arrested for trespass."[39] Peter Drummey was not a conventional librarian.

Aside from Drummey's improvements, the library had become a different type of facility in the 1980s and early 1990s with respect to usage. A more diverse body of researchers was visiting the library.

[38] The recataloguing of the manuscript collection was made possible through a grant of $100,000 from the William and Flora Hewlett Foundation. M.H.S., *Procs.*, 99(1987):191.

[39] M.H.S., *Procs.*, 103(1991):210.

There were more foreign students and a larger number of non-traditional researchers, such as archaeologists and documentary film makers. The researchers tended to be younger and less experienced than earlier users. Many were graduate students, and the gender balance was shifting. Whereas in the past the bulk of the patrons had been males, there was now nearly a 50–50 split between men and women.

While attendance in the library showed a gradual increase each year, the staff reported that a greater amount of their time was spent in servicing requests by correspondence, the telephone, or the facsimile machine. Possibly because of the exorbitant expense of travel and lodging in Boston, a number of out-of-state researchers were using the above-mentioned techniques for acquiring information. Some researchers ordered microfilm copies of materials, thereby avoiding a trip to Boston.

Just as Drummey changed the character of library operations, so did Conrad E. Wright, the second member of the dynamic duo, transform the publications and research division. His first goal was to expand publications, and the traditional annual publications, such as the *Proceedings*, *House Journals*, and the *Miscellany*, the Society's newsletter, were soon joined by a spate of special works. These ranged from a heavily-illustrated book on the portraits owned by the Society, one of the largest and most significant collections of early American art in the nation, to additions to the *Collections* series. Under the direction of the fiercely energetic Wright, the Society was able to bring to fruition many years of research, writing, and editing by longtime members, including Andrew Oliver, Ann Millspaugh Huff, and Robert E. Moody.[40]

In 1989, Wright initiated a new series, the Massachusetts Historical Society Studies in American History and Culture, which would include volumes based upon Society-sponsored academic conferences, which he organized. The first volume was *American Unitarianism, 1805–1865* (1989), based upon a 1987 conference on one of New England's most

[40] Oliver and Huff worked on the portrait catalogue cited earlier; and Moody edited the *Papers of Leverett Saltonstall, 1816–1845*, the fourth volume of which appeared in the *Collections* series in 1991. At the end of the bicentennial year, four more volumes of edited documents were in production: a final volume of the Saltonstall papers by Moody; volume 6 of the *Winthrop Papers*, edited by Malcolm Freiberg; and the first two volumes of the *Papers of Robert Treat Paine*, edited by Stephen T. Riley and Edward W. Hanson.

influential denominations. Wright organized a second conference in 1990, "New England and the Early Republic." A volume of essays followed this event. A third conference, "Puritanism in Old and New England," was held in Millersville, Pennsylvania, in 1991 under the co-sponsorship of the Society, Millersville University, and the Institute of Early American History and Culture.[41]

The completion of a long-running publication series in 1990 represented another milestone for Wright. In 1919, the Society had begun to reissue with a new introduction and index the *Journals of the House of Representatives of Massachusetts*, which had originally been published from 1715 to 1779. The project commenced during the editorship of Worthington C. Ford. Throughout the years, this publication was supported by a fund endowed in 1927 by William Bradford Homer Dowse, a member, and through a subsidy from the Commonwealth of Massachusetts. The state distributed the set, a valuable research source, throughout public libraries and similar institutions around the commonwealth. From 1919 to 1990, when the final volume was reprinted, the Society produced fifty-five volumes in a total of sixty-five parts.[42]

Wright also can be credited with reviving the *Sibley's Harvard Graduates* series, dormant since the death of Clifford K. Shipton in 1973. As an early American historian, he knew the importance of this seminal work, described by a reviewer in the *New England Quarterly* as "a monument to scholarship in America." In 1986, with the assistance of Edward Hanson and one to two part-time researchers, he began work on volume eighteen, which covered the classes of 1772 through 1774—132 graduates and 8 non-graduates. He hoped to produce the volume "around 1995."

Wright not only had a strong desire to publish books, he was also anxious to sell them. Like most small historical organizations in the United States, the Society had a difficult time finding buyers for its many published wares. It had no formal marketing system. As a result,

---

[41] The conference volume, *Puritanism: Transatlantic Perspectives on a Seventeenth-Century Anglo-American Faith*, edited by Francis J. Bremer, was published by the Society in 1993.

[42] A brief history of this project is given in its last volume, *Journals of the House of Representatives*, 55:vii-ix.

its basement and the space it rented in the New England Deposit Library was filled with unsold volumes.[43] The Society had a desperate need for an aggressive distributor.

In 1983, Tucker had made an agreement with the Northeastern University Press to market selected Society publications.[44] This arrangement worked to the financial advantage of the Society but, since the list was limited, the returns were minimal. What was needed was a more comprehensive arrangement.

In 1988, after consulting with the director, Wright effected the type of agreement with the Northeastern University Press that the Society had sought. The original contract was extended to include almost every publication the Society produced. Wright favored the relationship with Northeastern University Press, even though it was a small, local press. His reasoning was based upon the belief that the Society would receive "more particular attention to our active booklist than if the Society simply became yet another client of an older, more established press."

Wright's reasoning was accurate. The collaboration with the Northeastern University Press resulted in a successful partnership. There was a steady increase in the sales of Society publications, which were now distributed to a wider national audience than ever before. The Society welcomed the wider distribution as enthusiastically as it welcomed the hefty royalty payment it received annually from the press.

Even before the arrival of Wright, Tucker had made an agreement with University Microfilms International to market the Society's extensive and outstanding microfilm holdings. This firm was the international leader of microtext distribution and promotion. From a financial standpoint, this arrangement was eminently successful.

Wright also played a salient role in developing a vibrant short-term fellowship program. This type of scholarly incentive had become commonplace among the major independent research libraries of the nation by the 1970s, but the Society could not initiate one because of a lack of funds. The Society offered its first fellowship in the early 1980s through

---

[43] In 1933, Stewart Mitchell underwrote the cost of a "Handbook, or Descriptive List" of the Society's publications at his own expense in an effort to increase sales. "The cellar of the Society is full of books printed to be sold," Mitchell wrote, "the treasury is empty." Mitchell to Samuel E. Morison, Jan. 28, 1933 (Mitchell Papers, Boston Athenaeum).

[44] M.H.S., *Procs.*, 95(1983):177.

the courtesy of the Society of the Cincinnati.[45] The program expanded quickly when Wright arrived on the scene. By 1991, the Society was offering eighteen fellowships. The Andrew W. Mellon Foundation endowed ten of these in 1986.[46] The Oliver family endowed the Andrew Oliver Fellowship in 1989.[47] Generous support for other fellowships was provided by the Massachusetts Society of the Cincinnati, the Massachusetts Society of Colonial Wars, the Paul Revere Memorial Association, and the Unitarian Universalist Association. Through this effort scholars came to the Society from across the nation and from abroad to study a full range of subjects in American history and material culture.

Another of Wright's achievements was to make the Society the home base for the Boston Area Early American History Seminar, a program that brought together scholars and graduate students from colleges and universities throughout New England, public school teachers, and interested members of the public to discuss a wide range of topics in American history. This occurred in 1989. Previously, the seminar had met intermittently at Boston University in a sub-par physical setting. Attendance there was low and dwindling.

At the Society, the seminar convened in elegant Ellis Hall and, after the formal session, adjourned to the Oliver Room and Dowse Library where the Society provided a light dinner and libations, a feature that may have contributed to the attendance, consistently over forty participants. As Wright noted in 1990: "One result of the series was proof, if proof was necessary, of the proposition that hungry graduate students will go to meetings where free food is served. . . . As word circulated that the Society was serving a free buffet supper after each session, attendance swelled."[48]

Wright served as one of the coordinators of the seminar, planning the yearly programs in conjunction with history professors from Boston University, Tufts University, Boston College, and Wellesley College. The seminar was intended to present "work-in-progress" and provide an opportunity for authors to test new ideas and for

[45] M.H.S., *Procs.*, 96(1984):57.
[46] M.H.S., *Procs.*, 96(1984):57.
[47] M.H.S., *Procs.*, 102(1990):179–180.
[48] M.H.S., *Procs.*, 102(1990):193.

participants to explore new approaches to the study of American history from the colonial era to the Civil War. It encouraged a multidisciplinary approach to the study of American history and provided graduate students, in particular, with an opportunity to see how history "gets done."

Wright was a strong supporter of the concept of a Center for the Study of New England History to administer the fellowships, conferences, and seminars, now offered by the Society in growing numbers. When this division was established in the summer of the bicentennial year, he volunteered to become its acting director, in addition to carrying out his other responsibilities.

As the Society completed its second century of institutional life, it was at the highest point of development in its history. With an endowment of nearly $30 million, it rested on a sturdy financial foundation—for the first time in two hundred years. Its staff of about twenty-five full-time employees was the largest and best-trained in its history. Managed by three experienced administrators, the core units of library, publications, and Adams Papers editorial project were functioning efficiently. The newest unit in the table of organization, the Center for the Study of New England History, was in its initial stage of operation but already gave evidence of developing into a vibrant area of activity, with fellowships increasing, special publications either in the planning phase or in process, more historical conferences scheduled, the Boston Area Early American History Seminar firmly established, and database projects in prospect. The annual social-educational events for members, Fellows of the Library, and the general public (consisting of lectures at the Society and Boston Public Library, spring reception and exhibition, and annual dinner) went off with clock-work regularity.

And what of the immediate future? The Society faced two formidable and familiar challenges as it entered its third century: an imperative need for additional space and greater financial resources. The increase in staff and expansion of activities dictated the need for a larger physical plant. Library stacks, office space, an auditorium, lecture and seminar rooms, a facility in which to mount exhibitions—these were immediate, pressing needs. The addition of these resources, as well as the normal progressive development of the institution, would require a stronger financial base. A $30 million endowment would sustain the current operation, but it would not support the Society of the third century.

The history of the Society is replete with formidable challenges confronted and met, and the result is clear: the Society does have staying power. Jeremy Belknap never intended the institution as a passing indulgence. As long as there is a United States of America, there will be a need for the Massachusetts Historical Society.

Appendixes   *Index*

Appendix I

Members of the
Massachusetts Historical Society
1791–1991

Aaron, Daniel
Cambridge
R 845, December 12, 1975

Abbot, William Wright
Charlottesville, Virginia
C 720, April 11, 1985

Abbott, Wilbur Cortez
Cambridge
R 534, February 14, 1924
Died: February 3, 1947

Abt, Clark C.
Cambridge
R 1014, January 10, 1991

Adams, Brooks
Quincy
R 422, April 10, 1902
Died: February 13, 1927
Memoir: M.H.S. *Procs.*,
60(1926–1927):
345–358

Adams, Charles Francis, I
Boston
R 150, March 25, 1841
Died: November 21, 1886
Memoir: M.H.S. *Procs.*,
2d ser., 13(1899–
1900):198–207

Adams, Charles Francis, II
Lincoln
R 295, April 15, 1875
Died: March 20, 1915
Tributes: M.H.S. *Procs.*,
48(1914–1915):
383–423

Adams, Charles Francis, III
Concord
R 508, March 13, 1919
Died: June 10, 1954

Adams, Charles Francis, IV
Dover
R 742, April 14, 1960

Adams, Frederick Baldwin, Jr.
Princeton, New Jersey
C 595, April 11, 1963

Adams, George Burton
New Haven, Connecticut
C 452, October 13, 1921
Died: May 26, 1925

Adams, Henry, I
Washington, D.C.
C 347, December 9, 1880
Washington, D.C.
H 67, January 9, 1908
Died: March 27, 1918
Tributes: M.H.S. *Procs.*,
51(1917–1918):
313–319

Adams, Henry, II
Concord
R 563, October 9, 1930
Died: April 26, 1951
Memoir, M.H.S. *Procs.*,
70(1950–1953):
279–281

Adams, Henry Bigelow
Kansas City, Kansas
C 746, April 12, 1990

Adams, Herbert Baxter
Baltimore, Maryland
C 356, January 11, 1883
Died: July 30, 1901

Adams, James Truslow
Southport, Connecticut
C 454, May 11, 1922
Died: May 18, 1949

Adams, Jasper
Charleston, South Carolina
C 138, August 27, 1833
Died: October 25, 1841

Adams, John, I
Quincy
R 56, July 31, 1800
Died: July 4, 1826
Memoir: M.H.S. *Procs.*,
1(1791–1835):400–
407

Adams, John, II
Lincoln
R 636, February 8, 1945
H 93, December 12, 1963
Died: August 30, 1964
Memoir, M.H.S. *Procs.*,
76(1964):160–168

Adams, John Quincy, I
Quincy
R 65, April 27, 1802
Died: February 23, 1848
Memoir: M.H.S. *Procs.*,
2(1835–1855):395–
410

Adams, John Quincy, II
Dover
R 691, December 11, 1952
Died: July 20, 1987
Memoir, M.H.S. *Procs.*,
99(1987):177–178

Adams, John Weston
Dedham
R 919, May 24, 1984

Adams, Peter Boylston
Lincoln
R 975, October 13, 1988

Adams, Randolph Greenfield
Ann Arbor, Michigan
C 489, February 13, 1936
Died: January 4, 1951

Adams, Thomas Boylston
South Lincoln
R 674, December 13, 1951

Adams, Thomas Randolph
Providence, Rhode Island
C 594, March 14, 1963

Adams, William Howard
Washington, D.C.
C 665, May 8, 1975

Adelung, Friedrich von
Berlin, Germany
C 106, April 25, 1822
Died: January 30, 1843

Appendix I: Members

Agassiz, Alexander
Cambridge
R 387, March 12, 1896
Removed December 22, 1909
Died: March 27, 1910

Agassiz, George Russell
Newport, Rhode Island
C 442, March 13, 1919
Boston
R 594, May 14, 1936
Died: February 5, 1951

Ahlstrom, Sydney Elkman
New Haven, Connecticut
C 668, January 13, 1977
Died: July 3, 1984

Aiken, John Adams
Greenfield
R 501, May 10, 1917
Died: January 28, 1927
Memoir: M.H.S. *Procs.*, 60(1926–1927):309–312

Akins, Thomas Beamish
Halifax, Nova Scotia
C 302, October 15, 1869
Died: May 7, 1891

Alaman, Don Lucas
Mexico City, Mexico
C 220, February 28, 1850
Died: June 15, 1853

Alba. See Berwick y Alba, duque de

Alden, John Richard
Durham, North Carolina
C 629, December 12, 1968
Died: August 14, 1991

Alden, Timothy
Portsmouth, New Hampshire
C 51, October 1, 1801
Died: July 5, 1839

Aldrich, Bailey
Cambridge
R 846, December 12, 1975

Alison, Sir Archibald, baronet
Lanarkshire, Scotland
C 206, April 27, 1843
Died: May 23, 1867

Allen, Alexander Viets Griswold
Cambridge
R 352, December 9, 1886
Died: July 1, 1908
Memoir: M.H.S. *Procs.*, 44(1910–1911):355–362

Allen, Frederick Lewis
New York, New York
C 512, February 10, 1944
Died: February 13, 1954

Allen, Gardner Weld
Boston
R 467, December 8, 1910
Died: July 12, 1944

Allen, Joseph
Worcester
R 71, September 7, 1808
Died: September 2, 1827
Memoir: M.H.S. *Procs.*, 1(1791–1835):411–413

Allen, William
Brunswick, Maine
C 159, July 28, 1836
Died: July 16, 1868

Allen, William Francis
Madison, Wisconsin
C 353, February 9, 1882
Died: December 9, 1889

Allen, Zachariah
Providence, Rhode Island
C 345, September 9, 1880
Died: March 17, 1882

Allibone, Samuel Austin
New York, New York
C 272, May 9, 1861
Died: October 2, 1889

Allis, Frederick Scouller, Jr.
Andover
R 705, December 8, 1955

Allyn, John
Duxbury
R 52, October 29, 1799
Resigned May 5, 1831
Died: July 19, 1833
Memoir: M.H.S. *Colls.*, 3d ser., 5:245–252

Almack, Richard
Long Melford, England
C 203, November 17, 1842
Died: January 1, 1875

Alsop, Joseph Wright, Jr.
Washington, D.C.
C 707, May 12, 1983
Died: August 28, 1989

Altamira y Crevea, Rafael
Mexico City, Mexico
C 420, February 13, 1908
Died: June 1, 1951

Alvord, Clarence Walworth
Minneapolis, Minnesota
C 456, November 9, 1922
Died: January 25, 1928

Ames, Ellis
Canton
R 178, August 12, 1852
Resigned October 9, 1884
Died: October 30, 1884

Ames, Sir Herbert Brown
Brookline
C 505, February 13, 1941
Died: March 31, 1954

Ames, James Barr
Cambridge
R 701, November 10, 1954

Ames, Oliver Filley
Boston
R 812, March 12, 1970

Ames, Seth
Boston
R 259, December 8, 1864
Died: August 15, 1881
Memoir: M.H.S. *Procs.*, ,
20(1882–1883):35–36

Amory, Copley
Boston
R 702, May 12, 1955
Died: April 16, 1960

Amory, Thomas Coffin
Boston
R 230, September 8, 1859
Died: August 20, 1889
Memoir: M.H.S. *Procs.*,
2d ser., 5(1889–1890):
341–346

Amory, William
Boston
R 278, April 13, 1871
Died: December 8, 1888
Memoir: M.H.S. *Procs.*,
2d ser., 4(1887–1889):
414–417

Anderson, Robert
Edinburgh, Scotland
C 61, August 27, 1805
Died: February 20, 1830

Andrew, John Albion
Boston
R 263, February 8, 1866
Died: October 30, 1867
Memoir: M.H.S. *Procs.*,
18(1880–1881):41–64

**Andrews, Charles
McLean**
New Haven, Connecticut
C 460, February 14, 1924
Died: September 9, 1943

Angelis, Don Pedro de
Buenos Aires, Argentina
C 210, January 30, 1845
Died: 1860

Angell, James Burrill
Ann Arbor, Michigan
C 375, February 13, 1896
Died: April 1, 1916

Appleton, Francis Henry
Boston
R 561, April 10, 1930
Died: April 5, 1939

Appleton, John
Cambridge
R 269, January 14, 1869
Died: February 4, 1869
Memoir: M.H.S. *Procs.*,
15(1876–1877):365–
367

Appleton, Nathan
Boston
R 134, June 26, 1834
Died: July 14, 1861
Memoir: M.H.S. *Procs.*,
5(1860–1862):248–
308

Appleton, William
Boston
R 213, July 8, 1858
Died: February 15, 1862
Memoir: M.H.S. *Procs.*,
6(1862–1863):429–
469

**Appleton, William
Sumner, I**
Boston
R 271, May 13, 1869
Died: April 28, 1903
Memoir: M.H.S. *Procs.*,
2d ser., 17(1903):516–
531

**Appleton, William
Sumner, II**
Boston
R 498, February 8, 1917
Died: November 24, 1947
Memoir: M.H.S. *Procs.*,
69(1947–1950):422–
425

Arieli, Yehoshua
Jerusalem, Israel
C 754, December 13, 1990

Armstrong, John Borden
Hingham
R 894, January 8, 1981
Died: December 4, 1985
Memoir, M.H.S. *Procs.*,
98(1986):135–136

Armstrong, Rodney
Boston
R 840, April 10, 1975

Arnold, Samuel Greene
Providence, Rhode
Island
C 236, March 8, 1855
Died: February 12, 1880

**Ashley, Sir William
James**
Birmingham, England
C 393, November 14,
1901
Died: July 23, 1927

Aspinwall, Thomas
London
C 135, July 25, 1833
Boston
R 187, April 12, 1855
Died: August 11, 1876
Memoir: M.H.S. *Procs.*,
2d ser., 7(1891–1892):
32–38

**Atherton, Charles
Humphery**
Amherst, New
Hampshire
C 86, April 25, 1816
Died: January 8, 1853

Austin, James Trecothick
Boston
R 125, May 5, 1831
Resigned January 10,
1856
Died: May 8, 1870

**Avezac-Macaya, Marie
Armand Pascal d'**
Paris, France
C 313, March 14, 1872
Died: January, 1875

Appendix I: Members

Babson, John James
Gloucester
R 237, November 8, 1860
Died: April 13, 1886
Memoir: M.H.S. *Procs.*,
2d ser., 3(1886–1887):
138–143

Bacon, Gaspar Griswold
Dedham
R 581, June 8, 1933
Died: December 25, 1947
Memoir, M.H.S. *Procs.*,
69(1947–1950):426–
428

Bacon, Leonard
New Haven, Connecticut
C 175, July 26, 1838
Died: December 24, 1881

Bagdikian, Ben Haig
Washington, D.C.
C 644, December 10, 1970

Bailyn, Bernard
Cambridge
R 724, May 8, 1958

Baird, Henry Martyn
New York, New York
C 349, October 13, 1881
Died: November 11, 1906

Baker, Gardiner
New York, New York
C 24, August 17, 1795
Died: October, 1798

Baldwin, Simeon Eben
New Haven, Connecticut
C 385, March 8, 1900
Died: January 30, 1927

Bancroft, Frederic
Washington, D.C.
C 391, June 13, 1901
Died: February 22, 1945

Bancroft, George
Northampton
R 135, June 26, 1834
Washington, D.C.
C 219, February 28, 1850
Died: January 17, 1891

Bancroft, Hubert Howe
San Francisco, California
C 327, November 11,
1875
Died: March 3, 1918

Bangs, Edward
Boston
R 348, June 11, 1885
Died: February 16, 1894
Memoir: M.H.S. *Procs.*,
2d ser., 10(1895–
1896):311–314

Banks, Charles Edward
Vineyard Haven
R 541, November 12,
1925
Died: October 21, 1931
Memoir: M.H.S. *Procs.*,
68(1944–1947):437–
441

Banks, Gordon Thaxter
Shirley
R 710, February 9, 1956
Died: March 8, 1981
Memoir, M.H.S. *Procs.*,
93(1981):123–126

**Barbé-Marbois,
François de**
Paris, France
C 113, October 28, 1824
Died: February 12, 1837

Barbour, Thomas
Boston
R 587, November 8, 1934
Died: January 8, 1946

Barker, James Madison
Pittsfield
R 388, April 9, 1896
Died: October 3, 1905
Memoir: M.H.S. *Procs.*,
43(1909–1910):399–
401

Barnard, Daniel Dewey
Albany, New York
C 184, June 27, 1839
Died: April 24, 1861

Baron, Robert C.
Wayland
R 920, May 24, 1984
Golden, Colorado
C 726, December 11, 1986

Barrett, Clifton Waller
New York, New York
C 548, January 12, 1956
Died: November 6, 1991

Barry, John Stetson
Roxbury
R 188, November 8, 1855
Died: December 11, 1872
Memoir: M.H.S. *Procs.*,
13(1873–1875):136–
139

Barry, William
Lowell
R 176, January 31, 1850
Chicago, Illinois
C 310, January 11, 1872
Died: January 17, 1885

Bartlet, William Stoodley
Chelsea
R 208, April 8, 1858
Died: December 12, 1883
Memoir: M.H.S. *Procs.*,
2d ser., 2(1885–1886):
430–434

Bartlett, John Russell
Providence, Rhode
Island
C 244, May 8, 1856
Died: May 28, 1886

Bartlett, Josiah, I
Charlestown
R 46, April 24, 1798
Died: March 3, 1820
Memoir: M.H.S. *Procs.*,
1(1791–1835):323–
330

Bartlett, Josiah, II
Concord
R 142, August 30, 1836
Resigned March 12, 1857

Barton, Benjamin Smith
C 25, January 26, 1796
Died: December 19, 1815

Barton, William
Lancaster, Pennsylvania
C 55, October 26, 1802
Died: July 22, 1823

Barzun, Jacques
New York, New York
C 577, March 9, 1961

Bassett, John
Albany, New York
C 69, August 29, 1809
Died: September 4, 1824

Bassett, John Spencer
Northampton
R 475, May 9, 1912
Died: January 27, 1928

Bate, Walter Jackson
Cambridge
R 881, November 2, 1979

**Bath and Wells, Lord
Arthur Charles Hervey,
bishop of**
Wells, England
C 266, May 12, 1859
H 33, February 11, 1875
Died: June 9, 1894

**Bauer, Frederick
Edward, Jr.**
Holden
R 871, December 14, 1978
C 718, December 13, 1984

Baxter, James Phinney, I
Portland, Maine
C 414, January 10, 1907
Died: May 8, 1921

Baxter, James Phinney, II
Williamstown
R 562, May 8, 1930
A 10, February 11, 1965
C 614, January 11, 1968
Died: June 17, 1975

Bayard, Samuel
Princeton, New Jersey
C 89, April 24, 1817
Died: May 12, 1840

Baylies, Francis
Taunton
R 144, November 23,
1837
Resigned March 30, 1848
Died: October 28, 1852

Baylies, William
Dighton
R 9, January 24, 1791
Resigned April 20, 1815
Died: June 17, 1826

Beal, Boylston Adams
Boston
R 617, April 11, 1940
Died: July 27, 1944

Bear, James Adam, Jr.
Charlottesville, Virginia
C 706, January 13, 1983

Beardsley, Eben Edwards
New Haven, Connecticut
C 333, January 10, 1878
Died: December 21, 1891

Beck, Emily Morison
Canton
R 882, April 10, 1980

Beck, Theodric Romeyn
Albany, New York
C 223, May 29, 1851
Died: November 19, 1855

Beha, Ann
Boston
R 996, May 11, 1989

Belknap, Jeremy
Boston
R 1, January 24, 1791
Died: June 20, 1798
Memoir: M.H.S. *Colls.*,
1st ser., 6:x-xviii

Bell, Charles Henry
Exeter, New Hampshire
C 308, August 15, 1871
Died: November 11, 1893

Bell, James Brugler
Cambridge
R 875, January 11, 1979
Princeton, New Jersey
C 705, September 23,
1982

Bell, Luther V.
Charlestown
R 207, April 8, 1858
Died: February 11, 1862
Memoir: M.H.S. *Procs.*,
7(1863–1864):27–99

Bell, Whitfield Jenks, Jr.
New Haven, Connecticut
C 558, January 8, 1959

Bellows, Robert Peabody
Boston
R 688, May 8, 1952
Died: May 23, 1957

Bemis, George
Boston
R 261, July 13, 1865
Died: January 5, 1878
Memoir: M.H.S. *Procs.*,
16(1878):112–116

Bemis, Samuel Flagg
New Haven, Connecticut
C 500, December 14, 1939
Died: September 26, 1973
Memoir, M.H.S. *Procs.*,
85(1973):117–129

Bender, Wilbur Joseph
Cambridge
R 761, April 12, 1962
Died: March 31 1969

**Benson, Godfrey
Rathbone. See
Charnwood**

Bentinck-Smith, William
Groton
R 843, May 8, 1975

Appendix I: Members

Bentley, William
Salem
R 33, March 25, 1796
Died: December 29, 1819
Memoir: M.H.S. *Procs.*,
1(1791–1835):320–
323

Beranek, Leo Leroy
Winchester
R 929, May 9, 1985

Bercovitch, Sacvan
Cambridge
R 1003, April 12, 1990

Berkeley, Francis Lewis
Charlottesville, Virginia
C 562, May 13, 1959

Berlin, Sir Isaiah
Oxford, England
C 578, March 9, 1961

Berrien, John Macpherson
Savannah, Georgia
C 187, October 31, 1839
Died: January 1, 1856

Berwick y Alba, Jacobo Maria Del Pilar Carlos Manuel
Fitz-James Stuart, duque de
Madrid, Spain
C 491, March 11, 1937
H 88, January 8, 1953
Died: September 24, 1953

Beveridge, Albert Jeremiah
Indianapolis, Indiana
C 444, May 8, 1919
Died: April 27, 1927
Tribute: M.H.S. *Procs.*,
60(1926–1927):315–
318

Biddle, Richard
Pittsburgh, Pennsylvania
C 156, May 26, 1836
Died: July 7, 1847

Bigelow, Albert Francis
Brookline
R 607, April 14, 1938
Resigned: November 10,
1955
Died: June 19, 1958

Bigelow, Erastus Brigham
Boston
R 256, April 14, 1864
Died: December 6, 1879
Memoir: M.H.S. *Procs.*,
19(1881–1882):429–
437

Bigelow, George Tyler
Boston
R 222, February 10, 1859
Died: April 12, 1878
Memoir: M.H.S. *Procs.*,
2d ser., 5(1889–1890):
458–482

Bigelow, Jacob
Boston
R 203, February 11, 1858
Died: January 10, 1879
Memoir: M.H.S. *Procs.*,
17(1879–1880):383–
467

Bigelow, John
New York, New York
C 324, February 11, 1875
Died: December 19, 1911

Bigelow, Melville Madison
Cambridge
R 411, April 12, 1900
Died: May 4, 1921
Memoir: M.H.S. *Procs.*,
55(1921–1922):
328–338

Bigelow, William Sturgis
Boston
R 503, March 14, 1918
Died: October 6, 1926

Biggar, Henry Perceval
Toronto, Canada
C 459, December 13, 1923
Died: July 26, 1938

Bigsby, Robert
Ashby-de-la-Zouch,
England
C 222, March 27, 1851
Died: September 27, 1873

Billias, George Athan
Worcester
R 883, April 10, 1980

Billington, Ray Allen
Evanston, Illinois
C 565, January 14, 1960
Died: March 6–7, 1981
Memoir, M.H.S. *Procs.*,
93(1981):119–122

Binney, Horace
Philadelphia, Pennsylva-
nia
H 16, May 9, 1861
Died: August 12, 1875

Bird, Charles Sumner
Walpole
R 713, December 13, 1956
Died: May 13, 1980

Bixby, William Keeney
St. Louis, Missouri
C 438, December 14, 1916
Died: October 29, 1931

Black, Barbara Aronstein
New York, New York
C 744, January 11, 1990

Black, Henry
Quebec, Canada
C 195, October 29, 1840
Died: August 16, 1873

Blagden, George Washington
Boston
R 160, February 29, 1844
New York, New York
C 360, March 13, 1884
Died: December 17, 1884

Blake, Maurice Cary
Brookline
R 719, April 10, 1958
Died: February 20, 1969
Memoir, M.H.S. *Procs.*,
81(1969):212

Blakeslee, George Hubbard
Worcester
R 469, March 9, 1911
Resigned October 11, 1933

Blanck, Jacob Nathaniel
Chestnut Hill
R 782, March 11, 1965
Died: December 23, 1974
Memoir, M.H.S. *Procs.*, 86(1974):99–101

Bland, Theodoric
Annapolis, Maryland
C 120, August 28, 1827
Died: November 16, 1846

Bliss, Philip
Oxford, England
C 205, March 30, 1843
Died: November 18, 1857

Blount, William
Tennessee
C 26, October 25, 1796
Expelled July 20, 1797
Died: March 21, 1800

Blum, John Morton
New Haven, Connecticut
C 568, May 12, 1960

Bok, John
Boston
R 989, April 13, 1989

Bolton, Charles Knowles
Shirley
R 427, February 12, 1903
Died: May 19, 1950
Memoir, M.H.S. *Procs.*, 70(1950–1953): 271–273

Bomford, George
Washington, D.C.
C 193, July 30, 1840
Died: March 25, 1848

Bond, Henry
Philadelphia, Pennsylvania
C 226, September 8, 1853
Died: May 4, 1859

Bond, William Henry
Concord
R 781, February 11, 1965

Boorstin, Daniel J.
Washington, D.C.
C 748, May 10, 1990

Borgeaud, Charles
Geneva, Switzerland
C 423, October 8, 1908
Died: October 6, 1940

Bortman, Mark
Newton
R 664, February 8, 1951
Died: June 1, 1967
Memoir, M.H.S. *Procs.*, 79(1967):200–203

Botta, Carlo Giuseppe Guglielmo
Paris, France
C 100, October 26, 1820
Died: August 10, 1837

Boudinot, Elias
Burlington, New Jersey
C 77, April 29, 1813
Died: October 24, 1821

Bourbon-Orléans. See Paris, comte de,

Bourne, Edward Gaylord
New Haven, Connecticut
C 394, January 9, 1902
Died: February 24, 1908

Bowditch, Charles Pickering
Boston
R 406, November 9, 1899
Died: June 1, 1921
Memoir: M.H.S. *Procs.*, 56(1922–1923): 306–315

Bowditch, Harold
Brookline
R 640, November 8, 1945
Peterborough, New Hampshire
A 6, October 19, 1961
Died: August 6, 1964
Memoir, M.H.S. *Procs.*, 76(1964):157–159

Bowditch, Nathaniel Ingersoll
Boston
R 193, December 11, 1856
Died: April 16, 1861
Memoir: M.H.S. *Procs.*, 5(1860–1862):500–512

Bowdoin, James
Boston
R 102, August 27, 1821
Died: March 6, 1833
Memoir: M.H.S. *Colls.*, 3d ser., 9:224–225

Bowen, Francis
Cambridge
R 164, December 4, 1845
Resigned February 14, 1878
Died: January 21, 1890

Bowen, Richard Le Baron
East Providence, Rhode Island
C 526, March 10, 1949
Died: August 9, 1969

Bowers, Q. David
Wolfeboro, New Hampshire
C 728, January 8, 1987

Bowles, Francis Tiffany
Barnstable
R 540, October 8, 1925
Died: August 3, 1927
Memoir: M.H.S. *Procs.*, 64(1930–1932):415–421

Boyd, Julian Parks
Princeton, New Jersey
C 493, January 13, 1938
Died: May 28, 1980
Memoir, M.H.S. *Procs.*, 92(1980):160–163

Appendix I: Members

Bradford, Alden
Boston
R 25, January 2, 1793
Resigned January 27,
1820
Died: October 26, 1843
Memoir: M.H.S. *Procs.*,
55(1921–1922):
153–164

Bradford, Charles H.
Cambridge
R 937, January 9, 1986

Bradford, Gamaliel, I
Boston
R 40, October 31, 1797
Died: March 7, 1824
Memoir: M.H.S. *Colls.*,
3d ser., 1:202–209

Bradford, Gamaliel, II
Cambridge
R 109, April 28, 1825
Died: October 22, 1839
Memoir: M.H.S. *Colls.*,
3d ser., 9:224–225

Bradford, Gamaliel, III
Grantville
R 308, April 10, 1878
Died: August 20, 1911
Memoir: M.H.S. *Procs.*,
47(1913–1914):356–
368

Bradford, Gamaliel, IV
Wellesley
R 473, November 9, 1911
Died: April 11, 1932
Memoir: M.H.S. *Procs.*,
65(1932–1936):81–91

Bradford, John
Roxbury
R 43, January 30, 1798
Died: January 27, 1825
Memoir: M.H.S. *Procs.*,
1(1791–1835):382

Bradish, Luther
New York, New York
H 19, March 12, 1863
Died: August 30, 1863

Bradlee, Frederick Josiah
Beverly
R 735, May 14, 1959
Died: April 28, 1970
Memoir, M.H.S. *Procs.*,
82(1970):116–127

Bradley, Eleanor Cabot
Canton
R 901, May 14, 1981
Died: August 30, 1990
Memoir, M.H.S. *Procs.*,
102(1990):169–170

Bradley, Ralph
Canton
R 811, January 8, 1970
Died: August 28, 1970

**Bragdon, Henry
Wilkinson**
Exeter, New Hampshire
C 604, December 10, 1964
Died: March 15, 1980
Memoir, M.H.S. *Procs.*,
92(1980):146–150

Brattle, Thomas
Cambridge
R 38, April 25, 1797
Died: February 7, 1801
Memoir: M.H.S. *Colls.*,
1st ser., 8:82–85

**Braybrooke, Richard
Griffin Neville, baron**
Saffron Walden, England
C 214, May 7, 1846
Died: March 13, 1858

**Brayton, John
Summerfield**
Fall River
R 397, January 13, 1898
Died: October 30, 1904
Memoir: M.H.S. *Procs.*,
2d ser., 19(1905):268–
272

Brevoort, James Carson
New York, New York
C 264, March 10, 1859
Died: December 7, 1887

Brew, John Otis
Cambridge
R 736, May 14, 1959
Died: March 19, 1988

**Brewington, Marion
Vernon**
Salem
R 721, March 13, 1958
Died: December 8, 1974
Memoir, M.H.S. *Procs.*,
86(1974):95–98

Brewster, Ellis Wethrell
Plymouth
R 679, February 14, 1952
Died: March 17, 1978

Brewster, Kingman, Jr.
New Haven, Connecticut
C 695, May 14, 1981
Died: November 8, 1988

**Brewster, William
Souther**
Plymouth
R 938, January 9, 1986

Bridenbaugh, Carl
Williamsburg, Virginia
C 522, December 12, 1946

Briggs, LeBaron Russell
Cambridge
R 527, June 8, 1922
Died: April 24, 1934

**Brigham, Clarence
Saunders**
Worcester
R 535, June 12, 1924
Died: August 13, 1963

Brigham, F. Gorham, Jr.
Newton
R 1026, October 10, 1991

Brigham, Lincoln Flagg
Salem
R 347, May 14, 1885
Died: February 27, 1895
Memoir: M.H.S. *Procs.*,
2d ser., 16(1902):535–
538

Brigham, William
Boston
R 181, December 8, 1853
Died: July 9, 1869
Memoir: M.H.S. *Procs.*,
13(1873–1875):280–
281

Brimmer, Martin
Boston
R 342, March 13, 1884
Died: January 14, 1896
Memoir: M.H.S. *Procs.*,
2d ser., 10(1895–
1896):586–595

Brinton, Crane
Cambridge
R 667, March 8, 1951
Died: September 7, 1968

Broderick, Francis Lyons
Boston
R 817, December 10, 1970
C 664, April 10, 1975

Brodhead, John Romeyne
New York, New York
C 211, January 30, 1845
Died: May 6, 1873

Brogan, Denis William
Cambridge, England
C 541, March 11, 1954
Died: January 5, 1977

Brooke, Edward William
Newton Centre
R 816, May 14, 1970
Washington, D.C.
C 700, December 10, 1981

Brooks, Charles
Medford
R 210, May 13, 1858
Died: July 7, 1872
Memoir: M.H.S. *Procs.*,
18(1880–1881):174–
178

Brooks, Phillips
Boston
R 313, March 13, 1879
Died: January 23, 1893
Memoir: M.H.S. *Procs.*,
49(1915–1916):170–
175

Brooks, William Gray
Boston
R 242, April 11, 1861
Died: January 6, 1879
Memoir: M.H.S. *Procs.*,
17(1879–1880):98–
100

Brown, Alexander
Norwood, Virginia
C 370, March 12, 1891
Died: August 29, 1906

Brown, Andrew
Halifax, Nova Scotia
C 13, April 30, 1793
Died: February 19, 1834

Brown, Davenport
Boston
R 682, April 10, 1952
Died: March 17, 1973

Brown, Francis
New York, New York
C 535, December 11, 1952
R 860, March 10, 1977

Brown, John Carter
Providence, Rhode Island
C 233, August 10, 1854
Died: June 10, 1874

Brown, John Marshall
Portland, Maine
C 340, May 8, 1879
Died: July 20, 1907

Brown, John Nicholas, I
Providence, Rhode Island
C 371, March 8, 1894
Died: May 1, 1900

Brown, John Nicholas, II
Providence, Rhode Island
C 490, March 11, 1937
Died: October 9, 1979
Memoir, M.H.S. *Procs.*,
91(1979):232–234

Brown, Richard David
Hampton, Connecticut
C 721, April 11, 1985

Brown, Samuel Carson
Boston
R 899, April 9, 1981

Brown, Sanborn Conner
Lexington
R 832, May 10, 1973
C 676, March 10, 1977
Died: November 28, 1981

Brown, Thomas N.
Cambridge
R 995, May 11, 1989

Bruce, John
London, England
C 292, June 6, 1867
Died: October 28, 1869

Bruce, Philip Alexander
Charlottesville, Virginia
C 462, April 10, 1924
Died: August 16, 1933

Bryan, John Stewart
Williamsburg, Virginia
C 494, January 13, 1938
Died: October 16, 1944

Bryant, Douglas Wallace
Lexington
R 747, December 8, 1960

Bryant, John Winslow
Beverly Farms
R 773, April 9, 1964

Bryant, William Cullen
New York, New York
H 14, February 14, 1861
Died: June 12, 1878

Appendix I: Members

Bryce, James, viscount
London, England
C 354, September 14,
1882
H 57, October 8, 1896
Died: January 22, 1922

**Buchan, David Steuart
Erskine, earl of**
Edinburgh, Scotland
C 67, August 30, 1808
Died: April 19, 1829

Buck, Paul Herman
Cambridge
R 615, February 8, 1940
Died: December 23, 1978
Memoir, M.H.S. *Procs.*,
91(1979):217–220

**Buckminster, Joseph
Stevens**
Boston
R 75, April 25, 1811
Died: June 9, 1812
Memoir: M.H.S. *Colls.*,
2d ser., 2:271–274

Budington, William Ives
Charlestown
R 170, March 30, 1848
Brooklyn, New York
C 306, February 9, 1871
Died: November 29, 1879

Bugbee, James McKellar
Boston
R 335, November 9, 1882
Died: February 8, 1913
Memoir: M.H.S. *Procs.*,
46(1912–1913):372–
378

Buhler, Kathryn Clark
Brookline
R 847, December 12, 1975
Died: November 7, 1986
Memoir, M.H.S. *Procs.*,
98(1986):139–141

Bulfinch, Charles
Boston
R 64, October 1, 1801
Died: April 15, 1844

Bulger, William Michael
Boston
R 955, January 8, 1987

**Bullard, Frederic
Lauriston**
Melrose Highlands
R 631, March 9, 1944
Died: August 3, 1952
Memoir, M.H.S. *Procs.*,
70(1950–1953):290–
293

Bullard, Henry Adams
New Orleans, Louisiana
C 155, May 26, 1836
Died: April 17, 1851

Bullitt, Stimson
Seattle, Washington
C 708, May 12, 1983

**Bullock, Alexander
Hamilton**
Worcester
R 297, December 9, 1875
Died: January 17, 1882
Memoir: M.H.S. *Procs.*,
2d ser., 3(1886–1887):
322–339

Bundy, McGeorge
New York, New York
C 635, April 10, 1969

Burgess, George
Gardiner, Maine
C 278, February 12, 1863
Died: April 23, 1866

Burgin, C. Rodgers
Milton
R 753, April 13, 1961
Died: February 22, 1990

Burke, Sir John Bernard
Dublin, Ireland
C 322, April 9, 1874
Died: December 13, 1892

Burkhardt, Frederick H.
New York, New York
C 650, January 13, 1972

Burns, James MacGregor
Williamstown
R 822, January 14, 1971

Burns, Kenneth L.
Walpole, New Hamp-
shire
C 752, October 11, 1990

Burns, Thomas D.
Boston
R 1012, December 13,
1990

Burr, Francis Hardon
Ipswich
R 909, January 13, 1983

Burr, George Lincoln
Ithaca, New York
C 447, November 13,
1919
Died: June 27, 1938

Burrage, Henry Sweetser
Kennebunkport, Maine
C 458, April 12, 1923
Died: March 9, 1926

Burroughs, Charles
Portsmouth, New Hamp-
shire
C 200, February 24, 1842
Died: March 5, 1868

Burton, John Hill
Edinburgh, Scotland
H 46, December 12, 1878
Died: August 10, 1881

Bury, John Bagnell
Cambridge, England
C 419, January 9, 1908
Died: June 1, 1927

Bushman, Richard Lyman
Belmont
R 835, January 10, 1974
C 690, December 13, 1979

Butterfield, Lyman Henry
Williamsburg, Virginia
C 533, December 13, 1951
Boston
R 700, November 10,
1954
Died: April 25, 1982
Memoir, M.H.S. *Procs.*,
94(1982):99–114

Butterfield, Roger Place
New York, New York
C 599, March 12, 1964
Died: January 31, 1981
Memoir, M.H.S., *Procs.*
93(1981):115–118

Bynner, Edwin Lassetter
Boston
R 363, February 13, 1890
Died: August 5, 1893
Memoir: M.H.S. *Procs.*,
2d ser., 9(1894–1895):
173–179

Cabot, George Edward
Boston
R 585, June 14, 1934
Died: April 18, 1946
Memoir: M.H.S. *Procs.*
69(1947–1950):413–
415

Cabot, Godfrey Lowell
Boston
R 690, October 9, 1952
Died: November 2, 1962

Cabot, James Elliot
Brookline
R 304, November 8, 1877
Died: January 16, 1903
Memoir: M.H.S. *Procs.*,
2d ser., 20(1906–
1907):526–533

**Cabot, John Godfrey
Lowell**
Prides Crossing
R 981, January 12, 1989

Cabot, Samuel
Jamaica Plain
R 687, May 8, 1952
Died: September 8, 1967

Caldwell, Sir John
Quebec, Canada
C 145, February 26, 1835
Died: October 26, 1842

Campbell, Eleanor Lewis
Cambridge
R 1030, December 12
1991

Campbell, Levin Hicks
Cambridge
R 855, January 13, 1977

Campbell, Louisa Dresser
Worcester
R 828, December 14, 1972
C 701, December 10, 1981
R 828, April 14, 1983
Died: September 15, 1989

Canham, Erwin Dain
Boston
R 726, November 13,
1958
C 687, December 13, 1979
Died: January 3, 1982

Cappers, Elmer O.
Weston
R 959, May 14, 1987

Cappon, Lester Jesse
Williamsburg, Virginia
C 551, February 14, 1957
Died: August 24, 1981
Memoir, M.H.S. *Procs.*,
93(1981):127–128

Carlyle, Thomas
London, England
H 30, February 10, 1870
Died: February 4, 1881

Carr, Lucien
Cambridge
R 395, June 10, 1897
Died: January 27, 1915
Memoir: M.H.S. *Procs.*,
49(1915–1916):91–94

Carrington, Henry Beebee
New London, Connecti-
cut
C 350, October 13, 1881
Resigned 1886
Died: October 26, 1912

Carroll, Mark Sullivan
Lexington
R 795, January 11, 1968
C 674, March 10, 1977

Carter, Hodding, 3rd
Alexandria, Virginia
C 729, April 8, 1987

Cary, Thomas Greaves
Boston
R 215, August 11, 1858
Died: July 3, 1859
Memoir: M.H.S. *Procs.*,
18(1880–1881):166–
168

**Casgrain, Henry
Raymond**
Quebec, Canada
C 369, February 12, 1891
Died: February 11, 1904

Cass, Lewis
Detroit, Michigan
C 137, July 25, 1833
Died: June 17, 1866

Catanzariti, John
Princeton, New Jersey
C 734, April 14, 1988

Catlin, George
New York, New York
C 179, September 27,
1838
Died: December 23, 1872

**Caulkins, Frances
Manwaring**
Norwich, Connecticut
C 217, April 26, 1849
Died: February 3, 1869

Chadbourne, Paul Ansel
Williamstown
R 320, June 10, 1880
Died: February 23, 1883
Memoir: M.H.S. *Procs.*,
2d ser., 18(1903–
1904):448–453

Chadwick, French Ensor
Newport, Rhode Island
C 431, March 14, 1912
Died: January 27, 1919

Chafee, Zechariah, Jr.
Cambridge
R 606, April 14, 1938
Died: February 8, 1957
Memoir, M.H.S. *Procs.*,
71(1953–1957):429–
431

Appendix I: Members

Challinor, Joan Ridder
Washington, D.C.
C 751, October 11, 1990

Chalmers, George
London, England
C 85, April 25, 1816
Died: May 31, 1825

Chamberlain, Daniel Henry
West Brookfield
R 409, February 8, 1900
Died: April 13, 1907
Memoir: M.H.S. *Procs.*,
41(1907–1908):169–179

Chamberlain, Joshua Lawrence
Brunswick, Maine
C 430, February 8, 1912
Died: February 24, 1914

Chamberlain, Mellen
Chelsea
R 282, January 9, 1873
Died: June 25, 1900
Memoir: M.H.S. *Procs.*,
2d ser., 20(1906–1907):119–146

Chandler, Alfred Dupont, Jr.
Cambridge
R 851, May 13, 1976

Chandler, Peleg Whitman
Boston
R 159, January 25, 1844
Died: May 28, 1889
Tribute: M.H.S. *Procs.*,
2d ser., 4(1887–1889):
377–378; Memoir: 3
M.H.S. *Procs.*, 1

Channing, Edward
Cambridge
R 346, December 11, 1884
Died: January 7, 1931
Memoir: M.H.S. *Procs.*,
64(1930–1932):250–284

Channing, Henry
New London, Connecticut
C 130, May 5, 1831
Died: August 27, 1840

Channing, Henry Morse
Sherborn
R 693, January 8, 1953
Died: October 1, 1964

Chapin, Melville
Cambridge
R 964, October 8, 1987

Charnwood, Godfrey Rathbone Benson, baron
Lichfield, England
C 451, April 14, 1921
Died: February 3, 1945

Chase, George Bigelow
Boston
R 300, November 9, 1876
Died: June 2, 1902
Memoir: M.H.S. *Procs.*,
2d ser., 17(1903):117–127

Chase, Philip Putnam
Milton
R 565, December 11, 1930
Died: March 25, 1978
Memoir, M.H.S. *Procs.*,
90(1978):140–142

Chase, Theodore
Dover
R 738, December 10, 1959

Cheever, David
Boston
R 619, January 9, 1941
Died: August 13, 1955
Memoir, M.H.S. *Procs.*,
71(1953–1957):423–426

Chester, Joseph Lemuel
London, England
C 315, February 13, 1873
Died: May 28, 1882

Childs, Charles Dyer
Stow
R 683, April 10, 1952

Choate, Joseph Hodges
New York, New York
C 381, December 9, 1897
Died: May 14, 1917

Choate, Rufus
Boston
R 137, June 25, 1835
Died: July 13, 1859
Memoir: M.H.S. *Procs.*,
2d ser., 11(1896–1897):124–155

Chorley, Kenneth
Hopewell, New Jersey
C 540, February 11, 1954
Died: March 21, 1974

Churchill, Sir Winston Leonard Spencer
Westerham, England
H 81, December 9, 1943
Died: January 25, 1965

Circourt, Adolphe, comte de
Paris, France
H 12, November 8, 1860
Died: November 17, 1879

Claflin, William Henry, Jr.
Belmont
R 671, October 11, 1951
Died: March 4, 1982
Memoir, M.H.S. *Procs.*,
94(1982):85–87

Clap, Elisha
Boston
R 79, October 29, 1812
Died: October 22, 1830
Memoir: M.H.S. *Procs.*,
1(1791–1835):438–440

Clarke, Hermann Frederick
Brookline
R 597, December 10, 1936
Died: October 29, 1947
Memoir, M.H.S. *Procs.*,
  70(1950–1953):269–
  270

Clarke, James
Halifax, Nova Scotia
C 22, August 17, 1795
Died: October 13, 1802

Clarke, James Freeman
Boston
R 312, March 13, 1879
Died: June 8, 1888
Memoir: M.H.S. *Procs.*,
  2d ser., 4(1887–1889):
  320–335

Clarke, John
Boston
R 32, January 26, 1796
Died: April 2, 1798
Memoir: M.H.S. *Colls.*,
  1st ser., 6:iii–ix

Clay, Henry
Lexington, Kentucky
C 158, July 28, 1836
Died: June 29, 1852

Clement, Edward Henry
Brookline
R 445, February 8, 1906
Died: February 7, 1920
Memoir: M.H.S. *Procs.*,
  56(1922–1923):57–68

Clements, William Lawrence
Bay City, Michigan
C 461, March 13, 1924
Died: November 6, 1934

Clérel de Tocqueville, Charles Alexis Henri Maurice, comte de
Tocqueville, France
H 2, May 14, 1857
Died: April 16, 1859

Clifford, John Henry
New Bedford
R 180, October 13, 1853
Died: January 2, 1876
Memoir: M.H.S. *Procs.*,
  15(1876–1877):368–
  379

Clinton, DeWitt
New York, New York
C 83, April 28, 1814
Died: February 11, 1828

Clive, John Leonard
Cambridge
R 829, December 14, 1972
Resigned May 11, 1989;
  restored June 15, 1989
Died: January 7, 1990
Memoir, M.H.S. *Procs.*,
  102(1990):164–166

Cobb, Samuel Crocker
Boston
R 322, May 12, 1881
Died: February 18, 1891
Memoir: M.H.S. *Procs.*,
  2d ser., 7(1891–1892):
  318–330

Cochran, Andrew William
Quebec, Canada
C 172, February 22, 1838
Died: July 11, 1849

Cochrane, Francis Douglas
Milton
R 814, April 9, 1970

Codman, Charles Russell
Cotuit
R 374, April 13, 1893
Died: October 5, 1918
Memoir: M.H.S. *Procs.*,
  53(1919–1920):168–
  176

Codman, John
Dorchester
R 133, July 25, 1833
Died: December 23, 1847
Memoir: M.H.S. *Procs.*,
  5(1860–1862):
  411–427

Coffin, Joshua
Newbury
R 116, August 28, 1827
Removed 1835
Died: June 24, 1864

Coffin, Peleg, Jr.
Nantucket
R 21, August 13, 1792
Died: March 6, 1805
Memoir: M.H.S. *Procs.*,
  1(1791–1835):
  170–172

Coffin, Sir Isaac
London, England
C 108, October 31, 1822
Died: July 23, 1839

Cogan, John Francis, Jr.
Boston
R 1005, April 12, 1990

Cogswell, Willard Goodrich
Haverhill
R 668, March 8, 1951
Died: May 20, 1955
Memoir, M.H.S. *Procs.*,
  71(1953–1957):402–
  409

Cogswell, William
Boston
R 147, December 26, 1839
Removed 1841
Died: April 18, 1850

Cohen, I. Bernard
Cambridge
R 706, December 8, 1955

Cohen, Sheldon Samuel
Chicago, Illinois
C 745, January 11, 1990

Cole, Arthur Harrison
Cambridge
R 638, May 10, 1945
Died: November 11, 1974
Memoir, M.H.S. *Procs.*,
  86(1974):86–89

Appendix I: Members

Coles, Edward
Philadelphia, Pennsylvania
H 7, March 10, 1859
Died: July 7, 1868

Collier, Abram Thurlow
Weston
R 889, December 11, 1980
C 719, December 13, 1984

Collins, John Frederick
Jamaica Plain
R 827, April 13, 1972
Resigned December 13, 1990

Collins, Winifred Virginia
Lexington
R 844, May 8, 1975

Collinson, Patrick
Cambridge, England
C 749, May 10, 1990

Commager, Henry Steele
R 858, March 10, 1977
New York, New York
C 502, January 11, 1940

Conant, James Bryant
Cambridge
R 595, November 12, 1936
Randolph, New Hampshire
C 539, February 11, 1954
Died: February 11, 1978
Memoir, M.H.S. *Procs.*, 90(1978):122–130

Conway, Jill Ker
Northampton
R 923, December 13, 1984

Coolidge, Archibald Cary
Boston
R 403, February 9, 1899
Died: January 14, 1928
Memoir: M.H.S. *Procs.*, 64(1930–1932):394–403

Coolidge, Charles Allerton
Boston
R 525, December 8, 1921
Died: April 1, 1936

Coolidge, Daniel Jones
Boston
R 836, January 10, 1974

Coolidge, Francis Lowell
Boston
R 956, April 9, 1987

Coolidge, John Calvin
Northampton
R 538, March 12, 1925
Died: January 5, 1933

Coolidge, John Linzee
Boston
R 810, October 9, 1969

Coolidge, John Phillips
Cambridge
R 823, January 14, 1971

Coolidge, Joseph, Jr.
Boston
R 74, April 25, 1811
Died: November 19, 1840
Memoir: M.H.S. *Procs.*, 2(1835–1855):209–210

Coolidge, Nancy Rich
Boston
R 1016, April 11, 1991

Coolidge, Thomas Jefferson, I
Manchester
R 383, May 9, 1895
Died: November 17, 1920
Memoir: M.H.S. *Procs.*, 54(1920–1921):141–149

Coolidge, Thomas Jefferson, II
Brookline
R 604, January 13, 1938
Died: August 6, 1959
Memoir, M.H.S. *Procs.*, 72(1957–1960):373–378

Coolidge, Thomas Jefferson, III
Boston
R 953, January 8, 1987

Coolidge, William Appleton
Topsfield
R 803, November 14, 1968

Cooper, William Durrant
London, England
C 250, May 14, 1857
Died: December 28, 1875

Copley, John Singleton. See Lyndhurst

Coquillette, Daniel R.
Cambridge
R 914, December 15, 1983

Corning, Howard
Salem
R 591, April 11, 1935
Died: February 13, 1956

Costa de Macedo, Joaquim José da
Lisbon, Portugal
C 183, April 25, 1839
Died: 1873

Cott, Nancy Falik
Cambridge
R 997, May 11, 1989

Coupland, Sir Reginald
Oxford, England
C 495, February 10, 1938
Died: November 6, 1952

Courtenay, William Ashmead
Charleston, South Carolina
C 364, October 14, 1886
Resigned December 14, 1905

Cox, Archibald
Wayland
R 786, December 9, 1965

Cox, Gardner
Cambridge
R 876, January 11, 1979
Died: January 14, 1988

Cox, Jacob Dolson
Cincinnati, Ohio
C 373, November 8, 1894
Died: August 4, 1900

Crapo, William Wallace
New Bedford
R 384, November 14,
1895
Died: February 28, 1926
Memoir: M.H.S. *Procs.*,
60(1926–1927):41–48

Craven, Wesley Frank
Princeton, New Jersey
C 600, April 9, 1964
Died: February 10, 1981

Crawford, James Winfield
Brookline
R 945, October 9, 1986

**Creighton, Mandell. See
London**

Crittenden, John Jordan
Frankfort, Kentucky
H 6, February 10, 1859
Died: July 26, 1863

Croce, Benedetto
Naples, Italy
H 77, April 13, 1933
Died: November 20, 1952

Crocker, Uriel Haskell
Boston
R 341, February 14, 1884
Died: March 8, 1902
Memoir: M.H.S. *Procs.*,
2d ser., 19(1905):554–
565

Cross, Arthur Lyon
Ann Arbor, Michigan
C 463, October 8, 1925
Died: June 21, 1940

Cross, Robert Dougherty
New York, New York
C 596, May 9, 1963

**Crowninshield, Edward
Augustus**
Boston
R 219, December 9, 1858
Died: February 20, 1859
Memoir: M.H.S. *Procs.*,
17(1879–1880):356–
359

**Cullum, George
Washington**
New York, New York
C 359, February 14, 1884
Died: February 28, 1892

Cummings, Abbot Lowell
Boston
R 727, December 11, 1958
New Haven, Connecticut
C 713, January 12, 1984

**Cunliffe, Marcus
Faulkner**
Manchester, England
C 575, February 9, 1961
Died: September 2, 1990

**Cunningham, Henry
Winchester**
Milton
R 529, January 11, 1923
Died: October 27, 1930

Cunningham, William
Cambridge, England
C 384, May 11, 1899
Died: June 10, 1919

Current, Richard N.
South Natick
R 978, December 8, 1988

Currier, Thomas Franklin
Belmont
R 627, March 11, 1943
Died: September 14, 1946

**Curry, Jabez Lamar
Monroe**
Richmond, Virginia
C 361, March 12, 1885
Died: February 12, 1903

Curti, Merle Eugene
Madison, Wisconsin
C 560, April 9, 1959

Curtis, Benjamin Robbins
Boston
R 286, May 8, 1873
Died: September 15, 1874
Memoir: M.H.S. *Procs.*,
16(1878):16–35

Curtis, Charles Pelham
Boston
R 665, February 8, 1951
Died: December 23, 1959
Memoir, M.H.S. *Procs.*,
72(1957–1960):385–
394

Curtis, George Ticknor
West Roxbury
R 217, September 9, 1858
New York, New York
C 285, March 9, 1865
Died: March 28, 1894

Curtis, George William
West New Brighton, New
York
C 325, September 9, 1875
Died: August 31, 1892

Curtiss, Frederic Haines
Dover
R 634, November 9, 1944
Died: May 24, 1967

Curtiss, Mina Kirstein
Bethel, Connecticut
C 658, May 10, 1973
Died: November 1, 1985
Memoir, M.H.S. *Procs.*,
97(1985):160–
161

Curtius, Ernst
Berlin, Germany
H 54, May 12, 1887
Died: July 11, 1896

Cushing, Caleb
Newburyport
R 223, February 10, 1859
Died: January 2, 1879
Memoir: M.H.S. *Procs.*,
64(1930–1932):440–
447

Appendix I: Members

Cushing, Harvey
Brookline
R 542, April 8, 1926
New Haven, Connecticut
C 485, May 10, 1934
Removed April 12, 1934
Died: October 7, 1939

Cushing, John Daniel
Hingham
R 754, May 11, 1961
Died: September 17, 1987
Memoir, M.H.S. *Procs.*,
99(1987):168–174

Cutler, Manasseh
Ipswich
R 14, May 29, 1792
Resigned April 27, 1815
Died: July 28, 1823

Cutter, Richard Ammi
Cambridge
R 884, April 10, 1980

Dalton, Charles Henry
Boston
R 436, June 9, 1904
Died: February 23, 1908
Memoir: M.H.S. *Procs.*,
42(1908–1909):287–
312

Dalzell, Robert Fenton, Jr.
Williamstown
R 1031, December 12,
1991

**Dana, Henry Wadsworth
Longfellow**
Cambridge
R 658, March 10, 1949
Died: April 26, 1950

Dana, Richard Henry, I
Cambridge
R 218, September 9, 1858
Died: January 6, 1882
Memoir: M.H.S. *Procs.*,
19(1881–1882):197–
207; M.H.S., *Procs.*, 2d
ser., 6(1890–1891):
262–267

Dana, Richard Henry, II
Cambridge
R 471, June 8, 1911
Died: December 16, 1931

Dane, Nathan
Beverly
R 117, February 19, 1829
Died: February 15, 1835
Memoir: M.H.S. *Procs.*,
2(1835–1855):6–10

Darling, Arthur Burr
Andover
R 629, April 8, 1943
New Haven, Connecticut
C 552, April 11, 1957
Died: November 27, 1971

Daveis, Charles Stewart
Portland, Maine
C 237, May 10, 1855
Died: March 29, 1865

**Davenport, Charles
Milton**
Boston
R 608, April 14, 1938
Died: July 22, 1943
Memoir: M.H.S. *Procs.*
68(1944–1947):442–
443

**Davis, Andrew
McFarland**
Cambridge
R 402, October 13, 1898
Died: March 29, 1920
Memoir: M.H.S. *Procs.*,
54(1920–1921):204–
211

**Davis, Archibald
Kimbrough**
Winston-Salem, North
Carolina
C 669, January 13, 1977

Davis, Charles Thornton
Marblehead
R 569, October 8, 1931
Died: September 4, 1936

Davis, Daniel
Portland, Maine
R 16, May 29, 1792
Resigned June 26, 1834
Died: October 27, 1835

Davis, David Brion
New Haven, Connecticut
C 747, April 12, 1990

Davis, George Thomas
Greenfield
R 204, February 11, 1858
Portland, Maine
C 311, February 8, 1872
Died: June 17, 1877

Davis, Horace
San Francisco, California
C 403, April 9, 1903
Died: July 12, 1916

Davis, Isaac P.
Boston
R 121, August 24, 1830
Died: January 13, 1855
Memoir: M.H.S. *Procs.*,
11(1869–1870):94–99

Davis, John
Plymouth
R 13, December 21, 1791
Died: January 14, 1847
Memoir: M.H.S. *Colls.*,
3d ser., 10:186–203

Davis, Nathaniel Morton
Plymouth
R 149, July 30, 1840
Died: July 29, 1848
Memoir: M.H.S. *Colls.*,
4th ser., 4:492–494

Davis, Samuel
Plymouth
R 77, January 30, 1812
Died: July 10, 1829
Memoir: M.H.S. *Colls.*,
3d ser., 5:253–255

Davis, Walter Goodwin
Portland, Maine
C 534, January 10, 1952
Died: June 11, 1966

Davis, William Thomas
Plymouth
R 275, May 12, 1870
Resigned May 13, 1880
Died: December 3, 1907

Dawson, Henry Barton
Morrisania, New York
C 281, April 9, 1863
Died: May 23, 1889

Day, Thomas
Hartford, Connecticut
C 198, December 31, 1840
Died: March 1, 1855

De Peyster, Frederic
New York, New York
H 47, March 11 1880
Died: August 17, 1882

De Normandie, James
Boston
R 401, June 9, 1898
Died: October 6, 1924
Memoir: M.H.S. *Procs.*,
59(1925–1926):26–34

Dean, James
Burlington, Vermont
C 133, October 26, 1831
Died: January 20, 1849

Deane, Charles
Cambridge
R 174, October 25, 1849
Died: November 13, 1889
Memoir: M.H.S. *Procs.*,
2d ser., 7(1891–1892):
45–89

Dearborn, Henry
Alexander Scammell
Roxbury
R 131, January 26, 1832
Resigned after 1833
Died: July 29, 1851

Dechame, Stephen Pell
Boston
R 976, October 13, 1988

Demos, John Putnam
Waltham
R 865, May 12, 1977
New Haven, Connecticut
C 727, December 11, 1986
Resigned, April 12, 1990

Dennis, Rodney Gove
Cambridge
R 991, April 13, 1989

Denny, Henry Gardner
Boston
R 264, December 13, 1866
Died: September 19, 1907
Memoir: M.H.S. *Procs.*,
41(1907–1908):310–
314

Derby, Elias Hasket
Salem
R 60, April 28 1801
Resigned 1801
Died: September 16, 1826

Desaussure, Henry
William
Charleston, South Caro-
lina
C 32, April 25, 1797
Died: March 29, 1839

Desimoni, Cornelio
Genoa, Italy
C 358, March 8, 1883
Died: June 29, 1899

Devens, Charles
Worcester
R 294, March 11, 1875
Died: January 7, 1891
Memoir: M.H.S. *Procs.*,
2d ser., 7(1891–1892):
104–117

Dewing, Arthur Stone
Newton
R 655, May 13, 1948
Died: January 19, 1971
Memoir, M.H.S. *Procs.*,
83(1971):165–167

DeWitt, Benjamin
Albany, New York
C 44, July 18 1799
Died: September 10, 1819

Dexter, Aaron
Boston
R 15, May 29, 1792
Died: February 28, 1829
Memoir: M.H.S. *Procs.*,
1(1791–1835):421–
423

Dexter, Franklin
Bowditch
New Haven, Connecticut
C 339, May 8, 1879
Died: August 13, 1920

Dexter, George
Cambridge
R 305, November 8, 1877
Died: December 18, 1883
Memoir: M.H.S. *Procs.*,
2d ser., 1(1884–1885):
327–334

Dexter, Henry Martyn
Boston
R 272, August 12, 1869
Died: November 13, 1890
Memoir: M.H.S. *Procs.*,
7(1891–1892):90–103

Dexter, Julius
Cincinnati, Ohio
C 348, February 10, 1881
Died: October 21, 1898

Dexter, Morton
Boston
R 382, March 14, 1895
Died: October 29, 1910
Memoir: M.H.S. *Procs.*,
44(1910–1911):489–
492

Dicey, Albert Venn
Oxford, England
C 396, April 10, 1902
Died: April 7, 1922

Dickson, Brenton
Halliburton, 3rd
Weston
R 869, May 11, 1978
Died: August 29 1988
Memoir, M.H.S. *Procs.*,
100(1988):144–147

Appendix I: Members

Dike, Kenneth Onwuka
Belmont
R 856, January 13, 1977
C 702, December 10, 1981
Died: October 26, 1983

Diman, Jeremiah Lewis
Providence, Rhode Island
C 314, February 13, 1873
Died: February 3, 1881

Disney, John, I
Ingatestone, England
C 70, August 29, 1809
Died: December 26, 1816

Disney, John, II
Ingatestone, England
C 173, June 28, 1838
Died: May 6, 1857

Dix, John Adams
New York, New York
H 23, January 14, 1864
Died: April 21, 1879

Dodd, Edwin Merrick
Cambridge
R 635, November 9, 1944
Died: November 3, 1951
Memoir, M.H.S. *Procs.*,
70(1950–1953):282–
289

Dodge, Ernest Stanley
Danvers
R 644, October 10, 1946
Died: February 9, 1980
Memoir, M.H.S. *Procs.*,
92(1980):143–146

Dodge, Theodore Ayrault
Brookline
R 389, May 14, 1896
Died: October 26, 1909
Memoir: M.H.S. *Procs.*,
43(1909–1910):208–
221

Donald, David Herbert
Princeton, New Jersey
C 571, December 8, 1960
R 839, April 10, 1975

Donald, Elijah Winchester
Boston
R 412, May 10, 1900
Died: August 6, 1904
Memoir: M.H.S. *Procs.*,
44(1910–1911):460–
488

Donaldson, Thomas
Baltimore, Maryland
C 218, November 22,
1849
Died: October 4, 1877

Dow, George Francis
Topsfield
R 558, November 14,
1929
Died: June 5, 1936

Dow, Sterling
Cambridge
R 707, January 12, 1956

Dowse, William Bradford Homer
Sherborn
R 502, February 14, 1918
Died: April 19, 1928
Memoir: M.H.S. *Procs.*,
62(1928–1929):67–84

Doyle, John Andrew
Oxford, England
C 367, May 12, 1887
Died: August 4, 1907

Draper, Lyman Copeland
Madison, Wisconsin
C 277, December 12, 1861
Died: August 26, 1891

Du Ponceau, Peter Stephen
Philadelphia, Pennsylvania
C 92, January 29, 1818
Died: April 1, 1844

Dunbar, Charles Franklin
Cambridge
R 293, February 11, 1875
Died: January 29, 1900
Memoir: M.H.S. *Procs.*,
2d ser., 14(1900–
1901):218–228

Dunn, Charles William
Cambridge
R 939, January 9, 1986

Dunn, John
Killala, Ireland
C 36, December 1, 1797
Died: ?

Dunn, Mary Maples
Northampton
R 982, January 12, 1989

Dunn, Richard Slator
Philadelphia, Pennsylvania
C 723, May 8, 1986

Dunning, William Archibald
New York, New York
C 407, January 12, 1905
Died: August 25, 1922

Dupin, François Charles Pierre, baron
Paris, France
H 8, April 14, 1859
Died: January, 1873

DuPont, Henry Francis
Winterthur, Delaware
C 529, March 8, 1951
Died: April 10, 1969

Dupree, Anderson Hunter
Providence, Rhode Island
C 648, April 8, 1971

Durfee, Job
Tiverton, Rhode Island
C 171, October 26, 1837
Died: July 26, 1847

Duyckinck, Evert Augustus
New York, New York
C 286, December 14, 1865
Died: August 13, 1878

Dwight, Theodore, I
New York, New York
C 140, March 27, 1834
Died: June 12, 1846

Dwight, Theodore, II
New York, New York
C 141, March 27, 1834
Died: October 16, 1866

Dwight, Timothy
New Haven, Connecticut
C 35, October 31, 1797
Died: January 11, 1817

Eames, Wilberforce
New York, New York
C 415, April 11, 1907
Died: December 6, 1937

Eaton, Cyrus
Warren, Maine
C 228, September 8, 1853
Died: January 21, 1875

Ebeling, Christoph Daniel
Hamburg, Germany
C 16, October 28, 1794
Died: June 30, 1817

Eddy, Samuel
Providence, Rhode Island
C 62, August 27, 1805
Died: February 3, 1839

Edes, Henry Herbert
Cambridge
R 468, January 12, 1911
Died: October 13, 1922

Eliot, Andrew
Fairfield, Connecticut
C 41, October 30, 1798
Died: October 26, 1805
Memoir: M.H.S. *Colls.*,
10:188–189

Eliot, Charles William
Cambridge
R 288, October 9, 1873
Died: August 22, 1926
Memoir: M.H.S. *Procs.*,
60(1926–1927):2–15,
64(1930–1932):364–
368

Eliot, Ephraim
Boston
R 81, August 24, 1813
Resigned January 26,
1826
Died: Sept. 13, 1827

Eliot, John
Boston
R 2, January 24, 1791
Died: February 14, 1813
Memoir: M.H.S. *Colls.*,
2d ser., 1:211–248

Eliot, Samuel
Brookline
R 179, March 10, 1853
Hartford, Connecticut
Removed June 24, 1856
C 246, October 9, 1856
Boston
R 179, April 20, 1865
Died: September 14, 1898
Memoir: M.H.S., *Procs.*,
2d ser., 14(1900–
1901):105–126

Eliot, Samuel Atkins
Cambridge
R 579, April 13, 1933
Died: October 15, 1950
Memoir, M.H.S. *Procs.*,
70(1950–1953):274–
276

Eliot, William Greenleaf
St. Louis, Missouri
C 280, March 12, 1863
Died: January 23, 1887

Eller, Ernest McNeill
Annapolis, Maryland
C 567, February 11, 1960

Elliott, Byron Kauffman
Boston
R 930, May 9, 1985

Ellis, Arthur Blake
Boston
R 330, March 9, 1882
Burley, Washington
C 401, January 8, 1903
Died: December 25, 1923

Ellis, George Edward
Boston
R 153, October 28, 1841
Died: December 20, 1894
Memoir: M.H.S. *Procs.*, 2
ser., 10(1895–1896):
207–255

Emerson, Amelia Forbes
Concord
R 830, December 14, 1972
Died: October 24, 1979

Emerson, Edward Waldo
Concord
R 464, June 9, 1910
Died: January 27, 1930
Memoir: M.H.S. *Procs.*,
65(1932–1936):387–
390

Emerson, George Barrell
Boston
R 252, April 9, 1863
Died: March 4, 1881
Memoir: M.H.S. *Procs.*,
20(1882–1883):232–
259

Emerson, Ralph Waldo
Concord
R 280, June 15, 1871
Died: April 27, 1882
Memoir: M.H.S. *Procs.*,
2d ser., 2(1885–1886):
107–117

Emerson, William
Boston
R 62, July 13, 1801
Died: May 12, 1811
Memoir: M.H.S. *Colls.*,
2d ser., 1:254–258;
M.H.S., *Procs.*,
55(1921–1922):8–29

Emerton, Ephraim
Cambridge
R 429, April 9, 1903
Died: March 3, 1935
Memoir: M.H.S. *Procs.*
68(1944–1947):444–
445

Appendix I: Members

Emmet, Richard Stockton, Jr.
Westford
R 870, May 11, 1978

Endicott, William
Boston
R 446, March 8, 1906
Died: November 7, 1914
Memoir: M.H.S. *Procs.*,
48(1914–1915):243–
252

Endicott, William Crowninshield, I
Salem
R 257, April 14, 1864
Died: May 6, 1900
Memoir: M.H.S. *Procs.*,
2d ser., 15(1901–
1902):523–537

Endicott, William Crowninshield, II
Danvers
R 487, January 14, 1915
Died: November 28, 1936
Memoir: M.H.S. *Procs.*,
66(1936–1941):423–
426

Ernst, Harold Clarence
Boston
R 517, November 11,
1920
Died: September 7, 1922
Memoir: M.H.S. *Procs.*,
56(1922–1923):162–
166

Ernst, Roger
Brookline
R 694, January 8, 1953
Died: March 29, 1955

Erskine, David Stewart. See Buchan

Erskine, John
Edinburgh, Scotland
C 9, October 8, 1792
Died: January 19, 1803

Erving, George William
New York, New York
C 109, October 31, 1822
Died: July 22, 1850

Evarts, William Maxwell
New York, New York
H 43, November 9, 1876
Died: February 28, 1901

Everett, Alexander Hill
Boston
R 119, August 24, 1830
Removed 1841
Died: June 29, 1847

Everett, Edward
Cambridge
R 98, April 27, 1820
Died: January 15, 1865
Memoir: M.H.S. *Procs.*,
2d ser., 18(1903–
1904):91–117

Everett, William
Cambridge
R 299, March 8, 1876
Died: February 16, 1910
Memoir: M.H.S. *Procs.*,
49(1915–1916):43–58

Fainsod, Merle
Cambridge
R 777, October 8, 1964
Died: February 11, 1972

Fairbank, John King
Cambridge
R 789, January 12, 1967
Died: September 14, 1991

Fairbanks, Jonathan Leo
Westwood
R 924, December 13, 1984

Faribault, George Barthélemy
Quebec, Canada
C 248, January 8, 1857
Died: December 21, 1866

Farlow, John Woodford
Boston
R 507, January 9, 1919
Died: September 23, 1937
Memoir: M.H.S. *Procs.*
68(1944–1947):446–
448

Farmer, John
Amherst, New Hampshire
C 104, January 31, 1822
Died: August 13, 1838

Farnham, John Hay
Salem, Indiana
C 131, August 30, 1831
Died: July 10, 1833

Farrand, Max
New Haven, Connecticut
C 443, April 10, 1919
Died: June 17, 1945

Farwell, John Whittemore
Cohasset
R 536, January 8, 1925
Died: October 7, 1929

Faÿ, Bernard
Paris, France
C 484, April 13, 1933
Dropped March 9, 1944

Fay, Sidney Bradshaw
Cambridge
R 556, April 11, 1929
Died: August 29, 1967
Memoir: M.H.S. *Procs.*,
79(1967):206–208

Feiling, Sir Keith Grahame
London, England
H 87, January 8, 1953
Died: September 16, 1977

Felt, Joseph Barlow
Salem
R 123, August 24, 1830
Died: September 8, 1869
Memoir: M.H.S. *Procs.*,
14(1875–1876):113–
116

Felton, Cornelius Conway
Cambridge
R 191, March 13, 1856
Died: February 26, 1862
Memoir: M.H.S. *Procs.,*
10(1867–1869):352–
368

Fenn, William Wallace
Cambridge
R 532, December 13, 1923
Died: March 6, 1932
Memoir: M.H.S. *Procs.,*
65(1932–1936):503–
506

Ferguson, William Scott
Prince Edward Island,
Canada
C 474, May 8, 1930
Died: April 28, 1954

Fetchko, Peter
Salem
R 971, May 12, 1988

Field, Fred Tarbell
Newton
R 610, November 10,
1938
Died: July 23, 1950

Field, Walbridge Abner
Boston
R 378, April 12, 1894
Died: July 15, 1899
Memoir: M.H.S. *Procs.,*
2d ser., 19(1905):61–
82

Fiering, Norman Sanford
Providence, Rhode Island
C 714, May 24, 1984

Fillmore, Millard
Buffalo, New York
H 20, April 9, 1863
Died: March 7, 1874

Firth, Sir Charles Harding
Oxford, England
C 392, October 10, 1901
H 70, February 13, 1919
Died: February 19, 1936

Fisher, David Hackett
Wayland
R 1000, January 11, 1990

Fisher, George Park
New Haven, Connecticut
C 378, January 14, 1897
Died: December 20, 1909

**Fisher, Herbert Albert
Laurens**
London, England
C 445, June 12, 1919
H 79, March 11, 1937
Died: April 17, 1940

Fisher, Joshua Francis
Philadelphia, Pennsylva-
nia
C 162, October 27, 1836
Died: January 21, 1873

Fisk, Moses
White Pine, Tennessee
C 73, October 31, 1811
Died: July 26, 1840

Fisk, William
Waltham
R 39, April 25, 1797
Died: August 13, 1803
Memoir: M.H.S. *Colls.,*
1st ser., 9:206–207

Fiske, John
Cambridge
R 371, March 10, 1892
Died: July 4, 1901
Memoir: M.H.S. *Procs.,*
46(1912–1913):167–
174

Fitch, Ebenezer
Williamstown
R 49, October 30, 1798
Resigned April 24, 1817
Died: March 21, 1833

Fitz, Reginald Heber
Boston
R 478, April 10, 1913
Died: September 30, 1913
Memoir: M.H.S. *Procs.,*
52(1918–1919):104–
116

Fitzpatrick, Jane
Stockbridge
R 972, May 12, 1988

**Fitz-James Stuart. See
Berwick y Alba,**

Flather, Newell
Newton
R 966, January 14, 1988

Fleming, Donald H.
Cambridge
R 775, May 14, 1964

Fleming, Ronald Lee
Cambridge
R 977, October 13, 1988

Flint, Timothy
Red River, Louisiana
C 123, February 19, 1829
Died: August 16, 1840

Foley, Mason Allen
Hingham
R 797, February 8, 1968
Died: June 8, 1968

Folsom, Charles
Cambridge
R 245, May 9, 1861
Died: November 8, 1872
Memoir: M.H.S. *Procs.,*
13(1873–1875):26–42

Folsom, George
New York, New York
C 166, December 29, 1836
Died: March 27, 1869

Foote, Henry Wilder, I
Boston
R 291, November 12,
1874
Died: May 29, 1889
Memoir: M.H.S. *Procs.,*
2d ser., 8(1892–1894):
236–251

Foote, Henry Wilder, II
Cambridge
R 560, January 9, 1930
Died: August 27, 1964

Appendix I: Members

Forbes, Allan
Westwood
R 519, January 13, 1921
Died: July 9, 1955
Memoir, M.H.S. *Procs.*,
71(1953–1957):412–
422

Forbes, Allyn Bailey
Cambridge
R 586, June 14, 1934
Died: January 21, 1947
Memoir, M.H.S. *Procs.*,
70(1950–1953):267–
268

Forbes, Esther
Worcester
R 793, February 9, 1967
Died: August 12, 1967
Memoir, M.H.S. *Procs.*,
79(1967):204–205

**Forbes, Francis Murray,
Jr.**
Boston
R 739, January 14, 1960

**Forbes, Henry Ashton
Crosby**
Cambridge
R 808, April 10, 1969

Forbes, Robert Bennet
Milton
R 239, January 10, 1861
Died: November 23, 1889
Memoir: M.H.S. *Procs.*,
2d ser., 6(1890–1891):
197–202

Forbes, William Cameron
Norwood
R 522, June 9, 1921
Died: December 24, 1959

Force, Manning Ferguson
Cincinnati, Ohio
C 320, November 13,
1873
Died: May 8, 1899

Force, Peter
Washington, D.C.
C 245, August 14, 1856
Died: January 23, 1868

Ford, Franklin Lewis
Belmont
R 749, February 8, 1961
Resigned, June 15, 1989

**Ford, Worthington
Chauncey**
Cambridge
R 413, November 8, 1900
Removed October 10,
1902
C 400, December 11, 1902
R 413, February 11, 1909
Died: March 7, 1941
Memoir, M.H.S. *Procs.*,
69(1947–1950):407–
411

Forster, John
London, England
C 284, February 9, 1865
H 38, March 11, 1875
Died: February 2, 1876

**Foster, Charles Henry
Wheelwright**
Needham
R 768, April 11 1963
A 14, January 12, 1967
C 615 , January 11, 1968
R 768, December 10, 1981

Foster, Francis Apthorp
Vineyard Haven
R 496, May 11, 1916
Died: March 18, 1966

Foster, Theodore
Providence, Rhode Island
C 49, October 28, 1800
Died: January 13, 1828

Fothergill, Anthony
Bath, England
C 58, August 28, 1804
Died: May 11, 1813

**Fowler, William Morgan,
Jr.**
Reading
R 941, May 8, 1986

Fox, Dixon Ryan
Schenectady, New York
C 492, May 13, 1937
Died: January 30, 1945

Fox, Gustavus Vasa
Boston
R 306, December 13, 1877
Washington, D.C.
C 357, February 8, 1883
Died: October 29, 1883

Francis, Convers
Watertown
R 127, May 5, 1831
Died: April 7, 1863
Memoir: M.H.S. *Procs.*,
8(1864–1865):233–
253

Francis, Sir Frank Chalton
London, England
C 573, January 12, 1961
Died: October 15, 1988
Memoir, M.H.S. *Procs.*,
100(1988):147–148

Francis, John Wakefield
New York, New York
C 81, January 27, 1814
Died: February 8, 1861

Franklin, John Hope
Chicago, Illinois
C 601, October 8, 1964

Fraser, Charles
Charleston, South Caro-
lina
C 134, January 26, 1832
Died: October 5, 1860

Frédéricq, Paul
Ghent, Belgium
C 446, October 9, 1919
Died: March 30, 1920

Freeman, Constant
Washington, D.C.
C 72, April 25, 1811
Died: February 27, 1824

**Freeman, Douglas
Southall**
Richmond, Virginia
C 516, March 8, 1945
Died: June 13, 1953

Freeman, Edward Augustus
Oxford, England
H 31, September 11, 1873
Died: March 16, 1892

Freeman, James
Boston
R 3, January 24, 1791
Died: November 14, 1835
Memoir: M.H.S. *Colls.*, 3d ser., 5:255–271

Freeman, Nathaniel
Sandwich
R 24, October 23, 1792
Resigned October 25, 1808
Died: September 20, 1827

Freiberg, Malcolm
Belmont
R 725, May 8, 1958

Freidel, Frank Burt, Jr.
Belmont
R 729, February 12, 1959; October 9, 1986
C 696, October 8, 1981

French, Allen
Concord
R 546, March 10, 1927
Died: October 6, 1946
Memoir: M.H.S. *Procs.* 69(1947–1950):416–419

French, Benjamin Franklin
New Orleans, Louisiana
C 254, September 10, 1857
Died: May 30, 1877

Frese, Joseph Raphael
New York, New York
C 582, February 8, 1962

Freund, Paul Abraham
Cambridge
R 733, April 8, 1959

Friedlaender, Marc
Cambridge
R 785, October 14, 1965

Friedman, Lee Max
Boston
R 637, February 8, 1945
Died: August 7, 1957

Friedrichsthal, Emanuel, ritter von
Vienna, Austria
C 194, August 25, 1840
Died: March 3, 1842

Frost, Donald McKay
Boston
R 613, February 9, 1939
Died: April 14, 1958

Frothingham, Nathaniel Langdon
Boston
R 156, October 26, 1843
Died: April 4, 1870
Memoir: M.H.S. *Procs.*, 11(1869–1870):371–386

Frothingham, Octavius Brooks
Boston
R 354, February 10, 1887
Died: November 27, 1895
Memoir: M.H.S. *Procs.*, 2d ser., 10(1895–1896):207–255

Frothingham, Paul Revere
Boston
R 488, March 12, 1915
Died: November 27, 1926
Memoir: M.H.S. *Procs.*, 60(1926–1927):383–392

Frothingham, Richard
Charlestown
R 166, July 30, 1846
Died: January 29, 1880
Memoir: M.H.S. *Procs.*, 2d ser., 1(1884–1885):381–393

Frothingham, Thomas Goddard
Boston
R 521, March 10, 1921
Died: March 17, 1945

Froude, James Anthony
London, England
H 26, April 11, 1867
Died: October 20, 1894

Fuess, Claude Moore
Andover
R 551, February 9, 1928
Died: September 9, 1963
Memoir: M.H.S. *Procs.*, 76(1964):137–153

Fulton , John Farquhar
New Haven, Connecticut
C 566, January 14, 1960
Died: May 29, 1960

Fuñes, Gregorio
Cordova, Argentina
C 115, October 27, 1825
Died: January 11, 1829

Gabriel, Ralph Henry
New Haven, Connecticut
C 520, February 14, 1946
Died: April 21, 1987

Gage, Thomas Hovey
Worcester
R 568, April 9, 1931
Died: July 15, 1938

Galindo, Juan
Guatemala, Guatemala
C 154, January 28, 1836
Died: Before 1858

Gallatin, Albert
New York, New York
C 122, February 19, 1829
Died: August 12, 1849

Galvin, John Thomas
Boston
R 861, April 14, 1977

Gammell, William
Providence, Rhode Island
C 317, July 10, 1873
Died: April 3, 1889

Gannett, Caleb
Cambridge
R 41, October 31, 1797
Died: April 25, 1818
Memoir: M.H.S. *Colls.*, 2d ser., 8:277–285

Appendix I: Members

Gardiner, Robert Hallowell
Gardiner, Maine
H 10, May 12, 1859
Died: March 22, 1864

Gardiner, Samuel Rawson
Oxford, England
C 323, November 12, 1874
H 56, October 8, 1896
Died: February 23, 1902

Gardner, George Peabody
Brookline
R 744, May 12, 1960
Died: September 17, 1976
Memoir, M.H.S. *Procs.*, 88(1976):132–134

Gardner, John Lowell
Hamilton
R 866, May 12, 1977

Gardner, Samuel Pickering
Boston
R 108, August 24, 1824
Died: December 18, 1843
Memoir: M.H.S. *Procs.*, 2(1835–1855):282–283

Garnett, Richard
London, England
C 377, December 10, 1896
Died: April 13, 1906

Garraty, John Arthur
New York, New York
C 659, May 9, 1974

Garrett, Wendell Douglas
Cambridge
R 766, February 14, 1963
A 15, January 12, 1967
C 616, January 11, 1968

Gasparin, Agénor Etienne, comte du
Geneva, Switzerland
H 18, February 12, 1863
Died: June 4, 1871

Gay, Edwin Francis
Cambridge
R 477, December 12, 1912
Removed November 5, 1919
Pasadena, California
C 448, June 10, 1920
Brookline
R 477, November 13, 1924
Removed August 17, 1936
Died: February 7, 1946

Gay, Frederick Lewis
Brookline
R 480, January 8, 1914
Died: March 3, 1916
Memoir: M.H.S. *Procs.*, 50(1916–1917):110–117

Gay, Harry Nelson
Rome, Italy
C 470, December 13, 1928
Died: August 13, 1932

Gibbs, William
Lexington
R 141, August 30, 1836
Resigned March 27, 1851
Died: December 23, 1853

Gilbert, Edward Hooker
Ware
R 424, October 9, 1902
Died: October 7, 1921
Memoir: M.H.S. *Procs.*, 55(1921–1922):199–200

Gilbert, Helen Homans
Dover
R 927, April 11, 1985
Died: September 26, 1989

Gillerman, Gerald
Boston
R 998, December 14, 1989

Gilman, Daniel Coit
Baltimore, Maryland
C 388, January 10, 1901
Died: October 13, 1908

Gilmore, Myron Piper
Belmont
R 728, December 11, 1958
A 11, February 11, 1965
C 617, January 11, 1968
R 728, April 10, 1975
Died: October 27, 1978
Memoir, M.H.S. *Procs.*, 90(1978):146–151

Gilpin, Henry Dilworth
Philadelphia, Pennsylvania
C 265, April 14, 1859
Died: January 29, 1860

Gipson, Lawrence Henry
Rydal, Pennsylvania
C 561, April 9, 1959
Died: September 26, 1971

Gleason, Herbert
Boston
R 1032, December 12, 1991

Gleason, Sarell Everett
Washington, D.C.
C 598, December 12, 1963
Died: November 20, 1974
Memoir, M.H.S. *Procs.*, 86(1974):90–94

Goddard, Delano Alexander
Boston
R 290, October 8, 1874
Died: January 10, 1882
Memoir: M.H.S. *Procs.*, 19(1881–1882):429–437

Godine, David Richard
Milton
R 905, January 14, 1982

Gomes, Peter John
Cambridge
R 852, May 13, 1976

Gooch, George Peabody
London, England
C 453, December 8, 1921
H 86, December 13, 1951
Died: August 31, 1968

Goodell, Abner Cheney, Jr.
Salem
R 277, March 9, 1871
Died: July 19, 1914
Memoir: M.H.S. *Procs.*,
52(1918–1919):38–43

Goodhue, Jonathan
New York, New York
C 94, April 29, 1819
Died: November 24, 1848

Goodhue, Lydia Davis
Wellesley
R 960, May 14, 1987

Goodspeed, Charles Eliot
Shirley
R 612, December 8, 1938
Died: October 30, 1950
Memoir, M.H.S. *Procs.*,
71(1953–1957):362–
365

Goodspeed, George Talbot
Concord
R 662, December 14, 1950
Resigned
Died: January 28, 1970

Goodwin, Ezra Shaw
Sandwich
R 105, April 25, 1822
Died: February 5, 1833
Memoir: M.H.S. *Colls.*,
3d ser., 5:282–286

Goodwin, William Watson
Cambridge
R 350, October 14, 1886
Died: June 15, 1912
Memoir: M.H.S. *Procs.*,
51(1917–1918):233–
237

Gordon, George Angier
Boston
R 398, February 10, 1898
Died: October 25, 1929

Gore, Christopher
Waltham
R 42, January 30, 1798
Died: March 1, 1827
Memoir: M.H.S. *Colls.*,
3d ser., 3:191–209

Gräberg af Hemsö, Jacob, Conte
Florence, Italy
C 199, May 27, 1841
Died: 1847

Graebner, Norman A.
Charlottesville, Virginia
C 709, December 15, 1983

Graham, James Duncan
Richmond, Virginia
C 207, May 30, 1844
Died: December 28, 1865

Graham, Patricia Albjerg
Cambridge
R 1009, October 11, 1990

Grahame, James
London, England
C 128, October 29, 1829
Died: July 3, 1842
Memoir: M.H.S. *Colls.*,
3d ser., 9:2–41

Grant, Frederic D., Jr.
Boston
R 1021, May 9, 1991

Grant, Robert
Boston
R 490, June 10, 1915
Died: May 19, 1940

Grattan, Thomas Colley
London, England
C 209, December 26, 1844
Died: July 4, 1864

Graubard, Stephen R.
Cambridge
R 848, December 12, 1975

Gray, Edward
Milton
R 512, January 8, 1920
Died: October 14, 1923
Memoir: M.H.S. *Procs.*,
58(1924–1925):198–
200

Gray, Francis Calley
Boston
R 90, January 29, 1818
Died: December 29, 1856
Memoir: M.H.S. *Procs.*,
47(1913–1914):529–
534

Gray, Horace
Boston
R 243, April 11, 1861
Died: September 15, 1902
Memoir: M.H.S. *Procs.*,
2d ser., 18(1903–
1904):155–187

Gray, John Chipman, I
Boston
R 154, December 30, 1841
Died: March 3, 1881
Memoir: M.H.S. *Procs.*,
2d ser., 4(1887–1889):
22–27

Gray, John Chipman, II
Boston
R 399, March 10, 1898
Died: February 25, 1915
Memoir: M.H.S. *Procs.*,
49(1915–1916):387–
410

Gray, Roland
Cambridge
R 574, March 10, 1932
Died: November 23, 1957

Gray, Russell
Boston
R 504, April 11, 1918
Died: June 7, 1929

Gray, William
Boston
R 289, May 14, 1874
Resigned October 9, 1884
Died: February 11, 1892

Green, John Richard
London, England
C 329, November 9, 1876
Died: March 7, 1883

Appendix I: Members

Green, Samuel Abbott
Boston
R 234, January 12, 1860
Died: December 5, 1918
Tributes: M.H.S. *Procs.*,
52(1918–1919):45–55
Memoir: M.H.S. *Procs.*,
54(1920–1921):236–
242

Greene, Albert Gorton
Providence, Rhode Island
C 261, October 14, 1858
Died: January 4, 1868

**Greene, George
Washington**
Providence, Rhode Island
C 279, February 12, 1863
Died: February 2, 1883

Greene, Jack Phillip
Baltimore, Maryland
C 678, January 12, 1978

Greenleaf, Simon
Cambridge
R 143, November 23,
1837
Died: October 6, 1853
Memoir: M.H.S. *Procs.*,
2(1835–1855):563–
568

**Greenough, Charles
Pelham**
Brookline
R 457, April 9, 1908
Died: November 21, 1924
Memoir: M.H.S. *Procs.*,
58(1924–1925):395–
400

**Greenough, Chester
Noyes**
Cambridge
R 483, May 14, 1914
Died: February 26, 1938

**Greenough, William
Whitwell**
Boston
R 314, April 10, 1879
Died: June 17, 1899
Memoir: M.H.S. *Procs.*,
2d ser., 14(1900–
1901):468–482

Greenslet, Ferris
Boston
R 493, January 13, 1916
Died: November 19, 1959
Memoir, M.H.S. *Procs.*,
72(1957–1960):379–
384

**Greenwood, Francis
William Pitt**
Boston
R 110, April 28, 1825
Died: August 2, 1843
Memoir: M.H.S. *Procs.*,
2(1835–1855):272–
275

Grew, Joseph Clark
Washington, D.C.
C 475, October 9, 1930
Died: May 25, 1965

Griffin, Frederic
Montreal, Canada
C 232, August 10, 1854
Died: April 3, 1878

Grigsby, Hugh Blair
Norfolk, Virginia
C 270, February 14, 1861
H 35, February 11, 1875
Died: April 28, 1881

**Grinnell, Frank
Washburn**
Boston
R 557, October 10, 1929
Died: March 13, 1964
Memoir, M.H.S. *Procs.*,
76(1964):154–156

**Griswold, Erwin
Nathaniel**
Belmont
R 760, March 8, 1962
C 663, April 10, 1975

Gross, Charles
Cambridge
R 416, May 9, 1901
Died: December 3, 1909
Memoir: M.H.S. *Procs.*,
49(1915–1916):161–
166

Grote, George
London, England
H 21, May 14, 1863
Died: June 18, 1871

Grover, Wayne Clayton
Silver Spring, Maryland
C 585, May 10, 1962
Died: June 8, 1970

Guild, Curtis, Jr.
Boston
R 465, October 13, 1910
Died: April 6, 1915
Memoir: M.H.S. *Procs.*,
50(1916–1917):308–
312

**Guizot, François Pierre
Guillaume**
Paris, France
H 1, May 14, 1857
Died: September 12, 1874

Gummere, Richard Mott
Cambridge
R 722, April 10, 1958
Died: December 13, 1969
Memoir, M.H.S. *Procs.*,
81(1969):220–233

Gutheim, Marjorie Frye
Cambridge
R 890, December 11, 1980

**Hadley, Rollin van
Nostrand**
Boston
R 895, January 8, 1981
C 750, October 11, 1990

Hale, Edward Everett
Boston
R 238, January 10, 1861
Died: June 10, 1909
Memoir: M.H.S. *Procs.*,
55(1921–1922):307–
318

Hale, George Silsbee
Boston
R 267, April 11, 1867
Died: July 27, 1897
Memoir: M.H.S. *Procs.*,
2d ser., 12(1897–
1899):483–500

Hale, Horatio
Clinton, Ontario, Canada
C 363, March 11, 1886
Died: December 28, 1896

Hale, Judson
Dublin, New Hampshire
C 736, May 12, 1988

Hale, Nathan
Boston
R 96, January 27, 1820
Died: February 8, 1863
Memoir: M.H.S. *Procs.*,
18(1880–1881):270–
279

Hale, Philip
Brookline
R 528, November 9, 1922
Died: November 30, 1934

Hale, Richard Walden, Jr.
Chestnut Hill
R 672, October 11, 1951
Died: February 25, 1976
Memoir, M.H.S. *Procs.*,
88(1976):115–116

Haliburton, Thomas Chandler
Windsor, Nova Scotia
C 126, October 29, 1829
Died: August 27, 1865

Hall, David Drisko
Arlington
R 902, May 14, 1981

Hall, Edward Henry
Cambridge
R 407, December 14, 1899
Died: February 22, 1912
Memoir: M.H.S. *Procs.*,
54(1920–1921):358–
361

Hall, Granville Stanley
Worcester
R 386, February 13, 1896
Died: April 24, 1924

Hall, Hubert
London, England
C 411, December 14, 1905
Died: July 27, 1944
Memoir: M.H.S. *Procs.*
68(1944–1947):449–
450

Hall, Max Reddick
Cambridge
R 819, November 12,
1970

Hall, Michael Garibaldi
Austin, Texas
C 677, May 12, 1977

Hall, Thomas
Leghorn, Italy
C 50, April 28, 1801
Died: April 12, 1824

Hallam, Henry
London, England
C 230, May 11, 1854
Died: January 21, 1859

Halsey, Luther
Auburn, New York
C 168, March 30, 1837
Died: October 29, 1880

Hamer, Philip May
Bethesda, Maryland
C 563, May 13, 1959
Died: April 10, 1971

Hamilton, Edward Pierce
Milton
R 686, May 8, 1952
Died: May 22, 1972
Memoir, M.H.S. *Procs.*,
84(1972):113–117

Hammer, Roy A.
Cambridge
R 1017, April 11, 1991

Hammond, Mason
Boston
R 731, December 11, 1958

Hampton, Henry
Boston
R 999, December 14, 1989

Handlin, Lilian
Cambridge
R 936, December 12, 1985

Handlin, Oscar
Cambridge
R 684, April 10, 1952

Hanify, Edward Benno
Belmont
R 841, April 10, 1975

Hanotaux, Albert Auguste Gabriel
Paris, France
C 410, May 11, 1905
H 71, February 10, 1921
Died: April 11, 1944

Haring, Clarence Henry
Cambridge
R 548, May 12, 1927
Died: September 4, 1960
Memoir, M.H.S. *Procs.*,
72(1957–1960):397–
400

Harlow, Thompson Ritner
Hartford, Connecticut
C 543, April 8, 1954

Harnack, Adolf
Berlin, Germany
H 62, June 9, 1904
Died: June 15, 1930

Harris, Edward Doubleday
Cambridge
R 279, May 11, 1871
New York, New York
C 426, February 10, 1910
Died: March 2, 1919

Harris, Thaddeus Mason
Cambridge
R 17, August 13, 1792
Died: April 3, 1842
Memoir: M.H.S. *Colls.*,
4th ser., 2:130–155

Appendix I: Members

Harris, Thaddeus William
Cambridge
R 169, January 27, 1848
Died: January 16, 1856
Memoir: M.H.S. *Procs.*,
19(1881–1882):313–
322

**Harris, Wilhelmina
Sellers**
Quincy
R 903, May 14, 1981
Died: May 20, 1991
Memoir, M.H.S. *Procs.*,
103(1991):191–192

Harris, William
New York, New York
C 82, January 27, 1814
Died: October 18, 1829

Harrison, Frederic
London, England
C 390, March 14, 1901
Died: January 14, 1923

Harrison, William Henry
Harvard
R 685, April 10, 1952
Died: July 3, 1986

Hart, Albert Bushnell
Cambridge
R 357, January 10, 1889
Died: June 16, 1943
Tributes: M.H.S. *Procs.*,
66(1936–1941):434–
438; 68(1944–1947):
477–478

Hart, Charles Henry
Philadelphia, Pennsylvania
C 336, October 10, 1878
Died: July 29, 1918

Hart, Francis Russell
Boston
R 515, May 13, 1920
Died: January 18, 1938
Tribute: M.H.S. *Procs.*,
66(1936–1941):427–
433

Haskins, Charles Homer
Cambridge
R 437, December 8, 1904
Died: May 14, 1937

Haskins, George Lee
Philadelphia, Pennsylvania
C 559, February 12, 1959
Died: October 4, 1991

Hassam, John Tyler
Boston
R 326, November 10,
1881
Died: April 22, 1903
Memoir: M.H.S. *Procs.*,
53(1919–1920):85–91

Hatch, Francis Whiting, I
Castine, Maine
C 628, October 10, 1968
Died: May 14, 1975
Memoir, M.H.S. *Procs.*,
87(1975):145–153

Hatch, Francis Whiting, II
Beverly Farms
R 922, May 24, 1984

Hatch, Robert McConnell
Randolph, New Hampshire
C 660, May 9, 1974

Hauser, Henri
Paris, France
C 471, November 14,
1929
Died: May 27, 1946

**Haussonville, Joseph
Othenin Bernard de
Cléron, vicomte d'**
Paris, France
C 352, December 8, 1881
Died: May 28, 1884

**Haven, Nathaniel
Appleton, Jr.**
Portsmouth, New Hampshire
C 103, January 31, 1822
Died: June 3, 1826

Haven, Samuel Foster
Worcester
R 216, August 11, 1858
Died: September 5, 1881
Memoir: M.H.S. *Procs.*,
2d ser., 1(1884–1885):
394–405

Hawks, Francis Lister
New York, New York
C 174, July 26, 1838
Died: September 26, 1866

Hay, John Milton
Washington, D.C.
C 387, June 14, 1900
Died: July 1, 1905

**Haynes, Henry
Williamson**
Boston
R 316, June 12, 1879
Died: February 16, 1912
Memoir: M.H.S. *Procs.*,
48(1914–1915):128–
132

Hayward, Elijah
Columbus, Ohio
C 234, August 10, 1854
Died: September 22, 1864

Hazard, Ebenezer
Philadelphia, Pennsylvania
C 1, May 29, 1792
Died: June 13, 1817

Hazen, Charles Downer
Washington, D.C.
C 437, May 11, 1916
Died: September 18, 1941

Hedge, Frederic Henry
Brookline
R 202, January 14, 1858
Resigned November 9,
1876
Died: August 21, 1890

Hedge, Levi
Cambridge
R 84, August 29, 1815
Resigned January 25,
1827
Died: January 3, 1844

Hedges, James Blaine
Providence, Rhode Island
C 508, December 11, 1941
Died: October 13, 1965

Hennessey, Edward Francis
Needham
R 1002, January 11, 1990

Henry, William Wirt
Richmond, Virginia
C 351, November 10, 1881
Died: December 5, 1900

Herrick, Samuel Edward
Boston
R 368, March 12, 1891
Died: December 4, 1904
Memoir: M.H.S. *Procs.*,
41(1907–1908):65–70

Hervey, Lord Arthur Charles. See Bath and Wells

Heslin, James Joseph
New York, New York
C 586, May 10, 1962

Hiatt, Arnold S.
Weston
R 961, May 14, 1987

Hiatt, Jacob
Worcester
R 833, May 10, 1973

Higginson, Henry Lee
Boston
R 421, February 13, 1902
Died: November 14, 1919
Memoir: M.H.S. *Procs.*,
53(1919–1920):105–127

Higginson, Stephen, Jr.
Boston
R 66, January 25, 1803
Resigned August 25, 1812
Died: November 22, 1828

Higginson, Thomas Wentworth
Newport, Rhode Island
C 328, November 9, 1876
Cambridge
R 317, February 12, 1880
Died: May 9, 1911
Memoir: M.H.S. *Procs.*,
47(1913–1914):348–355

Hildreth, Richard
New York, New York
C 257, May 13, 1858
Died: July 11, 1865

Hill, Clement Hugh
Boston
R 332, May 11, 1882
Died: December 12, 1898
Memoir: M.H.S. *Procs.*,
2d ser., 13(1899–1900):130–141

Hill, David Jayne
Washington, D.C.
C 450, November 11, 1920
Died: March 2, 1932

Hill, Don Gleason
Dedham
R 439, February 9, 1905
Died: February 20, 1914
Memoir: M.H.S. *Procs.*,
48(1914–1915):163–166

Hill, Hamilton Andrews
Boston
R 364, March 13, 1890
Died: April 27, 1895
Memoir: M.H.S. *Procs.*,
2d ser., 11(1896–1897):188–196

Hill, Richard Devereaux
Marblehead
R 928, April 11, 1985

Hill, Thomas
Waltham
R 265, February 14, 1867
Portland, Maine
C 318, October 9, 1873
Died: November 21, 1891

Hillard, George Stillman
Boston
R 155, October 26, 1843
Died: January 21, 1879
Memoir: M.H.S. *Procs.*,
19(1881–1882):339–348

Hindle, Brooke
Washington, D.C.
C 679, January 12, 1978

Hitchings, Sinclair Hamilton
Boston
R 783, March 11, 1965

Hoadly, Charles Jeremy
Hartford, Connecticut
C 304, September 8, 1870
Died: October 19, 1900

Hoar, Ebenezer Rockwood
Concord
R 258, May 12, 1864
Died: January 31, 1895
Memoir: M.H.S. *Procs.*,
45(1911–1912):531–540

Hoar, George Frisbie
Worcester
R 351, November 11, 1886
Died: September 30, 1904
Memoir: M.H.S. *Procs.*,
2d ser., 19(1905):258–267

Hoar, Samuel
Concord
R 151, September 30, 1841
Died: November 2, 1856
Memoir: M.H.S. *Procs.*,
5(1860–1862):366–372

Hodges, Arthur C.
Essex
R 1001, January 11, 1990

Appendix I: Members

Hodges, George
Cambridge
R 470, May 11, 1911
Died: May 27, 1919
Memoir: M.H.S. *Procs.*,
53(1919–1920):131–
139

**Hodgkinson, Harold
Daniel**
Boston
R 765, January 10, 1963
Died: November 17, 1979
Memoir, M.H.S. *Procs.*,
91(1979):235–237

Hofer, Philip
Cambridge
R 751, March 9, 1961
Died: November 9, 1984

Hoffman, Robert David
New York, New York
C 613, October 19, 1967
Died: December 5, 1975

**Hoffman, Samuel
Verplanck**
New York, New York
C 428, January 12, 1911
Died: February 23, 1942

Hofstadter, Richard
New York, New York
C 569, October 13, 1960
Died: October 24, 1974

Holden, Harley Peirce
Cambridge
R 891, December 11, 1980

**Holdsworth, Sir William
Searle**
Oxford, England
H 80, March 9, 1939
Died: January 2, 1944

Holland, Josiah Gilbert
Springfield
R 209, May 13, 1858
New York, New York
Removed October 14,
1871
C 319, November 13,
1873
Died: October 12, 1881

**Hollingsworth, Zachary
Taylor**
Cohasset
R 482, April 9, 1914
Died: April 1, 1925
Memoir: M.H.S. *Procs.*,
58(1924–1925):459–
463

Holmes, Abiel
Cambridge
R 45, April 24, 1798
Died: June 4, 1837
Memoir: M.H.S. *Colls.*,
3d ser., 7:270–282

**Holmes, Oliver
Wendell, I**
Boston
R 198, September 10,
1857
Died: October 7 1894
Memoir: M.H.S. *Procs.*,
2d ser., 11(1896–
1897):47–66

**Holmes, Oliver
Wendell, II**
Boston
R 369, May 14, 1891
Died: March 6, 1935

**Holmes, Oliver
Wendell, III**
Washington, D.C.
C 605, January 14, 1965
Died: November 25, 1981
Memoir, M.H.S. *Procs.*,
94(1982):81–85

**Holst, Hermann Eduard
von**
Chicago, Illinois
C 338, February 13, 1879
Died: January 20, 1904

Holton, Gerald James
Lexington
R 778, December 10, 1964

**Holtzendorff, Joachim
Wilhelm Franz Philipp,
baron von**
Munich, Bavaria
H 40, October 14, 1875
Died: February 5, 1889

Homans, George Caspar
Cambridge
R 689, May 8, 1952
Died: May 29, 1989
Memoir, M.H.S. *Procs.*,
101(1989):128–129

Homer, Arthur
Cambridge, England
C 48, January 28, 1800
Died: July 2, 1806

Homer, Jonathan
Newton
R 51, April 30, 1799
Died: August 11, 1843
Memoir: M.H.S. *Procs.*,
2(1835–1855):275–
278

Hopkinson, Charles
Cambridge
R 720, March 13, 1958
Died: October 15, 1962

Hoppin, Nicholas
Cambridge
R 254, January 14, 1864
Died: March 8, 1886
Memoir: M.H.S. *Procs.*,
2d ser., 3(1886–1887):
299–308

Hornblower, Henry, 2nd
Brookline
R 708, January 12, 1956
Died: October 20, 1985
Memoir, M.H.S. *Procs.*,
97(1985):157–160

Hosack, David
New York, New York
C 80, January 27, 1814
Died: December 22, 1835

Hosmer, James Kendall
Minneapolis, Minnesota
C 418, October 10, 1907
Died: May 11, 1927

Hovgaard, William
Brookline
R 566, January 8, 1931
Summit, New Jersey
Removed June 15, 1934
C 486, December 13, 1934
Died: January 5, 1950

Howard, Joseph Jackson
Blackheath England
C 290, December 13, 1866
Died: April 18, 1902

Howay, Frederic William
New Westminster, British Columbia, Canada
C 468, December 8, 1927
Died: October 4, 1943

Howe, Henry Forbush
Cohasset
R 677, January 10, 1952
A 8, April 12, 1962
C 618, January 11, 1968
Chicago, Illinois
Died: March 6, 1977
Memoir, M.H.S. *Procs.*,
89(1977):184–186

Howe, Henry Saltonstall
Brookline
R 555, January 10, 1929
Died: March 2, 1931
Memoir: M.H.S. *Procs.*,
64(1930–1932):499–
504

Howe, Mark Antony DeWolfe
Boston
R 449, November 8, 1906
H 91, May 12, 1955
Died: December 6, 1960
Memoir, M.H.S. *Procs.*,
72(1957–1960):403–
408

Howe, Mark DeWolfe
Cambridge
R 642, December 13, 1945
Died: February 28, 1967
Memoir, M.H.S. *Procs.*,
79(1967):197–199

Howe, Parkman Dexter
Needham
R 653, February 12, 1948
Emeritus, March 13, 1969
Died: January 13, 1980

Howells, William White
Kittery Point, Maine
C 693, April 9, 1981

Howland, Llewellyn, 3rd
Jamaica Plain
R 862, April 14, 1977

Howland, Weston, Jr.
Weston
R 906, May 11, 1982
Resigned, December 8,
1988

Hubbard, Gilbert Harrison
Demerara, Guiana
C 27, November 18, 1796
Died: May 11, 1803

Hudson, Charles
Boston
R 227, June 9, 1859
Died: May 4, 1881
Memoir: M.H.S. *Procs.*,
2d ser., 4(1887–1889):
28–32

Huff, Ann Millspaugh
Saunderstown, Rhode
Island
C 715, May 24, 1984

Hugo, E. Harold
Meriden, Connecticut
C 554, December 11, 1959
Died: September 9, 1985
Memoir, M.H.S. *Procs.*,
97(1985):152–156

Humboldt, Friedrich Heinrich Alexander, freiherr von
Berlin, Germany
C 91, October 30, 1817
Died: May 6, 1859

Hunnewell, James Frothingham
Boston
R 408, January 11, 1900
Died: November 11, 1910
Memoir: M.H.S. *Procs.*,
45(1911–1912):571–
576

Hunnewell, James Melville
Boston
R 596, November 12,
1936
Died: March 22, 1954

Hunter, Joseph
London, England
C 202, November 17,
1842
Died: May 9, 1861
Memoir: M.H.S. *Procs.*,
17(1879–1880):300–
306

Hutchinson, Elisha
Birmingham, England
C 97, April 27, 1820
Died: June 24, 1824

Hutchinson, John
Blurton, England
C 119, August 28, 1827
Died: April 27, 1865

Hutchison, William Robert
Cambridge
R 892, December 11, 1980

Ide, Dora Donner
San Francisco, California
C 716, May 24, 1984

Iriye, Akira
Cambridge
R 1018, April 11, 1991

Irving, Washington
Tarrytown, New York
C 127, October 29, 1829
Died: November 28, 1859

Jackman, Sydney Wayne
Victoria, British Columbia, Canada
C 647, February 11, 1971

Appendix I: Members

Jackson, Charles, I
Boston
R 83, August 29, 1815
Resigned November 18, 1841
Died: December 13, 1855

Jackson, Charles, II
Dover
R 697, March 11, 1954
Died: September 19, 1969
Memoir, M.H.S. *Procs.*, 81(1969):217–219

Jackson, William Alexander
Cambridge
R 628, March 11, 1943
Died: October 18, 1964

James, Janet Wilson
Cambridge
R 868, January 12, 1978
Died: June 10, 1987
Memoir, M.H.S. *Procs.*, 99(1987):174–177

Jameson, John Franklin
Washington, D.C.
C 383, June 9, 1898
Died: September 28, 1937

Jantz, Harold Stein
Evanston, Illinois
C 510, November 18, 1943
Died: February 26, 1987

Jarvis, Edward
Louisville, Kentucky
C 188, October 31, 1839
Died: October 31, 1884

Jay, John
Bedford, New York
C 2, May 29, 1792
Died: May 17, 1829

Jay, William
Bedford, New York
C 143, June 26, 1834
Died: October 14, 1858

Jeffries, William Augustus
Milton
R 602, October 14, 1937
Died: February 20, 1948
Memoir: M.H.S. *Procs.* 69(1947–1950):429–430

Jenkins, Lawrence Waters
Salem
R 588, December 13, 1934
Died: April 20, 1961
Memoir, M.H.S. *Procs.*, 73(1961):107–109

Jenks, Henry Fitch
Boston
R 321, February 10, 1881
Died: January 31, 1920
Memoir: M.H.S. *Procs.*, 53(1919–1920):182–184

Jenks, William
Boston
R 101, August 27, 1821
Died: November 13, 1866
Memoir: M.H.S. *Procs.*, 10(1867–1869):105–112

Jenner, Edward
Berkeley, England
C 75, October 29, 1812
Died: January 26, 1823

Jennings, John Melville
Richmond, Virginia
C 579, April 13, 1961

Jensen, Merrill Monroe
Madison, Wisconsin
C 588, October 11, 1962
Died: January 30, 1980
Memoir, M.H.S. *Procs.*, 92(1980):140–143

Jervis, Thomas Best
Calcutta, India
C 212, March 27, 1845
Died: April 3, 1857

Johnson, Alden Porter
Worcester
R 732, February 12, 1959
Died: September 8, 1972

Johnson, Edward Crosby, 3rd
Boston
R 804, December 12, 1968

Johnson, Edward Francis
Woburn
R 377, February 8, 1894
Resigned October 9, 1913
Died: September 23, 1922

Johnson, William
New York, New York
C 59, May 28, 1805
Died: August 11, 1834

Johnston, Alexander
Princeton, New Jersey
C 365, November 11, 1886
Died: July 20, 1889

Jomard, Edmé François
Paris, France
H 9, April 14, 1859
Died: September 25, 1862

Jones, Howard Mumford
Cambridge
R 787, December 9, 1965
Died: May 11, 1980

Jones, Jacqueline
Wellesley
R 988, April 13, 1989

Jones, John Winter
London, England
C 294, December 12, 1867
Died: September 7, 1881

Jones, Matt Bushnell
Newton
R 582, June 8, 1933
Died: July 1, 1940

Jones, Sir William
Calcutta, India
C 18, January 27, 1795[1]
Died: April 27, 1794

Jordan, Daniel P.
Charlottesville, Virginia
C 725, October 9, 1986

Jordan, Henry Donaldson
Worcester
R 752, March 9, 1961
Died: December 20, 1972
Memoir, M.H.S. *Procs.*,
  84(1972):125–126

Jordan, Wilbur Kitchener
Cambridge
R 630, November 18,
  1943
Died: June 3, 1980

Jordan, Winthrop Donaldson
Berkeley, California
C 685, November 2, 1979

Joy, Benjamin
Boston
R 654, February 12, 1948
Died: September 10, 1968
Memoir, M.H.S. *Procs.*,
  81(1969):211

Joy, Michael
Chippenham, England
C 87, August 27, 1816
Died: July 10, 1825

Judd, Sylvester
Northampton
R 171, April 27, 1848
Died: April 17, 1860
Memoir: M.H.S. *Procs.*,
  18

Jusserand, Jean Adrien Antoine Jules
Paris, France
C 417, June 13, 1907
H 73, November 8, 1923
Died: July 18, 1932

Kammen, Michael Gedaliah
Ithaca, New York
C 670, January 13, 1977

Kaplan, Justin
Cambridge
R 948, October 9, 1986

Keeney, Barnaby Conrad
Providence, Rhode Island
C 576, February 9, 1961
Died: June 18, 1980

Kegan, Elizabeth Hamer
Alexandria, Virginia
C 651, January 3, 1972
Died: March 9, 1979

Kellen, William Vail
Boston
R 453, June 13, 1907
Died: December 20, 1942

Keller, Morton
Cambridge
R 872, December 14, 1978

Kellogg, Edmund Halsey
Lincoln
R 837, January 10, 1974
C 691, December 13, 1979

Kelly, Liam
Wellesley Hills
R 969, April 14, 1988

Kennan, George Frost
Princeton, New Jersey
C 609, February 10, 1966

Kennedy, Edward Moore
Boston
R 800, May 9, 1968

Kennedy, John Fitzgerald
Boston
R 755, May 11, 1961
Died: November 22, 1963
Memoir, M.H.S. *Procs.*,
  75(1963):113–117

Kennedy, John Pendleton
Baltimore, Maryland
C 262, October 14, 1858
Died: August 18, 1870

Kenny, Herbert
Manchester
R 849, December 12 1975

Kenyon, Cecelia Marie
Northampton
R 834, May 10, 1973
Died: January 22, 1990

Kerber, Linda K.
Iowa City, Iowa
C 758, May 9, 1991

Kilbourne, Payne Kenyon
Litchfield, Connecticut
C 216, November 23,
  1848
Died: July 19, 1859

Kilham, Daniel
Wenham
R 44, April 24, 1798
Resigned April 29, 1830
Died: October 12, 1841

Kilham, Walter Harrington
Boston
R 649, May 8, 1947
Died: September 11, 1948
Memoir, M.H.S. *Procs.*,
  69(1947–1950):431–
  434

King, John Glen
Salem
R 138, June 25, 1835
Died: July 26, 1857
Memoir: M.H.S. *Procs.*,
  18(1880–1881):37–40

King, Patricia Miller
Cambridge
R 867, May 12, 1977

---

[1] Word of the death of this man did not reach the Society until after he had been elected a corresponding member.

Appendix I: Members

King, Rufus
New York, New York
C 111, October 28, 1824
Died: April 29, 1827

Kingsley, James Luce
New Haven, Connecticut
C 176, August 28, 1838
Died: August 31, 1852

Kinnicutt, Lincoln Newton
Worcester
R 489, April 8, 1915
Died: December 13, 1921
Memoir: M.H.S. *Procs.*,
58(1924–1925):93–96

Kirk, John Foster
Berne, Switzerland
C 282, February 11, 1864
Dorchester
R 262, November 9, 1865
Philadelphia, Pennsylvania
C 282, December 8, 1870
Died: September 3, 1904

Kirkland, Edward Chase
Brunswick, Maine
C 531, April 12, 1951
Died: May 24, 1975
Memoir, M.H.S. *Procs.*,
87(1975):154–158

Kirkland, John Thornton
Boston
R 30, January 26, 1796
Resigned April 24, 1828
Died: April 26, 1840

Kittredge, George Lyman
Cambridge
R 456, March 12, 1908
Died: July 23, 1941

Klein, Milton M.
Knoxville, Tennessee
C 742, May 11, 1989

Knight, Russell W.
Marblehead
R 771, March 12, 1964

Knollenberg, Bernhard
Chester, Connecticut
C 504, January 9, 1941
Died: July 6, 1973
Memoir, M.H.S. *Procs.*,
86(1974):81–83

Knopf, Alfred A.
Purchase, New York
C 555, December 11, 1958
Died: August 11, 1984
Memoir, M.H.S. *Procs.*,
96(1984):41–43

Knox, Dudley Wright
Washington, D.C.
C 515, February 8, 1945
Died: June 11 1960

Kohl, John George
Bremen, Germany
C 260, August 11, 1858
Died: October 28, 1878

Kollock, Lemuel
Savannah, Georgia
C 33, April 25, 1797
Died: April; 1823

Kugler, Richard Cory
New Bedford
R 863, April 14, 1977

Kurtz, Stephen Guild
Williamsburg, Virginia
C 645, January 14, 1971
Resigned January 11,
1990

Labaree, Benjamin Woods
Cambridge
R 769, March 14, 1963
C 688, December 13, 1979

Labaree, Leonard Woods
New Haven, Connecticut
C 518, April 12, 1945
Died: May 5, 1980
Memoir, M.H.S. *Procs.*,
92(1980):156–160

Laboulaye, Edouard René Lefebvre
Paris, France
H 22, December 10, 1863
Died: May 25, 1883
Tribute: M.H.S. *Procs.*,
20(1882–1883):260–263

Lafayette, Marie Jean Paul Roch Yves Gilbert Motier, marquis de
Paris, France
C 114, October 28, 1824
Died: May 19, 1834

Lally, Francis Joseph
Roslindale
R 825, January 13, 1972
C 689, December 13, 1979
R 823, December 13, 1984
Died: September 3, 1987
Memoir, M.H.S. *Procs.*,
99(1987):183–186

Lamb, William Kaye
Ottawa, Ontario, Canada
C 587, May 10, 1962

Lamson, Alvan
Dedham
R 148, April 30, 1840
Died: July 18, 1864
Memoir: M.H.S. *Procs.*,
11(1869–1870):258–261

Lane, William Coolidge
Cambridge
R 459, June 10, 1909
Died: March 18, 1931

Langdon-Elwyn, Alfred
Philadelphia, Pennsylvania
C 344, May 13, 1880
Died: March 15, 1884

Langer, William Leonard
Cambridge
R 580, May 11, 1933
Died: December 26, 1977
Memoir, M.H.S. *Procs.*,
89(1977):187–195

Langlois, Charles Victor
Paris, France
C 464, April 8, 1926
Died: June 26, 1929

Larsen, Roy Edward
Fairfield, Connecticut
C 545, November 10,
1954
Died: September 9, 1979
Memoir, M.H.S. *Procs.*,
91(1979):228–231

Latham, Williams
Bridgewater
R 226, May 12, 1859
Died: November 6, 1883
Memoir: M.H.S. *Procs.*,
2d ser., 4(1887–1889):
195–198

Lathrop, John
Boston
R 443, December 14, 1905
Died: August 24, 1910
Memoir: M.H.S. *Procs.*,
44(1910–1911):703–
705

**Laughlin, Henry
Alexander**
Concord
R 743, April 14, 1960
Died: August 10, 1977
Memoir, M.H.S. *Procs.*,
90(1978):117–119

**Laval, Anne Adrien Pierre
Montmorency, duc de**
Paris, France
C 148, December 31, 1835
Died: June 16, 1837

Lavisse, Ernest
Paris, France
H 65, February 9, 1905
Died: August 18, 1922

Lawrence, Abbott, I
Boston
R 182, December 8, 1853
Died: August 15, 1855
Memoir: M.H.S. *Colls.*,
4th ser., 4:495–507;
M.H.S., *Procs.*,
3(1855–1858):67–82

Lawrence, Abbott, II
Boston
R 311, December 12, 1878
Died: July 6, 1893
Memoir: M.H.S. *Procs.*,
42(1908–1909): 41–47

Lawrence, Amos Adams
Brookline
R 247, October 10, 1861
Died: August 22, 1886
Memoir: M.H.S. *Procs.*,
2d ser., 12(1897–
1899):130–137

Lawrence, James, Jr.
Brookline
R 718, February 13, 1958

Lawrence, John Silsbee
Manchester
R 673, October 11, 1951
Emeritus, November 9,
1972
Died: December 14, 1973

Lawrence, Robert Means
Boston
R 516, June 10, 1920
Died: March 7, 1935
Memoir: M.H.S. *Procs.*
68(1944–1947):451–
454

Lawrence, William
Milton
R 380, June 14, 1894
Died: November 6, 1941

Lazarus, Maurice
Cambridge
R 963, October 8, 1987

Lea, Henry Charles
Philadelphia, Pennsylvania
C 326, October 14, 1875
H 61, October 9, 1902
Died: October 24, 1909

Leach, Douglas Edward
Nashville, Tennessee
C 625, January 11, 1968

**Lecky, William Edward
Hartpole**
London, England
H 52, September 14, 1882
Died: October 23, 1903

Lecuna, Vicente
Caracas, Venezuela
H 84, February 12, 1948
Died: February 20, 1954
Memoir, M.H.S. *Procs.*,
71(1953–1957):386

Lee, Henry, I
Boston
R 307, March 14, 1878
Died: November 24, 1898
Memoir: M.H.S. *Procs.*,
2d ser., 19(1905):228–
257

Lee, Henry, II
Boston
R 789, February 10, 1966

Lee, John
Edinburgh, Scotland
C 197, October 29, 1840
Died: May 2, 1859

Lee, Sir Sidney
London, England
C 404, January 14, 1904
Died: March 3, 1926

Lee, William
Washington, D.C.
C 107, August 27, 1822
Died: February 29, 1840

Lefavour, Henry
Boston
R 539, June 11, 1925
Died: June 16, 1946

Leland, Waldo Gifford
Newton
R 692, December 11, 1952
Washington, D.C.
H 92, October 19, 1961
Died: October 19, 1966

**LeMoine, Sir James
MacPherson**
Quebec, Canada
C 343, April 6, 1880
Died: February 5, 1912

Appendix I: Members

Lemon, Robert
London, England
C 208, September 26,
  1844
Died: January 3, 1867

Lenox, James
New York, New York
C 238, July 12, 1855
Died: February 17, 1880

Leopold, Richard William
Evanston, Illinois
C 556, December 11, 1958

Lettsom, John Coakley
London, England
C 17, January 27, 1795
Died: November 1, 1815

**Leuchtenburg, William
Edward**
Dobbs Ferry, New York
C 682, January 11, 1979

Leventhal, Norman
Boston
R 983, January 12, 1989

Levin, David
Charlottesville, Virginia
C 740, December 8, 1988

Levy, Leonard
Claremont, California
C 743, December 14, 1989

Lewis, Alonzo
Lynn
R 122, August 24, 1830
Resigned January 1, 1844
Died: January 21, 1861

Lewis, Anthony
Cambridge
R 880, November 2, 1979

Lewis, Wilmarth Sheldon
Farmington, Connecticut
C 643, November 12,
  1970
Died: October 7, 1979

Lieber, Francis
New York, New York
C 255, January 14, 1858
Died: October 2, 1872

Lincoln, Benjamin
Hingham
R 47, July 19, 1798
Died: May 9, 1810
Memoir: M.H.S. *Colls.*,
  2d ser., 3:233–255

Lincoln, Levi, Jr.
Worcester
R 220, January 13, 1859
Died: May 29, 1868
Memoir: M.H.S. *Procs.*,
  11(1869–1870):47–83

Lincoln, Solomon, I
Hingham
R 162, January 30, 1845
Died: December 1, 1881
Memoir: M.H.S. *Procs.*,
  19(1881–1882):381–
  384

Lincoln, Solomon, II
Boston
R 355, November 10,
  1887
Died: October 15, 1907
Memoir: M.H.S. *Procs.*,
  41(1907–1908):279–
  280

Lincoln, Waldo
Worcester
R 430, May 14, 1903
Died: April 7, 1933

Lincoln, William
Worcester
R 130, January 26, 1832
Died: October 5, 1843
Memoir: M.H.S. *Colls.*,
  3d ser., 10:225–235

**Lindsay, Franklin
Anthony**
Lincoln
R 900, April 9, 1981

Link, Arthur Stanley
Princeton, New Jersey
C 671, January 13, 1977

Lippman, Walter
Washington, D.C.
C 589, December 13, 1962
Died: December 14, 1974

Little, Bertram Kimball
Boston
R 680, February 14, 1952

Little, David Britton
Concord
R 703, May 12, 1955

Little, Nina Fletcher
Brookline
R 853, May 13, 1976

Livermore, George
Cambridge
R 175, November 22,
  1849
Died: August 30, 1865
Memoir: M.H.S. *Procs.*,
  10(1867–1869):415–
  468

**Livermore, Thomas
Leonard**
Boston
R 414, January 10, 1901
Died: January 9, 1918

Livermore, William Roscoe
Boston
R 393, April 8, 1897
Died: September 28, 1919
Memoir: M.H.S. *Procs.*,
  53(1919–1920):338–
  342

Lodge, George Cabot
Beverly
R 798, March 14, 1968

Lodge, Henry Cabot, I
Nahant
R 301, December 14, 1876
Died: November 9, 1924
Memoir: M.H.S. *Procs.*,
  58(1924–1925):324–
  376

Lodge, Henry Cabot, II
Beverly
R 652, November 13,
1947
Died: February 27, 1985
Memoir, M.H.S. *Procs.*,
97(1985):149–152

Lodge, Henry Sears
Beverly
R 915, December 15, 1983

**Lombard, Lawrence
Manuel**
Needham
R 824, March 11, 1971
Died: August 27, 1985

**London, Mandell
Creighton, bishop of**
London, England
C 366, January 13, 1887
H 58, December 9, 1897
Died: January 4, 1901

Long, John Davis
Hingham
R 438, January 12, 1905
Died: August 28, 1915
Memoir: M.H.S. *Procs.*,
53(1919–1920):10–16

**Longfellow, Henry Wads-
worth**
Cambridge
R 200, December 10, 1857
Died: March 24, 1882
Memoir: M.H.S. *Procs.*,
2d ser., 8(1892–1894):
152–167

**Longley, James
Wilberforce**
Halifax, Nova Scotia
C 421, March 12, 1908
Died: March 16, 1922

Lord, Arthur
Plymouth
R 329, February 9, 1882
Died: April 10, 1925
Memoir: M.H.S. *Procs.*,
58(1924–1925):378–
385; 61(1927–1928):
196–211

Lord, Milton Edward
Boxford
R 592, April 11, 1935
Died: February 12, 1985

Lord, Robert Howard
Wellesley
R 567, February 12, 1931
Died: May 22, 1954
Memoir, M.H.S. *Procs.*,
71(1953–1957):387–
389

**Loring, Augustus
Peabody, I**
Boston
R 600, May 13, 1937
Died: October 1, 1951

**Loring, Augustus
Peabody, II**
Pride's Crossing
R 676, January 10, 1952
Died: November 27, 1986
Memoir, M.H.S. *Procs.*,
98(1986):141–144

Loring, Caleb, Jr.
Pride's Crossing
R 916, December 15, 1983

Loring, Charles Greely, I
Boston
R 244, May 9, 1861
Died: October 8, 1867
Memoir: M.H.S. *Procs.*,
11(1869–1870):263–
291

Loring, Charles Greely, II
Boston
R 353, January 13, 1887
Died: August 18, 1902
Memoir: M.H.S. *Procs.*,
48(1914–1915):355–
360

Lossing, Benson John
Dover Plains, New York
C 275, July 11, 1861
Died: June 3, 1891

Lothrop, Francis Bacon
Manchester
R 776, May 14, 1964
Died: February 6, 1986

Lothrop, Isaac
Plymouth
R 12, October 11, 1791
Died: July 25, 1808
Memoir: M.H.S. *Colls.*,
2d ser., 1:258–260

Lothrop, Samuel Kirkland
Boston
R 184, June 8, 1854
Died: June 12, 1886
Memoir: M.H.S. *Procs.*,
2d ser., 3(1886–1887):
161–177

**Lothrop, Thornton
Kirkland**
Boston
R 358, April 11, 1889
Died: November 2, 1913
Memoir: M.H.S. *Procs.*,
47(1913–1914):425–
444

Loubat, Joseph Florimond
New York, New York
C 335, October 10, 1878
Died: March 1, 1927

Lovering, Henry Morton
Taunton
R 463, May 12, 1910
Died: January 21, 1918
Memoir: M.H.S. *Procs.*,
52(1918–1919):101–
103

Lovett, Robert Woodberry
Beverly
R 820, December 10, 1970

Lowell, Abbott Lawrence
Boston
R 366, December 11, 1890
Died: January 6, 1943

Lowell, Augustus
Boston
R 410, March 8, 1900
Died: June 22, 1900
Memoir: M.H.S. *Procs.*,
2d ser., 15(1901–
1902):169–179

Appendix I: Members

Lowell, Charles
Boston and Cambridge
R 82, August 29, 1815
July 14,, 1859
Resigned January 10,
1856
Died: January 20, 1861
Memoir: M.H.S. *Procs.*,
5(1860–1862):427–
440

Lowell, Edward Jackson
Boston
R 345, November 13,
1884
Died: May 11, 1894
Memoir: M.H.S. *Procs.*,
2d ser., 9(1894–1895):
541–549

Lowell, Francis Cabot
Boston
R 385, January 9, 1896
Died: March 6, 1911
Memoir: M.H.S. *Procs.*,
48(1914–1915):69–74

Lowell, James Russell
Cambridge
R 253, May 14, 1863
Died: August 12, 1891
Memoir: M.H.S. *Procs.*,
2d ser., 11(1896–
1897):75–102

Lowell, John, I
Boston
R 106, January 30, 1823
Died: March 12, 1840
Memoir: M.H.S. *Procs.*,
2(1835–1855):160–
169

Lowell, John, II
Newton
R 310, September 12,
1878
Died: May 14, 1897
Memoir, M.H.S. *Procs.*,
2d ser., 14(1900–
1901):177–188

Lowell, John, III
Nahant
R 873, December 14, 1978

Lowell, John Amory
Boston
R 189, November 8, 1855
Died: October 31, 1881
Memoir, M.H.S. *Procs.*,
2d ser., 12(1897–
1899):113–129

Lowell, Ralph
Westwood
R 639, May 10, 1945
Died: May 15, 1978

Lunt, William Parsons
Quincy
R 152, September 30,
1841
Died: March 21, 1857
Memoir: M.H.S. *Colls.*,
4th ser., 4:508–514;
M.H.S., *Procs.*,
3(1853–1858):207–
213

Lyman, Arthur Theodore
Waltham
R 418, October 10, 1901
Died: October 24, 1915
Memoir: M.H.S. *Procs.*,
52(1918–1919):36–37

Lyman, George Hinckley
Boston
R 564, November 13,
1930
Resigned November 15,
1938
Died: May 17, 1945
Memoir: M.H.S. *Procs.*
69(1947–1950):412

Lyman, Susan Storey
Boston
R 921, May 24, 1984
Charleston, South Caro-
lina
C 757, April 11, 1991

Lyman, Theodore, I
Boston
R 107, April 24, 1823
Resigned May 30, 1836
Died: July 17, 1849

Lyman, Theodore, II
Brookline
R 273, November 11,
1869
Died: September 9, 1897
Memoir: M.H.S. *Procs.*,
2d ser., 20(1906–
1907):147–177

**Lyndhurst, John
Singleton Copley,
baron**
Turville, England
H 3, February 11, 1858
Died: October 12, 1863

Lynn, Kenneth Schuyler
Cambridge
R 748, December 8, 1960
C 630, March 13, 1969

Lyons, Louis Martin
Cambridge
R 801, October 10, 1968
Died: April 11, 1982
Memoir, M.H.S. *Procs.*,
94(1982):90–93

**Macaulay, Thomas
Babington, lord**
London, England
C 229, May 11, 1854
Died: December 28, 1859

**MacCaffrey, Wallace
Trevethick**
Acton
R 886, May 8, 1980
Resigned, October 12,
1989

MacClure, David
East Windsor, Connecti-
cut
C 21, August 17, 1795
Died: June 25, 1820

MacDonald, William
Providence, Rhode Island
C 432, May 9, 1912
Died: December 15, 1938

MacLeish, Archibald
Washington, D.C.
C 506, February 13, 1941
Conway, N.H.
A 5, May 13, 1948
Boston
R 661, December 14, 1950
Died: April 20, 1982
Memoir, M.H.S. *Procs.*,
94(1982):93–98

MacNeil, Neil
Washington, D.C.
C 672, January 13, 1977

Magnusen, Finn
Copenhagen, Denmark
C 153, December 31, 1835
Died: December 24, 1847

Magnus-Allcroft, Sir Philip
Onibury, Shropshire,
England
C 653, February 10, 1972
Died: December 21, 1988

Mahan, Alfred Thayer
Washington, D.C.
C 372, May 10, 1894
H 66, January 10, 1907
Died: December 1, 1914

Mahoney, Thomas Henry Donald
Cambridge
R 784, April 8, 1965

Maier, Pauline R.
Cambridge
R 912, May 12, 1983

Maitland, Frederic William
Cambridge, England
C 382, April 14, 1898
Died: December 19, 1906

Major, Richard Henry
London, England
C 296, May 14, 1868
Died: June 25, 1891

Malone, Dumas
Lincoln
R 599, March 11, 1937
A 1, January 11, 1945
C 619, January 11, 1968
New York, New York
Died: December 27, 1986

Marcou, Jules
Paris, France
C 300, May 13, 1869
Died: April 17, 1898

Margry, Pierre
Paris, France
C 303, October 15, 1869
Died: May 27, 1894

Marsh, Ebenezer Grant
New Haven, Connecticut
C 56, September 1, 1803
Died: November 16, 1803
Memoir: M.H.S. *Colls.*,
9:108–111

Marsh, George Perkins
Rome, Italy
C 259, June 17, 1858
Burlington, Vermont
H 32, February 11, 1875
Died: July 23, 1882

Marshall, John
Richmond, Virginia
C 71, August 29, 1809
Died: July 6, 1835

Marshall, Megan
Newton
R 1034, December 12,
1991

Martin, Bon Louis Henri
Paris, France
H 45, October 10, 1878
Died: December 14, 1883

Marx, Leo
Boston
R 957, April 9, 1987

Mason, Charles
Boston
R 232, November 10,
1859
Died: March 23, 1862
Memoir: M.H.S. *Procs.*,
7(1863–1864):104–
114

Mason, Charles Ellis, Jr.
Chestnut Hill
R 893, December 11, 1980

Mason, Jeremiah
Portsmouth, New Hampshire
C 101, April 26, 1821
Died: October 14, 1848

Mason, Robert Means
Boston
R 270, January 14, 1869
Died: March 13, 1879
Memoir: M.H.S. *Procs.*,
18(1880–1881):302–
317

Masson, David
Edinburgh, Scotland
C 309, August 15, 1871
Edinburgh, Scotland
H 37, March 11, 1875
Died: October 6, 1907

Matthews, Albert
Boston
R 452, February 14, 1907
Died: April 13, 1946

Matthews, Nathan
Boston
R 506, June 13, 1918
Died: December 11, 1927

May, Ernest Richard
Cambridge
R 772, March 12, 1964

May, Henry F.
Berkeley, California
C 735, April 14, 1988

Mayer, Brantz
Baltimore, Maryland
C 291, June 6, 1867
Died: February 23, 1879

Appendix I: Members

Mayo, Lawrence Shaw
Newton
R 511, November 13,
1919
Died: July 23, 1947
Memoir: M.H.S. *Procs.*
69(1947–1950):420–
421

McAllister, Matthew Hall
San Francisco, California
C 191, November 26,
1839
Died: December 19, 1865

McCall, Hugh
Savannah, Georgia
C 90, October 30, 1817
Died: July 9, 1824

McCall, Samuel Walker
Winchester
R 460, January 13, 1910
Died: November 4, 1923
Memoir: M.H.S. *Procs.*,
57(1923–1924):503–
512

McCleary, Samuel Foster
Boston
R 349, February 11, 1886
Died: April 25, 1901
Memoir: M.H.S. *Procs.*,
2d ser., 15(1901–
1902):255–263

**McCord, David
Thompson Watson**
Boston
R 711, February 9, 1956

McCorison, Marcus Allen
Worcester
R 798, March 14, 1968

McCrady, Edward
Charleston, South Caro-
lina
C 397, May 8, 1902
Died: November 1, 1903

McCraw, Thomas Kincaid
Belmont
R 940, January 9, 1986

McCullough, David
Washington, D.C., and
West Tisbury
C 710, December 15, 1983

McGill, Ralph Emerson
Atlanta, Georgia
C 597, May 9, 1963
Died: February 3, 1969

**McIlwain, Charles
Howard**
Cambridge
R 533, January 10, 1924
Princeton, New Jersey
A 3, January 9, 1947
R 533, December 14, 1950
Died: June 1, 1968

McKean, Joseph
Boston
R 70, September 7, 1808
Died: March 17, 1818
Memoir: M.H.S. *Colls.*,
2d ser., 8:157–167

McKenzie, Alexander
Cambridge
R 327, December 8, 1881
Died: August 6, 1914
Memoir: M.H.S. *Procs.*,
48(1914–1915):304–
318

**McLaughlin, Andrew
Cunningham**
Ann Arbor, Michigan
C 412, March 8, 1906
Died: September 24, 1947

**McLoughlin, William
Gerald, Jr.**
Providence, Rhode Island
C 646, January 14, 1971

McMaster, John Bach
Philadelphia, Pennsylva-
nia
C 395, February 13, 1902
Died: May 24, 1932

McNiff, Philip James
Chestnut Hill
R 826, January 13, 1972

McPherson, James M.
Princeton, New Jersey
C 753, December 13, 1990

Mead, Edwin Doak
Boston
R 444, January 11, 1906
Died: August 17, 1937

Mease, James
Philadelphia, Pennsylva-
nia
C 142, June 26, 1834
Died: May 14, 1846

Medina, José Toribio
Santiago, Chile
H 74, May 8, 1924
Died: December 11, 1930

Meinecke, Friedrich
Berlin, Germany
H 78, March 14, 1935
Died: February 6, 1954
Memoir, M.H.S. *Procs.*,
71(1953–1957):376–
379

Mellen, John
Barnstable
R 23, October 23, 1792
Died: September 19, 1828
Memoir: M.H.S. *Procs.*,
1(1791–1835):420–
421

**Mendenhall, Thomas
Corwin**
Worcester
R 391, January 14, 1897
Resigned November 8,
1906
Died: March 22, 1924

**Mendenhall, Thomas
Corwin**
Northampton
R 745, May 12, 1960

Menou, Jules, comte de
Paris, France
H 4, April 8, 1858
Died: 1865

Merivale, Charles
Ely, England
H 53, October 14, 1886
Died: December 26, 1893

Merk, Frederick
Belmont
R 598, March 11, 1937
Died: September 24, 1977
Memoir, M.H.S. *Procs.*,
89(1977):181–183

Merriam, George Spring
Springfield
R 372, June 9, 1892
Resigned November 8,
1906
Died: January 22, 1914

Merrill, Benjamin
Salem
R 114, August 29, 1826
Died: July 30, 1847
Memoir: M.H.S. *Procs.*,
2(1835–1855):390–
392

Merrill, James Cushing
Boston
R 99, April 27, 1820
Died: October 4, 1853
Memoir: M.H.S. *Procs.*,
2(1835–1855):561–
563

Merriman, Roger Bigelow
Cambridge
R 435, February 11, 1904
Died: September 7, 1945

Metcalf, Keyes DeWitt
Belmont
R 609, November 10,
1938
Died: November 3, 1983
Memoir, M.H.S. *Procs.*,
95(1983):163–166

Metcalf, Theron
Boston
R 241, February 14, 1861
Died: November 13, 1875
Memoir: M.H.S. *Procs.*,
14(1875–1876):386–
393

Meyer, Eduard
Berlin, Germany
H 68, March 10, 1910
Died: August 31, 1930

Middlekauff, Robert
San Marino, California
C 732, January 14, 1988

Mignet, François Auguste Marie
Paris, France
H 11, April 12, 1860
Died: March 24, 1884

Miller, Lawrence Kelton
Pittsfield
R 896, January 8, 1981
Died: March 31, 1991

Miller, Perry
Cambridge
R 621, October 9, 1941
Died: December 9, 1963

Miller, Phineas
C 19, August 17, 1795
Died: December 7, 1803

Miller, Samuel
New York, New York
C 46, July 18, 1799
Died: January 7, 1850

Miller, William Davis
Wakefield, Rhode Island
C 501, December 14, 1939
Resigned November 12,
1956
Died: July 7, 1959

Milman, Henry Hart
London, England
H 15, April 11, 1861
Died: September 24, 1868

Minns, Thomas
Boston
R 434, January 14, 1904
Died: October 28, 1913

Minot, George Richards
Boston
R 10, January 24, 1791
Died: January 2, 1802
Memoir: M.H.S. *Colls.*,
1st ser., 8:86–109

Minot, Henry Whitney
Brookline
R 779, December 10, 1964
Died: April 30, 1971
Memoir, M.H.S. *Procs.*,
83(1971):176

Minot, James Jackson
Beverly
R 757, October 19, 1961
Died: September 6, 1985

Minot, Joseph Grafton
Boston
R 484, June 11, 1914
Santa Barbara, California
C 483, March 9, 1933
Died: June 19, 1939

Minot, William
Boston
R 158, November 23,
1843
Died: June 2, 1873
Memoir: M.H.S. *Procs.*,
13(1873–1875):255–
259

Mitchell, Nahum
Bridgewater
R 93, August 25, 1818
Died: August 1, 1853
Memoir: M.H.S. *Procs.*,
2(1835–1855):560–
561

Mitchell, Stewart
Boston
R 575, April 14, 1932
Died: November 3, 1957
Memoir, M.H.S. *Procs.*,
72(1957–1960):361–
363

Mitchill, Samuel Latham
New York, New York
C 38, January 30, 1798
Died: September 7, 1831

Moe, Henry Allen
New York, New York
C 593, February 14, 1963
Died: October 2, 1975

Appendix I: Members

Moerenhout, Jacob Antoine
Los Angeles, California
C 163, October 27, 1836
Died: July 11, 1879

Moireau, Auguste
Paris, France
C 402, February 12, 1903
Died: December 24, 1919

Mommsen, Theodor
Berlin, Germany
H 48, October 14, 1880
Died: November 1, 1903

Monaghan, Bernard Andrew
Birmingham, Alabama
C 697, December 10, 1981

Monroe, George Harris
Brookline
R 400, April 14, 1898
Died: October 15, 1903
Memoir: M.H.S. *Procs.*,
  50(1916–1917):30–36

Montague, Gilbert Holland
New York, New York
C 521, March 14, 1946
Died: February 4, 1961

Montmorency, Anne Adrien Pierre. See Laval

Moody, Robert Earle
Needham
R 656, May 13, 1948
Died: April 4, 1983
Memoir, M.H.S. *Procs.*,
  95(1983):161–162

Moore, Clarence Bloomfield
Philadelphia, Pennsylvania
C 425, June 10, 1909
Died: March 24, 1936

Moore, George Foot
Cambridge
R 472, October 11, 1911
Died: May 16, 1931
Memoir: M.H.S. *Procs.*,
  64(1930–1932):424–432

Moore, George Henry
New York, New York
C 268, June 9, 1859
Died: May 5, 1892

Moore, John Bassett
New York, New York
C 386, May 10, 1900
Died: November 12, 1947

Moore, Roger Allan
Boston
R 885, April 10, 1980
Died: June 4, 1990
Memoir, M.H.S. *Procs.*,
  102(1990):167–169

Moreau, César
Paris, France
C 149, December 31, 1835
Died: November 26, 1861

Moreño, Don Manuel
Buenos Aires, Argentina
C 116, October 27, 1825
Died: December 18, 1857

Morgan, Edmund Sears
Providence, Rhode Island
C 527, March 10, 1949

Morgan, Frank
Newton
R 994, May 11, 1989

Morgan, Henry Sturgis
New York, New York
C 487, March 14, 1935
Died: February 7, 1982

Morison, Elting Elmore
Cambridge
R 704, May 12, 1955
C 631, March 13, 1969

Morison, Samuel Eliot
Boston
R 485, November 12, 1914
H 91, January 12, 1956
Died: May 15, 1976
Memoir, M.H.S. *Procs.*,
  88(1976):121–131

Morley, John, viscount Morley of Blackburn
London, England
C 389, February 14, 1901
H 63, October 13, 1904
Died: September 23, 1923

Morris, Henry
Springfield
R 331, March 9, 1882
Died: June 4, 1888
Memoir: M.H.S. *Procs.*,
  2d ser., 4(1887–1889):209–212

Morris, Richard Brandon
Mt. Vernon, New York
C 607, January 13, 1966
Died: March 3, 1989

Morrison, Robert
Canton, China
C 88, October 31, 1816
Died: August 1, 1834

Morse, Horace Henry
Northfield
R 578, March 9, 1933
Died: June 17, 1959
Memoir, M.H.S. *Procs.*,
  72(1957–1960):371–372

Morse, Jedidiah
Charlestown
R 31, January 26, 1796
Removed 1819
Died: June 9, 1826

Morse, John Torrey, Jr.
Needham
R 302, January 11, 1877
Died: March 27, 1937
Tribute: M.H.S., *Procs.*,
  66(1936–1941):445–450

Motley, John Lothrop
Boston
R 192, October 9, 1856
Died: May 29, 1877
Memoir: M.H.S. *Procs.*,
16(1878):404–473

Moyers, Bill
New York, New York
C 738, October 13, 1988

**Mumford, Lawrence
Quincy**
Cleveland, Ohio
C 544, May 13, 1954
Died: August 15, 1982

Munro, William Bennett
Boston
R 523, October 13, 1921
Pasadena, California
C 476, November 13,
1930
Removed October 9, 1930
Died: September 4, 1957

Murdock, Harold
Brookline
R 462, March 10, 1910
Died: April 5, 1934
Memoir: M.H.S. *Procs.*
68(1944–1947):455–
458

**Murdock, Kenneth
Ballard**
Boston
R 544, January 13, 1927
Emeritus, April 10, 1975
Died: November 15, 1978

Murphy, William Francis
Brighton
R 1027, October 10, 1991

Nagel, Paul Chester
Athens, Georgia
C 686, November 2, 1979

Nash, Chauncey Cushing
Boston
R 626, November 12,
1942
Died: July 16, 1968
Memoir, M.H.S. *Procs.*,
80(1968):134

Nash, Norman Burdett
Boston
R 695, February 11, 1954
Died: January 3, 1963

Nash, Ray
Hanover, New Hamp-
shire
C 557, December 11, 1958
Died: May 21, 1982

Neill, Edward Duffield
St. Paul Minnesota
C 312, March 14, 1872
Died: September 26, 1893

Neilson, William Allan
Northampton
R 605, February 10, 1938
Falls Village, Connecticut
C 507, October 9, 1941
Removed May 8, 1941
Died: February 13, 1946

Nelson, David S.
Boston
R 979, December 8, 1988

Nettels, Curtis Putnam
Ithaca, New York
C 517, March 8, 1945
Died: October 19, 1981

**Neville, Richard Griffin.
See Braybrooke.**

Nevins, Allan
New York, New York
C 480, December 10, 1931
Died: March 5, 1971
Memoir, M.H.S. *Procs.*,
83(1971):175

Newell, William
Cambridge
R 185, December 14, 1854
Died: October 28, 1881
Memoir: M.H.S. *Procs.*,
2d ser., 1(1884–1885):
72–74

Newman, John
Salisbury, North Caroli-
na
C 52, April 27, 1802
Died: 1833

Newmyer, R. Kent
Storrs, Connecticut
C 730, May 14, 1987

Nichols, Benjamin Ropes
Salem
R 94, January 28, 1819
Died: April 30, 1848
Memoir: M.H.S. *Procs.*,
2(1835–1855):427

Nichols, Charles Lemuel
Worcester
R 499, March 8, 1917
Died: February 19, 1929
Memoir: M.H.S. *Procs.*,
62(1928–1929):144–
152

Nichols, John Gough
London, England
C 295, April 9, 1868
Died: November 14, 1873

Nicolson, Sir Harold
London, England
H 89, February 11, 1954
Died: May 1, 1968

Niles, Nathaniel
Fairlee, Vermont
C 12, January 2, 1793
Died: October 31, 1828

Nissenbaum, Stephen
Amherst
R 1019, April 11, 1991

Nobel, John
Boston
R 404, March 9, 1899
Died: June 10, 1909
Memoir: M.H.S. *Procs.*,
44(1910–1911):543–
561

**Norcross, Grenville
Howland**
Boston
R 423, October 9, 1902
Died: February 12, 1937

Northrop, George Norton
West Roxbury
R 645, January 9, 1947
Died: July 31, 1964

Appendix I: Members

Norton, Asahel Strong
Paris, New York
C 30, January 31, 1797
Died: May 10, 1853

Norton, Charles Eliot
Cambridge
R 236, June 14, 1860
Died: October 21, 1908
Memoir: M.H.S. *Procs.*,
48(1914–1915):57–68

Norton, Mary Beth
Ithaca, New York
C 711, December 15, 1983

Notestein, Wallace
New Haven, Connecticut
C 509, November 12,
1942
Died: February 2, 1969

Nott, Eliphalet
Schenectady, New York
C 76, April 29, 1813
Died: January 29, 1866

Nourse, Henry Stedman
Lancaster
R 361, November 14,
1889
Died: November 14, 1903
Memoir: M.H.S. *Procs.*,
2d ser., 18(1903–
1904):292–295

Nutter, George Read
Boston
R 571, December 10, 1931
Died: February 21, 1937
Memoir: M.H.S. *Procs.*
68(1944–1947):459–
465

O'Brien, Conor Cruise
Dublin, Ireland
C 755, January 10, 1991

O'Brien, Robert Lincoln
Brookline
R 524, November 10,
1921
Washington, D.C.
C 538, February 11, 1954
Died: November 23, 1955
Memoir, M.H.S. *Procs.*,
71(1953–1957):427–
428

**O'Callaghan, Edmund
Burke**
Albany, New York
C 252, September 10,
1857
Died: May 27, 1880

O'Connor, Thomas H.
Braintree
R 904, December 10, 1981

O'Keefe, Bernard J.
Wayland
R 950, December 11, 1986
Died: July 20, 1989

Oliver, Andrew, I
New York, New York
C 553, February 13, 1958
Boston
R 821, December 10, 1970
Died: October 20, 1981
Memoir, M.H.S. *Procs.*,
93(1981):128–132

Oliver, Andrew, II
Chevy Chase, Maryland
C 722, January 9, 1986

Oliver, Fitch Edward
Boston
R 298, January 13, 1876
Died: December 8, 1892
Memoir: M.H.S. *Procs.*,
2d ser., 8(1892–1894):
474–485

Oliver, Frederick Scott
London, England
C 440, May 9, 1918
Died: June 4, 1934

Oliver, George
Exeter, England
C 204, March 30, 1843
Died: March 23, 1861

Oliver, Peter
Mount Kisco, New York
C 536, January 8, 1953
Died: February 16, 1959

Olney, Richard
Boston
R 394, May 13, 1897
Died: April 8, 1917
Memoir: M.H.S. *Procs.*,
51(1917–1918):203–
208

**Oman, Sir Charles
William Chadwick**
Oxford, England
C 427, November 10,
1910
Died: June 24, 1946

Osgood, Russell
Ithaca, New York
C 741, January 12, 1989

Osgood, Samuel
New York, New York
C 251, July 9, 1857
Died: April 14, 1880

Osgood, William B.
Boston
R 716, March 14, 1957

**Oxford, William Stubbs,
bishop of**
Oxford, England
H 42, October 12, 1876
Died: April 22, 1901

Paige, Lucius Robinson
Cambridge
R 161, May 30, 1844
Died: September 2, 1896
Memoir: M.H.S. *Procs.*,
2d ser., 15(1901–
1902):240–254

Paine, John Bryant, Jr.
Weston
R 699, November 10,
1954
Died: May 11, 1976
Memoir, M.H.S. *Procs.*,
88(1976):117–120

Paine, Nathaniel
Worcester
R 415, March 14, 1901
Died: January 14, 1917
Memoir: M.H.S. *Procs.*,
51(1917–1918):109–
113

Paine, Richard Cushing
Brookline
R 712, May 10, 1956
Died: May 10, 1966
Memoir, M.H.S. *Procs.*,
78(1966):145–146

Paine, Stephen D.
Boston
R 947, October 9, 1986

Paine, Thomas Middleton
Wellesley
R 1022, May 9, 1991

Palfrey, Francis Winthrop
Boston
R 284, February 13, 1873
Died: December 5, 1889
Memoir: M.H.S. *Procs.*,
2d ser., 7(1891–1892):
39–44

Palfrey, John Carver
Boston
R 425, December 11, 1902
Resigned December 14,
1905
Died: January 29, 1906

Palfrey, John Gorham
Cambridge
R 111, April 28, 1825
Resigned June 28, 1838
R 111, June 30, 1842
Resigned April 17, 1854
Died: April 26, 1881

Palgrave, Sir Francis
London, England
C 136, July 25, 1833
Died: July 6, 1861

Palmer, Joseph
Boston
R 221, January 13, 1859
Died: March 3, 1871
Memoir: M.H.S. *Procs.*,
19(1881–1882):224–
229

Palmer, Robert Roswell
Princeton, New Jersey
C 581, October 19, 1961

Palmer, Stephen
Needham
R 88, August 27, 1816
Died: October 31, 1821
Memoir: M.H.S. *Procs.*,
1(1791–1835):343–
345

Paltsits, Victor Hugo
New York, New York
C 473, April 10, 1930
Died: October 3, 1952

**Paris, S.A.R. Louis
Philippe Albert
Bourbon-Orléans,
comte de**
Paris, France
H 41, December 9, 1875
Died: September 8, 1894

Park, Charles Edwards
Boston
R 494, March 9, 1916
Died: September 23, 1962

Park, Edwards Amasa
Andover
R 246, September 12,
1861
Died: June 4, 1900
Memoir: M.H.S. *Procs.*,
2d ser., 14(1900–
1901):446–467

Park, Lawrence
Groton
R 500, April 12, 1917
Died: September 28, 1924
Memoir: M.H.S. *Procs.*,
58(1924–1925):137–
144

Parker, Francis Edward
Boston
R 250, February 12, 1863
Died: January 18, 1886
Memoir: M.H.S. *Procs.*,
2d ser., 3(1886–1887):
247–252

Parker, Henry Tuke
London, England
C 274, June 13, 1861
Died: August 18, 1890

Parker, Joel
Cambridge
R 225, May 12, 1859
Keene, New Hampshire
C 196, October 29, 1840
Died: August 17, 1875
Memoir: M.H.S. *Procs.*,
14(1875–1876):172–
179

Parkman, Francis, I
Boston
R 177, February 26, 1852
Died: November 6, 1893
Memoir: M.H.S. *Procs.*,
2d ser., 8(1892–1894):
520–562

Parkman, Francis, II
Boston
R 573, February 11, 1932
Died: July 15, 1990

Parry, John Horace
Harvard
R 818, November 12,
1970
Died: August 25, 1982
Memoir, M.H.S. *Procs.*,
94(1982):114–117

Appendix I: Members

Parsons, Ebenezer
Boston
R 37, January 31, 1797
Died: November 27, 1819
Memoir: M.H.S. *Procs.*,
1(1791–1835):317–
320

Parsons, Theophilus
Cambridge
R 229, September 8, 1859
Resigned May 9, 1878
Died: January 26, 1882

Parsons, Usher
Providence, Rhode Island
C 164, November 24,
1836
Died: December 19, 1868

Parton, James
New York, New York
C 287, April 12, 1866
Died: October 17, 1891

Paterson, Stanley C.
Nahant
R 935, December 12, 1985

Paul, Oglesby
Dedham
R 1013, December 13,
1990

Paulding, James Kirke
New York, New York
C 157, June 30, 1836
Died: April 6, 1860

Paver, William
York, England
C 247, December 11, 1856
Died: June 1, 1871

Paxson, Frederic Logan
Berkeley, California
C 477, January 8, 1931
Died: October 24, 1948

Payson, William Lincoln
Cambridge
R 756, May 11, 1961
Died: July 17, 1980

Peabody, Andrew Preston
Portsmouth, New Hamp-
shire
C 258, May 13, 1858
Cambridge
R 240, February 14, 1861
Died: March 10, 1893
Memoir: M.H.S. *Procs.*,
2d ser., 11(1896–
1897):25–46

Peabody, Endicott
Hollis, New Hampshire
C 739, October 13, 1988

Peabody, George
London, England
H 25, August 9, 1866
Died: November 4, 1869

Peabody, James Bishop
Boston
R 854, May 13, 1976
Died: March 22, 1977

**Peabody, Oliver William
Bourn**
Boston
R 157, October 26, 1843
Removed 1845
Died: July 5, 1848

Peabody, Robert Ephraim
Jamaica Plain
R 646, January 9, 1947
Died: January 20, 1984

Pearson, Eliphalet
Andover
R 53, January 28, 1800
Resigned August 28,
1810
Died: September 12, 1826

Pearson, Henry Greenleaf
Boston
R 441, April 13, 1905
Died: December 28, 1939

Peck, William Dandridge
Cambridge
R 22, October 8, 1792
Died: October 3, 1822
Memoir: M.H.S. *Colls.*,
2d ser., 10:161–170

Peckham, Howard Henry
Ann Arbor, Michigan
C 666, May 8, 1975

Pedersen, Chevalier Peder
Copenhagen, Denmark
C 125, April 30, 1829
Died: ?

Pelikan, Jaroslav Jan
Hamden, Connecticut
C 712, December 15, 1983

**Pell, Stephen Hyatt
Pelham**
New York, New York
C 524, February 12, 1948
Died: June 22, 1950

Pemberton, Thomas
Boston
R 18, August 13, 1792
Died: July 5, 1807
Memoir: M.H.S. *Colls.*,
10:190–191

Perera, Guido Rinaldo
Boston
R 874, December 14, 1978

Perera, Lawrence T.
Boston
R 967, January 14, 1988

**Perkins, Augustus
Thorndike**
Boston
R 281, February 8, 1872
Died: April 21, 1891
Memoir: M.H.S. *Procs.*,
2d ser., 7(1891–1892):
426–437

Perkins, Bradford
Ann Arbor, Michigan
C 641, May 14, 1970

Perkins, Charles Callahan
Boston
R 292, December 10, 1874
Died: August 25, 1886
Memoir: M.H.S. *Procs.*,
2d ser., 3(1886–1887):
223–246

Perkins, Dexter
Rochester, New York
C 528, March 10, 1949
Died: May 12, 1984

Perkins, Elliott
Cambridge
R 648, February 13, 1947
Died: March 4, 1985

Perkins, James
Cap François, Haiti
C 3, May 29, 1792
Boston
R 34, March 25, 1796
Died: August 1, 1822
Memoir: M.H.S. *Procs.*,
   1(1791–1835):353–
   368

Perkins, John A.
Boston
R 973, May 12, 1988

Perkins, Palfrey
Boston
R 632, March 9, 1944
Died: March 12, 1976

**Perry, Alice de
   Vermandois Clarke**
Needham
R 925, December 13, 1984

Perry, Amos
Providence, Rhode Island
C 362, March 12, 1885
Died: August 10, 1899

Perry, Arthur Latham
Williamstown
R 339, May 10, 1883
Resigned December 8,
   1904
Died: July 9, 1905

Perry, Bliss
Milton
R 442, May 11, 1905
Exeter, New Hampshire
C 537, February 11, 1954
Died: February 13, 1954
Memoir, M.H.S. *Procs.*,
   71(1953–1957):380–
   385

Perry, Carroll
Ipswich
R 589, January 10, 1935
Died: October 2, 1937

Perry, John Curtis
Lincoln Center
R 1006, May 10, 1990

Perry, Lewis Frederick
Chestnut Hill
R 764, October 11, 1962
Died: August 24, 1973
Memoir, M.H.S. *Procs.*,
   86(1974):84–85

Peterson, Merrill Daniel
Charlottesville, Virginia
C 717, May 24, 1984

Petigru, James Louis
Charleston, South Caro-
   lina
H 13, February 14, 1861
Died: March 9, 1863

Pettit, Norman
Cambridge
R 946, October 9, 1986

Phillips, James Duncan
Topsfield
R 584, December 14, 1933
Died: October 19, 1954

Phillips, John Charles
Boston
R 328, January 12, 1882
Died: March 9, 1885
Memoir: M.H.S. *Procs.*,
   2d ser., 4(1887–1889):
   33–36

Phillips, John Marshall
New Haven, Connecticut
C 530, March 8, 1951
Died: May 7, 1953

Phillips, Stephen
Salem
R 750, February 8, 1961
Died: January 15, 1971
Memoir, M.H.S. *Procs.*,
   83(1971):161–164

Phillips, Stephen Willard
Salem
R 554, December 13, 1928
Died: July 6, 1955

Phillips, William
North Beverly
R 647, February 13, 1947
Died: February 23, 1968
Memoir, M.H.S. *Procs.*,
   80(1968):133

Pickering, John
Salem
R 91, January 29, 1818
June 25,, 1835 Boston
Resigned May 5, 1831
Died: May 5, 1846
Memoir: M.H.S. *Colls.*,
   3d ser., 10:204–224

Pickering, Timothy
Philadelphia, Pennsylva-
   nia
C 40, April 24, 1798
Died: January 29, 1829

Pickman, David Motley
Medford
R 1010, October 11, 1990

Pickman, Edward Motley
Bedford
R 549, November 10,
   1927
Died: May 9, 1959
Memoir, M.H.S. *Procs.*,
   72(1957–1960):364–
   370

Pier, Arthur Stanwood
Milton
R 552, March 8, 1928
Removed March 10, 1932
Concord, New Hamp-
   shire
C 481, April 14, 1932
Milton
A 2, December 13, 1945
R 552, December 14, 1950
Died: August 14, 1966
Memoir, M.H.S. *Procs.*,
   79(1967):189–196

Appendix I: Members

Pierce, Edward Lillie
Milton
R 373, March 9, 1893
Died: September 6, 1897
Memoir: M.H.S. *Procs.*,
2d ser., 18(1903–
1904):363–369

Pierce, Henry Lillie
Boston
R 390, November 12,
1896
Died: December 17, 1896
Memoir: M.H.S. *Procs.*,
2d ser., 11(1896–
1897):386–410

Pierce, John
Brookline
R 73, January 31, 1809
Died: August 24, 1849
Memoir: M.H.S. *Colls.*,
4th ser., 1:277–295

Pieronnet, Thomas
Demerara, Guiana
C 47, January 28, 1800
Died: ?

Pintard, John
New York, New York
C 79, October 28, 1813
Died: June 21, 1844

Pirenne, Henri
Ghent, Belgium
H 72, May 10, 1923
Died: October 24, 1935

Pirie, Robert S.
Hamilton
R 831, December 14, 1972

Pitkin, Timothy
Farmington, Connecticut
C 74, August 25, 1812
Died: December 18, 1847

Plimpton, George Arthur
New York, New York
C 441, February 13, 1919
Died: July 1, 1936

Plumer, William
Epping, New Hampshire
C 64, August 25, 1807
Died: December 22, 1850

Pomfret, John Edwin
San Marino, California
C 602, October 8, 1964
Died: November 26, 1981

Pond, Shepard
Winchester
R 624, January 8, 1942
Died: May 28, 1945
Memoir, M.H.S. *Procs.*,
71(1953–1957):359–
361

Poole, William Frederick
Chicago, Illinois
C 332, January 10, 1878
Died: March 1, 1894

Popkin, John Snelling
Boston
R 63, July 13, 1801
Resigned January 26,
1826
Died: March 2, 1852

Porter, Edward Griffin
Lexington
R 318, April 6, 1880
Died: February 5, 1900
Memoir: M.H.S. *Procs.*,
2d ser., 15(1901–
1902):55–68

Potter, Alfred Claghorn
Cambridge
R 570, November 12,
1931
Removed October 25,
1936
Died: November 1, 1940

Pound, Roscoe
Watertown
R 611, December 8, 1938
Died: July 1, 1964

Powicke, Sir Frederick Maurice
Oxford, England
H 82, November 13, 1947
Died: May 19, 1963

Preble, George Henry
Brookline
R 333, May 11, 1882
Died: March 1, 1885
Memoir: M.H.S. *Procs.*,
2d ser., 2(1885–1886):
132–135

Prescott, William Hickling
Boston
R 145, July 26, 1838
Died: January 28, 1859
Memoir: M.H.S. *Procs.*,
4(1858–1860):167–
205

Pressensé, Edmond de
Paris, France
C 298, February 11, 1869
Died: April 8, 1891

Preyer, Kathryn Lee Conway
Cambridge
R 842, April 10, 1975

Price, Don K., Jr.
Cambridge
R 788, May 12, 1966

Price, Ezekiel
Boston
R 28, April 30, 1793
Died: July 15, 1802
Memoir: M.H.S. *Colls.*,
1st ser., 8:85

Price, Jacob Myron
Ann Arbor, Michigan
C 704, May 11, 1982

Price, Lucien
Boston
R 759, February 8, 1962
Died: March 30, 1964

Prince, John
Salem
R 26, January 29, 1793
Died: June 7, 1836
Memoir: M.H.S. *Colls.*,
3d ser., 5:271–282

Proctor, Thomas Emerson
Died: August 19, 1973
Hamilton
R 715, February 14, 1957

Prothero, Sir George Walter
Rye, England
C 416, May 9, 1907
Died: July 10, 1922

Prucha, Francis Paul
Milwaukee, Wisconsin
C 652, January 13, 1972

Punchard, George
Boston
R 276, December 8, 1870
Died: April 2, 1880
Memoir: M.H.S. *Procs.*,
19(1881–1882):262–
264

Pusey, Nathan Marsh
Cambridge
R 696, February 11, 1954
C 673, March 10, 1977

Putnam, Franklin Delano
Boston
R 618, January 9, 1941
Died: January 8, 1943

Putnam, Frederic Ward
Cambridge
R 334, November 9, 1882
Died: August 14, 1915
Memoir: M.H.S. *Procs.*,
49(1915–1916):482–
487

Putnam, Herbert
Washington, D.C.
C 479, October 8, 1931
Died: August 14, 1955

Quincy, Edmund
Dedham
R 274, December 9, 1869
Died: May 17, 1877
Memoir: M.H.S. *Procs.*,
2d ser., 18(1903–
1904):401–416

Quincy, Josiah
Boston
R 36, July 26, 1796
Died: July 1, 1864
Memoir: M.H.S. *Procs.*,
9(1866–1867):83–156

Quincy, Josiah Phillips
Quincy
R 260, May 11, 1865
Died: October 31, 1910
Memoir: M.H.S. *Procs.*,
45(1911–1912):338–
346

Quint, Alonzo Hall
Jamaica Plain
R 214, July 8, 1858
Resigned December 9,
1880
Died: November 4, 1896

Rabb, Irving W.
Cambridge
R 949, December 11, 1986

Rafn, Carl Christian
Copenhagen, Denmark
C 124, April 30, 1829
Died: October 20, 1864

Ramsay, David
Charleston, South Caro-
lina
C 4, May 29, 1792
Died: May 8, 1815

Ramsay, Ephraim
Charleston, South Caro-
lina
C 34, April 25, 1797
Died: November 18, 1801

Ranck, George Washington
Lexington, Kentucky
C 342, December 11, 1879
Died: August 2, 1901

Rand, Arnold Augustus
Boston
R 450, December 13, 1906
Died: December 23, 1917
Memoir: M.H.S. *Procs.*,
53(1919–1920):30–36

Rand, Edward Kennard
Cambridge
R 553, April 12, 1928
Died: October 28, 1945

Rand, Isaac
Boston
R 48, July 19, 1798
Died: December 11, 1822
Memoir: M.H.S. *Procs.*,
1(1791–1835):368–
369

Randall, James Garfield
Urbana, Illinois
C 525, February 12, 1948
Died: February 20, 1953

Randolph, Edmund
Frederick County,
Virginia
C 11, October 23, 1792
Expelled July 20, 1797
Died: September 12, 1813

Ranke, Leopold von
Berlin, Germany
H 27, April 11, 1867
Died: May 23, 1886

Rantoul, Robert Samuel
Salem
R 455, February 13, 1908
Died: May 1, 1922

Rathbone, Perry Townsend
Cambridge
R 709, January 12, 1956

Read, John Meredith
Albany, New York
C 289, December 13, 1866
Died: December 27, 1896

Reardon, Paul Cashman
Hingham
R 864, April 14, 1977
Died: July 29, 1988
Memoir, M.H.S. *Procs.*,
100(1988):140–144

Reaves, George Madison
Boston
R 792, January 12, 1967
C 632, March 13, 1969
Died: August 11, 1972

Appendix I: Members

Redlich, Josef
Vienna, Austria
C 465, February 10, 1927
Died: November 11, 1936

Reischauer, Edwin Oldfather
Belmont
R 794, February 9, 1967
Died: September 1, 1990

Renwick, William Goodwin
Weston
R 669, April 12, 1951
C 620, January 11, 1968
Tucson, Arizona
A 7, October 19, 1961
Died: September 5, 1971

Reston, James Barrett
Washington, D.C.
C 610, March 10, 1966

Rhoads, James Berton
Lanham, Maryland
C 657, December 14, 1972

Rhodes, James Ford
Brookline
R 376, December 14, 1893
Died: January 22, 1927
Memoir: M.H.S. *Procs.*,
60(1926–1927):178–
192

Rice, Harry F.
Boston
R 1023, May 9, 1991

Rich, Obadiah
Boston
R 68, March 5, 1805
Died: January 20, 1850

Richards, James
Newark, New Jersey
C 84, January 26, 1815
Died: August 2, 1843

Richardson, Elliot Lee
Brookline
R 813, March 12, 1970
C 675, March 10, 1977

Richardson, George Shattuck
Brookline
R 887, May 8, 1980

Richardson, Robert Dale
Concord
R 723, April 10, 1958
Died: April 15, 1969
Memoir, M.H.S. *Procs.*,
81(1969):213–214

Richmond, Carleton Rubira
Milton
R 643, February 14, 1946
Emeritus, February 8,
1973
Died: December 13, 1975
Memoir, M.H.S. *Procs.*,
87(1975):165–166

Riker, James
Harlem, New York
C 225, November 11,
1852
Died: July 3, 1889

Riley, Stephen Thomas
Boston
R 659, November 10,
1949

Ripley, Samuel
Waltham
R 97, January 27, 1820
Died: November 24, 1847
Memoir: M.H.S. *Procs.*,
2(1835–1855):392–
394

Rives, William Cabell, I
Linsey's Store, Virginia
C 243, March 13, 1856
Died: April 25, 1868

Rives, William Cabell, II
Richmond, Virginia
C 368, November 10,
1887
Died: April 7, 1889

Rhizos Neroulos, Jakobos
Athens, Greece
C 170, October 26, 1837
Died: 1850

Robbins, Caroline
Rosemont, Pennsylvania
C 639, March 12, 1970

Robbins, Chandler
Boston
R 163, December 4, 1845
Died: September 11, 1882
Memoir: M.H.S. *Procs.*,
1st ser., 20(1882–
1883):403–417

Robbins, James Murray
Milton
R 235, June 14, 1860
Died: November 2, 1885
Memoir: M.H.S. *Procs.*,
2d ser., 3(1886–1887):
206–214

Robertson, John Jacob
Saugerties, New York
C 169, October 26, 1837
Died: October 6, 1881

Robertson, Priscilla Smith
North Anchorage,
Kentucky
C 724, October 9, 1986
Died: November 26, 1989

Robinson, Fred Norris
Cambridge
R 510, October 9, 1919
Died: July 21, 1966
Memoir, M.H.S. *Procs.*,
78(1966):147

Robinson, Raymond Henry
Wellesley Hills
R 878, May 10, 1979

Rochambeau, Achille Lacroix de Vimeux, marquis de
Vendôme, France
C 321, February 12, 1874
H 49, November 10, 1881
Died: September 4, 1897

Roche, John P.
Weston
R 954, January 8, 1987

Roelker, Nancy Lyman
East Greenwich, Rhode
Island
C 680, January 12, 1978

Roelker, William Greene
Providence, Rhode Island
C 523, December 12, 1946
Died: May 29, 1953

Rogers, Henry Munroe
Boston
R 559, December 12, 1929
Died: March 29, 1937

Rogers, John Smyth
Hartford, Connecticut
C 150, December 31, 1835
Died: March 30, 1851

Rogers, Rutherford David
New Haven, Connecticut
C 661, May 9, 1974
Resigned January 1, 1985

Romilly, Joseph
Cambridge, England
C 224, July 8, 1852
Died: August 7, 1864

Root, Elihu
New York, New York
C 449, October 14, 1920
Died: February 7, 1937

Ropes, John Codman
Boston
R 319, June 10, 1880
Died: October 28, 1899
Memoir: M.H.S. *Procs.*,
2d ser., 14(1900–
1901):229–254

Rose, John Holland
Cambridge, England
C 433, December 11, 1913
Died: March 3, 1942

**Rosebery, Archibald
Philip Primrose, earl of**
London, England
C 439, October 11, 1917
Died: May 21, 1929

**Rosenkrantz, Barbara
Gutmann**
Cambridge
R 931, May 9, 1985

Rosenthal, Arthur Jesse
Cambridge
R 913, May 12, 1983
Resigned, October 11,
1990

**Rostovtzeff, Michael
Ivanovich**
New Haven, Connecticut
H 75, January 13, 1927
Died: October 20, 1952

Rostow, Walt Whitman
Belmont
R 746, May 12, 1960
A 12, February 11, 1965
C 621, January 11, 1968

Rugg, Arthur Prentice
Worcester
R 505, May 9, 1918
Died: June 12, 1938

**Rumford, Benjamin
Thompson, Count**
Auteuil, France
C 39, January 30, 1798
Died: August 21, 1814

Rush, Richard
Philadelphia, Pennsylva-
nia
H 5, June 17, 1858
Died: July 30, 1859

Russell, George Robert
Jamaica, Plain
R 194, January 8, 1857
Died: August 5, 1866
Memoir: M.H.S. *Procs.*,
18(1880–1881):280–
281

**Russell, William
Goodwin**
Boston
R 344, November 13,
1884
Died: February 6, 1896
Memoir: M.H.S. *Procs.*,
2d ser., 14(1900–
1901):155–162

Ruzicka, Rudolph
Boston
R 737, October 8, 1959
Hanover, New Hamp-
shire
A 9, March 12, 1964
C 622, January 11, 1968
Died: July 20, 1978
Memoir, M.H.S. *Procs.*,
90(1978):143–145

Ryerson, Richard Alan
Boston
R 926, December 13, 1984

Sabine, Lorenzo
Framingham
R 186, December 14, 1854
Died: April 14, 1877
Memoir: M.H.S. *Procs.*,
17(1879–1880):371–
382

Sainsbury, William Noël
London, England
C 271, April 11, 1861
Died: March 9, 1895

Salazar, José Maria
Bogota, Colombia
C 117, October 27, 1825
Died: February, 1828

Salisbury, Harrison Evans
New York, New York
C 655, April 13, 1972

Salisbury, Stephen, I
Worcester
R 205, March 11, 1858
Died: August 24, 1884
Memoir: M.H.S. *Procs.*,
2d ser., 2(1885–1886):
89–100

Appendix I: Members

Salisbury, Stephen, II
Worcester
R 325, November 10,
1881
Died: November 16, 1905
Memoir: M.H.S. *Procs.*,
2d ser., 20(1906–
1907):412–419

Saltonstall, Endicott
Peabody
Newton
R 513, March 11, 1920
Died: December 19, 1922

Saltonstall, Leverett, I
Salem
R 87, August 27, 1816
Died: May 8, 1845
Memoir: M.H.S. *Colls.*,
3d ser., 9:117–125

Saltonstall, Leverett, II
Newton
R 212, June 17, 1858
Died: April 15, 1895
Memoir: M.H.S. *Procs.*,
2d ser., 11(1896–
1897):337–366

Saltonstall, Leverett, III
Dover
R 603, January 13, 1938
Died: June 17, 1979
Memoir, M.H.S. *Procs.*,
91(1979):225–227

Saltonstall, William
Gurdon
R 859, March 10, 1977
Exeter, New Hampshire
C 513, May 11, 1944
Died: December 18, 1989

Saltonstall, William
Lawrence
Manchester
R 806, March 13, 1969

Sampson, Ezra
Hudson, New York
C 53, August 26, 1802
Died: December 12, 1823

Samuels, Ernest
Evanston, Illinois
C 546, November 10,
1954

Sanborn, Franklin
Benjamin
Concord
R 426, January 8, 1903
Died: February 24, 1917
Memoir: M.H.S. *Procs.*,
51(1917–1918):307–
311

Sanford, John Elliot
Taunton
R 340, January 10, 1884
Died: October 11, 1907
Memoir: M.H.S. *Procs.*,
42(1908–1909):281–
286

Sargeant, Hélène S. Kazan-
jian
Wellesley Hills
R 917, December 15, 1983

Sargent, Lucius Manlius
West Roxbury
R 190, March 13, 1856
Died: June 2, 1867
Memoir: M.H.S. *Procs.*,
2d ser., 3(1886–1887):
309–312

Sargent, Winthrop, I
Philadelphia, Pennsylva-
nia
C 15, January 28, 1794
Died: June 3, 1820

Sargent, Winthrop, II
Philadelphia, Pennsylva-
nia
C 241, January 10, 1856
Died: May 18, 1870

Sargent, Winthrop, III
Philadelphia, Pennsylva-
nia
C 498, December 8, 1938
Died: July 9, 1968

Savage, James
Boston
R 80, January 28, 1813
Died: March 8, 1873
Memoir: M.H.S. *Procs.*,
16(1878):117–153; 2d
ser., 20
(1906–1907):232–244

Sawtelle, William Otis
Haverford, Pennsylvania
C 472, January 9, 1930
Died: September 24, 1939

Schaff, Morris
Cambridge
R 526, February 9, 1922
Died: October 19, 1929
Memoir: M.H.S. *Procs.*,
64(1930–1932):516–
521

Schinas, Constantine
Demetrius
Athens, Greece
C 181, October 25, 1838
Died: 1870

Schlegel, August Wilhelm
Copenhagen, Denmark
C 152, December 31, 1835
Died: May 12, 1845

Schlesinger, Arthur
Meier, I
Cambridge
R 545, February 10, 1927
Died: October 30, 1965
Memoir, M.H.S. *Procs.*,
77(1965):154–155

Schlesinger, Arthur
Meier, II
Cambridge
R 641, November 8, 1945
A 13, February 11, 1965
C 623 , January 11, 1968

Schouler, James
Boston
R 396, December 9, 1897
Intervale, New Hamp-
shire
C 408, February 9, 1905
Died: April 16, 1920
Memoir: M.H.S. *Procs.*,
54(1920–1921):283–
288

Schurz, Carl
New York, New York
H 55, December 8, 1887
Died: May 14, 1906

Schutz, John Adolph
Los Angeles, California
C 662, May 9, 1974

Schwab, John Christopher
New Haven, Connecticut
C 399, October 9, 1902
Died: January 12, 1916

Scott, Austin Wakeman
Cambridge
R 650, May 8, 1947
Died: April 9, 1981

Scott, Benjamin
Weybridge, England
C 307, February 9, 1871
Died: January 18, 1892

Scott, Peter R.
Weston
R 918, May 24, 1984

Scott, Sir Walter, baronet
Abbotsford, Scotland
C 105, January 31, 1822
Died: September 21 1832

Scott, Winfield
Washington, D.C.
H 17, November 14, 1861
Died: May 29, 1866

Scudder, Horace Elisha
Cambridge
R 323, May 12, 1881
Died: January 11, 1902
Memoir: M.H.S. *Procs.*,
2d ser., 17(1903):142–
161

Seamans, Robert C., Jr.
Cambridge
R 951, December 11, 1986

Sears, Barnas
Staunton, Virginia
C 301, July 8, 1869
H 39, September 9, 1875
Died: July 6, 1880

Sears, David
Boston
R 172, April 27, 1848
Died: January 14, 1871
Memoir: M.H.S. *Procs.*,
2d ser., 2(1885–1886):
405–429

Sears, Edmund Hamilton
Wayland
R 197, August 13, 1857
Died: January 19, 1876
Memoir: M.H.S. *Procs.*,
18(1880–1881):224–
239

Sears, John Winthrop
Boston
R 910, January 13, 1983

Seaver, Edwin Pliny
Newton
R 356, December 8, 1887
Died: December 8, 1917
Memoir: M.H.S. *Procs.*,
51(1917–1918):287–
288

Seaver, Henry Latimer
Lexington
R 572, January 14, 1932
H 94, October 14, 1965
Died: November 26, 1975
Memoir, M.H.S. *Procs.*,
87(1975):159–164,
90(1978):111–112

Sedgwick, Ellery
Beverly
R 486, December 10, 1914
Died: April 21, 1960
Memoir: M.H.S. *Procs.*,
72(1957–1960):395–
396

Sedgwick, Harold Bend
Lincoln Center
R 1007, May 10, 1990

Sedgwick, Henry Dwight
Dedham
R 531, November 8, 1923
Died: January 5, 1957

Sedgwick, John
Newton
R 1033, December 12,
1991

Seeley, Sir John Robert
Cambridge, England
H 51, February 9, 1882
Died: January 13, 1895

Senter, Isaac
Newport, Rhode Island
C 28, November 18, 1796
Died: December 20, 1799

Sewall, David
York, Maine
R 11, October 11, 1791
Died: October 22, 1825
Memoir: M.H.S. *Procs.*,
1(1791–1835):389–390

Sewall, Jonathan
Quebec, Canada
C 144, February 26, 1835
Died: November 12, 1839

Sewall, Samuel
Burlington
R 139, January 28, 1836
Resigned August 29,
1837
Died: February 18, 1868

Seward, William Henry
Auburn, New York
H 24, April 20, 1865
Died: October 10, 1872

Seymour, Charles
New Haven, Connecticut
C 496, April 14, 1938
Died: August 11, 1963

Appendix I: Members

Seymour, Horatio
Deerfield, New York
H 44, February 8, 1877
Died: February 12, 1886

Shannon, William Vincent
Brookline
R 907, May 11, 1982
Died: September 27, 1988

Shapiro, L. Dennis
Chestnut Hill
R 1011, October 11, 1990

Shattuck, Frederick Cheever
Boston
R 497, November 9, 1916
Died: January 11, 1929
Memoir: M.H.S. *Procs.*,
62(1928–1929):213–224

Shattuck, George Cheever
Brookline
R 717, January 9, 1958
Died: June 12, 1972
Memoir, M.H.S. *Procs.*,
84(1972):118–124

Shattuck, George Otis
Boston
R 359, June 13, 1889
Died: February 23, 1897
Memoir: M.H.S. *Procs.*,
2d ser., 14(1900–1901):361–368

Shattuck, Henry Lee
Boston
R 590, February 14, 1935
H 95, April 10, 1969
Died: February 2, 1971
Memoir, M.H.S. *Procs.*,
83(1971):168–174

Shattuck, Lemuel
Concord
R 120, August 24, 1830
Died: January 17, 1859
Memoir: M.H.S. *Procs.*,
18(1880–1881):155–165

Shaw, Lemuel
Boston
R 124, May 5, 1831
Died: March 30, 1861
Memoir: M.H.S. *Procs.*,
10(1867–1869):50–79

Shaw, Robert Gould
Wellesley
R 509, April 10, 1919
Died: April 10, 1931

Shaw, Samuel Savage
Boston
R 428, March 12, 1903
Died: September 24, 1915
Memoir: M.H.S. *Procs.*,
50(1916–1917):499–503

Shaw, William Smith
Boston
R 69, November 7, 1805
Died: April 25, 1826
Memoir: M.H.S. *Procs.*,
1(1791–1835):391–392

Shea, John Dawson Gilmary
New York, New York
C 239, July 12, 1855
Died: February 21, 1892

Sheldon, George
Deerfield
R 448, June 14, 1906
Died: December 23, 1916

Shelley, Fred
Kensington, Maryland
C 731, October 8, 1987

Shenton, Robert
Cambridge
R 974, May 12, 1988

Shepley, Hugh
Manchester
R 952, December 11, 1986
Resigned, January 10, 1991

Sherrill, Henry Knox
Boston
R 625, February 12, 1942
New York, New York
A 4, January 1, 1947
R 625, January 11, 1968
Died: May 11, 1980

Shipton, Clifford Kenyon
Shirley
R 614, December 14, 1939
Died: December 4, 1973
Memoir, M.H.S. *Procs.*,
85(1973):130–135

Shiverick, Nathan C.
Cambridge
R 984, January 12, 1989

Shurtleff, Nathaniel Bradstreet
Boston
R 167, March 25, 1847
Died: October 17, 1874
Memoir: M.H.S. *Procs.*,
13(1873–1875):389–395

Shurtleff, William Steele
Springfield
R 365, November 13, 1890
Died: January 14, 1896
Memoir: M.H.S. *Procs.*,
2d ser., 11(1896–1897):234–236

Sibley, John Langdon
Cambridge
R 165, January 1, 1846
Died: December 9, 1885
Memoir, M.H.S. *Procs.*,
2d ser., 2(1885–1886):487–507

Silliman, Benjamin
New Haven, Connecticut
C 68, September 7, 1808
Died: November 24, 1864

Silvestro, Clement Mario
Groton
R 958, April 9, 1987

Simpson, Alan
Little Compton, Rhode
Island
C 683, May 10, 1979

**Sioussat, St. George
Leakin**
Chevy Chase, Maryland
C 499, March 9, 1939
Died: August 3, 1960

Sizer, Theodore
New Haven, Connecticut
C 547, November 10,
1954
Died: June 21, 1967

Skelton, Raleigh Ashlin
London, England
C 591, January 10, 1963
Died: December 7, 1970
Memoir, M.H.S. *Procs.*,
82(1970):128–132

Slafter, Edmund Farwell
Boston
R 324, October 13, 1881
Died: September 22, 1906
Memoir: M.H.S. *Procs.*,
2d ser., 20(1906–
1907):591–596

Sloane, William Milligan
New York, New York
C 429, May 11, 1911
Died: September 11, 1928

Smith, Buckingham
St. Augustine, Florida
C 253, September 10,
1857
Died: January 5, 1871

Smith, Charles Card
Boston
R 266, April 11, 1867
Died: March 20, 1918
Memoir: M.H.S. *Procs.*,
51(1917–1918):345–
352

**Smith, Charles Llewellyn,
Jr.**
Cohasset
R 993, May 11, 1989
Died: November 4, 1990
Memoir, M.H.S. *Procs.*,
102(1990):170–172

Smith, Elihu Hubbard
New York, New York
C 37, December 1, 1797
Died: September 19, 1798

Smith, Erastus
New Haven, Connecticut
C 151, December 31, 1835
Died: October 8, 1878

Smith, Fitz-Henry, Jr.
Boston
R 514, April 8, 1920
Died: June 8, 1955
Memoir, M.H.S. *Procs.*,
71(1953–1957):410–
411

Smith, Goldwin
Toronto, Canada
C 283, October 13, 1864
H 64, December 8, 1904
Died: June 7, 1910

Smith, Henry Nash
Berkeley, California
C 592, January 10, 1963
Died: May 30, 1986

Smith, John Cotton
Sharon, Connecticut
C 78, April 29, 1813
Died: December 7, 1845

Smith, Jonathan
Clinton
R 451, January 10, 1907
Died: February 28, 1930
Memoir, M.H.S. *Procs.*,
68(1944–1947):466–
469

Smith, Justin Harvey
Boston
R 474, December 14, 1911
Resigned October 14,
1920
Died: March 21, 1930

Smith, Maurice Henry
Broxbourne, Hertford-
shire, England
C 684, May 10, 1979

**Smith, Philip Chadwick
Foster**
Salem
R 850, December 12, 1975
C 692, December 13, 1979

Smith, Theodore Clarke
Williamstown
R 440, March 9, 1905
Died: November 19, 1960
Memoir, M.H.S. *Procs.*,
72(1957–1960):401–
402

Smyth, Egbert Coffin
Andover
R 337, December 14, 1882
Died: April 12, 1904
Memoir: M.H.S. *Procs.*,
43(1909–1910):402–
411

**Snelling, Nathaniel
Greenwood**
Boston
R 92, January 29 1818
Resigned December 26,
1844
Died: September 7, 1858

Snow, Caleb Hopkins
Boston
R 112, August 29, 1826
Resigned February 26,
1835
Died: July 6, 1835

Snyder, Arthur F. F.
Boston
R 985, January 12, 1989

Solomon, Barbara Miller
Cambridge
R 877, January 11, 1979

Appendix I: Members

Somerby, Horatio Gates
London, England
C 267, May 12, 1859
Died: November 14, 1872
Memoir: M.H.S. *Procs.*,
2d ser., 1(1884–1885):
132–138

Southey, Robert
Keswick, England
C 95, April 29, 1819
Died: March 21, 1843

Southgate, William Scott
Scarborough, Maine
C 235, December 14, 1854
Died: May 21, 1899

Spang, Joseph Peter
Deerfield
R 1004, April 12, 1990

Spark, Alexander
Quebec, Canada
C 5, May 29, 1792
Died: March 7, 1819

Sparks, Jared
Cambridge
R 113, August 29, 1826
Died: March 14, 1866
Tribute: M.H.S. *Procs.*,
9(1866–1867):157–
176
Memoir: M.H.S. *Procs.*,
10(1867–1869):211–
310

Spaulding, Helen Bowdoin
Manchester
R 942, May 8, 1986

Spooner, John Jones
Martin's Brandon,
Virginia
C 14, November 26, 1793
Died: September 13, 1799

Spooner, William
Boston
R 35, April 26, 1796
Resigned May 28, 1835
Died: February 15, 1836

Spooner, William Jones
Boston
R 104, April 25, 1822
Died: October 17, 1824
Memoir: M.H.S. *Colls.*,
3d ser., 1:265–271

Sprague, Charles
Boston
R 249, February 13, 1862
Died: January 22, 1875
Memoir: M.H.S. *Procs.*,
14(1875–1876):39–51

Sprague, William Buell
Albany, New York
C 249, March 12, 1857
Died: May 7, 1876

Spring, Leverett Wilson
Williamstown
R 392, February 11, 1897
Died: December 23, 1917

Squier, Ephraim George
Chillicothe, Ohio
C 215, June 29, 1848
Died: April 17, 1888

Stampp, Kenneth Milton
Berkeley, California
C 667, May 8, 1975

Stanhope, Philip Henry Stanhope, earl
Kent, England
C 242, February 14, 1856
Died: December 24, 1875

Stanley, Arthur Penrhyn
London, England
H 29, January 14, 1869
Died: July 18, 1881

Stanwood, Edward
Brookline
R 432, October 8, 1903
Died: October 11, 1923
Memoir: M.H.S. *Procs.*,
57(1923–1924):212–
228

Staples, William Reed
Providence, Rhode Island
C 269, April 12, 1860
Died: October 19, 1868

Stearns, Foster
Exeter, New Hampshire
C 542, April 8, 1954
Died: June 4, 1956

Stearns, Raymond Phineas
Urbana, Illinois
C 564, October 8, 1959
Died: November 15, 1970
Memoir, M.H.S. *Procs.*,
83(1971):157–160

Stearns, William Augustus
Amherst
R 248, February 13, 1862
Resigned February 9,
1871
Died: June 8, 1876

Steinberg, Harvey
Framingham
R 968, January 14, 1988

Stephen, Sir Leslie
London, England
C 374, January 9, 1896
Died: February 22, 1904

Stephens, Henry Morse
Berkeley, California
C 422, April 9, 1908
Died: April 16, 1919

Stephens, John Lloyd
New York, New York
C 178, September 27,
1838
Died: October 10, 1852

Stern, Joseph S.
Cincinnati, Ohio
C 756, January 10, 1991

Stevens, Abbot
North Andover
R 678, January 10, 1952
Died: May 15, 1958

Stevens, Henry
London, England
C 227, September 8, 1853
Died: February 28, 1886

Stevens, John Austin
New York, New York
C 334, March 14, 1878
Died: June 16, 1910

Stevens, William Bacon
Philadelphia, Pennsylvania
C 192, July 30, 1840
Died: June 11, 1887

Stiles, Ezra
New Haven, Connecticut
C 10, October 23, 1792
Died: May 12, 1795

Stillé, Charles Janeway
Philadelphia, Pennsylvania
C 299, February 11, 1869
Died: August 11, 1899

Stimson, Frederic Jesup
Dedham
R 431, June 11, 1903
Died: November 19, 1943
Memoir: M.H.S. *Procs.*
68(1944–1947):470–
471

Stinehour, Roderick Douglas
Lunenburg, Vermont
C 611, March 10, 1966

Stone, Galen L.
Dedham
R 980, December 8, 1988

Stone, Lawrence
Princeton, New Jersey
C 656, April 13, 1972

Stone, William Leete
New York, New York
C 182, January 31, 1839
Died: August 15, 1844

Storer, Malcolm
Boston
R 476, June 13, 1912
Died: January 2, 1935

Storer, Robert Treat Paine, Jr.
Beverly Farms
R 986, April 13, 1989

Storey, Charles Moorfield
Jamaica Plain
R 620, April 10, 1941
Died: March 19, 1980
Memoir, M.H.S. *Procs.*,
92(1980):151–156

Storey, James M.
Boston
R 933, December 12, 1985

Storey, Moorfield
Boston
R 433, November 12,
1903
Died: October 24, 1929
Memoir: M.H.S. *Procs.*,
63(1929–1930):288–
301

Storrs, Richard Salter
Brooklyn, New York
C 330, December 14, 1876
Died: June 5, 1900

Story, Joseph
Salem
R 86, April 25, 1816
Died: September 10, 1845
Memoir: M.H.S. *Procs.*,
10(1867–1869):176–
205

Story, William Wetmore
Rome, Italy
C 297, January 14, 1869
Died: October 7, 1895

Strauss, Herbert Ranger
Chicago, Illinois
C 637, January 8, 1970
Died: February 11, 1974

Streeter, Henry Schofield
Wenham
R 796, January 11, 1968

Streeter, Thomas Winthrop
Morristown, New Jersey
C 497, December 8, 1938
Died: June 12, 1965
Memoir, M.H.S. *Procs.*,
77(1965):151–153

Strobel, Edward Henry
Cambridge
R 420, January 9, 1902
Died: January 15, 1908
Memoir: M.H.S. *Procs.*,
49(1915–1916):330–
346

Strong, Caleb
Northampton
R 57, July 31, 1800
Died: November 7, 1819
Memoir: M.H.S. *Procs.*,
1(1791–1835):290–
316

Stubbs, William. See Oxford

Sturgis, William
Boston
R 211, June 17, 1858
Died: October 21, 1863
Memoir: M.H.S. *Procs.*,
7(1863–1864):420–
473

Stuyvesant, Peter Gerard
New York, New York
C 167, March 30, 1837
Died: August 16, 1847

Sullivan, Charles M.
Cambridge
R 1028, October 10, 1991

Sullivan, Edward T.
Milton
R 970, April 14, 1988

Sullivan, James
Boston
R 4, January 24, 1791
Died: December 10, 1808
Memoir: M.H.S. *Colls.*,
2d ser., 1:252–254

Sullivan, John Langdon
Boston
R 59, April 28, 1801
Removed 1818
Died: February 10, 1865

Appendix I: Members

Sullivan, Thomas Russell
Boston
R 495, April 13, 1916
Died: June 28, 1916
Memoir: M.H.S. *Procs.*,
52(1918–1919):80–84

Sullivan, William
Boston
R 55, April 29, 1800
Died: September 3, 1839
Memoir: M.H.S. *Procs.*,
2(1835–1855):150–
160

Sumner, Charles
Boston
R 287, October 9, 1873
Died: March 11, 1874
Memoir: M.H.S. *Procs.*,
2d ser., 20(1906–
1907):538–549

Sumner, George
Boston
R 231, November 10,
1859
Died: October 6, 1863
Memoir: M.H.S. *Procs.*,
18(1880–1881):189–
223

Sumner, John Osborne
Boston
R 417, June 13, 1901
Died: February 20, 1938

Sumner, William Hyslop
Jamaica Plain
R 199, December 10, 1857
Died: October 24, 1861
Memoir: M.H.S. *Procs.*,
18(1880–1881):282–
286

Swain, David Lowry
Chapel Hill, North Caro-
lina
C 189, November 26,
1839
Died: September 3, 1868

Swift, Lindsay
Boston
R 447, April 12, 1906
Died: September 11, 1921

Syme, Sir Ronald
Oxford, England
C 570, October 13, 1960
Died: September 4, 1989

Syrett, Harold Coffin
New York, New York
C 590, December 13, 1962
Died: July 29, 1984
Memoir, M.H.S. *Procs.*,
96(1984):38–41

Taft, Henry Walbridge
Pittsfield
R 379, May 10, 1894
Died: September 22, 1904
Memoir: M.H.S. *Procs.*,
2d ser., 19(1905):390–
393

Tappan, Benjamin
Augusta, Maine
C 161, October 27, 1836
Died: December 23, 1863

Tate, Thaddeus W., Jr.
Williamsburg, Virginia
C 737, May 12, 1988

Tate, Vernon Dale
Hingham
R 657, May 13, 1948
Annapolis, Maryland
C 550, October 11, 1956
Died: September 30, 1989

**Taunay, Affonso De
Escragnolle**
Sao Paulo, Brazil
H 85, February 12, 1948
Died: March 20, 1958

Taylor, Charles Henry
Boston
R 593, April 11, 1935
Died: August 18, 1941

Taylor, Francis Henry
Worcester
R 714, January 10, 1957
Died: November 22, 1957

Taylor, Henry Osborn
New York, New York
C 435, October 14, 1915
Died: April 13, 1941

Taylor, John Ingalls
South Natick
R 897, January 8, 1981
Died: June 8, 1987
Memoir, M.H.S. *Procs.*,
99(1987):178–183

Taylor, Robert Joseph
Medford
R 838, January 10, 1974

Taylor, Robert Sundling
Marblehead
R 943, May 8, 1986

Taylor, William Davis
South Natick
R 908, May 11, 1982

Taylor, William O.
Medfield
R 992, May 11, 1989

Tefft, Israel Keech
Savannah, Georgia
C 186, October 31, 1839
Died: June 30, 1862

**Temperley, Harold
William Vazeille**
Cambridge, England
C 478, April 9, 1931
Died: July 11, 1939

Tenney, Samuel
Exeter, New Hampshire
C 8, October 8, 1792
Died: February 6, 1816

Ternaux-Compans, Henri
Paris, France
C 177, August 28, 1838
Died: December, 1864

Thacher, Peter
Boston
R 5, January 24, 1791
Died: December 16, 1802
Memoir: M.H.S. *Colls.*,
1st ser., 8:277–284

Thayer, James Bradley
Cambridge
R 360, October 10, 1889
Died: February 14, 1902
Memoir: M.H.S. *Procs.*,
52(1918–1919):133–
138

Thayer, Nathaniel
Boston
R 255, February 11, 1864
Died: March 7, 1883
Memoir: M.H.S. *Procs.*,
2d ser., 2(1885–1886):
51–63

Thayer, William Roscoe
Cambridge
R 381, October 11, 1894
Died: September 7, 1923
Tribute: M.H.S. *Procs.*,
57(1923–1924):15–17

Thernstrom, Stephan Albert
Lexington
R 898, January 8, 1981

Thiers, Louis Adolphe
Died: September 3, 1877
Paris, France
H 28, January 14, 1869

Thomas, Benjamin Franklin
Jamaica Plain
R 233, January 12, 1860
Died: September 27, 1878
Memoir: M.H.S. *Procs.*,
2d ser., 14(1900–
1901):297–302

Thomas, Isaiah
Worcester
R 76, April 25, 1811
Died: April 4, 1831
Memoir: M.H.S. *Procs.*,
1(1791–1835):440–
444

Thomas, Joshua
Plymouth
R 72, October 25, 1808
Died: January 10, 1821
Memoir: M.H.S. *Colls.*,
2d ser., 10:1–6

Thomas, Milton Halsey
Princeton, New Jersey
C 574, January 12, 1961
Died: July 7, 1977
Memoir, M.H.S. *Procs.*,
90(1978):115–116

Thompson, Benjamin Franklin
New York, New York
C 213, December 4, 1845
Died: March 22, 1849

Thompson, Benjamin. See Rumford

Thompson, F. Hugh
Guildford, Surrey, England
C 698, December 10, 1981

Thompson, Lovell
Boston
R 767, December 12, 1963
Died: December 18, 1986
Memoir, M.H.S. *Procs.*,
98(1986):144–147

Thomson, Charles
Philadelphia, Pennsylvania
C 6, May 29, 1792
Died: August 16, 1824

Thorndike, John L.
Dover
R 987, April 13, 1989

Thorndike, Samuel Lothrop
Boston
R 419, December 12, 1901
Died: June 18, 1911
Memoir: M.H.S. *Procs.*,
48(1914–1915):124–
127

Thorndike, W. Nicholas
Brookline
R 990, April 13, 1989

Thorne, Samuel Edmund
Cambridge
R 740, January 14, 1960

Thwaites, Reuben Gold
Madison, Wisconsin
C 398, October 9, 1902
Died: October 22, 1913

Ticknor, George
Boston
R 132, July 25, 1833
Died: January 26, 1871
Memoir: M.H.S. *Procs.*,
20(1882–1883):384–
391

Tilden, Joseph
Boston
R 78, January 30, 1812
Resigned April 25, 1816
Died: July 28, 1853

Tocqueville, Charles Alexis. See Clérel de Tocqueville.

Tolles, Frederick Barnes
Swarthmore, Pennsylvania
C 603, October 8, 1964
Died: April 18, 1975

Toppan, Robert Noxon
Cambridge
R 405, May 11, 1899
Died: May 10, 1901
Memoir: M.H.S. *Procs.*,
2d ser., 15(1901–
1902):480–492

Torrey, Henry Warren
Cambridge
R 224, March 10, 1859
Died: December 14, 1893
Memoir: M.H.S. *Procs.*,
2d ser., 9(1894–1895):
197–210

Tourtellot, Arthur Bernon
Westport, Connecticut
C 633, March 13, 1969
Died: October 18, 1977

Tout, Thomas Frederick
London, England
C 467, June 9, 1927
Died: October 23, 1929

Towner, Lawrence William
Chicago, Illinois
C 627, March 14, 1968

Appendix I: Members

Toynbee, Arnold Joseph
London, England
H 83, November 13, 1947
Died: October 22, 1975

Tozzer, Alfred Marston
Cambridge
R 537, February 12, 1925
Died: October 5, 1954
Memoir, M.H.S. *Procs.*,
71(1953–1957):399–
401

**Trafford, William
Bradford**
Wenham
R 770, December 12, 1963
Died: February 20, 1983
Memoir, M.H.S. *Procs.*,
95(1983):154–157

Trescot, William Henry
Charleston, South Caro-
lina
C 256, February 11, 1858
Died: May 4, 1898

**Trevelyan, George
Macaulay**
Cambridge, England
C 436, April 13, 1916
H 76, November 14, 1929
Died: July 21, 1962

**Trevelyan, Sir George
Otto, baronet**
London, England
C 346, December 9, 1880
H 59, November 9, 1899
Died: August 16, 1928

Trumbull, Benjamin
North Haven, Connecti-
cut
C 42, October 30, 1798
Died: February 2, 1820

**Trumbull, James
Hammond**
Hartford, Connecticut
C 221, June 27, 1850
Died: August 5, 1897

Trumbull, Jonathan
Lebanon, Connecticut
C 43, April 30, 1799
Died: August 7, 1809

**Tuchman, Barbara
Wertheim**
Cos Cob, Connecticut
C 654, February 10, 1972
Died: February 6, 1989

Tucker, Ichabod
Salem
R 89, August 26, 1817
Resigned April 25, 1844
Died: October 22, 1846

Tucker, Louis Leonard
Wellesley Hills
R 857, January 13, 1977

Tucker, St. George
Williamsburg, Virginia
C 23, August 17, 1795
Died: November 10, 1828

**Tuckerman, Henry
Theodore**
New York, New York
C 305, January 12, 1871
Died: December 17, 1871

Tudor, Frederic
Boston
R 201, January 14, 1858
Died: February 6, 1864

Tudor, William, I
Boston
R 6, January 24, 1791
Died: July 8, 1819
Memoir: M.H.S. *Colls.*,
2d ser., 8:285–325

Tudor, William, II
Boston
R 85, April 25, 1816
Died: March 9, 1830
Memoir: M.H.S. *Procs.*,
1(1791–1835):429–
433

Turell, Samuel
Boston
R 29, July 30, 1793
Expelled August 27, 1811
Died: January 17, 1818

Turner, Frederick Jackson
Madison, Wisconsin
C 405, April 14 1904
Cambridge
R 466, November 10,
1910
Pasadena, California
C 405, November 13,
1924
Died: March 14, 1932
Memoir: M.H.S. *Procs.*,
65(1932–1936):432–
440

Turner, Sharon
Winchmore Hill, England
C 146, June 25, 1835
Died: February 13, 1847

Tuttle, Charles Wesley
Boston
R 285, February 13, 1873
Died: July 18, 1881
Memoir: M.H.S. *Procs.*,
2d ser., 1(1884–1885):
406–412

Tuttle, Julius Herbert
Dedham
R 492, December 9, 1915
Died: February 10, 1945
Memoir, M.H.S. *Procs.*,
70(1950–1953):265–
266

**Twisleton, Edward
Turner Boyd**
London, England
C 316, March 13, 1873
Died: October 5, 1874

Tyler, John W.
Groton
R 1029, October 10, 1991

Tyler, Lyon Gardiner
Williamsburg, Virginia
C 424, February 11, 1909
Died: February 12, 1935

Tyler, Moses Coit
Ithaca, New York
C 337, February 13, 1879
Died: December 28, 1900

Tyler, William Royall
Washington, D.C.
C 649, April 8, 1971

Tyng, Dudley Atkins
Newburyport
R 27, April 30, 1793
Died: August 1, 1829
Memoir: M.H.S. *Colls.*,
3d ser., 2:280–295

Ulrich, Laurel Thatcher
Durham, New Hamp-
shire
C 759, October 10, 1991

Updike, Daniel Berkeley
Boston
R 576, May 12, 1932
Died: December 29, 1941

**Upham, Charles
Wentworth**
Salem
Resigned May 19, 1852
R 129, January 26, 1832
R 129, November 14,
1867
Died: June 15, 1875
Memoir: M.H.S. *Procs.*,
15(1876–1877):182–
221

Upham, William Phineas
Salem
R 296, November 11,
1875
Died: November 23, 1905
Tribute: M.H.S. *Procs.*,
2d ser., 191(1905):
413–415

Usher, Roland Greene
St. Louis, Missouri
C 511, January 13, 1944
Died: March 22, 1957

**Vail, Robert William
Glenroie**
Worcester
R 601, May 13, 1937
New York, New York
Removed January 15,
1940
C 503, March 14, 1940
Died: June 21, 1966

Vallancey, Charles
Dublin, Ireland
C 63, November 7, 1805
Died: August 8, 1812

Van Ravenswaay, Charles
Sturbridge
R 762, April 12, 1962
A 16, January 12, 1967
C 624, January 11, 1968
Died: March 20, 1990
Memoir, M.H.S. *Procs.*,
102(1990):166–167

**Van Tyne, Claude
Halstead**
Ann Arbor, Michigan
C 466, March 10, 1927
Died: March 21, 1930

Van Rensselaer, Stephen
Albany, New York
C 31, January 31, 1797
Died: January 26, 1839

**Van Winkle, William
Mitchell**
New York, New York
C 532, April 12, 1951
Died: November 14, 1965

Vapéreau, Louis Gustave
Paris, France
C 331, November 8, 1877
Died: April 18, 1906

Vaughan, John
Philadelphia, Pennsylva-
nia
C 54, August 26, 1802
Died: March 25, 1807

Vaux, Roberts
Philadelphia, Pennsylva-
nia
C 139, October 31, 1833
Died: January 7, 1836

**Vermuele, Cornelius
Clarkson, III**
Cambridge
R 780, January 14, 1965

**Verplanck, Gulian
Crommelin**
New York, New York
C 96, January 27, 1820
Died: March 18, 1870

Vershbow, Arthur E.
Newton
R 944, May 8, 1986

**Vidaurré, Manuel
Lorenzo**
Lima, Peru
C 121, February 19, 1829
Died: March 9, 1841

Viets, Henry Rouse
Brookline
R 616, March 14, 1940
Died: July 5, 1969
Memoir, M.H.S. *Procs.*,
82(1970):113–115

Villari, Pasquale
Florence, Italy
H 60, December 12, 1901
Died: December 7, 1917

**Vose, Robert Churchill,
Jr.**
Boston
R 932, May 9, 1985

**Wainwright, Nicholas
Biddle**
Philadelphia, Pennsylva-
nia
C 572, December 8, 1960
Died: October 25, 1986

Appendix I: Members

Walcott, Henry Pickering
Cambridge
R 370, June 11, 1891
Died: November 11, 1932
Memoir: M.H.S. *Procs.*,
  65(1932–1936):330–
  333

Walcott, Robert
Cambridge
R 675, December 13, 1951
Died: November 11, 1956

Waldeck, Jean Frédéric de
Paris, France
C 185, September 26,
  1839
Died: May 2, 1875

Walker, Francis Amasa
Boston
R 338, May 10, 1883
Died: January 5, 1897
Memoir: M.H.S. *Procs.*,
  2d ser., 13(1899–
  1900):303–309

Walker, James
Cambridge
R 196, May 14, 1857
Died: December 23, 1874
Memoir: M.H.S. *Procs.*,
  2d ser., 6(1890–1891):
  443–468

Wallcut, Thomas
Boston
R 7, January 24, 1791
Died: June 5, 1840
Memoir: M.H.S. *Procs.*,
  2(1835–1855):193–
  208

Wallenstein, Julius von
Berlin, Germany
C 112, October 28, 1824
Died: ?

Walpole, Sir Spencer
Hatfield, England
C 406, December 8, 1904
Died: July 8, 1907

Walsh, Michael Joseph
Hyde Park
R 663, December 14, 1950
Died: May 27, 1984
Memoir, M.H.S. *Procs.*,
  96(1984):34–37

Walsh, Robert
Philadelphia, Pennsylva-
  nia
C 98, August 29, 1820
Died: February 7, 1859

Ward, George Atkinson
New York, New York
C 201, November 17,
  1842
Died: September 22, 1864

Ward, John William
New York, New York
C 703, January 14, 1982
Died: August 3, 1985

Warden, David Bailie
Paris, France
C 129, January 28, 1830
Died: October 9, 1845

Ware, Henry, Jr.
Boston
R 103, January 31, 1822
Died: September 22, 1843
Memoir: M.H.S. *Procs.*,
  2(1835–1855):278–
  282

Warner, Charles G. K.
Cambridge
R 1008, May 10, 1990

Warner, Sam Bass, Jr.
Boston
R 965, October 8, 1987

Warren, Charles
Dedham
R 530, February 8, 1923
Washington, D.C.
C 514, November 9, 1944
H 90, March 11, 1954
Died: August 16, 1954
Memoir, M.H.S. *Procs.*,
  71(1953–1957):390–
  398

Warren, Charles Henry
Boston
R 195, March 12, 1857
Died: June 29, 1874
Memoir: M.H.S. *Procs.*,
  19(1881–1882):424–
  428

Warren, Howland Shaw
Nahant
R 730, January 8, 1959

Warren, John
Boston
R 550, December 8, 1927
Died: July 17, 1928

Warren, John Collins
Boston
R 461, February 10, 1910
Died: November 3, 1927

Warren, Joseph
Brookline
R 577, February 9, 1933
Died: September 19, 1942

Warren, Lowell A., Jr.
Wellesley
R 962, May 14, 1987

Warren, Winslow
Dedham
R 283, January 9, 1873
Died: April 3, 1930
Memoir: M.H.S. *Procs.*,
  64(1930–1932):50–65

**Washburn, Charles
Grenfill**
Worcester
R 479, December 11, 1913
Died: May 25, 1928
Memoir: M.H.S. *Procs.*,
  61(1927–1928):213–
  218

Washburn, Emory
Worcester
R 183, June 8, 1854
Died: March 18, 1877
Memoir: M.H.S. *Procs.*,
  17(1879–1880):23–32

Washburn, Henry Bradford
Cambridge
R 518, December 9, 1920
Died: April 25, 1962

Washburn, John Davis
Worcester
R 336, December 14, 1882
Died: April 4, 1903
Memoir: M.H.S. *Procs.*,
2d ser., 17(1903):511–
515

Washburn, Wilcomb E.
Washington, D.C.
C 733, January 14, 1988

Washburne, Elihu Benjamin
Chicago, Illinois
H 50, January 12, 1882
Died: October 22, 1887

Waters, Henry Fitz-Gilbert
Salem
R 362, January 9, 1890
Died: August 16, 1913
Memoir: M.H.S. *Procs.*,
47(1913–1914):118–
126

Waters, Thomas Franklin
Ipswich
R 481, February 12, 1914
Died: November 23, 1919
Memoir: M.H.S. *Procs.*,
53(1919–1920):61–64

Waterston, Robert Cassie
Boston
R 228, June 9, 1859
Died: February 21, 1893
Memoir: M.H.S. *Procs.*,
2d ser., 8(1892–1894):
292–302

Watson, Benjamin Marston
Plymouth
R 367, February 12, 1891
Died: February 19, 1896
Memoir: M.H.S. *Procs.*,
2d ser., 12(1897–
1899):253–258

Watson, Elkanah
Albany, New York
C 102, c. 1821
Died: December 5, 1842

Watson, John Fanning
Philadelphia, Pennsylvania
C 132, October 26, 1831
Died: December 23, 1860

Watson, Marston
Boston
R 54, April 29, 1800
Died: August 7, 1800
Memoir: M.H.S. *Colls.*,
1st ser., 8:80–81

Watson, Richard
Westmoreland, England
C 57, January 31, 1804
Died: July 4, 1816

Wayne, James Moore
Savannah, Georgia
C 190, November 26,
1839
Died: July 5, 1867

Webb, Thomas Hopkins
Quincy
R 173, September 28,
1848
Died: August 2, 1866
Memoir: M.H.S. *Procs.*,
19(1881–1882):336–
338

Webster, Sir Charles Kingsley
London, England
C 482, February 9, 1933
Died: August 21, 1961

Webster, Daniel
Boston
R 100, August 27, 1821
Died: October 24, 1852
Memoir: M.H.S. *Procs.*,
2(1835–1855):529–
531

Webster, Noah
New Haven, Connecticut
C 7, August 13, 1792
Died: May 28, 1843

Webster, Redford
Boston
R 20, August 13, 1792
Died: August 31, 1833
Memoir: M.H.S. *Procs.*,
1(1791–1835):490–
492

Wedgwood, Dame Cicely Veronica
Stoke-on-Trent, Staffordshire, England
C 608, January 13, 1966

Weeden, William Babcock
Providence, Rhode Island
C 376, November 12,
1896
Died: March 28, 1912

Weeks, John Wingate
Belmont
R 805, December 12, 1968

Weeks, Sinclair, Jr.
Concord
R 1020, April 11, 1991

Weis, Frederick Lewis
Lancaster
R 622, December 11, 1941
Dublin, New Hampshire
A 5, February 14, 1952
Died: April 11, 1966

Weld, Charles Richmond
Baltimore, Maryland
C 355, January 11, 1883
Died: September 11, 1918

Weld, Philip Saltonstall
Gloucester
R 879, May 10, 1979
Died: November 6, 1984
Memoir, M.H.S. *Procs.*,
96(1984):43–46

Weld, William Floyd
Cambridge
R 1024, May 9, 1991

Appendix I: Members

Welles, John
Boston
R 128, January 26, 1832
Died: September 25, 1855
Memoir: M.H.S. *Procs.*,
2d ser., 3(1886–1887):
98–100

Wells, William Vincent
San Francisco, California
C 288, May 10, 1866
Died: June 1, 1876

Wendell, Barrett
Boston
R 375, June 8, 1893
Died: February 8, 1921
Memoir: M.H.S. *Procs.*,
55(1921–1922):174–
184

**Wentworth, Sir Charles
Mary, baronet**
Halifax, Nova Scotia
C 60, May 28, 1805
Died: April 10, 1844

**Wertenbaker, Thomas
Jefferson**
Princeton, New Jersey
C 469, March 8, 1928
Died: April 22, 1966

**Wetmore, George
Peabody**
Newport, Rhode Island
C 434, May 14, 1914
Died: September 11, 1921

Wetmore, William
Boston
R 19, August 13, 1792
Resigned August 29,
1815
Died: November 25, 1830

**Wheatland, David
Pingree**
Topsfield
R 774, April 9, 1964
Resigned Oct. 25, 1979
Died: December 13, 1979

Wheatland, Henry
Salem
R 168, January 27, 1848
Died: February 27, 1893
Memoir: M.H.S. *Procs.*,
2d ser., 9(1894–1895):
276–300

Wheatland, Stephen
Brookline
R 666, February 8, 1951
Died: May 30, 1987

Wheeler, Warren Gage
Dedham
R 660, November 10,
1949
Died: March 9, 1982
Memoir, M.H.S. *Procs.*,
94(1982):88–90

Wheelock, John
Hanover, New Hamp-
shire
C 65, August 25, 1807
Died: April 4, 1817

White, Andrew Dickson
Ithaca, New York
C 341, September 11,
1879
H 69, March 9, 1911
Died: November 4, 1918

White, Daniel Appleton
Salem
R 140, May 26, 1836
Died: March 30, 1861
Memoir: M.H.S. *Procs.*,
6(1862–1863):262–330

White, Theodore Harold
Bridgewater, Connecticut
C 699, December 10, 1981
Died: May 15, 1986

Whitehill, Walter Muir
Andover
R 623, December 11, 1941
Died: March 5, 1978
Memoir, M.H.S. *Procs.*,
90(1978):131–139

Whitmore, William Henry
Boston
R 251, February 12, 1863
Died: June 14, 1900
Memoir: M.H.S. *Procs.*,
2d ser., 15(1901–
1902):96–104

**Whitney, George
Kirkpatrick**
Concord
R 734, April 8, 1959
Died: December 30, 1979
Memoir, M.H.S. *Procs.*,
91(1979):238–241

Whitney, Henry Austin
Boston
R 206, March 11, 1858
Died: February 21, 1889
Memoir: M.H.S. *Procs.*,
2d ser., 5(1889–1890):
424–429

Whitney, Hugh
Boston
R 681, March 13, 1952
Died: November 10, 1967
Memoir: M.H.S. *Procs.*,
79(1967):209–213

Whitney, Peter
Northborough
R 67, August 28, 1804
Died: February 29, 1816
Memoir: M.H.S. *Colls.*,
2d ser., 7:177–178

Whitridge, Arnold
Salisbury, Connecticut
C 584, March 8, 1962
Died: January 19, 1989

Wicker, Thomas Gray
Washington, D.C.
C 642, May 14, 1970

Wiggins, James Russell
Washington, D.C.
C 583, February 8, 1962

Wight, Crocker
Brookline
R 911, January 13, 1983

Wilberforce, Samuel
Oxford, England
C 240, August 9, 1855
Died: July 19, 1873

Wilbur, James Benjamin
Manchester, Vermont
C 457, January 11, 1923
Died: April 28, 1929

Wilder, Amos Niven
Cambridge
R 802, October 10, 1968

Wilkins, Raymond Sanger
Winchester
R 633, March 9, 1944
Died: May 12, 1971

Willard, Joseph
Lancaster
R 118, February 19, 1829
Died: May 12, 1865
Memoir: M.H.S. *Procs.,*
    9(1866–1867):276–
    298

Willcox, William Bradford
New Haven, Connecticut
C 640, April 9, 1970
Died: September 15, 1985

Williams, Alexander Whiteside
Boston
R 763, May 10, 1962
Died: August 9, 1983
Memoir, M.H.S. *Procs.,*
    95(1983):157–160

Williams, George Huntston
Belmont
R 1015, January 10, 1991

Williams, John
Deerfield
R 50, October 30, 1798
Died: July 27, 1816
Memoir: M.H.S. *Procs.,*
    1(1791–1835):260–
    262

Williams, Jonathan
Philadelphia, Pennsylvania
C 66, October 27, 1807
Died: May 16, 1815

Williams, Samuel
London, England
C 110, October 30, 1823
Died: September 19, 1853

Williams, William Trumbull
Lebanon, Connecticut
C 93, April 30, 1818
Died: December 16, 1839

Williamson, Hugh
Edenton, North Carolina
C 20, August 17, 1795
Died: May 22, 1819

Williamson, Joseph
Belfast, Maine
C 380, March 11, 1897
Died: December 4, 1902

Williamson, William Durkee
Bangor, Maine
C 165, November 24,
    1836
Died: May 27, 1846

Willis, William
Portland, Maine
C 231, May 11, 1854
Died: February 17, 1870

Willis, Zephaniah
Kingston
R 61, April 28, 1801
Resigned April 27, 1815
Died: March 6, 1847

Wilson, Thomas James
Cambridge
R 670, April 12, 1951
C 636, April 10, 1969
Died: June 27, 1969
Memoir, M.H.S. *Procs.,*
    81(1969):215–216

Wilson, Thomas Woodrow
Princeton, New Jersey,
    and Washington, D.C.
C 379, February 11, 1897
Died: February 3, 1924

Wiltse, Charles Maurice
Hanover, New Hampshire
C 638, January 8, 1970
Died: May 22, 1990

Winship, George Parker
Providence, Rhode Island
C 409, March 9, 1905
Dover
R 491, October 14, 1915
Died: June 22, 1952
Memoir, M.H.S. *Procs.,*
    71(1953–1957):366–
    375

Winship, Lawrence Leathe
Sudbury
R 809, April 10, 1969
Died: March 3, 1975

Winship, Thomas
South Lincoln
R 788, December 9, 1965

Winslow, Ola Elizabeth
Sheepscot, Maine
C 612, May 12, 1966
Died: September 27, 1977
Memoir, M.H.S. *Procs.,*
    90(1978):120–121

Winsor, Justin
Boston
R 303, June 14, 1877
Died: October 22, 1897
Memoir: M.H.S. *Procs.,*
    2d ser., 12(1897–
    1899):457–482

Winthrop, Adam
New Orleans, Louisiana
C 118, April 27, 1826
Died: November 24, 1846

Appendix I: Members

Winthrop, Beekman
New York, New York
C 413, June 14, 1906
Died: November 10, 1940

Winthrop, Benjamin Robert
New York, New York
C 263, February 10, 1859
Died: July 26, 1879

Winthrop, Francis Bayard
New Haven, Connecticut
C 147, October 29, 1835
Died: March 21, 1841

Winthrop, Frederic, I
Hamilton
R 454, January 9, 1908
Died: May 6, 1932
Memoir: M.H.S. *Procs.*,
65(1932–1936):361–367

Winthrop, Frederic, II
Hamilton
R 651, October 9, 1947
Died: February 16, 1979
Memoir, M.H.S. *Procs.*,
91(1979):221–224

Winthrop, Frederic, III
Ipswich
R 888, May 8, 1980

Winthrop, Grenville Lindall
Lenox
R 583, June 8, 1933
Died: January 19, 1943

Winthrop, James
Cambridge
R 8, January 24, 1791
Died: September 26, 1821
Memoir: M.H.S. *Colls.*,
2d ser., 10:77–80

Winthrop, John, I
New Orleans, Louisiana
C 180, October 25, 1838
Died: March 12, 1886

Winthrop, John, II
Greenwich, Connecticut
C 694, April 9, 1981

Winthrop, Nathaniel Thayer
New York, New York
C 626, February 8, 1968
Died: June 3, 1980
Memoir, M.H.S. *Procs.*,
92(1980):163–166

Winthrop, Robert
New York, New York
C 519, November 8, 1945

Winthrop, Robert Charles, I
Boston
R 146, October 31, 1839
Died: November 16, 1894
Tributes: M.H.S. *Procs.*,
2d ser., 9(1894–1895):
211–214

Winthrop, Robert Charles, II
Boston
R 315, May 8, 1879
Died: June 5, 1905
Memoir: M.H.S. *Procs.*,
2d ser., 20(1906–1907):178–200

Winthrop, Thomas Lindall
Boston
R 58, October 28, 1800
Died: February 22, 1841
Memoir: M.H.S. *Colls.*,
4th ser., 2:202–214

Winthrop, William, I
Cambridge
R 95, January 27, 1820
Died: February 5, 1825
Memoir: M.H.S. *Procs.*,
1(1791–1835):383

Winthrop, William, II
Valetta, Malta
C 273, May 9, 1861
Died: July 3, 1869

Wisner, Benjamin Blydenburg
Boston
R 126, May 5, 1831
Died: February 9, 1835
Memoir: M.H.S. *Procs.*,
2(1835–1855):4–6

Wistar, Caspar
Philadelphia, Pennsylvania
C 45, July 18, 1799
Died: January 22, 1818

Wolcott, Oliver
New York, New York
C 29, November 18, 1796
Died: June 1, 1833

Wolcott, Roger, I
Boston
R 343, April 10, 1884
Died: December 21, 1900
Memoir: M.H.S. *Procs.*,
2d ser., 18(1903–1904):86–90

Wolcott, Roger, II
Milton
R 547, April 14, 1927
Died: April 21, 1965
Memoir, M.H.S. *Procs.*,
77(1965):145–150

Wolf, Edwin, 2nd
Wyncote, Pennsylvania
C 606, February 11, 1965
Died: February 20, 1991

Wolfe, Albert B.
Boston
R 1025, May 9, 1991

Wolff, Robert Lee
Cambridge
R 758, January 11, 1962
Died: November 11, 1980

Wolkins, George Gregerson
Newton, Highlands
R 520, February 10, 1921
Died: March 2, 1951
Memoir, M.H.S. *Procs.*,
70(1950–1953):277–
278

Wood, Gordon Stewart
Barrington, Rhode Island
C 681, May 11, 1978

Woodbury, John
Canton
R 543, December 9, 1926
Died: January 4, 1940

Woodbury, Levi
Portsmouth, New Hampshire
C 160, July 28, 1836
Died: September 4, 1851

Woods, Henry Ernest
Boston
R 458, October 8, 1908
Died: October 11, 1919
Memoir: M.H.S. *Procs.*,
54(1920–1921):188–
192

Woods, Leonard
Brunswick, Maine
C 276, November 14,
1861
H 36, March 11, 1875
Died: December 24, 1878

Woodward, Comer Vann
Baltimore, Maryland
C 580, May 11, 1961

Woolsey, Theodore Dwight
New Haven, Connecticut
C 293, September 12,
1867
H 34, February 11, 1875
Died: July 1, 1889

Worcester, Joseph Emerson
Cambridge
R 115, April 26, 1827
Died: October 27, 1865
Memoir: M.H.S. *Procs.*,
18(1880–1881):169–
173

Wright, Charles Conrad
Cambridge
R 934, December 12, 1985

Wright, Louis Booker
Washington, D.C.
C 549, January 12, 1956
Died: February 26, 1984

Wrong, George MacKinnon
Toronto, Canada
C 455, June 8, 1922
Died: June 29, 1948

Wroth, Lawrence Counselman
Providence, Rhode Island
C 488, January 9, 1936
Died: December 25, 1970

Wroth, Lawrence Kinvin
Portland, Maine
C 634, March 13, 1969

Wylie, Craig
Cambridge
R 815, April 9, 1970
Died: December 6, 1976
Memoir, M.H.S. *Procs.*,
88(1976):135–140

Wyman, Jeffries
Cambridge
R 268, July 9, 1868
Died: September 4, 1874
Memoir: M.H.S. *Procs.*,
14(1875–1876):4–24

Wyzanski, Charles Edward, Jr.
Cambridge
R 698, November 10,
1954
Died: August 31, 1986
Memoir: M.H.S. *Procs.*,
98(1986):136–139

Yates, John Van Ness
Albany, New York
C 99, August 29, 1820
Died: January 10, 1839

Young, Alexander
Boston
R 136, June 25, 1835
Died: March 16, 1854
Memoir: M.H.S. *Colls.*,
4th ser., 2:241–245

Young, Benjamin Loring
Boston
R 741, April 14, 1960
Died: June 4, 1964

Young, Edward James
Cambridge
R 309, June 13, 1878
Died: June 23, 1906
Memoir: M.H.S. *Procs.*,
44(1910–1911):529–
542

Zobel, Hiller Bellin
Lexington
R 807, March 13, 1969

Appendix II

Officers and Principal Staff
of the Society
1791–1991

The Massachusetts Historical Society

Presidents

James Sullivan, 1791–1806
Christopher Gore, 1806–1818
John Davis, 1818–1835
Thomas Lindall Winthrop, 1835–1841
James Savage, 1841–1855
Robert Charles Winthrop, 1855–1885
George Edward Ellis, 1885–1894
Charles Francis Adams, 1895–1915
Henry Cabot Lodge, 1915–1924
Arthur Lord, 1925
George Foot Moore, 1925–1927
William Crowninshield Endicott, 1927–1936
Francis Russell Hart, 1937–1938
Henry Lefavour, 1938–1942
Albert Francis Bigelow, 1942–1950
John Adams, 1950–1957
Thomas Boylston Adams, 1957–1975
James Barr Ames, 1975–1978
Francis Douglas Cochrane, 1978–1987
Henry Lee, 1987–

Vice-Presidents

Jared Sparks, 1857–1866
David Sears, 1857–1862
Thomas Aspinwall, 1862–1870
John Chipman Gray, 1866–1869
Charles Francis Adams, 1869–1881
Emory Washburn, 1870–1877
George Edward Ellis, 1877–1885
Charles Deane, 1881–1889
Francis Parkman, 1885–1893
Charles Francis Adams, 1890–1895
Justin Winsor, 1894–1897
Samuel Abbott Green, 1895–1914
Thomas Jefferson Coolidge, 1898–1904
James Ford Rhodes, 1904–1922
John Davis Long, 1914–1915
Winslow Warren, 1915–1921
Arthur Lord, 1921–1924
Charles Homer Haskins, 1922–1932
George Foot Moore, 1925
William Crowninshield Endicott, 1926–1927
Henry Lefavour, 1927–1938
Roger Bigelow Merriman, 1932–1945
Joseph Warren, 1938–1942

Zechariah Chafee, Jr., 1945–1957
George Gregerson Wolkins, 1943–1947
Mark Antony DeWolfe Howe, 1947–1955
Keyes DeWitt Metcalf, 1955–1958
Stephen Wheatland, 1957–1966
Henry Latimer Seaver, 1958–1972
Mark DeWolfe Howe, 1966–1967
James Barr Ames, 1967–1975
Paul Abraham Freund, 1972–1982
Francis Douglas Cochrane, 1975–1978
George Kirkpatrick Whitney, 1978–1979
Kathryn Lee Conway Preyer, 1980–
Paul Reardon, 1982–1984
William Davis Taylor, 1984–1988
Charles Francis Adams, 1987–
Oliver Filley Ames, 1988–1990
Leo Leroy Beranek, 1990–

Recording Secretaries

Thomas Wallcut, 1791–1792
George Richards Minot, 1792–1793
James Freeman, 1793–1812
Joseph McKean, 1812–1818
Charles Lowell, 1818–1833
Gamaliel Bradford, 1833–1835
Joseph Willard, 1835–1857
Chandler Robbins, 1857–1864
Charles Deane, 1864–1877
Edmund Quincy, 1877
George Dexter, 1878–1883
Edward James Young, 1883–1906
Edward Stanwood, 1906–1923
Henry Winchester Cunningham, 1923–1930
Mark Antony DeWolfe Howe, 1930–1933
Frank Washburn Grinnell, 1933–1956
Walter Muir Whitehill, 1956–1978
Marc Friedlaender, 1978
William Bentinck-Smith, 1978–

Corresponding Secretaries

Jeremy Belknap, 1791–1798
John Eliot, 1798–1813
Abiel Holmes, 1813–1833

Appendix II: Officers and Principal Staff

Charles Lowell, 1833–1849
Alexander Young, 1849–1854
William Parsons Lunt, 1854–1857
Joseph Willard, 1857–1864
Chandler Robbins, 1864–1877
Charles Deane, 1877–1881
Justin Winsor, 1881–1894
William Watson Goodwin, 1894–1896
Henry Williamson Haynes, 1896–1912
William Roscoe Thayer, 1912–1923
Roger Bigelow Merriman, 1923–1932
Francis Russell Hart, 1932–1937
Matt Bushnell Jones, 1937–1940
Clarence Saunders Brigham, 1940–1943
Roger Wolcott, 1943–1957
Charles Pelham Curtis, 1957–1959
James Barr Ames, 1959–1967
Andrew Oliver, 1967–1981
Henry Lee, 1981–1987
Lilian Handlin, 1987–

Treasurers

William Tudor, 1791–1796
George Richards Minot, 1796–1799
William Tudor, 1799–1803
Josiah Quincy, 1803–1820
James Savage, 1820–1839
Nahum Mitchell, 1839–1845
Peleg Whitman Chandler, 1845–1847
Richard Frothingham, 1847–1877
Charles Card Smith, 1877–1907
Arthur Lord, 1907–1921
Allan Forbes, 1921–1928
George Gregerson Wolkins, 1928–1943
Augustus Peabody Loring, Jr., 1943–1951
Allan Forbes, 1951–1955
Charles Jackson, 1955–1957
John Bryant Paine, Jr., 1957–1970
Francis Murray Forbes, Jr., 1970–1979
John Lowell, 1979–1991
Arthur C. Hodges, 1991–

Cabinet-Keepers[1]

John Eliot, 1791–1793
George Richards Minot, 1793–1794
Samuel Turell, 1794–1808
Timothy Alden, 1808–1809
Joseph McKean, 1809–1810
Redford Webster, 1810–1833
Isaac P. Davis, 1834–1854
Nathaniel Bradstreet Shurtleff, 1854–1860
Samuel Abbott Green, 1860–1868
Henry Gardner Denny, 1868–1874
William Sumner Appleton, 1874–1880
Fitch Edward Oliver, 1880–1892
Samuel Foster McCleary, 1893–1898
Henry Fitch Jenks, 1898–1904
Grenville Howland Norcross, 1904–1937
Henry Wilder Foote, 1937–1949
Walter Muir Whitehill, 1949–1956
Edward Pierce Hamilton, 1956–1972
Theodore Chase, 1972–1990

Members-at-Large of the Council

George Richards Minot, April 1791–April 1793
Peter Thacher, April 1791–April 1802
James Winthrop, April 1791–April 1821
Redford Webster, April 1793–April 1810
John Davis, April 1798–April 1818
Josiah Quincy, April 1798–April 1802
William Tudor, April 1803–April 1807
William Emerson, April 1803–April 1809
John T. Kirkland, April 1806–April 1812
Thomas L. Winthrop, April 1810–April 1835
Abiel Holmes, April 1811–April 1813
James Freeman, April 1812–April 1826
John Pierce, April 1813–April 1834
James Savage, April 1818–April 1820
William Tudor, Jr., April 1820–April 1824

[1] This position was abolished with a change of the bylaws, Oct. 11, 1990.

Francis C. Gray, April 1821–April 1836

Nathan Hale, April 1824–April 1836

James Bowdoin, April 1826–April 1833

Jared Sparks, April 1833–April 1838

James T. Austin, April 1834–April 1838

James Savage, April 1835–April 1841

Nathan Appleton, April 1835

Convers Francis, April 1835–April 1852

John Davis, April 1836–April 1838

Alexander Young, April 1838–April 1852

Joseph B. Felt, April 1838–April 1839

Samuel P. Gardner, April 1838–April 1842

George Ticknor, April 1839–April 1852

Joseph Willard, April 1841–April 1852

Francis C. Gray, April 1842–April 1852

Edward Everett, April 1852–April 1853

George E. Ellis, April 1852–April 1853

George Livermore, April 1852–April 1854

Nathaniel B. Shurtleff, April 1852–April 1854

Charles Deane, April 1852–April 1856

Robert C. Winthrop, April 1853–April 1855

George W. Blagden, April 1853–April 1855

Lucius R. Paige, April 1854–April 1856

Chandler Robbins, April 1854–April 1857

John C. Gray, April 1855–April 1857

William Brigham, April 1855–April 1858

Francis Parkman, April 1856–April 1858

George Livermore, April 1856–April 1859

William P. Lunt, April 1857–March 1857

Thomas Aspinwall, April 1857–April 1859

Emory Washburn, April 1858–April 1860

Lorenzo Sabine, April 1858–April 1860

Charles Deane, April 1858–April 1861

Solomon Lincoln, April 1859–April 1861

Henry A. Whitney, April 1859–April 1861

Thomas Aspinwall, April 1860–April 1862

Leverett Saltonstall, April 1860–April 1862

Samuel K. Lothrop, April 1861–April 1863

Charles H. Warren, April 1861–April 1862

Robert C. Waterston, April 1861–April 1863

Emory Washburn, April 1862–April 1864

Thomas C. Amory, April 1862–April 1864

William G. Brooks. 1862–April 1865

George E. Ellis, April 1863–April 1866

Horace Gray, April 1863–April 1866

Charles E. Norton, April 1864–April 1865

Leverett Saltonstall, April 1864–April 1867

Charles Folsom, April 1865–April 1867

Amos A. Lawrence, April 1865–April 1867

Henry W. Torrey, April 1866–April 1868

Samuel Eliot, April 1866–April 1869

George E. Ellis, April 1867–April 1868

William C. Endicott, April 1867–April 1869

William G. Brooks, April 1867–April 1870

Charles C. Smith, April 1868–April 1870

George W. Blagden, April 1868–April 1871

James M. Robbins, April 1869–April 1871

Henry W. Torrey, April 1869–April 1871

Theodore Lyman, April 1870–April 1872

Henry M. Dexter, April 1870–April 1871

Edmund Quincy, April 1871–April 1873

George S. Hillard, April 1871–April 1873

George Punchard, April 1871–April 1872

Robert C. Waterston, April 1871–April 1874

Appendix II: Officers and Principal Staff

Nathaniel B. Shurtleff, April 1872–April 1875

Augustus T. Perkins, April 1872–April 1875

Robert M. Mason, April 1873–April 1876

William S. Appleton, April 1873–April 1874

Francis W. Palfrey, April 1874–April 1876

Edmund Quincy, April 1874–April 1877

William G. Brooks, April 1875–April 1877

Charles C. Smith, April 1875–April 1877

Henry W. Foote, April 1876–April 1878

George E. Ellis, April 1876–April 1877

Francis Parkman, April 1877–June 1877

Richard Frothingham, June 1877–April 1879

James Russell Lowell, April 1877–April 1878

Charles C. Perkins, April 1877–April 1879

Winslow Warren, April 1877–April 1880

Charles W. Tuttle, April 1878–April 1880

Leverett Saltonstall, April 1878–April 1881

Justin Winsor, April 1879–April 1881

Delano A. Goddard, April 1879–January 1882

George B. Chase, April 1880–April 1882

Henry Cabot Lodge, April 1880–April 1883

Phillips Brooks, April 1881–April 1883

Henry W. Haynes, April 1881–April 1884

Charles F. Adams, Jr., April 1882–April 1885

J. Elliot Cabot, April 1882–April 1884

John T. Morse, Jr., April 1883–April 1884

Clement Hugh Hill, April 1883–April 1885

William W. Greenough, April 1884–April 1886

Samuel C. Cobb, April 1884–April 1886

Abbott Lawrence, April 1884–April 1887

Abner C. Goodell, Jr., April 1885–April 1887

Mellen Chamberlain, April 1885–April 1888

William Everett, April 1886–April 1888

Robert C. Winthrop, Jr., April 1886–April 1889

John Lowell, April 1887–April 1890

John D. Washburn, April 1887–April 1889

George S. Hale, April 1888–April 1890

William W. Goodwin, April 1888–April 1891

Josiah P. Quincy, April 1889–April 1891

Roger Wolcott, April 1889–April 1892

Edward Bangs, April 1890–April 1892

Edward J. Lowell, April 1890–April 1893

Edward G. Porter, April 1891–April 1893

Henry F. Jenks, April 1891–April 1894

Horace E. Scudder, April 1892–April 1894

Solomon Lincoln, April 1892–April 1895

Alexander McKenzie, April 1893–April 1895

John Davis Washburn, April 1893–April 1896

Edmund F. Slafter, April 1894–April 1896

Arthur Lord, April 1894–April 1897

Edward L. Pierce, April 1895–April 1897

Stephen Salisbury, April 1895–April 1896

Thornton K. Lothrop, April 1896–April 1898

Abbott Lawrence Lowell, April 1896–April 1898

Charles R. Codman, April 1896–April 1899

William W. Crapo, April 1897–April 1899

William R. Thayer, April 1897–April 1898

Winslow Warren, April 1898–April 1900

Barrett Wendell, April 1898–April 1900

Morton Dexter, April 1898–April 1901

George B. Chase, April 1898–April 1901

James Schouler, April 1899–April 1902

James Ford Rhodes, April 1899–April 1903

Thornton K. Lothrop, April 1900–April 1903

James B. Thayer, April 1900–February 1902

Andrew McFarland Davis, April 1901– April 1904

Archibald Cary Coolidge, April 1901– April 1904

William Roscoe Thayer, April 1902– April 1905

Worthington C. Ford, April 1902–April 1903

Samuel L. Thorndike, April 1903–April 1905

James F. Hunnewell, April 1903–April 1906

James DeNormandie, April 1903–April 1906

Thomas Wentworth Higginson, April 1904–April 1907

Arthur Theodore Lyman, April 1904– April 1905

Albert B. Hart, April 1905–April 1907

Thomas Leonard Livermore, April 1905–April 1908

Roger B. Merriman, April 1905–April 1906

Samuel Savage Shaw, April 1906–April 1908

Nathaniel Paine, April 1906–April 1909

Charles P. Bowditch, April 1906–April 1907

Edward H. Hall, April 1907–April 1909

Roger B. Merriman, April 1907–April 1910

Melville M. Bigelow, April 1907–April 1910

Edwin D. Mead, April 1908–April 1911

Bliss Perry, April 1908–April 1909

John D. Long, April 1909–April 1911

Waldo Lincoln, April 1909–April 1912

William R. Livermore, April 1909–April 1912

Frederic Winthrop, April 1910–April 1913

Moorfield Storey, April 1911–April 1913

Robert S. Rantoul, April 1911–April 1914

Mark Antony DeWolfe Howe, April 1912–April 1914

William V. Kellen, April 1912–April 1915

Frederick J. Turner, April 1913–April 1915

Gamaliel Bradford, Jr., April 1913– April 1916

Charles P. Greenough, April 1914– April 1916

John Collins Warren, April 1914–April 1917

Charles G. Washburn, April 1915–April 1917

Samuel W. McCall, April 1915–April 1918

Barrett Wendell, April 1916–April 1918

Joseph Grafton Minot, April 1916– April 1919

Lincoln Newton Kinnicutt, April 1917– April 1919

William Crowninshield Endicott, April 1917–April 1920

Ephraim Emerton, April 1918–April 1920

Frederick C. Shattuck, April 1918–April 1921

Charles L. Nichols, April 1919–April 1921

William B. H. Dowse, April 1919–April 1922

William S. Bigelow, April 1920–April 1922

Roger B. Merriman, April 1920–April 1923

Russell Gray, April 1921–April 1923

John W. Farlow, April 1921–April 1924

Paul Revere Frothingham, April 1922– April 1924

Francis R. Hart, April 1923–April 1925

Robert Grant, April 1923–April 1925

Chester Noyes Greenough, April 1923– April 1926

Malcolm Storer, April 1924–April 1926

Harold Murdock, April 1924–April 1927

Appendix II: Officers and Principal Staff

William Cameron Forbes, April 1925–April 1927

Fred Norris Robinson, April 1925–April 1928

Frederic Winthrop, April 1926–April 1928

Samuel Eliot Morison, April 1926–April 1929

Francis R. Hart, April 1927–April 1929

Charles Grenfill Washburn, April 1927–May 1928

Charles K. Bolton, April 1928–April 1930

Allen French, April 1928–April 1930

Frederic Winthrop, April 1929–April 1931

Henry Greenleaf Pearson, April 1929–April 1931

Edward Motley Pickman, April 1929–April 1932

Frank Washburn Grinnell, April 1930–April 1932

Chester Noyes Greenough, April 1930–April 1933

Claude Moore Fuess, April 1931–April 1933

Francis R. Hart, April 1931–April 1932

Samuel Eliot Morison, April 1932–April 1934

Clarence Henry Haring, April 1932–April 1934

Frederic Winthrop, April 1932–April 1933

Clarence S. Brigham, April 1933–April 1935

George Read Nutter, April 1933–April 1935

Henry Wilder Foote, April 1933–April 1936

John Woodbury, April 1934–April 1936

James Phinney Baxter, 3d., April 1934–April 1937

Clarence S. Brigham, April 1935–April 1937

Matt Bushnell Jones, April 1935–April 1937

Fitz-Henry Smith, Jr., April 1936–April 1938

George Edward Cabot, April 1936–April 1939

Bliss Perry, April 1937–April 1938

Joseph Warren, April 1937–April 1938

Stephen Willard Phillips, April 1937–April 1940

Roger Wolcott, April 1938–April 1941

James M. Hunnewell, April 1938–April 1940

Clarence S. Brigham, April 1938–April 1941

Gaspar G. Bacon, April 1939–April 1941

Lawrence Waters Jenkins, April 1940–April 1942

Keyes DeWitt Metcalf, April 1940–April 1942

Milton E. Lord, April 1941–April 1943

Stewart Mitchell, April 1941–April 1943

Augustus P. Loring, Jr., April 1941–April 1943

James Duncan Phillips, April 1942–Oct. 1944

Henry Lefavour, April 1942–Oct. 1944

Charles E. Goodspeed, April 1943–Oct. 1945

Shepard Pond, April 1943–May 1945

Clarence S. Brigham, April 1943–Oct. 1946

Fred N. Robinson, Oct. 1944–Oct. 1946

Chauncy C. Nash, Oct. 1944–Oct. 1947

Philip P. Chase, Oct. 1944–Oct. 1947

David Cheever, Oct. 1945–Oct. 1948

Palfrey Perkins, Oct. 1945–Oct. 1948

Clarence S. Brigham, Oct. 1946–Oct. 1949

Walter Muir Whitehill, Oct. 1946–Oct. 1949

John Adams, Oct. 1947–Oct. 1950

Carleton Rubira Richmond, Oct. 1947–Oct. 1950

Henry Latimer Seaver, Oct. 1948–Oct. 1951

Chauncey Cushing Nash, Oct. 1948–Oct. 1951

Harold Bowditch, Oct. 1949–Oct. 1952

Ernest Stanley Dodge, Oct. 1949–Oct. 1952

Parkman Dexter Howe, Oct. 1950–Oct. 1953

Robert Earle Moody, Oct. 1950–Oct. 1953

James Duncan Phillips, Oct. 1951–Oct. 1954

Lee Max Friedman, Oct. 1951–Oct. 1954

Chauncey C. Nash, Oct. 1952–Oct. 1955

Charles Pelham Curtis, Oct. 1952–Oct. 1955

Clifford K. Shipton, Oct. 1953–Oct. 1956

Thomas Boylston Adams, Oct. 1953–Oct. 1956

Edward Pierce Hamilton, Oct. 1954–Oct. 1956

Henry Latimer Seaver, Oct. 1954–Oct. 1957

Henry Forbush Howe, Oct. 1955–Oct. 1958

John Bryant Paine, Oct. 1955–Oct. 1958

Charles Pelham Curtis, Oct. 1956–Oct. 1959

George Caspar Homans, Oct. 1956–Oct. 1959

Stephen Wheatland, Oct. 1956–Oct. 1957

Lyman H. Butterfield, Oct. 1957–Oct. 1960

William Henry Harrison, Oct. 1957–Oct. 1959

Paul Herman Buck, Oct. 1958–Oct. 1961

Thomas James Wilson, Oct. 1958–Oct. 1961

Clifford K. Shipton, Oct. 1959–Oct. 1962

Howland Shaw Warren, Oct. 1959–Oct. 1962

Maurice Cary Blake, Oct. 1959–Oct. 1960

Henry Alexander Laughlin, Oct. 1960–Oct. 1963

Mason Hammond, Oct. 1960–Oct. 1963

Frederick Scouller Allis, Oct. 1961–Oct. 1964

Bernard Bailyn, Oct. 1961–Oct. 1964

Paul H. Buck, Oct. 1962–Oct. 1965

Lyman H. Butterfield, Oct. 1962–Oct. 1965

Clifford K. Shipton, Oct. 1963–Oct. 1966

Thomas James Wilson, Oct. 1963–Oct. 1966

Harold Daniel Hodgkinson, Oct. 1964–Oct. 1967

Andrew Oliver, Oct. 1964–Oct. 1967

Douglas Wallace Bryant, Oct. 1965–Oct. 1968

Russell W. Knight, Oct. 1965–Oct. 1968

Augustus Peabody Loring, Oct. 1966–Oct. 1969

Howland Shaw Warren, Oct. 1966–Oct. 1969

George Caspar Homans, Oct. 1967–Nov. 1970

Lovell Thompson, Oct. 1967–Nov. 1970

Franklin Lewis Ford, Oct. 1968–Nov. 1971

Harold Daniel Hodgkinson, Oct. 1968–Nov. 1971

Henry Lee, Oct. 1969–Nov. 1972

William Lincoln Payson, Oct. 1969–Nov. 1972

Frank Burt Freidel, Nov. 1970–Nov. 1973

George Kirkpatrick Whitney, Nov. 1970–Nov. 1973

Oscar Handlin, Nov. 1971–Nov. 1974

Edward Crosby Johnson, 3d, Nov. 1971–Nov. 1974

Francis Douglas Cochrane, Nov. 1972–Nov. 1975

Philip James McNiff, Nov. 1972–Nov. 1975

Henry Lee, Nov. 1973–Nov. 1976

Robert S. Pirie, Nov. 1973–Nov. 1976

John Leonard Clive, Nov. 1974–Nov. 1977

George Kirkpatrick Whitney, Nov. 1974–Nov. 1977

Marc Friedlaender, Nov. 1975–Nov. 1978

Edward Crosby Johnson, 3d, Nov. 1975–Nov. 1978

William Bentinck-Smith, Nov. 1976–Nov. 1979

Philip James McNiff, Nov. 1976–Nov. 1979

Alfred DuPont Chandler, Jr., Nov. 1977–Dec. 1983

Kathryn Lee Conway Preyer, Nov. 1977–Nov. 1980

Paul Cashman Reardon, Nov. 1978–Nov. 1982

Hiller Bellin Zobel, Nov. 1978–Nov. 1981

Janet Wilson James, Nov. 1979–Nov. 1982

Appendix II: Officers and Principal Staff

Philip James McNiff, Nov. 1979–Nov. 1982

Max R. Hall, Nov. 1980–Dec. 1983

Charles Francis Adams, Nov. 1981–Oct. 1987

Oliver Filley Ames, Nov. 1982–Oct. 1988

Samuel Carson Brown, Nov. 1982–Oct. 1988

Emily Morison Beck, Nov. 1982–Oct. 1987

Russell W. Knight, Dec. 1983–Oct. 1986

W. Davis Taylor, Dec. 1983–Oct. 1984

Abram Thurlow Collier, Oct. 1984–Oct. 1986

Leo Leroy Beranek, Oct. 1986–Oct. 1991

Caleb Loring, Jr., Oct. 1986–

John Weston Adams, Oct. 1987–

Thomas Kincaid McCraw, Oct. 1987–

Helen B. Spaulding, Oct. 1988–

David R. Godine, Oct. 1988–

John G. L. Cabot, Oct. 1990–

Librarians[2]

John Eliot, 1791–1793

George Richards Minot, 1793–1795

John Eliot, 1795–1798

John Thornton Kirkland, 1798–1806

William Smith Shaw, 1806–1808

Timothy Alden, 1808–1809

Joseph McKean, 1809–1812

Joseph Tilden, 1812–1814

James Savage, 1814–1818

Nathaniel Greenwood Snelling, 1818–1821

Elisha Clap, 1821–1823

William Jenks, 1823–1832

James Bowdoin, 1832–1833

Joseph Willard, 1833–1835

Nahum Mitchell, 1835–1836

Joseph Barlow Felt, 1836–1837

Thaddeus Mason Harris, 1837–1842

Joseph Barlow Felt, 1842–1855

Samuel Kirkland Lothrop, 1855–1861

Nathaniel Bradstreet Shurtleff, 1861–1864

Thomas Coffin Amory, 1864–1868

Samuel Abbott Green, 1868–1918

Julius Herbert Tuttle, 1919–1934

Allyn Bailey Forbes, 1934–1940

Stephen Thomas Riley, 1947–1963

John Daniel Cushing, 1963–1982

Stephen T. Riley Librarians[3]

John Daniel Cushing, 1982–1987

Peter Drummey, 1987–

Editors[4]

Charles Card Smith, 1889–1907

Worthington Chauncey Ford, 1909–1929

Stewart Mitchell, 1929–1939

Allyn Bailey Forbes, 1940–1947

Stewart Mitchell, 1947–1957

Malcolm Freiberg, 1957–1984

Conrad Edick Wright, 1985–

Directors[5]

Allyn Bailey Forbes, 1940–1947

Stewart Mitchell, 1947–1957

Stephen Thomas Riley, 1957–1976

Louis Leonard Tucker, 1977–

Adams Papers Editors-in-Chief

Lyman Henry Butterfield, 1954–1975

Robert Joseph Taylor, 1975–1983

Richard Alan Ryerson, 1983–

[2] A by-law change (approved June 14, 1934) altered the status of the librarian from being an officer of the Society elected annually to a position appointed by the Council; if a resident member of the Society, the librarian would be an ex-officio member of the Council.

[3] A vote of the Council established the Stephen T. Riley Librarianship on Dec. 9, 1982.

[4] The position of editor has always been an appointed one and does not hold the rank of an officer of the Society.

[5] The position of director was established through a by-law change approved May 9, 1940. The director is an ex-officio member of the Council.

Appendix III

Endowments
1837–1991

The Massachusetts Historical Society

*Principal balances are given from the audit
for the Fiscal Year ending June 30, 1991*

Adams Editorial Fund (1954)

Established with gifts from *Time*, Inc. The principal and income may be used to support the general operations of The Adams Papers editorial project. The fund is administered by The Adams Papers Administrative Board.

Council Records, October 14, 1954
Principal: $261,741

Adams Fund (1920)

Receipts from the royalties on *Charles Francis Adams: An Autobiography* (1916) and *The Education of Henry Adams* (1918). This fund is unrestricted both as to principal and to income. The income of this fund, according to the vote of the Council, is to be applied to the general expenses of the Society until further order.

M.H.S., *Procs.*, 53(1919–1920):151
Principal: $111,855

Adams Microfilm Fund (1954)

Established with receipts from subscribing institutions for the microfilm edition of The Adams Papers. The principal is to remain intact and the income used for the care and maintenance of The Adams Papers. The fund is administered by The Adams Papers Administrative Board.

Council Records, October 14, 1954
Principal: $316,017

John Adams Memorial Fund (1965), formerly known as the Endowment Fund

"All gifts to the Society in response to the Appeal to Members, as well as to the Appeal to the Public, shall, unless otherwise designated by the donors, be placed in the Endowment Fund of the Society, only the income of which shall be available for use by the Council."

"All gifts which are specifically unrestricted by the donors shall be placed in the General Fund, the capital of which may be available to the Council in case of necessity." This fund includes a $10,000 bequest from President John Adams and $1,000 from the Fidelity Management and Research Corporation.

Council Records, April 12, 1951, April 8, 1965; M.H.S., *Procs.*, 77(1965):173
Principal: $688,622

Mary Ogden Adams Ames Fund (1990)

Established by a gift from James B. Ames. "Only the income is to be spent for the general purposes of the Society, and also that expenditures from the income of the fund may be made for any of the purposes of the Society, not only for the announced purposes of the present capital campaign."

Council Records, April 11, 1991
Principal: $30,386

William Amory Fund (1889)

Bequest of $3,000 under the will of William Amory, who died on December 8, 1888, the income to be "applied to the general purposes of the Society; or to such specified objects as may be directed from time to time."

M.H.S., *Procs.*, 2d ser., 4(1887–1889): 236; Council Records, January 10, 1889
Principal: $3,000

Anonymous Fund (1887)

Gift, in 1887, of $1,000 by a Resident Member and an additional gift of $250 in 1888, the income to be "added to the principal until the annual meeting in 1991." At the October 1992 meeting of the Council, it was voted "That the

Appendix III: Endowment Funds

capital of the so-called 'Anonymous Centenary Fund' be included as an independently named entity in the total of the Society's Bicentennial Fund and that the fund's accumulated interest hereafter be used for the purposes specified by the founder of the fund, George Bigelow Chase."

M.H.S., *Procs.*, 2d ser., 3(1886–1887): 277–278; 4(1887–1889):353; 13(1899–1900):66–67; Council Records, October 8, 1992
Principal: $982,023

Samuel Appleton Fund (1854)

Gift of $10,000 from the executors of Samuel Appleton "in accordance with what we believe to have been his wish"— "the income of the same . . . to be applied for ever exclusively to the procuring, preservation, preparation, and publication of historical papers."

M.H.S., *Procs.*, 2(1835–1855): 599–601
Principal: $12,203

Frederic Bancroft Fund (1936)

Three gifts of $1,000 each, December 1936, January 1941, and January 1943, from Frederic Bancroft, the income of which may be applied to the general expenses of the Society as the Council may direct. This fund is unrestricted both as to principal and to income.

M.H.S., *Procs.*, 67(1941–1944):628
Principal: $3,000

Bicentennial Fund (1986)

Created to support the Society's bicentennial program consisting of (1) an addition to the Society's physical plant; (2) a public exhibition of the Society's most important holdings, from manuscripts to art works; (3) a bicentennial banquet featuring a prominent speaker; (4) special publications relating to the Society's history and collections; and (5) the 1991 spring reception.

M.H.S., *Procs.*, 98(1986):154–155
Principal: $1,199,427

Erastus Brigham Bigelow Fund (1881)

Gift of $1,000 from Mrs. Helen Bigelow Merriman, "in grateful remembrance of [her father's] pleasant connection with the Historical Society." The income was added to the principal until 1893, when the capital amounted to $2,000. There is no restriction on the use of the income.

M.H.S., *Procs.*, 18(1880–1881):322–323; 2d ser., 8(1892–1894):187
Principal: $2,000

Robert Charles Billings Fund (1903)

Gift of $10,000 from the executors of Robert Charles Billings, "the income to be used only for publications."

M.H.S., *Procs.*, 2d ser., 17(1903):235; 18(1903–1904):276
Principal: $10,000

Robert Apthorp Boit Fund (1922)

Bequest of $5,000 under the will of Robert Apthorp Boit, of Brookline, "the income of which shall be used in relation to the journals and logbooks of my grandfather, John Boit, or in relation to my own journals and diaries, or for such other purposes as the Society may from time to time determine." At a meeting, July 18, 1956, it was decided that income from the Boit Fund, by strict interpretation, should accumulate to the year 1969, at which time the diaries of Robert Apthorp Boit were to be opened.

M.H.S., *Procs.*, 54(1920–1921):253
Principal: $5,000

Mark Bortman Fund (1952)

The fund was established by Mark Bortman. The income is to be used for the general purposes of the Society.

Council Records, Oct. 9, 1952; M.H.S., *Procs.*, 70(1950–1953):377, 382, 386
Principal: $2,500

Brattle Church Fund (1877)

Gift of $100, with the model of the building of the Old Brattle Square Church, by the proprietors through Henry F. Jenks and the Reverend Samuel Kirkland Lothrop, for its "care and preservation."

M.H.S., *Procs.*, 15(1876–1877):264; 41(1907–1908):13–14, 417–418; Manuscript records for April 1877
Principal: $100

Building Fund (1919)

This fund was initiated by the appointment of a committee in April 1919, to raise money to "erect and fit with modern library equipment a stack building, absolutely fire-proof, in which [the Society's] library and manuscripts will be placed." This fund has been closed, all of it having been used for remodeling the Society's building after 1947.

M.H.S., *Procs.*, 53(1919–1920):145

Lyman H. Butterfield Fund (1978)

The bequest of Lyman H. Butterfield, the fund is "to strengthen the Society's resources and operations in one of its main fields of activity: the acquisition of reference, bibliographical, documentary, and important monographic works."

Council Records, January 12, April 13, 1978
Principal: $29,250

George Edward Cabot Fund (1947)

Bequest of $10,000 under the will of George Edward Cabot, of Boston, the principal of this fund to be safely invested, the income, only, to be used as the Council may direct.

Council Records, February 1947
Principal: $10,000

Mary Endicott Carnegie Fund (1958)

Bequest of $3,000 under the will of Mary Endicott Carnegie with principal and income subject to the regulations applying to the Massachusetts Historical Society's Endowment Fund.

Council Records, October 9, 1958
Principal: $3,000

The Louisa Williams Case Fund (1947)

Bequest of $5,000 under the will of Miss Louisa W. Case, of Weston, Massachusetts, who died on October 9, 1946. This legacy is unrestricted both as to principal and to income.

Council Records, November 1947
Principal: $5,000

Mellen Chamberlain Fund (1903–1906)

Gift of $10,062.01 to defray the cost of publishing his *History of Chelsea*, the balance to be funded "as a perpetual memorial of the interest which our honored associate took in the work of the Society." It was voted in 1908 that the interest be allowed to "accumulate and compound" until all likely royalties from the *History of Chelsea* had been received. The income has been used for the purposes of the Society since April 1909.

M.H.S., *Procs.*, 41(1907–1908):13, 509; 42(1908–1909):242
Principal: $1,232

Henry Winchester Cunningham Fund (1932)

Bequest of $50,000 under the will of Henry Winchester Cunningham, of Boston, who died at Milton on October 27, 1930, "the principal to be kept safely invested and the income used for any purpose connected with the work of the Society."

Council Records, May 1932
Principal: $50,000

Appendix III: Endowment Funds

Charles Deane Fund (1944)

Bequest of $1,000 under the will of Henry Herbert Edes, who died on October 13, 1922, in memory of his friend, Charles Deane, "the income only to be used toward defraying the cost of the Society's publications or for the general, or any special, purposes of the Society, as it, or its Council, may from time to time determine." This legacy became available in October 1944.

Council Records, October 1944
Principal: $1,000

Thomas Dowse Fund (1857)

Gift of $10,000 by the executors of Thomas Dowse that his library may be "for ever preserved and used in accordance with the views of the donor, and the votes of the Society at the time the gift was accepted." The income each year is placed to the credit of the general account in accordance with what was understood to be the wish of the executors.

M.H.S., *Procs.*, 3(1855–1858): 107–109, 171–173; 2d ser., 8(1892–1894):334–335
Principal: $14,586

William Bradford Homer Dowse Fund (1927)

Two gifts, $20,000 (1927), and $5,000 (1928), from William Bradford Homer Dowse, the income to be used for the reprinting of the *Journals of the House of Representatives of Massachusetts* (1715–1780). At the conclusion of this publication project, the Council voted that beginning in the fiscal year 1992/1993 "and hereafter until further notice of this board, the accumulated interest of the W.B.H. Dowse Fund be used for publications pertaining to colonial New England and for short-term fellowships for research at the Massachusetts Historical Society, on colonial New England."

M.H.S., *Procs.*, 60(1926–1927):196; 61(1927–1928):132–133.

Council Records, October 8, 1992
Principal: $25,000

George Edward Ellis Fund (1895)

Bequest of $30,000 under the will of the Reverend George Edward Ellis, who died in Boston on December 20, 1894, and $1,666.66 added from the sale of personal property. "My wish and expectation are that the bequest in money will yield sufficient annual income to insure, maintain, and repair the property [in Marlborough Street]."

M.H.S., *Procs.*, 2d ser., 10(1895–1896): 148–150, 404;17(1903):218–219
Principal: $31,667

Ellis House Fund (1895)

The $25,000 realized from the sale of the house of the Reverend George Edward Ellis at 110 Marlborough Street, Boston, is invested in the Society's real estate at 1154 Boylston Street, Boston.

M.H.S., *Procs.*, 2d ser., 10(1895–1896): 154–159, 296, 556–557, 561

William Crowninshield Endicott Fund (1958)

Bequest of $100,000 under the will of William C. Endicott who died in 1936: "in memory of my father, William Crowninshield Endicott." This legacy is unrestricted both as to principal and income.

Council Records, October 9, 1958
Principal: $100,000

Max Farrand Fund (1945)

Bequest of $1,000 under the will of Max Farrand, of New Haven, Connecticut, who died on June 17, 1945, "as a token of my regard for the Society." This legacy is "unrestricted."

Council Records, October 1945
Principal: $1,000

John Whittemore Farwell Fund (1930)

Bequest of $5,000 under the will of John Whittemore Farwell, of Cohasset, who died on October 7, 1929. The "sum was entered in the accounts as a permanent fund, without restriction [as to income]."

M.H.S., *Procs.*, 64(1930–1932):168
Principal: $5,000

Esther and Robert Feer Fund (1985)

Bequest of $42,000 under the will of Mrs. Esther R. Feer to establish a book fund, the income of which shall be used for the purchase of books and manuscripts in American history.

Council Records, December 13, 1985;
M.H.S., *Procs.*, 97(1985):170
Principal: $47,597

Francis Apthorp Foster Fund (1975)

Bequest of $104,651 under the will of Francis Apthorp Foster. The legacy is unrestricted both as to principal and income.

M.H.S., *Procs.*, 87(1975):187
Principal: $113,417

Richard Frothingham Fund (1883)

Gift of $3,000 by the widow of Richard Frothingham. It was voted "to employ the interest of said fund ... under the direction and at the discretion of the Council."

M.H.S., *Procs.*, 20(1882–1883):174–175
Principal: $3,000

General Fund, formerly known as the Library Addition Fund (1963)

An anonymous donor gave $1,000, "looking forward to the time when an addition to the building would become necessary." The 1977 audit notes that this fund "Now functions as the General Fund of the Society," and it was so renamed the following year.

Council Records, October 10, 1963;
M.H.S., *Procs.*, 76(1964):188–189;
85(1973):150
Principal: $1,715,188

Sarah Louisa Guild Fund (1949)

Bequest of $10,000 under the will of Sarah Louisa Guild for the maintenance and care of the Curtis and Courtenay Guild Library and paintings. On February 9, 1956, Frank W. Grinnell, the Society's counsel, gave his opinion that accumulated income be used to purchase books for the Society library, to be labeled "gift from Sarah Louisa Guild Fund."

M.H.S., *Procs.*, 69(1947–1950):471, 477; 70(1950–1953):299

Memorandum from Frank W. Grinnell to the Council, January 31, 1956
Principal: $10,000

Edward Pierce Hamilton Fund (1960)

Began with a gift of $2,500 by Edward P. Hamilton in 1960. The Society is to receive future royalties from Hamilton's book in the Main Stream of America series and add to the fund. The principal of the fund is to be kept intact and the income made available for the Society's general purposes.

Council Records, May 12, 1960
Principal: $38,137

John Tyler Hassam Fund (1941)

Bequest of $10,000 under the will of Eleanor Hassam, of Salem, in memory of her father, John Tyler Hassam, the principal to be "safely invested and the income thereof expended for the general purposes of the Society."

Council Records, October 1941
Principal: $10,000

Appendix III: Endowment Funds

Harold D. Hodgkinson Fund (1979)

A bequest of $5,000 is "to be held, managed, invested and reinvested as a separate fund but with the right of commingling for investment purposes with other funds held by the Society, the income only thereof to be expended, in such manner as the duly authorized representatives of the Society shall determine, for the preparation of papers to be read at one of the regular meetings of the Society or at such other suitable occasions as said representatives shall in their like discretion from time to time determine, each such paper to be on a subject of current or recent history, preferably pertaining to the Greater Boston area."

Council Records, January 10, 1980
Principal: $5,178

E. Harold Hugo Fund (1986)

Established in memory of E. Harold Hugo. The income of this fund is used "to purchase prints, maps, and drawings, all of which were special interests of Mr. Hugo."

M.H.S., *Procs.*, 98(1986):155
Principal: $2,025

James Frothingham Hunnewell Fund (1910)

Gift of $5,000 from James F. Hunnewell, of Boston, who died on November 11, 1910, "the income to be used in purchase of the rarer books needed for the Society's library. If at a future date some of my books come to the Society, the income of this fund can be used for binding or repair of the same or obtaining books to supply deficiencies."

M.H.S., *Procs.*, 54(1920–1921):568
Principal: $5,000

Thomas Hutchinson Fund (1978)

Established with a gift of $1,600 from William Bentinck-Smith as a permanent endowment fund, the income of which is to assist in purchasing books and manuscripts for the library. The fund is named for Thomas Hutchinson (1711–1780), governor and historian of the Massachusetts Bay Colony.

Council Records, December 14, 1978
Principal: $11,937

Abbott Lawrence Fund (1894)

Bequest of $3,000 under the will of Abbott Lawrence, who died in Boston on July 6, 1893, the income to be "expended in publishing the *Collections* and *Proceedings* of the Society."

M.H.S., *Procs.*, 2d ser., 9(1894–1895):96
Principal: $3,000

Henry Lefavour Fund (1947)

Bequest of $10,000 under the will of Henry Lefavour, of Boston, who died on June 16, 1946, unrestricted as to income or principal.

Council Records, November 1947
Principal: $10,000

Library Fund (1958)

The fund was established by the Council, the income to be used for new acquisitions and other purposes of the library, and the capital to be used only by special vote of the Council. It was started with a gift of $1,000 from Henry L. Seaver. The $5,000 principal of this fund was used to partially create a new Library Fund in 1962.

Council Records, February 13, March 13, April 10, 1958; March 8, May 10, 1962

Library Fund (1962)

"By vote of the Council, 3,000 volumes on the Civil War were sold to Rice University for $45,000, and, with $5,000

transferred from the old Library Fund, a new permanent Library Fund of $50,000 was established, the income to be used for general purposes of the library and the principal to be used only by special vote of the Council."
M.H.S., Procs., 74(1962):116
Principal: $104,009

Helen Alvera Lake Lill Fund (1948)

Bequest of $5,806 under the will of Helen Alvera (Lake) Lill, of Seekonk, Massachusetts. Unrestricted as to principal and income.
Council Records, April 1948, February 10, 1955.
M.H.S., Procs., 69(1947–1950):462–463
Principal: $6,000

Henry Cabot Lodge Fund (1925)

Bequest of $5,000 as a "trust fund" under the will of Henry Cabot Lodge, of Nahant, who died at Cambridge on November 9, 1924, "one-fifth of the income of said fund to be added each year to the principal and the remaining four-fifths of the income of said fund to be expended for those purposes of the Society which the Council of said Society shall select and determine."
M.H.S., Procs., 59(1925–1926):269;
Council Records, October 11, 1956.
Principal: $13,383

John Lowell Fund (1897)

Bequest of $3,000 under the will of John Lowell, who died on May 14, 1897, the income to "be applied to such purposes as the Council may from time to time authorize."
M.H.S., Procs., 2d ser., 12(1897–1899):1
Principal: $3,000

Theodore Lyman Fund (1955)

Established by a gift of $5,005 from John Adams on December 19, 1955. The income is to be used for the general purposes of the Society.
M.H.S., Procs., 71(1953–1957):494, 497, 499
Principal: $5,005

Kingsmill Marrs Fund (1927)

Bequest of $2,000 under the will of Mrs. Kingsmill Marrs (Laura Norcross), "the income only to be used in the care and preservation of the library of Kingsmill Marrs," which his widow gave to the Society.
M.H.S., Procs., 60(1926–1927):195–196
Principal: $2,000

Massachusetts Historical Trust Fund (1855)

Gift of $2,000 by David Sears (1855), and of $500 by David Sears (1866), and of $500 by Nathaniel Thayer (1866), the annual income to be added to the principal until the sum should amount to $10,000, the Society thereafter annually to appropriate the income of said fund by vote at the May meeting.
M.H.S., Procs., 3(1855–1858):44–47; 10(1867–1869):10; 15(1876–1877):305; 19(1881–1882):386; 2d ser., 17(1903): 224
Principal: $10,000

Albert Matthews Fund (1948–1949)

Bequest of $1,000 by Albert Matthews. One-fourth of the annual income to be added to the principal and three-fourths to be expended for the purchase of books, pamphlets, newspapers, or manuscripts.
M.H.S., Procs., 69(1947–1950):484
Principal: $2,612

Andrew W. Mellon Fund (1977)

The Andrew W. Mellon Foundation awarded a $400,000 grant to the Society in 1977: "100,000 in expendable funds toward support of processing, microfilm-

Appendix III: Endowment Funds

ing, and conservation activities over a two-year period, and $300,000 in endowment funds, the income to be used for similar purposes thereafter."

M.H.S., *Proc.*, 89(1977):201, 210
Principal: $980,211

Elizabeth and Perry Miller Fund (1982–1983)

Began with a bequest of one-half of the estate Elizabeth Williams Miller of Cambridge. The income shall be used for the general purposes of the Society's library.

Council Records, June 15, 1982; January 13, 1983
Principal: $151,164

Thomas Minns Fund (1945)

Bequest of $44,129.49, under the will of Susan Minns, of Boston, according to a trust agreement dated December 30, 1921, which terminated on October 19, 1945, this fund to be named for her brother, Thomas Minns, "the income thereof only to be applied by the directors to the general purposes of the Society."

Council Records, December 1945
Principal: $44,129

Stewart Mitchell Fund (1940)

Bequest of $50,000 under the will of Mrs. Georgine (Holmes) Thomas, of New York City, who died on February 3, 1940, "to be held by said Society and invested by it and the income therefrom accumulated until the total fund, both principal and income, shall have a value of $100,000, and thereafter ... to use the income therefrom for the purposes of the Society. This fund shall be known as the Stewart Mitchell Fund."

Council Records, December 1940
Principal: $100,000

Clarence Bloomfield Moore Fund (1937)

Bequest of $2,500 under the will of Clarence B. Moore, of Philadelphia, who died on March 24, 1936. In May 1937, the Council voted to accept the legacy "without setting it aside irrevocably as a separate fund."

Council Records, May 1937
Principal: $2,500

Grenville Howland Norcross Fund, I (1927)

Bequest of $10,000 under the will of Mrs. Kingsmill Marrs (Laura Norcross), sister of Grenville Howland Norcross, "the income only to be used in the maintenance, upkeep and care of the Society's property and collections."

M.H.S., *Procs.*, 60(1926–1927):195–196
Principal: $10,000

Grenville Howland Norcross Fund, II (1937)

Bequest of $50,000 under the will of Grenville Howland Norcross, of Boston, who died on February 12, 1937, without restrictions as to capital or income, to be applied to the general expenses of the Society at the discretion of the Council.

Council Records, October 1937
Principal: $50,000

George Read Nutter Fund (1937)

Bequest of $2,500, under the will of George Read Nutter, who died at Boston on February 21, 1937, the income of which is to be applied to the general expenses of the Society, at the discretion of the Council.

Council Records, October 1938
Principal: $2,500

Paine Publication Fund (1957)

Principal donated by members of the Paine family. The Council voted that "all donations received by the Society for the Paine Publication Fund, together with accumulated income at the approximate annual rate received by the Society on the market value of its investments for its previous fiscal year, shall be used for the publication of a volume of *Collections* by the Society which shall contain selections from the Paine Papers...."

Council Records, October 10, 1957
Principal: $111,783

Maria Antoinette Parker Fund (1905)

Gift of the deposit book of Miss Maria Antoinette Parker, dated February 21, 1821, by Thomas Minns, who added sums of $800, in 1906, and $124.29, in 1908, the "interest on this gift to be used for the purchase of books for the library."

M.H.S., *Procs.*, 2d ser., 20(1906–1907): 215–216; 41(1907–1908):418
Principal: $1,000

George Peabody Fund (1867)

Gift of $20,000 by George Peabody, of London, Honorary Member, in bonds, the proceeds of which shall constitute a permanent trust fund of which the income "shall be appropriated to the publication and illustration of [the Society's] proceedings and memoirs and to the preservation of [the Society's] historical portraits."

M.H.S., *Procs.*, 9(1866–1867): 438–439; 13(1873–1875):274–275
Principal: $22,123

James Duncan Phillips Fund (1944)

Gift of $500 by James Duncan Phillips, of Topsfield, "the income thereof, only, to be used for the general purposes of the Society." Further sums added include $1,000 in November 1950; $500 in October 1951; and $500 in November 1951.

Council Records, December 1944
Principal: $6,986

Prince Society Fund (1944)

Gift by the Prince Society, of Boston, at the time of its dissolution, of the balance in its treasury, this gift to "be held as a permanent fund, the income only to be used towards the cost of publications of the Society."

Council Records, February 1944
Principal: $1,345

Publication Fund (1965)

The income of this fund may be used for any publication of the Society but the principal may be used only by special vote of the Council.

Council Records, April 8, May 13, 1965
Principal: $552,391

Stephen T. Riley Fund (1974)

The Council established the fund in 1974 with a sum of $5,000 and voted to credit to it $2,500 thereafter annually to the conclusion of Riley's directorship.

Council Records, November 15, 1974
Principal: $30,719

Stephen T. Riley Librarianship (1982)

This fund was established by a grant from the National Endowment for the Humanities in 1982. It is a permanent endowment for the librarianship of the Society: the Stephen T. Riley Librarian.

M.H.S., *Procs.*, 94(1982):136
Council Records, November 18, 1982
Principal: $265,821

Stephen Salisbury Fund (1907)

Bequest of $5,000 under the will of Stephen Salisbury, of Worcester, who died on November 16, 1905, the income of which is "applicable to the general purposes of the Society."

M.H.S., *Procs.*, 41(1907–1908):418–419
Principal: $5,000

Appendix III: Endowment Funds

Saltonstall Publication Fund (1959)

The income shall be accumulated and the fund used strictly for work being done in connection with the publication of a book relating to the Saltonstall papers.

Council Records, December 13, 1962
Principal: $60,860

James Savage Fund (1873–1887)

Bequest of $5,000 under the will of James Savage, of Boston, who died on March 8, 1873, and a profit of $1,000 gained by a change of investment in 1887, "of the income whereof no use shall be made except for the increase of said Society's library at the discretion of said Society's standing committee who shall annually make report of their doings herein."

M.H.S., *Procs.*, 13(1873–1875):50; 2d ser., 3(1886–1887):285; 4(1887–1889): 111
Principal: $6,000

James Schouler Fund (1922)

Bequest of $2,850 under the will of James Schouler, of Intervale, New Hampshire, who died on April 16, 1920, "the income of which is to be used for the purchase of historical manuscripts."

M.H.S., *Procs.*, 53(1919–1920):187; 55(1921–1922):294
Principal: $2,850

Henry Lee Shattuck Fund, I (1971)

Began with a bequest from Henry L. Shattuck. The income is to be used for salaries, maintenance and other operating expenses, but not for the purchase of expensive books, manuscripts or other library materials.

Council Records, February 11, 197; Will of Henry L. Shattuck, December 4, 1970
Principal: $1,489,914

Henry Lee Shattuck Fund, II (1971)

A bequest of $300,000 from Henry L. shattuck, the income of which is to be used for the general purposes of the Society without restriction.

Council Records, February 11, 1971; Will of Henry L. Shattuck, December 4, 1970
Principal: $300,000

Robert Gould Shaw Fund (1931)

Bequest of $5,000 under the will of Robert Gould Shaw, of Wellesley, who died at Boston on April 10, 1931, the income to be used for the general expenses of the Society at the discretion of the Council.

M.H.S., *Procs.*, 64(1930–1932):451; Council Records, October 1931
Principal: $5,000

Charlotte Augusta Sibley Fund (1903–1904)

Bequest of $22,509.48 under the will of Mrs. John Langdon Sibley, who died at Groton on January 22, 1902, "without any restrictions, to be used and appropriated for the purposes of its [the Society's] incorporation, in such manner as it shall deem expedient."

M.H.S., *Procs.*, 2d ser., 2(1885–1886): 168–170; 16(1902):20–23
Principal: $23,522

John Langdon Sibley Fund (1885–1904)

Bequest of $161,169.33 under the will of John Langdon Sibley, of Cambridge, who died on December 9, 1885, received by the Society after the death of Mrs. Sibley in 1902, "the income thereof to be applied to the publication of biographical sketches of the graduates of Harvard University, written in the same general manner as the sketches already published by me and in continuation thereof. If any income then remain, the same shall be applied first to the purchase of printed books, pamphlets, or manuscripts, the same being composed by graduates of Harvard University, or relating to such graduates; and next, to the general purposes of the Society." One-fourth of the total yearly income from the John Langdon Sibley Fund must be added annually to the principal of the fund until January 22, 2002. The Society may, "in its discretion, apply not exceeding one-half part of the said accumulated fund toward the erection of a new fire-proof building to be called by [Mr. Sibley's] name." A vote of the Council, Dec. 13, 1951, made Sibley Fund income available for general purposes after provision for publication of the next volume of *Sibley's Harvard Graduates*.

M.H.S., *Procs.*, 2d ser., 2(1885–1886): 168–170; 43(1909–1910):521, 537; 62(1928–1929):114
Principal: $734,186

Edmund Farwell Slafter Fund (1910)

Bequest of $1,000 under the will of the Reverend Edmund F. Slafter, of Boston, who died on September 22, 1906, "to form a library fund, or to be added to a library fund already existing, the income of which is to be expended for the increase and enrichment of the library of said Society."

M.H.S., *Procs.*, 43(1909–1910):520
Principal: $1,000

Charles Card Smith Fund (1910)

Bequest of $15,000 under the will of Mrs. Charles Card Smith, the income "to be applied by vote of the Council to promote the objects for which the Society was founded."

M.H.S., *Procs.*, 53(1919–1920):151; Council Records, April 16, 1919
Principal: $15,000

Malcolm Storer Fund (1935)

Bequest of $2,000 under the will of Malcolm Storer, who died at Boston on January 2, 1935, "the principal to be left intact, and the income to be used in whatever way its Council shall see fit. It is my hope, however, that the said income may be used in connection with the Society's collection of coins and medals, in which I have taken great interest."

Council Records, January 1936
Principal: $2,000

Tercentenary Fund (1978)

This fund was established by a $500 gift made by Alice and Stephen T. Riley in 1978. The income is to be added to principal annually until the year 2091, at which time the entire fund would be available for any use that might be designated by the Council of the Society.

Council Records, January 12, 1978
Principal: $5,765

Hermann Jackson Warner Fund (1974–1975)

A bequest under the will of Hermann Jackson Warner, unrestricted as to principal and income, provided the Society agreed to accept a gift of books and manuscripts and preserve them.

Council Records, December 12, 1974
Principal: $356,054

John Collins Warren Fund (1928)

Bequest of $1,000 under the will of John Collins Warren, who died on November 3, 1927, the income to be used for the general expenses of the Society at the discretion of the Council.

M.H.S., *Procs.*, 61(1927–1928):131–132
Principal: $1,000

Winslow Warren Memorial Fund (1947)

Gift of $2,500 from Charles Warren, of Washington, "as an initial gift toward establishing the Winslow Warren Memorial Fund."

Council Records, April 1947
Principal: $5,000

Charles Grenfill Washburn Fund (1929)

Bequest of $2,500 under the will of Charles Grenfill Washburn, who died

May 25, 1928, "to be expended as the Council of [the] Society may direct."

M.H.S., *Procs.*, 62(1928–1929):114; Council Records, January 1929
Principal: $2,500

Robert Cassie Waterston Fund, I (1900)

Bequest of $5,000 under the will of the Reverend Robert C. Waterston, of Boston, who died on February 21, 1893. The first charge on the income of this fund was the cost of publishing the *Catalogue of the Waterston Library*, issued by the Society in 1906. According to the will, the income must be used for the arrangement and safe-keeping of the Waterston books and manuscripts and "for the purchase from time to time of any autographic letters and papers of literary or historical interest or value, these letters and papers to be added to the [Waterston collection]."

M.H.S., *Procs.*, 2d ser., 8(1892–1894): 171–173; 14(1900–1901):163–164
Principal: $5,000

Robert Cassie Waterston Fund, II (1900)

Bequest of $10,000 under the will of Robert C. Waterston, "the income thereof to be used in the printing and publishing of any important or interesting Autograph, original Manuscripts, Letters or Documents which may be in possession of said Society"—"the volumes thus printed to be designated in the volume as published by said Fund."

M.H.S., *Procs.*, 2d ser., 8(1892–1894): 171–173
Principal: $10,000

Robert Cassie Waterston Fund, III (1894)

Bequest of $10,000 under the will of Robert C. Waterston, "the income thereof to be used as a publishing fund for the publication . . . of such papers and books as are best calculated to disseminate useful Historical, Biographical or Literary information"—any book so printed to contain a statement that it was paid for from the income of the fund.

M.H.S., *Procs.*, 2d ser., 8(1892–1894): 171–173; 9(1894–1895):241
Principal: $10,000

Robert Cassie Waterston Library Fund (1900)

Bequest of $10,000 under the will of Robert C. Waterston, to create a room or portion of the Society's building "in order for the commodious and safe-keeping of the books" Mr. Waterston left the Society. The surplus to be used for adding books to this collection "under the direction of the standing committee." For some years the Society used the capital of this surplus for the purchase of books to be added to the Waterston Library.

M.H.S., *Procs.*, 2d ser., 8(1892–1894): 171–173; 15(1901–1902):34–35
Principal: $3,875

Albert Whitin Fund (1937)

Bequest of $5,000 under the will of Albert Whitin, of Whitinsville, Massachusetts, and Paris, France, of which the sum of $4,550 was received by the Society.

Council Records, December 1937
Principal: $5,000

Winthrop Publication Fund (1949–1950)

The Frederic Winthrop Fund and the Robert Winthrop Fund were consolidated into one fund to be called the Winthrop Publication Fund since both funds were devoted to a single purpose.

M.H.S., *Procs.*, 70(1950–1953):299
Principal: $40,000

Frederic Winthrop Fund (1932)

Bequest of $25,000 under the will of Frederic Winthrop, of Hamilton, who died at

Boston on May 6, 1932, the income to be used to meet a certain part of the expenses of continuing the publication of the Society's chronological, definitive edition of the *Winthrop Papers*.

Consolidated with the Robert Winthrop Fund into the Winthrop Publication Fund, 1950.

Council Records, October 1932; M.H.S., *Procs.*, 70(1950–1953):299

Robert Winthrop Fund (1920–1925)

Gifts of $2,500 each, by Frederic Winthrop, Grenville Lindall Winthrop, and Beekman Winthrop, and of $2,500 by Frederic Winthrop in memory of his dead brother, Robert Dudley Winthrop (1861–1912), to set up the Robert Winthrop Fund in honor of their father, Robert Winthrop (1833–1892), "the income only to be used for the publication of papers written by members of the Winthrop Family, or of papers relating to the Winthrop Family in Massachusetts and in Connecticut, or for research relating to the Winthrop Family in England before and during the great Puritan emigration to New England in the seventeenth century"—any accumulated income to be added to the principal of the fund from time to time, as occasion may require. The sum of $5,000 was added in 1925 to the Robert Winthrop Fund by gifts of $2,500 each from Mrs. Hamilton Fish Kean and Mrs. Albertine van Roijen, daughters of Robert Winthrop.

Consolidated with the Frederic Winthrop Fund into the Winthrop Publication Fund, 1950.

M.H.S., *Procs.*, 53(1919–1920):187–189; 54(1920–1921):253; 59(1925–1926):269; 70(1950–1953):299

Robert Charles Winthrop Fund (1894–1924)

Bequest of $5,000 under the will of Robert Charles Winthrop, of Boston, who died on November 16, 1894. It was voted that the income "shall be expended for such purposes as the Council may from time to time direct." Also a bequest of $5,000 under the will of Robert Charles Winthrop, Jr., of Boston, who died on June 5, 1905, "to be added to and form part of the fund bequeathed ... by my father and called by his name." Also a bequest of $2,000 by Miss Elizabeth Winthrop received on November 8, 1924.

M.H.S., *Procs.*, 2d ser., 9(1894–1895): 241; 19(1905):304–305; 58(1924–1925): 256, 262
Principal: $12,000

Thomas Lindall Winthrop Fund (1837–1905)

The sum of $2,000 received from the sale, on April 9, 1905, at the direction of the Council, of Audubon's *Birds of America*, given to the Society in 1837 by Thomas Lindall Winthrop, was set aside as the Thomas Lindall Winthrop Fund. The income of this fund is available for the purchase of books.

M.H.S., *Procs.*, 2(1835–1855): 77, 80; 2d ser., 20(1906–1907):214–215
Principal: $2,365

William Winthrop Fund (1882–1905)

Bequest of $3,000 under the will of William Winthrop, of Malta, who died on July 3, 1869, the income to be applied and devoted "to the binding, for better preservation, of the valuable manuscripts and books appertaining to the Society." Also a bequest of $2,000 from Robert Charles Winthrop, Jr. (1905), with the request that the Society, in future, not spend any part of the income of the William Winthrop Fund "for binding miscellaneous printed matter of little value."

M.H.S., *Procs.*, 20(1882–1883):17–20; 2d ser., 19(1905):306
Principal: $5,000

Appendix IV

Massachusetts Historical Society
By-Laws Adopted October 11, 1990

The Massachusetts Historical Society

Article I

Members

1. Membership in the Society shall be of two classes: resident and corresponding. Resident members shall be elected from among citizens of Massachusetts who habitually reside a considerable part of each year within the Commonwealth. They shall cease to be resident members if they remove from the state, but temporary or official absence shall not operate as a forfeiture of membership. Corresponding members shall be elected from among residents of others states or countries, and their corresponding membership shall cease if they become permanent residents within the Commonwealth. The number of resident members and corresponding members may be fixed from time to time by the Council. Only members may vote at meetings of the Society. Resident Members who remove from the Commonwealth shall become Corresponding Members, and Corresponding Members who move to the Commonwealth shall become Resident Members.

2. A book shall be kept by the Recording Secretary in which any member may enter the name of a person regarded as suitable for nomination as a resident or corresponding member. The Membership Committee shall from time to time select from the names so entered a person or persons to be nominated as resident or corresponding member, and the names so selected shall be presented to the Council. The Council shall select from the names so presented nominees to be reported at the next meeting of the members. At the following meeting of the members a brief statement shall be made as to the qualifications of the person nominated, and a vote of the members shall be taken thereon in such manner as the Council may from time to time determine. No election shall be effective unless at least twenty votes are cast and unless three-fourths of the votes cast are in the affirmative. Unless the person so elected, after being duly notified by the Corresponding Secretary in writing, signifies acceptance in writing within six months, such election shall be void.

3. No initiation fee or dues shall be required of any corresponding member. The Council may from time to time establish such initiation fee, dues or classes of dues for resident members as it deems appropriate. Any member who fails to pay the initiation fee or dues within two months after a second notice that such fee or dues are payable shall cease to be a member; provided, however, that the Council may in its discretion, before or after the lapse of the two-month grace period, extend such period, generally or in a specific case, or may reduce or waive the obligation if such action appears warranted in any specific instance.

4. The annual meeting of the members shall be held in October, at least three other regular meetings of the members shall be held in each year, and special meetings may be called by the Council or President, and shall be called by the Recording Secretary upon the written request of at least five members, in each case at such time and place as shall be fixed by the Council and of which notice shall be given to the members at least fourteen days in advance.

5. Fifteen members shall constitute a quorum for all purposes except for the election of members and for amendment of the articles of incorporation or of these by-laws as provided in Article I, paragraph 2, and Article VII, paragraph 1, respectively. The President and Director shall determine the matters to be considered at meetings of the members, provided that any subject proposed by two members present at a meeting shall at their request be considered at the next meeting of the members. Only members present in person may vote at any meeting of the members.

Appendix IV: By-Laws, 1990

Article II

Council

1. The governing body of the Society shall be the Council, which shall be composed of the elective officers and six individual members duly elected by the members from the membership. Of these six individual members, three shall be elected annually for a two-year term. On completion of two consecutive two-year terms, one year must elapse before an individual may be elected to another term as an individual member of the Council. The individual members shall be chosen at the annual meeting of the members by a majority vote, either in person or, if the Council shall so determine, by proxy.

2. The Council shall have general management and control of the property, business, and work of the Society. It shall have and may exercise all the corporate powers of the Society provided for in these by-laws and in the laws of the Commonwealth of Massachusetts. The Council may by general resolution delegate to committees of their own number, to officers of the corporation or to members, such powers as they see fit.

3. Any member of the Council may resign at any time by giving written notice of such resignation to the Council.

4. Any vacancies on the Council (other than that of an elective officer) occurring during the year may be filled by the Council. Any member of the Council so chosen shall hold office until the next annual meeting, at which time the vacancy shall be filled by the normal elective process.

5. There shall be no fewer than six regular meetings of the Council during the calendar year. The time and place of each meeting shall be determined by the Council by standing or special order.

6. A special meeting may be held at any time by order of the President or the Council, or by written request from three or more members of the Council filed with the Recording Secretary.

7. Written notices of all Council meetings shall be sent to the members of the Council at least fourteen days prior to the scheduled meeting, unless waived in writing by all members of the Council.

8. At all meetings of the Council, one-half of all the then current members shall be necessary and sufficient to constitute a quorum for the transaction of business, and the act of a majority of the members present at any meeting at which there is a quorum shall be the act of the Council, except as may be otherwise specifically provided by statute or by these by-laws.

Article III

Officers

1. The officers of the Society shall be a President, two or more Vice Presidents (as determined by the Nominating Committee with the approval of the Council), a Treasurer, a Recording Secretary, a Corresponding Secretary, and such other officers with such powers and duties not inconsistent with these by-laws as may be appointed by the President and approved by the Council.

2. The President, Vice Presidents, Treasurer, Recording Secretary and Corresponding Secretary shall be elected annually for a one-year term at the annual meeting of the members. No such person shall hold the same or any other office for more than ten consecutive years, provided that this limitation shall not apply to those in office when these amendments take effect.

3. Should the office of the President become vacant, the first Vice President shall serve as President until the next annual meeting of the members. If there is a further vacancy in this office, the succession shall be in the order of other Vice Presidents, the Treasurer, the Recording Secretary, and the Corresponding Secretary.

4. The President shall be the principal officer of the Society, shall superintend

and conduct its prudential affairs with the advice of the Council, and shall preside at all meetings of the Council and of the Society. The President shall be an ex officio member of all committees of the Society. In the absence of the President the succession of officers who shall assume his or her responsibilities shall be in the order set forth in the preceding section.

5. Under the supervision of the Finance Committee, the Treasurer shall have charge of the management of all the invested property, funds, and financial affairs of the Society, and shall have full authority, in the name and behalf of the Society, to receive, collect, take charge of, and disburse all monies, and to give due acquittance thereof, and shall arrange for the custody or the deposit of the Society's investments and funds with the approval of the Council, and such investments may be held in the name of any nominee approved by the Council. With the approval of the Council other officers of the Society or members of the staff may be given the authority to withdraw bank deposits, either jointly or singly.

The Treasurer shall:

a. be responsible for keeping, in books belonging to the Society, full and accurate accounts of all receipts and disbursements, bequests and devises by will, and of the various funds and financial condition of the Society;

b. render a report at each annual meeting of the operations of the Treasurer's office for the year preceding and of the amount and condition of all property of the Society in his or her charge, with a detailed statement of all investments;

c. render periodic reports of receipts and expenditures to the Finance Committee and the Council, in such detail as they may direct;

d. furnish such bond at the expense of the Society for the faithful performance of the duties pertaining to the office as the Council may direct;

e. have authority, with the approval of the Finance Committee, to sell, transfer and deliver any securities, mortgages, or other intangible personal property of the Society; to invest and reinvest the funds of the Society; to accept unrestricted gifts and bequests paid otherwise than in cash; and to execute any contracts and instruments relating thereto.

The Treasurer shall have such assistance, including that of such professional advisors and upon such terms, as the Council may authorize on the recommendation of the Finance Committee.

6. The Recording Secretary shall be the clerk of the corporation, shall issue notices of the meetings, shall make and keep accurate records of the proceedings of the Council and of the meetings of the Society and shall have custody, except as otherwise provided, of the corporate seal, all papers and reports that are ordered to be placed on file, and all documents and letters relating to the official business of these bodies. The Recording Secretary shall perform the duties of the Corresponding Secretary in his or her absence or in the event of a vacancy in that office. All proceedings, documents, and records, or copies thereof, shall be kept on file at the Society's House.

7. The Corresponding Secretary shall inform all persons of their election as members of the Society and send to each a copy of the by-laws. The Corresponding Secretary shall perform the duties of the Recording Secretary in his or her absence or in the event of a vacancy in that office.

Article IV

Committees

1. Following the annual meeting of the members, the President, with the approval of the Council, shall appoint the following committees with powers and duties as hereinafter set forth.

2. The Membership Committee shall consider and report on nominees for election as members of the Society in accor-

dance with Article I, paragraph 2 of these by-laws.

3. The Nominating Committee prior to September 1 of each year shall report to the Recording Secretary its recommendations for candidates for offices to be filled at the annual meeting of the members in October. A candidate for any office to be filled at the annual meeting may also be nominated by a petition signed by not fewer than twenty members and filed with the Recording Secretary prior to September 1. The Nominating Committee shall report its nominations for such candidates to the Recording Secretary prior to September 1. Notice of all such nominations shall be sent to the membership at least fourteen days before the date set for the annual meeting. Only candidates nominated in the manner provided in this paragraph shall be eligible for election at the annual meeting. Election shall take place in such manner as may be determined by the Council from time to time.

4. The Finance Committee shall review, with the Director, the annual budget prior to its presentation to the Council; and shall review the budget of The Adams Papers with the Editor-in-Chief of The Adams Papers prior to its presentation to the Administrative Committee for The Adams Papers; review and evaluate any financing needed for new programs or capital expense for recommendation to the Council; be responsible, with the Treasurer, for the supervision of the Society's investments, as set forth in Article III, paragraph 5; and have such additional responsibilities as are determined from time to time by the Council.

5. The Audit Committee shall meet from time to time with the auditor to review the financial statements and accounting procedures of the Society, and shall meet from time to time with the Director to review the performance of the auditor. Prior to each annual meeting of the members the Audit Committee shall recommend to the Council the appoint-ment of an auditor for the coming year.

6. The Publications Committee shall meet periodically with the Society's Editor and advise him or her on policies and procedures relating to *Proceedings*, *Collections*, and other publications of the Society.

7. The President, with approval of the Council, may at any time appoint a Research Committee to meet periodically with a member of the staff designated by the Director to advise with respect to the organization and operation of fellowship programs and scholarly conferences, the preparation of *Sibley's Harvard Graduates*, and the administration of such other research activities as the Society may undertake.

8. The Administrative Committee for The Adams Papers shall meet from time to time with the Editor-in-Chief of the Adams Papers and advise with respect to the preparation and publication thereon.

9. The House Committee shall meet from time to time with the Director and advise with respect to renovation, maintenance and decoration of the Society's House and the security of the Society's property, and shall also advise with respect to the Society's collections other than books and manuscripts.

10. The Library Committee shall meet from time to time with the Librarian and advise with respect to important prospective acquisitions, proposed de-accessions and the preservation and care of the Society's collection of books and manuscripts.

11. The Meetings Committee shall advise the Director with respect to the choice of, and invitations to, speakers at regular and special meetings of the Society.

12. The Development Committee shall advise the Director and the Council as to fund-raising matters, including the conduct of the annual campaign and of any capital or other special campaign and the employment of consultants with respect thereto.

13. The President, with the approval of the Council, may from time to time appoint such special committees for such purposes and for such terms of office as may be specified. The members of such committees and of the Standing Committees described in this Article IV may include members of the Council and members or non-members of the Society, and shall serve at the pleasure of the Council.

14. The Council may establish support groups such as Friends and Fellows for such purposes and upon such terms (other than the right to vote as members) as the Council may determine.

Article V

Staff

1. The Council shall employ a Director, who shall serve for such compensation and upon such other terms of employment as the Council may determine. The Director shall administer the policies of the Society as established by the Council, shall be an ex officio member of all committees except the Finance Committee and the Administrative Committee for The Adams Papers, and shall have the power, subject to these by-laws, to hire, supervise and discharge, all employees of the Society and, upon consultation with the Editor-in-Chief of and the Administrative Committee for The Adams Papers, all the staff members of that project. If the Director is a resident member of the Society, he shall be a member of the Council ex officio.

2. The Society's Editor and the Librarian shall be appointed by the Director, with the approval of the Council.

3. The Editor-in-Chief of The Adams Papers shall be appointed by the Council, with the approval of the Administrative Committee for The Adams Papers.

4. The Council shall establish and maintain an affirmative action and equal opportunity plan for the employment of staff and personnel policies with respect to their employment.

Article VI

Indemnification and Personal Liability

1. The Society may, to the extent legally permissible, indemnify each of its members, officers and employees (hereinafter collectively referred to as "officer") while in office and thereafter (and the heirs, executors and administrators of such officer) against all expenses and liabilities which he or she has reasonably incurred in connection with or arising out of any action or threatened action, suit or proceeding in which he or she may be involved by reason of his or her being or having been an officer of the Society. Such expenses and liabilities shall include, but not be limited to, judgments, court costs and attorney's fees and the cost of reasonable settlements, provided that no such indemnification shall be made in relation to matters as to which such officer shall be finally adjudged in any such action, suit or proceeding not to have acted in good faith in the reasonable belief that his or her action was in the best interests of the Society. In the event that a settlement or compromise of such action, suit or proceeding is effected, indemnification may be had, but only if the Council shall have been furnished with an opinion of counsel for the Society to the effect that such settlement or compromise is in the best interests of the Society and that such officer appears to have acted in good faith in the reasonable belief that his or her action was in the best interests of the Society, and if the Council shall have adopted a resolution approving such settlement or compromise. Indemnification hereunder may, in the discretion of the Council, include payment by the Society of costs and expenses incurred in defending a civil or criminal action or proceeding in advance of the final disposition of such action or

proceeding, upon receipt of an undertaking by the person indemnified to repay such payment if he or she shall be adjudicated not to be entitled to indemnification hereunder.

2. The foregoing right of indemnification shall not be exclusive of other rights to which any such officer may be entitled as a matter of law.

3. The members of the Society and of the Council and the officers of the Society shall not be personally liable for any debt, liability or obligation of the Society. All persons, corporations or other entities extending credit to, or contracting with, or having any claim against, the Society, may look only to the funds and property of the Society for the payment of any such contract or claim, or for the payment of any debt, damages, judgment or decree, or of any money that may otherwise become due or payable to them from the Society.

Article VII
Amendments

1. The articles of incorporation and these by-laws may be amended by a two-thirds vote at any regular meeting of the Society at which at least twenty-five members are present, provided that notice of the proposed amendments, together with recommendations of the Council in regard thereto, shall be set forth in the call for such meeting.

2. A proposal to amend the articles of incorporation or these by-laws may be made by a petition signed by at least twenty members of the Society and received by the Secretary at least sixty days before the meeting at which it is proposed that such amendment be considered. Notice of any such proposal, and action with respect thereto, shall be taken in accordance with the preceding paragraph.

Appendix V

Acts Passed by the General Court of
Massachusetts Relating to the
Massachusetts Historical Society

The Massachusetts Historical Society

Acts, 1793—Chapter 36

An Act to incorporate a Society, by the name of the Massachusetts Historical Society

Whereas the collection & preservation of materials for a political and natural history of the United States is a desirable object, and the institution of a Society for those purposes will be of public utility.

Be it therefore enacted by the Senate and House of Representatives, in General Court assembled, & by the authority of the same, that William Baylies Esqr. Jeremy Belknap, D.D. the Rev. Alden Bradford, Peleg Coffin, Esqr. Manasseh Cutler, D.D. John Davis, Esqr., Daniel Davis, Esqr., Aaron Dexter, Doctor in Physic, the Rev. John Elliot, Nathaniel Freeman, Esqr. the Rev. James Freeman, the Rev. Thaddeus Mason Harris, Isaac Lothrop, Esqr., George Richards Minot, Esqr. the Rev. John Mellen, jun., Thomas Pemberton, William Dandridge Peck, the Rev. John Prince, Ezekiel Price, Esqr., James Sullivan, Esqr. David Sewell, Esqr., Peter Thacher, D.D. William Tudor, Esqr. Samuel Turell, Dudley Atkins Tyng, Esqr., James Winthrop, Esqr., Thomas Wallcut, Redford Webster, and William Wetmore, Esqr., who have associated for the purposes aforesaid, and have requested an Act of incorporation, be, and hereby are, formed into, & constituted a Society and Body Politic and Corporate, by the name of the Massachusetts Historical Society; and that they, and their successors, and such other persons as shall be legally elected by them, shall be and continue a body politic and corporate, by that name for ever.

And be it further Enacted by the authority aforesaid, That the members of said society shall have power to elect a President, & all other necessary officers; and that the said society shall have one common seal, & the same may break, change and renew at pleasure; & that the same society by the name aforesaid, as a Body politic and corporate, may sue and be sued, prosecute and defend suits to final judgment and execution.

And be it further Enacted, that the said society shall have power to make orders and bye laws for governing its members and property, not repugnant to the laws of this Commonwealth; and may expel, disfranchise, or suspend any member, who, by his misconduct, shall be rendered unworthy.

And be if further Enacted, that the said Society may from time to time establish rules for electing officers and members, & also times and places for holding meetings; and shall be capable to take and hold real or personal estate, by gift, grant, devise or otherwise, & the same, or any part thereof, to alien and convey: *Provided* that the annual income of any real estate, by said Society holden, shall never exceed the sum of five hundred pounds; & that the personal estate thereof, besides books, papers, and articles in the museum of said Society, shall never exceed the value of two thousand pounds.

And be it further Enacted, that the members of said Society shall never be more than sixty (except honorary members residing without the limits of this Commonwealth), & that James Sullivan, Esqr. be, and hereby is, authorized and empowered to notify and warn the first meeting of said Society; and that the same Society, when met, shall agree upon a method for calling future meetings, and may have power to adjourn from time to time, as may be found necessary.

And be it further enacted that either branch of the Legislature shall and may have free access to the library and museum of said Society.

Approved February 19, 1794.

Acts, 1855—Chapter 459

An Act in addition to an Act to incorporate the Massachusetts Historical Society

Be it enacted by the Senate and House of Representatives, in General Court as-

sembled, and by the authority of the same, as follows:—

Section 1. The Massachusetts Historical Society is hereby authorized to hold real and personal estate in addition to its Library to an amount not exceeding one hundred thousand dollars.

Section 2. This Act shall take effect from and after its passage.

Approved May 21, 1855.

Acts, 1857—Chapter 41

An Act in relation to the Massachusetts Historical Society

Be it enacted &c., as follows:—

Section 1. Nothing in the Act of Incorporation of the Massachusetts Historical Society shall prevent said Society from electing Associate or Corresponding Members residing without the limits of this Commonwealth, or Honorary Members residing either within or without said limits, or from having as many as one hundred Resident Members, at their discretion.

Section 2. This Act shall take effect from and after its acceptance by said Society.

Approved April 2, and accepted by the Society April 9, 1857.

Acts, 1877—Chapter 13

An Act in addition to an Act to incorporate the Massachusetts Historical Society

Be it enacted &c., as follows:—

Section 1. The Massachusetts Historical Society is hereby authorized to hold real and personal estate in addition to its Library to an amount of three hundred thousand dollars.

Section 2. This Act shall take effect upon its passage.

Approved February 16, 1877.

Acts, 1894—Chapter 55

An Act to authorize the Massachusetts Historical Society to hold additional real and personal estate

Be it enacted by the Senate and House of Representatives, in General Court assembled, and by the authority of the same, as follows:—

Section 1. The Massachusetts Historical Society is hereby authorized to hold real and personal estate, in addition to its Library and Library building and land, to an amount not exceeding six hundred thousand dollars.

Section 2. This Act shall take effect upon its passage.

Approved February 26, 1894.

Acts, 1920—Chapter 413

An Act to authorize the Purchase and Distribution of Copies of the Journals of the House of Representative of Massachusetts Bay from Seventeen Hundred and Fifteen to Seventeen Hundred and Eighty

Be it enacted by the Senate and House of Representatives, in General Court assembled, and by the authority of the same, as follows:—

Section 1. Whenever the journals of the house of representatives of Massachusetts Bay from seventeen hundred and fifteen to seventeen hundred and eighty, inclusive, in volumes covering three years, more or less, shall be reprinted accurately the Massachusetts Historical Society, in the manner and form of volume one, seventeen hundred and fifteen to seventeen hundred and seventeen, inclusive, now in the press, and approved by the secretary of the commonwealth, the secretary shall purchase from the society five hundred copies of the said journals at a price not exceeding two dollars and fifty cents a volume, but in no year shall there be expended more than twelve hundred and fifty dollars, provided that if the copies are plated, the plates shall be subject to use by the commonwealth.

Section 2. The volumes purchased as aforesaid shall be distributed by the secretary of the commonwealth as follows: One copy to the office of the said secretary; one to the state library; one to the free public library of each city and town in the commonwealth; one to each state and territorial library in the United States; one to the library of congress; one to each incorporated historical society in the commonwealth; one to the library of each college in the commonwealth; and one to any library not included in the above designation which has contributed to the work by allowing its original journals to be used in preparation of the said publication. The remainder shall be placed in the state library for purpose of exchange.

Approved May 6, 1920.

Acts, 1922—Chapter 164

An Act reducing the Number of Copies of the Journals of the House of Representatives of Massachusetts Bay from Seventeen Hundred and Fifteen to Seventeen Hundred and Eighty to be purchased and distributed by the State Secretary

Be it enacted, etc., as follows:—

Section one of chapter four hundred and thirteen of the acts of nineteen hundred and twenty is hereby amended by striking out, in the ninth line, the word "five" and inserting in place thereof the word:—three,—and also by striking out, in the twelfth line, the word "twelve" and inserting in place thereof the word: —seven,—so as to read as follows:—*Section 1.* Whenever the journals of the house of representatives of Massachusetts Bay from seventeen hundred and fifteen to seventeen hundred and eighty, inclusive, in volumes covering three years, more or less, shall be reprinted accurately by the Massachusetts Historical Society, in the manner and form of volume one, seventeen hundred and fifteen to seventeen hundred and seventeen, in-

clusive, now in the press and approved by the secretary of the commonwealth, the secretary shall purchase from the society there hundred copies of the said journals at a price not exceeding two dollars and fifty cents a volume, but in no year shall there be expended more than seven hundred and fifty dollars; provided that if the copies are plated, the plates shall be subject to use by the commonwealth.

Approved March 17, 1922.

Acts 1928—Chapter 92

An Act Authorizing the Massachusetts Historical Society to Hold Additional Real and Personal Estate

Be it enacted, etc., as follows:—

The Massachusetts Historical Society, a corporation organized under chapter thirty-six of the acts of seventeen hundred and ninety-three, as affected by chapter four hundred and fifty-nine of the acts of eighteen hundred and seventy-seven, and by chapter fifty-five of the acts of eighteen hundred and ninety-four, is hereby authorized to hold real and personal estate, in addition to its library and library building and land, to an amount not exceeding two million dollars, notwithstanding any limitation in said act of incorporation or in any act in amendment thereof of in addition thereto.

Approved March 1, 1928.

Acts, 1931—Chapter 187

An Act to clarify previous Acts as to the Purchase by the Commonwealth of Copies of the House Journals from 1715 to 1780 and their Distribution by the Secretary of the Commonwealth

Be it enacted, etc., as follows:—

Section one of chapter four hundred and thirteen of the acts of nineteen hundred and twenty, as amended by chapter one hundred and sixty-four of the acts of nineteen hundred and twenty-two, is hereby further amended by striking out

Appendix V: Acts Relating to the Society

the words "covering three years, more or less" in the fourth line thereof and substituting therefor the words:—each covering one year or more,—so as to read as follows:—*Section 1.* Whenever the journals of the house of representatives of Massachusetts Bay from seventeen hundred and fifteen to seventeen hundred and eighty, inclusive, in volumes each covering one year or more, shall be reprinted accurately by the Massachusetts Historical Society, in the manner and form of volume one, seventeen hundred and fifteen to seventeen hundred and seventeen, inclusive, now in the press, and approved by the secretary of the commonwealth, the secretary shall purchase from the society three hundred copies of the said journals at a price not exceeding two dollars and fifty cents a volume, but in no year shall there be expended more than seven hundred and fifty dollars; provided that if the copies are plated, the plates shall be subject to use by the commonwealth.

Approved April 9, 1931.

Acts, 1945—Chapter 75

An Act Relating to the Massachusetts Historical Society

Be it enacted, etc., as follows:—

Section 1. Nothing in the act of incorporation of The Massachusetts Historical Society, approved February nineteenth, seventeen hundred and ninety-four, or in chapter forty-one of the acts of eighteen hundred and fifty-seven, shall prevent said society from electing resident members, associate members, corresponding members and honorary members under such conditions, upon such terms and in such numbers as said society may from time to time prescribe by its by-laws.

Section 2. This act shall take full effect upon its acceptance by vote of said society, and the filing with the state secretary of a certified copy of said vote, but not otherwise.

Approved March 5, and accepted by the Society April 12, 1945.

Acts, 1953—Chapter 446

An Act relative to the purchase by the Commonwealth of certain copies of the House journals from 1715 to 1780

Be it enacted, etc., as follows:

Chapter 413 of the acts of 1920 is hereby amended by striking out section 1, as most recently amended by chapter 187 of the acts of 1931, and inserting in place thereof the following section:—*Section 1.* Whenever the journals of the house of representatives of Massachusetts Bay from seventeen hundred and fifteen to seventeen hundred and eighty, inclusive, in volumes each covering one year or more, shall be reprinted accurately by the Massachusetts Historical Society, in the manner and form of volume one, seventeen hundred and fifteen to seventeen hundred and seventeen, inclusive, now in the press, and approved by the secretary of the commonwealth, the secretary shall purchase from the society three hundred copies of the said journals at a price not exceeding seven dollars and fifty cents a volume, but in no year shall there be expended more than twenty-two hundred and fifty dollars; provided, that if the copies are plated, the plates shall be subject to the use of the commonwealth.

Approved June 8, 1953.

Acts, 1965—Chapter 190

An Act increasing the amount of property which may be held by the Massachusetts Historical Society

Be it enacted, etc., as follows:

The Massachusetts Historical Society, a corporation organized under chapter thirty-six of the acts of seventeen hundred and ninety-three, is hereby authorized to hold real and personal estate in addition to its library and library building and land, to an amount not exceeding twenty million dollars, to have and to hold the same upon the terms and for the purposes specified in its act of incorporation or in any act in amendment thereof of in addition thereto; and also upon such terms and for such purposes and trusts as may be expressed in any deed or instrument of conveyance of gift made to said corporation; provided, the same shall not be inconsistent with the purposes specified in its act of incorporation or in any act in amendment thereof of in addition thereto.

Approved March 26, 1965.

Index

Abbreviations Used:
AAS: American Antiquarian Society
MHS: Massachusetts Historical Society
NEHGS: New England Historic Genealogical Society

Index

Index

Index

Index

Index

Index

Index

Index

Index

Index

Coffin, Sir Isaac, 484
Coffin, Joshua, 484
Coffin, Peleg, 572
Coffin, Peleg, Jr., 484
Cogan, John Francis, Jr., 484
Coggswell, Joseph, 42
Cogswell, Mary E., 446
Cogswell, Willard Goodrich, 484
Cogswell, William, 70, 484
Cohen, I. Bernard, 484
Cohen, Sheldon Samuel, 484
Cole, Arthur Harrison, 484
Coles, Edward, 485
Collections, MHS, 35, 46, 205, 207, 236;
    beginning of, 30–32, 36, 149;
    importance of, 150; Stephen T. Riley
    and, 421
College of William and Mary, 441
Collier, Abram Thurlow, 485; as MHS
    member-at-large of the Council, 547
Collins, John Frederick, 485
Collins, Winifred Virginia, 428, 446, 485
Collinson, Patrick, 485
Colonial Society of Massachusetts,
    164–166, 334, 452
Columbia (ship), 461
Columbia University, 250, 275, 340, 422,
    445
Columbus, Christopher, 33–34, 96, 236
Commager, Henry Steele, 449, 485
Conant, James Bryant, 485
Confederate States of America, 76
Confederation of New England (1643),
    70–71
Connecticut, State of, Jonathan Trumbull
    papers and, 64–65, 316–318
Connecticut Historical Society, 71
Connecticut State Library, 65
Conway, Jill Ker, 485
Coolidge, Archibald Cary, 485; as MHS
    member-at-large of the Council, 544
Coolidge, Charles Allerton, 485
Coolidge, Daniel Jones, 485
Coolidge, Francis Lowell, 485
Coolidge, John Calvin, 485
Coolidge, John Linzee, 485
Coolidge, John Phillips, 485
Coolidge, Joseph, 417
Coolidge, Joseph, Jr., 485
Coolidge, Nancy Rich, 485

Coolidge, Thomas Jefferson (1831–1920),
    137, 417–418, 485; as MHS
    vice-president, 540
Coolidge, Thomas Jefferson (1893–1959),
    418, 485
Coolidge, William Appleton, 485
Cooper, William Durrant, 485
Copley, John Singleton (1738–1815),
    paintings of, 337, 402
Copley, John Singleton (1772–1863). *See*
    Lyndhurst, baron
Coquillette, Daniel R., 485
Cornell, William M., 123
Cornell University, 241, 363, 457
Cornhill, Boston, 115
Corning, Howard, 485
Cornwallis, Lord, 99
Costa de Macedo, Joaquim José da, 485
Cott, Nancy Falik, 485
Cotton, John, 48
Coupland, Sir Reginald, 485
Courtenay, William Ashmead, 485
Cowan, Richard, 335, 386
Cox, Archibald, 485
Cox, Gardner, 486
Cox, Henry, 209
Cox, Jacob Dolson, 486
Cox, Richard, 209
Crapo, William W., 486; as MHS
    member-at-large of the Council, 543
Craven, Catherine S., 446
Craven, Wesley Frank, 486
Crawford, James Winfield, 486
Creighton, Rt. Rev. Mandell, bishop of
    London, 214–215, 508
Crittenden, John J., 486
Croce, Benedetto, 486
Crocker, Uriel Haskell, 486
Cromwell, Oliver, 146
Cross, Arthur Lyon, 486
Cross, Robert Dougherty, 486
Crowninshield, Edward Augustus, 486
Cullum, George Washington, 486
Culpepper Foundation, 452
Cummings, Abbot Lowell, 486
Cunliffe, Marcus Faulkner, 486
Cunningham, Henry W., 384, 486; as
    MHS recording secretary, 540; fund,
    552
Cunningham, William, 486

Index

Index

Index

Index

Index

Friedlaender, Marc, 369, 370, 494; as MHS recording secretary, 540; as MHS member-at-large of the Council, 546

Friedman, Lee Max, 494; as MHS member-at-large of the Council, 546

Friedrichsthal, Emanuel, ritter von, 494

Fritz-Carlton Hotel, Boston, 224, 292; *See also* The Bostonian Hotel; Berklee College of Music; Carlton Hotel

Frost, Donald McKay, 494

Frothingham, Nathaniel Langdon, 494

Frothingham, Octavius Brooks, 89, 173–174, 494

Frothingham, Paul Revere, 494; as MHS Member-at-Large of the Council, 544

Frothingham, Richard, 79, 144, 201, 222, 494; General Court and, 66; as MHS treasurer, 541; as MHS member-at-large of the Council, 543; fund, 554

Frothingham, Thomas Goddard, 494

Froude, James Anthony, 129, 494

Fuess, Claude M., 494; as MHS member-at-large of the Council, 545

Fulham Palace, London, 208, 210, 212, 216; Library of, 204, 205, 207

Fuller, Horace, 292

Fulton, John Farquhar, 494

Fuñes, Gregorio, 494

G. P. Putnam's Sons, 276

Gabriel, Ralph Henry, 494

Gage, Thomas Hovey, 494

Galindo, Juan, 494

Gallatin, Albert, 494

Galvin, John Thomas, 494

Gammell, William, 494

Gannett, Caleb, 494

Gardiner, Robert Hallowell, 495

Gardiner, Samuel Rawson, 495

Gardner, George Peabody, 495

Gardner, John Lowell, 495

Gardner, Samuel P., 495; as MHS member-at-large of the Council, 542

Garfield, James, 210

Garnett, Richard, 495

Garraty, John A., 495

Garrett, Wendell Douglas, 454, 495

Garrity, Paul, 411

Gasparin, Agénor Etienne, comte du, 495

Gay, Edwin Francis, 495

Gay, Frederick Lewis, 495

Gay, Harry Nelson, 495

General Court. *See* Massachusetts, General Court of

General Fund, 554

George VI, king of Great Britain, 346

Georgia Historical Society, 71

Gerald R. Ford Library and Museum, 454

Gettysburg, Pa., 92, 352

Giamatti, A. Bartlett, 450

Gibbs, William, 495

Gibson, Charles Hammond, 373

Gilbert, Edward Hooker, 495

Gilbert, Helen Homans, 495

Giles, Henry, 70

Gillerman, Gerald, 495

Gilman, Daniel Coit, 495

Gilmore, Myron Piper, 495

Gilpin, Henry Dilworth, 495

Gipson, Lawrence Henry, 495

Gleason, Herbert, 495

Gleason, Sarell Everett, 495

Godard, George S., 318

Goddard, Delano A., 495; as MHS member-at-large of the Council, 543

Godine, David R., 495; as MHS member-at-large of the Council, 547

Goldsbury land title records, 397

Gomes, Peter John, 495

Gooch, George Peabody, 495

Goodell, Abner C., Jr., 157, 162, 496; as MHS member-at-large of the Council, 543

Goodhue, Jonathan, 496

Goodhue, Lydia Davis, 496

Goodspeed, Charles E., 496; as MHS member-at-large of the Council, 545

Goodspeed, George Talbot, 496

Goodwin, Ezra Shaw, 496

Goodwin, William W., 496; as MHS corresponding secretary, 541; as MHS member-at-large of the Council, 543

Gordon, Rev. George A., 138, 496

Gordon, Rev. William, 7–8

Gore, Christopher, 24, 96, 496; as MHS president, 540

Gore Hall, Harvard University, 83

Gosnold Memorial, 305

Gräberg af Hemsö, Jacob, conte, 496

Index

Index

Index

Harvard University (*continued*)
Wheelwright and, 187; Medical School
of, 245; Samuel A. Green and, 282;
Stewart Mitchell and, 330, 334;
history department of, 333; New
England Deposit Library and,
338–339; Bernard Faÿ and, 339, 340,
345; George Parker Winship and, 342;
Adams family papers and, 367; Law
School, 370; Lyman H. Butterfield at,
370; School of Education of, 422;
Divinity School of, 444; Graduate
School of Education of, 453
Harvard University Press, 368, 369, 388,
435, 444
Haskins, Charles Homer, 499; as MHS
vice-president, 540
Haskins, George Lee, 499
Hassam, John Tyler, 499; fund, 554
Hassam land title records, 397
Hatch, Francis Whiting (1897–1975), 499
Hatch, Francis Whiting (b. 1925), 499
Hatch, Robert McConnell, 499
Hauser, Henri, 499
Haussonville, Joseph Othenin Bernard de
Cléron, vicomte d', 499
Haven, Nathaniel Appleton, Jr., 499
Haven, Parkman B., 188
Haven, Samuel F., 71, 120, 208, 499
Hawks, Francis Lister, 499
Hawthorne, Nathaniel, 159
Hay, John Milton, 499
Haynes, Henry W., 61, 138–139, 499; as
MHS corresponding secretary, 541; as
MHS member-at-large of the Council,
543
Hayward, Elijah, 499
Hazard, Ebenezer, 8, 17, 42, 499; Jeremy
Belknap and, 11; *Historical Collections*
of, 45
Hazen, Charles Downer, 499
Healey, Mark, 257
Heath, William, 149, 234
Hebron Academy, 453
Hedge, Frederic Henry, 499
Hedge, Levi, 499
Hedges, James Blaine, 500
Heidelberg, University of, 242
Hemenway Apartments, 409–415, 443
Hennessey, Edward Francis, 500

Henry, William Wirt, 500
Henry E. Huntington Library, 315
Herrick, Samuel Edward, 500
Hervey, Lord Arthur Charles, 476
Heslin, James Joseph, 500
Hewlett Foundation. *See* William and Flora
Hewlett Foundation
Heywood, S. P., 84
Hiatt, Arnold S., 500
Hiatt, Jacob, 500
Higginson, Henry Lee, 500
Higginson, Stephen, Jr., 500
Higginson, Thomas Wentworth, 163, 500;
as MHS member-at-large of the
Council, 544
Hildreth, Richard, 115, 500
Hill, Clement Hugh, 500; as MHS
member-at-large of the Council, 543
Hill, David Jayne, 500
Hill, Don Gleason, 500
Hill, Hamilton Andrews, 500
Hill, Richard Devereaux, 500
Hill, Thomas, 500
Hillard, George S., 79, 500; as MHS
member-at-large of the Council, 542
Hindle, Brooke, 500
Historical and Philosophical Society of
Ohio. *See* Cincinnati Historical
Society
Historical profession, modernization of,
239–242, 269, 272–273; MHS and,
435–436
Historical Society of Pennsylvania, 54, 279
Hitchcock, Augusta Bruce, 351, 364
Hitchings, Sinclair Hamilton, 500
Hoadley, Charles Jeremy, 500
Hoar, Ebenezer R., 134, 195, 222, 500
Hoar, George F., 65–67, 207, 396, 500;
William Bradford manuscript and,
206, 211–215
Hoar, Rockwood, 79
Hoar, Samuel, 500
Hodges, Arthur C., 447, 500; as MHS
treasurer, 541
Hodges, George, 501
Hodgkinson, Harold D., 501; as MHS
member-at-large of the Council, 546;
fund, 555
Hofer, Philip, 501
Hoffman, Robert David, 501

Index

Index

Jamaica Plain, Mass., 100
Jamaica Pond Ice Company, 245
James, Janet Wilson, 503
James I, king of Great Britain, 209
Jameson, J. Franklin, 240, 268–269, 367,
    503; Worthington C. Ford and, 270,
    361
Jantz, Harold Stein, 503
Jarvis, Edward, 503
Jay, John, 503
Jay, William, 503
Jefferson, Thomas, 12, 418; papers of, 275,
    322, 363, 417, 452; *Papers of Thomas
    Jefferson* and, 370
Jeffries, William Augustus, 503
Jenkins, Lawrence Waters, 503; as MHS
    member-at-large of the Council, 545
Jenks, Henry F., 503; as MHS cabinet
    keeper, 541; as MHS member-at-large
    of the Council, 543
Jenks, Samuel, 42
Jenks, Rev. William, 42, 70, 95, 96, 503; as
    MHS librarian, 547
Jenner, Edward, 503
Jennings, John Melville, 503
Jensen, Merrill M., 421, 503
Jervis, Thomas Best, 503
Jesus College, Cambridge University, 332
John Carter Brown Library, 314, 315
The Johns Hopkins University, 241, 242,
    453
Johnson, Alden Porter, 503
Johnson, Edward Crosby, 3rd, 503; as MHS
    member-at-large of the Council, 546
Johnson, Edward Francis, 503
Johnson, Marilyn B. M., 370
Johnson, Dr. Samuel, 90, 115, 121, 287,
    421
Johnson, William, 503
Johnston, Alexander, 503
Jomard, Edmé François, 503
Jones, Howard Mumford, 503
Jones, Jacqueline, 503
Jones, John Winter, 503
Jones, Matt Bushnell, 503; as MHS
    corresponding secretary, 541; as MHS
    member-at-large of the Council, 545
Jones, Sir William, 504
Jordan, Daniel P., 504
Jordan, Henry Donaldson, 504

Jordan, Wilbur Kitchener, 504
Jordan, Winthrop Donaldson, 504
*Journals of the House of Representatives
    of Massachusetts*, 423, 463, 573–575
Joy, Benjamin, 504
Joy, Michael, 504
Judd, Sylvester, 58, 504
Jusserand, Jean Adrien Antoine Jules, 504
J. Wilson & Son, 84

Kammen, Michael G., 457–458, 504
Kaplan, Justin, 504
Keeney, Barnaby Conrad, 504
Kegan, Elizabeth Hamer, 428, 504
Kellen, William V., 326, 504; as MHS
    member-at-large of the Council, 544
Keller, Morton, 504
Kellogg, Edmund Halsey, 504
Kelly, Sir Fitzroy, 208
Kelly, Liam, 504
Kennan, George Frost, 504
Kennedy, Edward M., 406, 407, 457, 504
Kennedy, Jacqueline, 429
Kennedy, John F., 429, 434, 504; proposed
    fund, 430; Medal of, 432
Kennedy, John Pendleton, 504
Kenny, Herbert, 504
Kenyon, Cecelia Marie, 428, 504
Kerber, Linda K., 504
Kilbourne, Payne Kenyon, 504
Kilham, Daniel, 504
Kilham, Walter Harrington, 504
King, James Gore, 347
King, John G., 68, 504
King, Melvin, 412
King, Patricia Miller, 504
King, Rufus, 505
King Philip (Metacom), samp bowl of, 37
King's Chapel, Boston, 48, 99, 104, 222,
    312; MHS and, 89, 103–104, 151–152
King's College, New York, N.Y., 10
Kingsley, James Luce, 505
Kinnicutt, Lincoln Newton, 505; as MHS
    member-at-large of the Council, 544
Kirk, John Foster, 505
Kirkland, Edward Chase, 136, 505
Kirkland, John Thornton, 505; as MHS
    member-at-large of the Council, 541;
    as MHS librarian, 547
Kittredge, George Lyman, 505

Index

Index

Index

Index

Index

tions of, 43–44, 47–51, 72–74, 86–87, 102–103, 311, 396–397; John Winthrop's "History of New England" and, 45–46; James Bowdoin as librarian, 49; Dowse Library and, 76–77, 80, 84–90, 128, 227, 230, 289–290, 450; Julius H. Tuttle as assistant librarian and librarian, 89, 251, 254–255, 306, 310, 333–334, 547; Samuel A. Green as librarian, 89, 233–238, 244–245, 249–258, 260–262, 270, 277–296, 303–306, 334, 347, 547; Robert C. Winthrop, Jr., criticizes, 167–169; manuscript collection policy of, 169, 257, 321–323, 399, 404; Francis Bernard papers and, 233; manuscript collections of, 233–235, 397, 415–418; acquires Washington's "Newburgh Address," 234–235; increased staff of, 238–239; regular hours first maintained, 239; Robert C. Waterston Library, 259, 289–290; Worthington C. Ford and, 278–279, 286; oversight committee reviews, 280–281; professionalization of, 305–306; Jonathan Trumbull papers and, 316–318; Allyn B. Forbes as librarian, 333–334, 353, 547; MHS director and, 335–336; Stephen T. Riley as librarian, 348, 388–398, 403–409, 415–418, 460, 547, 558; Stewart Mitchell's contributions to, 353–354; Francis Russell Hart library and, 358; Paine family papers and, 358; Paul Revere papers and, 358; Adams family papers and, 358–370; librarianship established, 390; Library funds of, 397, 404, 406, 555–556; Fellows of the Library, 404–406; John D. Cushing as librarian, 409, 445, 449, 547; Thomas Jefferson papers and, 417–418; National Endowment for the Humanities and, 437; endowed chair for, 443, 449; Peter Drummey as librarian, 445–446, 460–461; administrative changes in, 460–461; computerization and, 460–461; female researchers at, 462; by-law changes regarding librarian, 547; librarians of, 547; Robert C. Waterston funds and, 561

Membership, 14, 16, 23, 36–37, 38–39, 52–58, 78–80, 131–142, 219, 263–267, 300–303, 339–345, 356–358, 378–379, 405, 407, 425–428, 447–448, 451–452, 472–538, 564, 573, 575; dues and fees, 16–17, 62, 262–263, 447–448; beans and corn for voting by, 36–38; expulsion of members, 38–39; female membership, 55–58, 425–428, 431; Daniel Webster and, 62; Charles Sumner and, 76; Richard Henry Dana (1851–1931) and, 139–142; Rt. Rev. Dr. Mandell Creighton as honorary member, 216; case of Bernard Faÿ, 339–345

Meetings and Social Life, meetings, 35–36, 51–52, 89–90, 143–144, 225–226, 227–232, 383–385, 451; women and, 52, 55–58, 71, 231, 237, 241, 252–253, 257, 350, 352–353, 355, 357, 407, 425–428, 431, 460, 462; John Quincy Adams delivers lecture at, 69; public criticism of, 73, 252–253, 253–254; golden age of, 78–80; social life of, 89–90, 142–143, 354–356, 403, 406–407, 428–432, 457; Prince of Wales visits, 98–99; Ulysses S. Grant visits, 101–102; Grand Duke Alexis of Russia visits, 102; Ralph Waldo Emerson and, 146–148; centennial celebration, 162–164; heraldry decorations and, 218–219; American Historical Association and, 225, 240–241, 290–292, 309–310, 327; annual dinner established, 354–355; spring reception, 355–356, 403; bicentennial celebration, 453–458

Museum Collection, 14, 39, 43–44, 307–308, 312, 350–352, 392–393, 399; cabinet keepers, 15, 39, 49–50, 56, 231–232, 337, 541; Jeremy Belknap and, 24–25; King Philip's samp bowl, 37; Timothy Alden as cabinet keeper, 39, 541; Redford Webster as cabinet keeper, 49–50; Isaac P. Davis as cabinet keeper, 56, 541; portrait collection of, 86, 88, 96, 236–237, 351, 402, 427; Prescott and Linzee swords, 100–101; Robert C. Winthrop, Jr., criticizes, 167–169;

Index

Index

207; MHS art catalogues and, 236;
Worthington C. Ford as editor of,
251–252, 270–272, 277–279, 285–286,
297, 313–316, 323–328, 444, 547;
criteria for editor of, 267–269; Julius
H. Tuttle as assistant editor of, 278,
286; "Photostat Americana" and,
313–316; Stewart Mitchell as editor
of, 323–333, 335, 547; *Winthrop
Papers* and, 324–325, 423; Council
and, 325; growth of, 326–327, 462;
MHS director and, 335–336;
Miscellany, 354; Malcolm Freiberg as
editor of, 387, 421–422; Stephen T.
Riley and, 421; finances of, 422–425,
443, 557–559, 561–562; National
Historical Publications and Records
Commission and, 424–425;
microfilming projects of, 437; Conrad
E. Wright as editor of, 444, 462–466;
Studies in American History and
Culture and, 462–463; Commonwealth
of Massachusetts and, 463; *Journals of
the House of Representatives of
Massachusetts* and, 463, 573–575;
distribution of, 463–464; Northeastern
University Press and, 463–464;
University Microfilms International
and, 464; editors of, 547
Society, founding of, 1–17; Jeremy
Belknap and, 1–35, 38, 52, 58–59, 149,
266, 540, 572; Julian Boyd and, 13;
committees of, 15, 47, 205, 220, 242,
280–281, 325, 566–568; name changes
of, 17, 23; Massachusetts Bank and,
18–19; statement of purpose, 23; act
of incorporation of, 23–24, 53, 572;
Massachusetts General Court and,
23–24, 53–55, 65–66, 104–106,
118–121, 123–125, 572–576; by-laws
of, 24, 53, 167, 236, 390, 547,
564–569; Maine Boundary dispute
and, 32; Christopher Columbus and,
34; Worthington C. Ford and, 37, 303;
Edward Everett and, 37–38, 67, 68,
95–97, 542; American Revolution and,
39; public and, 39, 46, 235–238, 254,
307–309, 324–325, 333, 405; City of
Boston and, 39–40, 107–108, 110,
189–190, 192–199, 202; fire and,

44–47, 110, 130–131, 313; James
Savage and, 45–46, 47, 49, 53, 54, 64,
67, 540, 541, 542, 547; Trumbull
manuscripts and, 45–46, 64–65, 149,
316–318; John Davis and, 46, 59, 61,
540, 541, 542; American Academy of
Arts and Sciences and, 47, 107, 109,
127, 171, 223, 230, 457; Boston
Athenaeum and, 47, 106, 110, 127,
165, 223; Josiah Quincy (1772–1864)
and, 47, 52–53; Massachusetts Medical
Society and, 47; Provident Institution
for Savings Bank and, 47, 49, 73;
Society of Natural History and, 50;
seal of, 58–61; *Boston Transcript* and,
63–64; David Sears and, 64; George
Peabody and, 64, 77; Massachusetts
Historical Trust Fund and, 64;
Nathaniel Thayer and, 64; Thomas
Dowse and, 64, 80–91; state of
Connecticut and, 64–65, 316–318;
David Trumbull and, 65; preservation
of public records and, 65–67; King's
Chapel and, 89, 103–104, 151–152;
Dowse Institute and, 94–95; Harvard
University and, 104, 170–173, 356,
448; Hutchinson papers controversy
and, 104–106; Suffolk Savings Bank
and, 106–108; real estate transaction
with City of Boston, 108, 110,
192–199, 202; NEHGS and, 111–126;
Samuel F. Drake and, 126; Fire of
1872 and, 128–131; New-York
Historical Society and, 135, 314, 315;
John Langdon Sibley gifts to, 151,
171–172, 193, 248, 259–260, 293, 423;
Leif Erickson statue and, 152–155;
opposes new monument to Boston
Massacre, 155–157; Walter-Sharples
portrait incident and, 158–162;
Colonial Society of Massachusetts and,
164–166; Justin Winsor and, 170–171;
Robert C. Waterston and, 171–172,
193; George E. Ellis and, 174–177,
182–187, 193; Adams family and,
180–181, 360, 363, 367–369, 378–379;
Quincy family and, 191; Josiah
Quincy (1859–1919) and, 193, 198,
199; William Bradford manuscript
and, 203–216; African Americans and,

Index

Index

Middlesex, archdeacon of. *See* Sinclair, Rev. John

Mignet, François Auguste Marie, 512

Miller, Arthur, 450

Miller, Elizabeth and Perry, 512; fund, 557

Miller, Lawrence Kelton, 512

Miller, Phineas, 512

Miller, Samuel, 512

Miller, William Davis, 512

Millersville University, 463

Millman, Henry Hart, 512

Milman, Canon, 209

Milton, John, 88

Minns, Thomas, 512; fund, 557

Minot, George Richards, 15, 20, 512, 572; as MHS recording secretary, 540; as MHS cabinet keeper, 541; as MHS member-at-large of the Council, 541; as MHS treasurer, 541; as MHS librarian, 547

Minot, Henry Whitney, 512

Minot, James Jackson, 512

Minot, Joseph Grafton, 512; as MHS member-at-large of the Council, 544

Minot, William, 512

Miscellany, 354

Mitchell, Jethro, 375

Mitchell, Nahum, 61, 512; as MHS treasurer, 541; as MHS librarian, 547

Mitchell, Samuel Latham, 512

Mitchell, Stewart, 333, 387, 438, 512; MHS and, 36, 60, 309–310, 333, 349, 353–355, 405; Frances Manwaring Caulkins and, 58; James Walter and, 161; Worthington C. Ford and, 297, 327, 333; as MHS editor, 323–333, 335, 547; biographical sketch of, 330–332; John Dos Passos and, 331, 353; Georgina Holmes Thomas and, 331–332, 335, 354, 386; *New England Quarterly* and, 332; Clifford K. Shipton and, 333; Julius H. Tuttle and, 333; Malcolm Freiberg and, 333; Samuel Eliot Morison and, 333, 357–358; criticism of, 334, 375; Samuel A. Green and, 334; American Historical Association and, 335; homosexuality of, 335; Richard Cowan and, 335, 386; Allyn B. Forbes and,

336, 348; Bernard Faÿ and, 339–345; George Parker Winship and, 342; Arthur M. Schlesinger, Sr., and, 347; as MHS director, 347–358, 371–372, 375–376, 381–382, 385–387, 547; American Antiquarian Society and, 348; renovates MHS Boylston Street headquarters, 350–353; MHS finances and, 353–354, 374–375, 377, 381; MHS membership criteria and, 356–358; Augustus P. Loring and, 375, 377; John Adams (1875–1964) and, 382; Stephen T. Riley and, 385–386, 390–391; death of, 386; health of, 386–387; personal life of, 386–387, 390–391; MHS publications and, 422, 464; as MHS member-at-large of the Council, 545; fund, 557

Moe, Henry Allen, 512

Moerenhout, Jacob Antoine, 513

Moireau, Auguste, 513

Mommsen, Theodor, 513

Monaghan, Bernard Andrew, 513

Monroe, George Harris, 513

Monroe, James, papers of, 275, 363

Montague, Gilbert Holland, 116, 513

Montague, William, 112

Montgomery, Susan, 457

Montmorency, Anne Adrien Pierre. *See* Laval, duc de

Moody, Robert E., 462; as MHS member, 513; as MHS member-at-large of the Council, 545

Moore, Charles, 319

Moore, Clarence Bloomfield, 513; fund, 557

Moore, George Foot, 377, 513; as MHS president, 540; as MHS vice-president, 540

Moore, George H., 161, 513

Moore, John Bassett, 513

Moore, Roger Allan, 513

Moreau, César, 513

Morely, John, viscount Morley of Blackburn, 513

Moreño, Don Manuel, 513

Morgan, Edmund S., 513

Morgan, Frank, 513

Morgan, Henry Sturgis, 513

Morison, Elting Elmore, 513

Index

Morison, Samuel Eliot, 377, 513; Samuel A. Green and, 255; *Winthrop Papers* and, 325–326; Worthington C. Ford and, 327, 361; *New England Quarterly* and, 332; Stewart Mitchell and, 333, 357–358; Barnard Faÿ and, 341; Adams family papers and, 361, 363; MHS finances and, 373; proposed John F. Kennedy fund and, 430; John Fitzgerald Kennedy Award and, 457; as MHS member-at-large of the Council, 545

Morley, John, 211

Morrell, William, 30

Morris, Henry, 513

Morris, Richard B., 513

Morrison, Robert, 513

Morse, Horace Henry, 513

Morse, Jedidiah, 32, 513

Morse, John T., Jr., 79, 90, 513; as MHS member-at-large of the Council, 543

Morton, Nathaniel, 203, 205

Motley, John Lothrop, 78, 79, 85, 514; William Bradford manuscript and, 208–209

Mount Auburn Cemetery, Cambridge, 98

Mount Vernon Ladies Association, 93

Moyers, Bill, 514

Mt. Desert, Me., 174

Mt. Vernon Seminary, 422

Mumford, Lawrence Quincy, 514

Mumstead Hall, 95

Munro, William Bennett, 514

Murdock, Harold, 514; as MHS member-at-large of the Council, 544

Murdock, Kenneth B., 339, 514

Murphy, William Francis, 514

Museum of Fine Arts, Boston, 161, 456, 457

Music Hall, Boston, 95

Nagel, Paul C., 298, 514

Napoleon I, 211

Nash, Chauncey C., 379, 514; MHS annual dinners and, 354; as MHS member-at-large of the Council, 545, 546

Nash, Norman Burdett, 514

Nash, Ray, 514

National Archives, 424

National Endowment for the Humanities, 434, 436–437, 448–449, 454

National Historical Publications and Records Commission, 424–425, 452

National Historical Publications Commission. *See* National Historical Publications and Records Commission

National Park Service, 367, 368

Nazis, 339–345

Neiley, Robert G., 450

Neil, Edward Duffield, 514

Neilson, William Allan, 514

Nelson, David S., 514

Nettels, Curtis P., 514

Neville, Richard Griffin. *See* Braybrooke, baron

Nevins, Allan, 274, 332, 422, 514

Newberry Library, 315

Newcastle, Duke of, 99

Newell, William, 514

New England Confederation, celebration of, 96

New England Conservatory of Music, 188, 224

New England Deposit Library, 338–339, 464

New England Historic Genealogical Society, 169, 307, 350; MHS and, 111–126; founding of, 112–113; MHS members join, 114–115; changes name, 116; *Register* of, 116–117; AAS and, 120; critical of MHS publications, 121–122; capture of Quebec celebration and, 125–126; opposes new memorial to Boston Massacre, 157; Peter Drummey at, 445–446; Edward W. Hanson at, 446

New England Library. *See* Prince, Thomas

New England Merchants National Bank, 406

New England Quarterly, 332, 334, 347, 409, 463

New England Society of New York, 213

New Hampshire Historical Society, 71

New London, Conn., 57

Newman, John, 514

Newmyer, R. Kent, 514

New North Church, Boston, 13

Newport, R.I., 4, 48

Index

Newton, Sir Isaac, 118

New York, N.Y., 8, 332; John Pintard and, 10; American Museum and, 12; American Tract Society in, 57; fire in, 128

New York Evening Post, 275

New York Herald, 275

New-York Historical Society, 63, 71, 161, 444; beginning of, 11; membership of, 54, 135; MHS and, 135, 314, 315; criticism of, 383; Stephen T. Riley and, 391

New York Ledger, 93

New York Public Library, 161, 315

New York Society Library, 4

New York State American Revolution Bicentennial Commission, 441

New York State Education Department, 441

New York State Historical Association, 454

The New York Times, 450

Nichols, Dr., 287

Nichols, Benjamin Ropes, 514

Nichols, Charles L., 514; as MHS member-at-large of the Council, 544

Nichols, John Gough, 514

Niles, Nathaniel, 514

Nissenbaum, Stephen, 514

Nobel, John, 514

Norcross, Grenville Howland, 298, 299, 514; as MHS cabinet keeper, 541; funds, 557

Northeastern University Press, 463–464

Northrop, George Norton, 514

Norton, Asahel Strong, 515

Norton, Charles Eliot, 262, 515; as MHS member-at-large of the Council, 542

Norton, Mary Beth, 515

Norwell, Mass., 461

Norwich, Conn., 55, 57

Norwich University, 408

Notestein, Wallace, 515

Nott, Eliphalet, 515

Nourse, Henry Stedman, 515

Nova-Anglia (1625), 30

Nova Scotia, 48, 69, 204

Nurse, Rebecca, 419

Nutter, George Read, 515; as MHS member-at-large of the Council, 545; fund, 557

O'Brien, Conor Cruise, 515

O'Brien, Robert Lincoln, 515

O'Callaghan, Edmund Burke, 515

OCLC, 460–461

O'Connor, Thomas H., 515

O'Keefe, Bernard J., 515

Old Granary Burial Ground, Boston, 19, 34, 48

Old South Church, Boston, 2, 28, 204, 208, 312; British occupation of, 5; Thomas Prince's library and, 5

Old South Meeting House, Boston, 40, 319

Old Sturbridge Village, Mass., 408

Oliver, Andrew (1906–1981), 397, 447, 462, 515; as MHS corresponding secretary, 541; as MHS member-at-large of the Council, 546

Oliver, Andrew (b. 1936), 515

Oliver, Fitch Edward, 515; as MHS cabinet keeper, 541

Oliver, Frederick Scott, 515

Oliver, George, 515

Oliver, Peter, 515

Oliver family, 394, 397, 465

Olivier, Laurence, 92

Olmsted, Frederick Law, 185

Olney, Richard, 515

Olsen, Carl E., 346

Olympic College, 440

Oman, Sir Charles William Chadwick, 515

Oregon Historical Society, 454

Osgood, Russell, 515

Osgood, Samuel, 63, 515

Osgood, William B., 430, 515

O'Shea, Kitty, 322

Otis, Harrison Gray, 39–40, 255, 361

Otis, James, 48, 234

Oxford, Bishop of. *See* Stubbs, William; Wilberforce, Samuel

Oxford University, 4

Oxford University Press, 421

Page, Alfred B., 251, 294

Paige, Lucius R., 156–157, 163, 515; as MHS member-at-large of the Council, 542

Paine, John Bryant, Jr., 420, 430, 516; as MHS treasurer, 541; as MHS member-at-large of the Council, 546

Index

Index

Index

Index

Index

Index

Shannon, William Vincent, 525

Shapiro, L. Dennis, 525

Sharples, James, 159–162

Shattuck, Frederick C., 525; as MHS member-at-large of the Council, 544

Shattuck, George Cheever, 402, 525

Shattuck, George Otis, 525

Shattuck, Henry Lee, 400–401, 406, 407; Stephen T. Riley and, 402; as MHS member, 525; funds, 559

Shattuck, Lemuel, 112, 525

Shaw, Lemuel, 95, 525

Shaw, Robert Gould, 525; fund, 559

Shaw, Samuel Savage, 142, 525; as MHS member-at-large of the Council, 544

Shaw, William Smith, 525; as MHS librarian, 547

Shays's Rebellion, 9–10, 15

Shea, John Dawson Gilmary, 525

Sheldon, George, 525

Shelley, Fred, 525

Shenton, Robert, 525

Shepley, Bulfinch, Richardson and Abbott, 398

Shepley, Hugh, 525

Sherborn, Mass., 81

Sherrill, Henry Knox, 525

Shipton, Clifford K., 387, 423, 431, 525; Stewart Mitchell and, 332–333, 386; American Antiquarian Society and, 347; Adams family papers and, 363; death of, 463; as MHS member-at-large of the Council, 546

Shirley, William, 25

Shiverick, Nathan C., 525

Shurtleff, Dr. Benjamin, 89

Shurtleff, Nathaniel B., 205, 525; as MHS librarian, 103, 236, 547; as MHS cabinet keeper, 541; as MHS member-at-large of the Council, 542, 543

Shurtleff, William Steele, 525

Sibley, Charlotte Augusta, 259, 260; fund, 559

Sibley, John Langdon, 150–151, 525; as librarian of Harvard University, 78; gifts to MHS and, 151, 171–172, 193, 248, 259–260, 293, 423; sketches of Harvard graduates and, 151, 363, 463;

Samuel A. Green and, 248, 260, 293; papers of, 311; fund, 423, 559–560

Sibley's Harvard Graduates, 151, 294, 363, 423, 463

Sidney L. Kumins, Inc., 414

"Sigma." *See* Sargent, Lucius

Sigourney, Lydia Huntley, 57

Silliman, Benjamin, 525

Silvestro, Clement Mario, 525

Simmons College, 224, 377

Simpson, Alan, 526

Sinclair, Rev. John, 208

Sioussat, St. George Leakin, 526

Sisti, Sebastian, 440

Sizer, Theodore, 526

Skelton, Raleigh Ashlin, 526

Skinner, Inc., 456

Slafter, Edmund F., 526; as MHS member-at-large of the Council, 543; fund, 560

Sloane, William Milligan, 526

Smibert, John, 337

Smith, Buckingham, 526

Smith, Charles C., 139, 270, 281, 526; MHS social life and, 89; MHS meetings and, 134, 135; Robert C. Winthrop, Jr., and, 137, 162, 256; Richard Henry Dana (1851–1931) and, 141; MHS endowments and, 151; City of Boston and, 158; MHS Boylston Street headquarters and, 186, 218; as MHS editor, 198, 262, 272, 547; as MHS treasurer, 198, 541; MHS Tremont Street headquarters and, 198, 199, 201, 202; Samuel A. Green and, 200; MHS manuscript collections and, 233; Charles Francis Adams (1835–1915) and, 260–262, 267–268; resignation of, 267–268; as MHS member-at-large of the Council, 542, 543; fund, 560

Smith, Charles Llewellyn, Jr., 526

Smith, Elihu Hubbard, 526

Smith, Erastus, 526

Smith, Fitz-Henry, Jr., 526; as MHS member-at-large of the Council, 545

Smith, Goldwin, 526

Smith, Henry Nash, 526

Smith, James M., 454

Smith, John Cotton, 526

Index

Index

Index

Thrale, Henry, 115

Thwaites, Reuben Gold, 268, 530

Ticknor, George, 53, 85, 100, 530; opposes MHS membership increase, 54; Prince of Wales and, 98; as MHS member-at-large of the Council, 542

Tilden, Joseph, 530; as MHS librarian, 547

Time, Inc., 369

Tocqueville, Charles Alexis de. *See* Clérel de Tocqueville

Tolles, Frederick B., 530

Tontine Crescent, Boston, 20–23, 35, 50, 67; Charles Bulfinch and, 21–22; space limitations of, 44, 48; fire and, 45, 47, 130; public use of MHS collections at, 239

Toppan, Robert Noxon, 530

Torrey, Henry W., 145, 530; as MHS member-at-large of the Council, 542

Tourtellot, Arthur B., 530

Tout, Thomas Frederick, 530

Towner, Lawrence William, 530

Toynbee, Arnold J., 531

Tozzer, Alfred Marston, 531

Trafford, William Bradford, 531

Trescot, William Henry, 531

Trevelyan, George Macaulay, 531

Trevelyan, Sir George Otto, baronet, 531

Tribolet, Harold, 409

Truman, Harry S, 346

Trumbull, Benjamin, 17, 266, 531

Trumbull, David, 65, 317

Trumbull, James Hammond, 216, 531

Trumbull, John, 64, 337

Trumbull, Gov. Jonathan, 531; papers of, 45–46, 64–65, 149, 316–318

Tuchman, Barbara W., 428, 531

Tucker, Ichabod, 531

Tucker, Louis Leonard, 531; biographical sketch of, 440–441; as MHS director, 440–467, 547; MHS fundraising and, 442, 443, 453; *Adams Papers* project and, 443–444; John D. Cushing and, 445; MHS membership and, 451–452; MHS bicentennial celebration and, 453–458; MHS administrative changes under, 459–460

Tucker, St. George, 531

Tuckerman, Henry Theodore, 531

Tudor, Frederic, 143, 531

Tudor, William (1750–1819), 13, 531, 572; as MHS treasurer, 15, 541; as MHS member-at-large of the Council, 541

Tudor, William, (1779–1830), 531; as MHS member-at-large of the Council, 541

Tufts University, 465

Tulane University, 370

Turell, Samuel, 38–39, 531, 572; as MHS cabinet keeper, 541

Turk's Head Inn, London, 90

Turner, Frederick Jackson, 251, 268, 270, 366, 531; MHS and, 280–281; as MHS member-at-large of the Council, 544

Turner, Sharon, 531

Turner Construction Company, 396

Turrell, Samuel, 344

Tuttle, Charles W., 531; as MHS member-at-large of the Council, 543

Tuttle, Julius H., 285, 291, 531; as MHS assistant librarian, 89, 251, 254–255; as MHS assistant editor, 278, 286; Worthington C. Ford and, 286, 333–334; Samuel A. Green and, 287–288, 295; as MHS librarian, 306, 310, 333–334, 547; MHS museum collection and, 308; Stewart Mitchell and, 333; William Crowninshield Endicott (1860–1936) and, 334

Twisleton, Edward Turner Boyd, 531

Tyler, Daniel P., 64, 65

Tyler, John W., 531

Tyler, Lyon Gardiner, 531

Tyler, Moses Coit, 241, 531

Tyler, William Royall, 532

Tyng, Dudley Atkins, 532, 572

Ulrich, Laurel Thacher, 532

Union Club, 129, 379

Union Pacific Railroad, 180

Unitarians, 15, 163, 449, 462–463; first Boston church of, 48; George E. Ellis and, 173; Caroline Healey Dall and, 257; Unitarian Universalist Association and, 465

United States Agricultural Society, 37–38

United Zinc and Chemical Company, 378

University Microfilms International, 464

University of California, Davis, 441

University of Chicago, 370

University of Cincinnati, 441

Index

Index

Index

Whitney, Henry A., 535; as MHS member-at-large of the Council, 542
Whitney, Hugh, 535
Whitney, Peter, 535
Whitridge, Arnold, 535
Wicker, Thomas Gray, 450, 535
Wieland, Christoph Martin, 363
Wiggins, James Russell, 434, 535
Wight, Crocker, 535
Wigwam. *See* American Museum
Wilberforce, Rt. Rev. Samuel, bishop of Oxford, 204–205, 207, 536
Wilbur, James Benjamin, 536
Wilder, Amos Niven, 536
Wilkes, John, 145
Wilkes, Laura E., 319
Wilkins, Raymond Sanger, 536
Willard, Joseph, 67, 116, 536; as MHS recording secretary, 540; as MHS corresponding secretary, 541; as MHS member-at-large of the Council, 542; as MHS librarian, 547
Willcox, William Bradford, 536
William and Flora Hewlett Foundation, 461
William L. Clements Library, 315
Williams, Alexander Whiteside, 536
Williams, George Huntston, 536
Williams, Israel, 234
Williams, John, 536
Williams, Jonathan, 536
Williams, Samuel, 536
Williams, William Trumbull, 536
Williamson, Hugh, 536
Williamson, Joseph, 536
Williamson, William Durkee, 536
Willis, William, 536
Willis, Zephaniah, 536
Wilson, Don, 454
Wilson, Thomas James, 536; as MHS member-at-large of the Council, 546
Wilson, Thomas Woodrow, 536
Wiltse, Charles M., 536
Winship, George Parker, 268, 342, 536
Winship, Lawrence Leathe, 536
Winship, Thomas, 536
Winslow, Edward, 236
Winslow, Ola Elizabeth, 427, 536
Winslow family, 99, 236
Winsor, Justin, 140, 142, 196, 245, 536; Leif Erickson and, 154; proposed MHS

move to Cambridge, 170–172; William Bradford manuscript and, 207–209, 210, 214; as Harvard University librarian, 214; as MHS vice-president, 540; as MHS corresponding secretary, 541; as MHS member-at-large of the Council, 543
Winterthur, Henry Francis du Pont Museum, 454
Winthrop, Adam, 536
Winthrop, Beekman, 537
Winthrop, Benjamin Robert, 537
Winthrop, Fitz-John, 351
Winthrop, Francis Bayard, 537
Winthrop, Frederic (1868–1932), 537; as MHS member-at-large of the Council, 544, 545; fund, 561–562
Winthrop, Frederic (1906–1979), 537
Winthrop, Frederic (b. 1940), 537
Winthrop, Grenville Lindall, 537
Winthrop, Hannah Fayerweather, 145
Winthrop, James, 13, 58–60, 537, 572; as MHS member-at-large of the Council, 541
Winthrop, Gov. John (1588–1649), 2, 40, 48, 215; "History of New England" of, 45–46, 99, 270; portrait of, 236, 351
Winthrop, Prof. John (1714–179), 13, 145
Winthrop, John (1809–1886), 537
Winthrop, John (b. 1936), 537
Winthrop, Nathaniel Thayer, 537
Winthrop, Robert (1833–1892), fund, 562
Winthrop, Robert (b. 1904), 537
Winthrop, Robert Charles (1809–1894), 178, 196, 201, 222, 229, 537; ear of corn and, 38; Edward Everett and, 38; as MHS president, 38, 48, 54, 76–79, 377, 540; MHS Tremont Street headquarters and, 48, 74, 103, 104, 107–109, 128, 172–173; MHS social life and, 52, 89, 143, 145; MHS membership and, 54–55, 131–136, 264; James Savage and, 56; gives MHS public lecture, 71; prejudice against Confederate supporters, 76; Dowse Library and, 76–77, 83–84, 86, 88; Charles Francis Adams (1835–1915) praises, 77, 180; oratorical powers of, 77; Washington Monument and, 77;

Index

Index